MODERN

CONCEPTS AND SKILLS

MANAGEMENT

ELEVENTH EDITION

Samuel C. Certo
Steinmetz Professor of Management
Roy E. Crummer Graduate School of Business
Rollins College

S. Trevis Certo
Dean's Council of 100 Scholars
W. P. Carey School of Business
Arizona State University

Pearson Ed

Acquisitions Editor: Kim Norbuta

Editorial Director: Sally Yagan

Director of Development: Steve Deitmer

Product Development Manager: Ashley Santora

Editorial Project Manager: Claudia Fernandes

Editorial Assistant: Elizabeth Davis

Marketing Manager: Nikki Jones

Marketing Assistant: Ian Gold

Permissions Project Manager: Charles Morris

Senior Managing Editor: Judy Leale

Associate Managing Editor: Suzanne DeWorken

Senior Operations Specialist: Arnold Vila

Creative Director: Christy Mahon

Art Director: Steve Frim

Designer: Maureen Eide

Cover Designer: Maureen Eide

Manager, Rights and Permissions: Zina Arabia

Manager, Visual Research: Beth Brenzel

Image Permission Coordinator: Kathy Gavilanes

Manager, Cover Visual Research & Permissions:
   Karen Sanatar

Composition: Integra Software Services

Full-Service Project Management:
   BookMasters, Inc.

Printer/Binder: Quebecor World Versailles

Typeface: 11/12.5 Perpetua

Credits and acknowledgments borrowed from other sources and reproduced, with permission, in this textbook appear on pages 607–608.

Microsoft® and Windows® are registered trademarks of the Microsoft Corporation in the U.S.A. and other countries. Screen shots and icons reprinted with permission from the Microsoft Corporation. This book is not sponsored or endorsed by or affiliated with the Microsoft Corporation.

If you purchased this book within the United States or Canada you should be aware that it has been wrongfully imported without the approval of the Publisher or the Author.

Pearson Education Ltd., London

Pearson Education Singapore, Pte. Ltd

Pearson Education, Canada, Inc.

Pearson Education–Japan

Pearson Education Australia PTY, Limited

Pearson Education North Asia, Ltd., Hong Kong

Pearson Educación de Mexico, S.A. de C.V.

Pearson Education Malaysia, Pte. Ltd

Pearson Education Upper Saddle River, New Jersey

Prentice Hall
is an imprint of

PEARSON

www.pearsonhighered.com

10 9 8 7 6 5 4 3 2 1

ISBN-13: 978-0-13-207425-4

ISBN-10: 0-13-207425-7

Samuel C. Certo

To Mimi: My compass for right living

....

S. Trevis Certo

To the Certos in the desert: Melissa, Skylar,
Lexie, and Landon

BRIEF CONTENTS

CONTENTS

PREFACE

For more than 25 years, *Modern Management* has helped to transform hundreds of thousands of students around the world like you into practicing managers. Over time, this book has established a reputation as a comprehensive text that synthesizes and integrates the most recent and influential management research. *Modern Management* discusses management research and concepts and helps you to develop the managerial skills necessary to succeed in the marketplace.

Overall, this book is a traditionally organized principles of management text that *comprehensively integrates* both useful management concepts and training in how to apply those concepts. To help you develop management skills, you will complete several types of innovative learning activities either in this text or online through a companion Web site at MyManagementLab.com.

We've spent countless hours gathering and interpreting the opinions of other management professors around the country for ideas on how to develop our concepts and skills approach to this book. In the following sections, we discuss some of the new concepts added to this edition as well as new text components designed to help you learn how to apply these concepts. The focus of this text is reflected in its complete name: *Modern Management: Concepts and Skills.*

MODERN MANAGEMENT, 11TH EDITION: THE CONCEPTS

From a content viewpoint, *Modern Management,* 11th edition, represents an exciting new book carefully crafted to incorporate the latest management concepts. To help us in this endeavor, we surveyed management professors throughout the United States to better understand their opinions about what concepts should be covered in this text. Perhaps the most significant additions to the concepts in this edition are three new chapters: *Corporate Culture, Management and Entrepreneurship* and *Controlling, Information, and Technology.* The highlights of the content changes in this new edition include the following:

- CHAPTER 1: INTRODUCING MODERN MANAGEMENT: CONCEPTS AND SKILLS We added a new discussion about management careers and on the skills that help managers to be successful. This chapter pinpoints management skills emphasized throughout the book and sets the stage for learning management concepts and developing related skills. A new Harry Potter case opens the chapter and current examples about Home Depot and Exxon-Mobile Corporation were also added.

- CHAPTER 2: MANAGING: HISTORY AND CURRENT THINKING New class discussion exercises focus on fostering safe behavior in the construction industry and how time studies might apply to career development. New examples look at conducting efficiency studies and building a new work environment at State Street Bank.

- CHAPTER 3: CORPORATE SOCIAL RESPONSIBILITY AND BUSINESS ETHICS New examples in this chapter focus on volunteerism, the chemical industry, the hospitality industry, and the communications industry. Nike's Code of Conduct provides an excellent example of how one company tries to positively influence practices of global partner organizations. Material on whistle-blowing was also added.

- CHAPTER 4: MANAGEMENT AND DIVERSITY New coverage regarding sexual harassment and settlements related to EEO lawsuits has been included. Also, new pro-diversity work climate research is highlighted along with discussion of diversity training that McDonald's offers its managers.

- CHAPTER 5: MANAGING IN THE GLOBAL ARENA New content related to expectations about leaders in multinational corporations has been added as well as the possible impact of the Chinese culture on management careers. Updated information describes U.S. investment abroad as well as where investment in the United States has been originating. Discussion of the top 10 global companies as ranked by *Forbes* is also included.

- NEW CHAPTER 6: MANAGEMENT AND ENTREPRENEURSHIP This new chapter focuses on the discovery, evaluation, and exploitation of opportunities. The end of the chapter includes a discussion of how individuals might create social—as opposed to economic—value through social entrepreneurship. It is our hope that this new chapter will help students to better understand the role of entrepreneurship in today's society and the value of entrepreneurial skills.

- CHAPTER 7: PRINCIPLES OF PLANNING We added extensive examples about Yahoo! and Microsoft to demonstrate the relevance of planning in the technology sector. We also added a table listing statements of purpose from several popular organizations.

- CHAPTER 8: MAKING DECISIONS We substantively revised this chapter to cover the latest research on decision making. New sections on bounded rationality, risk and uncertainty, intuition and decision making, and heuristics and biases include examples regarding Starbucks and News Corp. to demonstrate the relevance of decision making in the corporate world.

- CHAPTER 9: STRATEGIC PLANNING We revised our discussion of globalization as well as the industry environment in an effort to better communicate the importance of these topics.

- CHAPTER 10: PLANS AND PLANNING TOOLS We updated the discussion of the quantitative tools used in forecasting. A new table illustrates the tools used recently in the corporate world. Examples based on Wal-Mart and Toyota help students to better understand the role of planning tools in today's business environment.

- CHAPTER 11: FUNDAMENTALS OF ORGANIZING We updated this chapter to streamline our discussion of organizing through departmentalization. A new table in this chapter summarizes the advantages and disadvantages of the different types of departmentalization. New figures also demonstrate how Sony—the subject of this chapter's Challenge Case—might implement these new structures.

- CHAPTER 12: RESPONSIBILITY, AUTHORITY, AND DELEGATION Our new focus elaborates on the steps of successful delegation. We include an example of Countrywide Financial and the recent mortgage meltdown to illustrate the concept of responsibility.

- CHAPTER 13: MANAGING HUMAN RESOURCES We included examples from the world of management to demonstrate how companies such as Dell and Aetna use training and performance appraisals to increase organizational effectiveness.

- CHAPTER 14: ORGANIZATIONAL CHANGE: STRESS AND CONFLICT Content on employee attitudes toward change is new to this edition. Conflict as a major topic relating to organizational change is also covered. New discussion primarily emphasizes techniques for handling conflict: compromising, avoiding, forcing, and resolving.

- CHAPTER 15: FUNDAMENTALS OF INFLUENCING AND COMMUNICATION New discussion and in-depth examples of Genentech and Steelcase in this chapter focus on the potential impact of diversity on communication in foreign subsidiaries. This chapter also extends the discussion on emotional intelligence as well as how negative stereotypes that managers might have about employees can hinder organizational communication.

- CHAPTER 16: LEADERSHIP New material in this edition explores leaders and encouraging creativity as well as servant leadership. New extended leadership-related examples focus on General Electric, Lore International Institute, and Walt Disney Company in Asia Pacific.

- CHAPTER 17: MOTIVATION New coverage focuses on how punishment might relate to career building and monetary incentives for men vs. women. Ron Villone, a New York

Yankee pitcher, was highlighted to discuss how the needs-goal theory of motivation can relate to his job as a pitcher. American Airlines was also highlighted to show how equity theory might relate to events within the company. Recent events at Bank of America were added as an example of using extrinsic rewards within an organization. More depth was added to the discussion on behavior modification.

- CHAPTER 18: GROUPS AND TEAMS Discussion additions for this edition include more extended coverage of groupthink as well as predicting attributes of effective self-managed teams. New extended examples related to groups and teams include choosing members for committees at the University of North Dakota, building effective global teams, and building trust within teams at Burberry.

- **NEW** CHAPTER 19: CORPORATE CULTURE Corporate Culture is new to this edition. The chapter opens with a case that spotlights establishing a culture of safety at BP. Major topics include defining organization culture, the importance of culture, and building a high-performance organization culture. Special discussion emphasizes cultural artifacts: organizational values, myths, sagas, language, symbols, ceremonies, and rewards. Extended culture-related examples from the world of management emphasize a code of conduct at the Australian Wheat Board, an innovation culture at 3M, and building a healthy culture at Uchumi Supermarkets in Kenya, Africa.

- CHAPTER 20: CREATIVITY AND INNOVATION We revised this chapter to incorporate the latest research examining how companies can foster creativity and retain their most creative employees. We also included a new table that summarizes a recent ranking of the most innovative companies in the United States.

- **NEW** CHAPTER 21: CONTROLLING, INFORMATION, AND TECHNOLOGY This new chapter streamlines the most critical elements of two chapters from previous edition: *Principles of Controlling and Information Technology*. This new approach allows students to more clearly understand how managers use IT for controlling purposes.

- CHAPTER 22: PRODUCTION MANAGEMENT AND CONTROL This chapter includes new examples from the world of management to illustrate how production management and control concepts apply to companies such Wal-Mart, Cisco, and Intel.

MODERN MANAGEMENT, 11TH EDITION: YOUR SKILLS

This edition of *Modern Management* has a unique focus of developing your management skills in *all major areas of management*. Each chapter opens by identifying a specific management skill on which the chapter focuses. The remainder of the chapter contains a number of purposefully placed features designed to help you develop that skill.

This focus on skill development is consistent with the Association to Advance Collegiate Schools of Business (AACSB), a world renowned agency that provides higher education professionals with sound standards for maintaining excellence in management education. The latest AACSB standards indicate that excellence in modern management education is achieved when you acquire *both knowledge* about management concepts and *skill* in applying that knowledge. According to these standards, this book helps you to understand and appreciate both the "why" and the "how" of management. Specifically, each chapter includes *new* devices to help you learn skills more easily:

- CHAPTER TARGET SKILL: The introduction of each chapter identifies and defines the target management skill that you will study in that chapter.

- LINKING SKILLS TO THE REAL WORLD: Each chapter opens with an introductory **Challenge Case.** The purpose of each challenge case is to demonstrate to you the usefulness of management skills in today's business environment. Each case summarizes a set of issues for a manager within a company and queries you to ponder how to resolve the situation. We worked diligently to write challenge cases that include companies that you can identify, understand, and appreciate. In our experience, such companies provide for the most compelling in-class case discussions.

In addition to each Challenge Case, the end of each chapter includes an additional case, which is followed by a series of discussion questions. Examining the content and skills for each chapter in multiple real world contexts will help you to further develop expertise regarding the application of chapter material.

- LINKING CONTENT TO SKILLS: After each introductory challenge case, an **Exploring Your Management Skills** exercise appears. This exercise (self-scored or electronically scored) asks you a series of questions to help you to recognize the relationship between content and the targeted management skill in a chapter. After studying the chapter, you can answer the questions again to assess your learning.

- LINKING RESEARCH AND SKILLS: Each chapter includes a **Research Highlight** that focuses on a recent research article. These highlights end with focused questions to help you better understand the implications of recent management research on management skills.

- LINKING SKILLS AND CAREERS: Each chapter also includes a **Career Highlight** feature that helps you to understand the relationship between the targeted skill of a chapter and the development of your career. This new feature includes a number of questions designed to help you appreciate the importance of management skill in your career development. It is our belief that this new feature helps you to better understand how the material in the text will help you throughout their careers. Introducing you to these management skills, which will demonstrate the relevance and importance of your book, course, and instructor.

- HIGHLIGHTING PRACTICED SKILLS: Each chapter includes a number of **examples from the world of management** related to the chapter's targeted management skill. These examples will help you to understand the practical relevance of what you're learning.

- MANAGEMENT SKILLS PORTFOLIO: An activity at the end of each chapter is specially designed to allow you to demonstrate the management skill that you've learned in that chapter. Instructors may choose to have you turn in hard or electronic copies of this assignment. In addition, instructors may ask you to present your completed portfolio exercises in class. If completed online at MyManangementLab.com., you can accumulate this evidence and print a portfolio covering as many chapters as desired, including cover sheet, to help you win a job during an employment interview.

Taken together, the concepts/skills focus of *Modern Management,* 11th Edition. helps you by:

1. discussing current as well as traditional main points of the management literature.
2. presenting management concepts while helping you to develop related management skills.
3. including a number of creative learning tools within the text that aid in developing your management skills.
4. allowing you to better understand the importance of management skills for your career.

MODERN MANAGEMENT: YOUR LEARNING PROCESS

We would like to suggest a way for you to study this book in order to maximize learning. By using the components of *Modern Management* in a conscientious and systematic fashion, you can build your knowledge about management concepts and your skill to apply it. Although the components of *Modern Management* are flexible and can be used in numerous different ways, our suggested study process is discussed here.

As shown in Figure 1, you can start chapter study by experiencing Exploring Your Management Skill: Part 1. This exercise will introduce you to concepts and skills emphasized in the chapter and help you to assess how much you know in these areas before studying the chapter.

FIGURE 1 A systematic method for maximizing learning when studying Modern Management

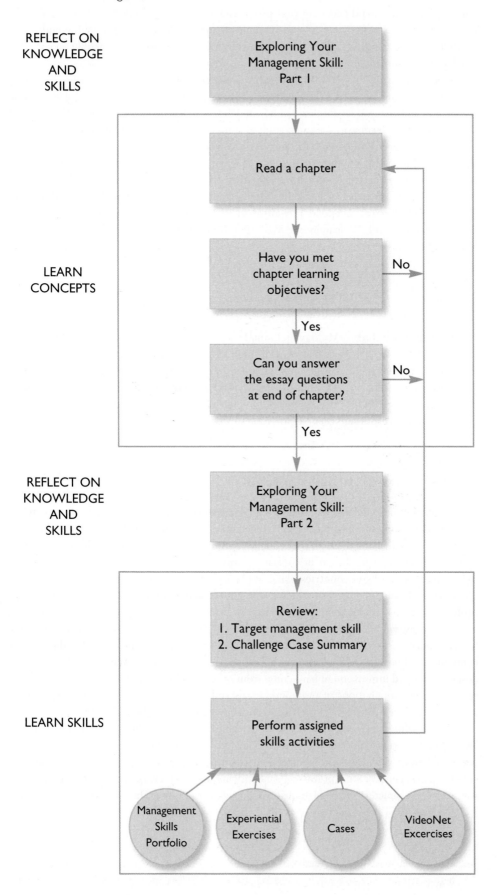

Once you have been introduced to the chapter via Exploring Your Management Skill: Part 1, you can start learning management concepts. You learn concepts by reading and studying the chapter and checking your progress in meeting learning objectives stated at the beginning of the chapter as well as being able to answer essay questions at the end of the chapter. By checking your learning progress, you can pinpoint areas in which further study is needed before moving forward.

Once you are satisfied that you have learned chapter content, you can experience Exploring Your Management Skill: Part 2. This exercise will reemphasize the knowledge and skills focus in the chapter and give you feedback about how much you've learned in the chapter. If you are not satisfied with your feedback, you can restudy chapter concepts in order to improve.

When you are satisfied with this feedback, you can focus more on learning management skills related to chapter content. You focus on learning how to apply management concepts by performing application exercises assigned by professors and still refer back to chapter content as often as necessary to further clarify concepts and how to apply them. You might also work on exercises independently, do work not assigned by your professor. Application exercises can include Management Skills Portfolio, Experiential Exercises, Cases, and VideoNet Exercises.

STUDENT SUPPLEMENTS

MyManagementLab—MyManagement Lab.com is an online learning solution with assessment and tutorial tools that provide practice and testing while personalizing course content. It creates a personalized interactive learning environment, where you can learn at your own pace and measure your progress. MyManagementLab includes a full eBook with a variety of multimedia resources available directly from selected examples and exercises on the page. All the resources you need for your success in the course are in one place.

ACKNOWLEDGMENTS

The overwhelming success of *Modern Management* has now continued for almost three decades. This book and its ancillaries have become a generally accepted academic standard for high-quality learning materials in colleges and universities throughout the world. These materials have been published in special "country editions," serving the special needs of management students in countries like Canada and India. *Modern Management* has also been published in foreign languages including Portuguese and Spanish and is commonly used in professional management training programs.

Obviously, we have received much personal satisfaction and professional recognition for the success of this text over the years. In truth, however, much of the credit for this success continues to rightfully belong to many of our respected colleagues. Many key ideas for text development and improvement have come from others. We're grateful for the opportunity to recognize the contributions of these individuals and extend to them our warmest personal gratitude for their professional insights and encouragement throughout the life of this project.

For this edition, several colleagues made valuable contributions through numerous activities like reviewing manuscript and providing unsolicited ideas for improvement. These individuals offered different viewpoints that required us to constructively question our work. Thoughtful comments, concern for student learning, and insights regarding instructional implications of the written word characterized the high-quality feedback we received. These individuals are:

Don Aleksy, Illinois Valley College

Karen Barr, Penn State University

Daniel Baugher, Pace University

Wayne Blue, Allegany College of Maryland

Elise A. Brazier, Northeast Texas Community College

Megan Endres, Eastern Michigan University

Joyce Ezrow, Anne Arundel Community College

William Brent Felstead, College of the Desert

Robert Freeland, Columbia Southern University

Adelina Gnanlet, California State University

Joseph Goldman, University of Minnesota

Heidi Helgren, Delta College

Jo Ann Hunter, Community College of Allegheny County

Dennis L. Kovach, Community College of Allegheny County

Loren Kuzuhara, University of Wisconsin

Gosia Langa, University of Maryland

Theresa Lant, New York University

Michelle Meyer, Joliet Junior College

Marcia Miller, George Mason University

Jennifer Morton, Ivy Tech Community College

Rhonda Palladi, Georgia State University

Donald Petkus, Indiana University

Johnny Shull, Central Carolina Community College

Denise M. Simmons, Northern Virginia Community College

Gregory Sinclair, San Francisco State University

L. Allen Slade, Covenant College

Dr. Peter Szende, Boston University

Tom Tao, Lehigh University

Don Tobias, Cornell University

Cindy W. Walter, Antelope Valley College

Over the years, many colleagues have made significant contributions to previous editions of this project that are still impacting this 11th edition. A list of such respected colleagues includes:

Dan Baugher, Pace University

Michael Carrell, Morehead State University

Lon Doty, San Jose State University

Steven E. Huntley, Florida Community College at Jacksonville

Robert E. Kemper, Northern Arizona University

Toni Carol Kind, Binghamton University

Maurice Manner, Marymount College

James I. Phillips, Northeastern State University

Richard Ratliff, Shari Tarnutzer, and their colleagues, Utah State University

Joe Simon, Casper College

Randi L. Sims, Nova Southern University

Charles I. Stubbart, Southern Illinois University Carbondale

Larry Waldorf, Boise State University

Gloria Walker, Florida Community College at Jacksonville

In addition, several colleagues have worked diligently on developing text ancillaries of only the highest quality. Such colleagues worked tirelessly to provide instructional aids to all of us. Such colleagues worked tirelessly to provide instructional aids to all of us and we thank them for their time and efforts.

We will always owe Professor Lee A. Graf, now retired from Illinois State University, a huge debt of gratitude for helping to build the success of *Modern Management*. Dr. Graf's countless significant contributions over the years in many different areas have certainly been instrumental in building the reputation and widespread acceptance of our materials. More important than our professional relationship, Dr. Graf is our friend.

Members of our Prentice Hall family deserve personal and sincere recognition. Our book team has been nothing but the best: Sally Yagan, Editorial Director; Kim Norbuta, Acquisitions Editor; Claudia Fernandes, Editorial Project Manager; Liz Davis, Editorial Assistant; Carol Samet, Production Project Manager; Judy Leale, Senior Managing Editor; and Nikki Jones, Marketing Manager. Needless to say, without our Prentice Hall colleagues, there would be no *Modern Management*.

Sam Certo would like to give special recognition to Craig McAllaster, Dean of the Crummer Graduate School of Business at Rollins College and Charles "Chuck" Steinmetz, entrepreneur extraordinaire. Personal and professional support demonstrated by these individuals over the years has helped to ensure the intensity, growth, and excitement necessary to maintain a vigorous, long-term writing schedule. Probably unknown to them, McAllaster and Steinmetz have been invaluable in the completion of this text.

Last and arguably most importantly, Sam Certo would like to thank his wife, Mimi, for her continual support throughout this revision. She constantly made personal sacrifices "beyond the call of duty" in support of the completion of this project. Thank you!

Trevis Certo would like to thank his colleagues at Arizona State University and Texas A&M University for their continued support. I would also like to thank my wife Melissa for her constant encouragement during our many years together. I could not have done this without you. I would also like to thank Skylar, Lexie, and Landon for humbling me every day. Finally, and most importantly, I would like to thank God for blessing me with a beautiful and healthy family.

SAMUEL C. CERTO

S. TREVIS CERTO

ABOUT THE AUTHORS

DR. SAMUEL C. CERTO is presently the Steinmetz Professor of Management at the Roy E. Crummer Graduate School of Business at Rollins College. Over his career, Dr. Certo has received many prestigious awards including the Award for Innovative Teaching from the Southern Business Association, the Instructional Innovation Award granted by the Decision Sciences Institute, and the Charles A. Welsh Memorial Award for outstanding teaching.

Dr. Certo has written several successful textbooks including *Modern Management, Strategic Management: Concepts and Applications,* and *Supervision: Concepts and Applications.* His textbooks have been translated into several foreign languages for distribution throughout the world. Having received six different teaching awards in the last four years alone, Dr. Certo constantly focuses on crafting all of his books to facilitate both the instructional and student learning processes. Dr. Certo's numerous publications include articles in such journals as *Academy of Management Review, The Journal of Change Management, Business Horizons, The Journal of Experiential Learning and Simulation,* and *Training.*

A past chairperson of the Management Education and Development Division of the Academy of Management, he has been honored by that group's Excellence of Leadership Award. Dr. Certo has also served as president of the Association for Business Simulation and Experiential Learning, as associate editor for *Simulation & Games,* and as a review board member of the *Academy of Management Review.* His consulting experience has been extensive with notable experience on boards of directors. He is presently chairperson of the compensation committee of both Federal Trust Bank and Federal Trust Corporation, a publicly traded American Stock Exchange company headquartered in Sanford, Florida.

DR. S. TREVIS CERTO is an associate professor and a Dean's Council of 100 Scholar in the W. P. Carey School of Business at Arizona State University. Dr. Certo holds a Ph.D. in strategic management from the Kelley School of Business at Indiana University. His research focuses on corporate governance, top management teams, initial public offerings (IPOs), and research methodology. Dr. Certo's research has appeared in the *Academy of Management Journal, Academy of Management Review, Strategic Management Journal, Journal of Management, California Management Review, Journal of Business Venturing, Entrepreneurship Theory and Practice, Business Ethics Quarterly, Journal of Business Ethics, Business Horizons, Journal of Developmental Entrepreneurship,* and *Across the Board.* Dr. Certo's research has also been featured in publications such as *Business Week, New York Times, Wall Street Journal, Washington Post,* and *Money* magazine.

Dr. Certo is a member of the Academy of Management and the Strategic Management Society and serves on the editorial review boards of the *Academy of Management Journal, Journal of Management, Entrepreneurship Theory and Practice, Journal of Management and Governance,* and *Business Horizons.* Prior to joining the faculty at Arizona State, he taught undergraduate, MBA, EMBA, and Ph.D. courses in strategic management, research methodology, and international business at Indiana University, Texas A&M University, Tulane University, and Wuhan University (China).

INTRODUCTION TO MODERN MANAGEMENT

1 Introducing Modern Management

CONCEPTS AND SKILLS

O B J E C T I V E S

TO HELP BUILD MY MANAGEMENT SKILL, WHEN STUDYING THIS CHAPTER, I WILL ATTEMPT TO ACQUIRE:

1. An understanding of the importance of management to society and individuals

2. An understanding of the role of management

3. An ability to define management in several different ways

4. An ability to list and define the basic functions of management

5. Working definitions of managerial effectiveness and managerial efficiency

6. An understanding of basic management skills and their relative importance to managers

7. An understanding of the universality of management

8. Knowledge of skills that help managers become successful

9. Insights concerning what management careers are and how they evolve

TARGET SKILL management skill: the ability to work with people and other organizational resources to accomplish organizational goals

NEW HARRY POTTER PARK AT UNIVERSAL

After months of speculation it's now official, the entertainment company Universal Studios is building a new Harry Potter theme park as part of its Universal Orlando Resort in the U.S. state of Florida. Harry Potter fans will soon be visiting the new park, "The Wizarding World of Harry Potter."

The new Harry Potter theme park is actually being developed as a partnership between Warner Bros. Entertainment Inc. and Universal Orlando Resort. The partner companies are planning to create the world's first fully immersive Harry Potter–themed environment based on the best-selling books by author J. K. Rowling and wildly successful feature films from Warner Bros. Rowling stated, "The plans I've seen look incredibly exciting, and I don't think fans of the books or films will be disappointed." The author has been working with a creative team to make sure the park resembles her work.[1]

Tom Williams, chairperson at Universal, said that I'm "still kind of pinching myself" over the deal. The pressure to build an attraction that is true to the Harry Potter brand, he said, will be intense, though the company is looking forward to creating the smells, sounds, and texture of the settings in the Rowling's

Bringing a massive project like a new Harry Potter theme park to life requires many types of management skills at all levels of the organization.

books. The power of the Harry Potter brand also impresses Williams. Rowling has sold more than 300 million Harry Potter books in more than 63 foreign languages. It is estimated that 8 out of 10 people already recognize the Harry Potter name, which is also an important customer draw.[2]

It seems clear that the new Harry Potter theme park is an attempt by Universal to better compete with Walt Disney World, another Orlando theme park. Universal reported attendances of just over 11 million last year, a drop on previous years, whereas Disney World, Orlando, has reported visiting figures of more than 45 million. Universal management feels sure that their new attraction will draw Potter pilgrims.[3]

For Universal, the idea of a Harry Potter theme park sounds fantastic. Going from an idea, however, to a reality of a profitably run theme park is a formidable challenge. The success of meeting this challenge rests squarely in the hands of management. Management must avoid classic mistakes such as recruiting the wrong employees, not creating a motivating work environment, and not keeping the development of the new park on schedule. Competent managers will meet the challenge whereas incompetent management will not. Only time will tell.

> "EXPLORE YOUR OWN MANAGEMENT SKILLS BY TAKING THE QUIZ ON THE NEXT PAGE"

Before studying this chapter, respond to the following questions regarding the type of advice that you would give to Universal's chairperson, Tom Williams, referenced in the Challenge Case. Then address the concerning management challenges that he presently faces within the company. You are not expected to be a "management" expert at this point. Answering the questions now can help you focus on important points when you study the chapter. Also, answering the questions again after you study the chapter will give you an idea of how much you have learned.

Record your answers here or online at MyManagement Lab.com. Completing the questions at MyManagement Lab.com will allow you to get feedback about your answers automatically. If you answer the questions in the book, look up answers in the Exploring Your Management Skill section at the end of the book.

FOR EACH STATEMENT CIRCLE:

- "Y" if you would give the advice to Williams.
- "N" if you would NOT give the advice to Williams.
- "NI" if you have no idea whether you would give the advice to Williams.

Mr. Williams, in meeting your management challenges at Universal, you should . . .

Before Study   *After Study*

1. make sure you understand how important management is in successfully building and operating the new Harry Potter park.

   Y, N, NI

2. keep in mind that building the new Potter park may not be consistent with goals of Universal as a whole.

   Y, N, NI

3. strive to manage people appropriately but understand that managing resources is generally not as important as managing people.

   Y, N, NI

4. focus mainly on planning and organizing to meet management challenges at Universal.

   Y, N, NI

5. use mainly the influencing function to make sure that people at Universal are managed appropriately.

   Y, N, NI

6. use the planning, organizing, influencing, and controlling functions together to reach Universal's organizational goals.

   Y, N, NI

7. use the management process to attain Universal's goals.

   Y, N, NI

8. almost always be aware of the status and use of Universal's resources.

   Y, N, NI

9. strive to be effective in reaching Universal's goals.

   Y, N, NI

10. focus on being an efficient manager, one who reaches organizational goals.

    Y, N, NI

11. ensure that an overabundance of managers in the exploration career stage is not involved in building the new Potter park.

    Y, N, NI

12. as CEO, have more technical skill than conceptual skill in building the new Potter park.

    Y, N, NI

13. focus mainly on building conceptual skill in managing Universal.

    Y, N, NI

14. rely on the universality of management principle as a worthwhile rationale for assigning only people with prior experience at Universal to build the new Potter park.

    Y, N, NI

THE MODERN MANAGEMENT CHALLENGE

The Challenge Case implies various modern management challenges that Universal management strives to meet, but primarily focuses on building a new Harry Potter theme park. The remaining material in this chapter explains the basic concepts of modern management and helps to develop the corresponding management skill that you will need to meet such challenges throughout your career. After studying chapter concepts, read the Challenge Case Summary at the end of the chapter to help you to relate chapter content to meeting modern management challenges at Universal.

THE IMPORTANCE OF MANAGEMENT

Managers influence all phases of modern organizations. Plant managers run manufacturing operations that produce the clothes we wear, the food we eat, and the automobiles we drive. Sales managers maintain a salesforce that markets goods. Personnel managers provide organizations with a competent and productive workforce. The "jobs available" section in the classified advertisements of any major newspaper describes many different types of management activities and confirms the importance of management (see Figure 1.1).

SR. MANAGEMENT DEVELOPMENT SPECIALIST

We are a major metropolitan service employer of over 5,000 employees seeking a person to join our management development staff. Prospective candidates will be degreed with 5 to 8 years experience in the design, implementation, and evaluation of developmental programs for first-line and mid-level management personnel. Additionally, candidates must demonstrate exceptional oral and written communications ability and be skilled in performance analysis, programmed instruction, and the design and implementation of reinforcement systems.

If you meet these qualifications, please send your résumé, including salary history and requirements to:

Box RS-653

An Equal Opportunity Employer

BRANCH MGR

$30,500. Perceptive pro with track record in administration and lending has high visibility with respected firm.

Box PH-165

AVIATION FBO MANAGER NEEDED

Sydney operation catering to corporate aviation. No maintenance or aircraft sales—just fuel and the best service. Must be experienced. Salary plus benefits commensurate with qualifications. Submit complete résumé to:

Box LJO688

DIVISION CREDIT MANAGER

Major mfg. corporation seeks an experienced credit manager to handle the credit and collection function of its largest division. Interpersonal skills are important, as is the ability to communicate effectively with senior management. Send résumé with current compensation to:

Box NM-43

ACCOUNTING MANAGER

Growth opportunity. Acctg. degree, capable of supervision. Responsibilities include G/L, financial statements, inventory control, knowledge of systems design for computer applications. Send résumé, incl. salary history to:

Box RJM-999

An Equal Opportunity Employer

FINANCIAL MANAGER

CPA/MBA (U of C) with record of success in management positions. Employed, now seeking greater opportunity. High degree of professionalism, exp. in dealing w/financial inst., strong communication & analytical skills, stability under stress, high energy level, results oriented. Age 34, 11 yrs. exper. incl. major public acctng., currently 5 years as Financial VP of field leader. Impressive references.

Box LML-666

MARKET MANAGER

Major lighting manufacturer seeks market manager for decorative outdoor lighting. Position entails establishing and implementing marketing, sales, and new product development programs including coordination of technical publications and related R&D projects. Must locate at Brisbane headquarters. Send résumé to

Box WM-214
No agencies please

GENERAL MANAGER

Small industrial service company, privately owned, located in Springfield, Missouri, needs aggressive, skilled person to make company grow in profits and sales. Minimum B.S. in Business, experienced in all facets of small business operations. Must understand profit. Excellent opportunity and rewards. Salary and fringes commensurate with experience and performance.

Box LEM-116

FOUNDRY SALES MANAGER

Aggressive gray iron foundry located in the U.S. Midwest, specializing in 13,000 tons of complex castings yearly with a weight range of 2 to 400 pounds, is seeking experienced dynamic sales manager with sound sales background in our industry. Salary commensurate with experience. excellent benefit package.

Box MO-948

HUMAN RESOURCE MANAGER

Publicly owned, national manufacturer with 12 plants, 700 employees, seeks first corporate personnel director. We want someone to administer programs in:

- Position and rate evaluation
- Employee safety engineering
- Employee training
- Employee communications
- Employee benefits
- Legal compliance

Qualifications: Minimum of 3–5 years personnel experience in mfg. company, ability to tactfully deal with employees at all levels from all walks of life, free to travel. Position reports to Vice President, Operations. Full range of company benefits, salary $32,000–$40,000. Reply in complete confidence to:

Box JK-236

FIGURE 1.1   The variety of management positions available

THE MANAGEMENT TASK

In addition to understanding the significance of managerial work to themselves and society and its related benefits, prospective managers need to know what the management task entails. The sections that follow introduce the basics of the management task through discussions of the role and definition of management, the management process as it pertains to management functions and organizational goal attainment, and the need to manage organizational resources effectively and efficiently.

Our society could neither exist as we know it today nor improve without a steady stream of managers to guide its organizations. Management expert Peter Drucker emphasized this point when he stated that effective management is probably the main resource of developed countries and the most needed resource of developing ones.[4] In short, all societies desperately need good managers.

Management is important to society as a whole as well as vital to many individuals who earn their livings as managers. Managers come from varying backgrounds and have diverse educational specialties. Many people who originally trained to be accountants, teachers, financiers, or even writers eventually make their livelihoods as managers. Although in the short term, the demand for managers varies somewhat, in the long term, managerial positions can yield high salaries, status, interesting work, personal growth, and intense feelings of accomplishment.

As an example, over the years, *Forbes* magazine has become well known for its periodic rankings of total compensation paid to top managers in the United States. Based upon the 2007 *Forbes* compensation study, Table 1.1 shows the names of the 10 highest paid chief U.S. executives, the companies they worked for, and the total compensations amounts they were paid. In the study, total compensation includes factors such as salary, bonuses, and stock options paid to executives.

An inspection of the list of highest paid executives in Table 1.1 reveals that these executives are all men. Based upon the results of a recent survey at the *Wall Street Journal,* Figure 1.2 illustrates a broad salary gap between men and women. According to Figure 1.2, while women and men make up roughly the same proportion of the workforce, men hold a disproportionate number of higher paying jobs.[5]

Predictably, concerns that certain managers are paid *too* much have been raised. For **an example from the world of management**, consider the notable criticism regarding the high salaries paid to **Robert R. Nardelli, Home Depot's** recently ousted chief executive officer.[6] Disapproval of the excessive compensation paid to Nardelli surfaced in the popular

| TABLE 1.1 | The 10 Highest Compensated Top Managers for 2007 |

Compensation Ranking	CEO Name	Company Name	Total Compensation ($ millions)
1	Steven P. Jobs	Apple	646.60
2	Ray R. Irani	Occidental Petroleum	321.64
3	Barry Diller	IAC/InterActiveCorp	295.14
4	William P. Foley II	Fidelity National Finl	179.56
5	Terry S. Semel	Yahoo!	174.20
6	Michael S. Dell	Dell	153.23
7	Angelo R. Mozilo	Countrywide Financial	141.98
8	Michael S. Jeffries	Abercrombie & Fitch	114.64
9	Kenneth D. Lewis	Bank of America	99.80
10	Henry C. Duques	First Data	98.21

Source: www.forbes.com.

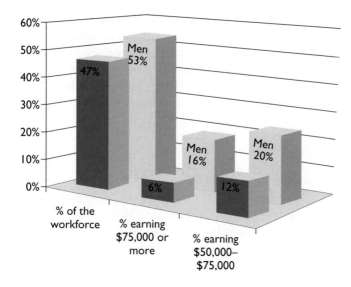

FIGURE 1.2
The salary gap between genders

press as well as in statements by stockholders. An article in *The Wall Street Journal,* for example, questioned whether Nardelli was worth the amount he received.[7] Nardelli had been paid $63.5 million during a five-year tenure during which Home Depot's shares lost 6 percent of their value. In the end, as with any manager, Nardelli's compensation should be determined by how much value he adds to the company. The more value he adds, the more compensation he deserves. As a result of the growing criticism about Nardelli's compensation and Nardelli's resistance to modify his compensation level, he was fired.

Some evidence suggests that societal concern about management compensation goes well beyond one manager at one company.[8] A recent U.S. Senate Commerce Committee meeting, for example, focused on justifying lavish pay programs for managers at companies such as Tyco International and American Airlines, whose companies were in financial trouble and laying off employees. By contrast, according to a recent report by the Institute for Policy Studies and United for a Fair Economy, the 20 highest-paid European executives made only a third as much as the 20 highest-paid U.S. executives. This Senate Committee meeting should be an important signal that U.S. managers who do not exercise judicious self-control about their salaries may face future legislative control.

class discussion highlight

YOUR SALARY AND YOUR CAREER

The preceding information could imply that career progress can be gauged by salary level; that is, the more salary that is received, the more progress made. In your mind, is salary history a valid measure of career progress? Why? List three other factors that you should use as measures of your career progress. To you, which is the most important in determining your progress? Why? How would you monitor changes in these factors as your career progresses?

The Role of Management

Essentially, the role of managers is to guide organizations toward goal accomplishment. All organizations exist for certain purposes or goals, and managers are responsible for combining and using organizational resources to ensure that their organizations achieve their purposes. Management moves an organization toward its purposes or goals by assigning activities that organization members perform. If the activities are designed effectively, the production of each individual worker will contribute to the attainment of organizational goals. Management strives to encourage individual activity that will lead to reaching organizational goals and to discourage individual activity that will hinder the accomplishment of those goals. Because the process of management emphasizes the achievement of goals, managers must keep organizational goals in mind at all times.[9]

Defining Management

Students of management should be aware that the term *management* can be, and often is, used in different ways. For instance, it can refer simply to the process that managers follow in order to accomplish organizational goals. It can also refer to a body of knowledge; in this context, management is a cumulative body of information that furnishes insights on how to manage. The term *management* can also refer to the individuals who guide and direct organizations or to a career devoted to the task of guiding and directing organizations. An understanding of the various uses and related definitions of the term will help you avoid miscommunication during management-related discussions.

As used most commonly in this text, **management** is the process of reaching organizational goals by working with and through people and other organizational resources. A comparison of this definition with the definitions offered by several contemporary management thinkers indicates broad agreement that management encompasses the following three main characteristics:

1. It is a process or series of continuing and related activities.
2. It involves and concentrates on reaching organizational goals.
3. It reaches these goals by working with and through people and other organizational resources.

A discussion of each of these characteristics follows.

The Management Process: Management Functions

The four basic **management functions**—activities that make up the management process—are described in the following sections.

Planning Planning involves choosing tasks that must be performed to attain organizational goals, outlining how the tasks must be performed, and indicating when they should be performed. Planning activity focuses on attaining goals. Through their plans, managers outline exactly what organizations must do to be successful. Planning is essential to getting the "right" things done.[10] Planning is concerned with organizational success in the near future (short term) as well as in the more distant future (long term).[11]

Organizing Organizing can be thought of as assigning the tasks developed under the planning function to various individuals or groups within the organization. Organizing, then, creates a mechanism to put plans into action. People within the organization are given work assignments that contribute to the company's goals. Tasks are organized so that the output of individuals contributes to the success of departments, which, in turn, contributes to the success of divisions, which ultimately contributes to the success of the organization. Organizing includes determining tasks and groupings of work.[12] Organizing should not be rigid, but adaptable and flexible to meet challenges as circumstances change.[13]

Influencing Influencing is another of the basic functions within the management process. This function—also commonly referred to as *motivating, leading, directing,* or *actuating*—is concerned primarily with people within organizations.* Influencing can be defined as guiding the activities of organization members in appropriate directions. An appropriate direction is any direction that helps the organization move toward goal attainment. The ultimate purpose of influencing is to increase productivity. Human-oriented work situations usually generate higher levels of production over the long term than do task-oriented work situations, because people find the latter type less satisfying.

Controlling   Controlling is the management function through which managers:

1. Gather information that measures recent performance within the organization.
2. Compare present performance to preestablished performance standards.
3. From this comparison, determine whether the organization should be modified to meet preestablished standards

Controlling is an ongoing process. Managers continually gather information, make their comparisons, and then try to find new ways of improving production through organizational modification.

History shows that managers commonly make mistakes when planning, organizing, influencing, and controlling. Figure 1.3 shows a number of such mistakes managers make related to each function. Studying this text carefully should help managers to avoid making such mistakes.

Management Process and Goal Attainment

Although we have discussed the four functions of management individually, planning, organizing, influencing, and controlling are integrally related and therefore cannot be separated in practice. Figure 1.4 illustrates this interrelationship and also indicates that managers use these

Planning
Not establishing objectives for all important organizational areas
Making plans that are too risky
Not exploring enough viable alternatives for reaching objectives
Not properly using the assistance of employee groups in making planning decisions
Not appropriately integrating both short-term and long-term planning

Organizing
Not establishing departments appropriately
Not emphasizing coordination of organization members
Establishing inappropriate spans of management
Not delegating appropriately
Establishing ineffective training programs

Influencing
Not taking the time to communicate properly with organization members
Establishing improper communication networks
Being a manager but not a leader
Not recognizing outstanding employee performance
Not managing organizational culture

Controlling
Not monitoring progress in carrying out plans
Not establishing appropriate performance standards
Not measuring performance to see where improvements might be made
Not monitoring productivity
Not improving production systems

FIGURE 1.3
Classic mistakes commonly made by managers in carrying out various management functions

*In early management literature, the term *motivating* was more commonly used to signify this people-oriented management function. The term *influencing* is used consistently throughout this text because it is broader and permits more flexibility in discussing people-oriented issues. Later in the text, motivating is discussed as a major part of influencing.

FIGURE 1.4
Relationships among the four functions of management used to attain organizational goals

activities solely for reaching organizational goals. Basically, these functions are interrelated because the performance of one depends on the performance of the others. For example, organizing is based on well-thought-out plans developed during the planning process, and influencing systems must be tailored to reflect both these plans and the organizational design used to implement them. The fourth function, controlling, involves possible modifications to existing plans, organizational structure, or the motivation system used to develop a more successful effort.

To be effective, a manager must understand how the four management functions are practiced, not simply how they are defined and related. Thomas J. Peters and Robert H. Waterman, Jr., studied numerous organizations—including Frito-Lay and Maytag—for several years to determine what management characteristics best describe excellently run companies. In their book *In Search of Excellence,* Peters and Waterman suggest that planning, organizing, influencing, and controlling should be characterized by a bias for action; a closeness to the customer; autonomy and entrepreneurship; productivity through people; a hands-on, value-driven orientation; "sticking to the knitting"; a simple organizational form with a lean staff; and simultaneous loose–tight properties.

This brief introduction to the four management functions will be further developed in Parts 3 through 6 of this text.

Management and Organizational Resources

Management must always be aware of the status and use of **organizational resources.** These resources, composed of all assets available for activation during the production process, are of four basic types:

1. Human
2. Monetary
3. Raw materials
4. Capital

As Figure 1.5 shows, organizational resources are combined, used, and transformed into finished products during the production process.

Human resources are the people who work for an organization. The skills they possess and their knowledge of the work system are invaluable to managers. Monetary resources are

FIGURE 1.5
Transformation of organizational resources into finished products through the production process

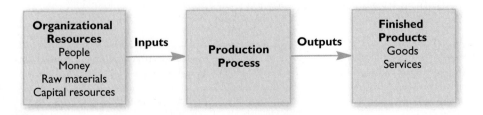

amounts of money that managers use to purchase goods and services for the organization. Raw materials are ingredients used directly in the manufacturing of products. For example, rubber is a raw material that Michelin would purchase with its monetary resources and use directly in manufacturing tires. Capital resources are machines used during the manufacturing process. Modern machines, or equipment, can be a major factor in maintaining desired production levels. Worn-out or antiquated machinery can make it impossible for an organization to keep pace with competitors.

Managerial Effectiveness As managers use their resources, they must strive to be both effective and efficient. **Managerial effectiveness** refers to management's use of organizational resources in meeting organizational goals. If organizations are using their resources to attain their goals, the managers are said to be effective. In reality, however, managerial effectiveness can be measured by degrees. The closer an organization comes to achieving its goals, the more effective its managers are considered to be. Managerial effectiveness, then, exists on a continuum ranging from *ineffective* to *effective*.

Managerial Efficiency **Managerial efficiency** is the proportion of total organizational resources that contribute to productivity during the manufacturing process.[14] The higher this proportion, the more efficient the manager. The more resources wasted or unused during the production process, the more inefficient the manager. In this situation, *organizational resources* refer not only to raw materials that are used in manufacturing goods or services but also to related human effort.[15] Like management effectiveness, management efficiency is best described as being on a continuum ranging from inefficient to efficient. *Inefficient* means that a small proportion of total resources contributes to productivity during the manufacturing process; *efficient* means that a large proportion of resources contributes to productivity.

As Figure 1.6 shows, the concepts of managerial effectiveness and efficiency are obviously related. A manager could be relatively ineffective—with the consequence that the organization is making little progress toward goal attainment—primarily because of major inefficiencies or poor utilization of resources during the production process. In contrast, a manager could be somewhat effective despite being inefficient if demand for the finished goods is so high that the manager can get an extremely high price per unit sold and thus absorb inefficiency costs. Thus a manager can be effective without being efficient, and vice versa. To maximize organizational success, however, both effectiveness and efficiency are essential.

FIGURE 1.6

Various combinations of managerial effectiveness and managerial efficiency

As **an example from the world of management**, think about efficiency and effectiveness at **British Petroleum**. Overall, British Petroleum Corporation engages in the exploration, production, transportation, and sale of crude oil and natural gas. Given the present high price at which crude oil is selling, the company can probably absorb many inefficiencies and be somewhat effective. As the price of oil drops, however, the company will earn less revenue, and inefficiencies or waste will have a more noticeable impact on company profits and therefore on effectiveness. Management in this situation has a chance to be somewhat effective despite its inefficiency. British Petroleum's management is constantly trying to improve its efficiency. The company uses benchmarking and best practices to develop targets for efficiency improvement.

THE UNIVERSALITY OF MANAGEMENT

Management principles are **universal**: That is, they apply to all types of organizations (businesses, churches, sororities, athletic teams, hospitals, etc.) and organizational levels.[16] Naturally, managers' jobs vary somewhat from one type of organization to another because each organizational type requires the use of specialized knowledge, exists in a unique working and political environment, and uses different technology. However, job similarities are found across organizations because the basic management activities—planning, organizing, influencing, and controlling—are common to all organizations.

The Theory of Characteristics

Henri Fayol, one of the earliest management writers, stated that all managers should possess certain characteristics, such as positive physical and mental qualities and special knowledge related to the specific operation.[17] B. C. Forbes emphasized the importance of certain more personal qualities, inferring that enthusiasm, earnestness of purpose, confidence, and faith in their own worthiness are primary characteristics of successful managers. Forbes has described Henry Ford as follows:

> At the base and birth of every great business organization was an enthusiast, a man consumed with earnestness of purpose, with confidence in his powers, with faith in the worthwhileness of his endeavors. The original Henry Ford was the quintessence of enthusiasm. In the days of his difficulties, disappointments, and discouragements, when he was wrestling with his balky motor engine—and wrestling likewise with poverty—only his inexhaustible enthusiasm saved him from defeat.[18]

Fayol and Forbes can describe desirable characteristics of successful managers only because of the universality concept: The basic ingredients of successful management are applicable to all organizations.

MANAGEMENT SKILL: THE KEY TO MANAGEMENT SUCCESS

Thus far, the introduction to the study of management has focused on discussing concepts such as the importance of management, the task of management, and the universality of management. This section continues the introduction to management by defining management skill and presenting both classic and more contemporary views of management skills thought to ensure management success.

Defining Management Skill

No introduction to the field of management would be complete without a discussion of management skill. **Management skill** is the ability to carry out the process of reaching organizational goals by working with and through people and other organizational resources.

Learning about management skill and focusing on developing it are of critical importance because possessing such skill is generally considered to be the prerequisite for management success.[19] Because management skills are so critical to the success of an organization, companies commonly focus on possible steps that can be taken to improve the skills of their managers.

As **an example from the world of management** illustrating how companies can focus on skill development of their managers, consider recent events at **PSA Peugeot Citroën**, Europe's number two automobile manufacturer.[20] PSA Peugeot Citroën is a noteworthy company, having sold 3.36 million vehicles worldwide in 2006 with continuing sales growth outside Europe, especially in Latin America and China. The company is fully aware of today's energy and environmental challenges and is focusing on reducing fuel consumption and greenhouse gas emissions. Recently, management decided that if the company's lofty goals were to be reached, management skills in the areas of motivating and inspiring work teams had to be improved. As a result, the company designed and is offering a special training program to its managers covering topics such as managing people, managing within the team, motivating the individual worker, and communication and coaching. Through this program, the company hopes to increase the skills of its managers in people-oriented areas.

Management Skill: A Classic View

Robert L. Katz has written perhaps the most widely accepted early article about management skill.[21] Katz states that managers' ability to perform is a result of their managerial skills. A manager with the necessary management skills will probably perform well and be relatively successful. One without the necessary skills will probably perform poorly and be relatively unsuccessful.

Katz indicates that three types of skills are important for successful management performance: technical, human, and conceptual skills.

- **Technical skills** involve the ability to apply specialized knowledge and expertise to work-related techniques and procedures. Examples of these skills are engineering, computer programming, and accounting. Technical skills are mostly related to working with "things"—processes or physical objects.

- **Human skills** build cooperation within the team being led. They involve working with attitudes and communication, individual and group interests—in short, working with people.

Technical skills, such as those one of these paper manufacturing employees is teaching the other, are among the types of skills necessary for successful management.

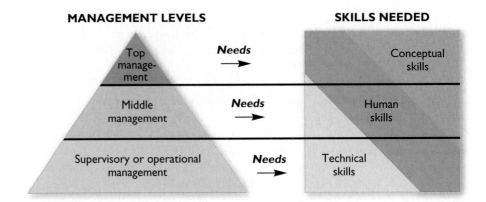

FIGURE 1.7
As a manager moves from the supervisory to the top-management level, conceptual skills become more important than technical skills, but human skills remain equally important

- **Conceptual skills** involve the ability to see the organization as a whole. A manager with conceptual skills is able to understand how various functions of the organization complement one another, how the organization relates to its environment, and how changes in one part of the organization affect the rest of the organization.

As one moves from lower-level management to upper-level management, conceptual skills become more important and technical skills less important (see Figure 1.7). The supportive rationale is that as managers advance in an organization, they become less involved with the actual production activity or technical areas and more involved with guiding the organization as a whole. Human skills, however, are extremely important to managers at top, middle, and lower (or supervisory) levels.[22] The common denominator of all management levels, after all, is people.

Management Skill: A Contemporary View

More current thought regarding management skills is essentially an expansion of the classic view list of skills that managers need in order to be successful. This expansion is achieved logically through two steps:

1. Defining the major activities that managers typically perform
2. Listing the skills needed to carry out these activities successfully

The major activities that modern managers typically perform are of three basic types.[23]

1. **Task-related activities** are management efforts aimed at carrying out critical management-related duties in organizations. Such activities include short-term planning, clarifying objectives of jobs in organizations, and monitoring operations and performance.
2. **People-related activities** are management efforts aimed at managing people in organizations. Such activities include providing support and encouragement to others, providing recognition for achievements and contributions, developing skill and confidence of organization members, consulting when making decisions, and empowering others to solve problems.
3. **Change-related activities** are management efforts aimed at modifying organizational components. Such activities include monitoring the organization's external environment, proposing new strategies and vision, encouraging innovative thinking, and taking risks to promote needed change.

Important management skills deemed necessary to carry out these management activities successfully appear in Figure 1.8. This figure pinpoints 12 such skills, ranging from empowering organization members to envisioning how to change an organization. Remember that Figure 1.8 is not intended as a list of *all* skills that managers need to be successful, but as

To increase the probability of being successful, managers should have competence in . . .

. . . Clarifying roles: assigning tasks and explaining job responsibilities, task objectives, and performance expectations

. . . Monitoring operations: checking on the progress and quality of the work, and evaluating individual and unit performance

. . . Short-term planning: determining how to use personnel and resources to accomplish a task efficiently, and determining how to schedule and coordinate unit activities efficiently

. . . Consulting: checking with people before making decisions that affect them, encouraging participation in decision making, and using the ideas and suggestions of others

. . . Supporting: acting considerate, showing sympathy and support when someone is upset or anxious, and providing encouragement and support when there is a difficult, stressful task

. . . Recognizing: providing praise and recognition for effective performance, significant achievements, special contributions, and performance improvements

. . . Developing: providing coaching and advice, providing opportunities for skill development, and helping people learn how to improve their skills

. . . Empowering: allowing substantial responsibility and discretion in work activities, and trusting people to solve problems and make decisions without getting prior approval

. . . Envisioning change: presenting an appealing description of desirable outcomes that can be achieved by the unit, describing a proposed change with great enthusiasm and conviction

. . . Taking risks for change: taking personal risks and making sacrifices to encourage and promote desirable change in the organization

. . . Encouraging innovative thinking: challenging people to question their assumptions about the work and consider better ways to do it

. . . External monitoring: analyzing information about events, trends, and changes in the external environment to identify threats and opportunities for the organizational unit

FIGURE 1.8
Skills for increasing the probability of management success

an important list containing many of the necessary skills. One might argue, for example, that skills such as building efficient operations or increasing cooperation among organization members are critical management skills and should have prominence in Figure 1.8.

Management Skill: A Focus of This Book

The preceding sections discussed both classic and contemporary views of management skills in modern organizations. A number of critical management skills were presented and related to top, middle, and supervisory management positions.

One common criticism of such management skill discussions is that although understanding such rationales about skills is important, skills categories—such as technical skill, human skill, and conceptual skill—are often too broad to be practical. Many management scholars believe that these broad skills categories contain numerous more narrowly focused skills that represent the more practical and essential abilities for successfully practicing management.[24] These more narrowly focused skills should not be seen as valuable in themselves, but as "specialized tools" that help managers to meet important challenges and successfully carry out the management functions of planning, organizing, influencing, and controlling. Table 1.2 summarizes the management functions and challenges covered in this book and corresponding management skills that help address them.

Because management skill is generally a prerequisite for management success, aspiring managers should strive to develop such skill. In developing such skill, however, managers should keep in mind that the value of individual management skills will tend to vary from manager to manager, depending upon the specific organizational situations faced. For example, managers facing serious manufacturing challenges might find that the skill to encourage

TABLE 1.2	Management Functions and Challenges Covered in This Text and Corresponding Management Skills Emphasized to Help Address Them

Introduction To Modern Management

Chapter 1—Management Skill: The ability to work with people and other organizational resources to accomplish organizational goals.

Chapter 2—Comprehensive Management Skill: The ability to collectively apply concepts from various major management approaches to performing a manager's job.

Modern Management Challenges

Chapter 3—Corporate Social Responsibility Skill: The ability to take action that protects and improves both the welfare of society and the interests of the organization.

Chapter 4—Diversity Skill: The ability to establish and maintain an organizational workforce that represents a combination of assorted human characteristics appropriate for achieving organization success.

Chapter 5—Global Management Skill: The ability to manage global factors as components of organizational operations.

Chapter 6—Entrepreneurship Skill: Involves the identification, evaluation, and exploitation of opportunities.

Planning

Chapter 7—Planning Skill: The ability to take action to determine the objectives of the organization as well as what is necessary to accomplish these objectives.

Chapter 8—Decision-Making Skill: The ability to choose alternatives that increase the likelihood of accomplishing objectives.

Chapter 9—Strategic Planning Skill: The ability to engage in long-range planning that focuses on the organization as a whole.

Chapter 10—Planning Tools Skill: The ability to employ the qualitative and quantitative techniques necessary to help develop plans.

Organizing

Chapter 11—Organizing Skill: The ability to establish orderly uses for resources within the management system.

Chapter 12—Responsibility and Delegation Skill: The ability to understand one's obligation to perform assigned activities and to enlist the help of others to complete those activities.

Chapter 13—Human Resource Management Skill: The ability to take actions that increase the contributions of individuals within the organization.

Chapter 14—Organizational Change Skill: The ability to modify an organization in order to enhance its contribution to reaching company goals.

Influencing

Chapter 15—Communication Skill: The ability to share information with other individuals.

Chapter 16—Leadership Skill: The ability to direct the behavior of others toward the accomplishment of objectives.

Chapter 17—Motivation Skill: The ability to create organizational situations in which individuals performing organizational activities are simultaneously satisfying personal needs and helping the organization attain its goals.

Chapter 18—Team Skill: The ability to manage a collection of people so that they influence one another toward the accomplishment of an organizational objective(s).

Chapter 19—Organization Culture Skill: The ability to establish is a set of shared values of organization members regarding the functioning and existence of their organization to enhance the probability of organizational success.

Chapter 20—Creativity and Innovation Skill: The ability to generate original ideas or new perspectives on existing ideas and to take steps to implement these new ideas.

Controlling

Chapter 21—Controlling Skill: The ability to use information and technology to ensure that an event occurs as it was planned to occur.

Chapter 22—Production Skill: The ability to transform organizational resources into products.

innovative thinking aimed at meeting these challenges is their most important skill. On the other hand, managers facing a disinterested workforce might find that the skill of recognizing and rewarding positive performance is their most valuable skill. Overall, managers should spend time defining the most formidable tasks they face and sharpening skills that will help to carry out these tasks successfully.

class discussion highlight

MODERN RESEARCH AND MANAGEMENT SKILL

Skills Needed to Manage in Vietnam[25]

A recent study by Neupert, Baughn, and Dao investigated the skills necessary to be a successful manager in Vietnam. The researchers focused on the opinions of practicing managers in Vietnam in generating their list of skills for managerial success.

To gather their information, the researchers used the critical incident method. This method asked managers in an interview format to tell the story of their *worst nightmare* or *biggest challenge* in their management positions. The researchers also asked managers their opinion about what skills were necessary to be a successful manager in Vietnam.

Through this critical incident process, a commonly used research technique, the researchers hoped to identify skills necessary to be a successful manager in Vietnam.

The researchers interviewed 50 local Vietnamese managers and 24 managers from other countries. Interviews lasted between 45 and 90 minutes and were conducted in English or Vietnamese, depending upon manager preference. The managers interviewed were from a number of firms in various industries from two major Vietnamese business centers: Hanoi and Ho Chi Minh City.

Do you think that the local Vietnamese and foreign managers suggested the same skills for managerial success in Vietnam? Why? If not, how do you think that the suggested skills differed? Why?

MANAGEMENT CAREERS

Thus far, this chapter has focused on outlining the importance of management to society, presenting a definition of management and the management process, and explaining the universality of management. Individuals commonly study such topics because they are interested in pursuing a management career. This section presents information that will help you preview your own management career. It also describes some of the issues you may face in attempting to manage the careers of others within an organization. The specific focus is on career definition, career and life stages and performance, and career promotion.

A Definition of Career

A **career** is a sequence of work-related positions occupied by a person over the course of a lifetime.[26] As the definition implies, a career is cumulative in nature: As people accumulate successful experiences in one position, they generally develop abilities and attitudes that qualify them to hold more advanced positions. In general, management positions at one level tend to be stepping-stones to management positions at the next higher level. In building a career, an individual should be focused on developing skills necessary to qualify for the next planned job and not simply taking a job with the highest salary.[27]

Career Stages, Life Stages, and Performance

Careers are generally viewed as evolving through a series of stages.[28] These evolutionary stages—exploration, establishment, maintenance, and decline—are shown in Figure 1.9, which highlights the performance levels and age ranges commonly associated with each stage. Note that the levels and ranges in the figure indicate what has been more traditional at each stage, not what is inevitable. According to the projections of census takers around the world, the number of people nearing retirement in developed countries is increasing rapidly.[29] As more workers beyond age 65 exist in the workforce, more careers will be maintained beyond the traditional benchmark age of 65 depicted in Figure 1.9.

Exploration Stage   The first stage in career evolution is the **exploration stage,** which occurs at the beginning of a career and is characterized by self-analysis and the exploration of different types of available jobs. Individuals at this stage are generally about 15 to 25 years old and are involved in some type of formal training, such as college or vocational education. They often pursue part-time employment to gain a richer understanding of what a career in a particular organization or industry might be like. Typical jobs held during this stage include cooking at fast-food restaurants like Quick, stocking at a B&Q home improvement store, and working as an office assistant at an ING Group insurance office.

FIGURE 1.9
The relationships among career stages, life stages, and performance

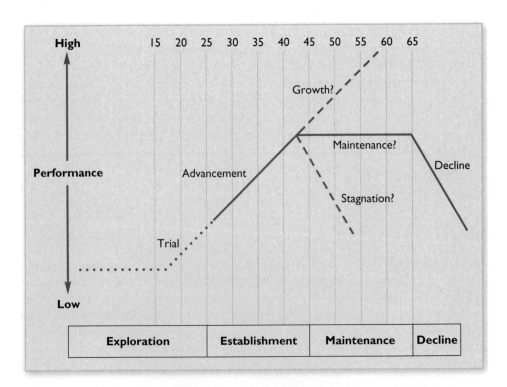

Establishment Stage The second stage in career evolution is the **establishment stage,** during which individuals about 25 to 45 years old start to become more productive, or higher performers (as Figure 1.9 indicates by the upturn in the dotted line and its continuance as a solid line). Employment sought during this stage is guided by what was learned during the exploration stage. In addition, the jobs sought are usually full-time. Individuals at this stage commonly move to different jobs within the same company, to different companies, or even to different industries.

Maintenance Stage The third stage in career evolution is the **maintenance stage.** In this stage, individuals who are about 45 to 65 years old show either increased performance (career growth), stabilized performance (career maintenance), or decreased performance (career stagnation).

From the organization's viewpoint, it is better for managers to experience career growth than maintenance or stagnation. For this reason, some companies such as IBM, Monsanto, and Brooklyn Union Gas have attempted to eliminate **career plateauing**—defined as a period of little or no apparent progress in a career.[30]

Decline Stage The last stage in career evolution is the **decline stage,** which involves people about 65 years old whose productivity is declining. These individuals are either close to retirement, semiretired, or fully retired. People in the decline stage may find it difficult to maintain prior performance levels, perhaps because they have lost interest in their careers or have failed to keep their job skills up-to-date.

As Americans live longer and stay healthier into late middle age, many of them choose to become part-time workers in businesses such as Publix supermarkets and McDonald's or in volunteer groups such as the Red Cross or Crescent. Some retired executives put their career experience to good social use by working with government-sponsored organizations such as the Service Corps of Retired Executives (SCORE) to offer management advice and consultation to small businesses trying to gain a foothold in their market.

Promoting Your Own Career

Both practicing managers and management scholars agree that careful formulation and implementation of appropriate tactics can enhance the success of a management career.[31] Planning your career path—the sequence of jobs that you will fill in the course of your working life—is the first step you need to take in promoting your career. For some people, a career path entails ascending the hierarchy of a particular organization. Others plan a career path within a particular profession or series of professions. Everyone, however, needs to recognize that career planning is an ongoing process, beginning with the career's early phases and continuing throughout the career.

In promoting your own career, you must be proactive and see yourself as a business that you are responsible for developing. You should not view your plan as limiting your options. First consider both your strengths and your liabilities and assess what you need from a career. Then explore all the avenues of opportunity open to you, both inside and outside the organization. Set your career goals, continually revise and update these goals as your career progresses, and take the steps necessary to accomplish these goals.

Another important tactic in promoting your own career is to work for managers who carry out realistic and constructive roles in the career development of their employees.[32] Table 1.3 outlines what career development responsibility, information, planning, and follow-through generally include. It also outlines the complementary career development role for a professional employee.

To enhance your career success, you must learn to be *proactive* rather than *reactive*.[33] That is, you must take specific actions to demonstrate your abilities and accomplishments. You must also have a clear idea of the next several positions you should seek, the skills you need to acquire to function appropriately in those positions, and plans for acquiring those

Promoting your own career may require you to continually demonstrate your skills and abilities. These Portaplayer, Inc. engineers in Santa Clara, CA are teleconferencing with project managers in India, although the time difference requires them to convene at 7:30 in the evening local time.

skills. Finally, you need to think about the ultimate position you want and the sequence of positions you must hold in order to gain the skills and attitudes necessary to qualify for that position.

Special Career Issues

In the business world of today, countless special issues significantly affect how careers actually develop. Two issues that have had a significant impact on career development in recent years are:

1.   Women managers
2.   Dual-career couples

The following sections discuss each of these factors.

Women Managers   Women in their roles as managers must meet the same challenges in their work environments that men do. However, because they have more recently joined the ranks of management in large numbers, women often lack the social contacts that are so important in the development of a management career. Another problem for women is that, traditionally, they have been expected to manage families and households while simultaneously handling the pressures and competition of paid

TABLE 1.3   Manager and Employee Roles in Enhancing Employee Career Development

Dimension	Professional Employee	Manager
Responsibility	Assumes responsibility for individual career development	Assumes responsibility for employee development
Information	Obtains career information through self-evaluation and data collection: What do I enjoy doing? Where do I want to go?	Provides information by holding up a mirror of reality: How manager views the employee How others view the employee How "things work around here"
Planning	Develops an individual plan to reach objectives	Helps employee assess plan
Follow-through	Invites management support through high performance on the current job by understanding the scope of the job and taking appropriate initiative	Provides coaching and relevant information on opportunities

employment. Finally, women are more likely than men to encounter sexual harassment in the workplace.

Interestingly, some management theorists believe that women may have an enormous advantage over men in future management situations.[34] They predict that networks of relationships will replace rigid organizational structures and star workers will be replaced by teams made up of workers at all levels who are empowered to make decisions. Detailed rules and procedures will be replaced by a flexible system that calls for judgments based on key values and a constant search for new ways to get the job done. Strengths often attributed to women—emphasizing interrelationships, listening, and motivating others—will be the dominant virtues in the corporation of the future.

Despite this optimism, however, some reports indicate that the proportion of men to women in management ranks seems to have changed little in the last 10 years.[35] This stabilized proportion can probably be explained by a number of factors. For example, perhaps women are not opting to move into management positions at a greater pace than men because of trade-offs they have to make, such as not having or delaying the birth of a baby. In addition, women often indicate that it's more difficult for them to move into management positions than men because of the lack of female mentors and role models in the corporate world. Table 1.4 lists seven steps that management can take to help women advance in an organization.[36]

Dual-Career Couples Because of the growing number of women at work, many organizations have been compelled to consider how dual-career couples affect the workforce.[37] The traditional scenario in which a woman takes a supporting role in the development of her spouse's career is being replaced by one of equal work and shared responsibilities for spouses. This arrangement requires a certain amount of flexibility on the part of the couple as well as the organizations for which they work. Today such burning issues as whose career takes precedence if a spouse is offered a transfer to another city and who takes the ultimate responsibility for family concerns point to the fact that dual-career relationships involve trade-offs and that it is difficult to "have it all."

How Dual-Career Couples Cope Studies of dual-career couples reveal that many cope with their career difficulties in one of the following ways.[38] The couple might develop a commitment to both spouses' careers so that when a decision is made, the right

---

TABLE 1.4	Seven Steps Management Can Take to Encourage the Advancement of Women in Organizations

1. *Make sure that women know the top three strategic goals for the company.*   Knowing these goals will help women focus their efforts on important issues. As a result, they'll be better able to make a meaningful contribution to goal attainment and become more likely candidates for promotion.

2. *Make sure that women professionals in the organization have a worthwhile understanding of career planning.*   Having a vision for their careers and a career planning tool at their disposal will likely enhance the advancement of women in an organization.

3. *Teach women how to better manage their time.*   The most effective managers are obsessed with using their time in the most valuable way possible. Helping women know where their time is being invested and how to make a better investment should better ready them for promotion.

4. *Assign outstanding mentors to women within the organization.*   Women continually indicate that mentors are important in readying themselves for promotion. Assigning outstanding leaders in an organization to women organization members should accelerate the process of readying women for management position.

5. *Have career discussions with women who have potential as managers.*   Career discussions involving both managers and women with the potential to be managers should be held regularly. Helping women to continually focus on their careers and their potential for upward mobility should help them to keep progressing toward management positions.

6. *Provide opportunities for women organization members to make contributions to the community.*   In today's environment, managers must be aware of and contribute to the community in which the organization exists. Experience within the community should help ready women for management positions.

7. *Encourage women to take the initiative in obtaining management positions.*   Women must be proactive in building the skills necessary to become a manager or be promoted to the next level of management. They should set career goals, outline a plan to achieve those goals, and then move forward with their plan.

of each spouse to pursue a career is taken into consideration. Both husband and wife are flexible about handling home- and job-oriented issues. They work out coping mechanisms, such as negotiating child care or scheduling shared activities in advance, to better manage their work and their family responsibilities. Often, dual-career couples find that they must limit their social lives and their volunteer responsibilities in order to slow their lives to a manageable pace. Finally, many couples find that they must take steps to consciously facilitate their mutual career advancement. An organization that wants to retain an employee may find that it needs to assist that employee's spouse in his or her career development as well.

{CHALLENGE CASE SUMMARY

The information just presented furnishes you, as CEO of Universal Studios, with insights concerning the significance of your role as manager. That role is important not only to society as a whole but to you as an individual. As a manager, you contribute to creating the standard of living that we all enjoy, and you earn corresponding rewards. Universal Studios is making societal contributions aimed at providing essentials such as food and clothing to people throughout the world. As its CEO, you would be helping Universal Studios in this endeavor. If you exert significant impact, the company's contribution to society, and your personal returns, will be heightened considerably.

The chapter emphasizes what management is and what managers do. According to this information, as CEO at Universal Studios, you must have a clear understanding of the company's objectives, and you must guide its operations in a way that helps the company reach those objectives. This guidance will involve your working directly with sales managers, other upper managers such as the vice president of human resources, and theme park personnel.

You must be sure that planning, organizing, influencing, and controlling are being carried out appropriately. You must be sure that jobs are designed to reach objectives, that these jobs are assigned to appropriate workers, that workers are encouraged to perform their jobs well, and that you make any changes necessary to ensure the achievement of company objectives. As you perform these four functions, remember that the activities themselves are interrelated and must blend together appropriately. Your wise use of Universal's organizational resources is critical. Strive to make sure that Universal managers are both effective and efficient, reaching company objectives without wasting company resources.

As is the case with managers of any company, the managers at Universal are at various stages of career development. As an example of how those stages might relate to managers at Universal, let us focus on one particular manager, Martin Plane. Assume that Martin Plane is a manager overseeing park visitor relations. He is 45 years old and is considered a member of middle management.

Plane began his career (exploration stage) in college by considering various areas of study and by working at a number of different types of part-time positions. He delivered pizzas for Domino's Pizza and worked for Scott's, a lawn care company. He began college at age 18 and graduated when he was 22.

Plane then moved into the establishment stage of his career. For a few years immediately after graduation, he held full-time trial positions in the retail industry as well as in the delivery industry. What he had learned during the career exploration stage helped him choose the types of full-time trial positions to pursue.

At the age of 26, he accepted a trial position as an assistant park visitor relations manager at Universal Studios in Orlando, Florida. Through this position he discovered that he wanted to remain in the theme park industry and more specifically with Universal Studios. From age 27 to age 45, he held a number of supervisory and management positions at Universal.

Now Plane is moving into an extremely critical part of his career, the maintenance stage. He could probably remain in his present position and maintain his productivity for several more years. However, he wants to advance his career. Therefore, he must emphasize a proactive attitude by formulating and implementing tactics aimed at enhancing his career success, such as seeking training to develop critical skills, or moving to a position that is a prerequisite for other, more advanced positions at Universal Studios.

In the future, as Plane approaches the decline stage of his career, it is probable that his productivity will decrease somewhat. From a career viewpoint, he may want to go from full-time employment to semiretirement. Perhaps he could work for Universal Studios or another theme park business such as Disney World on a part-time advisory basis or even pursue part-time work

in another industry. For example, he might be able to teach a management course at a nearby community college.

Focusing on developing management skills throughout a career would help any manager, including Plane, to ensure management success. Such skills include the ability to clarify organizational roles, encourage innovative thinking, and recognize worthwhile performance of organization members. Overall, such skills would help Plane to carry out task-, people-, and change-related activities.

MANAGEMENT SKILL ACTIVITIES

This section is specially designed to help you develop management skill. An individual's management skill is based upon an understanding of management concepts and the ability to apply those concepts in various organizational situations. The following activities are designed to both heighten your understanding of management concepts and to develop the ability to apply those concepts in a variety of organizational situations.

UNDERSTANDING MANAGEMENT CONCEPTS

This section is comprised of activities that will sharpen your understanding of management concepts. Answer essay questions as completely as possible. Also, remember that many additional true/false and multiple choice questions appear online at MyManagementLab.com to help you further refine your understanding of management concepts.

Essay Questions

1. Explain the relationships among the four functions of management.

2. How can controlling help a manager to become more efficient?

3. What is the value in having managers at the career exploration stage within an organization? Why? The decline stage? Why?

4. Discuss your personal philosophy for promoting the careers of women managers within an organization. Why do you hold this philosophy? Explain any challenges that you foresee in implementing this philosophy within a modern organization. How will you overcome these challenges?

5. List and define five skills that you think you'll need as CEO of a company. Why will these skills be important to possess?

Developing Management Skill

Learning activities in this section are aimed at helping you to develop management skill. Learning activities include Exploring Your Management Skill: Part 2, Your Management Skill Portfolio exercise, an experiential exercise, cases, and a VideoNet exercise.

EXPLORING YOUR MANAGEMENT SKILL: PART 2

As you recall, you completed Exploring Your Management Skill before you started to study this chapter. Your responses gave you an idea of how much you initially knew about modern management and helped you to focus on important points as you studied the chapter. Answer the Exploring Your Management Skill questions again now (p. 28) and compare your score to the first time you took it so that you get an idea of how much you have learned from studying this chapter and pinpoint areas for further clarification before you start studying the next chapter. Record your answers within the text or online at MyManagementLab.com. Completing the survey on MyManagementLab.com will allow you to grade and compare your test scores automatically. If you complete the test in the book, look up answers in the Exploring Your Management Skill section at the end of the book.

YOUR MANAGEMENT SKILLS PORTFOLIO

Your Management Skills Portfolio is a collection of activities specially designed to demonstrate your management knowledge and skill. By completing these activities online at MyManagementLab.com, you will be able to print, complete with cover sheet, as many activities as you choose. Be sure to save your work. Taking your printed portfolio to an employment interview could be helpful in obtaining a job.

*The portfolio activity for this chapter is **Managing the Blind Pig Bar**. Read the highlight about the Blind Pig and complete the activities that follow.*

You have just been hired as the manager of the Blind Pig, a bar in Cleveland, Ohio.[39] The Blind Pig has a local bar feel with downtown style, has 42 beers on tap, and offers games such as darts, foosball, and Silver Strike Bowling. Also available is a DJ to provide music and encourage dancing. Thursdays are Neighborhood & Industry Appreciation nights with half-priced drinks for those living or working in the area.

Given your five years of managerial experience in a similar bar in Cleveland, you know that managing a bar or club is a high-profile job. You also know that even with 12 employees, as manager you'll sometimes have to do everything from carrying kegs of beer up flights of stairs to handling irate customers. Naturally, as manager, you'll be responsible for the smooth bar operations and bar profitability. You start your new job in two weeks.

To get a head start on managing the Blind Pig, you decide to develop a list of issues within the bar that you'll check upon your arrival. You know that for your list to be useful, it must include issues related to bar planning, organizing, influencing, and controlling. Fill out the following form to indicate issues related to each management function that you'll check upon your arrival at the Blind Pig.

PLANNING ISSUES TO INSPECT

Example: The type of scheduling system used.

1. _____

2. _____

3. _____

4. _____

5. _____

Organizing Issues to Inspect

1. _____

2. _____

3. _____

4. _____

5. _____

Influencing Issues to Inspect

1. _____

2. _____

3. _____

4. _____

5. _____

Controlling Issues to Inspect

1. _____

2. _____

3. _____

4. _____

5. _____

Assuming that you change the scheduling system used at the Blind Pig, explain how that change affects your organizing, influencing, and controlling activities.

EXPERIENTIAL EXERCISE: ASSESSING INEFFICIENCY AT RYAN HOMES

Directions. Read the following scenario and then perform the listed activities. Your instructor may want you to perform the activities as an individual or within groups. Follow all of your instructor's directions carefully.

Ryan Homes is a home building company that has been building homes in more than 10 states in the northeastern part of the United States. The company has been in business since 1948 and has built major housing developments in Michigan, Ohio, Pennsylvania, and Virginia.

Your group, the newly established Ryan Homes Efficiency Team, is searching for ways to make your company more efficient. More specifically, you are to focus on making carpenters more efficient workers. In your company, the job of a carpenter is described as follows:

Carpenters are craftsmen who build things. The occupation rewards those who can combine precise detail work with strenuous manual labor. For Ryan, carpenters are involved with erecting and maintaining houses. Carpenters turn blueprints and plans into finished houses. Ryan's carpenters work with supervisors and construction managers on the production of houses containing different materials including fiberglass, drywall, plastic, and wood. Carpenters use saws, tape measures, drills, and sanders in their jobs. The job of a carpenter can entail long hours of physical labor in sometimes unpleasant circumstances. The injury rate among carpenters is above average. Some carpenters work indoors and are involved in maintenance and refinishing; others are involved in the creation frame and infrastructure.

Your team is to list five possible ways that carpenters at Ryan homes might be inefficient. In addition, assuming that each of your possible ways is a reality, suggest a corresponding action(s) that the company might take to eliminate this inefficiency.

CASES

NEW HARRY POTTER PARK AT UNIVERSAL

"New Harry Potter Park at Universal" (p. 27) and its related Challenge Case Summary were written to help you better understand the management concepts contained in this chapter. Answer the following discussion questions about the introductory case to better understand how fundamental management concepts can be applied in a company such as Universal Studios.

1. Do you think it will be difficult for you to become a successful manager? Explain.
2. What do you think you would like most about being a manager? What would you like least?
3. The case indicates that Tom Williams, chairperson at Universal, will face the challenge of building the new Harry Potter theme park. Assuming that you are Williams, list and describe five activities that you think you will have to perform as part of this job.

MANAGING ZINGERMAN'S COMMUNITY OF BUSINESSES

Read the following case and answer the questions. Studying this case will help you better understand how concepts relating to fundamental management concepts can be applied in a company such as Zingerman's Delicatessen.

In 1982, when Paul Saginaw and Ari Weinzweig opened Zingerman's Delicatessen in Ann Arbor, their goal was to make the best pastrami sandwich in Michigan—and beyond. "We wanted people to say about other sandwiches, 'This is a great sandwich, but it's not a Zingerman's,'" Saginaw says. By 1992, the deli was a popular Detroit Street destination, drawing crowds of food-lovers to its historic brick building near the local farmers market. That year, one of the deli managers helped open Zingerman's Bakehouse to provide the deli with fresh-baked breads and desserts.

However, even with the new bakery, annual sales were stagnating at the $5 million mark, and Saginaw feared that management complacency would allow competitors to take a bigger bite out of Zingerman's future sales and profits. The cofounders were unsure whether to keep their business small and local or to pursue a growth strategy. Could they move beyond the deli's roots without sacrificing the quality, intense customer focus, employee commitment, and community spirit that had made Zingerman's successful?

Saginaw and Weinzweig spent two years debating their company's direction. Arguing for change, Saginaw wanted to try new things and expand, possibly by opening delis in other cities. His partner understood the business case for growth but resisted the chain approach because he believed that trying to replicate the original would dilute the deli's uniqueness. The two continued to discuss alternatives and finally settled on a long-term concept they called the Zingerman's Community of Businesses. They envisioned a group of 12–15 businesses located in and around Ann Arbor, offering goods and services related to or in some way supporting Zingerman's Deli. "The key was having partners who were real owners," Weinzweig notes. "We wanted people who had visions of their own. Otherwise, whatever we did would be mediocre, and the whole idea was to elevate the quality of each element of the company." After the cofounders announced their plan in a letter to all employees, they found that not everyone agreed with the new direction. Faced with major changes to the company's culture, structure, and expectations, 80 percent of Zingerman's managers left during the first 18 months.

Saginaw and Weinzweig persisted and today, the Zingerman's Community of Businesses rings up more than $20 million annually from proceeds of the deli and bakery plus a mail order/Internet sales unit, a catering unit, a creamery, a restaurant, a mobile sandwich stand, a coffee company, and a training business. After the initial exodus of managers, the firm began attracting talented managers interested in new challenges. Consider Maggie Bayless, who worked at Zingerman's when the deli first opened. She left to complete an MBA and became a training consultant to corporations, but she wasn't completely satisfied: "I missed feeling that what I did was making a difference."

In 1994, Bayless returned to help Saginaw and Weinzweig start Zingerman's Training (ZingTrain), which shares the founders' management and food-service expertise through seminars and consulting. ZingTrain offers courses such as "3 Steps to Great Service" and "5 Steps to Implementing Change" for internal managers and for outside customers as well. Bayless remains excited about her work because "the more we share, the more we learn." Many ZingTrain customers take one course, go back to their jobs to apply what they learn, and then enroll in another. "Every time I go, I'm reenergized and recharged," comments the training coordinator of Michigan's First National Bank, which distinguishes itself on the basis of personal service.

Zingerman's, which *Inc.* magazine recently declared "The coolest small company in America," has not stopped growing. It currently employs more than 330 people and opens a new business approximately every 18 months. Just as important, Weinzweig and Saginaw are having fun and making money without compromising the principles that made their deli a regular stop for avid pastrami lovers all around Ann Arbor.

QUESTIONS

1. Which of the skills listed in Figure 1.8 did the cofounders apply when they made and implemented the decision to expand into the Zingerman's Community of Businesses?
2. Why was it important for Zingerman's to expand as a way to provide opportunities for employee and managers to develop their careers?
3. On which of the four types of resources do you think Saginaw and Weinzweig rely most heavily when planning a new business? Explain.

VIDEONET EXERCISE

Motivation: Ernst & Young

VIDEO HIGHLIGHTS

Ernst & Young, the third-largest U.S. accounting firm, increased its employee retention rate by 5 percent as a result of an HR initiative to put "People First." By creating a feedback-rich culture, building great resumes for its 160,000 people in New York City and around the world, and giving them time and freedom to pursue personal goals, Ernst & Young has reaped the benefits of a highly motivated workforce. The company uses mandatory goal setting, provides people with learning opportunities in areas of interest, and measures HR processes using an employee survey to evaluate the workplace environment.

While conceding that everyone is somewhat motivated by money, Jim Freer, Americas Vice Chair of People, believes that the way a person is treated is the determining factor in a person's level of performance.

Discussion Questions

1. Individual careers typically go through many different stages. How has Ernst & Young helped to encourage their employees to pass through these stages without leaving the company?
2. Robert Katz indicates three types of important managerial skills. According to the video, which of these is prioritized within the culture of Ernst & Young?
3. Using the four functions of management to analyze this video clip, which function is best displayed by the management team of Ernst & Young?

Internet Activity

Browse the Ernst & Young Web site at www.ey.com. Roam around the site. Look at the services offered, the career opportunities in your area, etc. Now click on the "About Us" link. Once there, read the statements listed about developing people. Next, follow the link listed on the right side of the page to "Our Values." Is this values statement consistent with the video clip? Of the four basic organizational resources, which does this statement emphasize? Would you be interested in working for this company? And if so, why?

2

Managing

HISTORY AND CURRENT THINKING

OBJECTIVES

TO HELP BUILD MY COMPREHENSIVE MANAGEMENT SKILL, WHEN STUDYING THIS CHAPTER, I WILL ATTEMPT TO ACQUIRE:

1. An understanding of the classical approach to management

2. An appreciation for the work of Frederick W. Taylor, Frank and Lillian Gilbreth, Henry L. Gantt, and Henri Fayol

3. An understanding of the behavioral approach to management

4. An understanding of the studies at the Hawthorne Works and the human relations movement

5. An understanding of the management science approach to management

6. An understanding of how the management science approach has evolved

7. An understanding of the system approach to management

8. Knowledge about the learning organization approach to management

9. An understanding of how triangular management and the contingency approach to management are related

TARGET SKILL comprehensive management skill: the ability to collectively apply concepts from various major management approaches to performing a manager's job

CHALLENGE CASE

HANDLING COMPETITORS AT BURGER KING

Burger King is a fast-food hamburger restaurant. Recent reports indicate that the company owns or franchises a total of 11,129 restaurants in 65 different countries, Burger King restaurants feature flame-broiled hamburgers, chicken, and other specialty sandwiches. Overall, the menu consists of hamburgers, cheeseburgers, and chicken and fish sandwiches. The menu also includes french fries, onion rings, salads, and desserts. Burger King is also known for its array of breakfast items.

Burger King and other fast-food companies are facing new competition from unlikely rivals. Specifically, "quick casual" restaurants, including Subway Sandwiches, Chipotle Mexican Grill, Cosi, and Panera Bread, are offering healthier food at higher prices. This combination has helped restaurants in this category to steal away traditional fast-food customers. Although executives in the fast-food industry initially believed that these new restaurants were attracting only older customers who could afford to pay higher prices, recent research reveals that the quick casual concept appeals to individuals between 18 and 34 years old, a key demographic for the fast-food industry.

One way Burger King management is trying to better compete is to operate the company in a way that is consistent with concerns of a customers in a modern society. For example, Burger King attacked this new competition by adding its own with healthier food offerings. The Chicken Whopper and a new Veggie Burger are examples of healthier meal alternatives. More recently, the company is offering other more socially conscious choices to customers. For example, in what animal welfare advocates are describing as a "historic advance," Burger King, the world's second-largest hamburger chain, has begun buying eggs and pork from suppliers that do not confine their animals in cages and crates.[1]

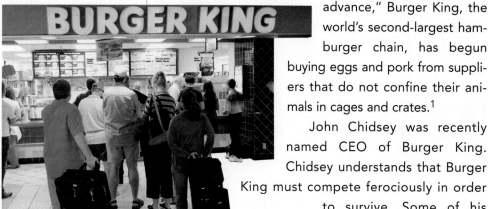

In the highly competitive fast-food market, Burger King managers use many management tools to attract and keep loyal customers, like these travelers at Miami Airport.

John Chidsey was recently named CEO of Burger King. Chidsey understands that Burger King must compete ferociously in order to survive. Some of his future challenges will be more traditional like building and maintaining store efficiency, while others will reflect more contemporary issues, such as managing the caloric content of the Burger King menu,[2] and dealing with illegal immigrant laborers.[3] For sure, Chidsey will have to meet these challenges by managing comprehensively, applying various management concepts collectively to management problems. For Burger King to be successful, Chidsey will have to successfully apply his comprehensive management skill.

"EXPLORE YOUR OWN MANAGEMENT SKILLS BY TAKING THE QUIZ ON THE NEXT PAGE"

Before studying this chapter, respond to the following questions regarding the type of advice that you would give to Burger King's CEO, John Chidsey, referenced in the Challenge Case. Then address the concerning comprehensive management skill challenges that he presently faces within the company. You are not expected to be a comprehensive management skill expert at this point. Answering the questions now can help you focus on important points when you study the chapter. Also, answering the questions again after you study the chapter will give you an idea of how much you have learned.

Record your answers here or online at MyManagement Lab.com. Completing the questions at MyManagement Lab.com will allow you to get feedback about your answers automatically. If you answer the questions in the book, look up answers in the Exploring Your Management Skill section at the end of the book.

FOR EACH STATEMENT CIRCLE:

- "Y" if you would give the advice to Chidsey.
- "N" if you would NOT give the advice to Chidsey.
- "NI" if you have no idea whether you would give the advice to Chidsey.

Mr. Chidsey, in meeting your comprehensive management skill challenges at Burger King, you should . . .

Before Study	After Study

1. keep in mind that there is probably "one best" way to do restaurant jobs.

   Y, N, NI

2. use motion study principles to manage lower-level jobs in restaurants such as cooks, but not upper-level jobs such as vice president of marketing.

   Y, N, NI

3. divide work among Burger King workers so that they can focus on special portions of tasks.

   Y, N, NI

4. not apply insights of the classical approach to management in concert with insights from the behavioral approach.

   Y, N, NI

5. focus on understanding how to increase production at Burger King through an understanding of people.

   Y, N, NI

6. not worry about some Burger King workers influencing other workers to disregard monetary incentives you offer.

   Y, N, NI

7. continually focus on building experience in determining what action to take at Burger King, depending upon what events occur.

   Y, N, NI

8. see Burger King as a series of interdependent parts functioning as a whole.

   Y, N, NI

9. build an understanding of Burger King as a closed system.

   Y, N, NI

10. visualize Burger King system inputs as directly leading to system outputs.

    Y, N, NI

11. feel free to change Burger King system inputs after considering system outputs but not system process.

    Y, N, NI

12. continually monitor customers to determine ways to make the Burger King system more responsive to customer needs.

    Y, N, NI

13. use the triangular management model as a guideline for understanding comprehensive management skill.

    Y, N, NI

14. analyze Burger King as a group of interrelated parts that may or may not function as a whole.

    Y, N, NI

15. use systems thinking at Burger King as a foundation for building the company as a learning organization.

    Y, N, NI

THE COMPREHENSIVE MANAGEMENT SKILL CHALLENGE

The Challenge Case illustrates many different comprehensive management skill challenges that management at Burger King must strive to meet. For Burger King to be successful, management must collectively apply insights from the classical, behavioral, management science, contingency, systems, and learning organization approaches to managing. The remaining material in this chapter explains these approaches and helps you to develop your comprehensive management skill. After studying chapter concepts, read the Challenge Case Summary at the end of the chapter to gain insights about using comprehensive management skill at Burger King.

Chapter 1 focused primarily on defining *management*. This chapter presents various approaches to analyzing and reacting to management situations, each characterized by a different method of analysis and a different type of recommended action.

Over the years, a variety of different approaches to management has popped up, along with wide-ranging discussions of what each approach entails. In an attempt to simplify the discussion of the field of management without sacrificing significant information, Donnelly, Gibson, and Ivancevich combined the ideas of Koontz, O'Donnell, and Weihrich with those of Haynes and Massie, and categorized three basic approaches to management:[4]

1. Classical approach
2. Behavioral approach
3. Management science approach

The following sections build on the work of Donnelly, Gibson, and Ivancevich in presenting the classical, behavioral, and management science approaches to analyzing the management task. The contingency approach is discussed as a fourth primary approach, while the system approach is presented as a recent trend in management thinking. The learning organization is continually evolving and is discussed as the newest form for analyzing management.

THE CLASSICAL APPROACH

The **classical approach to management** was the product of the first concentrated effort to develop a body of management thought. In fact, the management writers who participated in this effort are considered the pioneers of management study. The classical approach recommends that managers continually strive to increase organizational efficiency in order to increase production. Although the fundamentals of this approach were developed some time ago, contemporary managers are just as concerned with finding the "one best way" to get the job done as their predecessors were. To illustrate this concern, notable management theorists see striking similarities between the concepts of scientific management developed many years ago and the more current management philosophy of building quality into all aspects of organizational operations.[5]

For discussion purposes, the classical approach to management can be broken down into two distinct areas. The first, lower-level management analysis, consists primarily of the work of Frederick W. Taylor, Frank and Lillian Gilbreth, and Henry L. Gantt. These individuals studied mainly the jobs of workers at lower levels of the organization. The second area, comprehensive analysis of management, concerns the management function as a whole. The primary contributor to this category was Henri Fayol. Figure 2.1 illustrates the two areas in the classical approach.

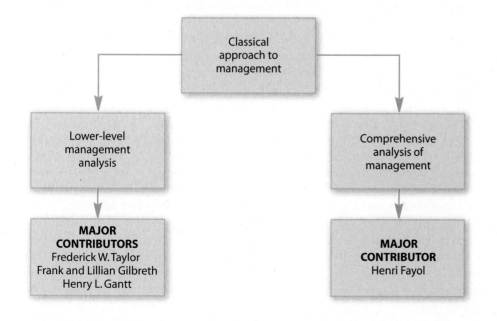

FIGURE 2.1
Division of classical approach to management into two areas and the major contributors to each area

Lower-Level Management Analysis

Lower-level management analysis concentrates on the "one best way" to perform a task; that is, it investigates how a task situation can be structured to get the highest production from workers. The process of finding this "one best way" has become known as the *scientific method of management,* or simply, **scientific management.** Although the techniques of scientific managers could conceivably be applied to management at all levels, the research, research applications, and illustrations relate mostly to lower-level managers. The work of Frederick W. Taylor, Frank and Lillian Gilbreth, and Henry L. Gantt is summarized in the sections that follow.

Frederick W. Taylor (1856–1915) Because of the significance of his contributions, Frederick W. Taylor is commonly called the "father of scientific management." His primary goal was to increase worker efficiency by scientifically designing jobs. His basic premise was that every job had one best way to do it and that this way should be discovered and put into operation.[6]

WORK AT BETHLEHEM STEEL CO. Perhaps the best way to illustrate Taylor's scientific method and his management philosophy is to describe how he modified the job of employees whose sole responsibility was shoveling materials at Bethlehem Steel Company.[7] During the modification process, Taylor made the assumption that any worker's job could be reduced to a science. To construct the "science of shoveling," he obtained answers—through observation and experimentation—to the following questions:

1. Will a first-class worker do more work per day with a shovelful of 5, 10, 15, 20, 30, or 40 pounds?
2. What kinds of shovels work best with which materials?
3. How quickly can a shovel be pushed into a pile of materials and pulled out properly loaded?
4. How much time is required to swing a shovel backward and throw the load a given horizontal distance at a given height?

As Taylor formulated answers to these types of questions, he developed insights on how to increase the total amount of materials shoveled per day. He raised worker efficiency by matching shovel size with such factors as the size of the worker, the weight of the materials, and the height and distance the materials were to be thrown. By the end of the third year after Taylor's shoveling efficiency plan was implemented, records at Bethlehem Steel showed that the total number of shovelers needed was reduced from about 600 to 140, the average number of tons shoveled per worker per day rose from 16 to 59, the average earnings per worker per day increased from $1.15 to $1.88, and the average cost of handling a long ton (2,240 pounds) dropped from $0.072 to $0.033—all in all, an impressive demonstration of the applicability of scientific management to the task of shoveling.[8]

For **an example from the world of management** relating to how modern managers might conduct efficiency studies consider **Pace Productivity,** a consulting company that offers time efficiency analysis services to managers. The company uses a proprietary instrument called a Timecorder, a handheld electronic device that allows employees to track their own time by pushing buttons associated with precoded work activities. When an employee presses a new button, time stops recording on the previous activity and begins recording on a new one. The Timecorder tracks how many times each activity occurs as well as how much time is cumulatively spent on each activity. Pace Productivity provides managers with summary reports concerning how many times work activities are performed, time spent on them, and suggestions for improving worker efficiency based upon the results of their study.

The human relations movement has made some important contributions to the study and practice of management. Advocates of this approach to management have continually stressed the need to use humane methods in managing people. Abraham Maslow, perhaps the best-known contributor to the human relations movement, believed that managers must understand the physiological, safety, social, esteem, and self-actualization needs of organization members. Douglas McGregor, another important contributor to the movement, emphasized a management philosophy built upon the views that people can be self-directed, accept responsibility, and consider work to be as natural as play.[29] The ideas of both Maslow and McGregor are discussed thoroughly in Chapter 17. As a result of the tireless efforts of theorists such as Maslow and McGregor, modern managers better understand the human component in organizations and how to appropriately work with it to enhance organizational success.

For **an example from the world of management** that illustrates management commitment to building a human-oriented work environment, consider recent events at **State Street Bank** in Quincy, in the U.S. state of Illinois. State Street Bank, founded in 1890, is the oldest community bank in Quincy. Since its founding, the bank has grown to five locations. Management believes that to serve customers well, employees must work in a human-oriented environment. One nontraditional method that management uses to create this human environment is to institute "laughing exercises" within the workplace. Because laughter is generally enjoyable and makes people feel better, employees are encouraged to attend and laugh together. Those employees who attend (on a volunteer basis) generally find the exercises invigorating; therefore, management believes that the exercises help employees to better enjoy their work environment and thereby take better care of customers.

class discussion highlight

MODERN RESEARCH AND COMPREHENSIVE MANAGEMENT SKILL

Fostering Safe Behavior Among Construction Workers[30]

The behavioral approach to management, presented as a major dimension of comprehensive management skill, emphasizes that managers should focus on solving organizational problems by incorporating a behavioral perspective into problem analysis and solution. This exercise focuses on the results of research relating to encouraging employees to act safely. Safe behavior is behavior that tends to keep employees from incurring injury while working. Although establishing a safe work environment admittedly contains classic, management science, contingency, and systems issues, this exercise focuses only on its behavioral issues.

A recent study by Teo, Ling, and Ong investigated various actions that construction site managers can use to foster safe behavior among construction site workers in Singapore. Many managers believe that

workers "don't know" and "don't care" what safe behaviors are and how to perform them. Managers would like to encourage safe behavior of workers so that projects can more easily be completed on schedule and medical costs due to injuries can be minimized. Workers are commonly injured on construction sites by falling, being struck by objects, being burned by fire, and experiencing bodily harm through explosions.

The researchers surveyed opinions of contractors in Singapore to see what they believed to be the most effective ways to increase the safe behavior of construction workers. The survey focused on three possible tools to increase this safe behavior: (1) rewarding employees for safe behavior, (2) disciplining (punishing) employees for unsafe behavior, and (3) training employees in how to be safe on a construction site. In the survey, discipline involved administering an undesired consequence when an employee performs unsafe behavior. Punishments studied include (1) fining employees who perform unsafe behaviors, (2) temporarily suspending workers performing unsafe behaviors, and (3) demoting employees who perform unsafe behaviors.

Which of these possible punishments do you think contractors seemed to value most in encouraging safe behavior of workers? Why? Which punishment do you think that they valued least? Why? Assuming that your thoughts are accurate, what hints can this research give you about developing your comprehensive management skill?

THE MANAGEMENT SCIENCE APPROACH

Churchman, Ackoff, and Arnoff define the management science, or operations research (OR), approach as (1) an application of the scientific method to problems arising in the operation of a system and (2) the solution of these problems by solving mathematical equations representing the system.[31] The **management science approach** suggests that managers can best improve their organizations by using the scientific method and mathematical techniques to solve operational problems.

The Beginning of the Management Science Approach

The management science, or operations research, approach can be traced to World War II, an era in which leading scientists were asked to help solve complex operational problems in the military.[32] The scientists were organized into teams that eventually became known as operations research (OR) groups. One OR group, for example, was asked to determine which gun sights would best stop German attacks on the British mainland. The term *management science* was actually coined by researchers of a UCLA–RAND academic complex featuring academic and industry researchers working together to solve operations problems.[33]

These early OR groups typically included physicists and other "hard" scientists who used the problem-solving method with which they had the most experience: the scientific method. The scientific method dictates that scientists:

1. Systematically *observe* the system whose behavior must be explained to solve the problem.
2. Use these specific observations to *construct* a generalized framework (a model) that is consistent with the specific observations and from which consequences of changing the system can be predicted.
3. Use the model to *deduce* how the system will behave under conditions that have not been observed but could be observed if the changes were made.
4. Finally, *test* the model by performing an experiment on the actual system to see whether the effects of changes predicted using the model actually occur when the changes are made.[34]

The OR groups proved successful at using the scientific method to solve the military's operational problems.

Management Science Today

After World War II, the world again became interested in manufacturing and selling products. The success of the OR groups in the military had been so obvious that managers were eager to try management science techniques in an industrial environment. After all, managers also had to deal with complicated operational problems.

By 1955, the management science approach to solving industrial problems had proved effective. Many people saw great promise in refining its techniques and analytical tools. Managers and universities alike pursued these refinements.

By 1965, the management science approach was being used in many companies and being applied to many diverse management problems, such as production scheduling, plant location, and product packaging.

In the 1980s, surveys indicated that management science techniques were used extensively in large, complex organizations. Smaller organizations, however, had not yet fully realized the benefits of using these techniques. Finding ways to apply management science techniques to smaller organizations is undoubtedly a worthwhile challenge for managers in the twenty-first century.[35]

Characteristics of Management Science Applications

Four primary characteristics are usually present in situations in which management science techniques are applied.[36] First, the management problems studied are so complicated that managers need help in analyzing a large number of variables. Management science techniques increase the effectiveness of the managers' decision making in such a situation. Second, a management science application generally uses economic implications as guidelines for making a particular decision, perhaps because management science techniques are best suited for analyzing quantifiable factors such as sales, expenses, and units of production.

Third, the use of mathematical models to investigate the decision situation is typical in management science applications. Models constructed to represent reality are used to determine how the real-world situation might be improved. The fourth characteristic of a management science application is the use of computers. The great complexity of managerial problems and the sophisticated mathematical analysis of problem-related information required are two factors that make computers especially valuable to the management science analyst.

Today managers use such management science tools as inventory control models, network models, and probability models to aid them in the decision-making process. Later parts of this text will outline some of these models in greater detail and illustrate their applications to management decision making. Because management science thought is still evolving, more and more sophisticated analytical techniques can be expected in the future.

THE CONTINGENCY APPROACH

In simple terms, the **contingency approach to management** emphasizes that what managers do in practice depends on, or is contingent upon, a given set of circumstances—a situation.[37] In essence, this approach emphasizes "if–then" relationships: "If" this situational variable exists, "then" a manager probably would take this action. For example, if a manager has a group of inexperienced subordinates, then the contingency approach would recommend that he or she lead in a different fashion than if the subordinates were experienced.[38]

In general, the contingency approach attempts to outline the conditions or situations in which various management methods have the best chance of success.[39] This approach is based on the premise that, although there is probably no one best way to solve a management problem in all organizations, there probably is one best way to solve any given management problem in any one organization. Perhaps the main challenges of using the contingency approach are the following:

1. Perceiving organizational situations as they actually exist
2. Choosing the management tactics best suited to those situations
3. Competently implementing those tactics

The notion of a contingency approach to management is not novel. It has become a popular discussion topic for contemporary management thinkers. The general consensus of their writings is that if managers are to apply management concepts, principles, and techniques successfully, they must consider the realities of the specific organizational circumstances they face.[40]

THE SYSTEM APPROACH

The **system approach to management** is based on general system theory. Ludwig von Bertalanffy, a scientist who worked mainly in physics and biology, is recognized as the founder of general system theory.[41] The main premise of the theory is that to understand fully the operation of an entity, the entity must be viewed as a system. A **system** is a number of interdependent parts functioning as a whole for some purpose. For example, according to general system theory, to fully understand the operations of the human body, one must understand the workings of its interdependent parts (ears, eyes, and brain). General system theory integrates the knowledge of various specialized fields so that the system as a whole can be better understood.

Types of Systems

According to von Bertalanffy, the two basic types of systems are closed systems and open systems. **Closed systems** are not influenced by, and do not interact with, their environments. They are mostly mechanical and have predetermined motions or activities that must be performed regardless of the environment. A clock is an example of a closed system. Regardless of its environment, a clock's wheels, gears, and so forth must function in a predetermined way if the clock as a whole is to exist and serve its purpose. The second type of system, the **open system,** is continually interacting with its environment. A plant is an example of an open system. Constant interaction with the environment influences the plant's state of existence and its future. In fact, the environment determines whether the plant will live.

Systems and "Wholeness"

The concept of "wholeness" is important in general system analysis. The system must be viewed as a whole and modified only through changes in its parts. Before modifications of the parts can be made for the overall benefit of the system, a thorough knowledge of how each part functions and the interrelationships among the parts must be present. L. Thomas Hopkins suggested the following six guidelines for anyone conducting system analysis:[42]

1. The whole should be the main focus of analysis, with the parts receiving secondary attention.
2. Integration is the key variable in wholeness analysis. It is defined as the interrelatedness of the many parts within the whole.
3. Possible modifications in each part should be weighed in relation to possible effects on every other part.
4. Each part has some role to perform so that the whole can accomplish its purpose.
5. The nature of the part and its function is determined by its position in the whole.
6. All analysis starts with the existence of the whole. The parts and their interrelationships should then evolve to best suit the purpose of the whole.

Because the system approach to management is based on general system theory, analysis of the management situation as a system is stressed. The following sections present the parts of the management system and recommend information that can be used to analyze the system.

The Management System

As with all systems, the **management system** is composed of a number of parts that function interdependently to achieve a purpose. The main parts of the management system are

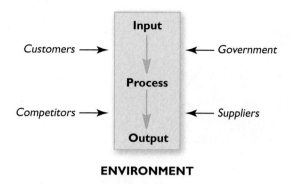

FIGURE 2.2
The open management system

organizational input, organizational process, and organizational output. As discussed in Chapter 1, these parts consist of organizational resources, the production process, and finished goods, respectively. The parts represent a combination that exists to achieve organizational objectives, whatever they may be.

The management system is an open system—that is, one that interacts with its environment (see Figure 2.2). Environmental factors with which the management system interacts include the government, suppliers, customers, and competitors. Each of these factors represents a potential environmental influence that could significantly change the future of the management system.

As **an example from the world of management** concerning how an environmental factor might impact organizational operations, consider recent events related to **e-signatures**. An e-signature is an electronic sound, symbol, or process associated with a contract and used as the legal equivalent of a written signature. A few years ago, a number of countries validated "electronic signatures" for use in doing business over the Internet. Since this validation, many companies are moving toward using e-signatures as a way to cut costs and reduce fraud. Managers must constantly be aware of how changes in the environment might impact the way an organization should function.

The critical importance of managers knowing and understanding various components of their organizations' environments is perhaps best illustrated by the constant struggle of supermarket managers to know and understand their customers. Hypermarket managers fight for the business of a national population that is growing by less than 1 percent per year. Survival requires that they know their customers better than the competition does. That is why many food retailers conduct market research to uncover customer attitudes about different kinds of foods and stores. Armed with a thorough understanding of their customers, gained from this kind of research, they hope to win business from competitors who are not benefiting from the insights made possible by such research.[43]

Information for Management System Analysis

As noted earlier, general system theory supports the use of information from many specialized disciplines to better understand a system. Information from any discipline that can increase the understanding of management system operations enhances the success of the system. Although this statement is a fairly sweeping one, managers can get this broad information from the first three approaches to management outlined in this chapter.

Thus the information used to discuss the management system in the remainder of this text comes from three primary sources:

1. Classical approach to management
2. Behavioral approach to management
3. Management science approach to management

The use of these three sources of information to analyze the management system is referred to as **triangular management.** Figure 2.3 presents the triangular management

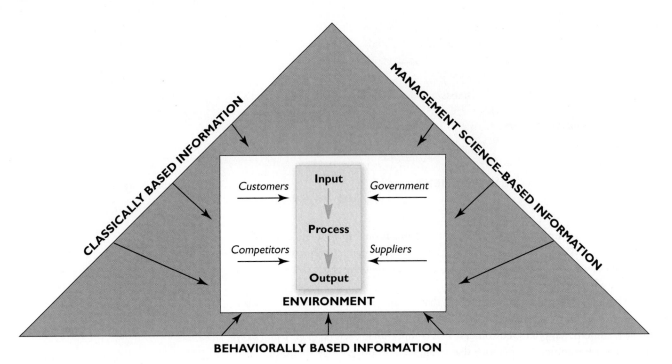

FIGURE 2.3   Triangular management model

model. The three sources of information depicted in the model are not meant to represent all the information that can be used to analyze the management system. Rather, these three types of management-related information are probably the most useful in analysis.

A synthesis of classically based information, behaviorally based information, and management science–based information is critical to effective use of the management system. This information is integrated and presented in subsequent parts of this book. These parts discuss management systems and planning (Chapters 7–10), organizing (Chapters 11–14), influencing (Chapters 15–20), and controlling (Chapters 21–22). In addition, a special part of the text focuses on modern challenges managers face when managing management systems (Chapters 3–6).

LEARNING ORGANIZATION: A NEW APPROACH?

The preceding material in this chapter provides a history of management by discussing a number of different approaches to management that have evolved over time. Each approach developed over a number of years and focused on the particular needs of organizations at the time.

In more recent times, managers seem to be searching for new approaches to management.[44] Fueling this search is a range of new issues that modern managers face but that their historical counterparts did not. These issues include a concern about the competitive decline of Western firms, the accelerating pace of technological change, the sophistication of customers, and an increasing emphasis on globalization.

A new approach to management that is evolving to handle this new range of issues can be called the *learning organization approach*. A **learning organization** is an organization that does well in creating, acquiring, and transferring knowledge, and in modifying behavior to reflect new knowledge.[45] Learning organizations emphasize systematic problem solving, experimenting with new ideas, learning from experience and past history, learning from the experiences of others, and transferring knowledge rapidly throughout the organization. Managers attempting to build a learning organization must create an environment conducive to learning and encourage the exchange of information among all organization members.[46] Honda, Corning, and General Electric are successful learning organizations.

The learning organization represents a specific, new *management paradigm,* or fundamental way of viewing and contemplating management. Peter Senge started serious discussion of learning organizations with his book *The Fifth Discipline: The Art & Practice of the Learning Organization.*[47] Senge, his colleagues at MIT, and many others have made significant progress in developing the learning organization concept. According to Senge, building a learning organization entails building five features within an organization:

1. **Systems thinking**—Every organization member understands his or her own job and how the jobs fit together to provide final products to the customer.
2. **Shared vision**—All organization members have a common view of the purpose of the organization and a sincere commitment to accomplish the purpose.
3. **Challenging of mental models**—Organization members routinely challenge the way business is done and the thought processes people use to solve organizational problems.
4. **Team learning**—Organization members work together, develop solutions to new problems together, and apply the solutions together. Working as teams rather than individuals will help organizations gather collective force to achieve organizational goals.
5. **Personal mastery**—All organization members are committed to gaining a deep and rich understanding of their work. Such an understanding will help organizations to successfully overcome important challenges that confront them.

{ CHALLENGE CASE SUMMARY

John Chidsey, the CEO of Burger King mentioned in the introductory case, could attempt to use a classical approach to management to stress organizational efficiency—the "one best way" to perform jobs at Burger King restaurants—in order to increase productivity. Focusing on efficiency could help Burger King to reduce costs, which would help the company contend with new competitors. To take a simplified example, Burger King's managers might want to check whether the dispenser used to apply mustard and ketchup is of the appropriate size to require only one squirt or whether more than one squirt is necessary to adequately cover a hamburger.

In the face of intense competition and the need to control costs, Chidsey could use motion studies to eliminate unnecessary or wasted motions by his employees. For example, are Whoppers, french fries, and drinks located for easy insertion into customer bags, or must an employee walk unnecessary steps during the sales process? Also, would certain Burger King employees be more efficient over an entire working day if they sat, rather than stood, while working?

The classical approach to management might also guide Chidsey to stress efficient scheduling. By ensuring that an appropriate number of people with the appropriate skills are scheduled to work during peak hours and that fewer such individuals are scheduled to work during slower hours, Burger King would maximize the return on labor costs.

Chidsey and other Burger King managers also might want to consider offering their employees some sort of bonus if they reach certain work goals. Management should make sure, however, that the goals it sets are realistic; unreasonable or impossible goals tend to make workers resentful and unproductive. For example, management might ask that certain employees reduce errors in filling orders by 50 percent during the next month. If and when these employees reached the goal, Burger King could give them a free lunch as a bonus.

The comprehensive analysis of organizations implies that John Chidsey might be able to further improve success at Burger King by evaluating the entire range of managerial performance—especially with regard to organizational efficiency, the handling of people, and appropriate management action. For example, Chidsey should make sure that Burger King employees receive orders from only one source (be sure that one manager doesn't instruct an employee to serve french fries moments before another manager directs the same employee to prepare milkshakes). Along the same lines, Chidsey might want to make sure that all Burger King employees are treated equally—that fry cooks, for example, don't get longer breaks than order takers.

The behavioral approach to management suggests that Chidsey strongly encourages Burger King managers to consider the people working for them and evaluate the impact of their employees' feelings and relationships on the productivity of Burger King restaurants. A Burger King manager, for example, should try to make the work more enjoyable, perhaps by allowing employees to work at different stations (grill, beverage, cash register, etc.) each day. A Burger King manager might also consider creating opportunities for employees to become more friendly with one another, perhaps through a Burger King employee picnic. In essence, the behavioral approach to management stresses that managers should recognize the human variable in their restaurants and strive to maximize its positive effects.

This chapter suggests that John Chidsey could enhance the success of Burger King by encouraging managers to use the management science approach to solve operational problems. According to the scientific method, a Burger King manager would first spend some time observing what takes place in a restaurant. Next, the manager would use these observations to outline exactly how the restaurant operates as a whole. Third, the manager would apply this understanding of Burger King's operations by predicting how various changes might help or hinder the restaurant as a whole. Before implementing possible changes, the manager would test them on a small scale to see whether they actually affected the restaurant as desired.

If Burger King's managers were to follow the contingency approach to management, their actions as managers would depend on the situation. For example, *if* some customers hadn't been served within a reasonable period because the equipment needed to make chocolate sundaes had broken down, *then* management probably would not hold employees responsible. But *if* management knew that the equipment had broken down because of employee mistreatment or neglect, *then* reaction to the situation would likely be different.

A Burger King manager could also apply the system approach and view a restaurant as a system, or a number of interdependent parts that function as a whole to reach restaurant objectives. Naturally, a Burger King restaurant would be viewed as an open system—one that exists in and is influenced by its environment. Major factors within the environment of a Burger King restaurant would be its customers, suppliers, competitors, and the government. For example, if a Burger King competitor significantly lowered its price for hamburgers to a point well below what Burger King was asking for a hamburger, Burger King management might be forced to consider modifying different parts of its restaurant system in order to meet or beat that price.

Last, a Burger King manager could apply the learning organization approach. Using this approach, a restaurant manager, for example, would see the restaurant as an organizational unit that needs to be good at creating, acquiring, and transferring knowledge, and modifying behavior to reflect new knowledge. For example, all Burger King employees at a restaurant would be involved in gathering new thoughts and ideas about running the restaurant and be on a team with management in which they possess a significant voice in establishing how the restaurant exists and operates.

MANAGEMENT SKILL ACTIVITIES

This section is specially designed to help you develop comprehensive management skill. An individual's comprehensive management skill is based upon an understanding of various approaches to management and the ability to apply that understanding to various management situations. The following activities are designed to both heighten your understanding of various approaches to management and to develop your ability to apply this understanding.

UNDERSTANDING APPROACHES TO MANAGEMENT CONCEPTS

This section is comprised of activities that will sharpen your understanding of approaches to management concepts.

Answer essay questions as completely as possible. Also, remember that many additional true/false and multiple choice questions appear online at MyManagementLab.com to help you further refine your understanding of management concepts.

Essay Questions

1. How will you be able to use the classical approach to management in your job as a manager?

2. How does Henri Fayol's contribution to management differ from the contributions of Frank and Lillian Gilbreth?

3. Discuss the primary limitation of the classical approach to management. Would this approach be more significant to managers of today than managers in the more distant past? Explain.

4. What is the "systems approach" to management? How do the concepts of closed and open systems relate to this approach?

5. Discuss the triangular management model as a tool for organizing how a manager should think about the management process.

Developing Management Skill

Learning activities in this section are aimed at helping you to develop comprehensive management skill. Learning activities include Exploring Your Management Skill: Part 2, Experiential Exercises, Cases, and a VideoNet Exercise.

EXPLORING YOUR MANAGEMENT SKILL: PART 2

As you recall, you completed Exploring Your Management Skill before you started to study this chapter. Your responses gave you an idea of how much you initially knew about various approaches to management and helped you to focus on important points as you studied the chapter. Answer the Exploring Your Management Skill questions again now (p. 54) and compare your score to the first time you took it. This comparison will give you an idea of how much you have learned from studying this chapter and pinpoint areas for further clarification before you start studying the next chapter. Record your answers within the text or online at MyManagementLab.com. Completing the survey at MyManagementLab.com will allow you to grade and compare your test scores automatically. If you complete the test in the book, look up answers in the Exploring Your Management Skill section at the end of the book.

YOUR MANAGEMENT SKILLS PORTFOLIO

Your Management Learning Portfolio is a collection of activities especially designed to demonstrate your management knowledge and skill. By completing these activities online at MyManagementLab.com, you will be able to print, complete with cover sheet, as many activities as you choose. Be sure to save your work. Taking your printed portfolio to an employment interview could be helpful in obtaining a job.

The portfolio activity for this chapter is Comprehensive Management Skill at Crocs. Read this highlight about Crocs Inc. and perform the activities that follow.

Crocs Inc. started when three Boulder, Colorado-based founders decided to develop and market an innovative type of footwear called Crocs™ shoes. Originally intended as a boating/outdoor shoe because of its slip-resistant, nonmarking sole, by 2003 Crocs had become a bona-fide phenomenon, universally accepted as an all-purpose shoe for comfort and fashion.

During 2003–2004 Crocs focused on accommodating remarkable growth while maintaining control. The company expanded its product line, added warehouses and shipping programs for speedy assembly and delivery, and hired a senior management team. Today, Crocs are available all over the world and on the Internet as the company continues to significantly expand all aspects of its business.

Despite rapid success, Crocs still stands behind its core values. The company is committed to making a lightweight, comfortable, slip-resistant, fashionable, and functional shoe that can be produced quickly and at an affordable price.

Crocs has also developed products that focus on the needs of specific industries. The company offers specialized footwear products that support the needs of the health care, hospitality, restaurant, and transportation industries. The stylish closed-toe designs, made from patented material, are nonmarking, slip resistant, and odor resistant. Ergonomically certified, company shoes provide arch support with circulation nubs designed to stimulate your feet while you work. Crocs purports that its shoes improve the health, safety, and overall well-being in the workplace.

Activity 1

You have just been appointed the new president of Crocs, Inc. To be successful, you will need to apply insights from many different approaches to management—your comprehensive management skill. Fill out the following form to help you organize your thoughts about how to examine Crocs, Inc., from a comprehensive management skill perspective.

PLANNING ISSUES TO INSPECT

Approach to Management	Issues to Be Examined at Crocs, Inc.
Behavioral Approach (managing by focusing on people)	Do employees get along with management? 1. _____ 2. _____ 3. _____ 4. _____
Systems Approach (managing by viewing the organization as a whole)	What major parts of Crocs, Inc., function together to achieve goals? 1. _____ 2. _____ 3. _____ 4. _____
Classical Approach (managing by finding the "one best way" to do jobs)	Do people have the right tools for performing their jobs? 1. _____ 2. _____ 3. _____ 4. _____

Activity 2

Assuming that you have gathered the information outlined in Activity 1, explain how the triangular management model would help you to organize your thoughts for enabling Crocs to maximize success.

_____

_____

_____

EXPERIENTIAL EXERCISE: ANALYZING A GOLF SWING

Directions. Read the following scenario and then perform the listed activities. Your instructor may want you to perform the activities as an individual or within groups. Follow all of your instructor's directions carefully.

Frank and Lillian Gilbreth recommended improving worker efficiency and effectiveness by searching for the "one best way" to perform work tasks. To discover this one best way, the Gilbreths would perform motion studies. A motion study would pinpoint those behaviors normally associated with a job well done and encourage workers to adopt those behaviors. As a result of one of the Gilbreths' motion studies, the number of motions needed to lay brick was reduced from 12 to 2. Obviously, the effectiveness and efficiency of bricklayers were significantly increased as a result of the motion study.

To gain some experience in performing a motion study, find two photos on the Internet. One photo should show Tiger Woods's golf swing and follow-through. The other photo should show an amateur's golf swing and follow-through. The form and follow-through of the amateur do not lead to the same golf success that Woods attains.

Activity 1: Compare Tiger Woods's follow-through and finish to that of the amateur. How are they the same? How are they different? Refer to specific behaviors in your comparison.

Activity 2: What advice would you give the amateur for improving his success in golf?

Activity 3: What are the strengths and limitations of your motion study results?

CASES

HANDLING COMPETITORS AT BURGER KING

"Handling Competitors at Burger King" (p. 53) was written to help you better understand the management concepts contained in this chapter. Answer the following discussion questions about the Challenge Case to better understand how concepts relating to management history can be applied in a company such as Burger King.

1. Based upon information in the introductory case, list three problems that you think future Burger King managers will have to solve.
2. What action(s) do you think the managers will have to take to solve these problems?
3. From what you know about fast-food restaurants, how easy would it be to manage a Burger King restaurant? Why?

FAMILY FEELING FACES CHALLENGES AT SMUCKER'S

Read the following case and answer the questions at the end. Studying this case will help you better understand how concepts relating to management history can be applied in a company such as Smucker's.

When Jerome M. Smucker founded his namesake company in 1897, he originally sold apple butter from the back of his horse-drawn wagon and then added a variety of fruity jams and jellies. During the 1980s, the company overtook its primary competitor, Welch's, to become the undisputed leader in jams and jellies. Now co-CEOs Tim and Richard Smucker—the founder's great-grandsons—have expanded the company's pantry of products even further. They spent $1 billion buying Jif peanut butter and Crisco shortening from Procter & Gamble and invested $840 million to acquire International Multifoods Corporation, with its Pillsbury cake mixes and frostings, Martha White flour, Hungry Jack pancake mixes, and other established brands. Yet the recent push to grow through acquisitions has also challenged the company's tradition of fostering a family feeling among the workforce, now nearly 5,000 employees strong.

For example, in 1994, just when many supermarkets began opening in-store bakeries, Smucker's agreed to buy the Mrs. Smith's frozen pie business from Kellogg. The company hoped to bring its winning recipe to other foods besides its mainstay jams and jellies, but the timing wasn't right. After two years of disappointing sales, management sold the pie business and refocused on Smucker's home-grown brands. Once Richard and Tim succeeded their father as CEO in 2001, they made a new shopping list for suitable acquisitions to expand into what Richard calls "icon brands." His brother Tim believes that "there is a limitation if you're only in one category. Growth has been one of our basic beliefs for 100 years." In short order, the co-CEOs purchased both Jif and Crisco, then arranged the Multifoods acquisition.

Today the company has become a major multinational corporation with more than $2 billion in annual sales and a multimillion-dollar marketing budget. Every day the giant Smucker's plant in Orrville, Ohio, where the company is headquartered, turns out 400,000 jars of marmalade, jams, and other spreadable treats. This factory—one of 28 factories in North America—along with the four overseas plants supply Smucker's foods to grocery stores in 60 countries. The Multifoods acquisition alone brought 2,300 additional employees into the Smucker's family.

For more than a century, the company's strategies and activities have been guided by five basic values: quality, growth, ethics, independence, and people. "'People' really embodies what we are all about," Tim Smucker says. "Our growth basic belief is not just about growing the company. It's about individual growth and the respect for individual ideas. So as people are involved in the decision-making process at every level of the organization, they have a sense of satisfaction for contributing to the growth of a company as a whole and to their individual growth." This approach to managing people helped put Smucker's at the top of *Fortune* magazine's list of 100 best companies to work for in 2004.

Yet the co-CEOs have also had to lay off managers and employees as they assimilate the latest acquisitions into the Smucker's organization. The process has been challenging for a company that believes in treating its employees with respect. When laying off employees in a California plant, the corporation stressed in a public statement that "this was a difficult decision and the company is committed to being fair

and thorough throughout this process in assisting all affected employees." The co-CEOs will continue to face tough choices in a world where many hungry consumers seek out low-carbohydrate foods rather than buying the kind of high-carbohydrate treats stocked in the Smucker's pantry.

Although the current top executives have demonstrated an appetite for major acquisitions, what would previous CEOs say about the company's expansion? "They would approve 100 percent," responds Tim Smucker. "They were very adventurous. They helped get us to where we are now. Now we're taking it the next step." But what will "the next step" mean for the family feeling that has meant so much to employees and managers over the years?

QUESTIONS

1. Does the human relations movement offer any insights for the co-CEOs as they move ahead with their expansion plans?
2. From the perspective of the systems approach to management, what potential problems might Smucker's encounter as a result of having only family members serve as CEOs?
3. Can Smucker's top executives learn from the classical approach to management in the context of the company's five basic values?

VIDEONET EXERCISE

Culture: American Apparel

VIDEO HIGHLIGHTS

American Apparel (www.americanapparel.net) is the largest T-shirt manufacturer in the United States. The company champions worker's rights and environmentalism. American Apparel is a Los Angeles-based T-shirt manufacturer headed by Dov Charney. The founder and CEO is a proponent of workers rights, innovative environmental solutions, and social responsibility. In an industry notorious for sweatshops and outsourcing, American Apparel's workers are paid a living wage. American Apparel also provides an onsite masseuse, health benefits, paid vacation, internship programs, and English classes. Its T-shirts are sweatshop-free, hip, sexy, and available online and at the company's retail stores. In 2007, American Apparel finalized the merger with Endeavor Acquisition, Corp. Students should be encouraged to think about how this might impact the strength of the firm.

Discussion Questions

1. What examples do you see of Fayol's general principles of management at work in the American Apparel organization?
2. In your opinion, would Charney and American Apparel believe more in the behavioral approach or the management science approach to management? Explain your answer.
3. Which of the characteristics of the learning organization do you think is best exhibited by American Apparel?

Internet Activity

Browse American Apparel's Web site at www.americanapparel.net. Click on the link entitled "About Us." Read about some of the company's political positions and browse any of the options available to you including the online store offerings, streaming videos, and press center articles. Make a point to check out the information on "Our Workers." What new benefits are listed as being offered to employees of American Apparel that were not mentioned in the video? In your opinion, what makes this company unique? How do the principles stated on the company's Web site support the concepts of the human relations movement?

MODERN MANAGEMENT CHALLENGES

3 Corporate Social Responsibility and Business Ethics

OBJECTIVES

TO HELP BUILD MY CORPORATE SOCIAL RESPONSIBILITY SKILL, WHEN STUDYING THIS CHAPTER, I WILL ATTEMPT TO ACQUIRE:

1. A thorough understanding of the term *corporate social responsibility*

2. An ability to argue both for and against the assumption of social responsibilities by business

3. Useful strategies for increasing the social responsiveness of an organization

4. Insights into the planning, organizing, influencing, and controlling of social responsibility activities

5. A practical plan for how society can help business meet its social obligations

TARGET SKILL corporate social responsibility skill: the ability to take action that protects and improves both the welfare of society and the interests of the organization

CHALLENGE CASE

IBM PROMOTES SOCIAL RESPONSIBILITY GOALS[1]

International Business Machines (IBM) Corporation provides business solutions to customers through the use of advanced information technology such as computers, software, and management information systems. Over the past decade, IBM has been arguably one of the largest corporate contributors of cash, equipment, and people to nonprofit organizations and educational institutions around the world. The company's central social responsibility focus is on helping people use information technology to improve the quality of life for themselves and others.

IBM believes that information technology innovations that are revolutionizing businesses can provide important break-throughs for improving the welfare of society as a whole. These innovations have the potential to help organizations in all segments of society to deliver better services, manage costs, maximize effectiveness, and implement exciting new programs.

Company commitment to providing solutions-oriented innovation for these organizations involves both monetary contributions and working hand-in-hand with the organizations themselves to design technology solutions that address specific problems. IBM's social responsibility activities are diverse and include a focus on improving education, enhancing the arts and culture, maintaining and improving the environment, and helping communities in need.

IBM is a long-standing corporate supporter of nonprofit and educational institutions around the world. Its KidSmart program provides technology to needy children in 50 countries.

One of IBM's more notable social responsibility programs is called KidSmart. This program is currently ongoing in 50 countries around the world and aims at providing technology resources to children in remote and needy communities. KidSmart aspires to develop children's social, innovative, and cognitive skills. A new KidSmart program recently launched in Egypt provided teachers with 50 computers specially designed by toy manufacturers to be colorful and appealing to children. The computer software was translated into Arabic, and helps teachers develop children's basic skills in mathematics, science, and creative writing and thinking. Egyptian officials are especially pleased with the KidSmart program not only because it helps children learn and develop skills, but it also spreads technology awareness within underprivileged communities.

The overall message from CEO Samuel J. Palmisano is clear: IBM strives to be a socially responsible member of the communities in which it does business.

"EXPLORE YOUR OWN MANAGEMENT SKILLS BY TAKING THE QUIZ ON THE NEXT PAGE"

Before studying this chapter, respond to the following questions regarding the type of advice that you would give to IBM's CEO Samuel J. Palmisano, referenced in the Challenge Case. Then address the concerning social responsibility challenges that he presently faces within the company. You are not expected to be a social responsibility expert at this point. Answering the questions now can help you focus on important points when you study the chapter. Also, answering the questions again after you study the chapter will give you an idea of how much you have learned.

Record your answers here or online at MyManagement Lab.com. Completing the questions at MyManagementLab.com will allow you to get feedback about your answers automatically. If you answer the questions in the book, look up answers in the Exploring Your Management Skill section at the end of the book.

FOR EACH STATEMENT CIRCLE:

- "Y" if you would give the advice to Palmisano.
- "N" if you would NOT give the advice to Palmisano.
- "NI" if you have no idea whether you would give the advice to Palmisano.

Mr. Palmisano, in meeting your social responsibility challenges at IBM, you should . . .

Before Study	*After Study*

1. pass the costs of social responsibility activities on to the consumer.

   Y, N, NI

2. be willing to have managers perform activities that result in good for society even though these activities might be outside the managers' normal area of expertise.

   Y, N, NI

3. require managers to perform most social responsibility activities required by law.

   Y, N, NI

4. normally require the performance of only a few social responsibility activities that benefit society but not IBM.

   Y, N, NI

5. monitor your country's health and safety bureau to keep current regarding safety and health legislation regarding conditions in nongovernmental workplaces.

   Y, N, NI

6. be socially responsible toward IBM's stakeholders.

   Y, N, NI

7. be careful to determine whether IBM has a social responsibility in a particular community before formulating and implementing programs to meet the needs of that community.

   Y, N, NI

8. put more focus on effectiveness than efficiency in carrying out social responsibility activities.

   Y, N, NI

9. determine whether the costs of performing social responsibility activities outweigh the benefits gained by performing them.

   Y, N, NI

10. implement a special planning process to focus only on formulating and implementing social responsibility activities.

    Y, N, NI

11. include environmental forecasts in determining future social responsibility activities of IBM.

    Y, N, NI

12. determine IBM's short-run social responsibility plans before determining IBM's long-run social responsibility plans.

    Y, N, NI

13. periodically perform a social audit to monitor IBM's social responsibility progress.

    Y, N, NI

14. make sure that you control social responsibility activities by making sure that they happen as planned.

    Y, N, NI

15. normally not worry about motivating IBM employees to perform social responsibility activities since "doing good works" will be enough reward.

    Y, N, NI

THE CORPORATE SOCIAL RESPONSIBILITY CHALLENGE

The Challenge Case illustrates different corporate social responsibility challenges that IBM strives to meet. The remaining material in this chapter explains corporate social responsibility concepts and helps to develop the corresponding corporate social responsibility skill that you will need to meet such challenges throughout your career. After studying chapter concepts, read the Challenge Case Summary at the end of the chapter to help you to relate chapter content to meeting corporate social responsibility challenges at IBM.

FUNDAMENTALS OF SOCIAL RESPONSIBILITY

The term *social responsibility* means different things to different people. For purposes of this chapter, however, **corporate social responsibility** is the managerial obligation to take action that protects and improves both the welfare of society as a whole and the interests of the organization. According to the concept of corporate social responsibility, a manager must strive to achieve societal as well as organizational goals.[2]

For **an example from the world of management** illustrating a manager's thoughts that are consistent with the concept of social responsibility, consider the ideas in a recent speech by **Michael E. Campbell**, top manager at **Arch Chemicals**.[3] Campbell's company excels in the production of water sanitization products. According to Campbell, water supplies are undergoing extreme swings in both developed and underdeveloped countries across the globe due to violent storms and floods. Campbell continued with the thought that water shortages are growing and in the near future will affect more than 450 million people. Also, according to Campbell, even when water is available, it is not unusual to find water sources that are too contaminated for people to drink without the risk of serious illness. Following the spirit of the social responsibility concept, Campbell pointed out that seeing both human need and, someday at least, profits, companies in the chemical industry have now begun developing a wide range of technologies that can help secure safe drinking water for the world's poor.

The amount of attention given to the area of social responsibility by both management and society has increased in recent years and probably will continue to increase.[4] The following sections present the fundamentals of social responsibility of businesses by discussing these topics:

1. The Davis model of corporate social responsibility
2. Areas of corporate social responsibility
3. Varying opinions on social responsibility
4. Conclusions about the performance of social responsibility activities by business

The Davis Model of Corporate Social Responsibility

A generally accepted model of corporate social responsibility was developed by Keith Davis.[5] Stated simply, Davis's model is a list of five propositions that describe why and how

An assistant manager at work in a Home Depot store. One area of social responsibility for Home Depot includes convincing its suppliers to protect forests in countries like Chile and Indonesia.

Source: Courtesy of Douglas Healey/*The New York Times*/Redux Pictures.

business should adhere to the obligation to take action that protects and improves the welfare of society as well as of the organization:

- **Proposition 1: Social responsibility arises from social power**—This proposition is derived from the premise that business has a significant amount of influence on, or power over, such critical social issues as minority employment and environmental pollution. In essence, the collective action of all businesses in the country primarily determines the proportion of minorities employed and the prevailing condition of the environment in which all citizens must live.

  Davis reasons that because business has this power over society, society can and must hold business responsible for social conditions that result from the exercise of this power. Davis explains that society's legal system does not expect more of business than it does of each individual citizen exercising personal power.

- **Proposition 2: Business shall operate as a two-way open system, with open receipt of inputs from society and open disclosure of its operations to the public**—According to this proposition, business must be willing to listen to what must be done to sustain or improve societal welfare. In turn, society must be willing to listen to business reports on what it is doing to meet its social responsibilities. Davis suggests that there must be ongoing, honest, and open communications between business and society's representatives if the overall welfare of society is to be maintained or improved.

- **Proposition 3: The social costs and benefits of an activity, product, or service shall be thoroughly calculated and considered in deciding whether to proceed with it**—This proposition stresses that technical feasibility and economic profitability are not the only factors that should influence business decision making. Business should also consider both the long- and short-term societal consequences of all business activities before undertaking them.

- **Proposition 4: The social costs related to each activity, product, or service shall be passed on to the consumer**—This proposition states that business cannot be expected to completely finance activities that may be socially advantageous but economically disadvantageous. The cost of maintaining socially desirable activities within business should be passed on to consumers through higher prices for the goods or services related to these activities.

- **Proposition 5: Business institutions, as citizens, have the responsibility to become involved in certain social problems that are outside their normal areas of operation**—This last proposition points out that if a business possesses the expertise to solve a social problem with which it may not be directly associated, it should be held responsible for helping society solve that problem. Davis reasons that because business eventually will reap an increased profit from a generally improved society, business should share in the responsibility of all citizenry to generally improve society.

Areas of Corporate Social Responsibility: Going Green

The areas in which business can act to protect and improve the welfare of society are numerous and diverse. Perhaps the most publicized of these areas are urban affairs, consumer affairs, community volunteerism, and employment practices. The one area that is arguably receiving the most recent attention is the area of ecology conservation, popularly called "going green."[6] An international effort sponsored by the United Nations is currently underway and growing to get large companies to start thinking seriously about ecosystems and how to maintain them. Companies are responding. For example, the Coca-Cola Company is exploring ways to maintain its bottling operation in India without using underground water; the Mohawk Home Company is developing a new line of bathroom rugs with all natural fibers;[7] and the foodmaker Kellogg's is developing environmentally sensitive products, such as its new organic cereals.[8] Pressure groups are also springing up to persuade companies to go green. One such group, The Center for

Health, Environment, and Justice, was founded and is led by a grassroots leader, Lois Gibbs.

The Modern Research and Social Responsibility Skill feature for this chapter focuses on implementing a community volunteer program within a financial services company.

class discussion highlight

MODERN RESEARCH AND SOCIAL RESPONSIBILITY SKILL

Volunteering at ABN-AMRO[9]

A recent study by Gilder, Schuyt, and Breedijk investigated the effects that employee volunteering have on the employees' attitudes and behaviors toward their employer. The researchers studied volunteerism within ABN-AMRO, a financial services company with a broad package of products and services in more than 70 different countries. The company actually established a Department of Community Involvement to provide a formal mechanism for helping employees identify and carry out volunteer activities in which they had interest. The company stipulated, however, that all volunteer activities had to focus in some way on the development of talents within young people. As stipulated by the program, an employee could spend one week on company time annually to perform his or her volunteer activities. Employees were NOT required to become volunteers. In essence, employees volunteered to be volunteers.

As one important question, researchers wanted to see whether those who did not participate in the volunteer program became somewhat disgruntled. This disgruntlement could exist because when volunteers were away from their jobs the same amount of work had to be completed within the company and those not participating in the volunteer programs would normally have to do extra work.

Do you think that the researchers found that employees NOT acting as volunteers in the community became somewhat disgruntled because of this extra work? Why? Assuming that your thoughts are accurate, what hints can this research give you about developing your *social responsibility skill*?

Varying Opinions on Social Responsibility

Although numerous businesses are already involved in social responsibility activities, much controversy remains about whether such involvement is necessary or even appropriate. The following two sections present some arguments for and against businesses performing social responsibility activities.[10]

Arguments *for* Business Performing Social Responsibility Activities

The best-known argument for the performance of social responsibility activities by business was alluded to earlier in this chapter. This argument begins with the premise that business as a whole is a subset of society, one that exerts a significant impact on the way society exists. Because business is such an influential member of society, the argument continues, it has the responsibility to help maintain and improve the overall welfare of society.[11] If society already puts this responsibility on its individual members, then why should its corporate members be exempt?

In addition, some people argue that business should perform social responsibility activities because profitability and growth go hand in hand with responsible treatment of employees, customers, and the community. This argument says, essentially, that performing social responsibility activities is a means of earning greater organizational profit.[12]

However, empirical studies have not demonstrated any clear relationship between corporate social responsibility and profitability. In fact, several companies that were acknowledged leaders in social commitment during the 1960s and 1970s—including Control Data Corporation, Atlantic Richfield, Dayton-Hudson, Levi Strauss, and Polaroid—experienced serious financial difficulties during the 1980s.[13] (No relationship between corporate social responsibility activities and these financial difficulties was shown, however.)

Arguments *Against* Business Performing Social Responsibility Activities The best-known argument against business performing social responsibility activities has been advanced by Milton Friedman, one of the world's most distinguished economists. Friedman argues that making business managers simultaneously responsible to business owners for reaching profit objectives and to society for enhancing societal welfare sets up a conflict of interest that could potentially cause the demise of business as it is known today. According to Friedman, this demise will almost certainly occur if business is continually forced to perform socially responsible actions that directly conflict with private organizational objectives.[14]

Friedman also argues that to require business managers to pursue socially responsible objectives may, in fact, be unethical, because it compels managers to spend money on some individuals that rightfully belongs to other individuals.

> In a free enterprise, private property system, a corporate executive is an employee of the owners of the business. He has direct responsibility to his employers. That responsibility is to conduct the business in accordance with their desires, which generally will be to make as much money as possible while conforming to the basic rules of society, both those embodied in law and those embodied in ethical custom. . . . Insofar as his actions reduce returns to stockholders, he is spending their money. Insofar as his actions raise the price to customers, he is spending the customers' money.[15]

An example that Friedman could use to illustrate his argument is the Control Data Corporation. Former chairman William Norris involved Control Data in many socially responsible programs that cost the company millions of dollars—from building plants in the inner city and employing a minority workforce to researching farming on the tundra. When Control Data began to incur net losses of millions of dollars in the mid-1980s, critics blamed Norris's "do-gooder" mentality. Eventually, a new chairman was installed to restructure the company and return it to profitability.[16]

Conclusions About the Performance of Social Responsibility Activities by Business

The preceding section presented several major arguments for and against businesses performing social responsibility activities. Regardless of which argument or combination of arguments particular managers embrace, they generally should make a concerted effort to do the following:

1. Perform all legally required social responsibility activities.
2. Consider voluntarily performing social responsibility activities beyond those legally required.
3. Inform all relevant individuals of the extent to which the organization will become involved in performing social responsibility activities.

Performing Required Social Responsibility Activities In some countries, legislation requires that businesses perform certain social responsibility activities. In the United States, for example, several government agencies have been established expressly to enforce such business-related legislation (see Table 3.1). The Environmental Protection Agency, for instance, has the authority to require businesses to adhere to certain socially responsible environmental standards.[17]

TABLE 3.1	Primary Functions of Several U.S. Agencies That Enforce Social Responsibility Legislation
Agency	**Primary Agency Functions**
Equal Employment Opportunity Commission	Investigates and conciliates employment discrimination complaints that are based on race, sex, or creed
Office of Contract Compliance Programs	Ensures that employers holding U.S. contracts grant equal employment opportunity to people regardless of their race or sex
Environmental Protection Agency	Formulates and enforces environmental standards in such areas as water, air, and noise pollution
Consumer Product Safety Commission	Strives to reduce consumer misunderstanding of manufacturers' product design, labeling, and so on, by promoting clarity of these messages
Occupational Safety and Health Administration	Regulates safety and health conditions in non-government workplaces
National Highway Traffic Safety Administration	Attempts to reduce traffic accidents through the regulation of transportation-related manufacturers and products
Mining Enforcement and Safety Administration	Attempts to improve safety conditions for mine workers by enforcing all mine safety and equipment standards

Voluntarily Performing Social Responsibility Activities

Adherence to legislated social responsibilities is the minimum standard of social responsibility performance that business managers must achieve. Managers must ask themselves, however, how far beyond the minimum they should go.

Determining how far to go is a simple process to describe, yet it is difficult and complicated to implement. It entails assessing the positive and negative outcomes of performing social responsibility activities over both the short and the long terms, and then performing only those activities that maximize management system success while making a desirable contribution to the welfare of society.

Events at the Sara Lee Bakery plant illustrate how company management can voluntarily take action to protect employees' health. Many employees at the plant began

Sara Lee Bakery took voluntary action to help employees who were developing the painful symptoms of carpal tunnel syndrome. Following a thorough investigation, the company asked its own engineers to design new tools for the workers that soon eliminated the symptoms.

to develop carpal tunnel syndrome, a debilitating wrist disorder caused by repeated hand motions. Instead of simply having its employees go through physical therapy—and, as the principal employer in the town in which it operated, watching the morale of the town drop—Sara Lee thoroughly investigated the problem. Managers took suggestions from factory workers and had their engineers design tools to alleviate the problem. The result was a virtual elimination of carpal tunnel syndrome at the plant within a short time.[18]

Sandra Holmes asked top executives in 560 major firms, in such areas as commercial banking, life insurance, transportation, and utilities, to state the possible negative and positive outcomes their firms could expect from performing social responsibility activities.[19] Table 3.2 lists these outcomes and indicates the percentage of executives questioned who expected them. Although this information furnishes managers with insights into how involved their organizations should become in social responsibility activities, it does not give them a clear-cut indication of what to do. Managers can determine the appropriate level of social responsibility involvement for a specific organization only by examining and reacting to specific factors related to that organization.

TABLE 3.2 Outcomes of Social Responsibility Involvement Expected by Executives and the Percent Who Expected Them	
Expected Outcomes	**Percent of Executives Expecting Them**
Positive Outcomes	
Enhanced corporate reputation and goodwill	97.4
Strengthening of the social system in which the corporation functions	89.0
Strengthening of the economic system in which the corporation functions	74.3
Greater job satisfaction among all employees	72.3
Avoidance of government regulation	63.7
Greater job satisfaction among executives	62.8
Increased chances for survival of the firm	60.7
Ability to attract better managerial talent	55.5
Increased long-term profitability	52.9
Strengthening of the pluralistic nature of society	40.3
Maintaining or gaining customers	38.2
Investor preference for socially responsible firms	36.6
Increased short-term profitability	15.2
Negative Outcomes	
Decreased short-term profitability	59.7
Conflict of economic or financial and social goals	53.9
Increased prices for consumers	41.4
Conflict in criteria for assessing managerial performance	27.2
Disaffection of stockholders	24.1
Decreased productivity	18.8
Decreased long-term profitability	13.1
Increased government regulation	11.0
Weakening of the economic system in which the corporation functions	7.9
Weakening of the social system in which the corporation functions	3.7

Communicating the Degree of Social Responsibility Involvement

Determining the extent to which a business should perform social responsibility activities beyond legal requirements is a subjective process. Despite this subjectivity, however, managers should have a well-defined position in this vital area and should inform all organization members of that position.[20] Taking these steps will ensure that managers and organization members behave consistently to support the position and that societal expectations of what a particular organization can achieve in this area are realistic.

Nike, the world famous athletic-gear manufacturer, recently felt so strongly that its corporate philosophy on social responsibility issues should be clearly formulated and communicated that the company created a new position, vice president of corporate and social responsibility. Maria Eitelto, a former public-relations executive at Microsoft, was hired to fill that position and is now responsible for clearly communicating Nike's thoughts on social responsibility both inside and outside the organization.[21]

class discussion highlight

SOCIAL RESPONSIBILITY SKILL AND YOUR CAREER

The preceding information implies that managers should communicate to other organization members the extent to which their organizations will be involved in performing social responsibility activities. Could the lack of such communication hinder your career success as a manger? Explain. As president of the school in which you are presently enrolled taking this management class, what would you say to professors and students regarding the overall position on social responsiblity that *you* would like for the school to embrace? What specific activities should be pursued corresponding to this position?

SOCIAL RESPONSIVENESS

The previous section discussed social responsibility, a business's obligation to take action that protects and improves the welfare of society along with the business's own interests. This section defines and discusses **social responsiveness,** the degree of effectiveness and efficiency an organization displays in pursuing its social responsibilities.[22] The greater the degree of effectiveness and efficiency, the more socially responsive the organization is said to be. The next three sections take up the following issues:

1. Determining whether a social responsibility exists
2. Social responsiveness and decision making
3. Approaches to meeting social responsibilities

Determining Whether a Social Responsibility Exists

One challenge facing managers who are attempting to be socially responsive is to determine which specific social obligations are implied by their business situation. Managers in the tobacco industry, for example, are probably socially obligated to contribute to public health by pushing for the development of innovative tobacco products that do less harm to people's health than present products do, but they are not socially obligated to help reclaim shorelines contaminated by oil spills.

Clearly, management has an obligation to be socially responsible toward its stakeholders. **Stakeholders** are all those individuals and groups that are directly or indirectly affected by an organization's decisions.[23] Managers of successful organizations typically have many different stakeholders to consider: stockholders, or owners of the organization; suppliers; lenders; government agencies; employees and unions; consumers; competitors; and local

TABLE 3.3	Stakeholders of a Typical Modern Organization and Examples of Social Obligations Managers Owe to Them
Stakeholder	**Social Obligations Owed**
Stockholders/owners of the organization	To increase the value of the organization
Suppliers of materials	To deal with them fairly
Banks and other lenders	To repay debts
Government agencies	To abide by laws
Employees and unions	To provide safe working environment and to negotiate fairly with union representatives
Consumers	To provide safe products
Competitors	To compete fairly and to refrain from restraints of trade
Local communities and society at large	To avoid business practices that harm the environment

communities as well as society at large. Table 3.3 lists these stakeholders and gives a corresponding example of how a manager is socially obligated to each of them.

Social Responsiveness and Decision Making

The socially responsive organization that is both effective and efficient meets its social responsibilities without wasting organizational resources in the process. Determining exactly which social responsibilities an organization should pursue and then deciding how to pursue them are the two most critical decisions for maintaining a high level of social responsiveness within an organization.

Figure 3.1 is a flowchart that managers can use as a general guideline for making social responsibility decisions that enhance the social responsiveness of their organization. This figure implies that for managers to achieve and maintain a high level of social responsiveness within an organization, they must pursue only those responsibilities their organization possesses and has a right to undertake. Furthermore, once managers decide to meet a specific social responsibility, they must determine the best way to undertake activities related to meeting this obligation. That is, managers must decide whether their organization should undertake the activities on its own or acquire the help of outsiders with more expertise in the area.

As **an example from the world of management** of how the guidelines in Figure 3.1 can be used profitably, consider a recent decision made by **Radisson Hotels International**. Radisson's management determined that the company had an obligation to help preserve the environment. To proactively meet this obligation, management initiated a new concept called Green Suites. Along with the normally expected suite appointments, Green Suites feature recycled paper goods because Radisson managers believe that by offering its customers recycled paper products, the company can discourage the unnecessary cutting of trees. In order for this decision to be considered truly socially responsible, however, it must actually help to preserve the environment by saving trees and attract customer dollars that will help Radisson Hotels International reach such organizational objectives as making a profit.[24]

Approaches to Meeting Social Responsibilities

Various managerial approaches to meeting social obligations are another determinant of an organization's level of social responsiveness. According to Lipson, a desirable and socially responsive approach to meeting social obligations does the following:[25]

1. Incorporates social goals into the annual planning process.
2. Seeks comparative industry norms for social programs.

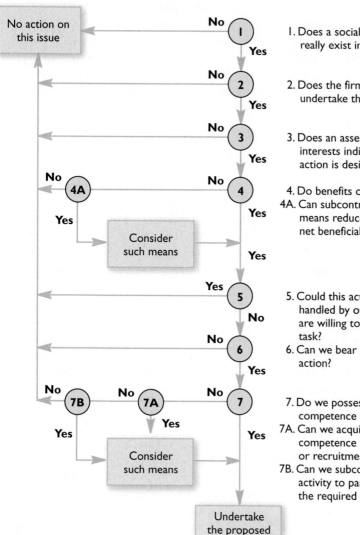

1. Does a social responsibility really exist in this case?
2. Does the firm have a right to undertake this action?
3. Does an assessment of all interests indicate that the action is desirable?
4. Do benefits outweigh costs?
4A. Can subcontracting or other means reduce the cost to a net beneficial level?
5. Could this action be better handled by other parties who are willing to undertake the task?
6. Can we bear the cost of this action?
7. Do we possess the managerial competence to do the job?
7A. Can we acquire needed competence through training or recruitment?
7B. Can we subcontract the activity to parties that possess the required competence?

FIGURE 3.1
Flowchart of social responsibility decision making that generally will enhance the social responsiveness of an organization

3. Presents reports to organization members, the board of directors, and stockholders on social responsibility progress.
4. Experiments with different approaches for measuring social performance.
5. Attempts to measure the cost of social programs as well as the return on social program investments.

S. Prakash Sethi presents three management approaches to meeting social obligations:[26]

1. Social obligation approach
2. Social responsibility approach
3. Social responsiveness approach

Each of these approaches entails behavior that reflects a somewhat different attitude toward performance of social responsibility activities by business. The **social obligation approach,** for example, considers business as having primarily economic purposes and confines social responsibility activity mainly to existing legislation. The **social responsibility approach** sees business as having both economic and societal goals. The **social responsiveness approach** considers business as having both societal and economic goals as well as the obligation to antici-pate potential social problems and work actively toward preventing their occurrence.

Organizations characterized by attitudes and behaviors consistent with the social responsive-ness approach are generally more socially responsive than organizations characterized by attitudes and behaviors consistent with either the social responsibility or the social obligation approach. And organizations that take the social responsibility approach usually achieve higher levels of social responsiveness than organizations that take the social obligation approach. In other words, as one moves along the continuum from social obligation to social responsiveness, one generally finds management becoming more proactive. Proactive managers do what is prudent from a business viewpoint to reduce liabilities regardless of whether such action is required by law.

SOCIAL RESPONSIBILITY ACTIVITIES AND MANAGEMENT FUNCTIONS

This section considers social responsibility as a major organizational activity subject to the same management techniques used in other major organizational activities, such as production, personnel, finance, and marketing. Managers have known for some time that to achieve desirable results in these areas, they must be effective in planning, organizing, influencing, and controlling. Achieving social responsibility results is no different. The following sections discuss planning, organizing, influencing, and controlling social responsibility activities.

Planning Social Responsibility Activities

Planning was defined in Chapter 1 as the process of determining how the organization will achieve its objectives, or get where it wants to go. Planning social responsibility activities, then, involves determining how the organization will achieve its social responsibility objectives, or get where it wants to go in the area of social responsibility. The following sections discuss how the planning of social responsibility activities is related to the organization's overall planning process and how its social responsibility policy can be converted into action.

The Overall Planning Process The model presented in Figure 3.2 illustrates how social responsibility activities can be handled as part of the overall planning process of the organization. As shown in this figure, social trends forecasts should be performed within the organizational environment along with the more typically performed economic, political, and technological trends forecasts. Examples of social trends are prevailing and future societal attitudes toward water pollution, safe working conditions, and the education system.[27] Each of the forecasts would influence the development of the organization's long-run plans, or plans for the more distant future, and short-run plans, or plans for the relatively near future.

Converting Organizational Policies on Social Responsibility into Action A *policy* is a management tool that furnishes broad guidelines for channeling management thinking in specific directions. Managers should establish organizational policies in the social responsibility area just as they do in some of the more generally accepted areas, such as hiring, promotion, and absenteeism.

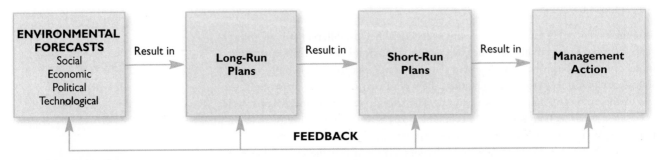

FIGURE 3.2   Integration of social responsibility activities and planning activities

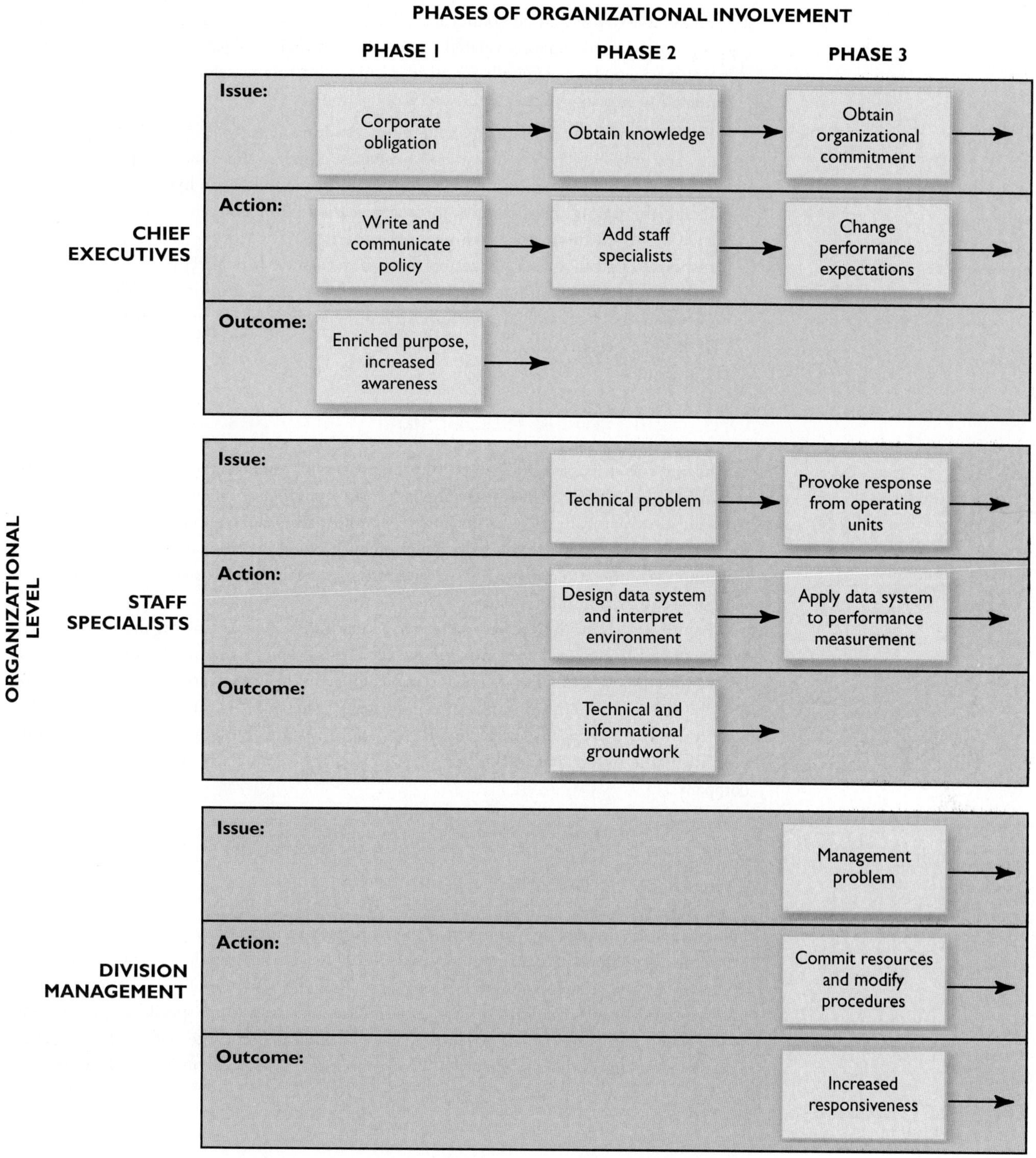

PHASES OF ORGANIZATIONAL INVOLVEMENT

	PHASE I	PHASE 2	PHASE 3

CHIEF EXECUTIVES

Issue:	Corporate obligation →	Obtain knowledge →	Obtain organizational commitment →
Action:	Write and communicate policy →	Add staff specialists →	Change performance expectations →
Outcome:	Enriched purpose, increased awareness →		

STAFF SPECIALISTS

Issue:		Technical problem →	Provoke response from operating units →
Action:		Design data system and interpret environment →	Apply data system to performance measurement →
Outcome:		Technical and informational groundwork →	

DIVISION MANAGEMENT

Issue:			Management problem →
Action:			Commit resources and modify procedures →
Outcome:			Increased responsiveness →

ORGANIZATIONAL LEVEL

FIGURE 3.3 Conversion of social responsibility policy into action

To be effective, social responsibility policies must be converted into appropriate action. As shown in Figure 3.3, this conversion involves three distinct and generally sequential phases.

- **Phase 1** consists of the recognition by top management that the organization has some social obligation. Top management then must formulate and communicate some policy about the acceptance of this obligation to all organization members.

- **Phase 2** involves staff personnel as well as top management. In this phase, top management gathers information related to meeting the social obligation accepted in phase 1. Staff personnel are generally involved at this point to give advice on technical matters related to meeting the accepted social obligation.

- **Phase 3** involves division management in addition to the organization personnel already involved from the first two phases. During this phase, top management strives to obtain the commitment of organization members to live up to the accepted social obligation and attempts to create realistic expectations about the effects of such a commitment on organizational productivity. Staff specialists encourage the responses within the organization necessary to meet the accepted social obligation properly; and division management commits resources and modifies existing procedures so that appropriate socially oriented activities can and will be performed within the organization.

Organizing Social Responsibility Activities

Organizing was discussed in Chapter 1 as the process of establishing orderly uses for all the organization's resources. These uses emphasize the attainment of management system objectives and flow naturally from management system plans. Correspondingly, organizing for social responsibility activities entails establishing for all organizational resources logical uses that emphasize the attainment of the organization's social objectives and that are consistent with its social responsibility plans.

Figure 3.4 shows how ChevronTexaco Corporation decided to organize for the performance of its social responsibility activities. The vice president for Health, Environment, and Safety has primary responsibility in the area of societal affairs and oversees the related activities of numerous individuals. This chart is intended only as an illustration of how a company might include its social responsibility area on its organization chart. Specific organizing in this area should always be tailored to the unique needs of a company.

Influencing Individuals Performing Social Responsibility Activities

Influencing was defined in Chapter 1 as the management process of guiding the activities of organization members to help attain organizational objectives. As applied to the social responsibility area, then, influencing is the process of guiding the activities of organization members to help attain the organization's social responsibility objectives. More specifically, to influence appropriately in this area, managers must lead, communicate, motivate, and work with groups in ways that result in the attainment of the organization's social responsibility objectives.

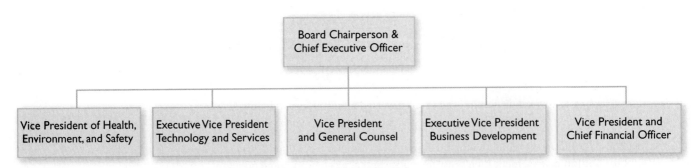

FIGURE 3.4 How ChevronTexaco Company includes social responsibility in its organization chart

Controlling Social Responsibility Activities

Controlling, as discussed in Chapter 1, is making things happen as they were planned to happen. To control, managers assess or measure what is occurring in the organization and, if necessary, change these occurrences in some way to make them conform to plans. Controlling in the area of social responsibility entails the same two major tasks. The following sections discuss various areas in which social responsibility measurement takes place and examine the social audit, a tool for determining and reporting progress in the attainment of social responsibility objectives.

Areas of Measurement Measurements to gauge organizational progress in reaching social responsibility objectives can be taken in any number of areas. The specific areas in which individual companies decide to take such measurements will vary according to the specific social responsibility objectives to be met. All companies, however, should take social responsibility measurements in at least the following four major areas:[28]

1. **The economic function area**—A measurement should be made of whether the organization is performing such activities as producing goods and services that people need, creating jobs for society, paying fair wages, and ensuring worker safety. This measurement gives some indication of the economic contribution the organization is making to society.
2. **The quality-of-life area**—The measurement of quality of life should focus on whether the organization is improving or degrading the general quality of life in society. Producing high-quality goods, dealing fairly with employees and customers, and making an effort to preserve the natural environment are all indicators that the organization is upholding or improving the general quality of life. As an example of degrading the quality of life, some people believe that cigarette companies, because they produce goods that can harm the health of society overall, are socially irresponsible.[29]
3. **The social investment area**—The measurement of social investment deals with the degree to which the organization is investing both money and human resources to solve community social problems. Here, the organization could be involved in assisting community organizations dedicated to education, charities, and the arts.
4. **The problem-solving area**—The measurement of problem solving should focus on the degree to which the organization deals with social problems, such as participating in long-range community planning and conducting studies to pinpoint social problems.

The Social Audit: A Progress Report A **social audit** is the process of measuring the present social responsibility activities of an organization to assess its performance in this area. The basic steps in conducting a social audit are monitoring, measuring, and appraising all aspects of an organization's social responsibility performance. Although some companies that pioneered concepts of social reporting, such as the retailing group Migros, in Switzerland, are still continuing their efforts, few companies, unfortunately, are joining their ranks.[30]

HOW SOCIETY CAN HELP BUSINESS MEET SOCIAL OBLIGATIONS

Although the point was made early in this chapter that there must be an open and honest involvement of both business and society in order for business to meet desirable social obligations, the bulk of the chapter has focused on what business should do in the area of social responsibility. This section emphasizes actions that society should take to help business accomplish its social responsibility objectives.

Jerry McAfee, board chair and CEO of Gulf Oil Corporation, says that although business has some responsibilities to society, society also has the following responsibilities to business:[31]

1. **Set rules that are clear and consistent**—This is one of the fundamental things that society, through government, ought to do. Although it may come as a surprise to some, I believe that industry actually needs an appropriate measure of regulation. By this I

mean that the people of the nation, through their government, should set the bounds within which they want industry to operate.

But the rules have got to be clear. Society must spell out clearly what it is it wants the corporations to do. The rules can't be vague and imprecise. Making the rules straight and understandable is what government is all about. One of my colleagues described his confusion when he read a section of a regulation that a regulatory representative had cited as the reason for a certain decision that had been made. "You're right," the official responded, "that's what the regulation says, but that's not what it means."

2. **Keep the rules technically feasible**—Business cannot be expected to do the impossible. Yet the plain truth is that many of today's regulations are unworkable. Environmental standards have on occasion exceeded those of nature. For example, a shale-oil development in the U.S. state of Colorado was delayed because air-quality standards, as originally proposed, required a higher quality of air than existed in the natural setting.

3. **Make sure the rules are economically feasible**—Society cannot impose a rule that society is not prepared to pay for because, ultimately, it is the people who must pay, either through higher prices or higher taxes, or both. Furthermore, the costs involved include not only those funds constructively spent to solve problems, but the increasingly substantial expenditures needed to comply with red-tape requirements. Although the total cost of government regulation of business is difficult to compute, it is enormous.

4. **Make the rules prospective, not retroactive**—Nowadays, there is an alarming, distressing trend toward retroactivity, toward trying to force retribution for the past. Certain patterns of taxation and some of the regulations and applications of the law are indications of this trend.

    As a case in point, the U.S. government recently filed a multimillion-dollar lawsuit against Borden Chemicals & Plastics, a company operating in the U.S. states of Louisiana and Illinois that produces various chemical products for construction, industrial, and agricultural markets.[32] The suit alleges that Borden released significant amounts of cancer-causing and other hazardous contaminants into the groundwater at its Louisiana complex. Borden maintains that recent changes to hazardous waste regulations are being applied retroactively to force the company to pay penalties for actions it took before the law existed. Borden charges that this type of action by the government violates the basic concepts of fairness and due process. Retroactive cleanup costs are an issue in many other countries, too, because they affect investors who could one day face higher health or cleanup costs unexpectedly.

    It is counterproductive to make today's rules apply retroactively to yesterday's ball game.

5. **Make the rules goal-setting, not procedure-prescribing**—The proper way for the people of the nation, through their government, to tell their industries how to operate is to set the goals, set the fences, set the criteria, set the atmosphere, but don't tell us how to do it. Tell us what you want made, but don't tell us how to make it. Tell us the destination we're seeking, but don't tell us how to get there. Leave it to the ingenuity of industry to devise the best, the most economical, the most efficient way to get there, for industry's track record in this regard has been good.

BUSINESS ETHICS

The study of ethics in management can be approached from many different directions. Perhaps the most practical approach is to view ethics as catalyzing managers to take socially responsible actions. The movement to include the study of ethics as a critical part of management education began in the 1970s, grew significantly in the 1980s, and is expected to continue growing in the twenty-first century. For example, John Shad, chair of the U.S. Securities and Exchange Commission during the 1980s when Wall Street was shaken by a number of insider trading scandals, recently pledged a $20 million trust fund to the Harvard Business School to create a curriculum in business ethics for MBA students. Television producer Norman Lear gave $1 million to underwrite the Business Enterprise Trust, which will give national awards to companies and "whistle blowers . . . who demonstrate courage, creativity, and social vision in the business world."[33]

The following sections define ethics, explain why ethical considerations are a vital part of management practices, discuss a workable code of business ethics, and present some suggestions for creating an ethical workplace.

A Definition of Ethics

The famous missionary physician and humanitarian Albert Schweitzer defined ethics as "our concern for good behavior. We feel an obligation to consider not only our own personal well-being, but also that of other human beings." This meaning is similar to the precept of the Golden Rule: Do unto others as you would have them do unto you.[34]

In business, **ethics** can be defined as the capacity to reflect on values in the corporate decision-making process, to determine how these values and decisions affect various stakeholder groups, and to establish how managers can use these observations in day-to-day company management.[35] Ethical managers strive for success within the confines of sound management practices that are characterized by fairness and justice.[36] Interestingly, using ethics as a major guide in making and evaluating business decisions is not only popular in Europe and the United States but also in the very different societies of India and Russia.[37]

Why Ethics Is a Vital Part of Management Practices

John F. Akers, former board chair of IBM, recently said that it makes good business sense for managers to be ethical. Unless they are ethical, he believes, companies cannot be competitive in either national or international markets. According to Akers:

> **Ethics and competitiveness are inseparable. We compete as a society. No society anywhere will compete very long or successfully with people stabbing each other in the back; with people trying to steal from one another; with everything requiring notarized confirmation because you can't trust the other person; with every little squabble ending in litigation; and with government writing reams of regulatory legislation, tying business hand and foot to keep it honest.[38]**

Although ethical management practices may not be linked to specific indicators of financial profitability, conflict is not inevitable between ethical practices and making a profit. As Akers's statement suggests, our system of competition presumes underlying values of truthfulness and fair dealing. The employment of ethical business practices can enhance overall corporate health in three important areas: productivity, stakeholder relations, and government regulation.

Productivity The employees of a corporation constitute one major stakeholder group that is affected by management practices. When management is resolved to act ethically toward stakeholders, then employees will be positively affected. For example, a corporation may decide that business ethics requires it to make a special effort to ensure the health and welfare of its employees. To this end, many corporations have established Employee Advisory Programs (EAPs) to help employees with family, work, financial, or legal problems, or with mental illness or chemical dependency. These programs have even enhanced productivity in some corporations. For instance, Control Data Corporation found that its EAP reduced health costs and sick-leave usage significantly.[39]

Stakeholder Relations The second area in which ethical management practices can enhance corporate health is by positively affecting "outside" stakeholders such as suppliers and customers. A positive public image can attract customers who view such an image as desirable. For example, Johnson & Johnson, the world's largest maker of health

We believe our first responsibility is to the doctors, nurses and patients, to mothers and fathers and all others who use our products and services. In meeting their needs everything we do must be of high quality. We must constantly strive to reduce our costs in order to maintain reasonable prices. Customers' orders must be serviced promptly and accurately. Our suppliers and distributors must have an opportunity to make a fair profit.

We are responsible to our employees, the men and women who work with us throughout the world. Everyone must be considered as an individual. We must respect their dignity and recognize their merit. They must have a sense of security in their jobs. Compensation must be fair and adequate, and working conditions clean, orderly, and safe. We must be mindful of ways to help our employees fulfill their family responsibilities. Employees must feel free to make suggestions and complaints. There must be equal opportunity for employment, development and advancement for those qualified. We must provide competent management, and their actions must be just and ethical.

We are responsible to the communities in which we live and work and to the world community as well. We must be good citizens—support good works and charities and bear our fair share of taxes. We must encourage civic improvements and better health and education. We must maintain in good order the property we are privileged to use, protecting the environment and natural resources.

Our final responsibility is to our stockholders. Business must make a sound profit. We must experiment with new ideas. Research must be carried on, innovative programs developed and mistakes paid for. New equipment must be purchased, new facilities provided and new products launched. Reserves must be created to provide for adverse times. When we operate according to these principles, the stockholders should realize a fair return.

FIGURE 3.5
Johnson & Johnson's Credo
Source: www.careers.jnj.com.

care products, is guided by "Our Credo" addressed more than 60 years ago by General Robert Wood Johnson to the company's employees and stockholders and members of its community (see Figure 3.5).

Government Regulation The third area in which ethical management practices can enhance corporate health is in minimizing government regulation. Where companies are believed to be acting unethically, the public is more likely to put pressure on legislators and other government officials to regulate those businesses or to enforce existing regulations.[40]

A Code of Ethics

A **code of ethics** is a formal statement that acts as a guide for the ethics of how people within a particular organization should act and make decisions. Ninety percent of *Fortune* 500 firms, and almost half of all other firms, have ethical codes. Moreover, many organizations that do not already have an ethical code are giving serious consideration to developing one.[41]

Codes of ethics commonly address such issues as conflict of interest, competitors, privacy of information, gift giving, and giving and receiving political contributions or business. A code of ethics recently developed by Nissan of Japan, for example, barred all Nissan employees from accepting almost all gifts or entertainment from, or offering them to, business partners and government officials. The new code was drafted by Nissan president Yoshikazu Hanawa and sent to 300 major suppliers.[42]

According to a recent survey, the development and distribution of a code of ethics is perceived as an effective and efficient means of encouraging ethical practices *within* organizations.[43] In addition, codes of conduct are also commonly used as vehicles for encouraging global ethical practices *outside* of organizations. Figure 3.6 contains an excerpt from the code of conduct that Nike, Inc. uses to influence the practices of global business partners, practices outside of Nike.

Managers cannot assume that merely because they have developed and distributed a code of ethics, organization members have all the guidelines they need to determine what is ethical and to act accordingly. It is impossible to cover all ethical and unethical conduct within an organization in one code. Managers should view codes of ethics as tools that must be evaluated and refined periodically so that they will be comprehensive and usable guidelines for making ethical business decisions efficiently and effectively.[44]

FIGURE 3.6
NIKE's Code of Conduct
Source: www.nike.com/nikebiz/ nikeresponsibility/tools/ Nike_Code_of_Conduct.pdf.

Wherever NIKE operates around the globe we are guided by this Code of Conduct and we bind our contractors to these principles. Contractors must post this Code in all major workspaces, translated into the language of the employee, and must train employees on their rights and obligations as defined by this Code and applicable local laws. While these principles establish the spirit of our partnerships, we also bind our partners to specific standards of conduct. The core standards are set forth below.

Forced Labor The contractor does not use forced labor in any form—prison, indentured, bonded or otherwise.

Child Labor The contractor does not employ any person below the age of 18 to produce footwear. The contractor does not employ any person below the age of 16 to produce apparel, accessories or equipment. If at the time Nike production begins, the contractor employs people of the legal working age who are at least 15, that employment may continue, but the contractor will not hire any person going forward who is younger than the Nike or legal age limit, whichever is higher. To further ensure these age standards are complied with, the contractor does not use any form of homework for Nike production.

Compensation The contractor provides each employee at least the minimum wage, or the prevailing industry wage, whichever is higher; provides each employee a clear, written accounting for every pay period; and does not deduct from employee pay for disciplinary infractions.

Benefits The contractor provides each employee all legally mandated benefits.

Hours of Work/Overtime The contractor complies with legally mandated work hours; uses overtime only when each employee is fully compensated according to local law; informs each employee at the time of hiring if mandatory overtime is a condition of employment; and on a regularly scheduled basis provides one day off in seven, and requires no more than 60 hours of work per week on a regularly scheduled basis, or complies with local limits if they are lower.

Environment, Safety and Health (ES&H) The contractor has written environmental, safety and health policies and standards, and implements a system to minimize negative impacts on the environment, reduce work-related injury and illness, and promote the general health of employees.

Documentation and Inspection The contractor maintains on file all documentation needed to demonstrate compliance with this Code of Conduct and required laws; agrees to make these documents available for Nike or its designated monitor; and agrees to submit to inspections with or without prior notice.

Creating an Ethical Workplace

Managers commonly strive to encourage ethical practices, not only to be morally correct, but to gain whatever business advantage lies in projecting an ethical image to consumers and employees.[45] Creating, distributing, and continually improving a company's code of ethics is one common step managers can take to establish an ethical workplace.

Another step many companies are taking to create an ethical workplace is to appoint a chief ethics officer. The chief ethics officer has the job of ensuring the integration of organizational ethics and values into daily decisions at all organizational levels. Such officers recommend, help implement, and reinforce strategies aimed at integrating appropriate conduct throughout all phases of company operations. Figure 3.7 gives the characteristics designated by the Ethics Officer Association that a person must have in order to be a successful chief ethics officer.

Another way to promote ethics in the workplace is to furnish organization members with appropriate training. GlaxoSmithKline, Rolls Royce, General Dynamics, McDonnell Douglas, Chemical Bank, and American Can Company are examples of corporations that conduct training programs aimed at encouraging ethical practices within their organizations.[46] Such programs do not attempt to teach managers what is moral or ethical, but to give them criteria they can use to help determine how ethical a certain action might be. Managers can feel confident that a potential action will be considered ethical by the general public if it is consistent with one or more of the following standards:[47]

1. **The golden rule**—Act in a way you would expect others to act toward you.
2. **The utilitarian principle**—Act in a way that results in the greatest good for the greatest number of people.
3. **Kant's categorical imperative**—Act in such a way that the action taken under the circumstances could be a universal law, or rule, of behavior.
4. **The professional ethic**—Take actions that would be viewed as proper by a disinterested panel of professional peers.
5. **The TV test**—Managers should always ask, "Would I feel comfortable explaining to a national TV audience why I took this action?"

FIGURE 3.7

Characteristics needed to be a successful chief ethics officer

Ethics officers come from diverse backgrounds such as legal, human resources, finance, auditing, security, or line operations, but share some common characteristics:

- Strong communicator—excellent and effective communication skills, including presentations, public speaking, and one-on-one interactions with employees of all levels
- Objective and thoughtful
- Ability to establish and maintain credibility and trust throughout organization
- Ability to quickly assimilate information relating to complex issues
- Ability to network on all levels of an organization
- Politically savvy
- Personal and professional maturity
- Rationality in tense interpersonal situations
- Organizational knowledge
- Working knowledge of applicable laws and regulations
- Experience with training and development including best practices in ethics and compliance education
- Solid and broad management skills
- Discreet and able to protect confidential information
- Able and willing to take a difficult or unpopular position if necessary
- Common sense
- Of the highest integrity

6. **The legal test**—Is the proposed action or decision legal? Established laws are generally considered minimum standards for ethics.

7. **The four-way test**—Managers can feel confident that a decision is ethical if they
can answer "yes" to the following questions: Is the decision truthful? Is it fair to all
concerned? Will it build goodwill and better friendships? Will it be beneficial to all
concerned?

Finally, managers can take responsibility for creating and sustaining conditions in
which people are likely to behave ethically and for minimizing conditions in which
people might be tempted to behave unethically. Two practices that commonly inspire
unethical behavior in organizations are to give unusually high rewards for good performance and unusually severe punishments for poor performance. By eliminating such factors, managers can reduce any pressure on employees to perform unethically in
organizations.

For **an example from the management world** illustrating how management
action can be debated from an ethical viewpoint, consider recent events at **Sprint,** the
third largest wireless provider in the United States with more than 53 million customers.[48] The company recently sent a letter to about 1,000 customers terminating their
contracts. These customers called Sprint with questions or needing help an average of 25
times a month, a rate 40 times higher than average customers. According to Sprint, these
customers were too costly to maintain at a time when cost control is a high company priority. Although Sprint cancels service of customers who do not pay their bills, it is the
first time the company has canceled customer contracts who call too much. Some would
argue that the company is being unethical due to its selfishness in this situation while others would argue that the company is being ethical because it is acting in the best interests
of stockholders. In the final analysis, management is responsible for evaluating its actions
from an ethical viewpoint and maintaining those activities that it deems ethical.

Following the Law

In the summer of 2001, outrageous management practices were discovered at several companies including Enron, WorldCom, and Tyco that seemed aimed at unjustifiably maximizing the personal wealth of top managers to the detriment of the well-being of other
organizational stakeholders. As an example, many of these managers used inaccurate
accounting reports to deceive employees, shareholders, legal authorities, the media, and
the general public. These reports grossly overstated the level of company performance,
allowing top managers to justify inflated salaries. Some employees were personally out-
raged by the deceitful management practices, and others experienced personal financial
disaster after being encouraged to invest in worthless company stock and company retirement programs. Needless to say, managers involved in such deceitful practices were pros-
ecuted to the full extent of the law.

Amid outcries of public outrage over such practices, the U.S. Sarbanes–Oxley Act of
2002 was passed to try to prevent such future deception in publicly owned companies.
The general thrust of this legislation focuses on promoting ethical conduct.[49] Areas covered include maintaining generally accepted accounting practices, evaluating executive
compensation, monitoring fundamental business strategies, understanding and mitigat-
ing major risk, and ensuring company structure and processes that enhance integrity and
reputation.

Managers who do not follow stipulations of the Sarbanes–Oxley Act face significant jail
time. Infractions such as securities fraud, impeding a financial investigation by regulators,
and mail fraud can result in up to 25 years of imprisonment. The Sarbanes–Oxley Act and
related significant infraction penalties create hope that grossly unethical behavior will be
significantly discouraged in the future.

The Sarbanes–Oxley Act seems to support whistle-blowing as a vehicle for both
discouraging deceptive management practices while encouraging ethical management

practices. **Whistle-blowing** is the act of an employee reporting suspected misconduct or corruption believed to exist within an organization. A **whistle-blower** is the employee who reports the alleged activities. Whistle-blowers can make their reports in a number of different ways, including reporting suspected organizational wrongdoings to proper legal authorities and/or proper management authorities. The Sarbanes–Oxley Act prohibits retaliation by employers against whistle-blowers.

One of the most famous whistle-blowers of modern times is Sherron Watkins, former vice president of Enron Corporation.[50] Watkins testified to the United States Congress that she was extremely alarmed by information she had received about Enron's finances, and warned then-chairman Kenneth Lay that investors were being duped by inflated profit statements. Watkins attempted, with no success, to persuade Lay to restate and reissue corporate financial statements after eliminating accounting misrepresentations. Enron, once the seventh largest corporation in the United States, declared bankruptcy in December 2001. The bankruptcy cost thousands of employees their jobs and retirement pensions and investors lost millions of dollars. A 2007 study by the consulting firm KPMG, found that 25 percent of 360 fraud incidents uncovered worldwide came to light thanks to a whistleblowing system put into place by companies. Nevertheless, internal fraud reporting systems are not widespread throughout the world.[51]

{ CHALLENGE CASE SUMMARY

Social responsibility is the obligation of management to take action that protects and improves the welfare of society in conjunction with the interests of the organization. Based on the Challenge Case, IBM protects and improves its communities through the use of information technology to improve the quality of life. IBM presently makes substantial contributions in employing technology in many different areas of community life and concern. According to Keith Davis's social responsibility model, making such investments in the welfare of society is essential to being a good business citizen. Corporations, however, must also take steps to protect their own interests while making social investments. For example, donating IBM equipment for use in educational programs could benefit the company by turning students into future IBM customers.

Following Davis's model of social responsibility further, IBM should commit to benefiting society because of the vast power the company possesses in creating such benefit. It should be remembered, however, that the costs of social responsibility activities can be passed to consumers, and action should be taken only if it is financially feasible. For IBM to invest in social responsibility activities to its own financial detriment would be socially irresponsible given the company's commitment to employees and stockholders.

IBM could become involved in many different areas of social responsibility. The company's present activities are clearly in education, arts and culture, community needs, the environment, and employee giving; other possibilities include women's rights, health, and racial equality. No matter how much IBM does in pursuing social responsibility goals, however, it will no doubt be criticized by someone for not doing enough. At this point, IBM's activities in the area of social responsibility appear to be highly significant.

Anything IBM does within the sphere of social responsibility could result in a short-run profit decrease simply because of the costs. Although, at first glance, such action might seem unbusinesslike, performing social responsibility activities could significantly improve IBM's public image and could be instrumental in generating increased sales.

Some social responsibility activities are legislated and therefore *must* be performed by businesses. Most of the legislated activities, however, are aimed at larger companies like IBM. Such legislation has to do with required levels of product safety and employee safety. Legislated support for community arts probably doesn't exist. Because IBM is not required by law to support things such as adult education or community arts, whatever it might contribute to such areas would be strictly voluntary. In making a decision about how to support society, IBM management should assess the positive and negative outcomes of such support over both the long and short terms, and then establish whatever support, if any, would maximize its success and offer some desirable contribution to society. IBM should communicate to all organization members, as well as society, those areas it will support, and why. The use of its Web site greatly facilitates this communication.

IBM should strive to maintain a relatively high level of social responsiveness in pursuing its social responsibility activities. To do this, management should make decisions focusing on IBM's established social responsibility areas and approach meeting those responsibilities in appropriate ways. In terms of supporting adult education, for example, management must first decide if IBM has a social responsibility to become involved, through the design and application of its products, in society's adult education problem. Assuming it was decided that IBM *has* such a responsibility, it must then determine how to accomplish the activities necessary to meet it. For example, IBM might employ its expertise to develop new, computer-based educational methods and content aimed specifically at adult learning needs. Making appropriate decisions will help IBM meet social obligations effectively and efficiently.

In terms of implementing an approach to meeting social responsibilities that will increase IBM's social responsiveness, management should try to view the company as having both societal and economic goals. In addition, management should attempt to anticipate social problems and actively work to prevent them. Managers at IBM should know that pursuing social responsibility objectives is a major management activity. Therefore, they must plan, organize, influence, and control IBM's social responsibility activities if the company is to be successful in reaching social responsibility objectives.

Regarding the planning of these activities, management should determine how IBM will achieve its objectives. By incorporating social responsibility planning into IBM's overall planning process, social trends forecasts can be made along with economic, political, and technological trends forecasts. In turn, these forecasts would influence the development of plans and, ultimately, the action taken by IBM in the area of social responsibility.

Management also must be able to turn IBM's social responsibility policy into action. For example, management may want to follow the policy of making IBM's laptop computers more affordable to customers, thereby facilitating the company's role in promoting education. To convert this goal into action, management should first communicate the policy to all organization members. Next, it must determine the best way to generate lower product costs that can ultimately be passed on to the customers. Finally, management should make sure everyone at IBM is committed to meeting this social

responsibility objective and that lower-level managers are allocating funds and establishing appropriate opportunities for organization members to help implement this policy.

In addition to planning social responsibility activities at IBM, management must organize, influence, and control them. To organize these activities, orderly use of all resources at IBM must be established to carry out the company's social responsibility plans. Developing an organization chart that shows the social responsibility area with corresponding job descriptions, responsibilities, and specifications for the positions would be an appropriate step for management to take.

To influence social responsibility activities, organization members should be guided in directions that will enhance the attainment of IBM's social responsibility objectives. Management must lead, communicate, motivate, and work with groups in ways that are appropriate for meeting those objectives.

To control, management must make sure that social responsibility activities occur as planned. If they do not, changes should be made to ensure that activities will be handled properly in the near future. One tool that can be used to check IBM's progress in meeting social responsibilities is the social audit. The audit will enable management to check and assess system performance in such areas as economic functions, quality of life, social investment, and problem solving.

As indicated earlier, no legislation requires IBM to support societal areas such as education or community arts. If such legislation were being developed, however, legislators could take certain steps to help management meet social responsibilities in these areas. For example, laws should be clear, consistent, and technically feasible, which would ensure that management knows what action is expected and that the means actually exist to take this action. Laws should also be economically feasible, emphasize the future, and allow flexibility. IBM should be able to follow them without going bankrupt and should not be penalized for past practices. It also should be given the flexibility to follow these laws to the best advantage of the company; IBM should not be told to conform to laws by following specific steps.

Assuming that management at IBM is ethical, its decisions would focus on enhancing the well-being of all company stakeholders. In essence, management should follow the Golden Rule by acting in a way that it would expect others to act toward it. Decisions at IBM will always be ethical if they are truthful and fair to all concerned, if they build goodwill and better friendships, and if they are beneficial to all concerned.

MANAGEMENT SKILL ACTIVITIES

This section is specially designed to help you develop corporate social responsibility skill. An individual's corporate social responsibility skill is based upon an understanding of social responsibility concepts and the ability to apply those concepts in management situations. The following activities are designed to both heighten your understanding of social responsibility concepts and to develop the ability to apply those concepts in a variety of management situations.

UNDERSTANDING CORPORATE SOCIAL RESPONSIBILITY CONCEPTS

This section is comprised of activities that will sharpen your understanding of social responsibility concepts. Answer essay questions as completely as possible. Also, remember that many additional true/false and multiple choice questions appear online at MyManagementLab.com to help you further refine your understanding of social responsibility concepts.

Essay Questions

1. What are the five propositions of the Davis model of corporate social responsibility? Which proposition would be the most valuable to you as a manager in guiding your social responsibility focus in an organization? Explain.

2. What is your personal position about businesses performing social responsibility activities now that you have studied the arguments "for" and "against" as presented in the chapter?

3. As a manager, would you use the social obligation, the social responsibility, or the social responsiveness approach in meeting your organization's social responsibilities? Why?

4. How can society help business meet social obligations?

5. What's the relationship between social responsibility and ethics?

Developing Management Skill

Learning activities in this section are aimed at helping you to develop social responsibility skill. Learning activities include Exploring Your Management Skill: Part 2, Experiential Exercises, Cases, and a VideoNet exercise.

EXPLORING YOUR MANAGEMENT SKILL: PART 2

As you recall, you completed Exploring Your Management Skill before you started to study this chapter. Your responses gave you an idea of how much you initially knew about social responsibility and helped you to focus on important points as you studied the chapter. Answer the Exploring Your Management Skill questions again now (p. 78) and compare your score to the first time you took it. This comparison will give you an idea of how much you have learned from studying this chapter and pinpoint

areas for further clarification before you start studying the next chapter. Record your answers within the text or online at MyManagementLab.com. Completing the survey at MyManagementLab.com will allow you to grade and compare your test scores automatically. If you complete the test in the book, look up answers in the Exploring Your Management Skill section at the end of the book.

YOUR MANAGEMENT SKILLS PORTFOLIO

Your Management Learning Portfolio is a collection of activities especially designed to demonstrate your management knowledge and skill. By completing these activities online at MyManagementLab.com, you will be able to print, complete with cover sheet, as many activities as you choose. Be sure to save your work. Taking your printed portfolio to an employment interview could be helpful in obtaining a job.

The portfolio activity for this chapter is Identifying Corporate Social Responsibilities. Read this highlight about the Bugaboo Strollers Company and answer the questions that follow.

Bugaboo is the brainchild of Dutch designer Max Barenburg and his physician brother-in-law Eduard Zanen. Together they wanted to invent a baby stroller that was functional, fashionable, appealing to both fathers and mothers, and would be able to function on different types of surfaces.

Their initial product was the Bugaboo Frog. Introduced in Holland in 1999, and named for it's "frog-like" suspension wheels that "jump" over obstacles in its path, the Frog became the "must have" stroller of celebrities and parents who wanted this elite stroller for their babies.

After years of customer feedback and further testing and development on the Frog, the pair realized that parents wanted more options and that different parents have different needs. In September of 2005, the pair introduced to the world the Bugaboo Cameleon, Bugaboo Gecko, and the Bugaboo Bee strollers to offer customers more choices.

Management of a company such as Bugaboo must clearly keep in mind the responsibilities that it has to society as a result of its business operations. The following list shows the four categories in which companies commonly have social responsibilities because of business operations. For each category, list the responsibilities to society that you believe Bugaboo has as a result of the products that it offers.

PLANNING ISSUES TO INSPECT

Category	Bugaboo's Responsibilities to Society
Social responsibilities related to the product itself	1. _____ 2. _____ 3. _____ 4. _____ 5. _____
Social responsibilities related to marketing practices	1. _____ 2. _____ 3. _____ 4. _____ 5. _____
Social responsibilities related to corporate philanthropy	1. _____ 2. _____ 3. _____ 4. _____ 5. _____
Social responsibilities related to employees	1. _____ 2. _____ 3. _____ 4. _____ 5. _____

EXPERIENTIAL EXERCISE: THE ENVIRONMENTAL IMPACT TEAM

Directions. Read the following scenario and then perform the listed activities. Your instructor may want you to perform the activities as an individual or within groups. Follow all of your instructor's directions carefully.

You are the head of a major British newspaper, *Guardian Unlimited,* and have just completed a social audit of your organization's business activities. Your company produces a progressive, enlightened newspaper and a Web site, and writes regularly about corporate social responsibility topics. You conducted your social audit to make sure that your company measures up to the high standards that your editorials expect of other companies. In the past, your company has won several social responsibility awards in areas such as encouraging diversity, innovation in social reporting, and employee giving to social responsibility causes.

Based upon the results of your audit, you have set a new social responsibility goal for your newspaper for the upcoming three-year period. This goal is simple: to persuade your readers to have a positive impact on the environment.

You have established a new team called the Environmental Impact Team to help you outline how your new goal will be accomplished. You are presently meeting with this new team for the first time. Lead your group in outlining plans, organization features, an influence system, and a control mechanism, all aimed at achieving this new goal.

CASES

IBM PROMOTES SOCIAL RESPONSIBILITY GOALS

"IBM Promotes Social Responsibility Goals" (p. 77) and its related Challenge Case Summary were written to help you better understand the management concepts contained in this chapter. Answer the following discussion questions about the Challenge Case to better understand how concepts relating to corporate social responsibility and business ethics can be applied in a company such as IBM.

1. Do you think that IBM has a responsibility to support adult education in the communities in which it does business? Explain.
2. Assuming that IBM has such a responsibility, in what instances would it be relatively easy for the company to be committed to living up to it?
3. Assuming that IBM has such a responsibility, in what instances would it be relatively difficult for the company to be committed to living up to it?

GAP GOES PUBLIC ON SOCIAL RESPONSIBILITY

Read the case and answer the questions that follow. Studying this case will help you better understand how concepts relating to corporate social responsibility and business ethics can be applied in a company such as Gap Inc.

Shortly after Paul Pressler became CEO of Gap Inc., his teenage daughter asked him, "Doesn't Gap use sweatshops?" The new CEO wasn't surprised at her reaction. Despite all the news coverage about the company's ups and downs, he realized that many customers, investors, and other stakeholders knew little about Gap's progress in monitoring and improving factory conditions. Gap operates 3,000 Gap, Banana Republic, and Old Navy stores in five countries, ringing up $16 billion in annual sales revenue. To keep its racks full of fashions, Gap's merchandise managers buy clothing and accessories from thousands of factories spread across North and South America, Eastern and Western Europe, Africa, India, Asia, and the Middle East.

Gap was going through a difficult time when Pressler came aboard. The company had lost money during the previous year and sales were stalled amid a sluggish economy. What's more, the stores were stuffed with inventory, mark-downs were squeezing profit margins, and competition among clothing retailers was fiercer than ever. To turn Gap around, the CEO and his management team carefully researched their customers, changed both stores and merchandise to sharpen distinctions among the three chains, and began using special software to support their pricing decisions.

In addition to these urgent challenges, Pressler knew that Gap had been wrestling with allegations that some of its suppliers mistreated workers, employed children, and tolerated other violations. Gap's senior management first developed labor, health, and safety standards for company suppliers to follow in 1992. Over the next decade, its executives toughened the rules, hired dozens of inspectors to visit factories, and investigated whether Gap's standards were being met. By the time Pressler became CEO, the company had created an independent Global Compliance department and was spending millions of dollars checking up on suppliers, then taking action. For example, in 2003 alone, Gap stopped buying from 136 overseas factories that repeatedly violated its rules.

Gap had been posting some information about factory standards on its company Web site for a few years. Now the CEO gave the go-ahead to publish a more comprehensive social responsibility report. The initial 40-page report noted that Gap had made progress in helping suppliers improve factory conditions and in forging ties with nongovernmental organizations to build momentum for sustainability. Candidly, the report admitted that Gap still had a way to go in achieving "transparency" and getting the entire industry to address factory conditions. In pushing for more transparency, the company invited representatives of several stakeholder groups to comment on its social responsibility results and suggest improvements.

Rather than keeping this feedback private, Gap reported both the compliments and the criticisms. It also printed its four social responsibility goals for the coming year, opening the door to closer stakeholder scrutiny of Gap's future performance in those areas.

While praising the company for going public with its results, some activists told the news media that Gap should be doing more to address factory conditions—and doing it more quickly. "We recognize and embrace our duty to take a leadership role" in promoting such changes, Pressler said in the report. He also mentioned the year's other social responsibility accomplishments, including donating $60 million to nonprofit groups, recycling 20,000 tons of cardboard and paper, and giving employees time off to volunteer 22,000 hours helping worthy causes.

Under Pressler, Gap returned to profitability and set ambitious financial goals for the future. Asked about Gap's ability to continue building sales and profits,

Pressler recently said, "We don't take yesterday's success as a guarantee for tomorrow." That's also true on the social responsibility side. No one company can overhaul conditions in every supplier's factories overnight, but Pressler is committed to making a difference in the lives of thousands of workers. Is the message getting out to Gap's stakeholders—and to his daughter?

QUESTIONS

1. Should Gap publicly report its social responsibility results in detail, even if every objective hasn't been completely achieved?
2. Do you think Gap's conversion of social responsibility policies into action is in phase 1, phase 2, or phase 3? Explain.
3. Is Gap's approach to social responsibility based on obligation, responsibility, or responsiveness? Support your answer.

VIDEONET EXERCISE

Social Responsibility at Terracycle

VIDEO HIGHLIGHTS

CEO Tom Szaky, self-proclaimed "eco-capitalist," gives us the scoop on starting his quickly growing company, which "manufactures potent, organic products that are not only made from waste, but are also packaged entirely in waste. TerraCycle Plant Food™ is made by feeding premium, organic waste to millions of worms. The worm poop is then liquefied into a powerful organic plant food and bottled directly in used soda bottles. This story gives the phrase 'earth-friendly' a whole new meaning." (Excerpt from TerraCycle's Web site.) Tom debunks the myth that doing the right thing costs more and explains how TerraCycle is different from other green businesses.

Discussion Questions

1. What argument does Tom Szaky use for his business performing socially responsible activities?
2. Using the Davis Model, discuss which of the five propositions of corporate responsibility you think are most applicable to TerraCycle.
3. Which management approach to meeting social obligations is being used by Szaky and TerraCycle?

Internet Activity

Go to the TerraCycle Web site at www.terracycle.net. Read the information on Ecocapitalism presented in the "Our Revolution" section, as well as the biography of Tom Szaky presented in the "Careers" section. Based on his theories and actions, do you see Szaky as a socially responsible manager? Overall, are his positions on social responsibility enhancing company success? Explain.

4

Management and Diversity

OBJECTIVES

TO HELP BUILD MY DIVERSITY SKILL, WHEN STUDYING
THIS CHAPTER, I WILL ATTEMPT TO ACQUIRE:

1. A definition of diversity
   and an understanding
   of its importance in the
   corporate structure

2. An understanding of the
   advantages of having a
   diverse workforce

3. An awareness of the challenges facing managers
   within a diverse workforce

4. An understanding of the
   strategies for promoting
   diversity in organizations

5. Insights into the role of the
   manager in promoting
   diversity in the organization

TARGET SKILL diversity skill: the ability to establish and maintain an organizational workforce that represents a combination of assorted human characteristics appropriate for achieving organizational success

CHALLENGE CASE

DENNY'S MAKES DIVERSITY ADVANCES

Advantica Restaurant Group, Inc., owns more than 1,800 Denny's restaurants. Denny's restaurants represent one of the largest U.S. family restaurant chains in market share and sales volume and has recently reached the benchmark of operating in all 50 states and five foreign countries. Advantica has 22 percent of its Denny's restaurants in the state of California, 11 percent in the state of Florida, and 9 percent in the state of Texas.

In the past, the Denny's chain has suffered some negative publicity regarding alleged racist employees. A black family is suing the Denny's restaurant chain for $10 million claiming that their group of 25 people was refused service. The suit alleges that the family waited for nearly two hours and was ultimately refused service based solely on their race. Rachelle Hood-Phillips, chief diversity officer for Advantica Restaurant Group, Inc., apologized for the poor service but asked that people not confuse a delay of service with discrimination. Back in 1994, Denny's settled a similar suit for $46 million that claimed black customers were denied service or forced to pay in advance.

Today, however, Denny's is receiving much recognition for its diversity improvements.[1] *Black Enterprise Magazine*

Advantica Restaurant Group is working to achieve diversity among its employees and (despite setbacks) to communicate an appreciation of diversity among its customers. Here Denny's president John Romandetti and diversity officer Rachelle Hood-Phillips celebrate the company's recent achievements in this area.

recently listed Denny's among the 40 best American companies for diversity. The recognition came as a happy surprise to Denny's top management, according to Hood-Phillips. Her job is to make sure the company is doing all it can to improve its diversity track record—one she readily admits was not always something to boast about.

Denny's made significant recent steps in establishing itself as a leader in diversity.[2] The company named Debra Smithart-Oglesby as its corporate board chairperson with more than half of the company's nine board members being minorities or female. The corporate board also hired a new chief executive, James B. Adamson, who is committed to improving Denny's diversity image. One of his first moves was to hire Hood-Phillips and charge her with improving the company's focus on diversity. In addition, several upper-level minority or female executives have been hired.

Despite its recent positive recognition, Denny's management is not about to consider its building diversity job finished. Instead, management has publicly proclaimed that it's nice to be known as a diversity leader, but to continue to be known as a leader it must be vigilant to stay on top and to get better.

> "EXPLORE YOUR OWN MANAGEMENT SKILLS BY TAKING THE QUIZ ON THE NEXT PAGE"

Before studying this chapter, respond to the following questions regarding the type of advice that you would give to James B. Adamson, the CEO referenced in the Challenge Case. Then address the concerning diversity challenges that he presently faces. You are not expected to be a diversity expert at this point. Answering the questions now can help you focus on important points when you study the chapter. Also, answering the questions again after you study the chapter will give you an idea of how much you have learned.

Record your answers here or online at MyManagement Lab.com. Completing the questions at MyManagement Lab.com will allow you to get feedback about your answers automatically. If you answer the questions in the book, look up answers in the Exploring Your Management Skill section at the end of the book.

FOR EACH STATEMENT CIRCLE:

- "Y" if you would give the advice to Adamson.
- "N" if you would NOT give the advice to Adamson.
- "NI" if you have no idea whether you would give the advice to Adamson.

Mr. Adamson, in meeting your diversity challenges at Denny's, you should . . .

Before Study	*After Study*

1. study the structure of minority and majority employee groups at Denny's.

   Y, N, NI

2. emphasize diversity at Denny's as a vehicle to gain, but not necessarily keep, market share.

   Y, N, NI

3. be willing to sacrifice some productivity at Denny's in order to build a diverse organization.

   Y, N, NI

4. be aware that Hispanics will likely have a higher percentage growth than blacks during 2010–2020 within the U.S. population.

   Y, N, NI

5. avoid ethnocentrism.

   Y, N, NI

6. use the "glass ceiling" to your advantage at Denny's.

   Y, N, NI

7. focus on eliminating the stereotyping of older workers at Denny's.

   Y, N, NI

8. use the strategy of improving mostly the skills of Denny's managers to improve company diversity.

   Y, N, NI

9. be careful of reverse discrimination at Denny's—employees' discrimination against managers.

   Y, N, NI

10. achieve excellent diversity at Denny's by using non-discrimination policies as guidelines for action, thereby reducing the need for diversity training of managers.

    Y, N, NI

11. control for diversity at Denny's by making sure that diversity efforts materialize as planned.

    Y, N, NI

12. follow the "Golden Rule" for business: "He who has the gold makes the rules."

    Y, N, NI

13. not forget that at Denny's you may have to eliminate resistance to change in order for diversity efforts to be successful.

    Y, N, NI

14. make sure that you are not being influenced by conscious incompetence in trying to build a pro-diversity climate a Denny's.

    Y, N, NI

15. organize your diversity efforts by offering incentives that employees will receive if they follow Denny's diversity guidelines.

    Y, N, NI

THE DIVERSITY CHALLENGE

The Challenge Case illustrates the diversity challenge that Denny's management strives to meet. The remaining material in this chapter explains diversity concepts and helps to develop the corresponding diversity skill that you will need to meet such challenges throughout your career. After studying chapter concepts, read the Challenge Case Summary at the end of the chapter to help you to relate chapter content to meeting diversity challenges at Denny's.

DEFINING DIVERSITY

Diversity refers to characteristics of individuals that shape their identities and the experiences they have in society. This chapter provides information about workforce diversity and discusses the strengths and problems of a diverse workforce. Understanding diversity is essential for managers today because managing diversity will undoubtedly constitute a large portion of the management agenda well into the twenty-first century.[3]

This chapter describes some strategies for promoting social diversity in organizations. It also explains how diversity is related to the four management functions. Given the nature of this topic, you will probably find yourself reflecting on diversity as you study future chapters.

The Social Implications of Diversity

Workforce diversity is not a new issue around the world or in the United States. People from various other regions and cultures have been immigrating to other countries for centuries, so the population has always been a mix of races, ethnicities, religions, social classes, physical abilities, and sexual orientations.[4] These differences—along with the basic human differences of age and gender—comprise diversity. The purpose of exploring diversity issues in a management textbook is to suggest how managers might include diverse employees equally, accepting their differences and utilizing their talents.[5]

Majority and Minority Groups Managers must understand the relationship between two groups in organizations: majority groups and minority groups. **Majority group** refers to that group of people in the organization who hold most of the positions that command decision-making power, control of resources and information, and access to system rewards. Note that the majority is not *always* the group with a numerical majority. **Minority group** refers to that group of people in the organization who are fewer or who lack critical power, resources, acceptance, and social status. Together, the minority and majority group members form the entire social system of the organization.

Note that the minority group is not *always* lesser in number than the majority group. For example, women are seen as a minority group in most organizations because they do not have the critical power to shape organizational decisions and to control resources. Moreover, they have yet to achieve full acceptance and social status in most workplaces. In most health care organizations, for instance, women outnumber men. Although men are numerical minorities, however, they are seldom denied social status because white males hold most positions of power in the health care system hierarchy, such as physician and health care administrator.

ADVANTAGES OF DIVERSITY IN ORGANIZATIONS

Managers are becoming more dedicated to seeking a wide range of talents from every group in their culture because they now realize that distinct advantages come from doing so.[6] For one thing, as you will see in Chapter 18, group decisions often improve the quality of decision making. For another, work groups or teams that can draw on the contributions of a multicultural membership gain the advantage of a larger pool of information and a richer array of approaches to work problems.

Ann Morrison carried out a comprehensive study of 16 private and public organizations in the United States. In the resulting book, *The New Leaders: Guidelines on Leadership Diversity in America,* she outlines the several other advantages of diversity, each of which is discussed here.[7]

Gaining and Keeping Market Share

Today managers must understand increasingly diverse markets. Failure to discern customers' preferences can cost a company business. Some people argue that one of the best ways to ensure that the organization is able to penetrate diverse markets is to include diverse managers among the organization's decision makers.[8]

Diversity in the managerial ranks has the further advantage of enhancing company credibility with customers. Employing a manager who is of the same gender or ethnic background as customers may imply to those customers that their day-to-day experiences will be understood. One African American female manager found that her knowledge of customers paid off when she convinced her company to change the name of a product it intended to sell at Wal-Mart. "I knew that I had shopped for household goods at Wal-Mart, whereas the CEO of this company, a white, upper-middle-class male, had not. He listened to me and we changed the name of the product."

Morrison cites a case in which one company lost an important opportunity for new business in a southwestern city's predominantly Hispanic community. The lucrative business ultimately went to a competitor that had put a Hispanic manager in charge of the project who solicited input from the Hispanic community.

For **an example from the world of management** illustrating a focus on gaining market share through diversity, consider events at **Safeway**, one of North America's largest food retailers. Several years ago with about 1,700 grocery stores, Safeway began facing increasingly stiff competition from companies such as Target and Wal-Mart. To cope with this competition, Safeway initiated a program to establish the company as an employer of choice. Additionally, because 70 percent of Safeway's customers were women, the company also wanted to expand the diversity of its workforce to make it more consistent with this customer base. Safeway recognized that a diverse workforce would help the company to better understand and respond to the needs of its customers and thereby afford a competitive edge in the marketplace. Because male leadership had been a tradition in the industry, Safeway's new program supporting women leaders was a deviation from the norm. Today, management openly credits its past diversity efforts as the foundation for present levels of both diversity and profitability.[9]

Recognizing that 70% of its customers are women, Safeway began a program to reflect this same gender diversity in its management group. As a result it has worked to become an employer of choice in the North American hypermarket industry.

Cost Savings

Companies incur high costs in recruiting, training, relocating, and replacing employees and in providing competitive compensation packages. According to Morrison, Corning Corporation's high turnover among women and people of color was costing the company an estimated $2 million to $4 million a year. Many managers who were questioned for her study felt that the personnel expenses associated with turnover—often totaling as much as two-thirds of an organization's budget—could be cut by instituting diversity practices that would give nontraditional managers more incentive to stay. When nontraditional managers remain with the organization, nontraditional employees at lower levels feel more committed to the company.

In addition to the personnel costs, executives are distressed by the high legal fees and staggering settlements resulting from lawsuits brought by employees who feel they have been discriminated against. For example, $17.7 million in damages was awarded to a woman employed by Texaco who claimed she had been passed over for a management promotion because of her gender. Executives are learning that such sums would be better spent on promoting diversity.

Increased Productivity and Innovation

Many executives quoted in Morrison's study believe productivity is higher in organizations that focus on diversity. These managers find that employees who feel valued, competent, and at ease in their work setting enjoy coming to work and perform at a high level.

Morrison also cites a study by Donna Thompson and Nancy DiTomaso, which concluded that a multicultural approach has a positive effect on employees' perception of equity. This, in turn, positively affects employees' morale, goal setting, effort, and performance. The managers in Morrison's study also saw innovation as a strength of a diverse workforce. In essence, diversity becomes the spark that ignites innovation.[10]

Better-Quality Management

Morrison also found that including nontraditional employees in fair competition for advancement usually improves the quality of management by providing a wider pool of talent. According to the research she cites, exposure to diverse colleagues helps managers develop breadth and openness.

The quality of management can also be improved by building more effective personnel policies and practices that, once developed, will benefit all employees in the organization, not just minorities. According to Morrison's study, many of the programs initially developed for nontraditional managers resulted in improvements that were later successfully applied throughout the organization. Ideas such as adding training for mentors, upgrading techniques for developing managers, and improving processes for evaluating employees for promotion—all concepts originally intended to help nontraditional managers—were later adopted for wider use. (See Table 4.1 for more information on the advantages of a diverse workforce.)

At first glance, the advantages of diversity to an organization seem undeniable. In a recent survey focusing on small to medium-sized enterprises, however, more managers surveyed disagreed that diversity contributed to performance than agreed.[11] These findings, however, do not dispute the overall conclusion that diversity contributes to organizational performance. Instead, the findings seem to indicate that many managers still need to be convinced of the benefits that accrue to an organization through diversity.

TABLE 4.1   Advantages of a Diverse Workforce

Improved ability to gain and keep market share
Cost savings
Increased productivity
A more innovative workforce
Minority and women employees who are more motivated
Better quality of managers
Employees who have internalized the message that "different" does not mean "less than"
Employees who are accustomed to making use of differing worldviews, learning styles, and approaches in the decision-making process and in the cultivation of new ideas
Employees who have developed multicultural competencies, such as learning to recognize, surface, discuss, and work through work-related issues pertaining to global, cultural, or intergroup differences
A workforce that is more resilient when faced with change

CHALLENGES THAT MANAGERS FACE IN WORKING WITH DIVERSE POPULATIONS

As you have seen, an organization may find numerous compelling reasons to encourage diversity in its workforce. For managers to fully appreciate the implications of promoting diversity, however, they must understand some of the challenges they face in managing a diverse workforce. Changing demographics and several issues arising out of these changes are discussed in the following sections.[12]

Changing Demographics

Demographics are statistical characteristics of a population. Demographics are an important tool that managers can use to study workforce diversity, and they are discussed further in Chapter 9. According to a report by the Hudson Institute, the workforce and jobs of the twenty-first century will parallel changes in society and in the economy. This report indicates that five demographic issues will be especially important to managers in developed countries in the twenty-first century:[13]

1. The population and the workforce will grow more slowly than at any time since the 1930s.
2. The average age of the population and the workforce will rise, and the pool of young workers entering the labor market will shrink.
3. More women will enter the workforce.
4. Minorities will make up a larger share of new entrants into the labor force.
5. Immigrants will represent the largest share of the increase in both the general population and the workforce.

The changing demographics of a population over an extended period can give managers insight regarding future diversity management challenges. For example, Figure 4.1 provides projections for average annual percent changes in various races in the U.S. population as an example. According to the projections, the black population in the United States will grow at more than twice the annual rate of change of the white population between 1995 and 2050. Through 2020, the Asian and Pacific Islander population group is projected to be the fastest-growing population segment. By the turn of the century, the Asian population will expand to more than 11 million, double its current size by 2020, and triple by 2040. The American Indian, Eskimo, and Aleut race segment is projected to grow, but not nearly as

Colleagues meet in a diversity council gathering at Levi Strauss & Company. The makeup of this group reflects the changing demographics of the workplace.

significantly as the Asian segment. Growth of the Hispanic population will also be a major element of the total population growth. Each year from now to 2050, the Hispanic segment is projected to add more people to the United States population than the white segment. Such demographic trends seem to indicate that the ability to handle diversity challenges will be valuable to both U.S. managers and managers around the world in the future.

Ethnocentrism and Other Negative Dynamics

The changing demographics described in the Hudson Institute's report set in motion certain social dynamics that can interfere with workforce productivity. If an organization is to be successful in diversifying, it must neutralize these dynamics.

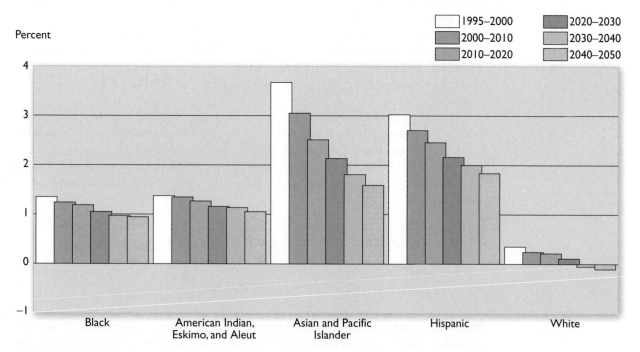

FIGURE 4.1 Average annual percentage changes in the U.S. population by race, 1995–2050

Ethnocentrism Our natural tendency is to judge other groups less favorably than our own. This tendency is the source of **ethnocentrism,** the belief that one's own group, culture, country, or customs are superior to others'. Two related dynamics are prejudices and stereotypes. A **prejudice** is a preconceived judgment, opinion, or assumption about an issue, behavior, or group of people.[14] A **stereotype** is a positive or negative assessment of members of a group or their perceived attributes. One modern possibility of stereotyping involves Muslims. Many Muslims living abroad fear that because some Muslims are high-profile terrorists, others might tend to stereotype all Muslims as terrorists. U.S. Muslims, for example, reason that they represent more than 6 percent of the U.S. population, are overwhelmingly college graduates, professionals and business owners, and contribute almost nothing to the crime rate. Thus, they argue that stereotyping all Muslims as terrorists is drastically unfair to them.[15]

Overall, it is important for managers to know about such negative dynamics as ethnocentrism and stereotyping so they can monitor their own perceptions and help their employees view diverse coworkers more accurately.

Discrimination When verbalized or acted upon, these negative dynamics can cause discomfort and stress for the judged individual. In some cases, there is outright discrimination. **Discrimination** is the act of treating an issue, person, or behavior unjustly or inequitably on the basis of stereotypes and prejudices. Consider the disabled person who is turned down for promotion because the boss feels this employee is incapable of handling the regular travel required for this particular job. The boss's prejudgment of this employee's capabilities on the basis of "difference," and implementation of the prejudgment through differential treatment, constitutes discrimination. Consider an older worker who is turned down for a job because the manger thinks the worker is too old for the job. The actual turning down of the potential employee based upon this managerial feeling could be considered age discrimination.[16]

Tokenism and Other Challenges Discrimination occurs when stereotypes are acted upon in ways that affect hiring, pay, or promotion practices—for example, where older employees are steered into less visible job assignments that are unlikely to provide opportunities for advancement. Other challenges facing minorities and women include the pressure to conform to the organization's culture, high penalties for mistakes, and tokenism. **Tokenism** refers to being one of few members of your group in the organization.[17] "Token" employees are given either very high or very low visibility in the organization. One African American male indicated that he was "discouraged" by his white female manager from joining voluntary committees and task forces within the company—but at the same time criticized in his performance appraisal by her for being "aloof" and taking a "low-profile approach."

In other cases, minorities are seen as representatives or "spokespeople" for all members of their group. As such, they are subject to high expectations and scrutiny from members of their own group. One Latino male employee described how other Latinos in his mostly white company "looked up to him" for his achievements in the organization. In general, ethnocentrism, prejudices, and stereotypes inhibit our ability to accurately process information.

Negative Dynamics and Specific Groups

The following sections more fully discuss these negative dynamics as they pertain to women, minorities, older workers, and workers with disabilities.

Women Rosabeth Kanter has researched the pressures women managers face. In her classic study of gender dynamics in organizations, she emphasized the high expectations women have of other women as one of those pressures.[18]

Gender Roles Women in organizations confront **gender-role stereotypes,** or perceptions about people based on what our society believes are appropriate behaviors for men and women. Both sexes find their self-expression constrained by gender-role stereotyping. For example, women in organizations are often assumed to be good listeners. This attribution is based on our societal view that women are nurturing. Although this assessment is a positive one, it is not true of all women or of any woman all the time—hence the negative side of this stereotypical expectation for women in the workplace.

Women professionals, for instance, often remark that they are frequently sought out by colleagues who want to discuss non–work-related problems. Women managers also describe the subtle sanctions they experience from both men and women when they do not fulfill expectations that they will be nurturing managers.

The Glass Ceiling and Sexual Harassment A serious form of discrimination affecting women in organizations has been dubbed the *glass ceiling*.[19] The glass ceiling refers to an invisible "ceiling," or barrier to advancement.[20] This term, originally coined to describe the limits confronting women, is also used to describe the experiences of other minorities in organizations. Although both women and men struggle to balance work and family concerns, it is still more common for women to assume primary responsibility for household management as well as their careers, and sometimes they are denied opportunities for advancement because of this stereotype.

Sexual harassment is another form of discrimination that affects female employees. *Sexual harassment* is defined as any unwanted sexual language, behavior, or imagery negatively affecting an employee.[21] Sexual harassment may include requests for sexual favors when such favors explicitly or implicitly become a term or condition of an individual's employment or education. Managers must keep in mind that although this discussion on sexual harassment has focused primarily on women, men can also be victims of sexual harassment in the workplace or educational settings.

class discussion highlight

DIVERSITY SKILL AND YOUR CAREER

Possible Negative Impact on Careers of Women

Based upon the preceding information, women may be negatively affected in their organizational lives simply because of their gender. A recent survey of professional women working in accounting companies seems to confirm this observation.[22] According to the survey, 59 percent of the respondents indicated that they were negatively affected by gender bias. Respondents believed that to an influential extent they were either given or not given their jobs because of their gender.

Could such gender bias affect your career if you are a woman? If you are a man? Could such bias have an impact on the success of an organization? Explain each answer fully. Summarize what you have learned about gender bias and building your career in an organization.

Minorities Racial, ethnic, and cultural minorities also confront inhibiting stereotypes about their group. Like women, they must deal with misunderstandings and expectations based on their ethnic or cultural origins.

Many members of ethnic or racial minority groups have been socialized to be members of two cultural groups—the dominant culture and their particular racial or ethnic culture. Ella Bell, professor of organizational behavior, refers to this dual membership as *biculturalism*. In her study of African American women, she identifies the stress of coping with membership in two cultures simultaneously as **bicultural stress**.[23] She also indicates that **role conflict** (having to fill competing roles because of membership in two cultures) and

role overload (having too many expectations to comfortably fulfill) are common characteristics of bicultural stress. Although these are problems for many minority groups, they are particularly intense for women of color because this group experiences negative dynamics affecting *both* minorities and women.

Internalized norms and values of one's culture of origin can lead to problems and misunderstandings in the workplace, particularly when a manager relies solely on the cultural norms of the majority group. According to the norms of Western culture, for example, it is acceptable—even positive—to publicly praise an individual for a job well done. However, in Eastern cultures that place primary value on group harmony and collective achievement, this way of rewarding an employee causes emotional discomfort because employees fear that, if praised publicly, they will "lose face" in their group.

Older Workers   Older workers are a significant and valuable component of today's labor force.[24] Over the next two decades, the number of people aged 50–64 in the EU will increase by 25 percent; the 20–29 age group will decrease 20 percent. In Japan, nearly 20 percent of the current population is over 65. The Japanese workforce is expected to shrink 16 percent over the next 25 years.[25]

Anticipating this future simultaneous shortage of younger workers and growth of older workers in the labor market, many managers recommend that now is the time to start recruiting older workers.[26] Successful tactics for recruiting older workers include asking for referrals by current employees, using employment agencies, contacting local senior citizens community groups, and surveying members of various churches. Advantages of hiring older workers include their willingness to work nontraditional schedules, their ability to serve as mentors, and their strong work ethic. Disadvantages of hiring older workers might include their lack of technology experience and possible increased benefits cost to the organization due to health care needs.

Once hired, management must focus on meeting the needs of older workers. For **an example from the world of management** that supports the importance of meeting the needs of older workers, consider the thoughts of **Sharon Birkman-Fink, president of Birkman International.** Birkman-Fink believes that management should continually focus on meeting the personal needs of older as opposed to younger workers. Management must understand issues such as job preferences, and personal needs of older versus younger workers are normally different. As a result, management will normally

Older workers have acquired skills, knowledge, and experience that make them valuable to the firm. That's one reason effective managers consider their special needs.

have to take special steps to meet the needs of older as opposed to younger workers. Such steps will help management to retain older workers and encourage older workers to be as productive as possible.[27]

Stereotypes and Prejudices Older workers present some specific challenges for managers. Stereotypes and prejudices link age with senility, incompetence, and lack of worth in the labor market. Jeffrey Sonnenfeld, an expert on senior executives and older workers, compiled research findings from several studies of older employees. He found that managers view older workers as "deadwood" and seek to "weed them out" through pension incentives, biased performance appraisals, and other methods.[28]

Actually, Sonnenfeld's compilation of research indicates that even though older managers are more cautious, less likely to take risks, and less open to change than younger managers, many are high performers. Studies that tracked individuals' careers over the long term conclude that a peak in performance occurs about age 45 to 50, and a second peak about age 55 to 60. Performance in some fields (e.g., sales) either improves with age or does not significantly decline.

It is the manager's responsibility to value older workers for their contributions to the organization and to see to it that they are treated fairly. This task requires an understanding of and sensitivity to the physiological and psychological changes that older workers are experiencing. Supporting older workers also requires paying attention to how performance appraisal processes, retirement incentives, training programs, blocked career paths, union insurance pensions, and affirmative action goals affect this segment of the workforce.

Workers with Disabilities People with disabilities are subject to the same negative dynamics that plague women, minorities, and older workers. For example, one manager confessed that before he attended diversity training sessions offered through a nearby university, he felt "uncomfortable" around disabled people. One disabled professional reported that she was always received warmly by phone and told that her background was exactly what companies were looking for, but when she showed up for job interviews, she was often rebuffed and informed that her credentials were insufficient.

Many companies are ignoring such negative dynamics and taking proactive steps to employ workers with disabilities as productive employees. As **an example from the world of management** illustrating how companies are proactively pursuing the hiring of workers with disabilities, consider recent events at **Walgreens Company,** operator of about 5,700 drug stores in the Unites States and Puerto Rico. The company recently unveiled its new 670,000 square foot distribution center in Anderson, South Carolina, servicing stores throughout the southeastern United States. The distribution center will employ about 700 employees, about 200 of which will have various sorts of disabilities. According to management, the new center has many features that can be adapted to meet the needs of workers with disabilities. Among the features are workstations that adjust for a workers' height and touch-screen computers to help perform tasks. According to Randy Lewis, senior vice president for distribution and logistics, "This is not charity. We didn't lower any of our [job performance] standards."[29]

STRATEGIES FOR PROMOTING DIVERSITY IN ORGANIZATIONS

This section looks at several approaches to diversity and strategies that managers can consider as they plan for promoting cultural diversity in their organizations. First, the six strategies for modern management offered by the Hudson Institute report focusing on the twenty-first–century workforce are explored. Then the requirements of the U.S. Equal Employment Opportunity Commission, which is legally empowered to regulate U.S. organizations to ensure that management practices enhance diversity, are discussed. Next, promoting diversity through various levels of commitment is covered. Finally, promoting diversity through pluralism is considered.

Promoting Diversity Through Hudson Institute Strategies

According to the Hudson Institute, six major issues demand the full attention of U.S. business leaders of the twenty-first century and require them to take the following actions:[30]

1. **Stimulate balanced world growth**—The United States must pay less attention to its share of world trade and more to the growth of the economies of other nations of the world, including those nations in Europe, Latin America, and Asia, with which the United States competes.
2. **Accelerate productivity increases in service industries**—Prosperity will depend much more on how fast output per worker increases in health care, education, retailing, government, and other services than on gains in manufacturing.
3. **Maintain the dynamism of an aging workforce**—As the age of the average American worker climbs toward 40, the nation must make sure that its workforce does not lose its adaptability and willingness to learn.
4. **Reconcile the conflicting needs of women, work, and families**—Despite a huge influx of women into the workforce in the last two decades, many organizational policies covering pay, fringe benefits, time away from work, pensions, welfare, and other issues do not yet reflect this new reality.
5. **Fully integrate African American and Hispanic workers into the economy**—The decline in the number of "traditional" white male workers among the young, the rapid pace of industrial change, and the rising skill requirements of the emerging economy make the full utilization of minority workers a particularly urgent challenge for the future.
6. **Improve the education and skills of all workers**—Human capital (knowledge, skills, organization, and leadership) is the key to economic growth and competitiveness.

As these key strategies for modern management suggest, many of the most significant managerial challenges that lie ahead for both U.S. managers and managers worldwide derive from dramatic demographic shifts and other complex societal issues. Organizations—and, ultimately, their leaders and managers—will need to clarify their own social values as they confront these dynamics. *Social values,* discussed further in Chapter 9, refer to the relative worth society places on different ways of existence and functions.

The six strategies outlined in the report strongly imply that organizations need to become more inclusive—that is, to welcome a broader mix of employees and to develop an organizational culture that maximizes the value and potential of each worker. As with any major initiative, commitment to developing an inclusive organization begins at the top of the organizational hierarchy. However, on a day-to-day operational basis, each manager's level of commitment is a critical determinant of how well or how poorly the organization's strategies and approaches will be implemented.

Promoting Diversity Through Equal Employment and Affirmative Action

The Equal Employment Opportunity Commission (EEOC) is the U.S. agency that enforces the laws regulating recruiting and other management practices. Chapter 13 contains a more extended discussion of the EEOC. Affirmative action programs in the United States are designed to eliminate barriers against and increase opportunities for underutilized or disadvantaged individuals. These programs are positive steps toward promoting diversity and have created career opportunities for both women and minority groups.

Unquestionably, complying with EEO legislation can help to promote diversity in organizations and, as a result, help organizations gain the many diversity-related advantages

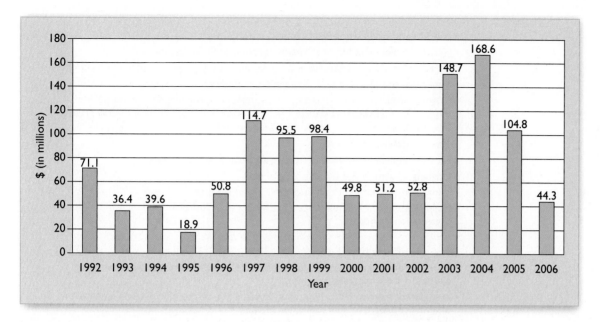

FIGURE 4.2 Total monetary settlements paid by companies for noncompliance with EEO legislation: 1992–2006

discussed earlier. On the other hand, not following the legislation can be expensive. As an example, consider the 15-year span of government data in Figure 4.2 of monetary settlements to employees who sued organizations for noncompliance with EEO legislation. Legal settlements to employees reached highs of $148.7 million in 2003 and $168.6 in 2004, but have since shown a decline. Overall, managers should view EEOC as a source of guidance on how to build organizational diversity and reap its related advantages rather than as a source of punishment when EEO legislation is not followed.

Still, organizations can do much more. For example, some employees are hostile toward affirmative action programs because they feel these programs have been misused to create **reverse discrimination**—that is, they discriminate against members of the majority group in order to help groups that are underrepresented in the organization. When management implements appropriate legal approaches but stops short of developing a truly multicultural organization, intergroup conflicts are highly likely.

Promoting Diversity Through Organizational Commitment

Figure 4.3 shows the range of organizational commitment to multiculturalism. At the top of the continuum are organizations that have committed resources, planning, and time to the ongoing shaping and sustaining of a multicultural organization. At the bottom of the continuum are organizations that make no efforts whatever to achieve diversity in their workforces. Most organizations fall somewhere between the extremes depicted in the figure.

Ignoring Differences Some organizations make no effort to promote diversity and do not even bother to comply with affirmative action and EEOC standards. They are sending a strong message to their employees that the dynamics of difference are unimportant. By ignoring EEOC policies, they are sending an even more detrimental message to their managers: that it is permissible to maintain exclusionary practices.

Complying with External Policies Some organizations base their diversity strategy solely on compliance with affirmative action and EEOC policies. They make no attempt to provide education and training for employees, nor do they use the organization's reward system to reinforce managerial commitment to diversity. Managers in some companies in

Broad-based diversity efforts based on:
- Effective implementation of affirmative action and EEOC policies
- Organization-wide assessment and management's top-down commitment to diversity
- Managerial commitment tied to organizational rewards
- Ongoing processes of organization assessment and programs for the purpose of creating an organizational climate that is inclusive and supportive of diverse groups

Diversity efforts based on:
- Effective implementation of affirmative action and EEOC policies
- Ongoing education and training programs
- Managerial commitment tied to organizational rewards
- Minimal attention directed toward cultivating an inclusive and supportive organizational climate

Diversity efforts based on:
- Narrowly defined affirmative action and EEOC policies combined with one-shot education and/or training programs
- Inconsistent managerial commitment; rewards not tied to effective implementation of diversity programs and goal achievement
- No attention directed toward organizational climate

Diversity efforts based on:
- Compliance with and enforcement of affirmative action and EEOC policies
- No organizational supports with respect to education, training
- Inconsistent or poor managerial commitment

Diversity efforts based on:
- Compliance with affirmative action and EEOC policies
- Inconsistent enforcement and implementation (those who breach policies may not be sanctioned unless noncompliance results in legal action)
- Support of policies is not rewarded; organization relies on individual managers' interest or commitment

No diversity efforts:
- Noncompliance with affirmative action and EEOC

FIGURE 4.3
Organizational diversity continuum

this category breach company affirmative action and EEOC policies with impunity. When top management does not punish them, the likelihood of costly legal action against the organization rises.

Enforcing External Policies Some organizations go so far as to enforce affirmative action and EEOC policies, but provide no organizational supports for education or training for diversity. Managerial commitment to a diverse workforce is either weak or inconsistent.

Responding Inadequately Other organizations fully comply with affirmative action and EEOC policies, but define these policies quite narrowly. Organizational systems and structures are inadequate to support real organizational change. Education and training in diversity are sporadic, and managerial rewards for implementing diversity programs are inconsistent or nonexistent. Although these organizations may design some useful programs, they are unlikely to result in any long-term organizational change, so the organizational climate never becomes truly receptive to diverse groups.

Implementing Adequate Programs Some organizations effectively implement affirmative action and EEOC policies, provide ongoing education and training programs pertaining to diversity, and tie managerial rewards to success in meeting diversity goals and addressing diversity issues. However, such companies make only a minimal attempt to cultivate the kind of inclusive and supportive organizational climate diverse populations of employees will feel comfortable in.

Taking Effective Action The most effective diversity efforts are based on managerial implementation of a country's diversity policies that are developed in conjunction with an organization-wide assessment of the company's systems and structures. Such an assessment is necessary to determine how these systems and structures support or hinder diversity goals.

Generally, for such a comprehensive assessment to take place, top management must "buy" the idea that diversity is important to the company. Actually, support from the top is critical to all successful diversity efforts and underlies tying organizational rewards to managers' commitment to diversity. Ongoing assessment and continuing programs are also necessary to create an organizational climate that is inclusive and supportive of diverse groups.

class discussion highlight

MODERN RESEARCH AND DIVERSITY SKILL

Pro-Diversity Work Climate and Intention to Leave an Organization[31]

A recent study of 7,000 managerial employees by McKay and colleagues investigated the relationship between employee intentions to voluntarily leave an organization and the degree to which employees viewed their work environment as being pro-diversity. A pro-diversity work environment was defined as an environment characterized by features such as recruiting employees from diverse sources, offering all people equal access to training, publicizing sound diversity principles, and having leaders who support principles of

sound diversity management. The researchers hypothesized that employees who did not see their organization as pro-diversity were more likely to voluntarily look for another job than those who did.

The researchers surveyed almost 7,000 managerial employees

- What do you think that the researchers found? Why?
- Do you believe that black, white, and Hispanic work groups all held similar opinions? Explain.
- What hints can this research give you about developing your diversity skill?

Promoting Diversity Through Pluralism

Pluralism refers to an environment in which differences are acknowledged, accepted, and seen as significant contributors to the entirety. A diverse workforce is most effective when managers are capable of guiding the organization toward achieving pluralism. Approaches, or strategies, to achieve effective workforce diversity have been classified into five major categories by Jean Kim of Stanford University:[32]

1. "Golden Rule" approach
2. Assimilation approach
3. "Righting-the-wrongs" approach
4. Culture-specific approach
5. Multicultural approach

Each approach is described briefly in the following sections.

"Golden Rule" Approach The "Golden Rule" approach to diversity relies on the biblical dictate, "Do unto others as you would have them do unto you."[33] The major strength of this approach is that it emphasizes individual morality. Its major flaw is that individuals apply the Golden Rule from their own particular frame of reference without knowing the cultural expectations, traditions, and preferences of the other person.

One African American male manager recalled a situation in which he was having difficulty scheduling a work-related event. In exasperation, he volunteered to schedule the event on Saturday. He was reminded by another employee that many of the company's Jewish employees went to religious services on Saturday. He was initially surprised—then somewhat embarrassed—that he had simply assumed that "all people" attended "church" on Sunday.

Assimilation Approach The assimilation approach advocates shaping organization members to fit the existing culture of the organization. This approach pressures employees who do not belong to the dominant culture to conform—at the expense of renouncing their own cultures and worldviews. The end result is the creation of a homogeneous culture that suppresses the creativity and diversity of views that could benefit the organization.

One African American woman in middle management said, "I always felt uncomfortable in very formal meetings. I tend to be very animated when I talk, which is not the norm for the company. Until I became more comfortable with myself and my style, I felt inhibited. I was tempted to try to change my style to fit in."

"Righting-the-Wrongs" Approach "Righting-the-wrongs" is an approach that addresses past injustices experienced by a particular group. When a group's history places its members at a disadvantage for achieving career success and mobility, policies are developed to create a more equitable set of conditions. Apartheid policies in South Africa are an example. Righting-the-wrongs approaches are designed to compensate for the damages people have suffered because of historical inequalities.

This approach most closely parallels the affirmative action policies to be discussed in Chapter 13. It goes beyond affirmative action, however, in that it emphasizes tapping the unique talents of each group in the service of organizational productivity.

Culture-Specific Approach The culture-specific approach teaches employees the norms and practices of another culture to prepare them to interact with people from that culture effectively. This approach is often used to help employees prepare for international assignments. The problem with it is that it usually fails to give employees a genuine appreciation for the culture they are about to encounter.

Stewart Black and Hal Gregerson, in their study of managers on assignment in foreign countries, found that some identify much more with their parent firm than with the local operation.[34] One male manager, for instance, after spending two years opening retail outlets throughout Europe, viewed Europeans as "lazy and slow to respond to directives." Obviously, his training and preparation had failed to help him adjust to European host countries or to appreciate their peoples and cultures.

Multicultural Approach The multicultural approach gives employees the opportunity to develop an appreciation for both differences of culture and variations in personal characteristics. This approach focuses on how interpersonal skills and attitudinal changes relate to organizational performance. One of its strengths is that it assumes the organization itself—as well as individuals working within it—will be required to change in order to accommodate the diversity of the organization's workforce.

The multicultural approach is probably the most effective approach to pluralism because it advocates change on the part of management, employees, and organization systems and structures. It has the added advantage of stressing the idea that equity

The multicultural approach to diversity commits the entire organization to appreciating both broad cultural variations and specific personal differences among employees. This woman works at a Nike factory.

demands making some efforts to "right the wrongs" so that underrepresented groups will be fairly included throughout the organization.

THE ROLE OF THE MANAGER

Managers play an essential role in tapping the potential capacities of each person within their departments. This task requires competencies that are anchored in the four basic management functions of planning, organizing, influencing, and controlling. In this context, planning refers to the manager's role in developing programs to promote diversity, while organizing, influencing, and controlling take place in the implementation phases of those programs.

Planning

Recall from Chapter 1 that planning is a specific action proposed to help the organization achieve its objectives. It is an ongoing process that includes troubleshooting and continually defining areas where improvements can be made. Planning for diversity may involve selecting diversity training programs for the organization or setting diversity goals for employees within the department.

Setting recruitment goals for members of underrepresented groups is a key component of diversity planning. If top management has identified a certain minority group as an underrepresented group within the company, every manager throughout the company will need to collaborate with the human resources department to achieve the organizational goal of higher representation. For example, a manager might establish goals and objectives for the increased representation of this group within five years. To achieve this five-year vision, the manager will need to set benchmark goals for each year.

Organizing

According to Chapter 1, organizing is the process of establishing orderly uses for all resources within the management system. To achieve a diverse workplace, managers have to work with human resource professionals in the areas of recruitment, hiring, and retention so that the best match is made between the company and the employees it hires. Managerial responsibilities in this area may include establishing task forces or committees to explore issues and provide ideas, carefully choosing work assignments to support the career development of all employees, and evaluating the extent to which diversity goals are being achieved.

After managers have begun hiring from a diverse pool of employees, they will need to focus on retaining them by paying attention to the many concerns of a diverse workforce. In the case of working women and men with families, skillfully using the organization's resources to support their need for day care for dependents, allowing flexible work arrangements in keeping with company policy, and assigning and reassigning work responsibilities equitably to accommodate family leave usage are all examples of managers applying the organizing function.

Influencing

According to Chapter 1, influencing is the process of guiding the activities of organization members in appropriate directions. Integral to this management function are an effective leadership style, good communication skills, knowledge about how to motivate others, and an understanding of the organization's culture and group dynamics. In the area of diversity, influencing organization members means that managers must not only encourage and support employees to participate constructively in a diverse work environment, but must themselves engage in the career development and training processes that will give them the skills to facilitate the smooth operation of a diverse work community.

Managers are accountable as well for informing their employees of breaches of organizational policy and etiquette. Let us assume that the diversity strategy selected by top management includes educating employees about organizational policies concerning diversity as well as providing workshops for employees on specific cultural diversity issues. The manager's role in this case would be to hold employees accountable for learning about company diversity policies and complying with them. They could accomplish this task by consulting with staff and holding regular group meetings and one-on-one meetings when necessary. To encourage participation in diversity workshops, the manager may need to communicate to employees the importance the organization places on this knowledge base. Alternatively, the manager might choose to tie organizational rewards to the development of diversity competencies. Examples of such rewards are giving employees public praise or recognition and providing workers with opportunities to use their diversity skills on desirable work assignments.

Controlling

Overseeing compliance with the legal stipulations of EEOC and affirmative action is one aspect of the controlling function in the area of diversity. According to Chapter 1, controlling is the set of activities that make something happen as planned. Hence the evaluation activities necessary to assess diversity efforts are part of the controlling role that managers play in shaping a multicultural workforce.

Managers may find this function the most difficult one of the four to execute. It is not easy to evaluate planned-change approaches in general, and it is particularly hard to do so in the area of diversity. Many times the most successful diversity approaches reveal more problems as employees begin to speak openly about their concerns. Moreover, subtle attitudinal changes in one group's perception of another group are difficult to measure. What *can* be accurately measured are the outcome variables of turnover; representation of women, minorities, and other underrepresented groups at all levels of the company; and legal problems stemming from inappropriate or illegal behaviors (e.g., discrimination and sexual harassment).

Managers engaged in the controlling function in the area of diversity need to continually monitor their units' progress with respect to diversity goals and standards. They must decide what control measures to use (e.g., indicators of productivity, turnover, absenteeism, or promotion) and how to interpret the information these measures yield in light of diversity goals and standards.

For example, a manager may need to assess whether the low rate of promotions for Muslim men in her department is due to subtle biases toward this group or group members' poor performance compared to others in the department. She may find she needs to explore current organizational dynamics, as well as create effective supports for this group. Such supports might include fostering greater social acceptance of Muslim men among other employees, learning more about the Muslim male's bicultural experience in the company, making mentoring or other opportunities available to members of this group, and providing them with some specific job-related training.

Management Development and Diversity Training

Given the complex set of managerial skills needed to promote diversity, it is obvious that managers themselves will need organizational support if the company is to achieve its diversity goals. One important component of the diversity strategy of a large number of companies is diversity training.[35] **Diversity training** is a learning process designed to raise managers' awareness and develop their competencies to deal with the issues endemic to managing a diverse workforce. More and more, managers are recognizing that a diverse workforce is critical to the exploration of new ideas and the creation of innovation in organizations and that diversity training is a valuable tool in achieving this diversity.[36] Figure 4.4 shows the array of diversity training programs that McDonald's offers its mangers.

Basic Themes of Diversity Training Training is the process of developing qualities in human resources that will make those employees more productive and better able to contribute to organizational goal attainment. Some companies develop intensive programs for management and less intensive, more generalized programs for other employees. Such programs are discussed further in Chapter 13 and generally focus on the following five components or themes:

1. Behavioral awareness
2. Acknowledgment of biases and stereotypes
3. Focus on job performance

FIGURE 4.4
Diversity training programs offered to McDonald's employees
Source: www.mcdonalds.com/corp/values/people/diversity/education.html.

4. Avoidance of assumptions
5. Modification of policy and procedure manuals

Stages in Managing a Diverse Workforce

Donaldson and Scannell, authors of *Human Resource Development: The New Trainer's Guide,* have developed a four-stage model to describe how managers progress in managing a diverse workforce.[37] In the first stage, known as "unconscious incompetence," managers are unaware of behaviors they engage in that are problematic for members of other groups. In the second stage, "conscious incompetence," managers go through a learning process in which they become conscious of behaviors that make them incompetent in their interactions with members of diverse groups.

The third stage is one of becoming "consciously competent": Managers learn how to interact with diverse groups and cultures by deliberately thinking about how to behave. In the last stage, "unconscious competence," managers have internalized these new behaviors and feel so comfortable relating to others different from themselves that they need to devote little conscious effort to doing so: Managers who have progressed to the "unconscious competence" stage will be the most effective with respect to interacting in a diverse workforce. Effective interaction is key to carrying out the four management functions previously discussed.

Table 4.2 summarizes our discussion of the challenges facing those who manage a diverse workforce. Managers, who are generally responsible for controlling organizational goals and outcomes, are accountable for understanding these diversity challenges and recognizing the dynamics described here. In addition to treating employees fairly, they must influence other employees to cooperate with the company's diversity goals.

TABLE 4.2	Organizational Challenges and Supports Related to Managing a Diverse Workforce
Organizational Challenges	**Organizational Supports**
Employee's Difficulties in Coping with Cultural Diversity	**Educational Programs and Training to Assist Employees in Working Through Difficulties**
Resistance to change	**Top-Down Management Support for Diversity**
Ethnocentrism	Managers who have diversity skills and competence
Lack of information and misinformation	Education and training
Prejudices, biases, and stereotypes	Awareness raising
Reasons Employees Are Unmotivated to Understand Cultural Differences	Peer support
Lack of time and energy and unwillingness to assume the emotional risk necessary to explore issues of diversity	Organizational climate that supports diversity
	Open communication with manager about diversity issues
Absence of social or concrete rewards for investing in diversity work (e.g., lack of peer support and monetary rewards, unclear linkage between multicultural competence and career mobility)	Recognition for employee development of diversity skills and competencies
	Recognition for employee contributions to diversity goals
Interpersonal and intergroup conflicts arising when diversity issues are either ignored or mismanaged	Organizational rewards for managers' implementation of organizational diversity goals and objectives
Work Group Problems	
Lack of cohesiveness	
Communication problems	
Employee stress	

Understanding and Influencing Employee Responses Managers cannot rise to the challenge of managing a diverse workforce unless they recognize that many employees have difficulties in coping with diversity. Among these difficulties are natural resistance to change, ethnocentrism, and lack of information and outright misinformation about other groups, as well as prejudices, biases, and stereotypes. Some employees lack the motivation to understand and cope with cultural differences, which requires time, energy, and a willingness to take some emotional risks.

Another problem is that employees often receive no social rewards (e.g., peer support and approval) or concrete rewards (e.g., financial compensation or career opportunities) for cooperating with the organization's diversity policies.

For all these difficulties, managers cannot afford to ignore or mismanage diversity issues because the cost of doing so is interpersonal and intergroup conflicts. These conflicts often affect the functioning of the work group by destroying cohesiveness and causing communications problems and employee stress.

Managers who are determined to deal effectively with their diverse workforce can usually obtain organizational support. One primary support is education and training programs designed to help employees work through their difficulties in coping with diversity. Besides recommending such programs to their employees, managers may find it helpful to enroll in available programs themselves.

Getting Top-Down Support Another important source of support for managers dealing with diversity issues is top management. Organizations that provide top-down support are more likely to boast the following features:

1. Managers skilled at working with a diverse workforce
2. Effective education and diversity training programs
3. An organizational climate that promotes diversity and fosters peer support for exploring diversity issues
4. Open communication between employees and managers about diversity issues
5. Recognition for employees' development of diversity skills and competencies
6. Recognition for employee contributions to diversity goals
7. Organizational rewards for managers' implementation of organizational diversity goals and objectives

CHALLENGE CASE SUMMARY

An organization such as Denny's that uses the diverse talents of a multicultural workforce can reap many rewards. Some experts believe that one of the best ways for a company such as Denny's to capture a diverse customer base is to make sure that its decision makers are a diverse group. For example, Denny's family restaurants could use menu offerings, internal décor, and employees that reflect the wants and desires of a diverse customer population. Promoting a diverse group of decision makers will ensure sensitivity to such issues, giving Denny's a better chance of establishing restaurants characterized by such diversity.

The progress of a company such as Denny's in its diversity program will enhance the productivity of its diverse workforce. An organization's diversity programs will help a diverse workforce to feel valued and at ease in their work setting, thereby performing better than workers who feel that their organization has little respect for them as people. As a result of its required diversity training, Denny's can retain employees, thereby lowering personnel costs related to recruiting and training.

Legislation and government involvement cannot provide complete direction for building diversity in organizations. Denny's management understands that organizations should not wait for laws and government to provide guidelines for building a diverse organization. Instead, management should recreate the company to reflect the environment in which it operates. For example, given demographics reflecting environmental population trends, Denny's will probably be recruiting and hiring a greater proportion of Asian and Hispanic employees.

If an organization such as Denny's increases the proportion of Asian and Hispanic employees, company diversity training programs should be modified to include a sensitivity toward factors relevant to the Asian and Hispanic cultures. This training should emphasize factors such as religion, values, and behavioral norms specific to these two groups. Such modification of diversity training at Denny's would be aimed at eliminating ethnocentrism within the company relating to these two demographic groups.

When management is committed to diversity, diversity programs are normally successful. Certainly, Denny's had to face difficult diversity-related issues as minority groups began to sue the company, alleging discriminatory practices against customers. Such allegations implied that one of Denny's major restaurant locations employed workers who discriminated against blacks. The continued commitment of Denny's management to diversity programs ultimately assisted the company in receiving the *Fortune* "Best Companies for Minorities" ranking.

In terms of the organizational diversity continuum, Denny's commitment to diversity seems broad based. This broad-based commitment is reflected in company-wide practices related to recruiting, hiring, and training a diverse workforce. The broad-based commitment is also evident through Denny's building of minority representation within influential company groups such as the board of directors. Consistent with diversity initiatives in most organizations, Denny's managers are given extensive diversity training. Managers in a company such as Denny's who know how to interact with people of different cultures will be the most successful in building productive multicultural teams in organizations. Overall, diversity training for managers at Denny's is aimed to help managers become more sensitive to other cultures and thereby more capable of using planning, organizing, influencing, and controlling skills to help organizations meet diversity goals.

In addition to managers, nonmanagers within organizations can be a focus of specially designed diversity training. As mentioned earlier, Denny's restaurant chain faced allegations of discriminatory practices against customers of color. Perhaps partially in attempting to make the chain more sensitive to customers of color as well as other minority groups, all of Denny's nonmanagement employees were required to complete a specially designed diversity training program. Focusing on workforce composition can help a restaurant chain such as Denny's to minimize discrimination against minority groups. Building a workforce more reflective of minority groups in the environment should help management of any organization to lessen discrimination against customers who are members of those groups. For example, building a workforce with notable proportions of African Americans, Hispanic Americans, and Asian Pacific Americans should help to lower the probability of customers from these groups being discriminated against.

MANAGEMENT SKILL ACTIVITIES

This section is specially designed to help you develop diversity skill. An individual's diversity skill is based upon an understanding of diversity concepts and the ability to apply those concepts in management situations. The following activities are designed to both heighten your understanding of diversity concepts and to develop the ability to apply those concepts in a variety of management situations.

UNDERSTANDING DIVERSITY CONCEPTS

This section is comprised of activities that will sharpen your understanding of diversity concepts. Answer essay questions as completely as possible. Also, remember that many additional true/false and multiple choice questions appear online at MyManagementLab.com to help you further refine your understanding of diversity concepts.

Essay Questions

1. When managing people, describe the significance of understanding both "minority" and "majority" groups as they exist in an organization.

2. Explain how average annual percentages changes in the U.S. population by race from 1995–2050 should influence today's diversity planning for organizations of the future.

3. Assume that you are ethnocentric. List three specific beliefs about your own culture that you might possess. Would such beliefs be a hindrance or a help in you becoming a successful manager? Explain.

4. Pinpoint five ways that discrimination might negatively affect an organization.

5. List five ways that you would promote diversity in an organization. How would you control your efforts to make sure they were successful?

Developing Management Skill

Learning activities in this section are aimed at helping you to develop diversity skill. Learning activities include Exploring Your Management Skill: Part 2, Your Management Skill Portfolio, Experiential Exercise, Cases, and a VideoNet exercise.

EXPLORING YOUR MANAGEMENT SKILL: PART 2

As you recall, you completed Exploring Your Management Skill before you started to study this chapter. Your responses gave you an idea of how much you initially knew about diversity and helped you to focus on important points as you studied the chapter. Answer the Exploring Your Management Skill questions again now (p. 106) and compare your score to the first time you took it. The comparison will give you an idea of how much you have learned from studying this chapter and pinpoint areas for further clarification before you start studying the next chapter. Record your answers within the text or online at MyManagementLab.com. Completing the survey at MyManagementLab.com will allow you to grade and compare your test scores automatically. If you complete the test in the book, look up answers in the Exploring Your Management Skill section at the end of the book.

YOUR MANAGEMENT SKILLS PORTFOLIO

Your Management Learning Portfolio is a collection of activities specially designed to demonstrate your management knowledge and skill. By completing these questions online at MyManagementLab.com, you will be able to print, complete with cover sheet, as many activities as you choose. Be sure to save your work. Taking your printed portfolio to an employment interview could be helpful in obtaining a job.

The portfolio activity for this chapter is Assessing Diversity at TECO Energy. Read this highlight about TECO Energy and answer the questions that follow.

TECO Energy is an energy company headquartered in Tampa, Florida. TECO Energy's five business units include (1) Tampa Electric, a regulated electric utility serving more than 635,000 customers in West Central Florida, (2) Peoples Gas System, Florida's largest natural gas distribution utility, (3) TECO Coal, producer of conventional coal and synthetic fuel, (4) TECO Transport, river and ocean waterborne transportation provider, and (5) TECO Guatemala, owner of two power plants in Guatemala. (You can learn more about the company by visiting www.tecoenergy.com). Over the years, TECO management has focused on building a diverse workforce. Management recently reported the results of a diversity study aimed at monitoring its diversity efforts by ascertaining the present characteristics of its workforce. Part of the results of that study appears in Exhibits 1, 2 and 3.

EXHIBIT 1 Gender of Workforce

Company	Female	Male
TECO Energy (corporate)	62%	38%
Tampa Electric	25%	75%
Peoples Gas	28%	72%
TECO Transport	10%	90%
TECO Coal	4%	96%
TECO Guatemala (corporate)	29%	71%
TECO Guatemala	12%	88%
Total Employees	970	4,122

EXHIBIT 2	Race/Ethnicity of Work Force			
Company	**Black**	**White**	**Hispanic**	**Other**
TECO Energy (corporate)	6%	84%	10%	0%
Tampa Electric	14%	73%	11%	2%
Peoples Gas	14%	70%	15%	1%
TECO Transport	12%	85%	2%	1%
TECO Coal	0%	100%	0%	0%
TECO Guatemala (corporate)	0%	43%	43%	14%
TECO Guatemala*				
Total Employees	522	3,993	399	178

*U.S. ethnicity codes not applicable to TECO Guatemala.

EXHIBIT 3	Leadership by Gender and Race					
Company	**Female**	**Male**	**Black**	**White**	**Hispanic**	**Other**
TECO Energy (corporate)	56%	44%	4%	87%	9%	0%
Tampa Electric	30%	70%	9%	77%	11%	3%
Peoples Gas	28%	72%	6%	80%	14%	0%
TECO Transport	20%	80%	6%	91%	2%	1%
TECO Coal	9%	91%	0%	100%	0%	0%
TECO Guatemala (corporate)	29%	71%	0%	43%	43%	14%
TECO Guatemala*	11%	89%	N/A	N/A	N/A	N/A
Total Employees	28%	72%	7%	79%	10%	4%

*U.S. ethnicity codes not applicable to TECO Guatemala.

QUESTIONS

1. List five major points that Exhibits 1, 2, and 3 tell management about TECO's workforce.

a) _____

b) _____

c) _____

d) _____

e) _____

2. How does management at TECO determine whether the present level of workforce diversity is appropriate for the company?

_____

_____

3. Assume that TECO management performs a similar study in five years. Name three new dimensions of diversity that you would like for the study to explore. Explain why you would like each dimension studied.

Dimension 1: _____

Why study this dimension?

_____

_____

Dimension 2: _____

Why study this dimension?

_____

_____

Dimension 3: _____

Why study this dimension?

_____

_____

EXPERIENTIAL EXERCISE: DEVELOPING A DIVERSITY PROFILE

Directions. Read the following scenario and then perform the listed activities. Your instructor may want you to perform the activities as an individual or within groups. Follow all of your instructor's directions carefully.

Your instructor will divide the class into groups of 4 or 5 people. The task of each group is to develop a diversity profile of your class as a whole. Perform this profile by summarizing the people dimensions of your class that comprise its diversity. As you know, some of the more traditional diversity dimensions are based upon factors such as age, gender, race, religion, cultural backgrounds, and

religion. Feel free to use any other factors that might help define the diversity of your class more accurately. Once you have completed your diversity profile, answer the following questions:

1. What are the main diversity characteristics of your class that an instructor should consider when teaching your class?
2. Should what an instructor does to teach your class be influenced by the main diversity characteristics of your class? Explain.
3. Can the quality of what an instructor does to teach your class be improved by utilizing the diversity of the class? Explain.

C A S E S

DENNY'S MAKES DIVERSITY ADVANCES

The case that introduces this chapter, "Denny's Makes Diversity Advances," and its related Challenge Case Summary were written to help you better understand the management concepts contained in this chapter. Answer the following discussion questions about the Challenge Case to better understand how concepts relating to management and diversity can be applied in an organization such as Denny's.

1. How important is having a diverse workforce to Denny's? Discuss fully.

2. How would you control diversity activities at Denny's if you were top management?
3. As Denny's top management, what steps would you take to build commitment for diversity throughout the organization? Be as specific as possible.

THE U.S. POSTAL SERVICE PUTS ITS STAMP ON DIVERSITY

Read the case and answer the questions that follow. Studying this case will help you better understand how concepts relating to management and diversity can be applied in a company like the U.S. Postal Service.

One of the largest U.S. employers is also one of the best at managing workforce diversity. With 780,000 employees and $68 billion in annual revenues, the U.S. Postal Service (USPS) is responsible for delivering mail to the country's homes and businesses. Over the years, the U.S. agency has become a leader in promoting diversity up and down the hierarchy. Its success has been recognized by a listing in *Fortune* magazine's "50 Best Companies for Diversity" ranking for five consecutive years.

The drive for diversity started in 1992. Top management carefully analyzed the demographic shifts within the United States and the USPS's growing involvement in global commerce, then created a Diversity Development department within the human resources function. The purpose was "to increase employees' awareness of and appreciation for ethnic and cultural diversity, both in the postal workplace and among customers," says Murry E. Weatherall, vice president of diversity development. Next, the USPS began training diversity specialists in career development and coaching skills so they could support and encourage diversity on the local level. The agency also initiated an Affirmative Employment Program to attract minority and female applicants as well as people with disabilities. In 1996, the USPS launched a National Awards Program for Diversity Achievement, inviting employees to nominate colleagues and teams that have made outstanding contributions to promoting diversity.

As a result of these activities, the composition of the USPS workforce reflects more diversity. In 1991, 34 percent of the workforce was female; by 2004, 38 percent was female. The proportion of minorities in the workforce has increased, from 32 percent in 1991 to nearly 37 percent in 2004. Now 59 percent of newly hired employees are members of minority groups and 24 percent of the top-salaried managers are members of minorities. No glass ceiling here: Women hold 42 percent of first-line management jobs, 31 percent of middle management jobs, and 27 percent of senior management jobs at the USPS.

The USPS keeps its diversity specialists up to date on the latest techniques and trends through National Diversity Network meetings and educational programs led by headquarters staff. A special events committee provides internal support for diversity-related programs such as National Hispanic Heritage month, Black History month, and National Asian Pacific American Heritage month. And to gauge internal reaction to diversity initiatives, the agency has an outside firm conduct a confidential survey of 25 percent of its employees every three months. The surveys ask for comments on discrimination, harassment, fairness, and other issues, providing feedback on how the workforce views the diversity situation.

Despite its success in managing diversity, the USPS must deal with a number of serious challenges. First, it is facing stronger competition from FedEx, UPS, and other domestic and international delivery firms. Second, relations between management and union members have been strained at times as the agency seeks ways to cut costs and as it keeps streamlining operations through new technology. Third, USPS managers must remain responsive to their customers' needs and priorities—while simultaneously complying with a complex set of government rules and regulations that limit their alternatives in making decisions about rates, facilities, transportation, and other key areas.

As the Postmaster General told a public hearing not long ago, "the status quo won't do" if the USPS is to operate both efficiently and effectively in the rapidly changing business environment. He is seeking the power to change the organization and "modernize with a vision of what America needs, not just today, but 10 to 15 to 30 years from now." Diversity plays such a vital role in shaping the USPS's future that top management has switched responsibility for succession planning from the human resources department to the diversity development department. Now "our corporate succession process is very inclusive and gives everybody—whether a minority or a woman—an opportunity to be considered," notes Murry Weatherall.

QUESTIONS

1. Describe the USPS's approach to pluralism, based on the information in this case study. Does this approach appear to be effective? Explain.
2. Of the challenges listed in Table 4.2, which do you think might be the most serious threats to the USPS's ability to manage its diverse workforce?
3. Would you recommend that the USPS strive to have its workforce mirror the demographic composition of the U.S. population? Why?

VIDEONET EXERCISE

Diversity at KPMG

VIDEO HIGHLIGHTS

We asked some provocative questions about diversity at KPMG and captured some interesting responses. Is it still necessary to focus on diversity? Yes, it is, and, you'll hear why. Get insights into people's personal experiences and understand what diversity means to the folks whose faces and stories bring diversity to life at KPMG. What diversity networks and initiatives do they participate in and why? How does KPMG ensure that diversity isn't treated like a buzzword and addressed with token gestures? Will we ever arrive at a post-diversity era because it's not an issue anymore?

Discussion Questions

1. What are some of the current and potential advantages KPMG might gain through their diversity efforts?
2. In what way has KPMG chosen to promote diversity in their organization?
3. How does KPMG use training to help manage their diversity?

Internet Activity

Go to the KPMG Web site at www.kpmg.com. What evidence can you discover that the organization is diverse? How do you think clients, customers, or potential job applicants would view this evidence?

Managing in the Global Arena

5

OBJECTIVES

TO HELP BUILD MY GLOBAL MANAGEMENT SKILL, WHEN STUDYING THIS CHAPTER, I WILL ATTEMPT TO ACQUIRE:

1. An understanding of international management and its importance to modern managers

2. An understanding of what constitutes a multinational corporation

3. Insights concerning the risk involved in investing in international operations

4. Insights into those who work in multinational corporations

5. Knowledge about managing multinational corporations

6. Knowledge about managing multinational organizations versus transnational organizations

7. An understanding of how ethics and the preparation of expatriates relate to managing internationally

TARGET SKILL

global management skill: the ability to manage global factors as components of organizational operations

CHALLENGE CASE

WAL-MART FACING GLOBAL PROBLEMS IN JAPAN

When Sam Walton opened the first Wal-Mart store in 1962, it was the beginning of an American success story that has become famous throughout the world. As evidence of the success of Wal-Mart, the company recently appeared on *Fortune* magazine's list of "The World's Most Admired Companies," a list compiled by surveying industry executives as well as Wall Street analysts. Today, Wal-Mart has about 3,800 stores scattered throughout 10 countries. The company is the world's largest private employer, with a staggering 1.1 million associates.

Through Walton's experience in operating variety stores in small U.S. towns, he was convinced that consumers would be drawn to a discount store offering a wide variety of merchandise that was accompanied by friendly service. Walton was absolutely correct.

In a few decades, Wal-Mart has become the world's number-one retailer. Company growth has come not only from the success of the original Wal-Mart concept, but also from diversified concepts such as the availability of grocery products to customers in Wal-Mart Supercenters and general merchandise being offered in countries such as Brazil, Argentina, and China. Also, SAM'S Clubs (a subsidiary of Wal-Mart) has undoubtedly aided company growth.

After Wal-Mart said it would spend $423 million to take control of troubled Japanese supermarket chain Seiyu Ltd., Wal-Mart International President and CEO John Menzer (C) met with Seiyu President Masao Kiuchi (L) and Sumitomo Corp. senior advisor Fumio Wada (R) in a joint press conference in Tokyo.

Upon Sam Walton's death in 1992, many company analysts were concerned that Wal-Mart was coming upon hard times. Analysts believed that Sam Walton was the personification of Wal-Mart's positive corporate culture and that without him it would erode. Time has shown, however, that the culture does not seem to have eroded, and indeed appears as strong or even stronger now than ever. Store openings are still conducted with high enthusiasm and operating stores look better than ever. The company cheer is still done regularly at store openings and meetings—the only difference is that now the cheer is done in many different countries and in many different languages.

Needless to say, Wal-Mart's CEO Lee Scott has approached global expansion with much excitement and enthusiasm. Today, Wal-Mart serves more than 176 million customers weekly in 13 countries worldwide including Argentina, Brazil, China, Japan, Mexico, and United States. Recent news, however, seems to cast doubt on Wal-Mart's ability to manage its Japanese stores.[1] Seiyu, Wal-Mart's Japanese brand, posted losses five times greater in the first half of 2006 than in the same period in 2005. Management, however, says that it remains committed to its 400 stores in Japan.[2] This news from Japan is especially ominous after the company recently pulled out of South Korea and Germany because of lagging sales, labor market obstacles, and local competition.

"EXPLORE YOUR OWN MANAGEMENT SKILLS BY TAKING THE QUIZ ON THE NEXT PAGE"

Before studying this chapter, respond to the following questions regarding the type of advice that you would give to Wal-Mart's CEO Lee Scott, referenced in the Challenge Case. Then address the concerning global management challenges that he presently faces within the company. You are not expected to be a global management expert at this point. Answering the questions now can help you focus on important points when you study the chapter. Also, answering the questions again after you study the chapter will give you an idea of how much you have learned.

Record your answers here or online at MyManagement Lab.com. Completing the questions at MyManagement Lab.com will allow you to get feedback about your answers automatically. If you answer the questions in the book, look up answers in the Exploring Your Management Skill section at the end of the book.

FOR EACH STATEMENT CIRCLE:

- "Y" if you would give the advice to Lee Scott.
- "N" if you would NOT give the advice to Lee Scott.
- "NI" if you have no idea whether you would give the advice to Lee Scott.

Mr. Scott, in meeting your global management challenges at Wal-Mart, you should . . .

Before Study	After Study

1. shy away from having Wal-Mart make direct foreign investment.

   Y, N, NI

2. start by building Wal-Mart into a transnational company and grow it into an international company.

   Y, N, NI

3. become familiar and react to various value systems of the citizens of countries in which Wal-Mart operates.

   Y, N, NI

4. not be concerned with physical distances among Wal-Mart's global business unit operations.

   Y, N, NI

5. remember that different laws in foreign countries may require different management responses from Wal-Mart managers regarding the same issue.

   Y, N, NI

6. train Wal-Mart host-country nationals more thoroughly than expatriates in local customs of a country such as Japan in which foreign operations exist.

   Y, N, NI

7. build an effective repatriation process at Wal-Mart to help retain returning expatriates.

   Y, N, NI

8. help Wal-Mart's newly located expatriates to deal with confusion, anxiety, and stress related to their new culture.

   Y, N, NI

9. consider market agreements when designing plans for Wal-Mart's foreign operations.

   Y, N, NI

10. focus on building an organization structure for Wal-Mart that primarily highlights foreign operations from either business function or territory viewpoints, but not both.

    Y, N, NI

11. usually avoid having an ethnocentric attitude, a feeling that home country policies and practices are superior to those of foreign countries.

    Y, N, NI

12. build systems to motivate Wal-Mart's organization members in foreign operations that consider the specific needs of individuals within host countries.

    Y, N, NI

13. thoroughly educate yourself in understanding the customs of foreign countries in which Wal-Mart does business.

    Y, N, NI

14. prepare Wal-Mart expatriates for foreign assignments through programs that emphasize how to adapt to a new culture more than how to perform their new jobs.

    Y, N, NI

15. emphasize expatriate preparation for foreign assignment at Wal-Mart slightly more than repatriation.

    Y, N, NI

THE GLOBAL MANAGEMENT CHALLENGE

The Challenge Case illustrates not only several steps that Wal-Mart has taken to maintain its growth over the years, but also the problem that the company presently faces regarding operation in Japan. The global management challenge for a manager such as Lee Scott at Wal-Mart includes understanding the need to manage internationally, managing a multinational corporation and its workforce, understanding management functions and multinational corporations and transnational organizations, and following through on special issues like maintaining ethics in international management situations and preparing expatriates for foreign assignments. After studying chapter concepts, read the Challenge Case Summary at the end of the chapter for added help in relating chapter content to meeting global management challenges at Wal-Mart.

MANAGING ACROSS THE GLOBE: WHY?

Most companies see great opportunities in the international marketplace today.[3] Although the population is growing slowly but steadily in developed countries such as the U.S., the population in many other countries is exploding. For example, it has been estimated that in 1990, China, India, and Indonesia together had more than 2 billion people, or 40 percent of the world's population.[4] Obviously, such countries offer a strong profit potential for aggressive businesspeople throughout the world.

This potential does not come without serious risk, however. Managers who attempt to manage in a global context face formidable challenges. Some of these challenges are the cultural differences among workers from different countries, different technology levels from country to country, and laws and political systems that can vary immensely from one nation to the next.

The remaining sections of this chapter deal with the intricacies of managing in a global context by emphasizing the following:

1. Fundamentals of international management
2. Categories of organizations by international involvement
3. Management functions and multinational corporations
4. International management: Special issues

FUNDAMENTALS OF INTERNATIONAL MANAGEMENT

International management is simply the performance of management activities across national borders.[5] It entails reaching organizational objectives by extending management activities to include an emphasis on organizations in foreign countries.[6] The trend toward increased international management, or *globalization,* is now widely recognized. The primary question for most firms is not *whether* to globalize, but *how* and *how fast* to do so and how to measure global progress over time.[7]

International management can take several different forms, from simply analyzing and fighting competition in foreign markets to establishing a formal partnership with a foreign company. AMP, Inc., for example, has been vigorously fighting competition in a foreign market. This company, a manufacturer of electrical parts, headquartered in Harrisburg, Pennsylvania, has achieved outstanding success by gaining significant control over a portion of its multinational market. The company built factories in 17 countries because experience showed management that competitors could best be beaten in foreign markets if AMP actually produced products within those markets. A message recently sent to AMP stockholders by company president William J. Hudson indicates that the company is continuing to make good progress in the international arena. Hudson has promised to persist in his efforts to develop AMP into a "globe-able" organization.[8]

For **an example from the world of management** of an international partnership, consider the partnership between **Toshiba Corporation** and **Time Warner**. Toshiba Corporation, a Japanese computer manufacturer, and Time Warner, a communications conglomerate that owns a major Hollywood film studio, formed a partnership to develop a new technology for presenting movies to consumers. This technology, now available in the marketplace, is called digital video disc (DVD). In a natural division of labor, Toshiba focused on making the hardware needed to deliver the new technology, and Time Warner provided the movies to be presented on DVD. Both companies hoped the partnership would give them an edge over formidable competitors such as Sony.[9]

The notable trend that already exists toward developing business relationships in and with foreign countries is expected to accelerate even more in the future. As Figure 5.1 illustrates, investment in foreign countries by developed countries continues to grow and is expected to continue growing, with only slight slowdowns or setbacks in

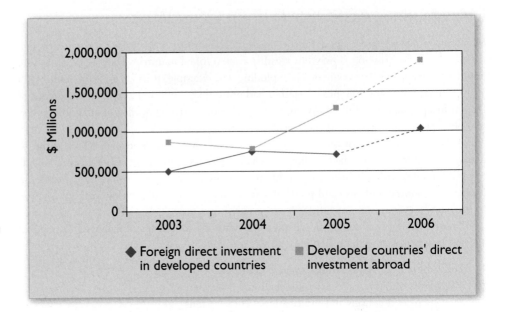

FIGURE 5.1

Investment by developed countries in foreign countries versus foreign investment in developed countries

Source: UNCTAD, *World Investment Report 2007* ; www.unctad.org/wir or www.unctad.org/fdistatistics.

recessionary periods. The bulk of FDI investments in less-developed countries seems to be associated with natural-resource-related investments. U.S. foreign investments have focused most heavily in European countries with Asian and Pacific countries and other Western Hemisphere countries being virtually tied for second place as Figure 5.2 shows. On the other hand, Figure 5.3 shows that European countries are by far the most significant foreign investors in the United States. Information of this nature has spurred both management educators and practicing managers to insist that knowledge of international management is necessary for a thorough understanding of the contemporary fundamentals of management.[10]

FIGURE 5.2

U.S. direct investment abroad by country

Source: U.S. Bureau of Economic Analysis.

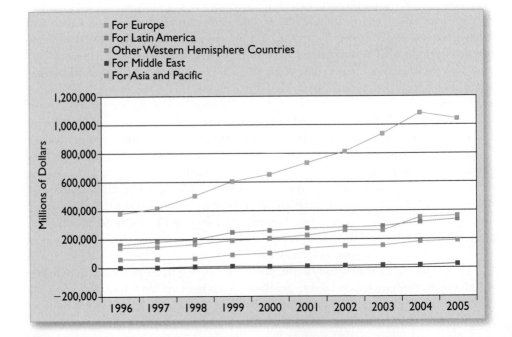

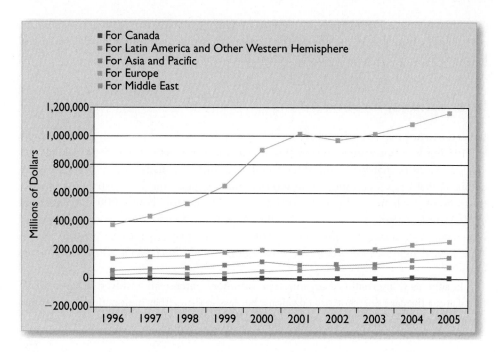

FIGURE 5.3
Foreign direct investment
in the United States by countries
Source: U.S. Bureau of Economic Analysis.

CATEGORIZING ORGANIZATIONS BY INTERNATIONAL INVOLVEMENT

A number of different categories have evolved to describe the extent to which organizations are involved in the international arena. These categories are domestic organizations, international organizations, multinational organizations, and transnational or global organizations. As Figure 5.4 suggests, this categorization format actually describes a continuum of international involvement, with domestic organizations representing the least and transnational organizations the most international involvement. Although the format may not be perfect, it is useful for explaining primary ways in which companies operate in the international realm.[11] The following sections describe these categories in more detail.

Domestic Organizations

Domestic organizations are organizations that essentially operate within a single country. These organizations normally not only acquire necessary resources within a single country but also sell their goods or services within that same country. Although domestic organizations may occasionally make an international sale or acquire some needed resource from a foreign supplier, the overwhelming bulk of their business activity takes place within the country where they are based.

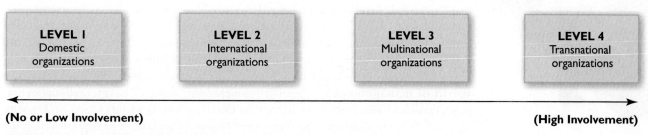

(No or Low Involvement)   **(High Involvement)**

FIGURE 5.4   Continuum of international involvement

Although this category is not determined by size, most domestic organizations today are quite small. Even smaller business organizations, however, are following the trend and becoming increasingly involved in the international arena.

International Organizations

International organizations are organizations that are based primarily within a single country but have continuing, meaningful international transactions—such as making sales and purchases of materials—in other countries. Nu Horizons is an example of a small company that can be classified as an international organization. This distributor of electronic goods made mainly by some 40 U.S. manufacturers has about 5,000 customers and is the fastest-growing company in Melville, New York. Nu Horizons is an international organization because an important part of its business is to act as the primary North American distributor of electronic components made by Japan's NIC Components Corp.[12]

In summary, international organizations are more extensively involved in the international arena than are domestic organizations, but less so than either multinational or transnational organizations.

Multinational Organizations: The Multinational Corporation

The *multinational organization,* commonly called the *multinational corporation* (MNC), represents the third level of international involvement. This section of the text defines the multinational corporation, discusses the complexities involved in managing such a corporation, describes the risks associated with its operations, explores the diversity of the multinational workforce, and explains how the major management functions relate to managing the multinational corporation.

With more than 30,000 restaurants in over 100 countries, McDonald's is a good example of a multinational corporation (MNC). This is its restaurant in the Plaza Flamingo shopping mall, Cancun, Mexico.

Defining the Multinational Corporation

The term *multinational corporation* first appeared in American dictionaries about 1970, and has since been defined in various ways in business publications and textbooks. For the purposes of this text, a **multinational corporation** is a company that has significant operations in more than one country. Essentially, a multinational corporation is an organization that is involved in doing business at the international level. It carries out its activities on an international scale that disregards national boundaries, and it is guided by a common strategy from a corporation center.[13]

Neil H. Jacoby explains that companies go through six stages to reach the highest degree of multinationalization. As Table 5.1 indicates, multinational corporations can range from slightly multinationalized organizations that simply export products to a foreign country to highly multinationalized organizations that have some of their owners in other countries. According to Alfred M. Zeien, CEO of Gillette Company, it can take up to 25 years to build a management team with the requisite skills, experience, and abilities to mold an organization into a highly developed multinational company.[14]

In general, the larger the organization, the greater the likelihood it participates in international operations of some sort. Companies such as Toyota, Lockheed, and DuPont, which have annually accumulated more than $1 billion from export sales, support this generalization. You will find exceptions, of course. As **an example from the world of management** of a smaller business being involved in international operations, consider **Viña Concha y Toro**. Viña Concha y Toro is a Chile-based winery with vineyards in Chile and Argentina. The company gets 80 percent of its revenues from the products its exports, and is one of Chile's leading exporters.[15] As noted earlier, an

TABLE 5.1	Six Stages of Multinationalization				
Stage 1	**Stage 2**	**Stage 3**	**Stage 4**	**Stage 5**	**Stage 6**
Exports its products to foreign countries	Establishes sales organizations abroad	Licenses use of its patterns and know-how to foreign firms that make and sell its products	Establishes foreign manufacturing facilities	Multinationalizes management from top to bottom	Multinationalizes ownership of corporate stock

increasing number of smaller organizations such as BRK Electronics are undertaking international operations.

Complexities of Managing the Multinational Corporation

From the discussion so far, it should be clear that international management and domestic management are quite different. Classic management thought indicates that international management differs from domestic management because it involves operating:[16]

1. Within different national sovereignties
2. Under widely disparate economic conditions
3. Among people living within different value systems and institutions
4. In places experiencing the industrial revolution at different times
5. Often over greater geographical distance
6. In national markets varying greatly in population and area

Figure 5.5 shows some of the more important management implications of these six variables and some of the relationships among them. Consider, for example, the first variable. Different national sovereignties generate different legal systems. In turn, each legal system implies a unique set of rights and obligations involving property, taxation, antitrust (control of monopoly) law, corporate law, and contract law. In turn, these rights and obligations require the firm to acquire the skills necessary to assess the international legal considerations. Such skills are different from those required in a purely domestic setting.

Risk and the Multinational Corporation

Developing a multinational corporation obviously requires a substantial investment in foreign operations. Normally, managers who make foreign investments expect that such investments will accomplish the following:[17]

1. Reduce or eliminate high transportation costs
2. Allow participation in the rapid expansion of a market abroad
3. Provide foreign technical, design, and marketing skills
4. Earn higher profits

Unfortunately, many managers decide to internationalize their companies without having an accurate understanding of the risks involved in making such a decision.[18] For example, political complications involving the **parent company** (the company investing in the international operations) and various factions within the **host country** (the country in which the investment is made) could prevent the parent company from realizing the desirable outcomes just listed. Some companies attempt to minimize this kind of risk by adding standard clauses to their contracts stipulating that in the event a business controversy cannot be resolved by the parties involved, they will agree to mediation by a mutually selected mediator.[19]

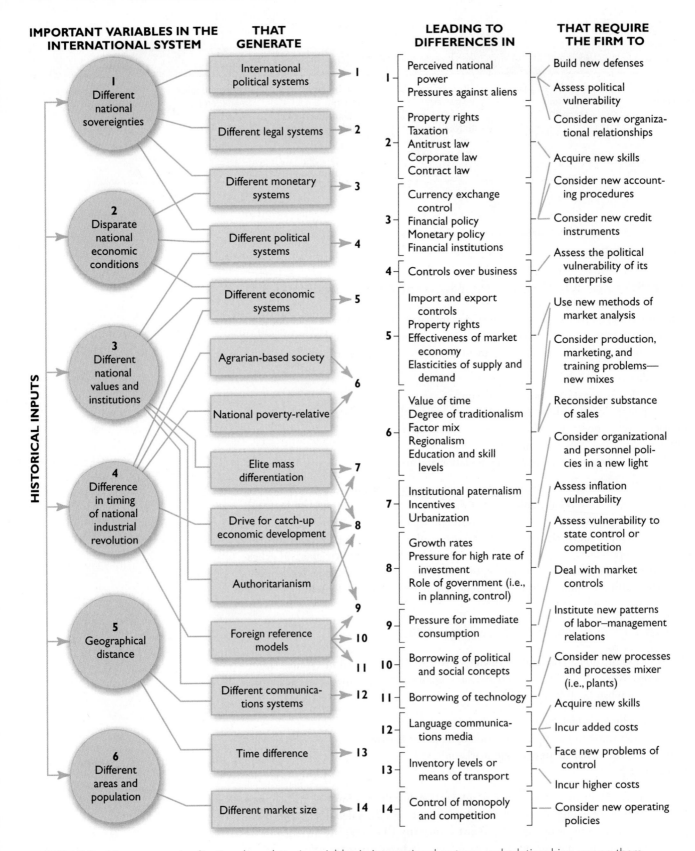

FIGURE 5.5 Management implications based on six variables in international systems and relationships among them

The likelihood of achieving desirable outcomes related to foreign investments will probably be somewhat uncertain and will certainly vary from country to country. Nevertheless, managers faced with making a foreign investment must assess this likelihood as accurately as possible. Obviously, a poor decision to invest in another country can cause serious financial problems for the organization.

The Workforce of Multinational Corporations

As organizations become more global, their organization members tend to become more diverse. Managers of multinational corporations face the continual challenge of building a competitive business team made up of people of different races who speak different languages and come from different parts of the world. The following sections perform two functions that should help managers build such teams:

1. They furnish details and related insights about the various types of organization members generally found in multinational corporations.
2. They describe the adjustments members of multinational organizations normally must make in order to become efficient and effective contributors to organization goal attainment, and they suggest how managers can facilitate these adjustments.

Types of Organization Members Found in Multinational Corporations
Workers in multinational organizations can be divided into three basic types:

- **Expatriates**—Organization members who live and work in a country where they do not have citizenship[20]
- **Host-country nationals**—Organization members who are citizens of the country in which the facility of a foreign-based organization is located[21]
- **Third-country nationals**—Organization members who are citizens of one country and who work in another country for an organization headquartered in still another country

Organizations that operate globally may employ all three types of workers. The use of host-country nationals, however, is increasing because they are normally the least expensive to employ. Such employees, for example, do not need to be relocated or undergo training in the culture, language, or tax laws of the country where the organization is doing business. Both expatriates and third-country nationals, on the other hand, would have to be relocated and normally undergo such training.

Workforce Adjustments
Working in a multinational corporation requires more difficult adjustments than working in an organization that focuses primarily on domestic activities. Probably the two most difficult challenges, which pertain to expatriates and third-country nationals rather than to host-country nationals, are adjusting to a new culture and repatriation.[22]

Adjusting to a New Culture
Upon arrival in a foreign country, many people experience confusion, anxiety, and stress related to the need to make cultural adjustments in their organizational and personal lives.[23] From a personal viewpoint, food, weather, and language may all be dramatically different, and driving may be done on the "wrong" side of the road. As an example of personal anxiety that can be caused by adjusting to a new culture, an expatriate recently working in Sao Paulo, Brazil, drove out of a parking lot by nudging his way into a terrible traffic jam. When a Brazilian woman allowed him to cut in front of her, the expatriate gave her the "ok" signal. To his personal dismay, he was told that in the Brazilian culture, forming a circle with one's first finger and thumb is considered vulgar.[24]

From an organizational viewpoint, workers may encounter different attitudes toward work and different perceptions of time in the workplace. To illustrate, the Japanese are

Clifford Mumm, project manager for the U.S. contractor Bechtel Corp., in the cramped prefab trailer camp for expatriate workers in Baghdad, where sandbags offer some protection from mortar and missile attacks.

renowned for their hard-driving work ethic, but Westerners take a slightly more relaxed attitude toward work. On the other hand, in many U.S. companies, working past quitting time is seen as exemplary, but in Germany, someone who works late is commonly criticized.

Members of multinational corporations normally have the formidable task of adjusting to a drastically new organizational situation. Managers must help these people adjust quickly and painlessly so they can begin contributing to organizational goal attainment as soon as possible.

class discussion highlight

MODERN RESEARCH AND GLOBAL MANAGEMENT SKILL

Expectations about Leaders in Multinational Corporations[25]

A recent study by Sergio Matviuk investigated expectations that individuals in multinational corporations have regarding how their leaders should behave. The researcher studied such expectations held by Mexicans versus Americans, all of whom were managers of a multinational corporation with production plants in the northern U.S. and central Mexico. Both groups were similarly represented by male and female members, managers from various organizational levels, age, and education.

The researcher conducted the study to help leaders in multinational corporations be more successful. The researcher reasoned that, if all other things are equal, leaders who behave as followers expect should have a better chance of overall success than leaders who

do not act as followers expect. As a result, leaders in multinational corporations should know whether managers from different countries might have different expectations about how leaders should behave and what those expectations difference are.

Leader expectations explored were quite specific. Managers filled out a survey asking the extent to which they expect leaders to (1) challenge existing processes, (2) inspire others to accomplish a shared vision, (3) enable others to act, (4) be a role model, and (5) encourage the "hearts" of others to do a good job.

Do you believe that study results showed that Mexican and American managers have different expectations about how a leader should act? If "yes," how might they differ? If "no," why not? If you were a Mexican manager in this company, would you want to know how American managers expected leaders to act? Why?

Repatriation **Repatriation** is the process of bringing individuals who have been working abroad back to their home country and reintegrating them into the organization's home-country operations.[26] Repatriation has its own set of adjustment problems, especially with people who have lived abroad for a long time. Some individuals become so accustomed to the advantages of an overseas lifestyle that they greatly miss it when they return home. Others idealize their homeland so much while they are abroad that they become disappointed when it fails to live up to their expectations upon their return. Still others acquire foreign-based habits that are undesirable from the organization's viewpoint and that are hard to break.

Managers must be patient and understanding with repatriates. Some organizations provide repatriates with counseling so that they will be better prepared to handle readjustment problems. Others have found that providing employees, before they leave for foreign duty, with a written agreement specifying what their new duties and career path will be when they return home reduces friction and facilitates the repatriate's adjustment.

The advantages of having organization members participate in an international experience in business are well known and growing. Organization members who have succeeded in the global environment are valuable assets to their organizations. One of the significant challenges to organizations is retaining these highly sought-after individuals through a successful repatriation process after they complete their overseas assignments.[27]

MANAGEMENT FUNCTIONS AND MULTINATIONAL CORPORATIONS

The sections that follow discuss the four major management functions—planning, organizing, influencing, and controlling—as they occur in multinational corporations.

Planning in Multinational Corporations

Planning was defined in Chapter 1 as determining how an organization will achieve its objectives. This definition is applicable to the management of both domestic and multinational organizations, but with some differences.

The primary difference between planning in multinational and domestic organizations is in the plans' components. Plans for the multinational organization include components that focus on the international arena, whereas plans for the domestic organization do not. For example, plans for multinational organizations could include the following:

1. Establishing a new salesforce in a foreign country
2. Developing new manufacturing plants in other countries through purchase or construction
3. Financing international expansion
4. Determining which countries represent the most suitable candidates for international expansion

Components of International Plans Although planning for multinational corporations varies from organization to organization, the following four components are commonly included in international plans:

* Imports/Exports
* License agreements
* Direct investing
* Joint ventures

This section discusses these four components as well as the responses of multinational corporations to international market agreements.

Imports/Exports Imports/exports planning components emphasize reaching organizational objectives by **importing** (buying goods or services from another country) or **exporting** (selling goods or services to another country).

Organizations of all sizes import and export. On one hand, companies such as Auburn Farms, Inc., a relatively small producer of all-natural, fat-free snack foods, imports products to be resold. Auburn Farms is the exclusive U.S. importer of Beacon Sweets & Chocolates of South Africa. Auburn sees its importing activities as a way of expanding and diversifying.[28] On the other hand, extremely large and complex organizations, such as Hitachi, export their products to a number of foreign countries.[29]

License Agreements A **license agreement** is a right granted by one company to another to use its brand name, technology, product specifications, and so on, in the manufacture or sale of goods and services. The company to which the license is extended pays some fee for the privilege. International planning components in this area involve reaching organizational objectives through either the purchase or the sale of licenses at the international level.

For example, the Tosoh Corporation recently purchased a license agreement from Mobil Research and Development Corporation to commercialize Mobil's newly developed process for extracting mercury from natural gas. Tosoh, a Japanese firm, will use its subsidiaries in Japan, the Netherlands, Greece, Canada, the United States, and the United Kingdom as bases of operations from which to profit from Mobil's new process.[30]

Upon entering into a license agreement, both companies should make absolutely sure that they understand the terms of the agreement. Some companies end up in litigation as a means of settling disagreements regarding specifics of the contents of a license agreement. Naturally, the cost of such litigation can be high and end up significantly diminishing the advantages that both companies thought they would gain as a result of entering into the agreement.[31]

Direct Investing **Direct investing** uses the assets of one company to purchase the operating assets (e.g., factories) of another company. International planning in this area emphasizes reaching organizational objectives through the purchase of the operating assets of another company in a foreign country.

A number of Japanese firms have recently been making direct investments abroad, including investments in the United States. In fact, many people believe that a new wave of direct Japanese investment in the United States is building. Several large Japanese companies

Licensing agreements allow one company to use another's brand name or images to manufacture products, like these Mickey Mouse toys being made in China, in exchange for a fee.

have announced plans to expand their U.S. production facilities. These planned direct invest-ments are focused on building competitive clout for Japanese companies in such core indus-tries as automobiles, semiconductors, electronics, and office products. Lower manufacturing wages and lower land costs in the United States are key attractions for the Japanese firms. For example, because the cost of building a factory was 30 percent cheaper in the United States than in Japan, Ricoh Company decided to spend $30 million to start making thermal paper products in the Southeastern United States. African countries and firms have typically been some of the largest recipients of direct foreign investments, with Morocco often leading the pack.[32]

Joint Ventures

Joint Ventures An **international joint venture** is a partnership formed by a com-pany in one country with a company in another country for the purpose of pursuing some mutually desirable business undertaking.[33] International planning components that include joint ventures emphasize the attainment of organizational objectives through partnerships with foreign companies.

Joint ventures between car manufacturers are becoming more and more common as companies strive for greater economies of scale and higher standards in product quality and delivery. For **an example from the world of management** of an inter-national joint venture between auto manufacturers, consider **Chang'an Suzuki**, a joint venture between **Chang'an Motors**, a Chinese company, and **Suzuki Motors**, which is based in Japan. The venture began in 1990, and in 1992, the joint company was formed. The two companies are involved in the assembly of inexpensive commer-cial trucks in China. Suzuki's has an international presence through its subsidiaries in Spain, Canada, Australia, New Zealand, Germany, France, Italy, Belgium, the Philippines, Pakistan, and Colombia makes the partnership desirable from the Chinese company's viewpoint. The lower expenses China offers are desirable from Suzuki's viewpoint.[34]

Planning and International Market Agreements

Planning and International Market Agreements In order to plan properly, managers of a multinational corporation, or any other organization participating in the international arena, must understand numerous complex and interrelated factors present within the organization's international environment. Managers should have a practical grasp of such international environmental factors as the economic and cultural conditions, and the laws and political circumstances, of foreign countries within which their companies operate.

One international environmental factor that affects strategic planning has lately received significant attention: An **international market agreement** is an arrange-ment among a cluster of countries that facilitates a high level of trade among these coun-tries. In planning, managers must consider existing international market agreements as they relate to countries in which their organizations operate. If an organization is from a country that is party to an international market agreement, the organization's plan should include steps for taking maximum advantage of that agreement. On the other hand, if an organization is from a country that is *not* party to an international market agreement, the organization's plan must include steps for competing with organizations from nations that are parties to such an agreement. The most notable international market agreements are discussed here.

The European Union (EU)

The European Union (EU) The European Union (EU) is an international market agreement established in 1994 dedicated to facilitating trade among member nations. To that end, the nations in the EU have agreed to eliminate tariffs among themselves and work toward meaningful deregulation in such areas as banking, insurance, telecommunications, and airlines. More recently, the nations are trying to develop a set of standardized accounting principles that will help facilitate business transactions among members.[35] Longer-term members of the EU include Denmark, the United Kingdom, Portugal, the Netherlands,

Belgium, Spain, Ireland, Luxembourg, France, Germany, Italy, and Greece. Member businesses are particularly excited about the EU because they are sure that membership will ultimately boost exports and encourage foreign investment from other member nations. The significance of the EU as an international environmental factor can only increase, since the number of member countries is expected to continue growing.[36]

Figure 5.6 identifies countries that are presently members of the EU as well as membership-candidate countries and applications-pending countries. Applications-pending countries are countries more in the initial stages of obtaining EU membership. Candidate countries are countries that have applied and have been chosen by the EU for more serious membership consideration.

North American Free Trade Agreement (NAFTA) The North American Free Trade Agreement is an international market agreement aimed at facilitating trade among member nations. Current NAFTA members are Canada, the United States, and Mexico.[37] To facilitate trade among themselves, these countries have agreed to such actions as the phasing out of tariffs on U.S. farm exports to Mexico, the opening up of Mexico to American trucking, and the safeguarding of North American pharmaceutical patents in Mexico.

FIGURE 5.6
The European Union: Members, candidates, and applicants

NAFTA has had significant impact since its implementation in January 1994. Recent figures show that since the agreement went into effect, Mexican exports to the United States increased 15 percent, and U.S. exports to Mexico increased 30 percent. Trade between Canada and the United States exploded since NAFTA took effect. As with the EU, the significance of NAFTA as an international environmental factor can only grow in the future as other countries in the Caribbean and South America apply for membership.[38]

Asian-Pacific Economic Cooperation (APEC) APEC was established in 1989 to further the economic growth and prosperity of the Asia-Pacific community. Since its beginning, APEC has worked to reduce tariffs and other trade barriers across the Asia-Pacific region. APEC is based upon the concept that free and open trade creates greater opportunities for international trade and related prosperity among member nations. The organization works diligently to create an environment in which goods can be transported safely and efficiently among countries. APEC has 21 members, including Canada, the People's Republic of China, Indonesia, and the United States. APEC entire country membership is depicted in Figure 5.7. Comparison of APEC and EU member countries shows that EU member countries are concentrated in Europe, while APEC member countries are spread throughout the globe.

To sum up, numerous countries throughout the world are already signatories to international market agreements. Moreover, the number of countries that are parties to such agreements should grow significantly in the future.

Organizing Multinational Corporations

Organizing was generally defined in Chapter 1 as the process of establishing orderly uses for all resources within the organization. This definition applies equally to the management of domestic and multinational organizations. Two organizing topics as they specifically relate to multinational corporations, however, bear further discussion. These topics are organization structure and the selection of managers.[39]

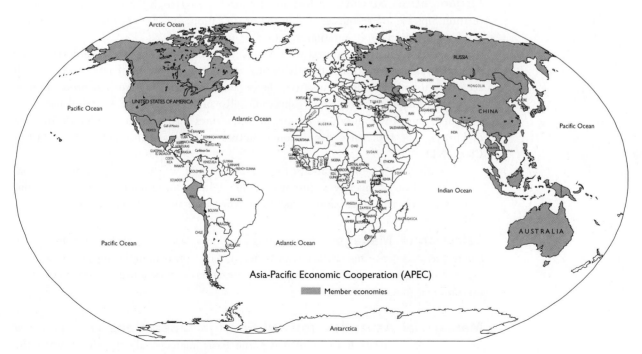

FIGURE 5.7 APEC member nations

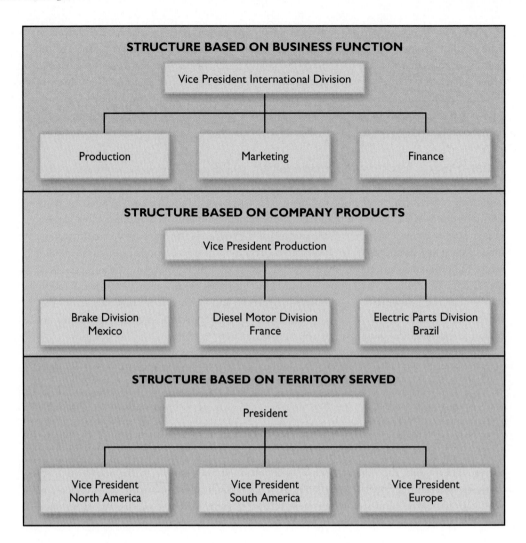

STRUCTURE BASED ON BUSINESS FUNCTION

Vice President International Division

Production | Marketing | Finance

STRUCTURE BASED ON COMPANY PRODUCTS

Vice President Production

Brake Division Mexico | Diesel Motor Division France | Electric Parts Division Brazil

STRUCTURE BASED ON TERRITORY SERVED

President

Vice President North America | Vice President South America | Vice President Europe

FIGURE 5.8
Partial multinational organization charts based on function, product, and territory

Organization Structure Basically, *organization structure* is the sum of all established relationships among resources within the organization, and the *organization chart* is the graphic illustration of organization structure.

Figure 5.8 illustrates several ways in which organization charts can be designed for multinational corporations. Briefly, multinational organization charts can be set up according to major business functions the organization performs, such as production or marketing; major products the organization sells, such as brakes or electrical parts; or, geographic areas within which the organization does business, such as South America or Europe. The topic of organization structure is discussed in much more detail in Chapter 11.

As with domestic organizations, there is no one best way to organize a multinational corporation. Instead, managers must analyze the multinational circumstances that confront them and develop an organization structure that best suits those circumstances.

Selection of Managers For multinational organizations to thrive, they must have competent managers. One characteristic believed to be a primary determinant of how competently managers can guide multinational organizations is their attitude toward how such organizations should operate.

Managerial Attitudes Toward Foreign Operations Over the years, management theorists have identified three basic managerial attitudes toward the operation of multinational corporations: ethnocentric, polycentric, and geocentric.

The **ethnocentric attitude** reflects the belief that multinational corporations should regard home-country management practices as superior to foreign-country management practices. Managers with an ethnocentric attitude are prone to stereotype home-country management practices as sound and reasonable and foreign management practices as faulty and unreasonable. The **polycentric attitude** reflects the belief that because foreign managers are closer to foreign organizational units, they probably understand them better, and therefore foreign management practices should generally be viewed as more insightful than home-country management practices. Managers with a **geocentric attitude** believe that the overall quality of management recommendations, rather than the location of managers, should determine the acceptability of management practices used to guide multinational corporations.[40]

Modern managers should continually monitor ethnocentric, polycentric, and geocentric attitudes that exist in organizations to make sure that they are consistent with global aspirations of the organization. One example of this monitoring involves the Coca-Cola Company where management constantly monitors its Chinese Web site. The purpose of this monitoring is to examine how Coca-Cola, the number one brand in the world, is using its Web site to communicate with management as well as the public in the world's largest market, China. Management wants to make sure that the Web site appropriately integrates ethnocentric and polycentric views in supporting the Chinese segment of the company's global strategy.[41]

Advantages and Disadvantages of Each Management Attitude It is extremely important to understand the potential advantages and disadvantages of these three attitudes within multinational corporations. The ethnocentric attitude has the advantage of keeping the organization simple, but it generally causes organizational problems because it prevents the organization from receiving feedback from its foreign operations. In some cases, the ethnocentric attitude even causes resentment toward the home country within the foreign society. The polycentric attitude permits the tailoring of foreign organizational segments to their cultures, which can be an advantage. Unfortunately, this attitude can lead to the substantial disadvantage of creating numerous foreign organizational segments that are individually run and rather unique, which makes them difficult to control.

The geocentric attitude is generally thought to be the most appropriate for managers in multinational corporations. This attitude promotes collaboration between foreign and home-country management and encourages the development of managerial skills regardless of the organizational segment or country in which managers operate. An organization characterized by the geocentric attitude generally incurs high travel and training expenses, and many decisions are made by consensus. Although the risks from such a wide distribution of power are real, the potential payoffs—better-quality products, worldwide utilization of the best human resources, increased managerial commitment to worldwide organizational objectives, and increased profit—generally outweigh the potential harm. Overall, managers with a geocentric attitude contribute more to the long-term success of the multinational corporation than managers with an ethnocentric or polycentric attitude.

Influencing People in Multinational Corporations

Influencing was generally defined in Chapter 1 as guiding the activities of organization members in appropriate directions through communicating, leading, motivating, and managing groups. Influencing people in a multinational corporation, however, is more complex and challenging than in a domestic organization.

Culture The factor that probably contributes most to this increased complexity and challenge is culture. **Culture** is the set of characteristics of a given group of people and their environment. The components of a culture that are generally designated as important are norms, values, customs, beliefs, attitudes, habits, skills, state of technology, level of education, and religion. As a manager moves from a domestic corporation involving basically one culture to a multinational corporation involving several, the task of influencing usually becomes more difficult.

To successfully influence employees, managers in multinational corporations should:

1. **Acquire a working knowledge of the languages used in countries that house foreign operations**—Multinational managers attempting to operate without such knowledge are prone to making costly mistakes.

2. **Understand the attitudes of people in countries that house foreign operations**—An understanding of these attitudes can help managers design business practices that are suitable for unique foreign situations. For example, Canadians generally accept competition as a tool to encourage people to work harder. As a result, Canadian business practices that include some competitive aspects seldom create significant disruption within organizations. Such practices could cause disruption, however, if introduced into either Japan or the typical European country.

3. **Understand the needs that motivate people in countries housing foreign operations**—For managers in multinational corporations to be successful at motivating employees in different countries, they must present these individuals with the opportunity to satisfy personal needs while being productive within the organization. In designing motivation strategies, multinational managers must understand that employees in different countries often have quite different personal needs. For example, the Swiss, Austrians, Japanese, and Argentineans tend to have high security needs; whereas Danes, Swedes, and Norwegians tend to have high social needs. People in Great Britain, the United States, Canada, New Zealand, and Australia tend to have high self-actualization needs.[42] Thus, to be successful at influencing, multinational managers must understand their employees' needs and mold such organizational components as incentive systems, job design, and leadership style to correspond to these needs.

class discussion highlight

The Chinese Culture and Your Career

You have just accepted a job with Nestlé and will soon be working in China as the manager of a plant with 300 employees making a new type of dog food. You know that Nestlé as a whole has about 250,000 employees, is made up of 100 different nationalities, and your China position looks to be a place where you can build an exciting international career.

You know that in your new job you will be managing mostly Chinese nationals. As such, you have read many articles about the Chinese culture and have found out the following:[43]

- Personal relationships are extremely important to the Chinese.

- The Chinese prefer working with friends.

- The Chinese avoid punishment and embarrassment.

- In China, gifts are used to build and strengthen personal relationships.

- Chinese businesses are built around family.

- The Chinese shy away from confrontational and direct conversation.

1. Is what you have found out about the Chinese culture important in building your career at Nestlé? Explain.

2. Would the way you manage in China change based upon your new understanding of the Chinese culture? How?

3. Would it be easy for you to make such changes? Why?

Controlling Multinational Corporations

Controlling was generally defined in Chapter 1 as making something happen the way it was planned to happen. As with domestic corporations, control in multinational corporations requires that standards be set, performance be measured and compared to standards, and corrective action be taken if necessary. In addition, control in such areas as labor costs, product quality, and inventory is important to organizational success regardless of whether the organization is domestic or international.

Special Difficulties Control of a multinational corporation involves certain complexities. First, to deal with the problem of different currencies, management must decide how to compare profits generated by organizational units located in different countries and therefore expressed in terms of different currencies. Another complication is that organizational units in multinational corporations are generally more geographically separated. This increased distance normally makes it difficult for multinational managers to keep a close watch on operations in foreign countries.

Improving Communication One action successful managers take to help overcome the difficulty of monitoring geographically separated foreign units is carefully designing the communication network or information system that links them. A significant part of this design requires all company units to acquire and install similar computer equipment in all offices, both foreign and domestic, to ensure the likelihood of network hookups when communication becomes necessary. Such standardization of computer equipment also facilitates communication among all foreign locations and makes equipment repair and maintenance easier and therefore less expensive.[44]

Transnational Organizations

Transnational organizations, also called *global organizations,* take the entire world as their business arena.[45] Doing business wherever it makes sense is primary; national borders are considered inconsequential. The transnational organization transcends any single home country, with ownership, control, and management being from many different countries. Transnational organizations represent the fourth, and maximum, level of international activity as depicted on the continuum of international involvement presented earlier in this chapter. Seeing great opportunities in the global marketplace, some MNCs have transformed themselves from home-based companies with worldwide interests into worldwide companies pursuing business activities across the globe and claiming no singular loyalty to any one country.

Perhaps the most commonly cited **example from the world of management** of a transnational organization is **Nestlé**.[46] Although Nestlé is headquartered in Vevey, Switzerland, its arena of daily business activity is truly the world. Nestlé has a diversified list of products that include instant coffee, cereals, pharmaceuticals, coffee creamers, dietetic foods, ice cream, chocolates, and a wide array of snack foods. Its recent acquisition of the French company Perrier catapulted Nestlé into market leadership in the mineral water industry. Nestlé has more than 210,000 employees and operates 494 factories in 71 countries worldwide, including Germany, Portugal, Brazil, France, New Zealand, Australia, Chile, the United States, and Venezuela. Of Nestlé's sales and profits, about 35 percent come from Europe, 40 percent from North and South America, and 25 percent from other countries. As with most transnational organizations, Nestlé has grown by acquiring companies rather than by expanding its present operations.[47]

INTERNATIONAL MANAGEMENT: SPECIAL ISSUES

The preceding section of this chapter discussed planning, organizing, influencing, and controlling multinational corporations. This section focuses on two special issues that can help to ensure management success in the international arena: maintaining ethics in international management, and preparing expatriates for foreign assignments.[48]

Maintaining Ethics in International Management

As discussed in Chapter 3, *ethics* is a concern for good behavior and reflects an obligation that forces managers to consider not only their own personal well-being, but that of other human beings as they lead organizations. Having a manager define what is ethical behavior can indeed be challenging. Defining what behavior is ethical becomes increasingly challenging as managers consider the international implications of management action. What seems ethical in a manager's home country can be unethical in a different country.

The following guidelines can help managers ensure that management action taken across national borders is indeed ethical. According to these guidelines, managers can ensure that such action is ethical by the following:

Respecting core human rights—This guideline underscores the notion that all people deserve an opportunity to achieve economic advancement and an improved standard of living. In addition, all people have the right to be treated with respect. Much effort has been made recently by major sporting goods companies, including Nike and Reebok, to ensure that this guideline is followed in business operations they are conducting in other countries.[49] These companies have joined forces to crack down on child labor, establish minimum wages comparable to existing individual country standards, establish a maximum 60-hour workweek with at least one day off, and support the establishment of a mechanism for inspecting apparel factories worldwide. These companies have also committed themselves to the elimination of forced labor, harassment, abuse, and discrimination in the workplace.

Respecting local traditions—This guideline suggests that managers hold the customs of foreign countries in which they conduct business in high regard. In Japan, for example, people have a long-standing tradition that those individuals who do business together exchange gifts. Sometimes, these gifts can be expensive. When Western managers started doing business in Japan, accepting a gift felt like accepting a bribe. As a result, many of these managers thought that the practice of gift giving might be wrong. As Western managers have come to know and respect this Japanese tradition, most have come to tolerate, and even encourage, the practice as ethical behavior in Japan. Some managers even set different limits on gift giving in Japan than they do elsewhere.

Determining right from wrong by examining context—This guideline suggests that managers should evaluate the specifics of the international situation confronting them in determining whether a particular management activity is ethical. Although some activities are wrong no matter where they take place, some that are unethical in one setting may be acceptable in another. For instance, the chemical EDB, a soil fungicide, is banned from use in some countries. In hot climates, however, it quickly becomes harmless through exposure to intense solar radiation and high soil temperatures. As long as the chemical is monitored, companies may be able to use EDB ethically in certain parts of the world.

Most managers and management scholars agree that implementing ethical management practices across national borders enhances organizational success. Although following the guidelines just described does not guarantee that management action taken across national borders will be ethical, it should increase the probability.

Preparing Expatriates for Foreign Assignments

The trend of companies forming joint ventures and other strategic alliances that emphasize foreign operations is increasing. As a result, the number of expatriates being sent from other countries is also rising.[50]

The somewhat casual approach of the past toward preparing expatriates for foreign duty is being replaced by the attitude that these managers need special tools to be able to succeed in difficult foreign assignments.[51] To help expatriates adjust, home companies are helping them find homes and high-quality health care in host countries. Companies are also responding to expatriate feelings that they need more help from home companies on career planning related to foreign assignments, career planning for spouses forced to go to the foreign assignment country to look for work, and better counseling for the personal challenges they will face during their foreign assignment.

Many companies prepare their expatriates for foreign assignments by using special training programs. Specific features of these programs vary from company to company, depending on the situation. Most of these programs, however, usually contain the following core elements:

- **Culture profiles**—Here, expatriates learn about the new culture in which they will be working.

- **Cultural adaptation**—Here, expatriates learn how to survive the difficulties of adjusting to a new culture.

- **Logistical information**—Here, expatriates learn basic information, such as personal safety, who to call in an emergency, and how to write a check.

- **Application**—Here, expatriates learn about specific organizational roles they will perform.

Expatriates generally play a critical role in determining the success of an organization's foreign operations. The tremendous personal and professional adjustments that expatriates must make, however, can delay their effectiveness and efficiency in foreign settings. Sound training programs can lower the amount of time expatriates need to adjust and can thereby help them become productive more quickly.

{CHALLENGE CASE SUMMARY

As the Challenge Case shows, Wal-Mart is an organization heavily involved in international management. The company now operates in countries such as China and Brazil, and has recently expanded into Japan. Manager Lee Scott will be performing international management activities in a number of countries and, given today's trend toward greater foreign investment, Wal-Mart is likely to continue to emphasize global expansion. In addition, it is likely that foreign companies will attempt to compete with Wal-Mart.

As Wal-Mart continues its international expansion it will become, and perhaps already is, more of a multinational corporation—an organization with significant operations in more than one country. In any company, management under international circumstances is a complex matter. As Wal-Mart continues to grow internationally, the complexity is related to the necessity for managing within different foreign countries that are separated by significant distances and that are characterized by different economic conditions, people, levels of technology, market sizes, and laws. Wal-Mart's success with foreign expansion illustrates the potential rewards to managers who can handle the complexity of doing business in other countries.

Management at Wal-Mart is attempting to minimize risk in its decisions to make foreign investments. Few managers would see expansion into a country such as Japan as too risky. This country is considered to be economically stable and safe for foreign investors, whereas expansion into a country characterized by civil upheaval and military action would certainly be risky.

The United States has normal trading relationships with Japan, and Wal-Mart may have much to gain by being successful merchandisers in Japan. Management must be aware, however, that the political situation between their countries and other countries can change rapidly. As a result, the company should constantly monitor the political relationship between the United

States and the countries in which it does business, in order to enable a quick response to any changes.

Wal-Mart management has apparently decided that foreign investment in Japan represents a tolerable amount of risk when weighed against the prospect of increased return from operations in Japan. Actual operation in Japan, however, is more recently furnishing feedback indicating that the decision might be riskier than they first thought.

Perhaps the most important variable in building the success of Japanese Wal-Marts is probably the people it employs. The company must establish the best combination of people to run the stores—expatriates, host-country nationals, or third-country nationals. Whatever blend of human resources is decided on, management must be sensitive in helping individuals adjust both personally and organizationally to the Japanese culture. In addition, if expatriates are involved in running the stores, Wal-Mart should be sensitive to helping them adjust when they are repatriated.

Planning is equally valuable to both domestic and international companies. The primary difference between planning for Wal-Mart as a domestic company and as an international company would be reflected in components of company plans. As an international corporation, Wal-Mart would have planning components that focus on the international sector, whereas a totally domestic organization would not. Such components could include establishing a partnership with a Japanese construction company to build Wal-Mart stores throughout Japan, building nearby training facilities that could provide well-trained employees for Japanese stores and stores in nearby countries, choosing additional store locations in other countries, and selling the rights to a foreign company to use the Wal-Mart name in mass merchandising.

In organizing a company such as Wal-Mart along international lines, organization structure generally should be based on one or more of the variables of function, product, territory, customers, or manufacturing process. Wal-Mart managers must consider all the variables within the situations that confront them and then design the organization structure that is most appropriate for those situations. Wal-Mart might organize internationally on a geographic basis, for example, with a CEO for its European division.

Over the long term, management at Wal-Mart should try to select for international positions the managers who possess geocentric attitudes, as opposed to polycentric or ethnocentric attitudes. Such managers would tend to build operating units in other countries, would use the best human resources available, and

would be highly committed to the attainment of organizational objectives.

As Wal-Mart becomes more multinational, influencing people within the company will become more complicated. The cultures of people in countries such as Japan and other countries in which Wal-Mart does international business must be thoroughly understood. Managers of foreign operations must have a working knowledge of the languages spoken in the host country and an understanding of the attitudes and personal needs that motivate individuals within the foreign workforce. If motivation strategy is to be successful for Wal-Mart as a whole, rewards used to motivate Japanese workers may need to be much different from the rewards used to motivate Wal-Mart's workers in other countries.

The control process at Wal-Mart should involve standards, measurements, and needed corrective action, just as it should within a purely domestic company. The different currencies used in countries such as Japan, however, tend to make control more complicated for an international organization than for a domestic one. The significant distance of countries such as Japan from the United States would also tend to complicate the issue of control at Wal-Mart.

Based on this information, managers at Wal-Mart should be concerned with promoting ethical behavior in the company's foreign operations, which include actions that respect the core human rights of foreign citizens, accommodate foreign local traditions, and reflect what is "right" in the particular foreign context. Examples of ethical behavior could be forbidding foreign children to be hired as employees, paying a fair wage that reflects foreign national wage levels, and eliminating abuse and discrimination in Wal-Mart stores.

In addition, Wal-Mart must properly prepare expatriates who are going to work in other countries, such as Japan, if these individuals are to be as productive as possible as quickly as possible. The company should take steps to help the expatriates find appropriate housing and health care, to explain how the assignment impacts the expatriates' long-term career at Wal-Mart, and to provide counseling for personal problems that the expatriates could face simply by living in Japan or elsewhere. Formal training of expatriates going to Japan should probably include a description of the Japanese culture; steps that expatriates can take to adapt to that culture; basic information about logistics of life in Japan, such as who to call in case of emergency; and specifics about the job they will be performing.

MANAGEMENT SKILL ACTIVITIES

This section is specially designed to help you develop global management skill. An individual's global management skill is based upon an understanding of global management concepts and the ability to apply those concepts in management situations. The following activities are designed to both heighten your understanding of global management concepts and to develop the ability to apply those concepts in a variety of management situations.

UNDERSTANDING CORPORATE GLOBAL MANAGEMENT CONCEPTS

This section is comprised of activities that will sharpen your understanding of global management concepts. Answer essay questions as completely as possible. Also, remember that many additional true/false and multiple choice questions appear online at MyManagementLab.com to help you further refine your understanding of social responsibility concepts.

Essay Questions

1. Discuss three similarities and three differences of international versus transnational organizations.
2. What are the risks and rewards of operating a multinational organization?
3. List and define the three types of organization members found in multinational organizations. Discuss the contribution that each type can bring to building the success of the organization.
4. What knowledge must a manager have to successfully influence organization members of multinational corporations? Would it be easy for a manager to acquire such knowledge? Why? How should the manager acquire the knowledge?
5. Is the preparation of expatriates more important than their repatriation? Explain fully.
6. Discuss the role of "examining context" in maintaining ethical practices in international management situations.

Developing Management Skill

Learning activities in this section are aimed at helping you to develop global management skill. Learning activities include Exploring Your Management Skill: Part 2, Your Management Skill Portfolio, Experiential Exercise, Cases, and a VideoNet exercise.

EXPLORING YOUR MANAGEMENT SKILL: PART 2

As you recall, you completed Exploring Your Management Skill before you started to study this chapter. Your responses gave you an idea of how much you initially knew about global management and helped you to focus on important points as you studied the chapter. Answer the Exploring Your Management Skill questions again now (p. 134) and compare your score to the first time you took it. This comparison will give you an idea of how much you have learned from studying this chapter and pinpoint areas for further clarification before you start studying the next chapter. Record your answers within the text or online at MyManagementLab.com. Completing the survey at MyManagementLab.com will allow you to grade and compare your test scores automatically. If you complete the test in the book, look up answers in the Exploring Your Management Skill section at the end of the book.

YOUR MANAGEMENT SKILLS PORTFOLIO

Your Management Learning Portfolio is a collection of activities especially designed to demonstrate your management knowledge and skill. By completing these activities online at MyManagementLab.com, you will be able to print, complete with cover sheet, as many activities as you choose. Be sure to save your work. Taking your printed portfolio to an employment interview could be helpful in obtaining a job.

The portfolio activity for this chapter is *Managing a Business in Japan.* Study this information and complete the exercises that follow.

You are an American-educated manager who believes in Western management philosophies. You have just accepted a job as a middle manager in a Toyota manufacturing plant in Tahara, slightly south of Osaka in Japan. The plant manufactures Toyota's new Lexus hybrid sedan. For your entire career, 10 years, you have worked as a middle manager in a General Motors plant in the United States and followed traditional American management practices. Toyota was clear, however, about expecting you to fit into its culture and following its management practices that have built company success. You know little about Japanese management practices and start to read as much as you can about how Japanese companies operate. During your reading you uncovered the following summary about the differences between the way Japanese and American companies are structured. Read and study this summary carefully.

Management and Corporate Structures in Asia and the West : 25 Key Differences

Large Western Firms	Large Asian Firms
1. Short time horizons in decision making	Long time horizons in decision making
2. The company is driven by profits and/or market share	The company is growth-driven
3. Corporate direction determined by overall corporate "vision" and strategy	Corporate direction determined by opportunity
4. Highly structured	Often poorly structured
5. Wide ownership (institutions)	Narrow ownership (family)
6. Professionally managed	Family managed
7. More concentrated	Highly diversified
8. Invest on the basis of research	Invest on the basis of connections
9. Minority shareholders well treated	Minority shareholders abused
10. Dispersed decision making	Centralized decision making
11. Relatively small number of units/companies	Large number of units/companies
12. Prefer accrual accounting	Prefer cash accounting
13. Lots of contracting out and buying in	High degree of vertical integration; lots of internal transactions
14. Reliant on external funding	Prefer internal funding
15. Services are important	Dislike services
16. R&D-intensive	Little or no R&D
17. Participative management	Patriarchal management
18. Senior management is relatively aloof	Senior management is hands-on
19. Well-defined career ladder for staff	Vague career ladder for staff
20. High priority given to transparency, auditing, and disclosure	Low priority given to transparency, auditing, and disclosure
21. Fringe benefits are generally a small part of total remuneration	Fringe benefits are a high component of salary (remuneration is paternalistic)
22. Staff training is formal and structured	Staff are trained informally and on the job
23. Employees tend to be promoted on the basis of their inherent productivity	Employees tend to be promoted on the basis of their connections and perceived loyalty
24. Job descriptions are precise and employees are encouraged to use initiative	Job descriptions are vague and employees work as directed
25. Staff initiative expected and rewarded	Staff initiative discouraged

Source: Michael Backman, *Asian Eclipse: Exposing the Dark Side of Business in Asia* (New York: John Wiley Publishers, 2001), 78.

Exercise 1: Overall, based upon the information given, list three major challenges that you will face as a manager at Toyota and steps you will take to meet these challenges.

Challenge 1: _____

What I will do to meet Challenge 1:

Challenge 2: _____

What I will do to meet Challenge 2:

_____

_____

_____

Challenge 3: _____

What will I do to meet Challenge 3:

_____

_____

_____

Exercise 2: Based upon the information given, to be successful in Japan, you will probably have to somewhat change the way you plan, organize, influence, and control. List the changes for each management function that you probably will have to make.

Changes to the way I will **plan** in Japan:

_____

_____

_____

Changes to the way I will **organize** in Japan:

_____

_____

_____

Changes to the way I will **influence** people in Japan:

_____

_____

_____

Changes to the way I will **control** in Japan:

_____

_____

_____

Exercise 3: Do you think that you would be successful in this job as manager at Toyota? Why?

_____

_____

Exercise 4: Overall, what did you learn from this experience?

_____

_____

EXPERIENTIAL EXERCISE: BUILDING A GLOBAL MANAGEMENT CURRICULUM

Directions. Read the following scenario and then perform the listed activities. Your instructor may want you to perform the activities as an individual or within groups. Follow all of your instructor's directions carefully.

You are the president of Fiat Lux, a small liberal arts school in Denver, Colorado. In recent years you have tried to provide leadership in building more of a business emphasis into your curriculum. Reflecting your lead, your faculty over the past four years has been developing courses in organizational studies that focus primarily on managing people in organizations with as well as how to organize and plan. Although you are pleased with the progress the school is making, you realize that the school's offerings should be expanded even more to offer a new major called Global Management.

Based upon your feelings, you've asked a few global business leaders from the community to help you develop a list of eight courses that could comprise this new major. Your goal is to propose is this new major and its related courses to your faculty as a vehicle they can use to prepare your undergraduate students for careers in global management.

You are presently leading a meeting of this business advisory group. Introduce your task for the group and lead discussion concerning what the eight courses should be. Be sure to get course titles as well as descriptions of what the courses should include and rationales for why the courses should be included in the new major. When completed, your eight courses should provide your students with the essential knowledge to begin and be successful in entry-level positions that include global management responsibilities.

CASES

WAL-MART FACING GLOBAL PROBLEMS IN JAPAN

"Wal-Mart Facing Global Problems in Japan" (p. 133) and its Challenge Case Summary were written to help you better understand the management concepts contained in this chapter. Answer the following discussion questions about the Challenge Case that relate to managing in the global arena and can be applied in a company such as Wal-Mart.

1. Do you think that at some point in your career you will become involved in international management? Explain.

2. Assuming that you are involved in managing a Wal-Mart store in Japan, what challenges do you think will be the most difficult for you in improving Japanese store success? Why?

3. Evaluate the following statement: Wal-Mart can learn to manage its U.S. operations better by studying how successful competitive operations are managed in other countries.

WHIRLPOOL'S WHIRLWIND OF GLOBAL BUSINESS

Read the case and answer the questions that follow. Studying this case will help you better understand how concepts relating to managing in the global arena can be applied in a company such as Whirlpool.

One world, many markets, many needs. The multinational giant Whirlpool faces a number of management challenges in selling home appliances such as washing machines, dryers, refrigerators, and stoves to customers in 170 countries. For example, CEO Jeff Fettig and his management team know, through research, that kitchen space in China is limited, so only small microwave ovens

will fit. In contrast, kitchens in U.S. homes are much larger, and customers are clamoring for microwave ovens nearly three times the size of those sold in China. They also know that refrigerators are symbols of affluence in India, and therefore are often displayed in living rooms. As a result, Whirlpool refrigerators intended for customers in the burgeoning Indian market are available in brighter colors and less angular profiles than those intended for customers in European markets.

Understanding the nuances of local culture is only the beginning for Whirlpool's executives, who direct an organization that rings up $12 billion in annual sales and employs 68,000 employees worldwide. They also face decisions about where to design and where to manufacture appliances to keep costs in line, tap talented employees, and boost profits. In most cases, they prefer to make products in factories located close to the destination market. For example, a Whirlpool factory in southern India makes basic washing machines designed specifically for that country, with reinforced wiring to withstand sporadic power surges. In addition, two factories in Ohio make energy-efficient, sophisticated top-loading washers for sale in the United States, while a soon-to-be expanded factory in Monterrey, Mexico, makes a variety of washers for sale across North America.

Unlike parts and finished products, technology and designs in progress can be moved anywhere at the click of a mouse—and Whirlpool takes advantage of such portability. In 1999, the company had no engineering and technical experts in Asia. Today, it employs more than 240 local experts in China and India and plans to hire 400 more within three years. "We're shifting quite a bit of our technology capacity to these countries from the higher-cost parts of the world, part of it from the United States and Europe," explains Whirlpool's regional vice president for Asia.

The company takes full advantage of time differences by transmitting computer-aided product designs in progress to China and India at the end of the U.S. work day. The engineers in Asia pick up where the U.S. engineers left off, then send the designs back at the end of their workday, speeding the design process along. This approach has boosted productivity and slashed development time dramatically. Now Whirlpool can bring new models from the idea stage to the brink of production in just 12–14 months, compared with 30–36 months under the old system.

Having headed the European division for three years before becoming president and then CEO of Whirlpool, Jeff Fettig is keenly aware of the realities of global competition. He knows that European and Asian appliance manufacturers are aggressively seeking market share, but he also puts a high priority on company profitability. For this reason, he has not allowed Whirlpool to get caught up in the discounting that many local manufacturers have used to attract buyers in China. In fact, Whirlpool was able to increase its profits even as it finally achieved its long-standing goal of becoming the number-one appliance company in Europe.

Doing business in so many countries means dealing with all kinds of problems, from currency devaluation in Brazil (which hurts income) to contract issues in China (which affects the price and quality of parts). To strengthen its position in Europe, Whirlpool is enlarging its factory in Poland to turn out a new line of refrigerators, dishwashers, and stoves. And North America remains a vital part of Whirlpool's global strategy. Top management recently decided to invest nearly $200 million in building new facilities and enhancing existing factories in the United States and Mexico in anticipation of continued growth—around the world.

QUESTIONS

1. Knowing that Whirlpool sells its appliances in 170 countries, should managers in the Michigan headquarters take an ethnocentric, a polycentric, or a geocentric attitude toward foreign operations? Why?

2. What are some of the challenges that Whirlpool might face in managing operations spread over so many time zones?

3. Whirlpool's organization structure is based on territory served. Do you agree with this decision, or would you suggest that Whirlpool use another structure? Why?

VIDEONET EXERCISE

Global Business at KPMG

VIDEO HIGHLIGHTS

KPMG spends hundreds of thousands of dollars sending interns on overseas assignments to ensure their potential future employees are globally savvy. Hard to believe it's a cost-effective practice, but they are the accounting experts after all. Aidan Walsh, Head of Global Mobility for KPMG, explains why interns and employees need global exposure to be effective in the financial services industry. How could a cultural misunderstanding potentially send ripples through the global economy? What are the biggest challenges of managing a global company in a global business environment?

Discussion Questions

1. Is KPMG an international or multinational corporation? What are some of the complexities associated with managing this type of organization?

2. How does KPMG's Global Mobility program help in the organization of their corporation?

3. Discuss three managerial challenges of linking more than 100,000 employees in 150 countries. How would you meet each challenge?

Internet Activity

Go to the KPMG Web site at www.kpmg.com. How is KPMG organized? What is the structure of this large multinational organization? How is this organization governed?

6 Management and Entrepreneurship

OBJECTIVES

TO HELP BUILD MY ENTREPRENEURSHIP SKILL, WHEN STUDYING THIS CHAPTER, I WILL ATTEMPT TO ACQUIRE:

1. An understanding of the three stages of entrepreneurship

2. An overall appreciation for the opportunity concept and an understanding of the primary types of entrepreneurial opportunities

3. An ability to distinguish between opportunity identification, evaluation, and exploitation

4. Insights regarding the various types of financing available to entrepreneurs

5. An appreciation for how existing organizations use corporate entrepreneurship

6. An understanding of and appreciation for the role of social entrepreneurship in society

TARGET SKILL entrepreneurship skill: involves the identification, evaluation, and exploitation of opportunities

GOOGLE ENTREPRENEURS WIN BIG

Larry Page and Sergey Brin were two typical computer science graduate students at Stanford University in the U.S. state of California.[1] Their reputations—and fortunes—changed dramatically, however, when they incorporated Google in 1998. Today, the company has proven so successful that many people refer to online searching as *googling*.

Google's founders challenged the conventional wisdom regarding Internet search by changing the way in which their search engine processed search requests. In particular, Google based search results on how many other pages linked

Google founders Larry Page (left) and Sergey Brin. Their exclusive focus on the search functions of their site have helped it garner a commanding market share.

to a particular Web page and how popular those Web pages were. If, for example, no other Web pages linked to the Web page with 20 instances of "automobile tires" and many Web pages linked to the Web page with one instance of "automobile tires," Google would provide higher search results for the latter and lower search results for the former.

Page and Brin also differentiated their company by changing the way they approached search. While other companies such as Yahoo! used their search engine primarily as a way to obtain new visitors to their Web sites, Google focused its efforts on search alone. Yahoo!, for example, used its search engine to draw visitors to its Web site that also includes news, entertainment, and weather information. In contrast, Google offers a simple Web site that focuses strictly on search and does not include other information that might distract search.

Even though the intense focus on search may seem curious at first, it is the search process that provides Google with its revenues and profits. When users enter search terms, Google places small text advertise-ments next to the search results. Each time users click on these small advertisements, Google receives money from the advertisers. Given these incentives for profits, Google continues to constantly improve the search process. This continuous improvement helps to explain why Google maintains approximately 64 percent of the market share for searches in the United States alone; this 64 percent is nearly three times as large as Google's biggest competitor, Yahoo! In other parts of the world, Google's market share is even higher.

Google's dominance in the search business has led to astounding performance. Although the company is just over 10 years old, it recently had revenues of $16 billion and profits of more than $4 billion.

Taken together, then, Google's founders identified an opportunity while they were graduate students at Stanford. After they evaluated the opportunity, they decided to start their own company. Just as IBM dominated mainframes and Microsoft dominated personal computer software, today Google has the potential to rule the Internet. How Page and Brin approach these next several years will largely determine Google's place in Internet—and corporate—history.

"EXPLORE YOUR OWN MANAGEMENT SKILLS BY TAKING THE QUIZ ON THE NEXT PAGE"

Before studying this chapter, respond to the following questions regarding the type of advice that you would give to Google's Larry Page and Sergey Brin, referenced in the Challenge Case. Then address the concerning entrepreneurship challenges that they presently face within the company. You are not expected to be an entrepreneurship expert at this point. Answering the questions now can help you focus on important points when you study the chapter. Also, answering the questions again after you study the chapter will give you an idea of how much you have learned.

Record your answers here or online at MyManagement Lab.com. Completing the questions at MyManagement Lab.com will allow you to get feedback about your answers automatically. If you answer the questions in the book, look up answers in the Exploring Your Management Skill section at the end of the book.

FOR EACH STATEMENT CIRCLE:

- "Y" if you would give the advice to Page and Brin.
- "N" if you would NOT give the advice to Page and Brin.
- "NI" if you have no idea whether you would give the advice to Page and Brin.

Messrs. Page and Brin, in meeting your entrepreneurship challenges at Google, you should . . .

Before Study   *After Study*

1. understand that because Google has become so large, they are no longer entrepreneurs and entrepreneurship concepts do not matter any longer to Google.

   Y, N, NI

2. recognize that entrepreneurship involves the identification, evaluation, and exploitation of opportunities.

   Y, N, NI

3. recognize that, on average, entrepreneurial ventures succeed, particularly in the United States.

   Y, N, NI

4. understand that, on average, entrepreneurial ventures started by teams of entrepreneurs tend to outperform entrepreneurial ventures started by solo entrepreneurs.

   Y, N, NI

5. recognize that five broad types of opportunities exist, and Google must continue to monitor these potential opportunities.

   Y, N, NI

6. understand that Google employees will be able to identify future opportunities equally.

   Y, N, NI

7. understand that their social networks will influence their ability to identify opportunities in the future.

   Y, N, NI

8. require Google employees to use feasibility analysis when evaluating new opportunities.

   Y, N, NI

9. understand the role of small numbers, which suggests that a small number of entrepreneurial ventures will succeed.

   Y, N, NI

10. recognize that Google will most likely require angel investors if the company is to continue to succeed in the future.

    Y, N, NI

11. understand that the objectives of venture capitalists, angel investors, and banks are all similar.

    Y, N, NI

12. communicate to Google employees the value of sustained regeneration and its importance as the most common form of strategic entrepreneurship.

    Y, N, NI

13. understand that *commercial entrepreneurship* and *social entrepreneurship* are two terms that have the same meaning.

    Y, N, NI

14. evaluate Google's social entrepreneurship activities without considering revenues and costs.

    Y, N, NI

15. recognize that corporate entrepreneurship is the most likely set of entrepreneurship activities to influence Google because it is a large company.

    Y, N, NI

THE ENTREPRENEURSHIP CHALLENGE

The Challenge Case illustrates different entrepreneurship challenges that Google strives to meet. The remaining material in this chapter explains entrepreneurship concepts and helps to develop the corresponding entrepreneurship skill that you will need to meet such challenges throughout your career. After studying the chapter concepts, read the Challenge Case Summary at the end of the chapter to help you relate chapter content to meeting entrepreneurship challenges at Google.

FUNDAMENTALS OF ENTREPRENEURSHIP

Entrepreneurship can be defined in a variety of ways. Most people believe that entrepreneurship entails an individual starting a new business to make money, but the meaning of the term is actually much broader. For our purposes, **entrepreneurship** refers to the identification, evaluation, and exploitation of opportunities.[2] Figure 6.1 illustrates this process. Opportunities in a general sense are appropriate or favorable occasions.[3] In the entrepreneurship context, though, the definition of *opportunity* is slightly different from this general definition. Specifically, **entrepreneurial opportunities** are occasions to bring into existence new products and services that allow outputs to be sold at a price greater than their cost of production.[4] In other words, entrepreneurial opportunities exist when individuals are able to sell new products and services at a price that produces a profit.

Although entrepreneurship has a broad definition, the term still involves starting new businesses. Understanding entrepreneurship is important;[5] studies suggest that somewhere between 20 to 50 percent of all individuals engage in entrepreneurial behaviors.[6] Despite these new businesses, the evidence suggests that entrepreneurs find it difficult to keep their businesses alive. Research reports, for example, that 34 percent of new businesses do not survive the first two years, 50 percent do not survive four years, and 60 percent do not survive six years.[7] Table 6.1 displays the results of some studies examining the failure rates of some new businesses.

Consistent with our framework, **entrepreneurs** are those individuals who identify, evaluate, and exploit opportunities. Many associate the term *entrepreneur* with one individual starting a new business, but it is not always the case. In fact, research suggests that approximately 75 percent of new organizations are started by entrepreneurial teams.[8] In other words, many entrepreneurs work with others when identifying, evaluating, and exploiting entrepreneurial opportunities. In fact, research suggests that organizations started by entrepreneurial teams tend to perform better than those started by individual entrepreneurs working by themselves.[9] Many attribute this "team advantage" to the combination of diverse skills, experiences, and relationships of the entrepreneurial team members.[10] In addition, as new organizations grow, they require leaders with new skills. Consequently, assembling a team makes it easier for entrepreneurs to add team members with these new skills as the venture expands.[11]

It is clear that entrepreneurship represents an important fabric of society. Taken together, then, these high business formation rates and high failure rates suggest that understanding the fundamentals of entrepreneurship represents an important activity. In the following sections, we highlight the primary issues as they pertain to identifying, evaluating, and exploiting entrepreneurial opportunities.

FIGURE 6.1
Stages of the entrepreneurship process

TABLE 6.1 A Summary of Entrepreneurial Failure Rates

Type of Businesses Studied	Failure Rate
Restaurants	Approximately 60% of new restaurants failed within the first 3 years.
New Businesses	Approximately 60% of new businesses failed within the first 6 years.
New Chemical Plants	Approximately 80% of new chemical plants failed within the first 10 years.

Sources: Based on data from Matthew Hayward, Dean Shepherd, and Dale Griffin, "A Hubris Theory of Entrepreneurship," *Management Science* 52, no. 2 (2006): 160–172; and H. G. Parsa, John Self, David Njite, and Tiffany King, "Why Restaurants Fail," *Cornell Hotel and Restaurant Administration Quarterly* 46, no. 3 (2005): 304–322.

Entrepreneurs are characterized by their ability to identify and exploit information pinpointing concrete business opportunities that others fail to see or capitalize on.

class discussion highlight

MODERN RESEARCH AND ENTREPRENEURSHIP SKILL

What Makes Entrepreneurs Quit?

The preceding discussion highlighted the fact that most new businesses tend to perform poorly. When firms perform poorly, entrepreneurs need to decide whether to continue with the firm or end the firm's existence. Given this rather systematic poor performance, why do some entrepreneurs quit while others continue down the path of poor performance?

Professors DeTienne, Shepherd, and Decastro examined this question in detail. The authors speculated that several factors may influence an entrepreneur's willingness to persist in the face of poor performance. They sampled 89 entrepreneurs and asked them how their willingness to continue down the path of poor performance was influenced by factors such as the resources available in the industry, the amount of money they invested in the venture, their previous successes, and the other career options available to the entrepreneurs.

Do you think such factors influenced their willingness to discontinue operations? Why or why not? If you were designing this study, what other factors would perhaps influence these decisions?

Source: This research highlight is based on D. R. DeTienne, D. A. Shepherd, and J. O. Decastro, "The Fallacy of 'Only The Strong Survive': The Effects of Extrinsic Motivation on the Persistence Decisions for Underperforming Firms," *Journal of Business Venturing*, 2007, in press.

OPPORTUNITIES

In the previous section, we defined entrepreneurship in terms of opportunities. In the following sections, we describe the different types of opportunities. In addition, we describe how entrepreneurs identify, evaluate, and exploit these opportunities.

Types of Opportunities

In his classic formulation of opportunities, Schumpeter described five different types of opportunities.[12] First, opportunities arise from the creation of new products or services. When a new type of medical device is created, for example, an opportunity exists in the form of convincing doctors to use the new device in their practices. In **an example from the world of management,** the creation of heart stents resulted in an entrepreneurial opportunity for companies such as **Boston Scientific** and **Abbott Laboratories.** These stents help doctors to clear and keep open patient's arteries, and in some cases, doctors use stents instead of using open heart surgery.[13]

Second, opportunities arise from the discovery of new geographical markets in which new customers will value the new product or service. As an example, suppose that an individual has exclusive rights to produce and distribute action figures based on a popular movie. After saturating the domestic market, the individual might begin to distribute the action figures in China. This scenario would represent an opportunity arising from the discovery of a new geographical market.

Third, opportunities may arise from the creation or discovery of new raw materials or after discovering alternative uses for existing raw materials. For example, ethanol, which can be produced from corn, represents a new use for corn. Although farmers typically sell corn to manufacturers of food products, ethanol provides farmers with another use for the corn they grow.

Fourth, opportunities may emerge from the discovery of new methods of production. According to Schumpeter, new methods of production allow entrepreneurs to produce goods or services at lower costs, which allows the entrepreneurs to satisfy the needs of customers more effectively. In **an example from the world of management, Dell Inc.** managed to use the Internet to transform the personal computer industry. By using the Internet to attract customers, Dell eliminated the need for retail outlets for its products. This new form of distribution allowed Dell to reduce the costs of the personal computers, which provided customers with lower-priced computers.

Finally, opportunities may arise from new methods of organizing. The emergence of the Internet provides an example of opportunities that arose from new methods of organizing. Specifically, the Internet allowed entrepreneurs to reach consumers without physical retail locations that required bricks and mortar.[14] In **an example from the world of management,** the Internet allowed **Netflix** to offer customers a new way to rent DVDs and video games. Instead of driving to a retail outlet such as Video Ezy, Netflix allows customers to choose their DVDs and video games without leaving their computers.

In sum, then, five different types of opportunities arise from the creation of new products or services, the discovery of new geographical markets, the discovery of new raw materials, the discovery of new methods of production, and the discovery of new methods of organizing. Table 6.2 summarizes and provides examples for each of these different types of

Not everyone can invent a new medical device or diagnostic technology. But entrepreneurial opportunities in the field of health care are broad, and they include the work of persuading doctors to use new discoveries to improve patient outcomes.

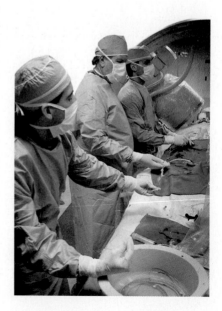

TABLE 6.2   Types of Opportunities

Opportunity Type	Example
New Product or Service	Nintendo developing and marketing the Wii gaming system
New Geographical Markets	Duetsche Bank providing services in China
New Raw Materials or New Uses for Raw Materials	Adidas' use of microfiber-based materials to make sports apparel
New Method of Production	Tyson Chicken raising chickens without antibiotics
New Method of Organizing	Amazon.com using the Internet to sell books

opportunities. In the following sections, we describe in detail how entrepreneurs identify, evaluate, and exploit these opportunities.

Opportunity Identification

Although an opportunity may exist, entrepreneurs will not be able to take advantage of this opportunity unless they are able to first identify the opportunity. Research suggests, though, that opportunities do not appear in a prepackaged form, and individuals differ in their ability to identify opportunities.[15] Intuitively, these differences in discernment make sense. If all individuals were equally able to identify opportunities, all individuals might rush to exploit the same opportunities.

Which factors help to determine whether individuals are able to identify opportunities? In the remainder of this section, we describe four factors that influence the ability of individuals to identify opportunities: entrepreneurial alertness, information asymmetry, social networks, and the ability to establish means-ends relationships.

First, individuals vary in terms of **entrepreneurial alertness,** which refers to an individual's ability to notice and be sensitive to new information about objects, incidents, and patterns of behavior in the environment.[16] When individuals have high levels of entrepreneurial alertness, they are more likely to identify potential entrepreneurial opportunities. In contrast, when individuals have low levels of entrepreneurial alertness, they are more likely to dismiss or ignore new information and overlook potential opportunities.

Second, individuals vary in terms of the information to which they have access, which is known as **information asymmetry.** This variation in information involves both new information and old information, and no two people share all of this information at the same time.[17] Two individuals, for example, may gain new market information regarding a potential entrepreneurial opportunity. Despite the fact that both of these individuals have gained access to this new information, only one of these individuals has access to addition information suggesting that other competitors are already moving to exploit this opportunity. As such, only one of these individuals will correctly identify this opportunity.

Third, individuals vary in terms of their **social networks,** which represent individuals' patterns of social relationships. Some individuals have extended social networks (i.e., many social relationships), while other individuals have narrow social networks (i.e., few social relationships). Research suggests that individuals with extended networks are more likely to identify potential entrepreneurial opportunities than those with more narrow social networks.[18] Moreover, the *type* of social network may influence opportunity identification. An individual with entrepreneurial family members, for example, may be better able to identify opportunities than an individual with family members who are not entrepreneurial.[19]

Fourth, individuals will vary in terms of their ability to assess means-ends relationships. In this context, the ability to assess means–end relationships refers to the ability of entrepreneurs to understand how to turn a new technology into a product or service that will be valued by consumers. For example, individuals may have access to technology, but they are unable to understand the potential commercial applications associated with the technology. When individuals are unable to see these relationships, they are unable to identify the opportunity. In an effort to help establish these means-ends relationships, several universities are working with individuals and researchers to help in identifying the commercial applications associated with new technologies.[20]

Taken together, then, a number of different factors influence opportunity identification. Figure 6.2 summarizes theses different factors.

Opportunity Evaluation

In the previous section, we discussed opportunity identification, which is the first step of the entrepreneurship process. In this section, we discuss the second stage of this process: opportunity evaluation. Opportunity evaluation occurs when an entrepreneur decides whether he or she has just a good idea or a viable opportunity that will provide the desired outcomes.[21] The evaluation step is "where the rubber meets the road," and it often presents a difficult challenge. When evaluating opportunities, entrepreneurs must be honest with themselves.[22] If not, the entrepreneurs may purposely ignore or accidentally overlook important factors that will limit the potential success of the opportunity.

To evaluate ideas, entrepreneurs will often engage in **feasibility analysis,** which is analysis that helps entrepreneurs understand whether an idea is practical.[23] In such a study, entrepreneurs will study customer demands, the structure of the industry, and the entrepreneur's ability to provide the new product or service. Although entrepreneurs have many ideas, not all of them are feasible; this analysis helps them to better understand the likelihood that their opportunity will provide the resources required.

Even if an idea is feasible, opportunities are associated with some risk. One of the central factors that entrepreneurs will examine in the evaluation stage is the opportunity's **entrepreneurial risk,** which is the likelihood and magnitude of the opportunity's downside loss. In this context, **downside loss** refers to the resources (i.e., money, relationships, etc.) that the entrepreneur could lose if the opportunity does not succeed. All else being equal, entrepreneurs are more likely to pursue opportunities with lower levels of entrepreneurial risk and less likely to pursue opportunities with higher levels of entrepreneurial risk.

Research suggests that two factors may adversely influence the accuracy of an entrepreneur's risk perceptions.[24] First, an entrepreneur's belief in the law of small numbers decreases the risk he or she perceive with an opportunity. The **law of small numbers** occurs when individuals rely on a small sample of information to inform their decisions. Because

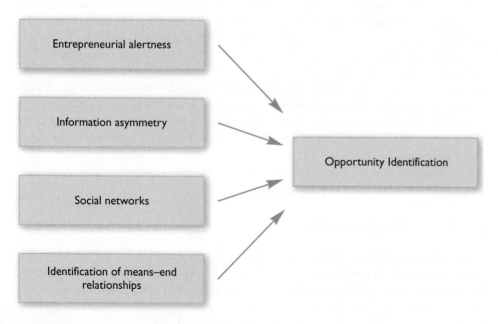

FIGURE 6.2
Determinants of opportunity identification

individuals are more likely to obtain good information (i.e., the success stories of other entrepreneurs) and less likely to obtain bad information (i.e., stories about the failures of other entrepreneurs), small samples of information are likely biased positively. Such beliefs tend to be common among entrepreneurs, because most entrepreneurs do not have access to large databases.[25] As such, to the extent that individuals believe in the law of small numbers, they are likely to obtain biased information and thus associate lower levels of risk to their ideas.

Second, the control that an entrepreneur feels with respect to the opportunity's outcome may influence perceptions of the idea's risk. **Illusion of control** exists when entrepreneurs overestimate the extent to which they can control the outcome of an opportunity.[26] The outcomes of some opportunities rely more on luck than entrepreneurial skill. In these situations, believing that one can control the outcomes is problematic.

Taken together, then, when entrepreneurs evaluate opportunities, they pay careful attention to entrepreneurial risk. It is important that entrepreneurs do not fall victim to the law of small numbers or the illusion of control when evaluating opportunities, because these two factors may negatively influence the accuracy of risk perceptions. In the following section, we discuss the final stage in the entrepreneurship process: opportunity exploitation.

Opportunity Exploitation

The third step in the entrepreneurship process involves exploiting an opportunity. **Exploitation** refers to the activities and investments committed to gain returns from the new product or service arising from the opportunity.[27] Simply stated, exploitation occurs when an entrepreneur (or group of entrepreneurs) decides that an opportunity is worth pursuing. When an entrepreneur, for example, decides that customers would highly value a new product, exploitation entails all of those activities (i.e., marketing, production, etc.) needed to sell the new product to consumers.

Several factors can help entrepreneurs decide whether they should exploit an opportunity.[28] First, entrepreneurs are more likely to exploit an opportunity when they believe that customers will value their new product or service. When customers value a new product or service, they provide market demand. This market demand, in turn, helps individuals to earn the resources (i.e., profits) necessary to support the opportunity exploitation.

Second, entrepreneurs are more likely to exploit an opportunity when they perceive that they have the support of important stakeholders. Stakeholders refer to groups such as employees, suppliers, investors, and other suppliers of capital (i.e., banks) who directly or indirectly influence organizational performance. When individuals perceive that these groups will provide support, they are more likely to exploit the opportunity. This tendency makes sense intuitively, because these stakeholders will help to ensure the success of the entrepreneur pursuing the opportunity. Conversely, it will likely prove difficult for entrepreneurs to succeed if they do not have the support of important stakeholders.

Finally, entrepreneurs are more likely to exploit opportunities when they perceive that their surrounding management team is capable. Qualified management teams will bring resources (i.e., ability, knowledge, information) to the opportunity, which will presumably enhance the prospects of the opportunity.[29] In contrast, when entrepreneurs feel as if their management teams are incapable, they are less likely to exploit the opportunity, because they feel they do not have access to the resources needed to ensure high levels of organizational performance.

In sum, then, several factors influence an entrepreneur's ability to exploit opportunities. Figure 6.3 summarizes these relationships.

Financing Exploitation

When entrepreneurs decide that an opportunity is worth exploiting, they often lack the capital (i.e., money) needed to exploit the opportunity. Although some entrepreneurs fund their operations with their own money or with credit cards, most entrepreneurs

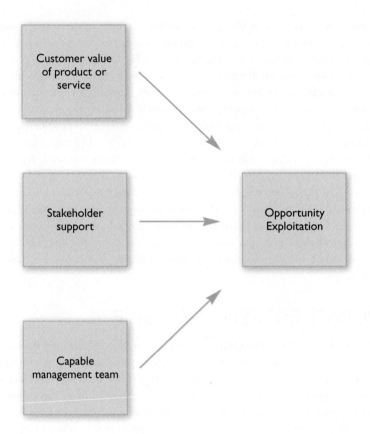

FIGURE 6.3
Factors influencing opportunity exploitation

require at least some money to fund operations. In this section we review three primary sources of external capital for entrepreneurs: angel investors, venture capitalists, and bank financing.

Angel investors are wealthy individuals who provide capital to new companies.[30] Angel investors may include an entrepreneur's family and friends, but angel investors are also private individuals who did not know the entrepreneur prior to funding the opportunity. Angel investors have existed for centuries. In **an example from the world of management, Henry Ford,** the founder of **Ford Motor, Inc.,** received a total of $41,500 from five angel investors in 1903. Within 15 years, the investment of the angel investors was worth $145 million.[31] Today, approximately 400,000 angel investors provide about $50 billion in capital to more than 50,000 companies each year.

Venture capitalists are firms that raise money from investors and then use this money to make investments in new firms. Many prominent companies such as Intel and Microsoft received investments from venture capitalists in their early days. The companies then used these funds to help acquire the resources (i.e., employees, equipment, etc.) that eventually made them the companies they are today. Although the use of venture capital peaked during the dot-com frenzy of 1998–2000, the venture capital industry today includes about $20 billion.[32]

It is important to note that both angel investors and venture capitalists provide money to entrepreneurs and in return receive a portion of the firm's equity. In other words, in return for their investment (money) in the entrepreneur's firm, the entrepreneur gives them partial ownership of the firm. As such, when the entrepreneur's firm does well and increases in value, the value of the investor's investment also increases. Likewise, when the entrepreneur's firm does poorly and decreases in value, the value of the investor's investment also decreases.

Although similar, angel investors and venture capitalists differ in a number of significant ways. In contrast to angel investors, venture capitalists make fewer investments,

Wealthy individuals who act as "angel" investors number about 400,000 today. Their financial backing helps some 50,000 companies get off the ground each year. What do you think "angels" would want to know about a firm they were considering financing?

but these investments are often larger than the investments made by angel investors. In fact, the average investment of venture capitalists is approximately $4 million, whereas the average investment of angel investors is about $75,000.[33] In addition, venture capitalists typically focus on a small number of industries. In contrast, angel investors tend not to focus on particular industries. Finally, venture capitalists typically invest in firms after the initial start-up stage. In other words, angel investors typically provide the initial financing to start-up ventures, and venture capitalists tend to provide more capital as the new venture becomes more established.

Bank financing occurs when an entrepreneur obtains financing from a financial institution in the form of a loan. It is important to note that unlike angel investors or venture capitalists, banks are not investors. Instead, banks make loans to entrepreneurs and in return expect repayment of the loans with interest. As such, banks are not concerned with the long-term potential for returns. Instead, these banks are more interested in ensuring that the entrepreneur's opportunity will survive long enough to ensure repayment. In other words, investors typically seek risk, but banks are more likely to minimize risk.

CORPORATE ENTREPRENEURSHIP

Until now, we have focused on entrepreneurial opportunities pursued by individuals or teams of individuals. It is important to note, though, that existing corporations can also identify, evaluate, and exploit opportunities. **Corporate entrepreneurship,** which refers to such activities, is the process in which an individual or group of individuals in an existing corporation create a new organization or instigate renewal or innovation within that corporation.[34] Although corporate entrepreneurship often involves establishing new organizations, these new organizations leverage the parent corporation's assets, market position, or other resources.[35] In other words, when corporate entrepreneurship results in new companies, these new companies often continue to work closely with the parent company.

It is important to recognize that corporate entrepreneurship does not necessarily require creating a new organization. Corporate entrepreneurship, for example, also involves creating new products, services, or technologies. In **an example from the world of management, 3M** allows engineers to spend as much as 15 percent of their time on projects of their own design. The thinking behind this policy is that this flexibility will provide the motivation needed for engineers to innovate successfully.[36] This flexibility may result in new products, services, or new organizations altogether.

Corporate entrepreneurship can be classified into four general types.[37] First, **sustained regeneration** occurs when firms develop new cultures, processes, or structures to support new product innovations in current markets as well as with existing products into new markets. Sustained regeneration, which refers to product innovation, is the most frequently used type of corporate entrepreneurship. In **an example from the world of management, Arm & Hammer** used sustained regeneration when it expanded the uses for baking soda by developing and introducing baking soda–based products such as toothpaste and deodorizing products.

Second, **organizational rejuvenation** involves improving the firm's ability to execute strategies and focuses on new processes instead of new products. In **an example from the world of the management, GE** successfully rejuvenated itself by changing policies and procedures within the company to support innovation.

Third, **strategic renewal** occurs when a firm attempts to alter its own competitive strategy. Unlike introducing a new product or service, strategic renewal occurs when the firm tries to offer a new strategy altogether. Of course, it remains quite difficult for a firm to change strategies. Wal-Mart, for example, is facing tremendous difficulties in trying to alter its strategy to focus on more affluent customers.[38]

Fourth, **domain definition** occurs when a firm proactively seeks to create a new product market position that competitors have not recognized. When pursuing domain definition, firms hope to become the first competitor in a market segment. In such situations, firms will enjoy the benefits of having no competitors. Amazon.com, for example, was one of the first companies to realize the potential of selling books online. It is important to note, though, that first movers do not always succeed. Apple's Newton, for example, was the first personal digital assistant (PDA), but this product no longer exists. Moreover, Apple's iPod was not the first digital music players on the market, but today the iPod dominates the marketplace.

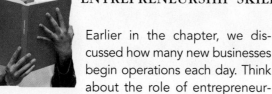

class discussion highlight

ENTREPRENEURSHIP SKILL AND YOUR CAREER

Earlier in the chapter, we discussed how many new businesses begin operations each day. Think about the role of entrepreneurship in your career. Have you given any thought to owning your own business one day? If you have not previously thought about being an entrepreneur, do the concepts in this chapter help you to identify potential entrepreneurial opportunities? How do the risks of being an entrepreneur compare to the risks of being a manager in a larger company? Finally, if you are planning to interview for a position in an established company, do you think your entrepreneurial ambitions may influence the company's perceptions of you as a potential employee? Why or why not?

SOCIAL ENTREPRENEURSHIP

The discussion of entrepreneurship so far in this chapter involves individuals or corporations that pursue entrepreneurial opportunities for the purposes of generating sales and profits, which we call **commercial entrepreneurship.** In recent years, researchers have begun to examine entrepreneurship in a social context. **Social entrepreneurship** involves the recognition, evaluation, and exploitation of opportunities that create social value as opposed to personal or shareholder wealth.[39] In this context, **social value** refers to the basic long-standing needs of society and has little to do with profits. Basic long-standing needs might include providing water, food, and shelter to those individuals in need. Social value might also refer to more specific needs such as providing playground equipment to needy school districts or seeing-eye dogs for those who are blind.

Recent reports suggest that that the growth in nonprofit organizations has increased at a faster pace than new businesses.[40] In **an example from the world of management, Muhammad Yunus** recently was awarded the Nobel Peace Prize for the organization he started, **Grameen Bank,** which specializes in providing small loans to entrepreneurs in third world countries.[41] Yunus realized that individuals in these developing countries needed only small loans to improve their financial situations—and lives—dramatically. Grameen Bank charges fairly low interest rates, because the organization is more interested in improving people's lives than making money.

How Do Commercial and Social Entrepreneurship Differ?

Although the two concepts share some similarities, substantive differences distinguish commercial entrepreneurship from social entrepreneurship. In the remainder of this section, we detail three differences with respect to mission, resources, and performance measurement.

Winner of the 2004 Nobel Peace Prize and Kenyan environmental activist Wangari Maatha helps to plant a valley oak in Capitol Park as part of the organization's social entrepreneurship effort. Like most such efforts, the project is driven by a desire to provide social value, but within an acceptable ratio of revenues and costs.

Perhaps the most fundamental difference between commercial and social entrepreneurship involves the entrepreneur's mission or purpose. The purpose of the commercial entrepreneurship is to create profits, while the purpose of social entrepreneurship is to create value for the public. Despite this difference in focus, it is important to note that social entrepreneurs cannot totally ignore issues surrounding sales and costs. If social entrepreneurs did ignore such important concepts they likely would not have the money needed to continue their pursuit of social value. As such, the goal of social entrepreneurship does not involve profits, but social entrepreneurs still need to monitor profit-oriented measures, including revenues and costs. In this sense, then, profits remain somewhat important, but social value dominates the goal structure of social entrepreneurs.[42]

A second primary distinction between commercial and social entrepreneurship involves the availability of resources such as funding and employees. Unlike commercial entrepreneurship, social entrepreneurs face more difficulties in attracting capital from angel investors, venture capitalists, or banks. Instead, most social entrepreneurs rely on donations as sources of funding. Also, social entrepreneurs often face difficulties in the form of hiring and compensating employees. Because social entrepreneurs often do not have the capital necessary to pay attractive salaries, they must focus on hiring employees who share the organization's purpose. When employees are able to share the organization's purpose, may be more likely to work for lower salaries. In fact, many social entrepreneurs rely on volunteers to help their organizations fulfill their missions.

Commercial and social entrepreneurship also differ in terms of performance measures. Commercial entrepreneurs, for example, focus on quantitative measures such as profits, shareholder wealth, revenues, and costs. In contrast, social entrepreneurs focus on less quantitative performance measures that are not related to money. For example, a soup kitchen needs to monitor costs, but the primary performance measure would deal with the number of meals served. In addition, though, a free meal may help the emotional state of someone who is homeless; this outcome is difficult to quantify.

Success Factors in Social Entrepreneurship

Although the topic of social entrepreneurship is fairly new from a research perspective, some studies look at the factors that influence the performance of social entrepreneurs.[43] In the remainder of this section, we describe three factors that influence the performance of social entrepreneurs: their networks of relationships, their capital bases, and the public's acceptance of the new venture.

Previously in this chapter, we described the importance of entrepreneurs' social networks. These networks are also important for social entrepreneurs. Large networks provide social entrepreneurs with potential sources of capital to fund their social missions. In addition, large social networks can help social entrepreneurs to identify potential employees and volunteers. In sum, then, large social networks improve the performance of social entrepreneurs.

Similar to commercial entrepreneurship, an organization's capital base is also important for social entrepreneurs. At the same time, capital is perhaps even more important for social entrepreneurs, because they do not have access to the venture capital and bank financing available to commercial entrepreneurs. Consequently, the capital raised through donations and other funding sources is extremely important for the success of social entrepreneurs.

Finally, the acceptance of a particular social entrepreneur's social value influences the performance of his organization. When a large segment of society supports a social entrepreneur's cause, the social entrepreneur is likely to gather the funds and employees or volunteers needed for success. In contrast, when only a small segment of society supports the social entrepreneur's cause, it is more difficult to gather the necessary resources. For example, the National Association of Parents of the Visually Impaired Children in Israel faced difficulties in raising the necessary resources because so few members of society found the organization worthy of support.[44]

{CHALLENGE CASE SUMMARY

The Challenge Case describes how Larry Page and Sergey Brin incorporated Google in 1998 and turned the company into the world's leading search engine. The story of Google provides an example of how entrepreneurship fundamentally changed an industry. Prior to Google, search engines operated by searching the text of Web pages on the Internet. If a Web page contained many instances of the search term, most search engines such as Yahoo! would give that Web page high search grades.

Page and Brin, however, thought that this method of searching was not ideal, which provided them with an opportunity. In other words, the situation represented an opportunity to bring a new service into the industry that customers would value. They believed they could build a search engine that would produce revenues that would exceed their cost of providing the new search engine. The founders believed that this new search engine would produce profits.

Page and Brin changed the search process by focusing more on Web page popularity than on the number of times that a given search term appeared on a Web page. They then linked search advertisements to these search results, which led in turn to extraordinary profits. By changing the nature of the search process, in retrospect it is clear that Page and Brin identified a valuable opportunity. Successful opportunity identification is not always the case, however, because research suggests that most new businesses fail.

According to Schumpeter's classic formulation of opportunities, Google would represent an opportunity that arose from a new product or service. The introduction of their new searching service has served many customers, but it is not the company's only new service. Google also provides Scholar Google, a Web site that allows academics and researchers to search for academic publications such as books, dissertations, and journal articles. Google also offers free software that allows users to complete basic tasks using word processing, spreadsheet, and presentation software.

When Google introduces international versions of its search engine, it is pursuing Schumpeter's second type of opportunity that arises from the discovery of new geographical markets. A modification of its search engine, for example, allows Google to enter markets in China. Of course, this market entry also allows Google to earn profits from selling advertisements in China. Today, Google offers a wide array of services to consumers. As the company progresses, it will continue to search for Schumpeter's other types of opportunities.

It is important to note that Page and Brin proceeded through the three steps of the entrepreneurial process when starting Google. First, the founders identified the opportunity; they understood that the search process could be improved, and they believed that they had the resources necessary to improve the process. It is clear that as graduate students, they had high levels of entrepreneurial alertness. In other words, they were able to notice and be sensitive to new information about objects, incidents, and patterns of behavior in the Internet environment.

After identifying the opportunity, Page and Brin also evaluated the opportunity. Specifically, they likely went through a process that helped them understand whether their idea was practical. For their analysis, they likely gathered information on the industry's current competitors and the functionality of their search engines to determine whether they could compete with the existing competitors. In addition, they almost certainly took note of the rapidly increasing usage of the Internet in the late 1990s; this information confirmed for them that they could potentially have a large customer base.

It was also important for Page and Brin to understand the entrepreneurial risk associated with their new search engine. In this case, the cost of creating Google was the cost of developing the new search engine. Other computer software companies face similar costs. If the search engine did not work effectively, they would largely lose the time they invested in the new project.

The potential loss for Google was dramatically different from starting a new company to compete with Carrefour and Auchan, for example. If a new company wanted to compete with Carrefour and Auchen, they would need to purchase or lease buildings throughout the world to sell their products. In addition, they would need to purchase all of the inventory needed to stock the shelves in these stores. Google, on the other hand, did not require such enormous expenditures, which helped Page and Brin to limit the downside risk.

After identifying and evaluating the opportunity, Page and Brin decided to exploit the opportunity. Stated differently, the first two stages of the process convinced the two founders that the idea was worth pursuing. To finance their exploitation, they first relied on an angel investor in the form of one of their professors at Stanford, who wrote them a check for $100,000. With this check in hand, they were able to raise another $900,000 from family members, friends, and acquaintances. A year later, Page and Brin needed more money, and they were able to raise $25 million from two prominent venture capital firms. Taken together, then, Google raised millions of dollars from both angel investors and venture capitalists; without such investors it is unlikely Google would have succeeded.

Although the company started small, today Google is worth hundreds of *billions* of dollars. As such it is difficult to think of Page and Brin as entrepreneurs today; instead they are leaders of one of the world's largest and most influential companies. Nonetheless, entrepreneurship remains important at Google, particularly corporate entrepreneurship. Instead of individuals pursuing opportunities, today Google as a corporation pursues opportunities. This culture of entrepreneurship has helped Google to maintain the diverse opportunities it pursues today. For example, today the company offers—among others—movie making software, picture editing software, mapping software, and social networking Web sites. In addition, Google even has an interface designed to respond to text message-based search queries from cell phones. It is this spirit of corporate entrepreneurship that Google will need to continue and thrive in an extremely competitive industry.

Finally, it is also important to note that Google developed Google.org to oversee the company's social entrepreneurship programs. The three broad missions of Google.org include addressing climate change, global public health, and economic development and poverty. To address climate change, Google.org is sponsoring initiatives to support alternative forms of transportation. Regarding global public health, Google.org has assembled the technology needed to more effectively communicate information regarding natural health disasters and other public health emergencies. To facilitate economic development and eliminate poverty, Google.org has provided grant money to support entrepreneurship programs in Africa and other parts of the world. Taken together, the company has donated millions of dollars to support these initiatives.

MANAGEMENT SKILL ACTIVITIES

This section is specially designed to help you develop entrepreneurship skill. An individual's management skill is based upon an understanding of management concepts and the ability to apply those concepts in management situations. As a result, the following activities are designed both to heighten your understanding of entrepreneurship concepts and to help you gain facility in applying these concepts in various management situations.

UNDERSTANDING ENTREPRENEURSHIP CONCEPTS

This section is comprised of activities that will sharpen your understanding of entrepreneurship concepts. Answer essay questions as completely as possible. Also, remember that many additional true/false and multiple choice questions appear at MyManagementLab.com to help you further refine your understanding of concepts related to entrepreneurship.

Essay Questions

1. Describe the main components of entrepreneurship.
2. Distinguish between the different types of opportunities.
3. Describe the differences between opportunity identification and opportunity exploitation.
4. Describe the main components of social entrepreneurship, and describe how social entrepreneurship differs from commercial entrepreneurship.
5. Describe the different types of corporate entrepreneurship and provide examples.

Developing Management Skill

Learning activities in this section are aimed at helping you to develop your entrepreneurship skill. Learning activities include Exploring Your Management Skill: Part 2, Experiential Exercise, Cases, and a VideoNet exercise.

EXPLORING YOUR MANAGEMENT SKILL: PART 2

As you recall, you completed Exploring Your Management Skill before you started to study this chapter. Your responses gave you an idea of how much you initially knew about entrepreneurship and helped you to focus on important points as you studied the chapter. Answer the Exploring Your Management Skill questions again now (p. 162) and compare your score to the first time you took it. This comparison will give you an idea of how much you

have learned from studying this chapter and pinpoint areas for further clarification before you start studying the next chapter. Record your answers within the text or online at MyManagementLab.com. Completing the survey at MyManagementLab.com will allow you to grade and compare your test scores automatically. If you complete the test in the book, look up answers in the Exploring Your Management Skill section at the end of the book.

YOUR MANAGEMENT SKILLS PORTFOLIO

Your Management Learning Portfolio is a collection of activities especially designed to demonstrate your management knowledge and skill. By completing these activities at MyManagementLab.com, you will be able to print, complete with cover sheet, as many activities as you choose. Be sure to save your work. Taking your printed portfolio to an employment interview could be helpful in obtaining a job.

The portfolio activity for this chapter is Serving up Drinks at BK. Study the information given here and complete the exercises that follow.[45]

Top management at Burger King has contacted you to help them enhance their business. In particular, top management has noticed a trend in the marketplace that the company is not capturing. Specifically, executives at Burger King are not sure that the company is making enough profits from sales of drinks due to its focus on food.

Given the success of companies such as Starbucks, some of Burger King's competitors are changing their menus to compete more effectively. McDonald's, for example, has begun marketing and selling drinks to compete with Starbucks. In fact, McDonald's claims that its new line of espresso drinks represents the most significant menu change for the company since it started serving breakfast in the 1970s. Sonic also started selling coffee-based beverages in addition to the many shakes and fruit slushes already on the menu.

Burger King would like you to help identify, evaluate, and form methods of exploitation for the company regarding drinks. In the following sections, answer the questions pertaining to the entrepreneurship process.

1. Identify a specific opportunity in the marketplace regarding drinks. It could be a new drink, a new line of drinks, a new type of retail outlet, or another type of opportunity.

_____

_____

_____

2. Evaluate your opportunity using feasibility analysis. In particular, focus on how *customers* might respond to the new opportunity, how other *industry competitors* are already exploiting this opportunity, and describe Burger King's *ability to exploit* this opportunity.

_____

_____

_____

3. How do you suggest that Burger King exploit this opportunity? Does the company have enough money to easily follow your suggestion(s), or should the company pursue other financing options? (Use the company's Web site to obtain more information if necessary.)

_____

_____

_____

EXPERIENTIAL EXERCISE: IDENTIFYING A SOCIAL ENTREPRENEURSHIP OPPORTUNITY

Directions. Read the following scenario and then perform the listed activities. Your instructor may want you to perform the activities as an individual or within groups. Follow all of your instructor's directions carefully.

The president of your institution has contacted your group in an effort to improve its outreach programs. In particular, the president would like your group to make a short presentation describing the concept of social entrepreneurship. In addition, the president would like your group to identify three potential social entrepreneurship opportunities that your institution can evaluate and potentially exploit. These opportunities might involve only the local community, but they might also apply to other portions of the country or world.

CASES

GOOGLE ENTREPRENEURS WIN BIG

"Google Entrepreneurs Win Big" (p. 161) and its Challenge Case Summary were written to help you better understand the management concepts contained in this chapter. Answer the following discussion questions about the Challenge Case that relate to entrepreneurship and how it can be applied in a company such as Google.

1. Do you think Google will be able to maintain its entrepreneurial culture in spite of its recent growth and increased size? Why or why not?

2. In your opinion, what were the key factors in determining the success of Google's entrepreneurial founders?

3. As you look into the future, what do you think represents a bigger threat to Google: established companies like Microsoft or smaller, entrepreneurial companies? Explain.

PURSUING A NEW OPPORTUNITY IN THE DRY CLEANING INDUSTRY

Read the case and answer the questions that follow. Studying this case will help you better understand how concepts relating to entrepreneurship and how it can be applied in a company such as Clothes Dr.

By the end of 2004, Chris Mendez was tempted to give up. The owner of a chain of dry cleaning stores in central Florida, Mendez had grown up in the industry, learning the business at his father's store in Apopka before striking out on his own in 1995. In just eight months, he broke even; by the end of 2003, he had six storefronts and his own 1,400-square-foot dry cleaning plant. But in his eighth year, Mendez's business, Clothes Dr., was spinning out of control: He was losing $130,000 a year on revenue of $1.2 million; he had completely leveraged his house; and he was physically and emotionally exhausted. "I couldn't sleep at night," he says. "How many more things could go wrong? How many more people could quit? When would the boiler explode again?" Did the dry cleaning business really have to be so difficult? Mendez wondered.

Mendez commiserated with his father. In February 2005, the two decided to attend a trade show in Miami, where they planned to research point-of-sale systems for their businesses. Updated technology, they reasoned, might help them clamp down on expenses, manage their employees, and keep better track of customer data. Mendez arrived in Miami with just a flicker of optimism. By the time he left, it had been stoked into a bona fide flame. He had Jason Loeb to thank for that.

Loeb is the CEO of Sudsies.com, a Miami-based dry cleaner that had all but abandoned the traditional storefront dry cleaner's model. Loeb's business, with approximately $3 million in revenue, was almost entirely Web-based. He had one storefront and 10 trucks on the road, picking up and delivering dry cleaning and laundry to customers who scheduled and tracked their orders on his Web site. Loeb wasn't a typical dry cleaner, removing spots or hovering over the steam cleaner in the back of his plant. Instead, he had gone to great lengths to create brand recognition, to train and engage his employees, and to cultivate relationships with his customers.

After talking to Loeb, Mendez found that business as usual looked less and less attractive. He was intrigued by the prospect of closing additional stores and investing in delivery trucks and a Web-based customer tracking system modeled on Loeb's. Such a move involved risk, to be sure. Loeb had invested $250,000 to change his business model and the venture was not instantly profitable. Mendez would need to build a Web site, master new technology, hire new staff, and retrain his existing employees. Trucks, however, would be far less expensive to run than storefronts, so he would vastly reduce his overhead while expanding his geographic reach. He also knew that door-to-door pickup and delivery was becoming increasingly popular among consumers; it could be just the way to differentiate his business from other dry cleaners.

In April 2005, two months after meeting Loeb, Mendez bought his first point-of-sale system with software customized for dry cleaners; by the end of the year, he had spent $56,000 on eight stations and a server. He began training one of his most trusted employees, Munic Datoo, to manage the new technology and, eventually, his new Web site. Three months later, he bought a new GMC truck, taking advantage of zero-percent financing; it was on the road serving customers by the end of the year.

Mendez is confident that his decision to change his business model was spot on. In fact, he recently invested in a 1,700-square-foot facility to run his trucks out of. Within five years, he'd like to have eight trucks and a drapery van serving 300 to 400 people per truck, with the majority of his best customers using Web-based pickup and delivery. But for now, he's satisfied with simpler pleasures. "This is the first time in 11 years that I've had people who work well together," he says. "Plus Merilyn and I can go out to dinner now and she doesn't have to pay."

QUESTIONS

1. Do you agree with Mendez's decision to change the primary way he engaged customers? Why or why not?
2. If you were Mendez, what primary factors would you consider when evaluating this opportunity?
3. In your opinion, what are the primary risks associated with Mendez's decision?

VIDEONET EXERCISE

Flying High in Small Business: Durango Pro-Focus Flight Training Center

VIDEO HIGHLIGHTS

Durango Pro-Focus Flight Training Center aims to be a high-flying small business. Working with Midland College and Mesa Airlines, the company provides classroom, simulator, and in-flight training for airline pilots. The entrepreneurial founder and his top managers have a passion for their business—working 80 hours per week or more at the outset—but also keep a critical eye on the market to be sure they are satisfying a real need. To start, management funded the purchase of a flight simulator and other equipment as well as the construction of an administrative wing for office space in anticipation of attracting future investors. Now Durango wants to expand by setting up training centers in other areas with good flying weather, a nearby airport, and a college partner.

Discussion Questions

1. What are some of the entrepreneurial characteristics displayed by president Phil Handley? In your opinion, which of the five different types of opportunities is being exploited by Durango?
2. According to the entrepreneurial exercise of opportunity evaluation, why were the social relationships with Mesa Airlines and Midland College critical to Durango's product development?
3. In your opinion, did Phil Handley rely on the law of small numbers? Explain your answer. How does he describe his personal theory of entrepreneurship? Do you agree with his ideas? Do his actions with Durango Pro-Focus support his theory?

Internet Activity

Browse Midland College's Web site area relating to the pilot training program at www.midland.edu/~pilots/about.html. Visit some of the many areas of information listed along the left side of the page. What are some of the specific facts concerning the program? Do you think this program would be attractive to students? Is the program well marketed on the Web site? In your opinion, did the entrepreneurs develop a service that successfully exploits the opportunity defined by Phil Handley and his partners?

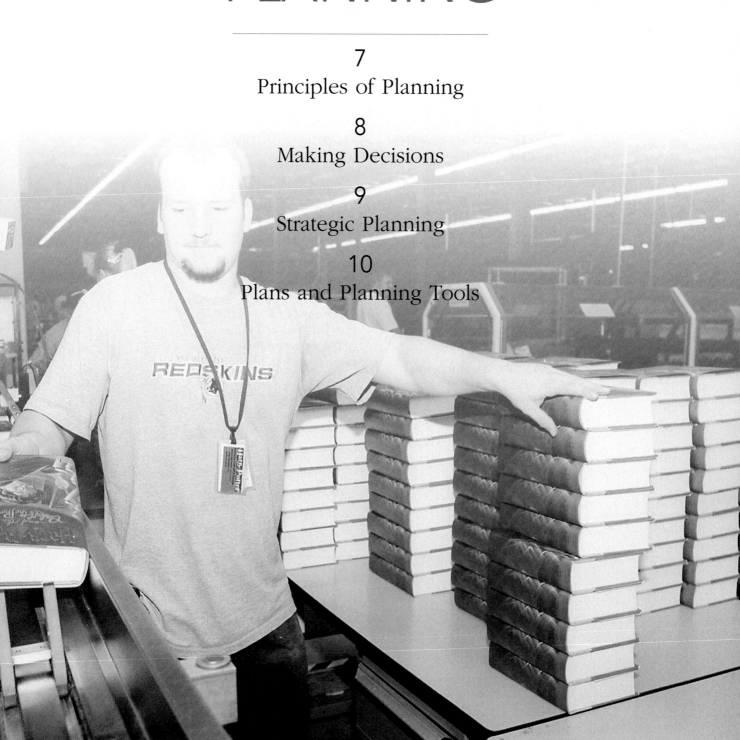

7 Principles of Planning

OBJECTIVES

TO HELP BUILD MY PLANNING SKILL, WHEN STUDYING THIS CHAPTER, I WILL ATTEMPT TO ACQUIRE:

1. A definition of planning and an understanding of the purposes of planning

2. Insights into how the major steps of the planning process are related

3. An understanding of the relationship between planning and organizational objectives

4. A knowledge of the areas in which managers should set organizational objectives

5. An appreciation for the potential of a management-by-objectives (MBO) program

6. A knowledge of how the chief executive relates to the planning process

7. An understanding of the qualifications and duties of planners and how planners can be evaluated

TARGET SKILL

planning skill: the ability to take action to determine the objectives of the organization as well as what is necessary to accomplish these objectives

CHALLENGE CASE

PLANNING FOR A REBOUND AT VOLKSWAGEN

Volkswagen AG, based in Germany, is one of the largest automobile manufacturers in the world. Historically, Volkswagen has prospered while manufacturing reliable and affordable cars such as the Jetta and the Golf for the average consumer. In fact, Volkswagen literally means "the people's car." Despite Volkswagen's past success as a company that produces mid-priced automobiles, the company's leaders modified the company's direction.

During a recent study of the automobile industry, Volkswagen's executives attempted to better understand the company's product line. The executives listed all of the different model segments in the automobile industry such as "big SUVs (sports-utility vehicles)" and "hatchbacks" and compared the list against all of the automobiles that Volkswagen produced. Study results clearly showed that Volkswagen did not offer products in the luxury market to compete with other German automobile manufacturers such as BMW and Mercedes-Benz.

Based upon the study, VW introduced a new line of luxury automobiles. One of the company's luxury models, known as the Phaeton, included a driver's seat with a lower-back massager. The Phaeton also had Italian leather seats and solar cells in the sunroof that controlled the car's ventilation system. Despite all of these features, the company was surprised when consumers purchased only a fraction of the company's

When its attempt to enter the luxury-car market faltered, Volkswagen revised its plan and returned to its tried-and-true lower-cost cars, including a new VW Rabbit.

projected sales. After a few years of disappointing sales, VW discontinued the Phaeton altogether.

The plan to enter the luxury segment did not meet the expectations of VW's leadership. In fact, the poor performance of the Phaeton caused VW's new CEO, Martin Winterkorn, to formulate a different plan for the company. Specifically, the introduction of the luxury cars caused consumers to think that VW had abandoned its roots as a company for the "common" consumer. In fact, VW's research suggests that some consumers believe that the company's automobiles are too expensive for entry-level buyers. To undo these perceptions, VW has introduced a new plan to focus on its popular, low-cost models such as the Rabbit, Jetta, and Beetle. Using a series of marketing techniques, the company hopes to remind consumers that VW produces high quality—yet affordable—automobiles.

The evidence suggests that VW's plan to enter the luxury segment did not reach objectives. To reverse the company's fortunes, VW's new CEO has instituted a new plan that focuses the company's efforts on its historical strengths. When preparing, reviewing, and modifying this new plan, perhaps VW's new management team will be able to review the pitfalls of the Phaeton plan, because organizational leaders can learn from both planning successes as well as planning failures.[1]

"EXPLORE YOUR OWN MANAGEMENT SKILLS
BY TAKING THE QUIZ ON THE NEXT PAGE"

Before studying this chapter, respond to the following questions regarding the type of advice that you would give to Volkswagen's Martin Winterkorn referenced in the Challenge Case. Then address the concerning planning challenges that he presently faces within the company. You are not expected to be a planning expert at this point. Answering the questions now can help you focus on important points when you study the chapter. Also, answering the questions again after you study the chapter will give you an idea of how much you have learned.

Record your answers here or online at MyManagement Lab.com. Completing the questions at MyManagement Lab.com will allow you to get feedback about your answers automatically. If you answer the questions in the book, look up answers in the Exploring Your Management Skill section at the end of the book.

FOR EACH STATEMENT CIRCLE:

- "Y" if you would give the advice to Martin Winterkorn.
- "N" if you would NOT give the advice to Martin Winterkorn.
- "NI" if you have no idea whether you would give the advice to Martin Winterkorn.

Mr. Winterkorn, in meeting your planning challenges at VW, you should . . .

Before Study	After Study

1. understand that there are only advantages—and no disadvantages—to planning at VW.

   Y, N, NI

2. encourage VW's employees to spend more time organizing, influencing, and controlling as opposed to planning.

   Y, N, NI

3. establish broad and ambiguous objectives so that it will be difficult to tell whether VW reached the objectives.

   Y, N, NI

4. formulate both alternatives and premises when establishing plans for VW.

   Y, N, NI

5. begin the planning process by establishing VW's organizational objectives.

   Y, N, NI

6. focus more on long-term objectives than short-term or intermediate-term objectives.

   Y, N, NI

7. establish objectives that are related only to VW's profitability rather than those related to areas such as innovation, productivity, and public responsibility.

   Y, N, NI

8. create objectives alone and resist the opinions of other employees in VW.

   Y, N, NI

9. pinpoint expected results so that VW employees will understand when an objective is or is not reached.

   Y, N, NI

10. form unreachable objectives, because higher goals always lead to higher performance.

    Y, N, NI

11. specify a timeline for achieving the objectives.

    Y, N, NI

12. realize the potential effectiveness of MBO programs for VW, because MBO programs work only in for-profit organizations.

    Y, N, NI

13. understand the importance of giving rewards in improving the effectiveness of MBO programs.

    Y, N, NI

14. understand that as VW's CEO, you are responsible for determining the overall direction of the firm.

    Y, N, NI

15. appreciate the fact that as VW's central planner, no one will review your planning performance.

    Y, N, NI

THE PLANNING CHALLENGE

The Challenge Case focuses on events at Volkswagen AG. The case ends with the implication that sound planning is necessary to successfully resolve the problems associated with the introduction of new luxury automobiles such as the Phaeton. Material in this chapter will help managers like those at Volkswagen to understand why planning is so important not only for ensuring the success of a new luxury automobile, but for carrying out any other organizational activity. The fundamentals of planning are described in this chapter. More specifically, this chapter (1) outlines the general characteristics of planning, (2) discusses steps in the planning process, (3) describes the planning subsystem, (4) elaborates upon the relationship between organizational objectives and planning, (5) discusses the relationship between planning and the chief executive, and (6) summarizes the qualifications of planners and explains how planners can be evaluated.

GENERAL CHARACTERISTICS OF PLANNING

The first part of this chapter is a general introduction to planning. The sections in this part discuss the following topics:

1. Definition of planning
2. Purposes of planning
3. Advantages and potential disadvantages of planning
4. Primacy of planning

Defining Planning

Planning is the process of determining how the organization can get where it wants to go, and what it will do to accomplish its objectives. In more formal terms, planning is "the systematic development of action programs aimed at reaching agreed-upon business objectives by the process of analyzing, evaluating, and selecting among the opportunities which are foreseen."[2]

Planning is a critical management activity regardless of the type of organization being managed. Modern managers face the challenge of sound planning in small and relatively simple organizations as well as in large, more complex ones, and in nonprofit organizations such as libraries as well as in for-profit organizations such as Volkswagen.[3]

Purposes of Planning

Over the years, management writers have presented several different purposes of planning. For example, a classic article by C. W. Roney indicates that organizational planning has two purposes: protective and affirmative. The protective purpose of planning is to minimize risk by reducing the uncertainties surrounding business conditions and clarifying the consequences of related management actions. The affirmative purpose is to increase the degree of organizational success.[4] For **an example in the world of management** of this affirmative purpose, consider **Whole Foods Market**, a health food chain in the U.S. state of Texas. This company uses planning to ensure success as measured by the systematic opening of new stores. Company head John Mackey believes that increased company success is not an accident, but a direct result of careful planning.[5] Still another purpose of planning is to establish a coordinated effort within the organization. Where planning is absent, coordination and organizational efficiency are also often absent.

The fundamental purpose of planning, however, is to help the organization reach its objectives. As Koontz and O'Donnell put it, the primary purpose of planning is "to facilitate the accomplishment of enterprise and objectives."[6] All other purposes of planning are spin-offs of this fundamental purpose.

Planning: Advantages and Potential Disadvantages

A vigorous planning program produces many benefits. First, it helps managers to be future-oriented. They are forced to look beyond their everyday problems to project what situations may confront them in the future.[7] Second, a sound planning program enhances decision coordination. No decision should be made today without some idea of how it will affect a decision that might have to be made tomorrow. The planning function pushes managers to coordinate their decisions. Third, planning emphasizes organizational objectives. Because organizational objectives are the starting points for planning, managers are continually reminded of exactly what their organization is trying to accomplish.[8]

Overall, planning is advantageous to an organization.[9] According to an often-cited survey, as many as 65 percent of all newly started businesses are not around to celebrate a fifth anniversary. This high failure rate seems primarily a consequence of inadequate planning. Successful businesses have an established plan, a formal statement that outlines the objectives the organization is attempting to achieve. Planning does not eliminate risk, of course, but it does help managers identify and deal with organizational problems before they cause havoc in a business.[10]

The downside is that if the planning function is not well executed, planning can have several disadvantages for the organization. For example, an overemphasized planning program can take up too much managerial time. Managers must strike an appropriate balance between time spent on planning and time spent on organizing, influencing, and controlling. If they don't, some activities that are extremely important to the success of the organization may be neglected.[11]

Overall, the advantages of planning definitely outweigh the disadvantages. Usually, the disadvantages of planning result from using the planning function incorrectly.

class discussion highlight

MODERN RESEARCH AND PLANNING SKILL

The Influence of Team Plans

A recent study by Mathieu and Schulze examined the influence of planning skills on performance in the team context. The study's authors used teams of business school students to better understand the influence of planning skills on team performance. Specifically, the teams all took part in a simulation that helped determine their grade in a course. In this particular simulation, each group represented a simulated firm's top management team. Team members occupied different functional roles (i.e., marketing, accounting, etc.), and the team collectively made decisions. Presumably, the better the decisions that each team made, the better would be the team's performance in the simulation as compared to the other student teams.

Prior to the simulation, each team created a formal plan outlining the steps needed to ensure success in the simulation. The authors then examined the relationship between the quality of the pre-simulation plan and the group's performance in the simulation. The authors then attempted to find a relationship between the quality of the plan and performance in the simulation. Do you think the study's results suggest that quality of the plan helped in understanding team performance? Why? Assuming that you are correct, what guidance can this research give you about developing your **planning skill**?[12]

Primacy of Planning

Planning is the primary management function—the one that precedes and is the basis for the organizing, influencing, and controlling functions of managers. Only after managers have developed their plans can they determine how they want to structure their organization, place their people, and establish organizational controls. As discussed in Chapter 1, planning, organizing, influencing, and controlling are interrelated. Planning is the foundation function and the first one to be performed. Organizing, influencing, and controlling are all based on the results of planning. Figure 7.1 shows this interrelationship.

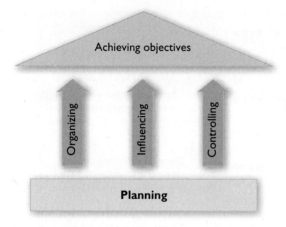

STEPS IN THE PLANNING PROCESS

The planning process consists of the following six steps. It is important to note, though, that the planning process is dynamic; in other words, effective planners will continuously revisit the planning process.

1. **State organizational objectives**—Because planning focuses on how the management system will reach organizational objectives, a clear statement of those objectives is necessary before planning can begin. Often planners examine important elements of the environment of their organizations, such as the overall economy or competitors, when forming objectives. In essence, objectives stipulate those areas in which organizational planning must occur.[13]
2. **List alternative ways of reaching objectives**—Once organizational objectives have been clearly stated, a manager should list as many available alternatives as possible for reaching those objectives.
3. **Develop premises on which to base each alternative**—To a large extent, the feasibility of using any one alternative to reach organizational objectives is determined by the premises, or assumptions, on which the alternative is based. For example, two alternatives a manager could generate to reach the organizational objective of increasing profit might be to (a) increase the sale of products presently being produced, or (b) produce and sell a completely new product. Alternative (a) is based on the premise that the organization can gain a larger share of the existing market. Alternative (b) is based on the premise that a new product would capture a significant portion of a new market. A manager should list all of the premises for each alternative.
4. **Choose the best alternative for reaching objectives**—An evaluation of alternatives must include an evaluation of the premises on which the alternatives are based. A manager usually finds that some premises are unreasonable and can therefore be excluded from further consideration. This elimination process helps the manager determine which alternative would best accomplish organizational objectives. The decision making required for this step is discussed more fully in Chapter 8.
5. **Develop plans to pursue the chosen alternative**—After an alternative has been chosen, a manager begins to develop strategic (long-range) and tactical (short-range) plans.[14] More information about strategic and tactical planning is presented in Chapters 9 and 10.
6. **Put the plans into action**—Once plans that furnish the organization with both long-range and short-range direction have been developed, they must be implemented. Obviously, the organization cannot directly benefit from the planning process until this step is performed. Figure 7.2 shows the sequencing of the six steps of the planning process.

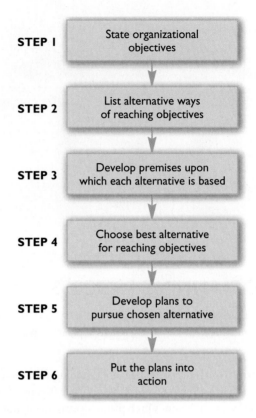

STEP 1 — State organizational objectives

STEP 2 — List alternative ways of reaching objectives

STEP 3 — Develop premises upon which each alternative is based

STEP 4 — Choose best alternative for reaching objectives

STEP 5 — Develop plans to pursue chosen alternative

STEP 6 — Put the plans into action

FIGURE 7.2
Elements of the planning process

THE PLANNING SUBSYSTEM

Once managers thoroughly understand the basics of planning, they can take steps to implement the planning process in their organization. Implementation is the key to a successful planning process. Even though managers might be experts on facts related to planning and the planning process, if they cannot transform this understanding into appropriate action, they will not be able to generate useful organizational plans.

One way to approach implementation is to view planning activities as an organizational subsystem. A subsystem is a system created as part of the overall management system. Figure 7.3 illustrates the relationship between the overall management system and a subsystem. Subsystems help managers organize the overall system and enhance its success.

Figure 7.4 presents the elements of the planning subsystem. The purpose of this subsystem is to increase the effectiveness of the overall management system by helping managers identify, guide, and direct planning activities within the overall system.[15]

Obviously, only a portion of organizational resources can be used as input in the planning subsystem. This input is allocated to the planning subsystem and transformed into output through the steps of the planning process.

FIGURE 7.3
Relationship between overall management system and subsystem

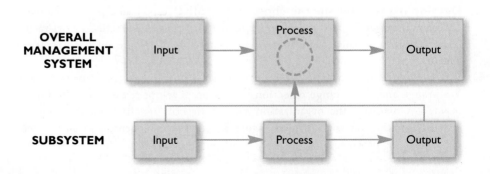

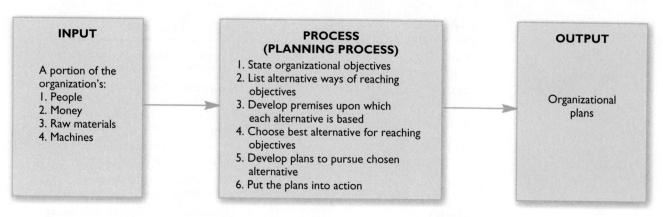

FIGURE 7.4   The planning subsystem

ORGANIZATIONAL OBJECTIVES: PLANNING'S FOUNDATION

The previous section made the point that managers start planning by stating or formulating organizational objectives. Only after they have a clear view of organizational objectives can they appropriately carry out subsequent steps of the planning process. Organizational objectives serve as the foundation upon which all subsequent planning efforts are built. The following sections focus on organizational objectives, a critical component of the planning process:

1. Defining organizational objectives
2. Pinpointing areas in which organizational objectives should be established
3. Illustrating how managers work with organizational objectives
4. Discussing management by objectives, an approach to management based mainly on organizational objectives

Definition of Organizational Objectives

Organizational objectives are the targets toward which the open management system is directed. Organizational input, process, and output—topics discussed in Chapter 2—all exist to reach organizational objectives (see Figure 7.5). Properly developed organizational

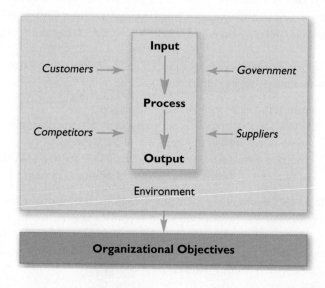

FIGURE 7.5

How an open management system operates to reach organizational objectives

TABLE 7.1   Examples of Statements of Organizational Purpose

Campbell Soup Company	Together we will build the world's most extraordinary food company.
Eli Lily & Company	We provide customers "Answers That Matter" through innovative medicines, information, and exceptional customer service that enable people to live longer, healthier, and more active lives.
Nike	To bring inspiration and innovation to every athlete in the world.
Charles Schwab	Our mission is to provide the most useful and ethical financial services in the world.
Wendy's	Our mission is to deliver superior quality products and services for our customers and communities through leadership, innovation, and partnerships.

Former CEO Gordon M. Bethune stated his objectives for Continental Airlines clearly—cut costs while improving service. He maintained that management can achieve both goals if the company becomes more market-savvy and more customer-oriented, as well as less willing to let strictly financial considerations dictate marketing decisions.

objectives reflect the purpose of the organization—that is, they flow naturally from the organization's mission. The **organizational purpose** is what the organization exists to do, given a particular group of customers and customer needs. Table 7.1 contains several statements of organizational purpose, or mission, as developed by actual companies.[16] If an organization is accomplishing its objectives, it is accomplishing its purpose and thereby justifying its reason for existence.

Organizations exist for various purposes and thus have various types of objectives. A hospital, for example, may have the primary purpose of providing high-quality medical services to the community. Therefore, its objectives are aimed at furnishing this assistance. The primary purpose of a business organization, in contrast, is usually to make a profit. The objectives of the business organization, therefore, concentrate on ensuring that a profit is made. Some companies, however, assume that if they focus on such organizational objectives as producing a quality product at a competitive price, profits will be inevitable. In **an example from the world of management,** although the **Lincoln Electric Company** is profit oriented, management has stated organizational objectives in the following terms.[17]

> The goal of the organization must be this—to make a better and better product to be sold at a lower and lower price. Profit cannot be the goal. Profit must be a by-product. This is a state of mind and a philosophy. Actually, an organization doing this job as it can be done will make large profits which must be properly divided between user, worker, and stockholder. This takes ability and character.

In a 1956 article that has become a classic, John F. Mee suggested that organizational objectives for businesses can be summarized in three points:[18]

1. Profit is the motivating force for managers.
2. Service to customers by the provision of desired economic values (goods and services) justifies the existence of the business.
3. Managers have social responsibilities in accordance with the ethical and moral codes of the society in which the business operates.

Deciding on the objectives for an organization, then, is one of the most important actions managers take. Unrealistically high objectives are frustrating for employees, while objectives that are set too low do not push employees to maximize their potential. Managers should establish performance objectives that they know from experience are within reach for employees, but not within *easy* reach.[19]

Areas for Organizational Objectives

Peter F. Drucker, one of the most influential management writers of modern times, believed that the survival of a management system was endangered when managers emphasized only the profit objective because this single-objective emphasis encourages managers to take action that will make money today with little regard for how a profit will be made tomorrow.[20]

Managers should strive to develop and attain a variety of objectives in all areas where activity is critical to the operation and success of the management system. Following are the eight key areas in which Drucker advised managers to set management system objectives:

1. **Market standing**—Management should set objectives indicating where it would like to be in relation to its competitors.
2. **Innovation**—Management should set objectives outlining its commitment to the development of new methods of operation.
3. **Productivity**—Management should set objectives outlining the target levels of production.
4. **Physical and financial resources**—Management should set objectives regarding the use, acquisition, and maintenance of capital and monetary resources.
5. **Profitability**—Management should set objectives that specify the profit the company would like to generate.
6. **Managerial performance and development**—Management should set objectives that specify rates and levels of managerial productivity and growth.
7. **Worker performance and attitude**—Management should set objectives that specify rates of worker productivity as well as desirable attitudes for workers to possess.
8. **Public responsibility**—Management should set objectives that indicate the company's responsibilities to its customers and society and the extent to which the company intends to live up to those responsibilities.

According to Drucker, the first five goal areas relate to tangible, impersonal characteristics of organizational operation, and most managers would not dispute their designation as key areas. Designating the last three as key areas, however, could arouse some managerial opposition because these areas are more personal and subjective. Regardless of this potential opposition, an organization should have objectives in all eight areas to maximize its probability of success.

As **an example of management in the world,** consider the appointment of **Jerry Yang** as CEO of **Yahoo!**[21] One of Yang's most important organizational objectives is improving the quality of the company's search engine. Yahoo!'s ability to reach this objective will help the company compete more effectively against Google in the market for Internet advertising.

Working with Organizational Objectives

Appropriate objectives are fundamental to the success of any organization. Theodore Levitt noted that some leading industries could be facing the same financial disaster as the railroads in some countries faced years earlier because their objectives were inappropriate for their organizations.[22]

Managers should approach the development, use, and modification of organizational objectives with the utmost seriousness. In general, an organization should set three types of objectives:[23]

1. **Short-term objectives**—targets to be achieved in one year or less
2. **Intermediate-term objectives**—targets to be achieved in one to five years
3. **Long-term objectives**—targets to be achieved in five to seven years

The necessity of predetermining appropriate organizational objectives has led to the development of a management guideline called the principle of the objective. This principle holds that before managers initiate any action, they should clearly determine, understand, and state organizational objectives.

As **an example from the world of management**, consider the case of **Craig Mundie**, chief research and strategy officer at **Microsoft**. Mundie is responsible for planning that relates to the company's long-term objectives. According to Mundie, he views his job "as making sure that the company supports the things that take time but end up being big."[24] With this long-term outlook, then, Mundie helps the company pursue long-term objectives.

Developing a Hierarchy of Objectives   In practice, an organizational objective must be broken down into subobjectives so that individuals at different levels and sections of the organization know what they must do to help reach the overall organizational objective.[25] An organizational objective is attained only after the subobjectives have been reached.

The overall organizational objective and the subobjectives assigned to the various people or units of the organization are referred to as a hierarchy of objectives. Figure 7.6 presents a sample hierarchy of objectives for a medium-sized company.

Suboptimization is a condition wherein subobjectives are conflicting or not directly aimed at accomplishing the overall organizational objective. Suboptimization is possible within the company whose hierarchy of objectives is depicted in Figure 7.6 if the first subobjective for the finance and accounting department clashes with the second subobjective for the supervisors. This conflict would occur if supervisors needed new equipment to

TOP MANAGEMENT
1. Represent stockholders' interests—net profits of 10% or more
2. Provide service to consumers—provide reliable products
3. Maintain growth of assets and sales—double each decade
4. Provide continuity of employment for company, personnel—no involuntary layoffs
5. Develop favorable image with public

PRODUCTION DEPARTMENT
1. Keep cost of goods no more than 50% of sales
2. Increase productivity of labor by 3% per year
3. Maintain rejects at less than 2%
4. Maintain inventory at 6 months of sales
5. Keep production rate stable with no more than 20% variability from yearly average

SALES DEPARTMENT
1. Introduce new products so that over a 10-year period, 70% will be new
2. Maintain a market share of 15%
3. Seek new market areas so that sales will grow at a 15% annual rate
4. Maintain advertising costs at 4% of sales

FINANCE AND ACCOUNTING DEPARTMENT
1. Borrowing should not exceed 50% of assets
2. Maximize tax write-offs
3. Provide monthly statements to operating departments by 10th of following month
4. Pay dividends at rate of 50% of net earnings

SUPERVISORS
1. Handle employee grievances within 24 hours
2. Maintain production to standard or above
3. Keep scrappage to 2% of materials usage

DISTRICT SALES MANAGER
1. Meet weekly sales quotas
2. Visit each large customer once each month
3. Provide sales representatives with immediate follow-up support

OFFICE MANAGERS
1. Maintain cycle billing within 3 days of target date
2. Prepare special reports within 1 week of request

FIGURE 7.6   Hierarchy of objectives for a medium-sized organization

maintain production and the finance and accounting department couldn't approve the loan without the company's borrowing surpassing 50 percent of company assets. In such a situation, in which established subobjectives are aimed in different directions, a manager would have to choose which subobjective would better contribute to obtaining overall objectives and should therefore take precedence.

Controlling suboptimization in organizations is part of a manager's job. Managers can minimize suboptimization by developing a thorough understanding of how various parts of the organization relate to one another and by ensuring that subobjectives properly reflect these relations.

Guidelines for Establishing Quality Objectives

The quality of goal statements, like that of all humanly developed commodities, can vary drastically. Here are some general guidelines that managers can use to increase the quality of their objectives:[26]

1. **Let the people responsible for attaining the objectives have a voice in setting them**—Often the people responsible for attaining the objectives know their job situation better than the managers do and can therefore help to make the objectives more realistic. They will also be better motivated to achieve objectives they have had a say in establishing. Work-related problems that these people face should be thoroughly considered when objectives are being developed.[27]

2. **State objectives as specifically as possible**—Precise statements minimize confusion and ensure that employees have explicit directions for what they should do.[28] Research shows that when objectives are not specific, the productivity of individuals attempting to reach those objectives tends to fluctuate significantly over time.

3. **Relate objectives to specific actions whenever necessary**—In this way, employees do not have to infer what they should do to accomplish their goals.

4. **Pinpoint expected results**—Employees should know exactly how managers will determine whether an objective has been reached.

5. **Set goals high enough that employees will have to strive to meet them, but not so high that employees give up trying to meet them**—Managers want employees to work hard but not to become frustrated.

6. **Specify when goals are expected to be achieved**—Employees must have a time frame for accomplishing their objectives. They then can pace themselves accordingly.

7. **Set objectives only in relation to other organizational objectives**—In this way, suboptimization can be kept to a minimum.

8. **State objectives clearly and simply**—The written or spoken word should not impede communicating a goal to organization members.

class discussion highlight

PLANNING SKILL AND YOUR CAREER

The previous section discusses the role of objectives in the planning process. Understanding the importance of objectives will help you to further develop your planning skill. As you think about your academic career thus far, describe the role of your own objectives in determining your course grades. Do you have objectives regarding your course grades? Now, think about your career in the future. Do you think that employers will find your planning skills attractive? Thinking longer term, how do you think your planning skills will influence your career progression?

MANAGEMENT BY OBJECTIVES (MBO)

Some managers find organizational objectives such an important and fundamental part of management that they use a management approach based exclusively on them. This approach, called management by objectives (MBO), was popularized mainly through the writings of Peter Drucker. Although mostly discussed in the context of profit-oriented companies, MBO is also a valuable management tool for nonprofit organizations such as libraries and community clubs. The MBO strategy has three basic parts:[29]

1. All individuals within an organization are assigned a specialized set of objectives that they try to reach during a normal operating period. These objectives are mutually set and agreed upon by individuals and their managers.[30]
2. Performance reviews are conducted periodically to determine how close individuals are to attaining their objectives.
3. Rewards are given to individuals on the basis of how close they come to reaching their goals.

The MBO process consists of five steps (see Figure 7.7):

1. **Review organizational objectives**—The manager gains a clear understanding of the organization's overall objectives.
2. **Set worker objectives**—The manager and worker meet to agree on worker objectives to be reached by the end of the normal operating period.
3. **Monitor progress**—At intervals during the normal operating period, the manager and worker check to see whether the objectives are being reached.
4. **Evaluate performance**—At the end of the normal operating period, the worker's performance is judged by the extent to which the worker reached the objectives.
5. **Give rewards**—Rewards given to the worker are based on the extent to which the objectives were reached.

Factors Necessary for a Successful MBO Program

Certain key factors are essential to the success of an MBO program. First, top management must be committed to the MBO process and set appropriate objectives for the organization. Because all individual MBO goals will be based on these overall objectives, if the overall objectives are inappropriate, individual MBO objectives will also be inappropriate and related individual work activity will be nonproductive. Second, managers and subordinates together must develop and agree on each individual's goals. Both managers and subordinates must feel

FIGURE 7.7
The MBO process

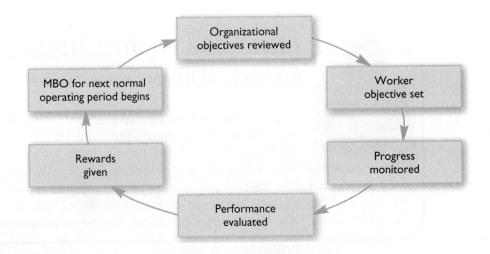

that the individual objectives are just and appropriate if each party is to seriously regard them as a guide for action. Third, employee performance should be conscientiously evaluated against established objectives. This evaluation helps determine whether the objectives are fair and if appropriate means are being used to attain them. Fourth, management must follow through on employee performance evaluations by rewarding employees accordingly.

If employees are to continue striving to reach their MBO program objectives, managers must reward those who do reach, or surpass, their objectives more than those whose performance falls short of their objectives. It goes without saying that such rewards must be given out fairly and honestly. Managers must be careful, though, not to conclude automatically that employees have produced at an acceptable level simply because they have reached their objectives. The objectives may have been set too low in the first place, and managers may have failed to recognize it at the time.[31]

MBO Programs: Advantages and Disadvantages

Experienced MBO managers claim that the MBO approach has two advantages. First, MBO programs continually emphasize what should be done in an organization to achieve organizational goals. Second, the MBO process secures employee commitment to attaining organizational goals. Because managers and subordinates have developed objectives together, both parties are sincerely interested in reaching those goals.

MBO managers also admit that MBO has certain disadvantages. One is that the development of objectives can be time consuming, leaving both managers and employees less time in which to do their actual work. Another is that the elaborate written goals, careful communication of goals, and detailed performance evaluations required in an MBO program increase the volume of paperwork in an organization.

On balance, however, most managers believe that MBO's advantages outweigh its disadvantages. Therefore, they find MBO programs beneficial.

PLANNING AND THE CHIEF EXECUTIVE

More than two decades ago, Henry Mintzberg pointed out that the top managers—the chief executives—of organizations have many different roles to perform.[32] As organizational figureheads, they must represent their organizations in a variety of social, legal, and ceremonial situations. As leaders, they must ensure that organization members are properly guided toward achieving organizational goals. As liaisons, they must establish themselves as links between their organizations and factors outside their organizations. As monitors, they must assess organizational progress. As disturbance handlers, they must settle disputes between organization members. And as resource allocators, they must determine where resources should be placed to benefit their organizations best.[33]

Final Responsibility

In addition to these many varied roles, chief executives have the final responsibility for organizational planning. As the scope of planning broadens to include a larger portion of the management system, it becomes increasingly important for chief executives to get involved in the planning process.

As planners, chief executives seek answers to the following broad questions:[34]

1. In what direction should the organization be going?
2. In what direction is the organization going now?
3. Should something be done to change this direction?
4. Is the organization continuing in an appropriate direction?

Keeping informed about social, political, and scientific trends is of utmost importance in helping chief executives to answer these questions.

Richard Branson, CEO and founder of the innovative Virgin Atlantic Airways, has continued to strike out in new business directions. While some planners have their hands full managing one type of business, Branson has achieved success in widely different business ventures due to his superb planning skills.

Planning Assistance

Given the necessity to participate in organizational planning while performing other time-consuming roles, more and more top managers have established the position of organization planner to obtain the planning assistance they require. Just as managers can ask others for help and advice in making decisions, so can they involve others in formulating organizational plans.[35]

The chief executive of a substantial organization almost certainly needs planning assistance.[36] The remainder of this chapter assumes that the organization planner is an individual who is not the chief executive of the organization, but rather a manager inside the organization who is responsible for assisting the chief executive on organizational planning issues.[37] Where the planner and the chief executive are the same person, however, the following discussion of the planner can, with slight modifications, be applied to the chief executive.

THE PLANNER

The planner is probably the most important input in the planning subsystem.[38] This individual combines all other inputs and influences the subsystem process so that its output is effective organizational plans. The planner is responsible not only for developing plans but also for advising management on what actions should be taken to implement those plans. Regardless of who actually does the planning or what organization the planning is being done in, the qualifications, duties, and evaluations of the planner are all important considerations for an effective planning subsystem.

Qualifications of Planners

Planners should have four primary qualifications:

* First, they should have considerable practical experience within their organization. Preferably, they should have been executives in one or more of the organization's major departments. This experience will help them develop plans that are both practical and tailor-made for the organization.

- Second, planners should be capable of replacing any narrow view of the organization they may have acquired while holding other organizational positions with an understanding of the organization as a whole. They must know how all parts of the organization function and interrelate. In other words, they must possess an abundance of the conceptual skills mentioned in Chapter 1.

- Third, planners should have some knowledge of and interest in the social, political, technical, and economic trends that could affect the future of the organization. They must be skillful in defining those trends and possess the expertise to determine how the organization should react to the trends to maximize its success. This qualification cannot be overemphasized.[39]

- The fourth and last qualification for planners is that they be able to work well with others. Their position will inevitably require them to work closely with several key members of the organization, so it is essential that they possess the personal characteristics necessary to collaborate and advise effectively. The ability to communicate clearly, both orally and in writing, is one of the most important of these characteristics.[40]

Evaluation of Planners

Planners, like all other organization members, should be evaluated according to the contribution they make toward helping the organization achieve its objectives.[41] The quality and appropriateness of the planning system and the plans that the planner develops for the organization are the primary considerations in this evaluation. Because the organizing, influencing, and controlling functions of managers all vitally depend on the fundamental planning function, an accurate evaluation of the planner is critically important to the organization.

Objective Indicators Although the assessment of planners is necessarily somewhat subjective, several objective indicators can be used. The use of appropriate techniques is one objective indicator. A planner who uses appropriate techniques is probably doing an acceptable job. The degree of objectivity displayed by the planner is another indicator. The planner's advice should be largely based on a rational analysis of appropriate information.[42] The assessment of this indicator is not to say that planners should abandon subjective judgment altogether, only that their opinions should be based chiefly on specific and appropriate information.

Malik suggests that a planner is doing a reputable job if the following objective criteria are met:[43]

1. Organizational plan is in writing.
2. Plan is the result of all elements of the management team working together.
3. Plan defines present and possible future business of the organization.
4. Plan specifically mentions organizational objectives.
5. Plan identifies future opportunities and suggests how to take advantage of them.
6. Plan emphasizes both internal and external environments.
7. Plan describes the attainment of objectives in operational terms whenever possible.
8. Plan includes both long- and short-term recommendations.

These eight criteria furnish objective guidelines for evaluating the performance of planners. However, management's evaluation of planners should never be completely objective. Important subjective considerations include how well planners get along with key members of the organization, the amount of organizational loyalty they display, and their perceived potential.

{ CHALLENGE CASE SUMMARY

It seems apparent from facts in the introductory case that Volkswagen managers must focus heavily on planning if the company's new strategy is to be successful. Such a process should help to determine issues such as what types of new equipment must be purchased to implement the new plan, who maintains the equipment once purchased, and how to change the organization's culture to focus on VW's strength of producing cars for common individuals. This process should also focus on how to improve the quality of Volkswagen's products.

Because of the many related benefits of planning, Volkswagen managers should make certain that the planning process is thorough and comprehensive, one particularly notable benefit of which is the probability of increased profits. To gain the benefits of planning, however, Volkswagen managers must be careful that the planning function is well executed and not overemphasized.

Volkswagen management should also keep in mind that planning is the primary management function. Thus managers should not begin to organize, influence, or control until planning for this new strategy is completed. Planning is the foundation management function upon which all other management functions at Volkswagen should be based.

Managers like those at Volkswagen who are refocusing their strategies should use their planning process to produce a practical plan for the activities. The process of developing this plan should consist of six steps. It should begin with a statement of an organizational objective to successfully design the plan and end with guidelines for putting the new plans into action. In this case, the ultimate organizational objective involves refocusing the company to build on its historical strengths.

To implement a planning process, managers should view planning as a subsystem that is part of the process of the overall management system. Thus they should use a portion of all the organizational resources available for the purpose of their planning. In this example, the output of this subsystem would be the actual plans to be used to introduce and produce new automobiles that are more affordable for consumers. Integrating the production of other Volkswagen brands such as the Golf or the Jetta would probably be emphasized. Naturally, a comprehensive planning effort at Volkswagen would focus on many other organizational areas such as obtaining needed funds and improving overall product quality.

Planning at Volkswagen, as at any other company, begins with a statement of organizational objectives, the targets at which the overall organization is aiming. These targets should be consistent with the purpose of Volkswagen, the reason that the company exists. Objectives for a company such as Volkswagen normally include profit targets, product quality targets, and social responsibility targets. Other organizational objectives would normally focus on market standing, innovation, productivity, and worker performance and attitude. Overall objectives for a company such as Volkswagen should be of three basic types: short-term objectives that are to be achieved in a year or less; intermediate objectives to be achieved in one to five years; and long-term objectives to be achieved in five to seven years. Additionally, Volkswagen and companies like it would normally develop a hierarchy of objectives so that individuals at different levels of the organization know what they must do to help reach organizational targets.

Planning for the strategic refocusing at Volkswagen should emphasize how to implement activities to help reach various organizational targets. Overall, Volkswagen's planning as it pertains to its automobiles should focus on enhancing the accomplishment of Volkswagen's short-term, intermediate-term, and long-term objectives that exist throughout the company's hierarchy of objectives.

Planning activities at a company such as Volkswagen tend to be more valuable the higher the quality of the organizational objectives. To increase the quality of objectives at Volkswagen, managers can take steps that allow people responsible for attaining objectives to have a voice in setting them, that state objectives as clearly and simply as possible, and that pinpoint results expected when objectives are achieved.

Management at Volkswagen might be so committed to managing via organizational targets that MBO becomes the primary management approach within the company. Such an approach would involve Volkswagen management monitoring the progress workers are making in reaching established objectives and using rewards and punishments to hold workers accountable for actually reaching the objectives. An MBO program might be advantageous to Volkswagen because it would continually emphasize what needs to be accomplished to reach organizational targets. On the other hand, an MBO program might be disadvantageous to Volkswagen because the process itself can be time-consuming.

Technically, the chief executive officer (CEO) at Volkswagen is responsible for planning for the organization as a whole and for performing such related time-consuming functions as keeping abreast of internal and external trends that could affect the future of the company. Because planning requires so much time, and because the chief executive officer of Volkswagen has many other responsibilities within the company, the CEO might want to consider appointing a director of planning.

The director of planning at Volkswagen would need certain qualities. Ideally, the planner should have some experience at Volkswagen, be able to see the company as an entire organization, have some ability to gauge and react to major trends that probably will affect the company's future, and be able to work well with others. The planner must oversee the planning process, evaluate developed plans, and solve planning problems. An evaluation of the Volkswagen organization planner would be based on both objective and subjective appraisals of his or her performance. Perhaps the first issue that a new company planner at Volkswagen should address is the introduction of its new luxury automobiles.

MANAGEMENT SKILL ACTIVITIES

This section is specially designed to help you develop management skill. An individual's planning skill is based upon an understanding of management concepts and the ability to apply those concepts in management situations. As a result, the following activities are designed both to heighten your understanding of principles of planning and to help you gain facility in applying these concepts in various management situations.

UNDERSTANDING PLANNING CONCEPTS

This section is comprised of activities that will sharpen your understanding of planning concepts. Answer essay questions as completely as possible. Also, remember that many additional true/false and multiple choice questions appear online at MyManagementLab.com to help you further refine your understanding of planning concepts.

Essay Questions

1. Summarize the primary advantages and disadvantages regarding planning. In your opinion, what is the most prominent advantage of planning? What is the largest disadvantage of planning?
2. Describe the various stages involved in the planning process. Use an example to illustrate these stages.
3. Explain the characteristics of effective objectives. Relying on these characteristics, provide an example of an effective objective for a not-for-profit organization of your choice.
4. Describe the relationship between planning and the other general functions of management (organizing, controlling, and influencing). In your opinion, which of the four functions is most important?
5. Describe the concept of a hierarchy of objectives. Why is developing such a hierarchy important for managers?

Developing Management Skill

Learning activities in this section are aimed at helping you to develop planning skill. Learning activities include Exploring Your Management Skill: Part 2, Experiential Exercises, Cases, and a VideoNet exercise.

EXPLORING YOUR MANAGEMENT SKILL: PART 2

As you recall, you completed Exploring Your Management Skill before you started to study this chapter. Your responses gave you an idea of how much you initially knew about planning and helped you to focus on important points as you studied the chapter. Answer the Exploring Your Management Skill questions again now (p. 182) and compare your score to the first time you took it. This comparison will give you an idea of how much you learned from studying this chapter and pinpoint areas for further clarification before you start studying the next chapter. Record your answers within the text or online at MyManagementLab.com. Completing the survey at MyManagementLab.com will allow you to grade and compare your test scores automatically. If you complete the test in the book, look up answers in the Exploring Your Management Skill section at the end of the book.

YOUR MANAGEMENT SKILLS PORTFOLIO

Your Management Learning Portfolio is a collection of activities especially designed to demonstrate your management knowledge and skill. By completing these activities at MyManagementLab.com, you will be able to print, complete with cover sheet, as many activities as you choose. Be sure to save your work. Taking your printed portfolio to an employment interview could be helpful in obtaining a job.

The portfolio activity for this chapter is Developing Your Planning Skills. Read the following highlight about Darden Restaurants, and answer the questions that follow.

Darden Restaurants Inc., which operates chains such as Red Lobster, Olive Garden, and Bahama Breeze, is one of the largest casual dining restaurant companies in the world. Darden is exploring potential opportunities for growth, and you have been hired to develop a new restaurant concept for the company. Executives at Darden are particularly interested in concepts that are consistent with the company's mission, which is "To nourish and delight everyone we serve." Darden has committed the funds necessary to test your new concept restaurant in an area around your school. If the new concept works well in your area, Darden may seek to expand the concept in a larger geographical area.

Your mission involves establishing a plan to introduce this new concept restaurant. After deciding on your new concept restaurant, Darden wants you to work through the first five steps of the planning process: (1) state organizational objectives; (2) list alternative ways of reaching objectives; (3) develop premises on which to base each alternative; (4) choose the best alternative for reaching objectives; and (5) develop plans to pursue the chosen alternative. In the space provided here, respond to the following inquiries regarding the first five steps of the planning process.

1. Briefly describe the most important characteristics of your new concept for Darden.

2. Develop three organizational objectives for your new restaurant.

3. Choose one of the three objectives to explore in more detail. List three alternative ways to reach this objective.

4. Develop premises to evaluate each of these three alternatives.

_____

_____

_____

5. Based on these premises, choose the alternative that is most likely to reach the objective.

_____

_____

_____

6. As you think about this alternative, list the significant steps needed to implement this alternative.

_____

_____

_____

EXPERIENTIAL EXERCISE: DEVELOPING OBJECTIVES FOR THE DON CESAR

Directions. Read the following scenario and then perform the listed activities. Your instructor may want you to perform the activities as an individual or within groups. Follow all of your instructor's directions carefully.

You have just been hired as the new assistant manager at the Don Cesar Beach Resort (www.doncesar.com) in St. Petersburg, Florida. This resort, which opened in 1928, has a storied history. Nonetheless, the manager of the resort has assigned you and your team the task of identifying new objectives for the resort. He thinks that your fresh perspective might help the organization to thrive for the next 100 years. Lead your group by outlining five objectives for the resort. Then, use the "Guidelines for Establishing Quality Objectives" listed on page 191 to better understand the quality of the five objectives that your team developed. Based on these guidelines, which objective was the best? Which objective was the worst? Why?

CASES

SOUND PLANNING AT VOLKSWAGEN?

"Planning for a Rebound at Volkswagen" (p. 181) was written to help you better understand the management concepts contained in this chapter. Answer the following discussion questions about the Challenge Case to better understand how principles of planning can be applied in a company like Volkswagen.

1. What special challenges would Volkswagen face in introducing a new SUV? What steps would you take to meet these challenges?

2. Would you have the Volkswagen CEO or an appointed planning executive do the planning for the new SUV? Why?

3. List three criteria that you would use to evaluate the planning for SUVs at Volkswagen. Explain why you chose each criterion.

HSBC PLANS TO MAKE A DIFFERENCE

Read the case and answer the questions that follow. Studying this case will help you better understand how principles of planning can be applied in a company such as HSBC.

Founded as a small Hong Kong bank in 1865, HSBC Holdings has followed a series of growth plans to emerge today as one of the world's largest financial services firms. The London-based company serves 110 million customers through 9,500 offices in 79 countries, offering an extensive array of banking, investment, insurance, and credit services. Under a five-year strategic plan launched in 1998, HSBC enjoyed a number of outstanding financial accomplishments, including increasing corporate profits by 41 percent between 2002 and 2003. In 2002, the company also introduced a five-year plan to protect the environment by donating $50 million to conservation causes and lending 2,000 employees to work on ecological projects. Despite careful planning, however, some HSBC divisions weren't always able to overcome severe economic pressures or other adverse conditions to achieve the intended results throughout the five-year period. For example, the investment banking unit's performance was so disappointing in 2001 that management did not give bankers and analysts any bonuses for that year.

Now Sir John Bond, HSBC's chairperson, is challenging corporate, division, and unit managers to set more ambitious objectives in line with a five-year "Managing for Growth" strategic plan initiated in 2003. This long-term plan builds on the foundation laid by the previous plan and establishes broad organizational priorities in key areas such as revenues and expenditures, customer service, shareholder return, competitive standing, productivity through teamwork, and corporate responsibility. In turn, these priorities guide objective-setting at all levels so managers can formulate and implement plans that will make a difference in the company's future, in its communities, and in the natural environment.

In their quest to secure the market leadership position that HSBC's mission envisions, Bond and his managers are applying each division's resources and strengths, which include sophisticated technology, human resources talent, customer knowledge, financial and risk management, and enduring business relationships. In the course of the previous strategic plan, corporate planners identified certain markets as especially promising for growth. Now they are coordinating divisional objectives and plans to make the most of profitable opportunities. For example, HSBC acquired or started banks as part of its lucrative expansion in the United States, Mexico, and France. Looking ahead, management is opening or buying more banks to serve consumers and business customers in these areas.

At the operational level, HSBC's country managers and branch managers are supporting corporate and divisional objectives by setting objectives for opening new accounts and other banking activities. HSBC Bank Malaysia's one-year objectives, as an example, are to issue 20 percent more credit cards and increase deposits by 20 percent. Similarly, the Hong Kong unit wants to expand its credit card base by 10 percent within a year—but "It's not just about competing in terms of the number of cards; profitability is more important," notes that unit's general manager. In Thailand, the local HSBC unit is targeting more affluent people in a short-term drive to open 300 new accounts within three months. And in the United States, the corporation applied for a national bank charter as one step in a long-term campaign to open dozens of new branches and bring in millions of dollars in deposits.

In addition, HSBC executives are developing measurement and reporting mechanisms so they can monitor the company's environmental impact and formulate appropriate long- and short-term objectives for greenhouse gas emissions, water consumption, energy consumption, and recycling. They are also examining interim results of HSBC's unprecedented $50 million environmental philanthropy project, designed to achieve objectives such as saving endangered plants, battling water pollution, preserving forests, and educating the public about the importance of conservation. Social responsibility objectives and plans are not easy to formulate or achieve, but the HSBC workforce is excited about the commitment. "The environment is something that people feel very strongly about, and the reality is that we can make some difference there because of our scale," says the HSBC manager in charge.

QUESTIONS

1. What are the arguments for and against HSBC managers making public their short-term and intermediate-term objectives, unit by unit or division by division?

2. Would you recommend that HSBC use the MBO process to reward investment bankers and analysts according to results, even though key factors influencing performance can't be precisely predicted or controlled? Explain.

3. Which stakeholders might be affected by HSBC's plan to invest $50 million in environmental conservation? Should the company continue this plan, regardless of short-term financial performance?

VIDEONET EXERCISE

Skate Park

VIDEO HIGHLIGHTS

When Oklahoma City set out to build a world-class skateboard/bike park, they had many obstacles to face—the least of which was they had never built one before! This included the entire team: the city planners, the architect, and the construction company. This video follows the planning and construction phases using a reality TV-type format as the players battle weather, budgets, hidden agendas, and each other. The seven steps of planning are incorporated into the story, which is edited in a fun, cutting-edge style. Despite delays ranging from unseasonable weather to problems with skaters sneaking in at night, success is ultimately achieved. The video culminates with a successful test run of the park by Mat Hoffman, world-champion vertical bike stunt rider.

Discussion Questions

1. The first step in the planning process is to state organizational objectives. Do you think Oklahoma City and Stan Carroll (architect) had clear objectives for the skate park? List some of the possible objectives for this type of project.
2. In what way were subsystem groups used to complete the skate park?
3. Which types of objectives were used in this project? Give specific examples of each.

Internet Activity

Browse the Oklahoma City skate park Web site at www.okc.gov/Parks/skatepark/index.html. What is your opinion of the Web site and the skate park, in general? Do you think the skate park is accomplishing the objectives originally established by the Oklahoma City officials and architect, Stan Carroll? Why do you think Oklahoma City chose to name the park after Mat Hoffman?

8 Making Decisions

O B J E C T I V E S

TO HELP BUILD MY DECISION-MAKING SKILL, WHEN STUDYING THIS CHAPTER, I WILL ATTEMPT TO ACQUIRE:

1. A fundamental understanding of the term *decision*

2. An understanding of each element of the decision situation

3. An ability to use the decision-making process

4. An appreciation for the various situations in which decisions are made

5. An understanding of probability theory and decision trees as decision-making tools

6. Insights into groups as decision makers

TARGET SKILL decision-making skill: the ability to choose alternatives that increase the likelihood of accomplishing objectives

CHALLENGE CASE

MAKING DIFFICULT DECISIONS AT TOYS"R"US

Gerald Storch is the CEO of Toys"R"Us, a retailer of toys, children's books, and children's apparel. Over the years, Toys"R"Us prospered and became the number one toy seller in the United States. Recently, however, Wal-Mart surpassed Toys"R"Us to become the number one toy retailer. Since Wal-Mart's emergence as the toy-selling superpower, other prominent toy companies such as F.A.O Schwartz and KB Toys have filed for bankruptcy, and Toys"R"Us' profits decreased more than 50 percent. As such, Storch has made a number of decisions that will hopefully help Toys"R"Us to better compete against Wal-Mart.

On becoming CEO of Toys"R"Us, Gerald Storch made a number of important decisions, including changing the entire executive team.

One of Storch's first decisions was to change the company's entire executive team. In his opinion, the pressure from Wal-Mart made the company's employees defensive instead of offensive, and he needed to change the corporate culture. In order to change these attitudes, he assembled a new executive team by hiring industry experts from companies such as The Home Depot, Sony, Limited Brands, Target, and Avon. With these new top executives on board, Storch is introducing a new slogan that Toys"R"Us is "playing to win," which is a far cry from the company's previous more defensive attitude.

Storch also decided to further differentiate Toys"R"Us as a toy seller. Although Wal-Mart routinely offers lower prices than Toys"R"Us, Storch has decided to use Toys"R"Us's position as a toy seller to its advantage. Specifically, Storch has invested in Toys"R"Us employees. Through increased training and development, Storch hopes that employees can help customers in ways that Wal-Mart's employees cannot. As a company that sells only toys, Storch believes that the employees of Toys"R"Us can learn more about toys than employees of Wal-Mart, who are forced to know about many other store departments (i.e., clothing, sporting goods, home improvement, etc.). Storch thinks that this increased knowledge of toys will help employees better serve customers.

It is clear that Storch has made some courageous decisions to improve the performance of Toys"R"Us. By hiring new executives, changing the corporate culture, and training employees, Storch hopes that Toys"R"Us will soon overtake Wal-Mart. Although this is an admirable objective, Storch knows that Wal-Mart will not go down without a tremendous fight. As such, Storch will most likely have to continue making tough decisions for Toys"R"Us to win the war of toy-selling supremacy.[1]

"EXPLORE YOUR OWN MANAGEMENT SKILLS BY TAKING THE QUIZ ON THE NEXT PAGE"

Before studying this chapter, respond to the following questions regarding the type of advice that you would give to Toys"R"Us CEO Gerald Storch, referenced in the Challenge Case. Then address the concerning decision-making challenges that he presently faces within the company. You are not expected to be a decision-making expert at this point. Answering the questions now can help you focus on important points when you study the chapter. Also, answering the questions again after you study the chapter will give you an idea of how much you have learned.

Record your answers here or go to MyManagement Lab.com. Recording your answers in MyManagement Lab will allow you to get immediate results and see how your score compares to your classmates. If you answer the questions in the book, look up answers in the Exploring Your Management Skill section at the end of the book.

FOR EACH STATEMENT CIRCLE:

- "Y" if you would give the advice to Gerald Storch.
- "N" if you would NOT give the advice to Gerald Storch.
- "NI" if you have no idea whether you would give the advice to Gerald Storch.

Mr. Storch, in meeting your decision-making challenges at Toys"R"Us, you should . . .

Before Study	*After Study*

1. realize that nonprogrammed decisions typically take less time to make than programmed decisions.

   Y, N, NI

2. understand that as decisions at Toys"R"Us affect more levels of the total management system, the scope of the decision increases.

   Y, N, NI

3. recognize that at Toys"R"Us, decision makers with exploitative orientations are more likely to ask others for advice as compared to decision makers with receptive orientations.

   Y, N, NI

4. understand that all employees at Toys"R"Us will employ the rational decision-making process when making decisions.

   Y, N, NI

5. teach other employees at Toys"R"Us that the rational decision-making process ends when an alternative has been chosen.

   Y, N, NI

6. understand that *risk* and *uncertainty* represent two terms that have the same meaning.

   Y, N, NI

7. realize that managers often operate in a state of bounded rationality, which suggests that managers often make decisions without all of the necessary information.

   Y, N, NI

8. understand that decision makers at Toys"R"Us will always satisfice, which means that employees will always choose the best available alternative.

   Y, N, NI

9. understand that decision makers at Toys"R"Us will often rely on heuristics, or rules of thumb, when making decisions.

   Y, N, NI

10. teach others that decisions will not be biased if decision makers are respectful of individuals with diverse backgrounds.

    Y, N, NI

11. be prepared to use probability theory to make important decisions at Toys"R"Us.

    Y, N, NI

12. realize that decisions made by groups are always better than decisions made by individuals.

    Y, N, NI

13. teach others to use both brainstorming and barnstorming techniques to improve group decision-making processes.

    Y, N, NI

14. realize that *risk* is a subjective term, and different managers at Toys"R"Us may associate different levels of risk with a particular decision.

    Y, N, NI

15. communicate to Toys"R"Us managers that they are responsible for identifying organizational problems, and lower-level employees are not qualified to identify problems.

    Y, N, NI

THE DECISION-MAKING CHALLENGE

The Challenge Case focuses on events at Toys"R"Us. The information in this chapter discusses specifics surrounding a decision-making situation and provides insights about the steps that management at Toys"R"Us might have taken in making these decisions. This chapter discusses (1) the fundamentals of decisions, (2) the decision-making process, (3) various decision-making conditions, (4) decision-making tools, and (5) group decision making. These topics are critical to managers and other individuals who make decisions.

FUNDAMENTALS OF DECISIONS

Definition of a Decision

A **decision** is a choice made between two or more available alternatives. *Decision making* is the process of choosing the best alternative for reaching objectives. Decision making is covered in the planning section of this text, but because managers must also make decisions when performing the other three managerial functions—organizing, influencing, and controlling—the subject requires a separate chapter.

We all face decision situations every day. A decision situation may involve simply choosing whether to spend the day studying, swimming, or golfing. It does not matter which alternative is chosen, only that a choice is made.[2]

Managers make decisions affecting the organization daily and communicate those decisions to other organization members.[3] Not all managerial decisions are of equal significance to the organization. Some affect a large number of organization members, cost a great deal of money to carry out, or have a long-term effect on the organization. Such significant decisions can have a major impact, not only on the management system itself, but on the career of the manager who makes them. Other decisions are fairly insignificant, affecting only a small number of organization members, costing little to carry out, and producing only a short-term effect on the organization.

Types of Decisions

Decisions can be categorized according to how much time a manager must spend in making them, what proportion of the organization must be involved in making them, and the organizational functions on which they focus. Probably the most generally accepted method of categorizing decisions, however, is based on computer language; it divides all decisions into two basic types: programmed and nonprogrammed.[4]

Programmed decisions are routine and repetitive, and the organization typically develops specific ways to handle them. A programmed decision might involve determining how products will be arranged on the shelves of a supermarket. For this kind of routine, repetitive problem, standard-arrangement decisions are typically made according to established management guidelines.

Nonprogrammed decisions, in contrast, are typically one-shot decisions that are usually less structured than programmed decisions. An example of the type of nonprogrammed decision that more and more managers are having to make is whether to expand operations into the "forgotten continent" of Africa.[5] Another example is deciding whether a hypermarket should carry an additional type of bread. The manager making this decision must consider whether the new bread will merely stabilize bread sales by competing with existing bread carried in the store or actually increase bread sales by offering a desired brand of bread to customers who have never before bought bread in the store. These types of issues must be dealt with before the manager can finally decide whether to offer the new bread. Table 8.1 shows traditional and modern ways of handling programmed and nonprogrammed decisions.

Programmed and nonprogrammed decisions should be thought of as being at opposite ends of the decision programming continuum, as illustrated in Figure 8.1. As the figure indicates, however, some decisions are neither programmed nor nonprogrammed, falling somewhere between the two. One of the key distinctions between programmed versus nonprogrammed decisions is that programmed decisions typically require less time and effort as compared to nonprogrammed decisions.

The Responsibility for Making Organizational Decisions

Many different kinds of decisions must be made within an organization—such as how to manufacture a product, how to maintain machines, how to ensure product quality, and how to establish advantageous relationships with customers. Because organizational decisions are

	Decision-Making Techniques	
Types of Decisions	**Traditional**	**Modern**

Programmed:
Routine, repetitive decisions
Organization develops specific processes for handling them
	1. Habit
	2. Clerical routine:
	    Standard operating procedures
	3. Organization structure:
	    Common expectations
	    A system of subgoals
	    Well-defined information channels
		1. Operations research:
		    Mathematical analysis models
		    Computer simulation
		2. Electronic data processing

Nonprogrammed:
One-shot, ill-structured, novel policy decisions
Handled by general problem-solving processes
	1. Judgment, intuition, and creativity
	2. Rules of thumb
	3. Selection and training of executives
		1. Heuristic problem-solving techniques applied to:
		    Training human decision makers
		    Constructing heuristic
		    computer programs

TABLE 8.1   Traditional and Modern Ways of Handling Programmed and Nonprogrammed Decisions

so varied, some type of rationale must be developed to stipulate who within the organization has the responsibility for making which decisions.

One such rationale is based primarily on two factors: the scope of the decision to be made and the levels of management. The **scope of the decision** is the proportion of the total management system that the decision will affect. The greater this proportion, the broader the scope of the decision is said to be. *Levels of management* are simply lower-level management, middle-level management, and upper-level management. The rationale for designating who makes which decisions is that the broader the scope of a decision, the higher the level of the manager responsible for making that decision. Figure 8.2 illustrates this rationale.

In **an example from the world of management,** Howard Schultz, the CEO of **Starbucks,** recently made a decision to increase drink prices by almost 10 cents per drink.[6] As CEO of the company, Schultz is in charge of making decisions that affect the entire Starbucks organization. In contrast, lower levels of management are responsible for making decisions that do not affect the entire organization.

The manager who is responsible for making a particular decision can ask the advice of other managers or subordinates before settling on an alternative. In fact, some managers prefer to use groups to make certain decisions.

Consensus is one method a manager can use in getting a group to arrive at a particular decision. **Consensus** is an agreement on a decision by all the individuals involved in making that decision. It usually occurs after lengthy deliberation and discussion by members of the decision group, who may be either all managers or a mixture of managers and subordinates.[7]

The manager who asks a group to produce a consensus decision must bear in mind that groups will sometimes be unable to arrive at a decision. Lack of technical skills or poor

FIGURE 8.1

Decision programming continuum

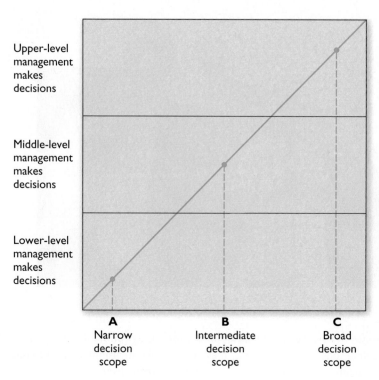

FIGURE 8.2
Level of managers responsible for making decisions as decision scope increases from A to B to C

interpersonal relations may prove insurmountable barriers to arriving at a consensus. When a group is stalemated, a manager needs to offer assistance in making the decision or simply make it herself.

Decisions arrived at through consensus have both advantages and disadvantages. One advantage of this method is that it focuses "several heads" on the decision. Another is that employees are more likely to be committed to implementing a decision if they helped make it. The main disadvantage of this method is that it often involves time-consuming discussions relating to the decision, which can be costly to the organization.

Elements of the Decision Situation

Wilson and Alexis isolate several basic elements in the decision situation.[8] Five of these elements are defined and discussed in this section.

The Decision Makers Decision makers, the first element of the decision situation, are the individuals or groups that actually make the choice among alternatives. According to Ernest Dale, weak decision makers usually have one of four orientations: receptive, exploitative, hoarding, and marketing.[9]

Decision makers who have a *receptive* orientation believe that the source of all good is outside themselves, and therefore they rely heavily on suggestions from other organization members. Basically, they want others to make their decisions for them.

Decision makers with an *exploitative* orientation also believe that the source of all good is outside themselves, and they are willing to steal ideas as necessary in order to make good decisions. They build their organizations on others' ideas and typically hog all the credit, extending little or none to the originators of the ideas.

The *hoarding* orientation is characterized by the desire to preserve the status quo as much as possible. Decision makers with this orientation accept little outside help, isolate themselves from others, and are extremely self-reliant. They are obsessed with maintaining their present position and status.

Store manager Gary Rains (right) leads Wal-Mart employees in the company cheer at the end of the regular morning staff meeting. Such actions are aimed at helping the manager build commitment to implementing decisions the manager and the team have made together.

Marketing-oriented decision makers look upon themselves as commodities that are only as valuable as the decisions they make. Thus they try to make decisions that will enhance their value and are highly conscious of what others think of their decisions.

The ideal decision-making orientation emphasizes the realization of the organization's potential as well as that of the decision maker. Ideal decision makers try to use all of their talents when making a decision and are characterized by reason and sound judgment. They are largely free of the qualities of the four undesirable decision-making orientations just described.

Goals to Be Served The goals that decision makers seek to attain are another element of the decision situation. In the case of managers, these goals should most often be organizational objectives. (Chapter 7 discussed the specifics of organizational objectives.)

Relevant Alternatives The decision situation is usually composed of at least two relevant alternatives. A **relevant alternative** is one that is considered feasible for solving an existing problem and for implementation. Alternatives that will not solve an existing problem *or* cannot be implemented are irrelevant and should be excluded from the decision-making situation.

Ordering of Alternatives The decision situation requires a process or mechanism for ranking alternatives from most desirable to least desirable. This process can be subjective, objective, or some combination of the two. Past experience of the decision maker is an example of a subjective process, and the rate of output per machine is an example of an objective process.

Choice of Alternatives The last element of the decision situation is the actual choice between available alternatives. This choice establishes the decision. Typically, managers choose the alternative that maximizes long-term return for the organization.

The Rational Decision-Making Process

A decision is a choice of one alternative from a set of available alternatives. The **rational decision-making process** comprises the steps the decision maker takes to arrive at this choice. The process a manager uses to make decisions has a significant impact on the quality

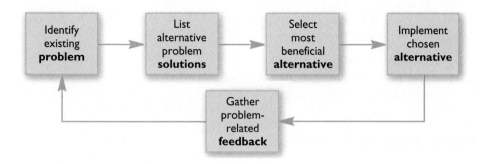

FIGURE 8.3
Model of the decision-making process

of those decisions. If managers use an organized and systematic process, the probability that their decisions will be sound is higher than if they use a disorganized and unsystematic process.[10]

A model of the decision-making process that is recommended for managerial use is presented in Figure 8.3. In order, the decision-making steps this model depicts are as follows:

1. Identify an existing problem.
2. List possible alternatives for solving the problem.
3. Select the most beneficial of these alternatives.
4. Implement the selected alternative.
5. Gather feedback to find out whether the implemented alternative is solving the identified problem.

The paragraphs that follow elaborate on each of these steps and explain their interrelationships.[11]

This model of the decision-making process is based on three primary assumptions.[12] First, the model assumes that humans are economic beings with the objective of maximizing satisfaction or return. Second, it assumes that within the decision-making situation all alternatives and their possible consequences are known. Its last assumption is that decision makers have some priority system to guide them in ranking the desirability of each alternative. If each of these assumptions is met, the decision made will probably be the best possible one for the organization. In real life, unfortunately, one or more of these assumptions is often not met, and therefore the decision made is less than optimal for the organization.

Identifying an Existing Problem

Decision making is essentially a problem-solving process that involves eliminating barriers to organizational goal attainment. The first step in this elimination process is identifying exactly what the problems or barriers are, for only after the barriers have been adequately identified can management take steps to eliminate them. In **an example from the world of management,** several years ago **Molson,** a Canadian manufacturer of beer as well as of cleaning and sanitizing products, faced a barrier to success: a free-trade agreement that threatened to open Canadian borders to U.S. beer. Although the borders were not due to open for another five years, Molson decided to deal with the problem of increased beer competition from the United States immediately by increasing production and sales of its specialty chemical products. Within four years, Molson's chemical sales exceeded its beer sales. Essentially, the company identified its problem—the threat of increased U.S. competition for beer sales—and dealt with it by emphasizing sales in a different division.[13]

Chester Barnard has stated that organizational problems are brought to the attention of managers mainly by the following means:[14]

1. Orders issued by managers' supervisors
2. Situations relayed to managers by their subordinates
3. The normal activity of the managers themselves

Listing Alternative Solutions

Once a problem has been identified, managers should list the various possible solutions. Few organizational problems are solvable in only one way. Managers must search out the numerous available alternative solutions to most organizational problems.

Before searching for solutions, however, managers should be aware of five limitations on the number of problem-solving alternatives available:[15]

1. Authority factors (e.g., a manager's superior may have told the manager that a certain alternative is not feasible)
2. Biological or human factors (e.g., human factors within the organization may be inappropriate for implementing certain alternatives)
3. Physical factors (e.g., the physical facilities of the organization may be inappropriate for certain alternatives)
4. Technological factors (e.g., the level of organizational technology may be inadequate for certain alternatives)
5. Economic factors (e.g., certain alternatives may be too costly for the organization)

Figure 8.4 presents additional factors that can limit a manager's decision alternatives. This diagram uses the term *discretionary area* to depict all the feasible alternatives available to managers. Factors that limit or rule out alternatives outside this area are legal restrictions, moral and ethical norms, formal policies and rules, and unofficial social norms.[16]

Selecting the Most Beneficial Alternative

Decision makers can select the most beneficial solution only after they have evaluated each alternative carefully. This evaluation should consist of three steps. First, decision makers should list, as accurately as possible, the potential effects of each alternative as if the alternative had already been chosen and implemented. Second, they should assign a probability factor to each of the potential effects; that is, indicate how probable the occurrence of the

FIGURE 8.4

Additional factors that limit a manager's number of acceptable alternatives

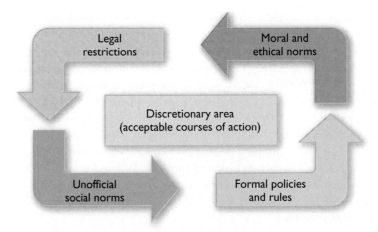

Scholastic, Inc., the publisher of the Harry Potter series of books, decided to honor the request of author J.K. Rowling that no one be allowed to see a copy of any new book before its publication date. Implementing that decision required gaining the cooperation of booksellers all over the globe. Here an Amazon.com employee prepares copies of "Harry Potter and the Order of the Phoenix" for shipping.

effect would be if the alternative were implemented. Third, keeping organizational goals in mind, decision makers should compare each alternative's expected effects and the respective probabilities of those effects.[17] After these steps have been completed, managers will know which alternative seems most advantageous to the organization.

class discussion highlight

MODERN RESEARCH AND DECISION-MAKING SKILL

The Influence of Advice on Decision Making

One key to effective decision making is gathering as much useful information as possible. Often, decision makers ask colleagues, friends, and family for advice before making decisions. A recent study by Yaniv and Milyavsky examined the extent to which individuals use the advice of others when improving the judgments needed for making decisions.[18]

In their study, the authors asked individuals to answer a series of 24 questions such as "In what year was the Suez Canal first opened for use?" After the individuals responded to these questions, the authors then provided the best estimates that other participants provided regarding the same questions. For example, after one student answered "1890," the study authors provided the student with two other responses: "1905" and "1830." After receiving this information, the participants answered the same questions one more time; this second opportunity allowed participants to revise their initial estimates if they desired to do so.

According to the study's findings, do you think that the participants used the advice of others when revising their initial estimates? If so, do you think this information helped or harmed the participants' subsequent answers? What implications might this study have for your own decision making?

Implementing the Chosen Alternative

The next step is to put the chosen alternative into action. Decisions must be supported by appropriate action if they are to have a chance of success.

Gathering Problem-Related Feedback

After the chosen alternative has been implemented, decision makers must gather feedback to determine the effect of the implemented alternative on the identified problem. If the identified problem is not being solved, managers need to seek out and implement some other alternative.

BOUNDED RATIONALITY

In the previous section, we described the rational decision-making process. Herbert Simon, however, questioned the ability of managers to make rational decisions. In his opinion, managers are not able to make perfectly rational decisions. Instead, Simon put forth the idea that managers deal with **bounded rationality,** which refers to the fact that managers are bounded in terms of time, computational power, and knowledge when making decisions.[19] In other words, managers do not always have access to the resources required to make rational decisions. As a result of bounded rationality, Simon suggests that managers **satisfice,** which occurs when an individual makes a decision that is not optimal but is "good enough." For example, a manager may hire the first employee who is acceptable according to the hiring criteria without interviewing the remaining candidates. In this example, a better candidate may exist, but the manager has satisfied by selecting the first "acceptable" candidate.

DECISION-MAKING AND INTUITION

As already discussed, the rational decision-making process includes a sequence of five steps. We also noted, however, that researchers have highlighted the potential influence of bounded rationality on this process. More recently, research suggests that individuals may also rely on additional processes when making decisions. In fact, Stanovich and West suggest that individuals use two different processes when making decisions.[20] According to their framework, the rational decision-making process discussed in the previous section is known as "System 2."

Complementing this formal system of decision making, Stanovick and West suggest that individuals also rely on a less formal process based on intuition to make decisions; they refer to this process as "System 1." Consistent with their framework, System 2 is a process described as being slow, comprehensive, and deliberate, while System 1 is described as being fast, automatic, and intuitive. **Intuition,** in fact, refers to an individual's inborn ability to synthesize information quickly and effectively.[21] Taken together, some researchers suggest that individuals employ the more sophisticated System 2 process to monitor or override the more automatic System 1 process. Often, however, System 2 does not monitor effectively; in such cases intuition drives decision making.

Decision-Making Heuristics and Biases

Daniel Kahneman and Amos Tversky were awarded the Nobel Prize for further examining the role of intuition in decision making. In particular, their ground-breaking research examined how individuals use **heuristics,** or simple rules of thumb, to make decisions. In addition, Kahneman and Tveresky examined how these heuristics introduce bias in decision-making processes. **Bias** refers to departures from rational theory that produce suboptimal decisions. In other words, when managers rely on rules of thumb when making decisions, these decisions are often flawed. Kahneman and Tversky's work spurred a great deal of interest in the discovery and examination of a number of decision-making biases. Researchers have discovered many other decision-making biases; Table 8.2 summarizes some of the more prominent biases examined by decision-making researchers.

TABLE 8.2	Common Decision-Making Biases
Name of Bias	**Brief Description**
Bandwagon Effect	The tendency to believe certain outcomes (i.e., stock markets will increase) because others believe the same
Confirmation Bias	The tendency to search for information that supports one's preconceived beliefs and to ignore information that contradicts those beliefs
Loss Aversion	Characteristic of individuals who tend to more strongly prefer avoiding losses rather than acquiring gains
Overconfidence	When assessing our ability to predict future events, the tendency to believe that our forecasts are better than they truly are
Unrealistic Optimism	Individuals' tendency to believe that they are less susceptible to risky events (i.e., earthquakes, disease transmission, etc.) than others

Source: For a complete review of research involving heuristics and biases, see T. Gilovich, D. Griffin, and D. Kahneman, *Heuristics and Biases: The Psychology of Intuitive Judgment* (Cambridge: Cambridge University Press, 2002).

Decision-Making Conditions: Risk and Uncertainty

In most instances, it is impossible for decision makers to know exactly what the future consequences of an implemented alternative will be. The word *future* is the key in discussing decision-making conditions. Because organizations and their environments are constantly changing, future consequences of implemented decisions are not perfectly predictable. In general, the two different conditions under which decisions are made are risk and uncertainty. Although many managers use them interchangeably, these two terms are in fact different.

Frank Knight distinguished between risk and uncertainty almost a century ago.[22] According to his framework, **risk** refers to situations in which statistical probabilities can be attributed to alternative potential outcomes. For example, the probabilities associated with the potential outcomes of roulette are known to individuals in advance. In contrast, **uncertainty** refers to situations where the probability that a particular outcome will occur is not known in advance. A manager, for instance, may be unable to articulate the probability that building a new manufacturing facility will increase a firm's sales in five years.

Despite this distinction between risk and uncertainty, it is important to note that objective standards are not always available when examining a situation with alternative potential outcomes. Specifically, two managers may attribute differing levels of uncertainty or risk to the same or similar decisions. For example, suppose that the managers of two competing firms—Alpha Inc. and Beta Inc.—are each considering opening new manufacturing facilities in China but are unsure whether the new plants will improve profitability. Suppose, however, that the manager of Alpha Inc. has previously opened 12 new facilities in China, but the manager of Beta Inc. has no experience opening such facilities. As such, the manager of Alpha Inc. has more information about opening these plants and might be able to better estimate the risk probabilities associated with profitability versus failure as compared to the manager of Beta Inc. In fact, the manager of Beta Inc. might not be able to estimate any risk probabilities and instead view this plant with complete uncertainty.

Now that we have distinguished between risk and uncertainty, the question remains: Why do we need to distinguish between these two terms? Research suggests that individuals dislike uncertainty even more than they dislike risk.[23] Vague or unknown probabilities of success are more likely to discourage managers from undertaking actions. This negative influence of uncertainty has implications for all sorts of decisions such as hiring new employees, introducing new products, or acquiring other firms.

class discussion highlight

DECISION-MAKING SKILL AND YOUR CAREER

The preceding discussion highlights the importance of decision making and describes a number of factors that influence decision making. Describe a scenario in which poor decision-making skills could hinder your career as a manager. What are some strategies you might employ to improve your decision-making skill? Explain. Describe two examples from your life that help you to communicate your decision-making skill to potential employers.

DECISION-MAKING TOOLS

Most managers develop an intuition about what decisions to make—a largely subjective feeling, based on years of experience in a particular organization or industry, that gives them insights into decision making for that industry or organization.[24] Although intuition is often an important factor in making a decision, managers generally emphasize more objective decision-making tools. The two most widely used such tools are probability theory and decision trees.[25]

Probability Theory

Probability theory is a decision-making tool used in risk situations—situations in which decision makers are not completely sure of the outcome of an implemented alternative.[26] *Probability* refers to the likelihood that an event or outcome will actually occur. It is estimated by calculating an expected value for each alternative considered. Specifically, the **expected value (EV)** for an alternative is the income (*I*) that alternative would produce, multiplied by its probability of producing that income (*P*). In formula form, $EV = I \times P$. Decision makers generally choose and implement the alternative with the highest expected value.[27]

An example will clarify the relationship of probability, income, and expected value. A manager is trying to decide where to open a store that specializes in renting surfboards. She is considering three possible locations (A, B, and C), all of which seem feasible. For the first year of operation, the manager has projected that, under ideal conditions, her company would earn $90,000 in Location A, $75,000 in Location B, and $60,000 in Location C. After studying historical weather patterns, however, she has determined that there is only a 20 percent chance—or a .2 probability—of ideal conditions occurring during the first year of operation in Location A. Locations B and C have a .4 and a .8 probability, respectively, for ideal conditions during the first year of operations. Expected values for each of these locations are as follows: Location A—$18,000; Location B—$30,000; Location C—$48,000. Figure 8.5 shows the situation this decision maker faces. According to her probability analysis, she should open a store in Location C, the alternative with the highest expected value.

FIGURE 8.5
Expected values from locating surfboard rental store in each of three possible locations

Alternative (locations)	Potential income	Probability of income	Expected value of alternatives
A	$90,000	.2	$18,000
B	75,000	.4	30,000
C	60,000	.8	48,000

I	x	P	=	EV

VIDEONET EXERCISE

Decision Making at Insomnia Cookies

VIDEO HIGHLIGHTS

Insomnia Cookies recently decided that their business model would be composed of 50 percent retail sales and 50 percent delivery sales in any given geography. Previously, the retail component was not a given. The COO explains the thinking behind this decision and talks about how Insomnia Cookies approaches the decision-making process as it relates to new opening stores/operations in new locations/geographies. The CEO and director of marketing also chime in.

Discussion Questions

1. Who makes the decisions at Insomnia Cookies? Is this effective?
2. What is the most likely decision-making condition when Insomnia Cookies is trying to determine whether to enter a new market? Explain.
3. Which group decision process best describes the decision-making method at Insomnia Cookies?

Internet Activity

Go to Insomnia Cookies' home page at www.insomnia-cookies.com. How many locations are currently under operation? How will the decision-making process change as this organization continues to grow?

9 Strategic Planning

OBJECTIVES

TO HELP BUILD MY STRATEGIC PLANNING SKILL, WHEN STUDYING THIS CHAPTER, I WILL ATTEMPT TO ACQUIRE:

1. Definitions of both *strategic planning* and *strategy*

2. An understanding of the strategic management process

3. A knowledge of the impact of environmental analysis on strategy formulation

4. Insights into how to use critical question analysis

and SWOT analysis to formulate strategy

5. An understanding of how to use business portfolio analysis and industry analysis to formulate strategy

6. Insights into what tactical planning is and how strategic and tactical planning should be coordinated

TARGET SKILL strategic planning skill: the ability to engage in long-range planning that focuses on the organization as a whole

CHALLENGE CASE

BARNES & NOBLE CHANGES STRATEGY

Barnes & Noble, Inc., owns and operates approximately 800 retail bookstores, making it the largest book retailer in the world. In the book retailing business, bookstores such as Barnes & Noble purchases books from book publishers and then sells these books to individual consumers. Despite Barnes & Noble's impressive presence, the company's chairperson, Leonard Riggio, understands that the company faces tremendous competitive pressures.

Over the past several years, traditional book retailers have faced competition from new rivals. For example, Barnes & Noble faces new competitors from Internet retailers such as Amazon.com and Half.com. Recent studies estimate that approximately 10 percent of all books are sold online, and some suggest that this percentage will only grow in the future, as these online competitors have recently introduced lower-priced shipping offers to consumers. In addition to online competitors, Barnes & Noble faces competition from discount retailers such as Carrefour and Wal-Mart, and price clubs such as METRO Cash & Carry and Costco. In fact, today consumers purchase more books from non-bookstore (i.e., Wal-Mart, Target, etc.) retail outlets than from bookstores such as Barnes & Noble.

To counter these new competitors, Barnes & Noble has decided to enter the book publishing industry. Specifically, the company has decided to publish and sell in its stores copies of classic books. According to Riggio,

As part of its strategic plan, Barnes & Noble decided to tackle the competition by becoming a book publisher in its own right and now produces a line of well-known classics.

Barnes & Noble is following a retail strategy that grocery stores have adopted for years. Riggio hopes to sell copies of Barnes & Noble's new "store brand" books for less while boosting the company's profits. However, the strategy is not without risks. For example, such a strategy is likely to upset other book publishers. This move will essentially turn Barnes & Noble into a competitor of traditional book publishers. At the same time, these traditional book publishers are Barnes & Noble's suppliers.

In addition, Barnes & Noble has instituted the Barnes & Noble Member Program, which the company hopes will build customer loyalty. This program, which costs consumers $25 annually to join, allows program members to save as much as 40 percent on some purchases. Although this program has helped Barnes & Noble to increase sales, the steep discounts have damaged the firm's profits. Nonetheless, Riggio sees the loyalty program as a way to lock in the company's best customers.

As competition in the book industry increases, Riggio will need to monitor continuously the strategy of Barnes & Noble. In particular, he will need to review the mechanisms needed to maintain and increase buyer loyalty. Even though he understands that strategies such as loyalty programs could possibly improve Barnes & Noble's competitive position, the recent decrease in firm profits demonstrates the difficulties associated with implementing such a strategy.[1]

"EXPLORE YOUR OWN MANAGEMENT SKILLS BY TAKING THE QUIZ ON THE NEXT PAGE"

Before studying this chapter, respond to the following questions regarding the type of advice that you would give to Barnes & Noble's Leonard Riggio, referenced in the Challenge Case. Then address the concerning planning challenges that he presently faces within the company. You are not expected to be a strategic planning expert at this point. Answering the questions now can help you focus on important points when you study the chapter. Also, answering the questions again after you study the chapter will give you an idea of how much you have learned.

Record your answers here or online at MyManagement Lab.com. Completing the questions at MyManagement Lab.com will allow you to get feedback about your answers automatically. If you answer the questions in the book, look up answers in the Exploring Your Management Skill section at the end of the book.

FOR EACH STATEMENT CIRCLE:

- "Y" if you would give the advice to Leonard Riggio.
- "N" if you would NOT give the advice to Leonard Riggio.
- "NI" if you have no idea whether you would give the advice to Leonard Riggio.

Mr. Riggio, in meeting your strategic planning challenges at Barnes & Noble, you should . . .

	Before Study	After Study

1. ensure that Barnes & Noble's top executives engage in the strategic planning process once per year.

   Y, N, NI

2. implement Barnes and Noble's strategy prior to establishing the firm's organizational direction.

   Y, N, NI

3. make sure that strategic controls are in place to assess the strategic management process.

   Y, N, NI

4. focus primarily on the economic component when analyzing Barnes & Noble's general environment.

   Y, N, NI

5. understand that Barnes & Noble's general environment will exert a larger influence on its performance than its industry environment.

   Y, N, NI

6. use Porter's Five Forces model to better understand the attractiveness of the book-selling industry.

   Y, N, NI

7. establish an effective mission statement to effectively guide the overall direction of Barnes & Noble.

   Y, N, NI

8. review the firm's mission statement when determining how to allocate resources such as capital and employees.

   Y, N, NI

9. allocate resources equally among Barnes & Noble's different strategic business units (SBUs).

   Y, N, NI

10. use resources generated by Barnes & Noble's dogs to support and further develop the company's cash cows.

    Y, N, NI

11. consult both the BCG Growth-Share Matrix and the GE Multifactor Portfolio Matrix when evaluating the performance of Barnes & Noble's SBUs.

    Y, N, NI

12. understand that differentiation strategies lead to better firm performance than cost leadership strategies.

    Y, N, NI

13. consider divestitures when examining Barnes & Noble's underperforming divisions.

    Y, N, NI

14. oversee Barnes & Noble's tactical planning and delegate strategic planning to lower-level employees.

    Y, N, NI

15. understand that strategic planning is long term, and tactical planning is more focused on the short term.

    Y, N, NI

THE STRATEGIC PLANNING CHALLENGE

The Challenge Case highlights the new competitive course taken by Barnes & Noble. Developing a new course of this sort is actually part of Barnes & Noble's strategic planning process. The material in this chapter explains how developing a competitive strategy fits into strategic planning and discusses the strategic planning process as a whole. Major topics included in this chapter are (1) strategic planning, (2) tactical planning, (3) comparing and coordinating strategic and tactical planning, and (4) planning and levels of management.

STRATEGIC PLANNING

If managers are to be successful strategic planners, they must understand the fundamentals of strategic planning and how to formulate strategic plans.

Fundamentals of Strategic Planning

This section presents the basic principles of strategic planning. In doing so, it discusses definitions of both *strategic planning* and *strategy* in detail.

Defining Strategic Planning **Strategic planning** is long-range planning that focuses on the organization as a whole.[2] In doing strategic planning, managers consider the organization as a total unit and ask themselves what must be done in the long term to attain organizational goals.[3] *Long range* is usually defined as a period of time extending about three to five years into the future. Hence, in strategic planning, managers try to determine what their organization should do to be successful three to five years from now. The most successful managers tend to be those who are capable of encouraging innovative strategic thinking within their organization.[4]

Managers may have a problem trying to decide exactly how far into the future they should extend their strategic planning. As a general rule, they should follow the **commitment principle,** which states that managers should commit funds for planning only if they can anticipate, in the foreseeable future, a return on planning expenses as a result of long-range planning analysis. Realistically, planning costs are an investment and therefore should not be incurred unless a reasonable return on that investment is anticipated.

Defining Strategy **Strategy** is defined as a broad and general plan developed to reach long-term objectives. Organizational strategy can, and generally does, focus on many different organizational areas, such as marketing, finance, production, research and development, and public relations. It gives broad direction to the organization.[5]

Strategy is actually the end result of strategic planning. Although larger organizations tend to be more precise in developing organizational strategy than smaller organizations are, every organization should have a strategy of some sort.[6] For a strategy to be worthwhile, though, it must be consistent with organizational objectives, which, in turn, must be consistent with organizational purpose. Table 9.1 illustrates this relationship between organizational

TABLE 9.1	Examples of Organizational Objectives and Related Strategies for Three Organizations in Different Business Areas		
Company	**Type of Business**	**Sample Organizational Objectives**	**Strategy to Accomplish Objectives**
Ford Motor Company	Automobile manufacturing	1. Regain market share recently lost to Toyota	1. Resize and downsize present models
		2. Regain quality reputation that was damaged because of Pinto gas tank explosions	2. Continue to produce subintermediate, standard, and luxury cars
			3. Emphasize use of programmed combustion engines instead of diesel engines
Quick	Fast food	1. Increase productivity	1. Increase people efficiency
			2. Increase machine efficiency
CP Railroad	Transportation	1. Continue company growth	1. Modernize
		2. Continue company profits	2. Develop valuable real estate holdings
			3. Complete an appropriate railroad merger

objectives and strategy by presenting sample organizational objectives and strategies for three well-known business organizations.

Strategic Management

Strategic management is the process of ensuring that an organization possesses and benefits from the use of an appropriate organizational strategy. In this definition, an appropriate strategy is one best suited to the needs of an organization at a particular time.

The strategic management process is generally thought to consist of five sequential and continuing steps:[7]

1. Environmental analysis
2. Establishment of an organizational direction
3. Strategy formulation
4. Strategy implementation
5. Strategic control

The relationships among these steps are illustrated in Figure 9.1.

Environmental Analysis The first step of the strategic management process is environmental analysis. Chapter 2 presented organizations as open management systems that are continually interacting with their environments. In essence, an organization can be successful only if it is appropriately matched to its environment. **Environmental analysis** is the study of the organizational environment to pinpoint environmental factors that can significantly influence organizational operations. Managers commonly perform environmental analyses to help them understand what is happening both inside and outside their organizations and to increase the probability that the organizational strategies they develop will appropriately reflect the organizational environment.

In order to perform an environmental analysis efficiently and effectively, a manager must thoroughly understand how organizational environments are structured. For purposes of environmental analysis, the environment of an organization is generally divided into three distinct levels: general environment, operating environment, and internal environment.[8] Figure 9.2 illustrates the positions of these levels relative to one another and to the organization; it also shows the important components of each level. Managers must be well aware of these three environmental levels, understand how each level affects organizational performance, and then formulate organizational strategies in response to this understanding.

THE GENERAL ENVIRONMENT The level of an organization's external environment that contains components having broad long-term implications for managing the organization is the **general environment.** The components normally considered part of the general environment are economic, social, political, legal, and technological.

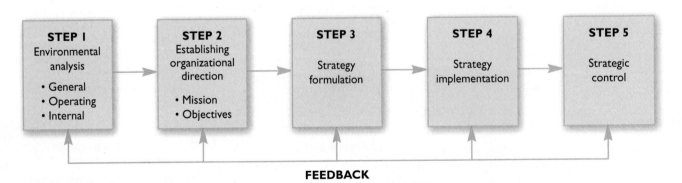

FIGURE 9.1 Steps of the strategic management process

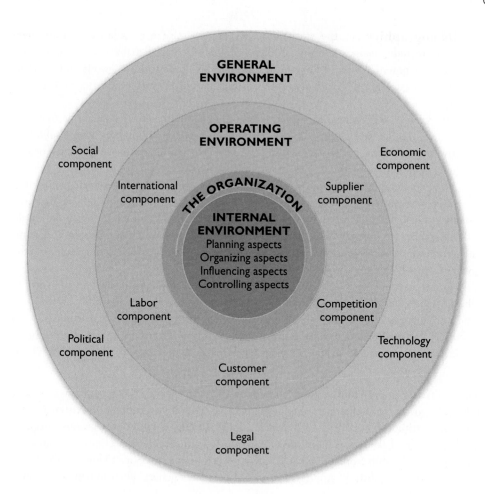

FIGURE 9.2
The organization, the levels of its environment, and the components of those levels

The economic component The economic component is that part of the general environment that indicates how resources are being distributed and used within the environment. This component is based on **economics,** the science that focuses on understanding how people of a particular community or nation produce, distribute, and use various goods and services. Important issues to be considered in an economic analysis of an environment are generally the wages paid to labor, inflation, the taxes paid by labor and businesses, the cost of materials used in the production process, and the prices at which produced goods and services are sold to customers.

These economic issues can significantly influence the environment in which a company operates, and the ease or difficulty the organization experiences in attempting to reach its objectives. For example, it should be somewhat easier for an organization to sell its products at higher prices if potential consumers in the environment are earning relatively high wages and paying relatively low taxes than if these same potential customers are earning relatively low wages and have significantly fewer after-tax money to spend.

Organizational strategy should reflect the economic issues in the organization's environment. To build on the preceding example, if the total amount of after-tax income that potential customers earn has significantly declined, an appropriate organizational strategy might be to lower the price of goods or services to make them more affordable. Such a strategy should be evaluated carefully, however, because it could have a serious impact on organizational profits.

The social component The social component is part of the general environment that describes the characteristics of the society in which the organization exists. Two important features of a society commonly studied during environmental analysis are demographics and social values.[9]

Consumer tastes and preferences are among the factors that firms consider in their environmental analysis. For instance, will this fragrance from Singapore appeal to Western customers? Its manufacturer will try to answer that question in planning its export strategy.

Demographics are the statistical characteristics of a population. These characteristics include changes in numbers of people and income distribution among various population segments. Such changes can influence the reception of goods and services within the organization's environment and thus should be reflected in organizational strategy.

For example, the demand for retirement housing would probably increase dramatically if both the number and the income of retirees in a particular market area doubled.[10] Effective organizational strategy would include a mechanism for dealing with such a probable increase in demand within the organization's environment.

An understanding of demographics is also helpful for developing a strategy aimed at recruiting new employees to fill certain positions within an organization. Knowing that only a small number of people have a certain type of educational background, for example, would tell an organization that it should compete more intensely to attract these people. To formulate a recruitment strategy, managers need a clear understanding of the demographics of the groups from which employees eventually will be hired.

Social values are the relative degrees of worth that society places on the ways in which it exists and functions. Over time, social values can change dramatically, causing significant changes in how people live. These changes alter the organizational environment and, as a result, have an impact on organizational strategy. It is important for managers to remember that although changes in the values of a particular society may come either slowly or quickly, they are inevitable.

The political component The political component is that part of the general environment related to government affairs. Examples include the type of government in existence, government's attitude toward various industries, lobbying efforts by interest groups, progress on the passage of laws, and political party platforms and candidates. The reunification of Germany and the shift from a Marxist-Socialist government in the Soviet Union in the 1980s illustrate how the political component of an organization's general environment can change at the international level.

The legal component The legal component is that part of the general environment that contains passed legislation. This component comprises the rules or laws that society's members must follow. Some examples of legislation specifically aimed at the operation of organizations are clean air regulations, which focuses on minimizing air pollution, occupational safety regulations, and product-safety regulations. Over time, new laws are passed and some old ones are amended or eliminated.

The technology component The technology component is that part of the general environment that includes new approaches to producing goods and services. These approaches can be new procedures as well as new equipment. The trend toward exploiting robots to improve productivity is an example of the technology component. The increasing use of robots in the next decade should vastly improve the efficiency of many industries.

The international component The international component is the operating environment segment that is composed of all the factors relating to the international implications of organizational operations. Although not all organizations must deal with international issues, the number that have to do so is increasing dramatically and continually in the early twenty-first century. Significant factors in the international component include other countries' laws, culture, economics, and politics.[11] Important variables within each of these four categories are presented in Table 9.2.

THE INDUSTRY ENVIRONMENT The level of an organization's external environment that contains components normally having relatively specific and immediate implications for managing the organization is the **industry environment.** The **Five Forces Model**, perhaps the best-known tool for industry analysis, was developed by internationally acclaimed strategic management expert Michael E. Porter.[12] Essentially, Porter's model

TABLE 9.2   Important Aspects of the International Component of the Organization's Operating Environment

Legal Environment	Cultural Environment
Legal tradition	Customs, norms, values, beliefs
Effectiveness of legal system	Language
Treaties with foreign nations	Attitudes
Patent and trademark laws	Motivations
Laws affecting business firms	Social institutions
	Status symbols
Economic Environment	Religious beliefs
Level of economic development	
Population	**Political System**
Gross national product	Form of government
Per capita income	Political ideology
Literacy level	Stability of government
Social infrastructure	Strength of opposition parties and groups
Natural resources	Social unrest
Climate	Political strife and insurgency
Membership in regional economic blocs (EEC, LAFTA, etc.)	Government attitude toward foreign firms
	Foreign policy
Monetary and fiscal policies	
Nature of competition	
Currency convertibility	
Inflation	
Taxation system	
Interest rates	
Wage and salary levels	

outlines the primary forces that determine competitiveness within an industry and illustrates how those forces are related.

Porter's model is presented in Figure 9.3. According to the model, the attractiveness of an industry is determined by five alternative forces. First, the **threat of new entrants** refers to the ability of new firms to enter an industry; as the threat of new entrants increases, the attractiveness of an industry decreases. Second, **buyer power** refers to the power that customers have over the firms operating in an industry; as buyer power increases, the attractiveness of an industry decreases. Third, **supplier power** denotes the power that suppliers have over the firms operating in an industry. As supplier power increases, industry attractiveness decreases. Fourth, the **threat of substitute products** refers to the extent to which customers may use products or services from another industry instead of the focal industry. As the threat of substitutes increases, which implies that customers have more choices, the attractiveness of an industry decreases. Finally, **intensity of rivalry** refers to the intensity of competition among the organizations in an industry. As the intensity of rivalry increases, the attractiveness of an industry decreases.

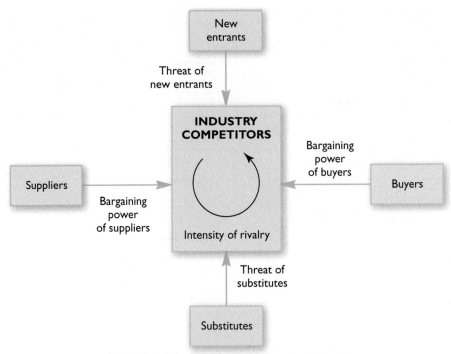

FIGURE 9.3
Porter's model of factors that determine competitiveness within an industry

DETERMINANTS OF SUBSTITUTION THREAT
Relative price performance of substitutes
Switching costs
Buyer propensity to substitute

class discussion highlight

MODERN RESEARCH AND PLANNING SKILL

The Influence of the Industry Environment[13]

Researchers in strategic management have devoted a great deal of attention to examining the influence of the industry environment on a firm's performance. Specifically, does the performance of a firm depend on the industry in which it operates? In other words, does a rising tide lift all boats?

To examine this question, Professor Misangyi and colleagues examined more than 1,500 U.S.–based corporations operating in approximately 75 industries over a 16-year time frame. Using a sophisticated statistical technique known as multilevel modeling, the authors were able to examine the influence of industry on firm profitability. According to their findings, what percentage of firm profitability is explained by industry membership? Explain how you arrived at your answer. Do you think that this percentage will remain constant across different countries?

THE INTERNAL ENVIRONMENT The level of an organization's environment that exists inside the organization and normally has immediate and specific implications for managing the organization is the **internal environment.** In broad terms, the internal environment includes marketing, finance, and accounting. From a more specific management viewpoint, it includes planning, organizing, influencing, and controlling within the organization.

Establishing Organizational Direction The second step of the strategic management process is establishing organizational direction. Through an interpretation of information gathered during environmental analysis, managers can determine the direction in which an organization should move. Two important ingredients of organizational direction are organizational mission and organizational objectives.

DETERMINING ORGANIZATIONAL MISSION The most common initial act in establishing organizational direction is determining an organizational mission. **Organizational mission** is the purpose for which—the reason why—an organization exists. In general, the firm's organizational mission reflects such information as what types of products or services it produces, who its customers tend to be, and what important values it holds. Organizational mission is a broad statement of organizational direction and is based on a thorough analysis of information generated through environmental analysis.[14]

DEVELOPING A MISSION STATEMENT A **mission statement** is a written document developed by management, normally based on input by managers as well as nonmanagers, that describes and explains what the mission of an organization actually is.[15] The mission is expressed in writing to ensure that all organization members will have easy access to it and thoroughly understand exactly what the organization is trying to accomplish.

THE IMPORTANCE OF ORGANIZATIONAL MISSION An organizational mission is important to an organization because it helps management increase the probability that the organization will be successful. There are several reasons why it does this. First, the existence of an organizational mission helps management focus human effort in a common direction. The mission makes explicit the major targets the organization is trying to reach and helps managers keep these targets in mind as they make decisions. Second, an organizational mission serves as a sound rationale for allocating resources. A properly developed mission statement gives managers general, but useful, guidelines about how resources should be used to best accomplish organizational purpose. Third, a mission statement helps management define broad but important job areas within an organization and therefore critical jobs that must be accomplished.[16]

THE RELATIONSHIP BETWEEN MISSION AND OBJECTIVES Organizational objectives were defined in Chapter 7 as the targets toward which the open management system is directed. Sound organizational objectives reflect and flow naturally from the purpose of the organization. The organization's purpose is expressed in its mission statement. As a result, useful organizational objectives must reflect and flow naturally from an organizational mission that, in turn, was designed to reflect and flow naturally from the results of an environmental analysis.[17]

Strategy Formulation: Tools After managers involved in the strategic management process have analyzed the environment and determined organizational direction through the development of a mission statement and organizational objectives, they are ready to formulate strategy. **Strategy formulation** is the process of determining appropriate courses of action for achieving organizational objectives and thereby accomplishing organizational purpose.

Managers formulate strategies that reflect environmental analysis, lead to fulfillment of organizational mission, and result in reaching organizational objectives. Special tools they can use to assist them in formulating strategies include the following:

1. Critical question analysis
2. SWOT analysis
3. Business portfolio analysis
4. Porter's Model for Industry Analysis

These four strategy development tools are related but distinct. Managers should use the tool or combination of tools that seems most appropriate for them and their organizations.

CRITICAL QUESTION ANALYSIS A synthesis of the ideas of several contemporary management writers suggests that formulating appropriate organizational strategy is a process of **critical question analysis**—answering the following four basic questions:[18]

- **What are the purposes and objectives of the organization?** The answer to this question will tell management where the organization should be going. As indicated earlier, appropriate strategy reflects both organizational purpose and objectives. By answering this question during the strategy formulation process, managers are likely to remember this important point and thereby minimize inconsistencies among the organization's purposes, objectives, and strategies.

- **Where is the organization presently going?** The answer to this question can tell managers whether the organization is achieving its goals and, if it is, whether the level of progress is satisfactory. Whereas the first question focuses on where the organization should be going, this one focuses on where the organization is actually going.

- **In what kind of environment does the organization now exist?** Both internal and external environments—factors inside and outside the organization—are covered in this question. For example, assume that a poorly trained middle-management team and a sudden influx of competitors in a market are factors in, respectively, the internal and external environments of an organization. Any strategy formulated, if it is to be appropriate, must deal with these factors.

- **What can be done to better achieve organizational objectives in the future?** It is the answer to this question that results in the strategy of the organization. The question should be answered, however, only *after* managers have had an adequate opportunity to reflect on the answers to the previous three questions. Managers cannot develop an appropriate organizational strategy unless they have a clear understanding of where the organization wants to go, where it is going, and in what environment it exists.

SWOT ANALYSIS **SWOT analysis** is a strategic development tool that matches internal organizational strengths and weaknesses with external opportunities and threats. (SWOT is an acronym for a firm's **S**trengths and **W**eaknesses and its environmental **O**pportunities and **T**hreats.) It is important to note that when using SWOT analysis, strengths and weaknesses refer to the manager's firm, and opportunities and threats refer to the firm's external environment. SWOT analysis is based on the assumption that if managers carefully review such strengths, weaknesses, opportunities, and threats, a useful strategy for ensuring organizational success will become evident to them.[19]

Because it must be set at the highest level of the firm, the company's direction is the responsibility of the CEO. Xerox CEO Anne Mulcahy is shown here speaking in Washington, D.C. She has overseen the company's successful return to profitability by shifting its focus from being a photocopier company to being a supplier of document-management tools and services.

class discussion highlight

STRATEGIC PLANNING SKILL AND YOUR CAREER

SWOT analysis represents an important tool for your strategic planning skill. Using SWOT analysis, top executives can better understand the strengths and weaknesses of their organization as well as the opportunities and threats in the external environment. Suppose that you are interviewing for a position in an organization. How might SWOT analysis help you prepare for an interview? Now suppose that you have just started working at an organization. How might SWOT analysis help you better understand your position and role in the organization?

BUSINESS PORTFOLIO ANALYSIS Business portfolio analysis is another strategy development tool that has gained wide acceptance. **Business portfolio analysis** is an organizational strategy formulation technique that is based on the philosophy that organizations should develop strategy much as they handle investment portfolios. Just as sound financial investments should be supported and unsound ones discarded, sound organizational activities should be emphasized and unsound ones deemphasized. Two business portfolio tools are the BCG Growth-Share Matrix and the GE Multifactor Portfolio Matrix.

The BCG Growth-Share Matrix The Boston Consulting Group (BCG), a leading manufacturing consulting firm, developed and popularized a portfolio analysis tool that helps managers develop organizational strategy based on market share of businesses and the growth of markets in which businesses exist.

The first step in using the BCG Growth-Share Matrix is identifying the organization's strategic business units (SBUs). A **strategic business unit** is a significant organization segment that is analyzed to develop organizational strategy aimed at generating future business or revenue. Exactly what constitutes an SBU varies from organization to organization. In larger organizations, an SBU could be a company division, a single product, or a complete product line. In smaller organizations, it might be the entire company. Although SBUs vary drastically in form, each has the following four characteristics:[20]

1. It is a single business or collection of related businesses.
2. It has its own competitors.
3. It has a manager who is accountable for its operation.
4. It is an area that can be independently planned for within the organization.

After SBUs have been identified for a particular organization, the next step in using the BCG Matrix is to categorize each SBU within one of the following four matrix quadrants (see Figure 9.4):

*   **Stars**—SBUs that are "stars" have a high share of a high-growth market and typically need large amounts of cash to support their rapid and significant growth. Stars also generate large amounts of cash for the organization and are usually segments in which management can make additional investments and earn attractive returns.

*   **Cash Cows**—SBUs that are cash cows have a large share of a market that is growing only slightly. Naturally, these SBUs provide the organization with large amounts of cash, but because their market is not growing significantly, the cash is generally used

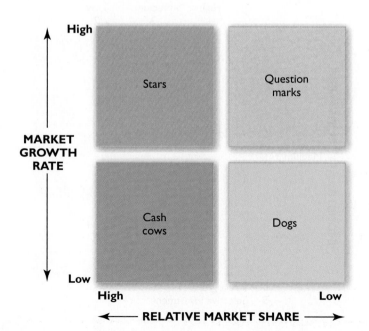

FIGURE 9.4
The BCG Growth-Share Matrix

to meet the financial demands of the organization in other areas, such as the expansion of a star SBU.

- **Question Marks**—SBUs that are question marks have a small share of a high-growth market. They are dubbed "question marks" because it is uncertain whether management should invest more cash in them to gain a larger share of the market or deemphasize or eliminate them. Management will choose the first option when it believes it can turn the question mark into a star, and the second when it thinks further investment would be fruitless.

- **Dogs**—SBUs that are dogs have a relatively small share of a low-growth market. They may barely support themselves; in some cases, they actually drain off cash resources generated by other SBUs. Examples of dogs are SBUs that produce typewriters or cash registers.

Companies such as Royal Dutch Shell and Westinghouse have successfully used the BCG Matrix in their strategic management processes. This technique, however, has some potential pitfalls. For one thing, the matrix does not consider such factors as (1) various types of risk associated with product development, (2) threats that inflation and other economic conditions can create in the future, and (3) social, political, and ecological pressures. These pitfalls may be the reason for recent research results indicating that the BCG Matrix does not always help managers make better strategic decisions.[21] Managers must remember to weigh such factors carefully when designing organizational strategy based on the BCG Matrix.

The GE Multifactor Portfolio Matrix With the help of McKinsey and Company, a leading consulting firm, the General Electric Company (GE) developed another popular portfolio analysis tool. Called the GE Multifactor Portfolio Matrix, this tool helps managers develop organizational strategy that is based primarily on market attractiveness and business strengths. The GE Multifactor Portfolio Matrix was deliberately designed to be more complete than the BCG Growth-Share Matrix.

Its basic use is illustrated in Figure 9.5. Each of the organization's businesses or SBUs is plotted on a matrix in two dimensions: industry attractiveness and business strength. Each of these two dimensions is actually a composite of a variety of factors that each firm must

FIGURE 9.5
GE's Multifactor Portfolio Matrix

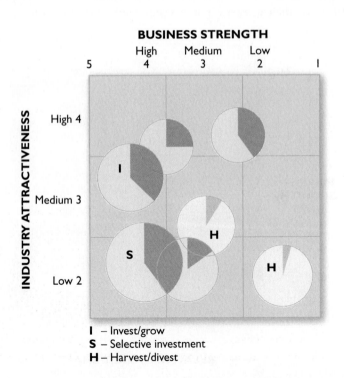

I – Invest/grow
S – Selective investment
H – Harvest/divest

determine for itself, given its own unique situation. As examples, industry attractiveness might be determined by such factors as the number of competitors in an industry, the rate of industry growth, and the weakness of competitors within an industry; while business strengths might be determined by such factors as a company's financially solid position, its good bargaining position over suppliers, and its high level of technology use.

Several circles appear on Figure 9.5, each representing a company line of business or SBU. Circle size indicates the relative market size for each line of business. The shaded portion of a circle represents the proportion of the total SBU market that a company has captured.

Specific strategies for a company are implied by where their businesses (represented by circles) fall on the matrix. Businesses falling in the cells that form a diagonal from lower left to upper right are medium-strength businesses that should be invested in only selectively. Businesses above and to the left of this diagonal are the strongest and the ones that the company should invest in and help to grow. Businesses in the cells below and to the right of the diagonal are low in overall strength and are serious candidates for divestiture.

Portfolio models are graphic frameworks for analyzing relationships among the businesses of an organization, and they can provide useful strategy recommendations. However, no such model yet devised gives managers a universally accepted approach for dealing with these issues. Portfolio models, then, should never be applied in a mechanistic fashion, and any conclusions they suggest must be carefully considered in light of sound managerial judgment and experience.

STRATEGY FORMULATION: TYPES Understanding the forces that determine competitiveness within an industry should help managers develop strategies that will make their companies more competitive within the industry. Porter has developed three generic strategies to illustrate the kind of strategies managers might develop to make their organizations more competitive.[22]

Differentiation **Differentiation,** the first of Porter's strategies, focuses on making an organization more competitive by developing a product or products that customers perceive as being different from products offered by competitors. Differentiation includes uniqueness in such areas as product quality, design, and level of after-sales service. Examples of products that customers commonly purchase because they perceive them as being different are Nike's Air Jordan shoes (because of their high-technology "air" construction) and Honda automobiles (because of their high reliability).

Cost leadership **Cost leadership** is a strategy that focuses on making an organization more competitive by producing products more cheaply than competitors can. According to the logic behind this strategy, by producing products more cheaply than its competitors do, an organization will be able to offer products to customers at lower prices than competitors can, and thereby increase its market share. Examples of tactics managers might use to gain cost leadership are obtaining lower prices for product parts purchased from suppliers and using technology such as robots to increase organizational productivity.

Focus **Focus** is a strategy that emphasizes making an organization more competitive by targeting a particular customer. Magazine publishers commonly use a focus strategy in offering their products to specific customers. *Working Woman* and *Ebony* are examples of magazines that are aimed, respectively, at the target markets of employed women and African Americans.

SAMPLE ORGANIZATIONAL STRATEGIES Analyzing the organizational environment and applying one or more of the strategy tools—critical question analysis, SWOT analysis, business portfolio analysis, and Porter's model—will give managers a foundation on which to formulate an organizational strategy. The four common organizational strategies that evolve this way are

Wal-Mart has adopted a consistent and tough-to-beat low-price strategy, as these signs show.

growth, stability, retrenchment, and divestiture. The following discussion of these organizational strategies features business portfolio analysis as the tool used to arrive at the strategy, although the same strategies could result from critical question analysis, SWOT analysis, or Porter's model.

Growth **Growth** is a strategy adopted by management to increase the amount of business that an SBU is currently generating. The growth strategy is generally applied to star SBUs or question mark SBUs that have the potential to become stars. Management generally invests substantial amounts of money to implement this strategy and may even sacrifice short-term profit to build long-term gain.[23]

Managers can also pursue a growth strategy by purchasing an SBU from another organization. As **an example from the world of management, Black & Decker,** not satisfied with being an international power in power tools, purchased **General Electric's** small-appliance business. Through this purchase, Black & Decker hoped that the amount of business it did would grow significantly over the long term. Similarly, President Enterprises, the largest food company in Taiwan, recently bought the American Famous Amos brand of chocolate chip cookies. Despite a downturn in the U.S. cookie market, management at President saw the purchase as important for company growth because it gave the company a nationally recognized product line in the United States.[24]

Stability **Stability** is a strategy adopted by management to maintain or slightly improve the amount of business that an SBU is generating. This strategy is generally applied to cash cows, because these SBUs are already in an advantageous position. Management must be careful, however, that in its pursuit of stability it does not turn cash cows into dogs.

Retrenchment In this section, *retrench* is used in the military sense: to defend or fortify. Through **retrenchment** strategy, management attempts to strengthen or protect the amount of business an SBU is generating. This strategy is generally applied to cash cows or stars that are beginning to lose market share.

Douglas D. Danforth, the chief executive of **Westinghouse,** provides **an example from the world of management.** Danforth is convinced that retrenchment is an important strategy for his company. According to Danforth, bigger profits at Westinghouse depend not only on fast-growing new products but also on the revitalization of Westinghouse's traditional businesses of manufacturing motors and gears.[25]

Divestiture **Divestiture** is a strategy adopted to eliminate an SBU that is not generating a satisfactory amount of business and that has little hope of doing so in the near future. In essence, the organization sells or closes down the SBU in question. This strategy is usually applied to SBUs that are dogs or question marks that have failed to increase market share but still require significant amounts of cash.

Strategy Implementation   **Strategy implementation,** the fourth step of the
strategic management process, is putting formulated strategies into action.[26] Without successive implementation, valuable strategies developed by managers are virtually worthless.[27]

The successful implementation of strategy requires four basic skills:[28]

1. **Interacting skill** is the ability to manage people during implementation. Managers who are able to understand the fears and frustrations others feel during the implementation of a new strategy tend to be the best implementers. These managers empathize with organization members and bargain for the best way to put a strategy into action.
2. **Allocating skill** is the ability to provide the organizational resources necessary to implement a strategy. Successful implementers are talented at scheduling jobs, budgeting time and money, and allocating other resources that are critical for implementation.
3. **Monitoring skill** is the ability to use information to determine whether a problem has arisen that is blocking implementation. Good strategy implementers

set up feedback systems that continually tell them about the status of strategy implementation.

4. **Organizing skill** is the ability to create throughout the organization a network of people who can help solve implementation problems as they occur. Good implementers customize this network to include individuals who can handle the special types of problems anticipated in the implementation of a particular strategy.

Overall, then, the successful implementation of a strategy requires handling people appropriately, allocating resources necessary for implementation, monitoring implementation progress, and solving implementation problems as they occur. Perhaps the most important requirements are knowing which people can solve specific implementation problems and being able to involve them when those problems arise.

Strategic Control **Strategic control,** the last step of the strategic management process, consists of monitoring and evaluating the strategic management process as a whole to ensure that it is operating properly. Strategic control focuses on the activities involved in environmental analysis, organizational direction, strategy formulation, strategy implementation, and strategic control itself—checking that all steps of the strategic management process are appropriate, compatible, and functioning properly.[29] Strategic control is a special type of organizational control, a topic that is featured in Chapters 21 and 22.

TACTICAL PLANNING

Tactical planning is short-range planning that emphasizes the current operations of various parts of the organization. *Short range* is defined as a period of time extending about one year or less into the future. Managers use tactical planning to outline what the various parts of the organization must do for the organization to be successful at some point one year or less into the future.[30] Tactical plans are usually developed in the areas of production, marketing, personnel, finance, and plant facilities.

Comparing and Coordinating Strategic and Tactical Planning

In striving to implement successful planning systems within organizations, managers must remember several basic differences between strategic planning and tactical planning:

1. Because upper-level managers generally have a better understanding of the organization as a whole than lower-level managers do, and because lower-level managers generally have a better understanding of the day-to-day organizational operations than upper-level managers do, strategic plans are usually developed by upper-level management and tactical plans by lower-level management.
2. Because strategic planning emphasizes analyzing the future and tactical planning emphasizes analyzing the everyday functioning of the organization, facts on which to base strategic plans are usually more difficult to gather than are facts on which to base tactical plans.
3. Because strategic plans are based primarily on a prediction of the future and tactical plans on known circumstances that exist within the organization, strategic plans are generally less detailed than tactical plans.
4. Because strategic planning focuses on the long term and tactical planning on the short term, strategic plans cover a relatively long period of time whereas tactical plans cover a relatively short period of time.

These major differences between strategic and tactical planning are summarized in Table 9.3.

TABLE 9.3 Major Differences Between Strategic and Tactical Planning

Area of Difference	Strategic Planning	Tactical Planning
Individuals involved	Developed mainly by upper-level management	Developed mainly by lower-level management
Facts on which to base planning	Facts are relatively difficult to gather	Facts are relatively easy to gather
Amount of detail in plans	Plans contain relatively little detail	Plans contain substantial amounts of detail
Length of time plans cover	Plans cover long periods of time	Plans cover short periods of time

Despite their differences, tactical planning and strategic planning are integrally related. As Russell L. Ackoff states, "We can look at them separately, even discuss them separately, but we cannot separate them in fact."[31] In other words, managers need both tactical and strategic planning programs, and these programs must be closely related to be successful. Tactical planning should focus on what to do in the short term to help the organization achieve the long-term objectives determined by strategic planning.

PLANNING AND LEVELS OF MANAGEMENT

An organization's top management is primarily responsible for seeing that the planning function is carried out. Although all management levels are involved in the typical planning process, upper-level managers usually spend more time planning than lower-level managers do. Lower-level managers are highly involved in the everyday operations of the organization and therefore normally have less time to contribute to planning than top managers do. Middle-level managers usually spend more time planning than lower-level managers, but less time than upper-level managers. Figure 9.6 shows how planning time increases as a manager moves from lower-level to upper-level management. In small as well as large organizations, determining the amount and nature of the work that each manager should personally handle is extremely important.

The type of planning done also changes as a manager moves up in the organization. Typically, lower-level managers plan for the short term, middle-level managers for the somewhat longer term, and upper-level managers for the even longer term. The expertise of lower-level managers in everyday operations makes them the best planners for what can be done in the short term to reach organizational objectives—in other words, they are best equipped to do tactical planning. Upper-level managers usually have the best understanding of the whole organizational situation and are therefore better equipped to plan for the long term—or to develop strategic plans.[32]

FIGURE 9.6

Increase in planning time as manager moves from lower-level to upper-level management

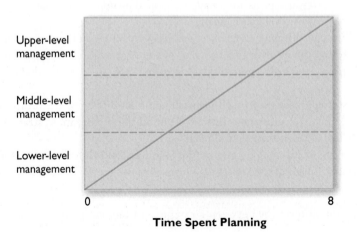

Time Spent Planning

{ CHALLENGE
CASE
SUMMARY

In developing a plan to compete in its industry, management at Barnes & Noble would normally begin by thinking strategically. That is, management should try to determine what can be done to ensure that Barnes & Noble will be successful at some point three to five years in the future. Developing a loyalty program, for example, that best suits the marketplace is part of this thinking. Barnes & Noble management must be careful, however, to spend funds on strategic planning only if they can anticipate a return on these expenses in the foreseeable future.

The end result of Barnes & Noble's overall strategic planning will be a strategy—a broad plan that outlines what must be done to reach long-range objectives and carry out the organizational purpose of the company. This strategy will focus on many organizational areas, one of which will be competing with other companies that develop similar book publishing strategies. Once the strategy has been formulated using the results of an environmental analysis, Barnes & Noble management must conscientiously carry out the remaining steps of the strategic management process: strategy implementation and strategic control.

As part of the strategy development process, Barnes & Noble management should spend time analyzing the environment in which the organization exists. Naturally, they should focus on Barnes & Noble's general, operating, and internal environments. Environmental factors that probably would be important to consider as it pursues strategic planning include the number of companies with which Barnes & Noble competes and knowing whether this number will be increasing or decreasing, strengths and weakness of its products when compared to competitive companies, the reasons that people shop at bookstores versus discount retailers, and the methods competitors such as Amazon.com are using to promote their products to their customers. Obtaining information about environmental issues such as these will increase the probability that any strategy developed for Barnes & Noble will be appropriate for the environment in which the company operates and that the company will be successful in the long term.

Based upon the previous information, after Barnes & Noble has performed its environmental analysis, it must determine the direction in which the organization will move regarding its competitive position. Issues such as

entering the book publishing business will naturally surface. Developing a mission statement with related objectives would be clear signals to all Barnes & Noble employees about the role of book publishing in the organization's future. Barnes & Noble management has several tools available to assist them in formulating strategy. If they are to be effective in this area, however, they must use the tools in conjunction with environmental analysis. One of the tools, critical question analysis, would require management to analyze the purpose of Barnes & Noble, the direction in which the company is going, the environment in which it exists, and how the goals might be better achieved.

SWOT analysis, another strategy development tool, would require management to generate information regarding the internal strengths and weaknesses of Barnes & Noble as well as the opportunities and threats that exist within the company's environment. Management probably would classify the technological innovations from online competitors such as Amazon.com as threats and significant factors to be considered in the strategy development process.

One approach to business portfolio analysis would suggest that Barnes & Noble management classify each major product line (SBU) within the company as a star, cash cow, question mark, or dog, depending on the growth rate of the market and the market share the Barnes & Noble product line possesses. Management could decide, for example, to consider the new book publishing business and each of its major businesses as a unit for SBU analysis and categorize them according to the four classifications. As a result of this categorization process, they could develop, perhaps for each different product line that they offer, growth, stability, retrenchment, or divestiture strategies. Barnes & Noble management should use whichever strategy development tools they think would be most useful. Their objective in this case, of course, is to develop an appropriate strategy for the development of Barnes & Noble's product lines.

To be successful at using the strategy that they develop, management at Barnes & Noble must apply its interacting skill, allocating skill, monitoring skill, and organizing skill. In addition, management must be able to improve the strategic management process when necessary.

In addition to developing strategic plans for its organization, Barnes & Noble management should consider tactical, or short-range, plans that would complement its strategic plans. Tactical plans for Barnes & Noble should emphasize what can be done within approximately the next year to reach the organization's three- to five-year objectives and to steal competition from its competitors. For example, Barnes & Noble could devote more resources to aggressive, short-range advertising campaigns, or increase sales by aggressively reducing the introductory prices of new books.

In addition, Barnes & Noble management must closely coordinate strategic and tactical planning within the company. They must keep in mind that strategic planning and tactical planning are different types of activities that may involve different people within the organization and result in plans with different degrees of detail. Yet they must also remember that these two types of plans are interrelated. While lower-level managers would be mostly responsible for developing tactical plans, upper-level managers would mainly spend time on long-range planning and developing strategic plans that reflect company goals.

MANAGEMENT SKILL ACTIVITIES

This section is specially designed to help you develop strategic planning skill. An individual's management skill is based upon an understanding of management concepts and the ability to apply those concepts in management situations. As a result, the following activities are designed both to heighten your understanding of strategic planning concepts and to help you gain facility in applying these concepts in various management situations.

UNDERSTANDING STRATEGIC PLANNING CONCEPTS

This section is comprised of activities that will sharpen your understanding of strategic planning concepts. Answer essay questions as completely as possible. Also, remember that many additional true/false and multiple choice questions appear online at MyManagementLab.com to help you further refine your understanding of concepts related to strategic planning.

Essay Questions

1. Describe the five steps involved with the strategic management process. In your opinion, which step is most important?

2. Compare and contrast the different strategy formulation tools. In your opinion, which tool is best suited for large organizations? Explain.

3. Describe how an organization might use the BCG Growth-Share Matrix to evaluate its different strategic business units. Now, explain how an organization might use the GE Multifactor Portfolio Matrix to evaluate its strategic business units.

4. Describe Porter's generic business strategies and provide an example of each strategy.

5. Describe Porter's Five Forces model. Why do organizations use Porter's Five Forces?

Developing Management Skill

Learning activities in this section are aimed at helping you to develop your strategic planning skill. Learning activities include Exploring Your Management Skill: Part 2, Experiential Exercise, Cases and a VideoNet exercise.

EXPLORING YOUR MANAGEMENT SKILL: PART 2

As you recall, you completed Exploring Your Management Skill before you started to study this chapter. Your responses gave you an idea of how much you initially knew about strategic planning and helped you to focus on important points as you studied the chapter. Answer the Exploring Your Management Skill questions again now (p. 226) and compare your score to the first time you took it. This comparison will give you an idea of how much you have learned from studying this chapter and pinpoint areas for further clarification before you start studying the next chapter. Record your answers within the text or online at MyManagementLab.com. Completing the survey at MyManagementLab.com will allow you to grade and compare your test scores automatically. If you complete the test in the book, look up answers in the Exploring Your Management Skill section at the end of the book.

YOUR MANAGEMENT SKILLS PORTFOLIO

Your Management Learning Portfolio is a collection of activities especially designed to demonstrate your management knowledge and skill. By completing these activities online at MyManagementLab.com, you will be able to print, complete with cover sheet, as many activities as you choose. Be sure to save your work. Taking your printed portfolio to an employment interview could be helpful in obtaining a job.

The portfolio activity for this chapter is Strategic Planning at the Washington Post. Study the information and complete the exercises that that follow.[33]

Strategic Planning at the Washington Post

The Washington Post Company is one of the most respected news and educational organizations in the world. Although known primarily for the *Washington Post* newspaper, the company is also involved in additional markets such as television, cable, education, and magazine publishing.

Despite the popularity and prestige associated with the *Washington Post* newspaper, the company's CEO, Donald Graham, is facing a difficult operating environment. Specifically, the emergence of the Internet and forms of digital news threaten the existence of the traditional newspaper industry. As a result, the Washington Post is generating lower levels of circulation; this decrease in circulation has also caused a dip in advertising. In sum, the profitability of the newspaper industry is decreasing.

Donald Graham has contacted you to help the company develop a new strategic plan. The following sections will help you to apply the strategic planning process to a real scenario.

1. Perform an environmental analysis for the Washington Post Company. Which segment of the environment is causing the company's problem(s)?

2. Based on this analysis, develop a mission statement for the company. Also develop three objectives that will help the company fulfill its mission.

3. Review Porter's generic strategies. Which one of these strategies would you recommend for the Washington Post Company? Explain.

4. Which of the four strategy implementation skills do you think will be most important for the company as it moves forward? Why?

EXPERIENTIAL EXERCISE

Directions. Read the following scenario and then perform the listed activities. Your instructor may want you to perform the activities as an individual or within groups. Follow all of your instructor's directions carefully.

Michael Dell, the CEO of Dell Inc., has contacted your group for consulting purposes. In particular, Dell is concerned about the current state of the personal computer industry. He would like your group to use Porter's Model for Industry Analysis to analyze the personal computer industry. What are the most important factors affecting each of the five forces in Porter's model? After performing this analysis, describe the most important threat. In addition, describe whether your group finds the personal computer industry attractive.

CASES

BARNES & NOBLE'S NEW STRATEGY: PUBLISHING BOOKS

"Barnes & Noble Changes Strategy" (p. 225) and its related Challenge Case Summary sections were written to help you better understand the management concepts contained in this chapter. Answer the following discussion questions about the Challenge Case to better understand how strategic planning concepts can be applied in a company such as Barnes & Noble.

1. For Barnes & Noble's management, is adding a book publishing unit a strategic management issue? Explain.

2. Give three factors in Barnes & Noble's internal environment that management should be assessing in determining the company's organizational direction. Why are these factors important?

3. Using the business portfolio matrix, categorize the new book publishing unit as a dog, question mark, star, or cash cow. From a strategic planning viewpoint, what do you recommend that Barnes & Noble management do as a result of this categorization? Why?

UNILEVER REVITALIZES ITS MISSION AND STRATEGY

Read the case and answer the questions that follow. Studying this case will help you better understand how strategic planning concepts can be applied in a company such as Unilever.

It's not every day that a corporate giant changes its mission statement. Then again, Unilever is not an everyday company. Formed from the 1930 merger of the British soap manufacturer Lever Brothers and the Dutch margarine firm Margarine Unie, Unilever still maintains headquarters in both countries. It operates in 150 nations and sells 150 million items every day, ranging from Dove soaps and Calvin Klein perfumes to Slim-Fast diet foods and Ben & Jerry's ice cream. With $53 billion in annual revenues and 234,000 employees, Unilever's size, scope, and skills provide strength for ongoing competition with Procter & Gamble, Colgate-Palmolive, Danone, Reckitt Benckiser, Nestlé, and other major manufacturers of food, household, and personal care products.

Niall FitzGerald, Unilever's former chairperson, changed the mission as the company neared the end of its 2000–2005 "Path to Growth" strategy, which called for annual revenue growth of 5 to 6 percent and significant improvement in profit margins. When the strategy was first implemented, FitzGerald arranged the $24 billion acquisition of Bestfoods to bring in such blockbuster product lines as Hellmann's mayonnaise and Knorr soups. At the same time, he began the process of selling off 140 business units representing more than 1,000 brands (including Mentadent, Pond's, and Elizabeth Arden) so he could focus Unilever's organizational

resources on a core portfolio of 400 brands capable of maintaining lucrative, market-leading performance for the long term. As an example, he authorized higher advertising budgets for the top brands and larger investments to develop new fragrances and other high-margin products.

By the time FitzGerald was ready to retire in 2004, the strategy was showing some success. Where Unilever had just four $1 billion-a-year brands in 1999, it now had 12 such brands; moreover, its profit margins had doubled within the past four years. However, revenue growth was stalled well below the targeted 5–6 percent level and some brands were having difficulty coping with critical environmental elements. For instance, Slimfast's managers were slow to recognize the threat posed by growing consumer interest in low-carbohydrate diets. By the time they introduced products with lower carbohydrate content, Slimfast's sales had fallen 22 percent. Also, sales of Unilever's prestigious fragrance products, including Calvin Klein perfumes, were lower than expected due to weak economic conditions and fewer travelers passing through airports worldwide, where the fragrances enjoy good distribution.

To guide development of a new strategy for 2005–2010, FitzGerald decided to revamp the corporate mission statement. After analyzing important trends such as increased urbanization in many countries, the aging population, and increased consumer interest in healthy living, the Fitzgerald and Unilever's managers crafted a statement declaring that "Unilever's new mission is to add vitality to life. We meet everyday needs for nutrition, hygiene, and personal care with products that help people feel good, look good, and get more out of life." This broad statement helps managers and employees connect their work activities with the well-being of the customers and communities they serve. It also suggests how Unilever will differentiate itself from rivals within the pressured global marketplace.

Now FitzGerald's successor, Patrick Cescau, has taken over the process of implementing the "Unilever 2010" strategy. He's giving the corporate name more prominence by ensuring that it appears on all company products, communications, and promotional materials. Instead of publicly explaining the corporation's growth goals in detail, he's talking more generally about a range of assumptions for sales, profits, costs, and debt. He's continuing the former CEO's policy of benchmarking shareholder return against a peer group of 20 competitors to check its performance. On the competitive front, Cescau has to deal with Reckitt Benckiser's strength in product innovation, Procter & Gamble's marketing power, and Nestlé's brand-building abilities. And he must keep Unilever's brands at the top of their categories to retain prime shelf space in Wal-Mart and other big retail chains.

QUESTIONS

1. How effectively do you think Unilever's mission statement establishes the company's direction and important values? What changes, if any, would you recommend, and why?

2. Identify one or more of Unilever's strengths, weaknesses, opportunities, and threats. How might Cescau use the strengths to counteract the threats?

3. Where on the BCG Matrix would you place Unilever's 400 remaining brands? Where would you place any newly developed products being introduced? Explain.

VIDEONET EXERCISE

Student Advantage

VIDEO HIGHLIGHTS

Most teenagers are familiar with the student advantage discount card, saving them up to 50 percent on everyday purchases on and off campus, including transportation on US Airways, Amtrak, and Greyhound. Keeping pace with the growing consumer base among high school and college students, Student Advantage, Inc., has successfully implemented an aggressive growth strategy. Working with hundreds of colleges, universities, campus organizations, and more than 15,000 merchant locations, the company reaches customers offline through the Student Advantage Membership and online through its Web site. Eleven acquisitions in its 10 years of existence have taught this company and its young CEO, Ray Sozzi, that communication is the key to successful organizational change.

Discussion Questions

1. Use the SWOT tool to analyze Student Advantage.
2. Using the BCG Growth Matrix, how would you classify Student Advantage? Why?
3. Analyze the Student Advantage industry using Porter's Model for Industry Analysis.

Internet Activity

Go to the Student Advantage Web site at www.studentadvantage.com. Browse the page, and become familiar with the product and services offered by this company. Based on information from both the Web page and video clip, write a mission statement for Student Advantage. Be prepared to defend your statement. Has the mission at Student Advantage changed as it has grown?

10 Plans and Planning Tools

OBJECTIVES

TO HELP BUILD MY PLANNING TOOLS SKILL, WHEN STUDYING THIS CHAPTER, I WILL ATTEMPT TO ACQUIRE:

1. A complete definition of a plan

2. Insights regarding various dimensions of plans

3. An understanding of various types of plans

4. Insights into why plans fail

5. A definition of forecasting

6. An ability to see the advantages and disadvantages of various methods of sales forecasting

7. A definition of scheduling

8. An understanding of Gantt charts and PERT

TARGET SKILL planning tools skill: the ability to employ the qualitative and quantitative techniques necessary to help develop plans

CHALLENGE CASE

FORD PLANS A U-TURN

In addition to producing cars and trucks, Ford Motor Company and its subsidiaries conduct business in other areas such as manufacturing automotive components, financing vehicle purchases for customers, and renting vehicles. The company's vehicle brand names include Ford, Mercury, Lincoln, Volvo, and Jaguar.

In recent years Ford has struggled to compete in the automobile industry. In particular, foreign competitors such as Toyota and Honda have produced more reliable automobiles that consumers have favored; this consumer preference has helped these companies to steal market share from Ford. Increased competition has damaged Ford's ability to generate sales and profits. In fact, in one recent year Ford *lost* $12.7 billion.

To increase Ford's profitability, Alan Mulally was hired as the company's new CEO. Prior to joining Ford, Mulally was the top executive for Boeing's commercial airline division. When asked about the challenges he faces at Ford, Mulally quipped that automobiles contain approximately 10,000 moving parts. Airplanes, on the other hand, contain about 2 million

Under the leadership of new CEO Alan Mulally, Ford plans to reverse its recent decline.

moving parts—and airplanes have to stay in the air. He used this comparison to demonstrate his ability to handle the challenges at Ford.

Mulally has implemented a new plan to help reverse Ford's recent decline. One component of this plan involves introducing a small automobile that can be sold around the globe. Currently, the company has different models for different countries. Another component of the plan involves selling more automobiles in China. In fact, one recent forecast suggests that Ford will soon increase sales in China by more than 30 percent. A final element of the plan involves potentially selling its Premier Automotive Group, the division that houses its luxury brands (i.e., Jaguar, Volvo, and Land Rover). Although five years ago management projected that this division would account for a large portion of Ford's profits, the division has instead led to larger losses.

It is clear that Alan Mulally faces a tough task in turning around Ford's fortunes. Ford's success will in large part depend on Mulally's new plan and the ability of Ford's employees to execute this new plan.[1]

"EXPLORE YOUR OWN MANAGEMENT SKILLS BY TAKING THE QUIZ ON THE NEXT PAGE"

Before studying this chapter, respond to the following questions regarding the type of advice that you would give to Ford's Alan Mulally referenced in the Challenge Case. Then address the concerning planning challenges that he presently faces within the company. You are not expected to be a planning tools expert at this point. Answering the questions now can help you focus on important points when you study the chapter. Also, answering the questions again after you study the chapter will give you an idea of how much you have learned.

Record your answers here or go to MyManagementLab. com. Recording your answers in MyManagementLab will allow you to get immediate results and see how your score compares to your classmates. If you answer the questions in the book, the answers are located in the Exploring Your Management Skill Appendix at the end of the book.

FOR EACH STATEMENT CIRCLE:

- "Y" if you would give the advice to Alan Mulally.
- "N" if you would NOT give the advice to Alan Mulally.
- "NI" if you have no idea whether you would give the advice to Alan Mulally.

Mr. Mulally, in meeting your planning tools challenges at Ford, you should . . .

	Before Study	After Study

1. understand that plans at Ford will vary in terms of repetitiveness, time, scope, and level.

   Y, N, NI

2. recognize that *policy*, *procedure*, and *rule* are different words that describe the same concept.

   Y, N, NI

3. communicate to Ford employees that large companies such as Ford only establish standing plans and avoid single-use plans.

   Y, N, NI

4. delegate responsibility for planning solely to the planning department.

   Y, N, NI

5. recognize that in addition to forming your own plans, it is important to operate by plans established by managers.

   Y, N, NI

6. communicate to employees that when forming site selection plans, "living conditions" is always the most important variable to consider.

   Y, N, NI

7. understand that Ford's human resource planning depends primarily upon three factors: employee turnover within Ford, the nature of the present workforce, and Ford's growth rate of the organization.

   Y, N, NI

8. require Ford employees to rely solely on the jury of executive opinion method for sales forecasts.

   Y, N, NI

9. realize that of all of the different forecasting methods, forecasters on average are most familiar with the moving average method.

   Y, N, NI

10. understand that qualitative and quantitative forecasts will always produce the same results in the automobile industry.

    Y, N, NI

11. require Ford employees to favor quantitative rather than qualitative forecasting methods when forecasting future automobile sales.

    Y, N, NI

12. realize that scheduling is often more important than forecasting.

    Y, N, NI

13. communicate to Ford's employees that Gantt charts have no real weaknesses.

    Y, N, NI

14. encourage Ford's employees to use both Gantt Charts and PERT to prepare long-term forecasts of automobile sales.

    Y, N, NI

15. stress the importance of both activities and events when using PERT for scheduling purposes.

    Y, N, NI

THE CHALLENGE OF USING PLANNING TOOLS

The Challenge Case ends with the notion that management at Ford Motor Company has been planning to improve its performance. This chapter emphasizes several fundamental issues about plans that should be useful to managers such as those at Ford who are involved in such planning. This chapter describes what plans are and discusses several valuable tools that can be used in actually developing plans.

PLANS: A DEFINITION

A **plan** is a specific action proposed to help the organization achieve its objectives. A critical part of the management of any organization is developing logical plans and then taking the steps necessary to put the plans into action.[2] Regardless of how important experience-related intuition may be to managers, successful management actions and strategies typically are based on reason. Rational managers are crucial to the development of an organizational plan.

Dimensions of Plans

Kast and Rosenzweig identify a plan's four major dimensions as follows:[3]

1. Repetitiveness
2. Time
3. Scope
4. Level

Each dimension is an independent characteristic of a plan and should be considered during plan development.

Repetitiveness The **repetitiveness dimension** of a plan is the extent to which the plan is used over and over again. Some plans are specially designed for one situation that is relatively short term in nature. Plans of this sort are essentially nonrepetitive. Other plans, however, are designed to be used time after time for long-term recurring situations. These plans are basically repetitive in nature.

Time The **time dimension** of a plan is the length of time the plan covers. In Chapter 9, strategic planning was defined as long term in nature, while tactical planning was defined as short term. It follows, then, that strategic plans cover relatively long periods of time and tactical plans cover relatively short periods of time.

Scope The **scope dimension** of a plan is the portion of the total management system at which the plan is aimed. Some plans are designed to cover the entire open management system: the organizational environment, inputs, process, and outputs. Such a plan is often referred to as a *master plan*. Other plans are developed to cover only a portion of the management system. An example of the latter would be a plan that covers the recruitment of new workers—a portion of the organizational input segment of the management system. The greater the portion of the management system that a plan covers, the broader the plan's scope is said to be.

To manage its planned expansion abroad, such as this new store in Beijing, Carrefour Hypermarkets, the French supermarket giant, prepares a master plan that is both deep and broad.

Level The **level dimension** of a plan is the level of the organization at which the plan is aimed. Top-level plans are those designed for the organization's top management, whereas middle- and lower-level plans are designed for middle and lower management, respectively. Because all parts of the management system are interdependent, however, plans designed for any level of the organization have some effect on all other levels.

Figure 10.1 illustrates the four dimensions of an organizational plan. This figure indicates that when managers develop a plan, they should consider the degree to which it will be used over and over again, the period of time it will cover, the parts of the management system on which it focuses, and the organizational level at which it is aimed.

Types of Plans

With the repetitiveness dimension as a guide, organizational plans are usually divided into two types: standing and single-use. **Standing plans** are used over and over again because they focus on organizational situations that occur repeatedly. **Single-use plans** are used only once—or, at most, several times—because they focus on unique or rare situations

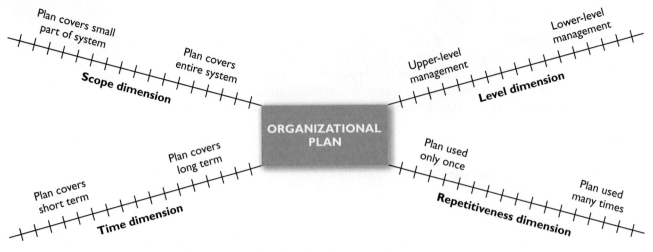

FIGURE 10.1 Four major dimensions to consider when developing a plan

within the organization. As Figure 10.2 illustrates, standing plans can be subdivided into policies, procedures, and rules and single-use plans into programs and budgets.

Standing Plans: Policies, Procedures, and Rules
A **policy** is a standing plan that furnishes broad guidelines for taking action consistent with reaching organizational objectives. For example, an organizational policy relating to personnel might be worded as follows: "Our organization will strive to recruit only the most talented employees." This policy statement is broad, giving managers only a general idea of what to do in the area of recruitment. The policy is intended to emphasize the extreme importance management attaches to hiring competent employees and to guide managers' actions accordingly.

As another example of an organizational policy, consider companies' responses to violence in the workplace, which the International Labour Organization (ILO) has said to be a worldwide problem. A sample policy could be: "Management strongly discourages any employee from bringing a weapon to work." This policy would encourage managers to deal forcefully and punitively with employees who bring weapons into the workplace for aggressive purposes.[4]

In **an example from the world of management, Wal-Mart** recently adopted a new policy regarding shoplifting.[5] According to the company's new policy, store managers are now directed to call the parents of shoplifters. Moreover, if parents do not appear quickly, managers are now directed to contact the police and prosecute first-time shoplifters as young as 16 years old.

FIGURE 10.2
Standing plans and single-use plans

STANDING PLAN PROGRAM

FIGURE 10.3
A successful standing plan program with mutually supportive policies, procedures, and rules

A **procedure** is a standing plan that outlines a series of related actions that must be taken to accomplish a particular task. In general, procedures outline more specific actions than policies do. Organizations usually have many different sets of procedures covering the various tasks to be accomplished. Managers must be careful to apply the appropriate organizational procedures for the situations they face and to apply them properly.[6]

A **rule** is a standing plan that designates specific required action. In essence, a rule indicates what an organization member should or should not do and allows no room for interpretation. An example of a rule some companies in parts of the world are now establishing is No Smoking. The concept of rules may become clearer if one thinks about the purpose and nature of rules in such games as Scrabble and Monopoly.

Although policies, procedures, and rules are all standing plans, they are different from one another and have different purposes within the organization. As Figure 10.3 illustrates, however, for the standing plans of an organization to be effective, policies, procedures, and rules must be consistent and mutually supportive.

class discussion highlight

MODERN RESEARCH AND PLANNING SKILL

Policies, Procedures, and Corporate Crime[7]

"White-collar" crime—crime committed by employees—is an important issue in management. When employees commit illegal acts, the company loses resources. How can companies reduce white-collar crime? Karen Schnatterly tried to answer this question by examining the extent to which company policies and procedures can help to reduce white-collar crime. According to her logic, clear policies and procedures help to communicate to employees the "rules of the game." In contrast, polices and procedures that are vague may encourage employees to engage in criminal activity.

To address this question, Professor Schnatterly examined documents available to the public—such as annual reports and proxy statements—and assessed whether these documents referred to the firm's policies and procedures. Documents that referred to such policies and procedures were given high scores, and documents that made no mention of these policies and procedures were given low scores. She then investigated the influence of these policies and procedures on corporate crimes.

Do you think she found a relationship between policies and procedures and corporate crime? If so, what type of association (i.e., positive or negative) would you expect between policies and procedure and corporate crime? Explain.

One-time events require multiple layers of single-use plans. The 2012 Summer Olympics, for instance, will be held in London. The Games will challenge the U.K. to prepare, adapt, and even build new athletic and housing facilities to accommodate hundreds of unique competitions, each with its own set of physical and environmental requirements, and all without disrupting the normal life and commerce of the city.

Single-Use Plans: Programs and Budgets A **program** is a single-use plan designed to carry out a special project within an organization. The project itself is not intended to remain in existence over the entire life of the organization. Rather, it exists to achieve some purpose that, if accomplished, will contribute to the organization's long-term success.

A common example is the management development program found in many organizations. This program exists to raise the skill levels of managers in one or more of the areas mentioned in Chapter 1: technical, conceptual, or human relations skills. Increasing managerial skills, however, is not an end in itself. The end or purpose of the program is to produce competent managers who are equipped to help the organization be successful over the long term. In fact, once managerial skills have been raised to a desired level, the management development program can be deemphasized. Activities on which modern management development programs commonly focus include understanding and using the computer as a management tool, handling international competition, and planning for a major labor shortage.[8]

A **budget** is a single-use financial plan that covers a specified length of time. It details how funds will be spent on labor, raw materials, capital goods, information systems, marketing, and so on, as well as how the funds will be obtained.[9] Although budgets are planning devices, they are also strategies for organizational control. They are discussed in more detail in Chapter 22.

Why Plans Fail

If managers know why plans fail, they can take steps to eliminate the factors that cause failure and thereby increase the probability that their plans will be successful. A study by K. A. Ringbakk determined that plans fail when:[10]

1. Corporate planning is not integrated into the total management system.
2. There is a lack of understanding of the different steps of the planning process.
3. Managers at different levels in the organization have not properly engaged in or contributed to planning activities.
4. Responsibility for planning is wrongly vested solely in the planning department.
5. Management expects that plans developed will be realized with little effort.
6. In starting formal planning, too much is attempted at once.
7. Management fails to operate by the plan.
8. Financial projections are confused with planning.
9. Inadequate inputs are used in planning.
10. Management fails to grasp the overall planning process.

Planning Areas: Input Planning

As discussed earlier, organizational inputs, process, outputs, and environment are major factors in determining how successful a management system will be. Naturally, a comprehensive organizational plan should focus on each of these factors. The following two sections cover planning in two areas normally associated with the input factor: plant facilities planning and human resource planning. Planning in these areas is called **input planning**—the development of proposed action that will furnish sufficient and appropriate organizational resources for reaching established organizational objectives.

Plant Facilities Planning **Plant facilities planning** involves determining the type of buildings and equipment an organization needs to reach its objectives. A major part of this determination is called **site selection**—deciding where a plant facility should be located. Table 10.1 lays out several major areas to be considered in plant site selection and gives sample questions that can be asked as these areas are being explored. The specifics of site selection will vary from organization to organization.[11]

TABLE 10.1	Major Areas of Consideration When Selecting a Plant Site and Sample Exploratory Questions to Be Asked
Major Areas of Consideration in Site Selection	**Sample Questions to Be Asked**
Profit	
Market location	Where are our customers in relation to the site?
Competition	What competitive situation exists at the site?
Operating costs	
Suppliers	Are materials available near the site at reasonable cost?
Utilities	What are utility rates at the site? Are utilities available in sufficient amounts?
Wages	What wage rates are paid by comparable organizations near the site?
Taxes	What are tax rates on income, sales, property, and so on for the site?
Investment costs	
Land/development	How expensive are land and construction at the site?
Others	
Transportation	Are airlines, railroads, highways, and so on accessible from the site?
Laws	What laws related to zoning, pollution, and so on will influence operations if the site is chosen?
Labor	Does an adequate labor supply exist around the site?
Unionization	What is the degree of unionization in the site area?
Living conditions	Are housing, schools, and so on around the site appropriate?
Community relations	Does the community support the organization's moving into the area?

One factor that significantly influences site selection is foreign location. Management in a foreign country planning to select a site must deal with such issues as differences among foreign governments in time taken to approve site purchases and political pressures that may slow down or prevent the purchase of a site. For example, Japanese investors who locate businesses abroad tend to select, among other things, areas that have low unionization rates, low employment rates, relatively impoverished populations, and the highest possible educational levels under those conditions. Japanese managers believe that these factors enhance the chances of success.[12]

In **an example from the world of management, Toyota** recently opened a new plant in the U.S. state of Texas, to build its popular Tundra pickup trucks.[13] That way, when a Toyota truck is manufactured and sold in the United States, the purchase is not consider an import; a massive amount of Toyota imports may upset U.S. lawmakers. In addition, manufacturing in the United States provides jobs to U.S. citizens, which also helps to satisfy U.S. lawmakers.

Many organizations use a weighting process to compare site differences among foreign countries. Basically, this process involves the following steps:

1. Deciding on a set of variables critical to obtaining an appropriate site
2. Assigning each of these variables a weight reflecting its relative importance
3. Ranking alternative sites according to how they reflect these different variables

TABLE 10.2 Results of Weighting Seven Site Variables for Six Countries

Criteria	Maximum Value Assigned	Sites					
		Japan	Chile	Jamaica	Australia	Mexico	France
Living conditions	100	70	40	45	50	60	60
Accessibility	75	55	35	20	60	70	70
Industrialization	60	40	50	55	35	35	30
Labor availability	35	30	10	10	30	35	35
Economics	35	15	15	15	15	25	25
Community capability and attitude	30	25	20	10	15	25	15
Effect on company reputation	35	25	20	10	15	25	15
Total	**370**	**260**	**190**	**165**	**220**	**275**	**250**

Table 10.2 shows the results of such a weighting process for seven site variables in six countries. In this table, "living conditions" are worth 100 points and are the most important variable; "effect on company reputation" is worth 35 points and is the least important variable. The six countries are given a number of points for each variable, depending on the importance of the variable and how well it is reflected within the country. The table shows that, using this particular set of weighted criteria, Japan, Mexico, and France are more desirable sites than Chile, Jamaica, and Australia.

Human Resource Planning Human resources are another area of concern to input planners. Organizational objectives cannot be attained without appropriate personnel. Future needs for human resources are influenced mainly by employee turnover, the nature of the present workforce, and the rate of growth of the organization.[14]

The following are representative of the kinds of questions personnel planners should try to answer:

1. What types of people does the organization need to reach its objectives?
2. How many of each type are needed?
3. What steps should the organization take to recruit and select such people?
4. Can present employees be further trained to fill future needed positions?
5. At what rate are employees being lost to other organizations?

Figure 10.4 shows the human resource planning process developed by Bruce Coleman. According to his model, **human resource planning** involves reflecting on organizational objectives to determine overall human resource needs; comparing these needs to the existing human resource inventory to determine net human resource needs; and, finally, seeking appropriate organization members to meet the net human resource needs.[15]

Ferenc Vissi, the head of human resources for **Raba,** a truck manufacturer in Hungary, provides **an example from the world of management.**[16] Specifically, Vissi explains the difficulties that his country's culture presents for human resource planning. According to Vissi, "The lack of labor mobility is a fact. It's part of the culture of the Hungarian population that they don't like to move." This lack of qualified labor presents a problem for the company, as human resource planners such as Vissi are forced to find foreign workers to work in the company's newest facilities.

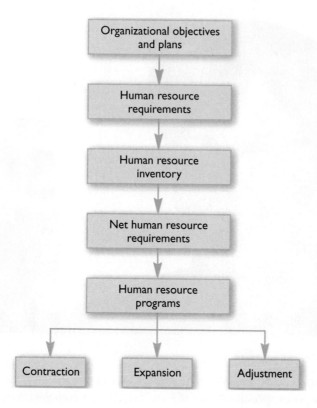

FIGURE 10.4
The human resource planning process

PLANNING TOOLS

Planning tools are techniques managers can use to help develop plans. The remainder of this chapter discusses forecasting and scheduling, two of the most important of these tools.

Forecasting

Forecasting is the process of predicting future environmental happenings that will influence the operation of the organization. Although sophisticated forecasting techniques have been developed only rather recently, the concept of forecasting can be traced at least as far back in the management literature as Fayol. The importance of forecasting lies in its ability to help managers understand the future makeup of the organizational environment, which, in turn, helps them formulate more effective plans.[17] Despite the importance of forecasting, a recent survey of manufacturers suggests that forecasting is an imprecise science.[18] According to this survey, on average, sales forecasts are off by approximately 20 percent. As such, managers continue to search for more accurate forecasting tools. In the following sections, we describe the forecasting process, and then we list a number of tools that managers might use to improve forecasts.

How Forecasting Works William C. House, in describing the Insect Control Services Company, developed an excellent illustration of how forecasting works. In general, Insect Control Services forecasts by attempting to do the following:[19]

1. Establish relationships between industry sales and national economic and social indicators.
2. Determine the impact government restrictions on the use of chemical pesticides will have on the growth of chemical, biological, and electromagnetic energy pest-control markets.
3. Evaluate sales growth potential, profitability, resources required, and risks involved in each of its market areas (commercial, industrial, institutional, governmental, and residential).
4. Evaluate the potential for expansion of marketing efforts in domestic geographical areas as well as in foreign countries.
5. Determine the likelihood of technological breakthroughs that would make existing product lines obsolete.

Forecasting is essential but never easy. Here, PepsiCo president and CEO Indra Nooyi addresses her first-ever press conference in India. Her position requires her to constantly make and revise predictions about the company's future, not only to assist in planning PepsiCo's strategy but also to inform the company's many stakeholders and the public about its position.

Types of Forecasts In addition to the general type of organizational forecasting done by Insect Control Services, specialized types of forecasting, such as economic, technological, social trends, and sales forecasting, are available. Although a complete organizational forecasting process should, and usually does, include all these types of forecasting, sales forecasting is considered the key organizational forecast. A *sales forecast* is a prediction of how high or low sales of the organization's products or services will be over the period of time under consideration. It is the key forecast for organizations because it serves as the fundamental guideline for planning. Only after the sales forecast has been completed can managers decide, for example, whether more salespeople should be hired, whether more money for plant expansion must be borrowed, or whether layoffs and cutbacks in certain areas are necessary. Managers must continually monitor forecasting methods to improve them and to reformulate plans based on inaccurate forecasts.[20]

Methods of Sales Forecasting Modern managers have several different methods available for forecasting sales. The two broad types of sales forecasting methods are qualitative and quantitative. In the following sections, we highlight popular qualitative (i.e., jury of executive opinion, salesforce estimation) and quantitative (i.e., moving average, regression, product stages) forecasting methods.

QUALITATIVE METHODS

Jury of executive opinion method The **jury of executive opinion method** of sales forecasting is straightforward. Appropriate managers within the organization assemble to discuss their opinions on what will happen to sales in the future. Because these discussion sessions usually revolve around hunches or experienced guesses, the resulting forecast is a blend of informed opinions.

A similar, more recently developed forecasting method, called the *Delphi method,* also gathers, evaluates, and summarizes expert opinions as the basis for a forecast, but the procedure is more formal than that for the jury of executive opinion method.[21] The basic Delphi method employs the following steps:

STEP 1 Various experts are asked to answer, independently and in writing, a series of questions about the future of sales or whatever other area is being forecasted.

STEP 2 A summary of all the answers is then prepared. No expert knows how any other expert answered the questions.

STEP 3   Copies of the summary are given to the individual experts with the request that they modify their original answers if they think it necessary.

STEP 4   Another summary is made of these modifications, and copies again are distributed to the experts. This time, however, expert opinions that deviate significantly from the norm must be justified in writing.

STEP 5   A third summary is made of the opinions and justifications, and copies are once again distributed to the experts. Justification in writing for *all* answers is now required.

STEP 6   The forecast is generated from all of the opinions and justifications that arise from step 5.

Salesforce estimation method The **salesforce estimation method** is a sales forecasting technique that predicts future sales by analyzing the opinions of salespeople as a group. Salespeople continually interact with customers, and from this interaction they usually develop a knack for predicting future sales. As with the jury of executive opinion method, the resulting forecast normally is a blend of the informed views of the group.

The salesforce estimation method is considered to be a valuable management tool and is commonly used in business and industry throughout the world. Although the accuracy of this method is generally good, managers have found that it can be improved by taking such simple steps as providing salespeople with sufficient time to forecast and offering incentives for accurate forecasts. Some companies help their salespeople to become better forecasters by training them to better interpret their interactions with customers.[22]

Quantitative Methods

Moving average The **moving average method** utilizes historical data to predict future sales levels. Specifically, forecasters compute average sales levels for *x* historical time periods; forecasters are able to choose the number of time periods that best fit their situations. Suppose, for example, that forecasters at Toyota are using a five-year moving average to predict future automobile sales. In 2009, they would select the five most recent years—2004 to 2008—and compute average automobile sales during that period. In 2010, they would rely on sales data from 2005 to 2009, and in 2011 they would rely on sales data from 2006 to 2010. Because the five-year time period changes each year to reflect the five most recent years, this method is referred to as a "moving" average.

Regression The **regression method** predicts future sales by analyzing the historical relationship between sales and time.[23] Using this information, analysts can use regression to forecast future sales. Specifically, regression provides forecasters with a trend-line that best explains the historical relationship between sales and time. Forecasters can use this trend-line, then, to predict future sales. Figure 10.5 illustrates an example of a trend-line that can be used to forecast future sales. Managers often use statistical programs such as SPSS or SAS to conduct regression analysis.

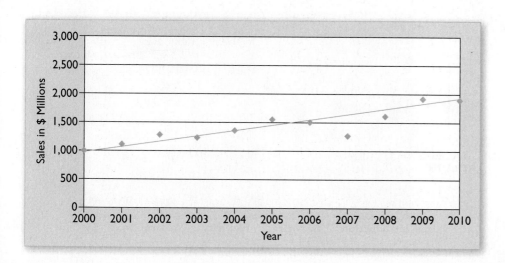

FIGURE 10.5
Regression analysis method

Although the actual number of time periods included in regression will vary from company to company, as a general rule, managers should include as many time periods as necessary to ensure that important sales trends do not go undetected. In **an example from the world of management, management** at the **Coca-Cola Company** believes that in order to validly predict the annual sales of any one year, it must chart annual sales in each of the 10 previous years.[24]

Product stages The data in Figure 10.5 indicate steadily increasing sales for B. J.'s Men's Clothing over time. However, because in the long term products generally go through what is called a product life cycle, the predicted increase based on the last decade of sales should probably be considered overly optimistic. A **product life cycle** is the five stages through which most products and services pass. These stages are introduction, growth, maturity, saturation, and decline.[25] The **product stages method** predicts future sales by using the product life cycle to better understand the history and future of the product.

Figure 10.6 shows how the five stages of the product life cycle are related to sales volume for seven products over a period of time. In the introduction stage, when a product is brand new, sales are just beginning to build (Web-capable cell phones). In the growth stage, the product has been in the marketplace for some time and is becoming more accepted, so product sales continue to climb (e.g., cellular phones and MP3 players). During the maturity stage, competitors enter the market, and although sales are still climbing, they are climbing at a slower rate than they did in the growth stage (e.g., personal computers). After the maturity stage comes the saturation stage, when nearly everyone who wanted the product has it (e.g., refrigerators and microwaves). Sales during the saturation stage typically are due to the need to replace a worn-out product or to population growth. The last product life cycle stage—decline—finds the product being replaced by a competing product (e.g., conventional, or not high-definition, televisions).

Managers may be able to prevent some products from entering the decline stage by improving product quality or by adding innovations. Other products, such as scissors, may never reach this last stage of the product life cycle because there are no competing products to replace them.

Evaluating Sales Forecasting Methods The sales forecasting methods just described are not the only ones available to managers. Other, more complex methods include the statistical correlation method and the computer simulation method.[26] The methods just discussed, however, do provide a basic foundation for understanding sales forecasting.

In practice, managers find that each sales forecasting method has distinct advantages and disadvantages. Before deciding to use a particular sales forecasting method, a manager must carefully weigh these advantages and disadvantages as they relate to the manager's organization. The best decision may be to use a combination of methods to forecast sales rather than just one.

FIGURE 10.6

Stages of the product life cycle

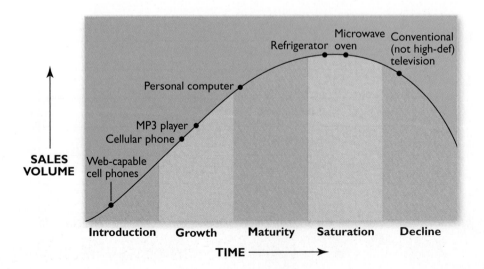

TABLE 10.3	Familiarity with Forecasting Methods		
	1980s	1990s	2000s
Qualitative Methods			
Jury of Executive Opinion	87%	82%	74%
Salesforce Estimation	84	85	83
Quantitative Methods			
Moving Average	92%	98%	100%
Regression	80	88	97

Note: The numbers in this table reflect the percentage of respondents who were "familiar" or "somewhat familiar' with the corresponding forecasting method.

Whatever method or methods are finally adopted, the manager should be certain the framework is logical, fits the needs of the organization, and can be adapted to changes in the environment.

A recent study surveyed forecasters to gauge their familiarity with using these forecasting methods.[27] The authors of the study then compared these familiarity statistics with two similar studies conducted in the 1980s and 1990s. The results of the study, which are displayed in Table 10.3, revealed some interesting trends. First, these results suggest the increasing popularity of quantitative forecasting methods; in fact, 100 percent of forecasters polled in the 2000s were familiar with the moving average method. In contrast, familiarity with qualitative methods—especially the jury of executive opinion method—has decreased over time.

Scheduling

Scheduling is the process of formulating a detailed listing of activities that must be accomplished to attain an objective, allocating the resources necessary to attain the objective, and setting up and following timetables for completing the objective. Scheduling is an integral part of every organizational plan. Two popular scheduling techniques are Gantt charts and the program evaluation and review technique (PERT).

Gantt Charts The **Gantt chart,** a scheduling device developed by Henry L. Gantt, is essentially a bar graph with time on the horizontal axis and the resource to be scheduled on

Scheduling is an important type of forecasting and is accomplished in many ways. These x-ray technicians in a U.S. hospital rely on the scheduling board behind them to coordinate their work with a steady stream of patients undergoing tests of many different types.

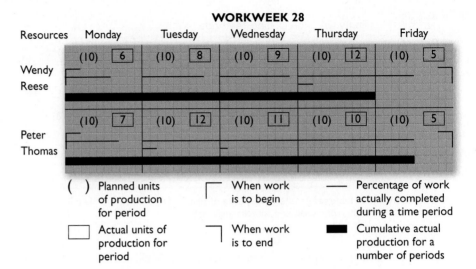

FIGURE 10.7
Completed Gantt chart

the vertical axis. It is used for scheduling resources, including management system inputs such as human resources and machines.

Figure 10.7 shows a completed Gantt chart for a work period entitled "Workweek 28." The resources scheduled over the five workdays on this chart were the human resources Wendy Reese and Peter Thomas. During this workweek, both Reese and Thomas were supposed to produce 10 units a day. Note, however, that actual production deviated from planned production. There were days when each of the two workers produced more than 10 units, as well as days when each produced fewer than 10 units. Cumulative actual production for workweek 28 shows that Reese produced 40 units and Thomas 45 units over the five days.

FEATURES Although simple in concept and appearance, the Gantt chart has many valuable managerial uses.[28] First, managers can use it as a summary overview of how organizational resources are being employed. From this summary, they can detect such facts as which resources are consistently contributing to productivity and which are hindering it. Second, managers can use the Gantt chart to help coordinate organizational resources. The chart can show which resources are not being used during specific periods, thereby allowing managers to schedule those resources for work on other production efforts. Third, the chart can be used to establish realistic worker output standards. For example, if scheduled work is being completed too quickly, output standards should be raised so that workers are scheduled for more work per time period.

Program Evaluation and Review Technique (PERT)
The main weakness of the Gantt chart is that it does not contain any information about the interrelationship of tasks to be performed. Although all tasks to be performed are listed on the chart, it is not possible to tell whether one task must be performed before another can be started. The **program evaluation and review technique (PERT),** a technique that evolved partly from the Gantt chart, is a scheduling tool that does emphasize the interrelationship of tasks.

DEFINING PERT PERT is a network of project activities showing both the estimates of time necessary to complete each activity and the sequence of activities that must be followed to complete the project. This scheduling tool was developed in 1958 for designing and building the Polaris submarine weapon system. The people who were managing this project found Gantt charts and other existing scheduling tools of little use because of the complicated nature of the Polaris project and the interdependence of the tasks to be performed.[29]

The PERT network contains two primary elements: activities and events. **Activities** are specified sets of behavior within a project, and **events** are the completions of major project tasks. Within the PERT network, each event is assigned corresponding activities that must be performed before the event can materialize.[30]

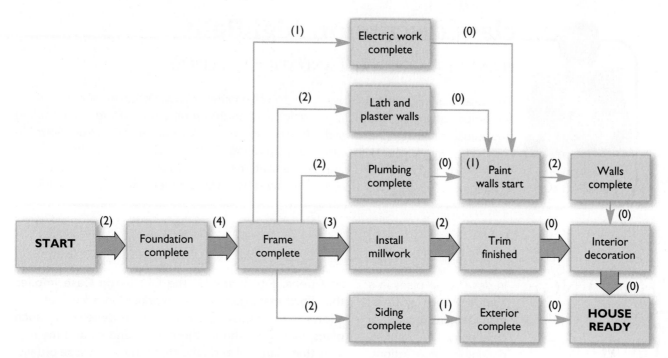

FIGURE 10.8 PERT network designed for building a house

FEATURES A sample PERT network designed for building a house is presented in Figure 10.8. Events are symbolized by boxes and activities by arrows. To illustrate, the figure indicates that after the event "Foundation Complete" (represented by a box) has materialized, certain activities (represented by an arrow) must be performed before the event "Frame Complete" (represented by another box) can materialize.

Two other features of the network shown in Figure 10.8 should be emphasized. First, the left-to-right presentation of events shows how the events interrelate or the sequence in which they should be performed. Second, the numbers in parentheses above each arrow indicate the units of time necessary to complete each activity. These two features help managers ensure that only necessary work is being done on a project and that no project activities are taking too long.[31]

CRITICAL PATH Managers need to pay close attention to the **critical path** of a PERT network—the sequence of events and activities requiring the longest period of time to complete. This path is called *critical* because a delay in completing this sequence results in a delay in completing the entire project. The critical path in Figure 10.8 is indicated by thick arrows; all other paths are indicated by thin arrows. Managers try to control a project by keeping it within the time designated by the critical path. The critical path helps them predict which features of a schedule are becoming unrealistic and provides insights into how those features might be eliminated or modified.[32]

STEPS IN DESIGNING A PERT NETWORK When designing a PERT network, managers should follow four primary steps:[33]

STEP 1 List all the activities/events that must be accomplished for the project and the sequence in which these activities/events should be performed.

STEP 2 Determine how much time will be needed to complete each activity/event.

STEP 3 Design a PERT network that reflects all of the information contained in steps 1 and 2.

STEP 4 Identify the critical path.

class discussion highlight

PLANNING TOOLS SKILL AND YOUR CAREER

The previous section describes the importance of scheduling tools such as Gantt charts and PERT. How might your skills with Gantt charts and PERT help your career? In particular, imagine a job that you would like to obtain after school, and think of a scenario in which you might employ one of these scheduling tools. Can you think of an example from your life (e.g., previous jobs, previous appointments with organizations on campus, etc.) that might have benefited from using either Gantt charts or PERT?

{ CHALLENGE CASE SUMMARY

In developing plans in a company such as Ford, management is actually developing recommendations for future actions. As such, plans should be action oriented; they should state precisely what management is going to do in order to achieve its goals.

In developing the plans, managers such as those at Ford should consider how often the plans will be used and the length of time they will cover. Will a plan be implemented only once or be used on a long-term basis to handle an ongoing issue, such as maintaining product quality? A plan similar to Ford's plan to improve product quality might not be used often by most companies and would be designed to cover a specific amount of time.

In addition, managers should consider what part of the organization the plans they develop will be aimed at and on what level the plans will focus. For instance, a plan to cut costs may encompass all Ford operations, whereas a plan to improve product quality may affect only one part of the production process, such as parts involving the company's luxury automobiles. Similarly, a plan to cut costs may be aimed at top-level management, whereas a product-quality plan may be aimed toward lower-level management and the auto assemblers themselves. Managers such as those at Ford must realize that management systems are interdependent, which means that any plans they implement will affect the system as a whole.

Managers would normally use both standing plans and single-use plans in a company. Standing plans include policies, procedures, and rules and should be developed for situations that occur repeatedly. For example, one policy Ford management could develop might focus on the level of product quality they want to emphasize with employees.

Single-use plans include programs and budgets and should be developed to help manage less repetitive situations. For example, the Challenge Case implies that Ford management has worked on a budget that allows it to improve its Explorer. In developing such plans, managers should thoroughly understand the reasons that plans fail and take steps to avoid those pitfalls.

Plant facilities planning and human resource planning are two types of planning that managers commonly pursue. In the case of Ford, plant facilities planning would entail developing the types of factories the company needs to reach its objectives. Automotive companies often focus on plant facilities planning. Such planning addresses questions such as where a new plant should be located, how to expand and remodel an existing factory, and how to lay out a plant to best facilitate the effective and efficient production of vehicles.

Human resource planning involves obtaining or developing the personnel an organization needs to reach its objectives. In this area, for example, Ford management might discuss the types of engineers needed to improve existing products or design new products that meet specified safety requirements. Discussion would inevitably focus on issues such as how many new employees, if any, Ford will need as economic conditions vary; in what areas they will be needed; when these employees would be needed; how they will be obtained; and how they will be trained appropriately.

One of the planning tools available to Ford management is forecasting, which involves predicting future environmental events that could influence the operation of the company. Although various specific types of forecasting—such as economic, technological, and social trends forecasting—are available to them, Ford management would probably use sales forecasting as its key, because it will predict how high or low their sales will be during the time period they are considering. Although the sales of the company have been decreasing, the changes instituted by Ford's new management may help to reverse this trend.

In order to forecast sales, managers should follow the jury of executive opinion method by having Ford executives discuss their opinions of future sales. This method would be quick and easy to use and, assuming that Ford executives have a good feel for product demand, might be as valid as any other method the company might use.

Ford management could also ask its auto retailers (salesforce) for opinions on predicted sales. Although the opinions of such car dealers may not be completely reliable, these people are closest to the market and must ultimately make the sales.

Finally, Ford management could use the regression analysis method by analyzing the relationship between sales and time. Although this method takes into account the cyclical patterns and past history of sales, it also assumes the continuation of these patterns in the future without considering outside influences such as economic downturns, which could cause the patterns to change.

Because each sales forecasting method has advantages and disadvantages, managers at Ford should carefully analyze them before deciding which method or combination of methods should be used.

Scheduling is another planning tool available to Ford management. It involves the detailed listing of activities that must be accomplished to reach an objective. For example, if Ford's goal is to have all of its employees working proficiently on updated equipment within two years, management needs to schedule activities such as installing the equipment, training the employees, and establishing new output standards.

Two scheduling techniques available to Ford management are Gantt charts and PERT. To schedule employee production output, the managers might want to use Gantt charts—bar graphs with time on the horizontal axis and the resource to be scheduled on the vertical axis. They might also find these charts helpful for evaluating worker performance and setting new production standards.

If managers at Ford want to see the relationships among tasks, they could use PERT to develop a flowchart showing activities, events, and the amount of time necessary to complete each task. For example, a PERT network would be helpful in scheduling the installation of new machines; this type of schedule would allow management to see which equipment needed to be installed first, the amount of time each installation would require, and how other activities in renovating an existing factory would be affected before the installation was completed. PERT would also help the managers to discern the critical path they must follow for successful installation. This path represents the sequence of activities and events requiring the longest amount of time to complete, and it indicates the total time it will take to finish the project. If, for example, new welding machinery takes longer to install than other types of equipment, management should target the completion of the entire equipment installation on the basis of this equipment's installation time.

MANAGEMENT SKILL ACTIVITIES

This section is specially designed to help you develop planning tools skill. An individual's management skill is based upon an understanding of management concepts and the ability to apply those concepts in management situations. As a result, the following activities are designed both to heighten your understanding of planning tools concepts and to help you gain facility in applying these concepts in various management situations.

UNDERSTANDING PLANNING TOOLS CONCEPTS

This section is comprised of activities that will sharpen your understanding of plans and planning tools concepts. Answer essay questions as completely as possible. Also, remember that many additional true/false and multiple choice questions appear online at MyManagementLab.com to help you further refine your understanding of concepts related to plans and planning tools.

Essay Questions

1. Describe the four dimensions of plans.
2. Describe the differences between policies, rules, and procedures. Provide examples of each.
3. Compare and contrast qualitative versus quantitative sales forecasting methods.
4. Describe the differences between Gantt charts and PERT. In your opinion, which one is better for organizations? Explain.
5. Explain five of the primary reasons why plans fail. In your opinion, which one of these reasons is most important? Why?

Developing Management Skill

Learning activities in this section are aimed at helping you to develop your plans and planning tools skill. Learning activities include Exploring Your Management

Skill: Part 2, Experiential Exercises, Cases, and a VideoNet exercise.

EXPLORING YOUR MANAGEMENT SKILL: PART 2

As you recall, you completed Exploring Your Management Skill before you started to study this chapter. Your responses gave you an idea of how much you initially knew about plans and planning tools and helped you to focus on important points as you studied the chapter. Answer the Exploring Your Management Skill questions again now (p. 248) and compare your score to the first time you took it. This comparison will give you an idea of how much you have learned from studying this chapter and pinpoint areas for further clarification before you start studying the next chapter. Record your answers within the text or online at MyManagementLab.com. Completing the survey at MyManagementLab.com will allow you to grade and compare your test scores automatically. If you complete the test in the book, look up answers in the Exploring Your Management Skill section at the end of the book.

YOUR MANAGEMENT SKILLS PORTFOLIO

Your Management Learning Portfolio is a collection of activities especially designed to demonstrate your management knowledge and skill. By completing these activities online at MyManagementLab.com, you will be able to print, complete with cover sheet, as many activities as you choose. Be sure to save your work. Taking your printed portfolio to an employment interview could be helpful in obtaining a job.

The portfolio activity for this chapter is Forecasting Sales at Best Buy. Study the following information and complete the exercises that that follow.[34]

Forecasting Sales at Best Buy

Best Buy is a retailer that specializes in consumer electronics, entertainment software, appliances, and home office products. In addition, Best Buy has established a number of services, such as its popular Geek Squad, to help consumers install, use, and troubleshoot the products they purchase in Best Buy stores. Although Circuit City is Best Buy's most direct competitor, the company also competes with larger and more general retailers such as Wal-Mart and Target.

Best Buy sells a number of different products and services, but personal computers (PCs) represent a substantial source of the company's sales each year. Because of the importance of PCs for Best Buy's performance, Robert Willett, Best Buy's chief information officer, has contacted you. Mr. Willett would like you to forecast Best Buy's PC sales for next year.

Explain how you would apply the five forecasting methods described in the chapter to help Mr. Willett better understand future personal computer sales. Assume that Mr. Willett has provided you with information that details Best Buy's PC sales over the past 10 years. You do not need to perform the actual calculations, but explain how you would use that information with the following methods. Keep in mind that some of these methods may not require the use of such information.

1. Jury of Executive Opinion Method

2. Salesforce Estimation Method

3. Moving Average Method

4. Regression Method

_____

_____

_____

5. Product Stages Method

_____

_____

_____

EXPERIENTIAL EXERCISE

Directions. Read the following scenario and then perform the listed activities. Your instructor may want you to perform the activities as an individual or within groups. Follow all of your instructor's directions carefully.

Jeff Fettig is the CEO of Whirlpool Corporation, a manufacturer of home appliances such as refrigerators, dishwashers, washers and dryers, microwaves, and stoves. Recently, a customer called and reported that the interior walls of his new Whirlpool refrigerator were cracking, such that the cracks looked like spider webs. Fettig is concerned that this problem may appear in other refrigerators around the world. As such, Fettig has contacted your group to form a procedure to handle similar customer calls in the future. Specifically, your group should develop a procedure that details the steps a customer service agent should utilize when fielding such calls. Steps in the procedure, for example, might include taking digital pictures, sending service agents to the location, and so on. The final steps in the procedure should outline potential solutions, which may include doing nothing, fixing the cracks with tape, or replacing the refrigerator. For each step in the procedure, identify the associated major costs.

CASES

FORD PLANS A U-TURN

"Ford Plans a U-Turn" (p. 247) and its related Challenge Case Summary were written to help you better understand the management concepts contained in this chapter. Answer the following discussion questions about the Challenge Case to better understand how concepts relating to plans and planning tools can be applied in a company such as Ford.

1. Should Ford's plan to improve the company's performance be related to its human resource planning? Explain.
2. Explain this statement: "The quality of Ford's decision about how to improve the company's performance is largely determined by product improvement planning."
3. Do you think that Ford management should use forecasted sales as a component of product improvement planning? Explain.

PLANNING FOR FAST FASHION AT ZARA

Read the case and answer the questions that follow. Studying this case will help you better understand how concepts relating to plans and planning tools can be applied in a company such as Zara.

Today's styles can become history overnight in the fast-paced world of women's fashion, as managers of the Zara retail company know all too well. Owned by Spain's Industria de Diseno Textil (Inditex), Zara was founded 30 years ago by Amancio Ortega Gaona, who remains chairman. From one small store selling popularly priced women's clothing in La Coruña, Spain, Zara has now blossomed into a powerful 600-store chain with a presence in more than 40 nations.

Staying on top of ever-changing and unpredictable fashion trends requires careful planning and forecasting. When a celebrity brings a certain style into the spotlight or a designer makes a splash with an innovative look, Zara competitors such as the Swedish retailer Hennes & Mauritz and the U.S. retailer Gap might need as long as six months to order the right fabric, design the garment and accessories, have everything manufactured, and ship the merchandise to their stores. In contrast, Zara follows a "fast fashion" strategy and can create, produce, and deliver an entirely new product line to store shelves in a matter of weeks.

"We don't want to miss out on the latest trend, which means a fast response to the demands of our customers and the market," explains Raul Estravera, one of Zara's communication managers. "Having our own factories allows us this flexibility—15 days from product decision to delivery and twice-weekly shipments of fresh merchandise—and there is less chance of error." To keep costs down and avoid holding mountains of merchandise that might suddenly turn into yesterday's fashions, Zara manufactures only what each store needs, based on forecasting. Yet because the company makes most of the clothing it sells, its managers can more tightly control crucial planning details such as production schedules, staffing, and budgets.

Zara's planners prepare store-by-store sales forecasts and tailor each store's assortment of merchandise to local tastes and trends, not an easy task for a company offering 12,000 styles every year. However, these initial forecasts are simply starting points. If a garment's early sales point to a big hit or store employees report unusually positive customer reaction to a particular style, the planners reforecast short-term sales, reorder immediately, and send shipments to stores where demand is highest.

Moving merchandise quickly is Zara's strength: Its state-of-the-art distribution center in Zaragoza, Spain, can handle 80,000 garments every *hour*, and management insists that stores receive deliveries no more than 35 hours after shipments leave the center. The company trucks merchandise to stores within one day's drive of Zaragoza and ships by air to more distant stores. As efficient as this system may be for the European stores, it could limit Zara's expansion in the United States, where the company now has 10 stores. Inditex's CEO notes that sending a cargo jet filled with merchandise to New York twice a week would enable Zara to stock up to 50 U.S. stores.

Meanwhile, Zara's managers continue to scout locations for new stores, analyzing local demographics and shopping patterns, examining the competition, estimating leasing and renovation or construction costs, and assessing local legal and regulatory issues. However, they can't always find the kind of facilities they want. For instance, Zara is seeking to expand in Ireland, but Mike Shearwood, that territory's executive, can't easily locate sufficiently large stores at affordable rents in good shopping districts.

Once he selects a site, Shearwood has a renovation budget of about $2 million and will make the most of the space by allocating about 85 percent for retail purposes, leaving just 15 percent for back-office operations. He also has to plan for the grand opening, not knowing exactly how things will go. When Shearwood opened a new store in Dublin, customer reaction was so enthusiastic that, he says, "We almost sold out and had to arrange a special delivery to be shipped in to ensure we had sufficient stock for the weekend."

QUESTIONS

1. Which of the three sales forecasting methods would you recommend that Zara's planners use for projecting sales item by item? Why?
2. What kinds of procedures, policies, and rules would Zara's management be likely to establish to guide planning for the grand opening of a new store?
3. If you were designing a PERT network for a Zara store opening, what type of activities would you consider part of the critical path? Explain.

VIDEONET EXERCISE

Mullen PR

VIDEO HIGHLIGHTS

Mullen is a full-service advertising and public relations firm located north of Boston and housed in a 1920s mansion. Its staff of 300 employees bills $640 million a year and has created some of America's most compelling commercials and print ads. Mullen's clients include Nextel, Arby's, Fortune Magazine, and GM. Since the dot.com bust, concurrent control has been replaced by preventive control— "account planning" in the advertising industry. Although he acknowledges the importance of measuring the bottom line, chief creative director Edward Boches, who began his career in the 1970s, still maintains allegiance to the corporate mission: "To generate enduring creative ideas, to do beautifully crafted work, and to expect the best."

Discussion Questions

1. Which type of plans do you think would be most appropriate for the advertising and public relations industry?

2. Using the planning process as the basis for your answer, why do you think a marketing campaign developed by Mullen PR may fail in its attempt to increase buyer awareness of a product or service?
3. In your own words, explain the "steering control" method of planning discussed in the video. How does this compare to the concept of forecasting discussed in the chapter?

Internet Activity

Browse the Web site for Mullen PR at www.mullenpr.com. Visit some of the links listed on the left side of the page. Specifically, click on the link for the company's "philosophy." Are you surprised by what you see there? Is this philosophy consistent with what you have learned about this company from the video? Now check out Monster.com, and compare the two Web sites. Which site would you remember visiting the most? Why? What is the new Monster.com slogan? Explain how the concepts of planning discussed in the video have aided in the success of Monster.com.

11 Fundamentals of Organizing

TO HELP BUILD MY ORGANIZING SKILL, WHEN STUDYING THIS CHAPTER, I WILL ATTEMPT TO ACQUIRE:

1. An understanding of the organizing function

2. An appreciation for the complexities of determining appropriate organizational structure

3. An understanding of the distinction between vertical and horizontal dimensioning

4. Insights into the advantages and disadvantages of division of labor

5. A working knowledge of the relationship between division of labor and coordination

6. An appreciation for the advantages and disadvantages associated with the different types of departmentalization

7. An understanding of span of management and the factors that influence its appropriateness

8. An understanding of scalar relationships

TARGET SKILL organizing skill: the ability to establish orderly uses for resources within the management system

CHALLENGE CASE

SONY ORGANIZES FOR SUCCESS

Sony Corporation designs, manufactures, and sells electronic equipment and devices to both consumers and companies. Although the electronics division accounts for a majority of its sales, Sony also develops, manufactures, and sells other entertainment products such as film, music, and videogame hardware and software. In addition, Sony also has a financial services division, which accounts for a majority of its income. Given the broad array of products and services that Sony offers, Sony's executives have faced some difficulties in determining the company's optimal organizational structure, which has resulted in some financial problems that jeopardize the company's operations.

Sir Howard Stringer, Sony's chief executive officer, has implemented several organizational structure changes to address the problem. One of the main causes for Sony's recent lackluster performance is the company's electronics division. In the past, Sony has relied on this division to produce new, innovative products such as the Sony Walkman. Recently, however, Sony has faced more difficulties in producing innovative products.

To face these challenges in the electronics division, Stringer has promised to change elements of the division's structure. In particular, he has vowed to restructure the electronics division to allow more communication. Hopefully, increased communication will lead to more innovations and, consequently, new Sony products. This increased communication will also improve coordination

Sony has implemented changes in its organizational structure to reduce financial problems that threatened to jeopardize its operations.

between the different units. At one point, for example, three different divisions within Sony were developing their own digital music players.[1]

Sony has also restructured its music business to improve the company's overall performance. Specifically, the company has reduced a large number of support positions in sales, manufacturing, and distribution. According to Sony, many employees in these positions were performing similar activities. By eliminating some of this overlap, Sony can redirect money to develop new artists, which is a crucial activity in the music business.

Finally, Sony will continue to search for new ways to combine its music, film, and electronics businesses with its videogame business. Sony's videogame business, which develops and sells its PlayStation III gaming system, represents Sony's largest profit driver. By developing linkages among Sony's businesses, the company may be better able to leverage its success in the videogame market. For example, when Sony first released its PlayStation Portable in the United States, the first million units were packaged with copies of Spider-Man 2, a movie produced by Sony's entertainment division.

Some questions remain as to whether Sony can rebound from its current downturn. According to Stringer, Sony's ability to restructure represents a key determinant of the company's future success. What organizing challenges do you see in Stringer's future?

"EXPLORE YOUR OWN MANAGEMENT SKILLS BY TAKING THE QUIZ ON THE NEXT PAGE"

Before studying this chapter, respond to the following questions regarding the type of advice that you would give to Sir Howard Stringer, Sony's CEO discussed in the Challenge Case. Then address the concerning organizing challenges that he presently faces within the company. You are not expected to be an organizing expert at this point. Answering the questions now can help you focus on important points when you study the chapter. Also, answering the questions again after you study the chapter will give you an idea of how much you have learned.

Record your answers here or go to MyManagementLab. com. Recording your answers in MyManagementLab will allow you to get immediate results and see how your score compares to your classmates. If you answer the questions in the book, the answers are located in the Exploring Your Management Skill Appendix at the end of the book.

FOR EACH STATEMENT CIRCLE:

- "Y" if you would give the advice to Stringer.
- "N" if you would NOT give the advice to Stringer.
- "NI" if you have no idea whether you would give the advice to Stringer.

Mr. Stringer, in meeting your organizing challenges at Sony, you should . . .

Before Study	*After Study*

1. design organizing activities to be more closely related to controlling activities than planning activities.
   Y, N, NI

2. concentrate more on clearly outlining an organization chart and less on how characteristics of people will affect the success of the chart.
   Y, N, NI

3. design an organization chart to reflect authority, responsibility, and informal communication patterns.
   Y, N, NI

4. know subordinates well because their makeup should influence the type of organization to be established.
   Y, N, NI

5. create more and more specialization within jobs in order to make jobs more interesting, and thereby make workers more productive.
   Y, N, NI

6. make sure that managers at lower levels of the organization have more individuals to supervise than those at upper levels of the organization.
   Y, N, NI

7. decide to manage more organization members if the members are performing complex jobs than if performing simple jobs.
   Y, N, NI

8. increase the height of an organization chart to help managers manage people performing jobs of high complexity.
   Y, N, NI

9. emphasize organizing as a means of putting controls into action.
   Y, N, NI

10. commonly establish situations in which organizations have more than one boss.
    Y, N, NI

11. ensure that authority is properly scaled within the organization chart.
    Y, N, NI

12. establish division of labor to increase worker efficiency and worker interest level in jobs.
    Y, N, NI

13. focus on using primary organizational inputs such as money, people, raw materials, and plans.
    Y, N, NI

14. encourage peer level members of different departments to communicate directly with one another without going through their managers in order to enhance organizational efficiency.
    Y, N, NI

15. use division of labor to minimize time wasted by organization members moving from location to location to perform different jobs.
    Y, N, NI

THE ORGANIZING CHALLENGE

The Challenge Case illustrates many different organizing challenges that Stringer, the CEO, will have to meet if Sony is to be successful. The remaining material in this chapter explains organizing concepts and helps to develop the corresponding organizing skill that you will need to meet organizing challenges throughout your career. After studying chapter concepts, read the Challenge Case Summary at the end of the chapter to help you relate chapter content to meeting organizing challenges at Sony.

DEFINITIONS OF ORGANIZING AND ORGANIZING SKILL

Organizing is the process of establishing orderly uses for resources within the management system. Correspondingly, **organizing skill** is the ability to establish orderly uses for resources within the management system. This chapter focuses on organizing and helping you to develop the target skill for this chapter, organizing skill.

Orderly uses of resources emphasize the attainment of management system objectives and assist managers not only in making objectives apparent but in clarifying which resources will be used to attain them.[2] A primary focus of organizing is determining both what individual employees will do in an organization and how their individual efforts should best be combined to advance the attainment of organizational objectives.[3] *Organization* refers to the result of the organizing process. Fayol presents a number of guidelines for effective organizations; these guidelines are displayed in Figure 11.1.

The Importance of Organizing

The organizing function is extremely important to the management system because it is the primary mechanism managers use to activate plans.[4] Organizing creates and maintains relationships between all organizational resources by indicating which resources are to be used for specified activities and when, where, and how they are to be used. A thorough organizing effort helps managers minimize costly weaknesses, such as duplication of effort and idle organizational resources.

Some management theorists consider the organizing function so important that they advocate the creation of an organizing department within the management system. Typical responsibilities of this department would include three primary responsibilities.[5] First, the department should periodically formulate reorganization plans that make the management system more effective and efficient. Companies, for example, typically restructure to devote

---

In essence, each organizational resource represents an investment from which the management system must get a return. Appropriate organization of these resources increases the efficiency and effectiveness of their use. Henri Fayol developed 16 general guidelines for organizing resources:

1. Judiciously prepare and execute the operating plan.
2. Organize the human and material facets so that they are consistent with objectives, resources, and requirements of the concern.
3. Establish a single competent, energetic guiding authority (formal management structure).
4. Coordinate all activities and efforts.
5. Formulate clear, distinct, and precise decisions.
6. Arrange for efficient selection so that each department is headed by a competent, energetic manager, and all employees are placed where they can render the greatest service.
7. Define duties.
8. Encourage initiative and responsibility.
9. Offer fair and suitable rewards for services rendered.
10. Make use of sanctions against faults and errors.
11. Maintain discipline.
12. Ensure that individual interests are consistent with the general interests of the organization.
13. Recognize the unity of command.
14. Promote both material and human coordination.
15. Institute and effect controls.
16. Avoid regulations, red tape, and paperwork.

FIGURE 11.1

Keys to organization: Fayol's guidelines

more resources to profitable divisions and less resources to divisions losing money. Second, the department should foster and support an advantageous organizational climate within the management system.

Finally, the department should develop plans to improve managerial skills to fit current management system needs. In **an example from the world of management**, **General Electric** (GE) is world-renowned for its ability to develop managerial talent. Although GE is famous for its products and services ranging from lightbulbs to television, many suggest that the key to GE's success is due primarily to the company's ability to identify and develop managers.[6]

The Organizing Process

The five main steps of the organizing process are presented in Figure 11.2: reflect on plans and objectives, establish major tasks, divide major tasks into subtasks, allocate resources and directives for subtasks, and evaluate the results of implemented organizing strategy.[7] As the figure implies, managers should continually repeat these steps. Through repetition, they obtain feedback that will help them improve the existing organization.[8]

The management of a restaurant can serve as an illustration of how the organizing process works. The first step the restaurant manager would take to initiate the organizing process would be to reflect on the restaurant's plans and objectives. Because planning involves determining how the restaurant will attain its objectives, and organizing involves determining how the restaurant's resources will be used to activate plans, the restaurant manager must start to organize by understanding planning.

The second and third steps of the organizing process focus on tasks to be performed within the management system. The manager must designate major tasks or jobs to be done within the restaurant. Two such tasks are serving customers and cooking food. Then the tasks must be divided into subtasks. For example, the manager might decide that serving customers includes the subtasks of taking orders and clearing tables.

The fourth organizing step is determining who will take orders, who will clear the tables, and what the details of the relationship between these individuals will be. The size of tables and how they are to be set are other factors to be considered at this point.

In the fifth step, evaluating the results of the implemented organizing strategy, the manager gathers feedback on how well the strategy is working. This feedback should furnish information that can be used to improve the existing organization. For example, the manager may find that a particular type of table is not large enough and that larger ones must be purchased if the restaurant is to attain its goals.

FIGURE 11.2
The five main steps of the organizing process

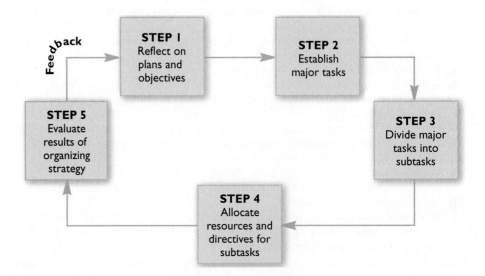

To organize any large project, like this study of the effect of chemicals on plant growth at Limburger Hof research station, managers must establish objectives (or in this case a hypothesis) and major tasks. Then they break tasks into smaller sub-tasks, allocate resources to each task, and finally evaluate the results.

CLASSICAL ORGANIZING THEORY

Classical organizing theory comprises the cumulative insights of early management writers on how organizational resources can best be used to enhance goal attainment. The following sections discuss three major components of classical organizing theory: Weber's bureaucratic model, division of labor, and structure.

Weber's Bureaucratic Model

The writer who probably had the most profound influence on classical organizing theory was Max Weber. Most agree that Weber's most notable contribution to classical organizing theory was his concept of bureaucracy.[9] Specifically, Weber used the term **bureaucracy** to label the management system that includes three primary components: detailed procedures and rules, a clearly outlined organizational hierarchy, and impersonal relationships among organization members.

Although he firmly believed in the bureaucratic approach to organizing, he was concerned that managers were inclined to overemphasize the merits of a bureaucracy. He cautioned that a bureaucracy is not an end in itself, but rather a means to the end of management system goal attainment. The main criticism of Weber's bureaucracy model, as well as the concepts of other classical organizing theorists, is that they give short shrift to the human variable within organizations. In fact, it is recognized today that the bureaucratic approach without an appropriate emphasis on the human variable is almost certainly a formula for organizational failure.[10]

Another criticism of bureaucracy is that it may negatively influence organizational effectiveness.[11] For an example of bureaucracy negatively influencing organizational effectiveness, consider the following scenario. In **an example from the world of management,** when Mark Hurd took over as the CEO of **Hewlett Packard** (HP), a worldwide computer product manufacturer and consulting services provider, he developed concerns about the potential negative influence of HP's bureaucracy. A meeting with his vice president of sales revealed that members of the sales team were spending only about one-third of their time with customers, while they spent the remainder of their time dealing with HP's bureaucracy. The sales team could not be effective in handling customers because too much time was spent on activities that included filing various HP forms and reporting responsibilities to bosses. Consequently, one of Hurd's first objectives was to eliminate components of HP's bureaucracy in order to improve effectiveness in dealing with customers.[12] Even though appropriate organization can improve efficiency and effectiveness, this example illustrates the potential problems associated with inappropriate organization.

Division of Labor

A primary consideration of any organizing effort is how to divide labor. **Division of labor** is the assignment of various portions of a particular task among a number of organization members.[13] Rather than one individual doing the entire job, several individuals perform different parts of it. Production is divided into a number of steps, with the responsibility for completing various steps assigned to specific individuals. The essence of division of labor is that individuals specialize in doing part of a task rather than the entire task.[14]

A commonly used illustration of division of labor is the automobile production line. Rather than one person assembling an entire car, specific portions of the car are assembled by various workers. Although most associate division of labor with automobiles, division of labor plays an important role in a variety of businesses. In **an example from the world of management,** division of labor plays an important role in the manufacturing of art in China. At some manufacturing facilities, several artists help to paint copies of the same picture. When individuals finish painting their particular sections, they pass the painting on to other members to finish their own sections.[15] This approach allows Chinese galleries such as the **Ji Yi Yuang Gallery** to sell paintings for lower prices. It is clear, then, that the division of labor influences a variety of organizations. The following sections discuss the advantages and disadvantages of division of labor, the relationship between division of labor and coordination, and Mary Parker Follett's coordination guidelines.

Advantages and Disadvantages of Division of Labor
Even the peerless physicist Albert Einstein, famous for his independent theorizing, believed that division of labor could be advantageous in many undertakings.[16] Several explanations have been offered for the usefulness of division of labor. First, when workers specialize in a particular task, their skill at performing that task tends to increase. Second, workers who have one job and one place in which to do it do not lose valuable time changing tools or locations. Third, when workers concentrate on performing only one job, they naturally try to make the job easier and more efficient. Lastly, division of labor creates a situation in which workers need only to know how to perform their part of the work task rather than the entire process for producing the end product. The task of understanding their work, therefore, does not become too burdensome.

Arguments have also been presented against the use of an extreme division of labor.[17] Essentially, these arguments contend that division of labor focuses solely on efficiency and economic benefit and overlooks the human variable in organizations. Work that is extremely specialized tends to be boring and therefore will eventually cause production rates to go down as workers become resentful of being treated like machines. Clearly, managers need to find a reasonable balance between specialization and human motivation.

Division of Labor and Coordination
In a division-of-labor situation, the importance of effective coordination of the different individuals doing portions of the task is obvious. Mooney has defined **coordination** as "the orderly arrangement of group effort to provide unity of action in the pursuit of a common purpose." In essence, coordination is a means for achieving any and all organizational objectives.[18] It involves encouraging the completion of individual portions of a task in a synchronized order that is appropriate for the overall task. Groups cannot maintain their productivity without coordination.[19] Part of the synchronized order of assembling an automobile, for example, is that seats are installed only after the floor has been installed; adhering to this order of installation is an example of coordination.

Establishing and maintaining coordination may require close supervision of employees, though managers should try to break away from the idea that coordination can only be achieved this way.[20] They can, instead, establish and maintain coordination through bargaining, formulating a common purpose for the group, or improving on specific problem solutions so the group will know what to do when it encounters those problems. Each of these efforts is considered a specific management tool.

Follett's Guidelines on Coordination Mary Parker Follett provided valuable advice on how managers can establish and maintain coordination within the organization. First, Follett said that coordination can be attained with the least difficulty through direct horizontal relationships and personal communications. In other words, when a coordination problem arises, peer discussion may be the best way to resolve it. Second, Follett suggested that coordination be a discussion topic throughout the planning process. In essence, managers should plan for coordination. Third, maintaining coordination is a continuing process and should be treated as such. Managers cannot assume that because their management system shows coordination today it will show coordination tomorrow.

Follett also noted that coordination can be achieved only through purposeful management action—it cannot be left to chance. Finally, she stressed the importance of the human element and advised that the communication process is an essential consideration in any attempt to encourage coordination. Primary considerations include employee skill levels, employee motivation levels, and the effectiveness of the human communication process used during coordination activities.[21]

Structure

In any organizing effort, managers must choose an appropriate structure. **Structure** refers to the designated relationships among resources of the management system. Its purpose is to facilitate the use of each resource, individually and collectively, as the management system attempts to attain its objectives.[22] The two basic types of structure within management systems are formal and informal structures. **Formal structure** is defined as the relationships among organizational resources as outlined by management; formal structure is represented primarily by the organization chart. In contrast, **informal structure** is defined as the patterns of relationships that develop because of the informal activities of organization members. It evolves naturally and tends to be molded by individual norms and values and social relationships. Essentially, an organization's informal structure is the system or network of interpersonal relationships that exists within, but is not usually identical to, the organization's formal structure.[23]

Organization structure is represented primarily by means of a graphic illustration called an **organization chart.** Traditionally, an organization chart is constructed in pyramid form, with individuals toward the top of the pyramid having more authority and responsibility than those toward the bottom.[24] The relative positioning of individuals within boxes on the chart indicates broad working relationships, and lines between boxes designate formal lines of communication between individuals. In addition to specifying formal relationships within the firm, an organization chart can also communicate to outsiders the complexity of the organization. In **an example from the world of management, Ted Terrazas,** an entrepreneur in the health care industry, displays the organizational chart for his company, **TerraHealth,** on the company's Web site. Although his company is quite small, the organizational chart helps potential customers to understand the complexity and professionalism of his company.[25]

Structure involves two primary dimensions: the vertical dimension and the horizontal dimension. The following sections discuss each dimension in detail.[26]

Vertical Dimensioning **Vertical dimensioning** refers to the extent to which an organization uses vertical levels to separate job responsibilities. Vertical dimensioning is directly related to the concept of **scalar relationships**—the chain of command. Every organization is built on the premise that the individual at the top possesses the most authority and that other individuals' authority is scaled downward according to their relative position on the organization chart. The lower a person's position on the organization chart, then, the less authority that person possesses.[27]

The scalar relationship, or chain of command, is related to the unity of command. **Unity of command** is the management principle that recommends that an individual have only one boss. If too many bosses give orders, the result will probably be confusion, contradiction, and frustration—a sure recipe for ineffectiveness and inefficiency in an organization. Although the unity-of-command principle made its first appearance in management literature well over 75 years ago, it is still discussed today as a critical ingredient of successful organizations.[28]

SPAN OF MANAGEMENT When examining the vertical dimensioning of an organizational chart, it is important for managers to consider the influence of **span of management**— the number of individuals a manager supervises. The more individuals a manager supervises, the greater the span of management. Conversely, the fewer individuals a manager supervises, the smaller the span of management. The span of management has a significant effect on how well managers carry out their responsibilities. Span of management is also called *span of control, span of authority, span of supervision,* and *span of responsibility.*[29]

The central concern of span of management is to determine how many individuals a manager can supervise effectively.[30] To use the organization's human resources effectively, managers should supervise as many individuals as they can best guide toward production quotas. If they are supervising too few people, however, they are wasting a portion of their productive capacity. If they are supervising too many, they are losing part of their effectiveness.

DESIGNING SPAN OF MANAGEMENT: A CONTINGENCY VIEWPOINT As reported by Harold Koontz, several important situational factors influence the appropriateness of the size of an individual's span of management:[31]

- **Similarity of functions**—the degree to which activities performed by supervised individuals are similar or dissimilar. As the similarity of subordinates' activities increases, the span of management appropriate for the situation widens. The converse is also generally true.

- **Geographic continuity**—the degree to which subordinates are physically separated. In general, the closer subordinates are physically, the more of them managers can supervise effectively.

These employees at a Bangalore, India, call center all perform essentially the same customer-service function, which means the span of management for their department can be relatively wide.

- **Complexity of functions**—the degree to which workers' activities are difficult and involved. The more difficult and involved the activities are, the more difficult it is to manage a large number of individuals effectively.

- **Coordination**—the amount of time managers must spend synchronizing the activities of their subordinates with the activities of other workers. The greater the amount of time that must be spent on such coordination, the smaller the span of management should be.

- **Planning**—the amount of time managers must spend developing management system objectives and plans and integrating them with the activities of their subordinates. The more time managers must spend on planning activities, the fewer individuals they can manage effectively.

Table 11.1 summarizes the factors that tend to increase and decrease the span of management.

GRAICUNAS AND SPAN OF MANAGEMENT Perhaps the best-known contribution to span-of-management literature was made by the management consultant V. A. Graicunas.[32] He developed a formula for determining the number of *possible* relationships between a manager and subordinates when the number of subordinates is known. **Graicunas's formula** is as follows:

$$C = n\left(\frac{2^n}{2} + n - 1\right)$$

C is the total number of possible relationships between manager and subordinates, and *n* is the known number of subordinates. As the number of subordinates increases arithmetically, the number of possible relationships between the manager and those subordinates increases geometrically.

A number of criticisms have been leveled at Graicunas's work. Some have argued that he failed to take into account a manager's relationships outside the organization and that he considered only *potential* relationships rather than *actual* relationships. These criticisms have some validity, but the real significance of Graicunas's work lies outside them. His main contribution involved pointing out that span of management is an important consideration that can have a far-reaching impact on the organization.[33]

HEIGHT OF ORGANIZATION CHART Span of management directly influences the height of an organization chart. Normally, the greater the height of the organization chart, the smaller the span of management, and the lower the height of the chart, the greater the span of management.[34] Organization charts with little height are usually referred to as *flat*, while those with much height are usually referred to as *tall*.[35]

Figure 11.3 is a simple example of the relationship between organization chart height and span of management. Organization chart A has a span of management of six, and organization chart B has a span of management of two. As a result, chart A is flatter than chart B.

TABLE 11.1	Major Factors That Influence the Span of Management	
Factor	**Factor Has Tendency to Increase Span of Management When—**	**Factor Has Tendency to Decrease Span of Management When—**
1. Similarity of functions	1. Subordinates have similar functions	1. Subordinates have different functions
2. Geographic contiguity	2. Subordinates are physically close	2. Subordinates are physically distant
3. Complexity of functions	3. Subordinates have simple tasks	3. Subordinates have complex tasks
4. Coordination	4. Work of subordinates needs little coordination	4. Work of subordinates needs much coordination
5. Planning	5. Manager spends little time planning	5. Manager spends much time planning

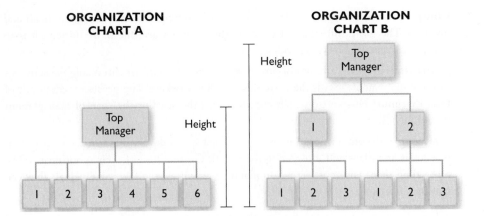

FIGURE 11.3
Relationship between organization chart height and span of management

Note that both charts have the same number of individuals at the lowest level. The larger span of management in A is reduced in B merely by adding a level to B's organization chart.

An organization's structure should be built from top to bottom to ensure that appropriate spans of management are achieved at all levels. Increasing spans of management merely to eliminate certain management positions and thereby reduce salary expenses may prove to be a short-sighted move. Increasing spans of management to achieve such objectives as speeding up organizational decision making and building a more flexible organization is more likely to help the organization achieve success in the long run.[36] A survey of organization charts of the 1990s reveals that top managers were creating flatter organizational structures than top managers used in the 1980s. Overall, managers seem to be using flatter organizational structures now than in the past.

In **an example from the world of management, Nucor Corp.,** a steel manufacturer, illustrates the benefits of flatter organizational structures. In recent years, the company increased its layers of management, which resulted in increased employee costs. In an effort to decrease these costs and improve efficiencies, the company drastically reduced its layers of management. Although some of its competitors had as many as 30 layers of management, Nucor reduced its structure to include only four layers of management. This reduction in layers of management reduced costs, but it has also increased the satisfaction of its employees at lower levels now that they are less removed from the top layer of the organization.[37]

class discussion highlight

ORGANIZING SKILL AND YOUR CAREER

The preceding section discusses vertical dimensioning, an important aspect of organizing skill. Assume that you are interviewing with a company for a potential job. Given your major, the classes you have taken so far, and your general interests, how might the vertical characteristics of the organization with which you are interviewing influence your career prospects and projected overall job satisfaction if working within the organization? Should you find out the vertical characteristics of organization structure of a potential employer before you start working for the company? Why?

Horizontal Dimensioning The **horizontal dimensioning** of an organization refers to the extent to which firms use lateral subdivisions or specialties within an organization. Overall, to build organizations horizontally, organizations establish departments. A **department** is a unique group of resources established by management to perform some organizational task. **Departmentalizing** is the process of establishing departments within the management system. Typically, these departments are based on, or contingent upon, such situational factors as the work functions being performed, the product or service being offered, the territory being covered, and the customer being targeted. In **an example from the world of management,** Pfizer, the world's largest company, recently announced a plan to restructure the company.[38] Management suggests that this new organizational structure, which includes five new horizontal departments, will help the company to increase future profitability.

The following sections highlight several different ways in which managers may departmentalize their organizations. In particular, the following illustrate how Sony, the company highlighted in the Challenge Case, might employ the various departmental structures discussed. Table 11.2 summarizes the major advantages and disadvantages associated with each type of departmentalization.

DEPARTMENTS BASED ON FUNCTION Perhaps the most widely used basis for establishing departments within the formal structure is the type of *work functions* (activities) being performed within the management system.[39] Functions are typically divided into the major categories of marketing, production, and finance. Figure 11.4 is an organization chart showing structure based primarily on function for Sony.

Functional departmentalizing brings with it both advantages and disadvantages. Perhaps the primary advantage of functional departmentalizing is the control conferred to the

TABLE 11.2   Advantages and Disadvantages of Departmentalization Modes

Departmentalization	Advantages	Disadvantages
Functional	• Power of functional heads promotes consistency (i.e., consistent marketing messages) • Relatively easy to assign blame or credit for the performance of a function (i.e., the performance of the company's marketing program)	• May prove difficult to coordinate between various functions • Difficult to assign credit or blame when a product performs well or poorly
Product	• Allows managers to focus on the products sold by the company • Relatively easy to assign credit or blame on the performance of a product	• Focus on product may force managers to miss differences in customers or geographic regions • May be difficult to coordinate across products
Geographic	• Managers can focus on the various regions (and their differences) served by the company • Allows firms to develop human resources by rotating managers across different regions	• May prove difficult to coordinate between various regions • May prove difficult to assign credit or blame based on the performance of a particular product
Customer	• Allows managers to focus on and cater to the most important customers • Relatively easy to assign blame or credit regarding customer relationships	• May prove difficult to coordinate across various customers • May introduce complexities as customers span different products and geographic areas
Matrix	• Allows firm to pool human resources for both short-term and long-term projects • Allows firm to maintain flexibility over time	• Difficult for employees to understand power structure within the firm • Difficult for employees to prioritize responsibilities based on multiple authority figures

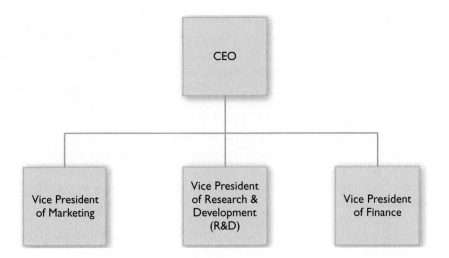

FIGURE 11.4
Departments by function at Sony

various functional heads. The vice president of marketing for Sony, for example, is able to control and coordinate the marketing plan for all of the organization's products, geographic regions, and customers. This structure allows for consistent marketing messages throughout the company. At the same time, however, the marketing plan emanating from such a structure may not be differentiated enough to suit the needs of Sony's diverse products, geographic regions, and customers. In other words, this structure may implicitly impose functional standardization that may not optimize the needs of the organization's various products and services.

DEPARTMENTS BASED ON PRODUCT OR SERVICE Organization structure based primarily on *product or service* departmentalizes resources according to the products or services being offered. As more and more products are offered by a company, it becomes increasingly difficult for management to coordinate activities across the organization. Organizing according to product or service permits the logical grouping of resources necessary to produce and market each product or service. Figure 11.5 is an organization chart for Sony showing structure based primarily on product.

Product or service departmentalizing also has both advantages and disadvantages. One of the primary advantages is the ability to focus the organization's efforts on each of the firm's products or services. With this structure, for example, the vice president of

Most hospitals are organized into departments based on the services they provide, such as radiology, surgery, or obstetrics. This doctor works in the emergency room, a critical department in most medical facilities.

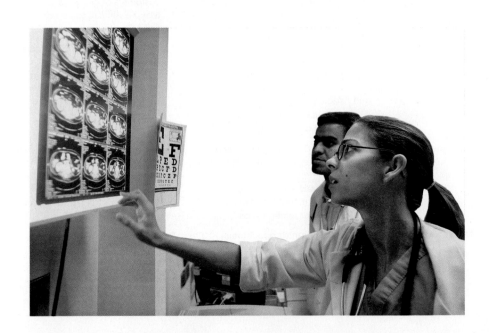

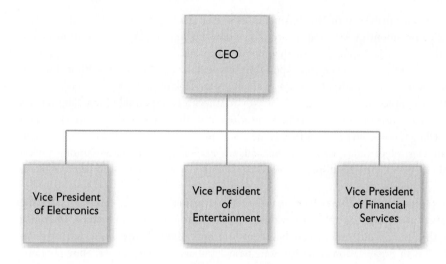

FIGURE 11.5
Departments by product at Sony

electronics for Sony has the power and authority to control all aspects of the electronics business. Moreover, this type of structure directly associates responsibility for each of the firm's products. If the electronics division does not perform well, for example, it is relatively easy for Sony's CEO to determine responsibility for the poor performance.

One of the primary disadvantages of this structure, though, is that the different units may result in some duplication of efforts, which may lead to higher costs. Continuing the example of Sony, the managers of the electronics division and the music division may both request more capital for marketing expenditures. Moreover, they may both create marketing positions within their units to aid in the marketing efforts. Taken together, these types of requests may strain the organization's resources.

DEPARTMENTS BASED ON GEOGRAPHY Structure based primarily on *territory* departmentalizes according to the places where the work is being done or the geographic markets on which the management system is focusing. The physical distances can range from quite short (between two points in the same city) to quite long (between two points in the same province, in different province, or even in different countries).[40] As market areas and work locations expand, the physical distances between places can make the management task extremely cumbersome. To minimize this problem, resources can be departmentalized according to territory. Figure 11.6 is an organization chart for Sony based primarily on territory.

Several advantages and disadvantages are associated with geographic departmentalizing. One of the primary advantages of this structure is that it helps the organization to focus equally on the organization's various geographic locations. For a company such as Sony, for

FIGURE 11.6
Departments by geography at Sony

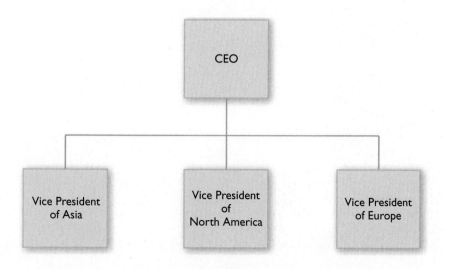

example, the vice president of North America is in charge of operations in North America, and the vice president of Asia is in charge of operations in Asia. The organization defines clearly the individuals responsible for these various regions.

At the same time, however, this type of departmentalizing also brings with it disadvantages. One of the main disadvantages, for example, is the lack of focus on products and services. In this example, the vice president for North America is responsible for selling movies, electronics, and music in North America. At the same time, the vice president of Asia is responsible for selling these same products in Asia; no single manager is responsible for the performance of movies, electronics, or music. Instead, the responsibility is shared among various divisional vice presidents; this dispersion of responsibility may produce coordination problems.

DEPARTMENTS BASED ON CUSTOMER Structure based primarily on the *customer* establishes departments in response to the organization's major customers. This structure, of course, assumes that major customers can be identified and divided into logical categories. Figure 11.7 is an organization chart for Sony based primarily on customers. Sony obviously can clearly identify its customers and divide them into logical categories.

Like the previously discussed organizational structures, customer departmentalization has both advantages and disadvantages. One of the primary advantages of customer departmentalization is that the firm focuses explicitly on its customers. Sony, for example, could follow this structure and include a vice president for each of its largest customers. This structure increases the likelihood that Sony will maintain its focus on its most important sources of sales. At the same time, however, this structure may also create some redundancies and increased costs. For example, the vice presidents may require their own marketing departments, which increases the likelihood for duplicated efforts.

DEPARTMENTS BY MATRIX The previous sections discussed several different types of departmentalizing. Moreover the potential advantages and disadvantages associated with each type were highlighted. These potential disadvantages have in part driven research examining "postbureaucratic" forms of organization.[41] These various organizational forms have arisen as a way to circumvent the possible disadvantages of the previously mentioned types of departmentalizing.

One of the most popular examples of postbureaucratic organizational forms is referred to a matrix structure. The matrix structure is best understood by first visualizing a more traditional form of organization structure. Figure 11.4, for example, shows a more traditional organizational form for Sony departmentalized by function. Figure 11.8 adds a series of projects (PlayStation III, Spiderman 3, and Portable Digital Music Player) and a manager for each project to the original organization structure to form a matrix organization for Sony. Essentially, a matrix organization is one in which a project

FIGURE 11.7
Departments by customer at Sony

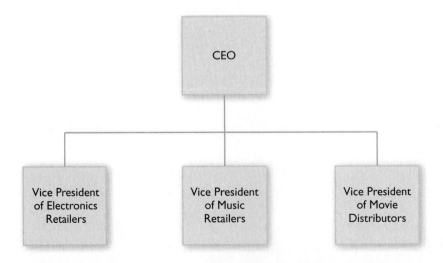

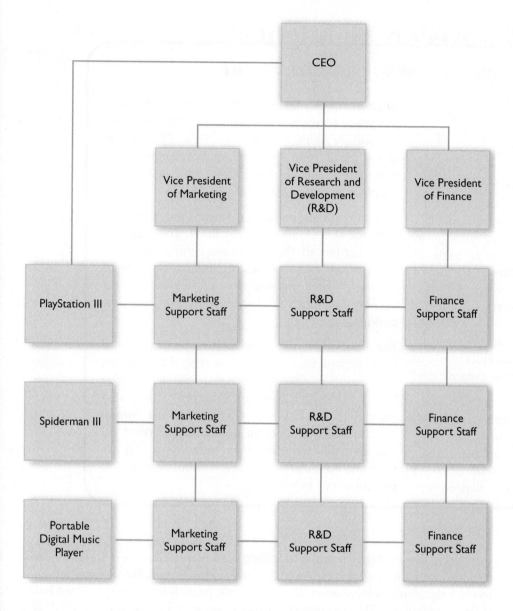

FIGURE 11.8
Matrix departments at Sony

manager(s) borrows workers from various parts of the organization to complete some specific project.[42] For this reason, matrix organizations are also called *project organizations.* The project itself may be either long term or short term, and once finished, the employees borrowed to complete it return to their original jobs. Within a matrix structure, the workers are responsible for their original activities along with project activities. Because of the importance of matrix structure projects, project managers generally report directly to the company CEO.

As with other types of departmentalizing, departmentalizing by matrix has both advantages and disadvantages. Perhaps the chief advantage of the matrix structure is that it allows the organization to focus on various projects simultaneously. For example, the matrix structure in Figure 11.8 allows Sony to focus on PlayStation III, Spiderman 3, and the Portable Digital Music Player at the same time.

As with any organization structure, the matrix structure also has disadvantages. For example, the matrix structure can be confusing, and employees may not be able to effectively cope with two bosses. In the Sony example, assume that the PlayStation III project manager and the VP of marketing both ask the same employee to complete different tasks. Which task should the employee complete first? Issues such as these can make matrix structure confusing.

class discussion highlight

RESEARCH FOR DEVELOPING ORGANIZING SKILL

Is a Formal Structure Always Best?

The preceding information has focused on formally establishing organization structure. Scholars have long debated whether formal organizational structures always lead to better firm performance. To examine this issue, researchers distinguish between mechanistic and organic organizational structures. **Mechanistic structures** are formal organizational structures such as those discussed in this chapter, and **organic structures** are less formal and represent loosely coupled networks of workers. Some researchers suggest that mechanistic structures are better suited for stable industries, but organic structures are better in more dynamic and uncertain industries.

A recent study by Sine, Mitsuhashi, and Kirsch examined this relationship in more detail. They attempted to answer the question: Which structures are best suited for smaller, entrepreneurial firms? Although some researchers suggest that organic structures are better for such firms, the authors of this study suggest that mechanistic structures are particularly helpful for smaller firms. The authors argue that formal structures make younger firms look more legitimate to outsiders such as customers, suppliers, and investors.

To examine their research question, they collected data for almost 500 Internet firms. The research team contacted the top management teams of these companies and asked them a number of questions about the structures of their companies. In addition, they collected measures of firm performance.

The authors examined several measures relating to each organization and top management team. They found that bigger firms were associated with higher levels of firm performance. They also examined the extent to which the firm's formal structure influenced firm performance. What do you think that the researchers found regarding the relationship between formal structure and firm performance? Why?

Forces Influencing Formal Structure   According to Shetty and Carlisle, the formal structure of a management system is continually evolving. Four primary forces influence this evolution: forces in the manager, forces in the task, forces in the environment, and forces in the subordinates.[43] The evolution of a particular organization is actually the result of a complex and dynamic interaction among these forces.

Forces in the manager are the unique way in which a manager perceives organizational problems.[44] Naturally, background, knowledge, experience, and values influence the manager's perception of what the organization's formal structure should be or how it should be changed.

Forces in the task include the degree of technology involved in performing the task and the task's complexity. As task activities change, a force is created to change the existing organization. Forces in the environment include the customers and suppliers of the management system, along with existing political and social structures. Forces in the subordinates include the needs and skill levels of subordinates. Obviously, as the environment and subordinates change, forces are created simultaneously to change the organization.

Fayol's Advice on Using Formal Structure   Preceding discussion has emphasized how to establish organization structure and related chain of command. Should a manager always adhere to established organization structure and related chain of command? Fayol has indicated that strict adherence to a particular chain of command is not always advisable.[45] Figure 11.9 explains his rationale. If individual F needs information from individual G and follows the concept of chain of command, F has to go through individuals D, B, A, C, and E before reaching G. The information would get back to F only by going from

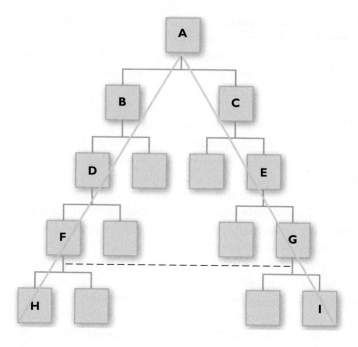

FIGURE 11.9
Sample organization chart showing that adhering to the chain of command is not advisable

G through E, C, A, B, and D. Obviously, this long, involved process can be time consuming and therefore expensive for the organization.

To avoid this lengthy process, Fayol recommended that in some situations a bridge, or **gangplank,** be used to allow F to go directly to G for information. This bridge is represented in Figure 11.9 by the dotted line connecting F and G. Managers should be careful in allowing the use of these organizational bridges, however, because although F might get the information from G more quickly and cheaply that way, individuals D, B, A, C, and E would be excluded from the communication channel, and their ignorance might prove more costly to the organization in the long run than would following the established chain of command. When managers allow the use of an organizational bridge, they must be extremely careful to inform all other appropriate individuals within the organization of any information received that way.

{ **CHALLENGE CASE SUMMARY**

The Challenge Case at the beginning of the chapter generally describes how Sony is being organized in order to be more competitive. Concepts in this chapter would be useful to a manager such as Sir Howard Stringer, Sony's CEO, in meeting organizing challenges similar to those discussed in the case.

In contemplating how Sony should be organized, a manager such as Stringer can focus on answering several important questions. These questions should be aimed at establishing an orderly use of Sony's organizational resources. Because these resources represent an investment on which he must get a return, Stringer's questions should be geared toward gaining information that will be used to maximize this return. Overall, such questions should focus on determining the use of Sony's resources that will best accomplish its goals.

Some preliminary questions could be as follows:

1. What organizational objectives exist at Sony? For example, does Sony want to focus more on international markets or focus its attention on Japanese consumers? Does Sony want to grow or maintain its present size?

2. What plans does Sony have to accomplish these objectives? Is Sony going to open more offices in international locations? Are additional training programs being added to enable employees to understand how to best work in international locations?

3. What are the major tasks Sony must go through to establish profitable linkages between its different divisions? For example, how many steps are involved in developing a videogame based on one of its current movies?

4. What resources does Sony have to run its operations? Answers to this question focus on issues such as the number of employees, financial resources available, equipment being used, and so on.

In order to develop a sound organizing effort, a manager should take classical organizing theory into consideration. Stringer, for example, should examine Sony's structure and how it influences working relationships among all Sony employees. In order to develop an effective organizational structure, Stringer must analyze situational factors in the company, such as functions, products, geographic locations, customers, and processes involved in offering its products to customers.

Within the case there is information indicating that Stringer's organization structure for Sony is based primarily upon products or services being offered. For example, two of the main areas at Sony are "music" and "videogames." In essence, Sony is arranging its resources to focus on its main product/service areas. A manager typically uses an organization chart to represent organization structure. Such a chart would not only allow Stringer to see the lines of authority and responsibility at Sony but also to understand the broad working relationships among his employees.

In developing the most appropriate way to organize Sony employees, a manager can reflect upon another major element in classical organizing theory, division of labor. Stringer could decide, for example, that instead of having one person do all the work involved in servicing a retail outlet such as Best Buy or Circuit City, the labor could be divided so that for each business customer one person would make the initial contact, another would assess the communication needs of the organization, and a third would explore the alternative ways that Sony could offer to meet those needs. In this way, employees could work more quickly and can specialize in one area of business customer relations, such as business needs assessment or meeting business customer needs.

In considering the appropriateness of division of labor at Sony, a manager could also consider creating a mechanism for enhancing coordination. In order to develop such a mechanism, Stringer must have a thorough understanding of how various Sony business processes occur so he can divide various tasks and maintain coordination within the various Sony divisions. In addition, a manager like Stringer must stress communication as a prerequisite for coordination. Without Sony employees continually communicating with one another, coordination will be virtually impossible. In taking action aimed at enhancing organizational coordination, Stringer must also continually plan for and take action toward maintaining such coordination.

The last two major elements in classical organizing theory that a manager could reflect upon are span of management and scalar relationships. Span of management focuses on the number of subordinates that managers in various roles at Sony can successfully supervise. In thinking about span of management Stringer might explore several important situational factors, such as similarities among various Sony activities, the extent to which Sony workers being managed are physically separated, and the complexity of various Sony work activities.

For example, Stringer should consider that distributing CDs to consumer outlets can be fairly simple and that developing new videogames can be much more involved and complicated. Therefore, the span of management for workers doing the former job should generally be larger than the span of management for workers doing the latter job. Other important factors Stringer should consider in determining spans of management for various Sony managers are the amount of time managers must spend coordinating workers' activities and the amount of time managers spend planning. With all this information, Stringer should be quite capable of determining appropriate spans of management for his managers.

MANAGEMENT SKILL ACTIVITIES

This section is specially designed to help you develop organizing skill. An individual's organizing skill is based upon an understanding of organizing concepts and the ability to apply those concepts in management situations. The following activities are designed both to heighten your understanding of organizing fundamentals and to develop your ability to apply those concepts in various management situations.

UNDERSTANDING ORGANIZING CONCEPTS

This section is comprised of activities that will sharpen your understanding of organizing concepts. Answer essay questions as completely as possible. Also, remember that additional true/false and multiple choice questions appear online at MyManagementLab.com to help you further refine your understanding of organizing.

Essay Questions

1. Describe the fundamental components of the organizing process. In your opinion, which of these components is most important? Which is least important? Explain.

2. Discuss the roles of vertical and horizontal differentiation as they relate to organizational structure. In your opinion, which of these concepts is most important for an effective organizational structure?

3. Compare and contrast the various types of departmentalization. In your opinion, which type of departmentalization is best?

4. Assume that you are the manager for Green Furniture, a company operating a number of furniture stores operating throughout the United States. Illustrate how the various types of departmentalization might apply to this company. In other words, discuss the various advantages and disadvantages of these types of departmentalization as they apply to Green Furniture.

5. Discuss the advantages and disadvantages associated with the concept of division of labor. How is the concept of span of management related to division of labor?

Developing Management Skill

Learning activities in this section are aimed at helping you to develop your strategic planning skill. Learning activities include Exploring Your Management Skill: Part 2, Experiential Exercise, Cases, and a VideoNet exercise.

EXPLORING YOUR MANAGEMENT SKILL: PART 2

As you recall, you completed Exploring Your Management Skill before you started to study this chapter. Your responses gave you an idea of how much you initially knew about organizing and helped you to focus on important points as you studied the chapter. Answer the Exploring Your Management Skill questions again now (p. 270) and compare your score to the first time you took it. This comparison will give you an idea of how much you have learned from studying this chapter and pinpoint areas for further clarification before you start studying the next chapter. Record your answers within the text or online at MyManagementLab.com. Completing the survey at MyManagementLab.com will allow you to grade and compare your test scores automatically. If you complete the test in the book, look up answers in the Exploring Your Management Skill section at the end of the book.

YOUR MANAGEMENT SKILLS PORTFOLIO

Your Management Skills Portfolio is a collection of activities especially designed to demonstrate your management knowledge and skill. By completing these activities at MyManagementLab.com, you will be able to print, complete with cover sheet, as many activities as you choose. Be sure to save your work. Taking your printed portfolio to an employment interview could be helpful in obtaining a job.

The portfolio activity for this chapter is Organizing Skill: Examining Organization Charts. Examine the organization chart shown and then answer the questions that follow.

1. Is the organization chart of the Department of Health and Human Services based mainly on function, product, geography, or customer? Argue why this basis might be an appropriate for its tasks.

2. Does this organization chart reflect a division of labor emphasis? Explain.

3. Give an illustration of how coordination is important to the success of the Department of Health and Human Services.

_____

_____

4. Present an argument discussing why the span of management for the Secretary is appropriate or inappropriate.

_____

_____

EXPERIENTIAL EXERCISE

Directions. Read the following scenario and then perform the listed activities. Your instructor may you to perform the activities as an individual or within groups. Follow all of your instructor's directions carefully.

Your company, Frogs of the World, has been manufacturing and selling plastic toy frogs for more than 15 years. Overall, the company has been successful and has become a market leader in the toy industry. Exploring the introduction of a new product, top management has just decided to begin manufacturing and selling a paper frog that hops. Mr. Hopper is the name of the new product. Your instructor will distribute design specifications for producing Mr. Hopper.

Top management has informed your group that it will immediately begin manufacturing Mr. Hopper. The department will only include people in your group. At some point, your instructor will appoint a leader for your group, give each member the raw materials needed to produce Mr. Hopper, and instruct you to actually begin the production process.

Your team will be judged by the number and quality of the Mr. Hoppers that you produce.

C A S E S

SONY ORGANIZES FOR SUCCESS

"Sony Organizes for Success" (p. 269) was written to help you better understand the organizing concepts contained in this chapter. Answer the following discussion questions about the Challenge Case to better understand how basic organization principles can be applied in a company such as Sony.

1. Does it seem reasonable that Stringer is attempting to better organize Sony in order to remain more competitive? Explain.
2. List five questions that Stringer should ask himself in exploring how best to organize Sony.
3. Explain why it would be important for Stringer to ask each of the questions you listed.

REORGANIZING FOR A NEW ERA AT NEWELL RUBBERMAID

Read the case and answer the questions that follow. Studying this case will help you better understand how concepts relating to fundamentals of organizing can be applied in a company such as Newell Rubbermaid.

Pots and pans, plastic tubs, permanent markers, pipe wrenches, and window shades are five distinctly different types of products that coexist under the Newell Rubbermaid corporate umbrella. Since Newell acquired Rubbermaid in 1999, management has been trying to find a structure that makes the most of the combined company's resources and well-known brands. Newell began life in 1902 as a manufacturer of window hardware. It went on a buying spree during the 1990s, picking up firms that make all kinds of household products, including Sanford (pens and markers), Kirsch (window treatments), Calphalon (cookware), and Goody (hair accessories). This growth strategy worked well; Newell's executives took advantage of increased manufacturing efficiencies and expanded marketing power to cut costs and build sales. Once acquired, the units remained loosely connected; as long as revenue growth continued, top management didn't even insist that all units report their results in the same way.

Meanwhile, Rubbermaid earned a global reputation for innovation as it pumped out a never-ending series of durable, handy products for home and office. During the mid-1990s, the company was launching at least one new product every day, for months on end. Eyeing Rubbermaid's new product prowess and its established retail relationships, Newell's top management became convinced that the two companies would fit well together. Only after the merger did they recognize how closely Rubbermaid's costs were tied to the fast-rising price of resin, a key ingredient in the manufacture of plastic products. Rubbermaid's bottom line was feeling the effects of eroding profit margins despite a deluge of new products.

Joseph Galli was appointed Newell Rubbermaid's CEO in 2001 and was charged with turning "two entities into a seamless whole," in the words of a corporate director. For his part, Galli saw "an unmatched portfolio of global brands," as well as some real challenges: "I didn't realize that Newell wasn't even measuring manufacturing productivity, let alone trying to improve it," he said. Galli immediately tackled several critical areas: He implemented a corporate-wide program for improving operational efficiency; developed a framework for tying tactics to goals and measuring progress toward interim targets; and began paring the portfolio to focus attention on the most promising units and products.

Galli set out to align what were once 26 diverse units into a more streamlined, collaborative structure. He divested underperforming units such as Mirro Cookware, got rid of 100 of Newell Rubbermaid's 500 brands, and outsourced some production to offshore facilities. The remaining units were organized into four distinct divisions identified by major brand, then reorganized into five divisions grouped according to type of product. These include the cleaning and organization group, the home and family group, the home fashions group, the office products group, and the tools and hardware group. Within each division, units are organized by brand and geography.

Just as important, Galli created a single corporate headquarters in the U.S. state of Georgia, replacing three head offices formerly located in the U.S. states of Illinois and Wisconsin. Before, arranging interdivisional meetings was a big headache; now, with dozens of executives in one place, Galli can call a meeting on the spur of the moment or consult with individual managers as needed. Moreover, he set up a Paris-based design center to support the new product efforts of all five divisions.

The new structure is starting to make a difference. Newell Rubbermaid units are combining forces to design and make products aimed at specific customer needs. For instance, the Rubbermaid unit recently developed an under-bed storage tub featuring an erasable surface created by the Sanford unit, enabling users to list the contents on the tub. However, the company has not yet met Galli's projections of aggressive growth. Although annual revenues are approaching $8 billion, the company recently experienced two years of multimillion-dollar losses due to reorganization costs. Looking ahead, Galli faces competition from Tupperware and other rivals, in addition to the challenges of rebuilding profits and getting more products into major retail chains worldwide.

QUESTIONS

1. Do you think that Newell Rubbermaid's departmentalization structure puts the company in a strong position for profitable growth? Explain.
2. How is Galli applying Mary Parker Follett's guidelines on coordination to Newell Rubbermaid?
3. Which of Fayol's 16 general guidelines would you recommend that Galli emphasize in using organization to address Newell Rubbermaid's challenges?

VIDEONET EXERCISE

Organizational Structure and Design at Insomnia Cookies

VIDEO HIGHLIGHTS

How does a small, quickly growing company develop and plan for a new structure that can expand with the company? Currently, the Insomnia Cookies headquarters consists of three to four people who oversee operations on 14 different college campuses. Each campus has its own manager and staff. Within the next year, Insomnia plans to open retail and delivery operations on six more campuses or locations. The following year, they will continue to launch in new locations. More people will have to be added to the senior management team to accommodate this level of growth, but Insomnia Cookies is grappling with how and when to bring on new people to help run the company. CEO Seth Berkowitz is determined to keep

the company from becoming top-heavy. Learn from the top management team at Insomnia as they take their own crash course on organizational structure and design.

Discussion Questions

1. What do you think the current organizational chart at Insomnia Cookies looks like? Is this structure appropriate for their needs? Explain.
2. What forces have most influenced the structure of Insomnia Cookies?
3. Describe CEO and founder Seth Berkowitz's span of management.

Internet Activity

Go to the Insomnia Cookies Web site at www.insomnia-cookies.com. In reviewing the site, list three organizational issues that top management must monitor to be successful in the future. How important will this be to company success? Why?

12 Responsibility, Authority, and Delegation

OBJECTIVES

TO HELP BUILD MY RESPONSIBILITY AND DELEGATION SKILL, WHEN STUDYING THIS CHAPTER, I WILL ATTEMPT TO ACQUIRE:

1. An understanding of the relationship of responsibility, authority, and delegation

2. Information on how to divide and clarify the job activities of individuals working within an organization

3. Knowledge of the differences among line authority, staff authority, and functional authority

4. An appreciation for the issues that can cause conflict in line and staff relationships

5. Insights into the value of accountability to the organization

6. An understanding of how to delegate

TARGET SKILL responsibility and delegation skill: the ability to understand one's obligation to perform assigned activities and to enlist the help of others to complete those activities

HUGGER MUGGER FACES ORGANIZING CHALLENGES

Nearly 20 years ago, Sara Chambers started to practice yoga. As her appreciation for yoga grew, she recognized that traditional exercise clothing was not ideal for those practicing yoga because it never seemed to fit quite right. Chambers, a skilled seamstress and designer, decided to address the problem. With two sewing machines, she began to design and manufacture exercise clothing especially for yoga, and she called her company Hugger Mugger Yoga Products.

Hugger Mugger makes clothing especially designed for the physical demands of yoga class.

Hugger Mugger's products included specially designed shorts with elastic on the legs that allowed the shorts to hug the legs during the upside down poses that are often a part of yoga. Due to the practicality of its products, the company experienced tremendous demand for its products. In fact, Hugger Mugger's products were featured on popular television programs and ordered by celebrities. To meet the increasing demand, the small company was forced to move three times to larger locations, and the payroll grew to 40 employees.

Recently, more and more people in the West have begun to practice yoga, and the once-small market for yoga products is growing quickly. A recent survey estimates that approximately 3 million people in the United States, for example, practice yoga at least twice per week; this represents a 133 percent increase from 2001. Moreover, in the most recent year tracked, Americans spent almost $3 billion on yoga classes and yoga-related products. Because of this increasing popularity, Hugger Mugger is facing new competition in the form of large, established companies such as Nike and Reebok. In fact, Nike is marketing its new cross-training shoe as a perfect yoga shoe. In addition, Liz Claiborne recently purchased Prana, a company specializing in yoga-related clothing; this purchase will help Liz Claiborne to tap into this growing market.

In the face of this growing market and increasing competition, Chambers must determine how Hugger Mugger will survive. Lacking formal business training, Chambers recently signed on a marketing expert as a managing partner. Until recently, Hugger Mugger products were sold only via catalog, online, or in specialty stores. With the marketing expert's help, however, the company has introduced a new line of lower-priced yoga products known as YogaBasics and sells them in chain stores. In addition, the company has created a catalog and an online store.

As the company progresses, Chambers must decide in which direction the company should move. As the company continues to grow and change, however, Chambers should recognize that she will not be able to control all facets of the company. How well she delegates responsibility to others within the organization may determine whether Hugger Mugger survives for another 20 years. Hugger Mugger's company motto is to "Celebrate The Journey." Chambers's decisions in the coming years will influence how much she—and her employees—will be celebrating.[1]

"EXPLORE YOUR OWN MANAGEMENT SKILLS BY TAKING THE QUIZ ON THE NEXT PAGE"

Before studying this chapter, respond to the following questions regarding the type of advice that you would give to Hugger Mugger's Sara Chambers, referenced in the Challenge Case. Then address the concerning human resource management challenges that she presently faces within the company. You are not expected to be a responsibility and delegation expert at this point. Answering the questions now can help you focus on important points when you study the chapter. Also, answering the questions again after you study the chapter will give you an idea of how much you have learned.

Record your answers here or go to MyManagementLab.com. Recording your answers in MyManagementLab will allow you to get immediate results and see how your score compares to your classmates. If you answer the questions in the book, the answers are located in the Exploring Your Management Skill Appendix at the end of the book.

FOR EACH STATEMENT CIRCLE:

- "Y" if you would give the advice to Sara Chambers.
- "N" if you would NOT give the advice to Sara Chambers.
- "NI" if you have no idea whether you would give the advice to Sara Chambers.

Ms. Chambers, in meeting your responsibility and delegation challenges at Hugger Mugger, you should . . .

Before Study	After Study

1. clarify the responsibilities of each employee at Hugger Mugger.

   Y, N, NI

2. make sure that one person is responsible for performing all of the activities that take place in Hugger Mugger.

   Y, N, NI

3. eliminate responsibility gaps when dividing job activities.

   Y, N, NI

4. communicate to employees that *responsibility* and *authority* are essentially interchangeable terms that have the same meaning.

   Y, N, NI

5. understand that throughout Hugger Mugger, authority does not necessarily imply that employees will follow the instructions of managers.

   Y, N, NI

6. realize that several factors—such as ability, communication, and consistency—will determine whether employees accept a manager's authority.

   Y, N, NI

7. focus primarily on line authority and not worry about the staff authority at Hugger Mugger, because the company is rather small.

   Y, N, NI

8. hold employees accountable for their job responsibilities in some circumstances, but should understand that accountability often backfires as a management approach.

   Y, N, NI

9. should hesitate to delegate responsibilities, because delegation will often reduce quality at Hugger Mugger.

   Y, N, NI

10. give employees freedom to pursue tasks in their own way when delegating at Hugger Mugger.

    Y, N, NI

11. recognize that neither centralization nor decentralization always works and instead should take into account the context of Hugger Mugger when considering these two organizing alternatives.

    Y, N, NI

12. recognize that as Hugger Mugger's products become more diverse, centralization becomes more effective.

    Y, N, NI

13. understand that as Hugger Mugger grows, decentralization becomes more effective.

    Y, N, NI

14. realize that as Hugger Mugger's customers become more diverse (in terms of tastes, geographic location, etc.), centralization becomes more effective.

    Y, N, NI

15. understand that in different circumstances, either supervisors or subordinates may provide obstacles in the delegation process.

    Y, N, NI

THE RESPONSIBILITY AND DELEGATION CHALLENGE

The Challenge Case describes Hugger Mugger's recent growth and expansion. As a small company like Hugger Mugger grows, management must constantly focus on organizing resources appropriately so that goals can be attained. To attain such organization, Sara Chambers, the founder of Hugger Mugger, must answer questions such as How should responsibility be established at Hugger Mugger? How should authority be distributed within the organization? Information in this chapter should be of great value to a manager in answering such questions.

RESPONSIBILITY

Perhaps the most fundamental method of channeling the activity of individuals within an organization, **responsibility** is the obligation to perform assigned activities. It is the self-assumed commitment to handle a job to the best of one's ability. The source of responsibility lies within the individual. A person who accepts a job agrees to carry out a series of duties or activities or to see that someone else carries them out.[2] The act of accepting the job means that the person is obligated to a superior to see that job activities are successfully completed. Even though a manager may delegate a task to another employee, the manager still remains responsible for the completion of the task. In other words, responsibility is in a sense shared by both the manager and the employee.

Nonetheless, responsibility is often difficult to identify. **An example from the world of management** illustrates this difficulty. **Countrywide Financial** is a company that engages in mortgage lending—when individuals need a loan to purchase a house, Countrywide is one of many companies to make these loans. Recently, Countrywide received negative attention from the press, because the company made loans to individuals who could not afford them, a practice known as "subprime" lending. When those individuals could not pay back their loans, the company lost a great deal of money and was forced to lay off employees. In this example, although the chief executive officer certainly bears some responsibility for the company's actions, the employees within the company who made loans to these individuals also bear some responsibility.[3]

The Job Description

An individual's job activities within an organization are usually summarized in a formal statement called a **job description**—a list of specific activities that must be performed by whoever holds the position. Unclear job descriptions can confuse employees and may cause them to lose interest in their jobs. On the other hand, a clear job description can help employees to become successful by focusing their efforts on the issues that are important for their position. When properly designed, job descriptions communicate job content to employees, establish performance levels that employees must maintain, and act as a guide that employees should follow to help the organization reach its objectives.[4]

Job activities are delegated by management to enhance the accomplishment of management system objectives. Management analyzes its objectives and assigns specific duties that will lead to reaching those objectives. A sound organizing strategy delineates specific job activities for every individual in the organization. Note, however, that as objectives and other conditions within the management system change, so will individual job activities.

The three areas related to responsibility include dividing job activities, clarifying the job activities of managers, and being responsible. Each of these topics is discussed in the sections that follow.

Dividing Job Activities

Obviously, one person cannot be responsible for performing all of the activities that take place within an organization. Because so many people work in a given management system, organizing necessarily involves dividing job activities among a number of individuals. Some method of distributing these job activities is essential.

The Functional Similarity Method The **functional similarity method** is, according to many management theorists, the most basic method of dividing job activities.

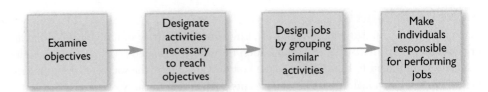

FIGURE 12.1
Sequence of activities for the functional similarity method of dividing job activities

Simply stated, the method suggests that management should take four basic interrelated steps to divide job activities in the following sequence:

1. Examine management system objectives
2. Designate appropriate activities that must be performed to reach those objectives
3. Design specific jobs by grouping similar activities
4. Make specific individuals responsible for performing those jobs

Figure 12.1 illustrates this sequence of activities.

Functional Similarity and Responsibility

At least three additional guides can be used to supplement the functional similarity method.[5] The first of these supplemental guides suggests that overlapping responsibility should be avoided when making job activity divisions. **Overlapping responsibility** refers to a situation in which more than one individual is responsible for the same activity. Generally speaking, only one person should be responsible for completing any one activity. When two or more employees are unclear about who should do a job because of overlapping responsibility, it usually leads to conflict and poor working relationships.[6] Often the job does not get done because each employee assumes the other will do it.

The second supplemental guide suggests that responsibility gaps should be avoided. A **responsibility gap** exists when certain tasks are not included in the responsibility area of any individual organization member. In this situation, nobody within the organization is obligated to perform certain necessary activities.[7]

The third supplemental guide suggests that management should avoid creating job activities for accomplishing tasks that do not enhance goal attainment. Organization members should be obligated to perform *only* those activities that lead to goal attainment.

The absence of clear, goal-related, nonoverlapping responsibilities undermines organizational efficiency and effectiveness.[8]

When job responsibilities are distributed inappropriately, the organization will have both responsibility gaps and overlapping responsibilities.

The effects of responsibility gaps on product quality are obvious, but overlapping responsibilities also impair product quality. When two (or more) employees are uncertain as to who is responsible for a task, four outcomes are possible:

1. One of the two may perform the job. The other may either forget to or choose not to do the job—and neither of these is a desirable outcome for product quality control.
2. Both employees may perform the job. At the least, this situation results in duplicated effort, which dampens employee morale. At worst, one employee may diminish the value of the other employee's work, resulting in a decrement in product quality.
3. Neither employee may perform the job because each assumed the other would do it.
4. The employees may spend valuable time negotiating each aspect and phase of the job to carefully mesh their job responsibilities, thus minimizing both duplication of effort and responsibility gaps. Though time consuming, this is actually the most desirable option in terms of product quality.

Note that each of these outcomes negatively affects both product quality and overall productivity.

Each member of a train crew performs separate tasks, eliminating the possibility of overlapping responsibilities.

class discussion highlight

RESPONSIBILITY AND DELEGATION SKILL AND YOUR CAREER

The preceding discussion highlights the role of responsibility in management. To manage other people, individuals must accept responsibility. Think about, for example, the various responsibilities of managers of your favorite retail store or the responsibilities of the chief executive officer of a large company. Given the role of responsibility in management, can you think of some examples that demonstrate your ability to accept responsibility? How has accepting responsibility helped your career? How might you integrate these examples into interview discussions? If you are currently employed, think of your responsibilities with your current employer. How might these responsibilities help you to advance in the company?

Clarifying Job Activities of Managers

Clarifying the job activities of managers is even more important than dividing the job activities of nonmanagers because managers affect greater portions of resources within the management system. Responsibility gaps, for instance, usually have a more significant impact on the management system when they relate to managers than when they relate to nonmanagers.

One process used to clarify management job activities "enables each manager to actively participate with his or her superiors, peers, and subordinates in systematically describing the managerial job to be done and then clarifying the role each manager plays in relationship to his or her work group and to the organization."[9] The purpose of this interaction is to eliminate overlaps or gaps in perceived management responsibilities and to ensure that managers are performing only those activities that lead to the attainment of management system objectives. Although this process is typically used to clarify the responsibilities of managers, it can also be effective in clarifying the responsibilities of nonmanagers.

Management Responsibility Guide A specific tool developed to implement this interaction process is the **management responsibility guide,** some version of which is used in most organizations. This guide helps management to describe the various responsibility relationships that exist in the organization and to summarize how the responsibilities of various managers relate to one another.

The seven main organizational responsibility relationships covered by the management responsibility guide are listed in Table 12.1. Once it is decided which of these

---

TABLE 12.1 Seven Responsibility Relationships Among Managers, as Used in the Management Responsibility Guide

1. **General Responsibility**—The individual who guides and directs the execution of the function through the person accepting operating responsibility

2. **Operating Responsibility**—The individual who is directly responsible for the execution of the function

3. **Specific Responsibility**—The individual who is responsible for executing a specific or limited portion of the function

4. **Must Be Consulted**—The individual whose area is affected by a decision and must be called on to render advice or relate information before any decision is made or approval is granted (This individual does not, however, make the decision or grant approval.)

5. **May Be Consulted**—The individual who may be called on to relate information, render advice, or make recommendations before the action is taken

6. **Must Be Notified**—The individual who must be notified of any action that has been taken

7. **Must Approve**—The individual (other than persons holding general and operating responsibility) who must approve or disapprove the decision

TABLE 12.2 Four Key Dimensions of Responsible Management Behavior

Attitude Toward and Conduct with Subordinates	Behavior with Upper Management	Behavior with Other Groups	Personal Attitudes and Values
Responsible managers—	Responsible managers—	Responsible managers—	Responsible managers—
1. Take complete charge of their work groups	1. Accept criticism for mistakes and buffer their groups from excessive criticism	1. Make sure that any gaps between their areas and those of other managers are securely filled	1. Identify with the group
2. Pass praise and credit along to subordinates	2. Ensure that their groups meet management expectations and objectives		2. Put organizational goals ahead of personal desires or activities
3. Stay close to problems and activities			3. Perform tasks that offer no immediate reward but help subordinates, the company, or both
4. Take actions to maintain productivity and are willing to terminate poor performers if necessary			4. Conserve corporate resources as if the resources were their own

relationships exist within the organization, the relationships between these responsibilities can be defined.

Responsible Managers Managers can be described as responsible if they perform the activities they are obligated to perform.[10] Because managers have more impact on an organization than nonmanagers, responsible managers are a prerequisite for management system success. Several studies have shown that responsible management behavior is highly valued by top executives because the responsible manager guides many other individuals within the organization in performing their duties appropriately.

The degree of responsibility that a manager possesses can be determined by appraising the manager on the following four dimensions:

1. Attitude toward and conduct with subordinates
2. Behavior with upper management
3. Behavior with other groups
4. Personal attitudes and values

Table 12.2 summarizes what each of these dimensions entails.

AUTHORITY

Individuals are assigned job activities to channel their behavior within the organization appropriately. Once they have been given specific assignments, they must be given a commensurate amount of authority to perform those assignments satisfactorily.

Authority is the right to perform or command. It allows its holder to act in certain designated ways and to directly influence the actions of others through orders. It also allows its holder to allocate the organization's resources to achieve organizational objectives.[11]

Authority on the Job

The following example illustrates the relationship between job activities and authority. Two primary tasks for which a particular service station manager is responsible are pumping gasoline and repairing automobiles. The manager has the authority necessary to perform both of these tasks, or he or she may choose to delegate automobile repair to the assistant manager. Along with the activity of repairing, the assistant should also be delegated the authority to order parts, to command certain attendants to help, and to do anything else necessary to perform repair jobs. Without this authority, the assistant manager may find it impossible to complete the delegated job activities.

Practically speaking, authority merely increases the probability that a specific command will be obeyed.[12] The following excerpt emphasizes that authority does not always exact obedience:[13]

> **People who have never exercised power have all kinds of curious ideas about it. The popular notion of top leadership is a fantasy of capricious power: the top man [or woman] presses a button and something remarkable happens; he [or she] gives an order as the whim strikes him [or her], and it is obeyed. Actually, the capricious use of power is relatively rare except in some large dictatorships and some small family firms. Most leaders are hedged around by constraints—tradition, constitutional limitations, the realities of the external situation, rights and privileges of followers, the requirements of teamwork, and most of all, the inexorable demands of large-scale organization, which does not operate on capriciousness. In short, most power is wielded circumspectly.**

Acceptance of Authority

As Chapter 11 showed, the positioning of individuals on an organization chart indicates their relative amount of authority. Those positioned toward the top of the chart possess more authority than those positioned toward the bottom. Chester Barnard writes, however, that the exercise of authority is determined less by formal organizational decree than by acceptance among those under the authority. According to Barnard, authority exacts obedience only when it is accepted.

In line with this rationale, Barnard defines *authority* as the character of communication by which an order is accepted by an individual as governing the actions that individual takes within the system. Barnard maintains that authority will be accepted only under the following conditions:

1. The individual can understand the order being communicated.
2. The individual believes the order is consistent with the purpose of the organization.
3. The individual sees the order as compatible with his or her personal interests.
4. The individual is mentally and physically able to comply with the order.

The fewer of these four conditions that are present, the lower the probability that authority will be accepted and obedience be exacted.

Barnard offers some guidance on what managers can do to raise the odds that their commands will be accepted and obeyed. He maintains that more and more of a manager's commands will be accepted over the long term if:[14]

1. The manager uses formal channels of communication and these are familiar to all organization members.
2. Each organization member has an assigned formal communication channel through which orders are received.
3. The line of communication between manager and subordinate is as direct as possible.
4. The complete chain of command is used to issue orders.
5. The manager possesses adequate communication skills.
6. The manager uses formal communication lines only for organizational business.
7. A command is authenticated as coming from a manager.

Types of Authority

Three main types of authority can exist within an organization: line authority, staff authority, and functional authority. Each type exists only to enable individuals to carry out the different types of responsibilities with which they have been charged.[15]

Line authority, such as this sewing factory supervisor holds, defines the superior–subordinate relationship.

Line and Staff Authority **Line authority,** the most fundamental authority within an organization, reflects existing superior–subordinate relationships. It consists of the right to make decisions and to give orders concerning the production-, sales-, or finance-related behavior of subordinates. In general, line authority pertains to matters directly involving management system production, sales, and finance and, as a result, the attainment of objectives. People directly responsible for these areas within the organization are delegated line authority to assist them in performing their obligatory activities.[16]

Whereas line authority involves giving orders concerning production activities, **staff authority** consists of the right to advise or assist those who possess line authority as well as other staff personnel. Staff authority enables those responsible for improving the effectiveness of line personnel to perform their required tasks. Examples of organization members with staff authority are people working in the accounting and human resource departments. Obviously, line and staff personnel must work together closely to maintain the efficiency and effectiveness of the organization. To ensure that line and staff personnel do work together productively, management must make sure both groups understand the organizational mission, have specific objectives, and realize that they are partners in helping the organization reach its objectives.[17]

Size is perhaps the most significant factor in determining whether an organization will have staff personnel. Generally speaking, the larger the organization, the greater the need and ability to employ staff personnel. As an organization expands, it usually needs employees with expertise in diversified areas. Although small organizations may also require this kind of diverse expertise, they often find it more practical to hire part-time consultants to provide it as needed than to hire full-time staff personnel, who may not always be kept busy.

Line–Staff Relationships Figure 12.2 shows how line–staff relationships can be presented on an organization chart. The plant manager on this chart has line authority over each immediate subordinate—the human resource manager, the production manager, and the sales manager. However, the human resource manager has staff authority in relation to the plant manager, meaning the human resource manager possesses the right to advise the plant manager on human resource matters. Still, final decisions concerning human resource matters are in the hands of the plant manager, the person holding line authority. Similar relationships exist

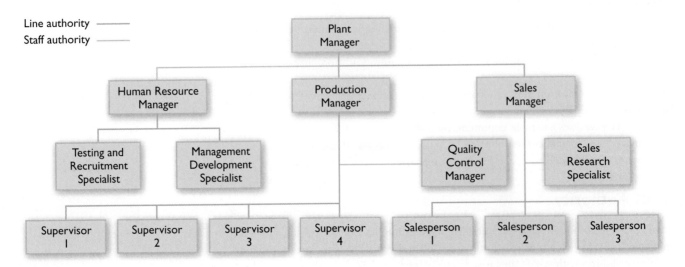

FIGURE 12.2 Possible line–staff relationships in selected organizational areas

between the sales manager and the sales research specialist, as well as between the production manager and the quality control manager.

Roles of Staff Personnel Harold Stieglitz has pinpointed three roles that staff personnel typically perform to assist line personnel:[18]

1. **The advisory or counseling role**—In this role, staff personnel use their professional expertise to solve organizational problems. The staff personnel are, in effect, internal consultants whose relationship with line personnel is similar to that of a professional and a client. For example, the staff quality control manager might advise the line production manager on possible technical modifications to the production process that will enhance the quality of the organization's products.
2. **The service role**—Staff personnel in this role provide services that can more efficiently and effectively be provided by a single centralized staff group than by many individuals scattered throughout the organization. This role can probably best be understood if staff personnel are viewed as suppliers and line personnel as customers. For example, members of a human resource department recruit, employ, and train workers for all organizational departments. In essence, they are the suppliers of workers, and the various organizational departments needing workers are their customers.
3. **The control role**—In this role, staff personnel help establish a mechanism for evaluating the effectiveness of organizational plans. Staff personnel exercising this role are representatives, or agents, of top management.

These three are not the only roles performed by staff personnel, but they are the major ones. In the final analysis, the roles of staff personnel in any organization should be specially designed to best meet the needs of that organization. In some organizations, the same staff people must perform all three major roles.

Conflict in Line–Staff Relationships Most management practitioners readily admit that a noticeable amount of organizational conflict centers around line–staff relationships.[19] From the viewpoint of line personnel, conflict is created because staff personnel tend to assume line authority, do not give sound advice, steal credit for success, fail to keep line personnel informed of their activities, and do not see the whole picture. From the viewpoint of staff personnel, conflict is created because line personnel do not make proper use of staff personnel, resist new ideas, and refuse to give staff personnel enough authority to do their jobs.

Staff personnel can often avert line–staff conflicts if they strive to emphasize the objectives of the organization as a whole, encourage and educate line personnel in the appropriate use of staff personnel, obtain any necessary skills they do not already possess, and deal intelligently with resistance to change rather than view it as an immovable barrier. Line personnel can do their part to minimize line–staff conflict by using staff personnel wherever possible, making proper use of the staff abilities, and keeping staff personnel appropriately informed.[20]

Functional Authority **Functional authority** consists of the right to give orders within a segment of the organization in which this right is normally nonexistent. This authority is usually assigned to individuals to complement the line or staff authority they already possess. Functional authority generally covers only specific task areas and is operational only for designated amounts of time. Typically, it is given to individuals who, in order to meet responsibilities in their own areas, must be able to exercise some control over organization members in other areas.

In **an example from the world of management,** Michael Schlotman, the chief financial officer for the **Kroger Company**, is an example of someone with functional authority. Among his basic responsibilities is the obligation to monitor the financial situation of the whole management system. To do so requires having appropriate financial information continually flowing in from various segments of the organization. The vice president

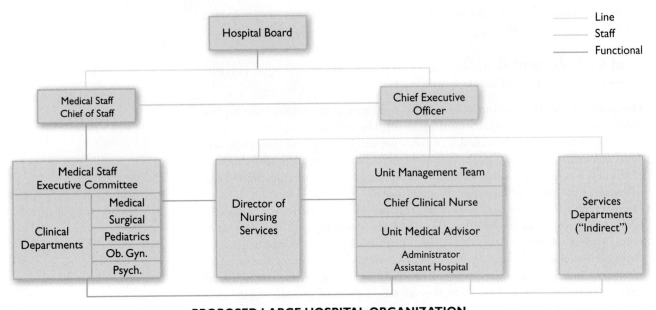

Line
Staff
Functional

**PROPOSED LARGE HOSPITAL ORGANIZATION
AUTHORITY AND RELATIONSHIPS**

FIGURE 12.3 Proposed design for incorporating three types of authority in a hospital

for finance, therefore, is usually delegated the functional authority to order various departments to furnish the kinds and amounts of information he or she needs to perform an analysis. In effect, this functional authority allows the vice president for finance to give orders to personnel within departments in which he or she normally cannot give orders.

From this discussion of line authority, staff authority, and functional authority, it is logical to conclude that although authority can exist within an organization in various forms, these forms should be used in a combination that will best enable individuals to carry out their assigned responsibilities and thereby best help the management system accomplish its objectives. When trying to decide on an optimal authority combination for a particular organization, managers should be aware that each type of authority has both advantages and disadvantages. The organization chart illustrated in Figure 12.3 shows how the three types of authority could be combined for the overall benefit of a hospital management system.

Accountability

Accountability refers to the management philosophy whereby individuals are held liable, or accountable, for how well they use their authority and live up to their responsibility of performing predetermined activities.[21] The concept of accountability implies that if an individual does not perform predetermined activities, some type of penalty, or punishment, is justifiable.[22] The punishment theme of accountability has been summed up by one company executive: "Individuals who do not perform well simply will not be around too long."[23] The accountability concept also implies that some kind of reward will follow if predetermined activities are performed well.

DELEGATION

So far in this chapter we have discussed responsibility and authority as complementary factors that channel activity within the organization. **Delegation** is the actual process of assigning job activities and corresponding authority to specific individuals within the organization.[24] This section focuses on the steps in the delegation process, obstacles to the delegation process, elimination of obstacles to the delegation process, and centralization and decentralization.

Steps in the Delegation Process

According to Newman and Warren, the delegation process consists of three steps, all of which may be either observable or implied.[25] The first step is assigning specific duties to the individual. In all cases, the manager must be sure that the subordinate assigned to specific duties has a clear understanding of what these duties entail. Whenever possible, the activities should be stated in operational terms so the subordinate knows exactly what action must be taken to perform the assigned duties. The second step of the delegation process involves granting appropriate authority to the subordinate—that is, the subordinate must be given the right and power within the organization to accomplish the duties assigned. The last step involves creating the obligation for the subordinate to perform the duties assigned. The subordinate must be aware of the responsibility to complete the duties assigned and must accept that responsibility. Table 12.3 offers several guidelines that managers can follow to ensure the success of the delegation process.

Obstacles to the Delegation Process

Obstacles that can make delegation within an organization difficult or even impossible can be classified into three general categories: (1) obstacles related to the supervisor, (2) obstacles related to subordinates, and (3) obstacles related to organizations.

An example of the first category is the supervisor who resists delegating his authority to subordinates because he cannot bear to part with any authority. Two other supervisor-related obstacles are the fear that subordinates will not do a job well and the suspicion that surrendering some authority may be seen as a sign of weakness. Moreover, if supervisors are insecure in their jobs or believe certain activities are extremely important to their personal success, they may find it hard to put the performance of these activities into the hands of others.

Supervisors who do wish to delegate to subordinates may encounter several subordinate-related roadblocks. First, subordinates may be reluctant to accept delegated authority because they are afraid of failing, lack self-confidence, or feel the supervisor doesn't have confidence in them.[26] These obstacles will be especially apparent in subordinates who have never before used delegated authority. Other subordinate-related obstacles are the fear that the supervisor will be unavailable for guidance when needed and the reluctance to exercise authority that may complicate comfortable working relationships.[27]

TABLE 12.3 Guidelines for Making Delegation Effective

- Give employees freedom to pursue tasks in their own way.
- Establish mutually agreed-upon results and performance standards for delegated tasks.
- Encourage employees to take an active role in defining, implementing, and communicating progress on tasks.
- Entrust employees with completion of whole projects or tasks whenever possible.
- Explain the relevance of delegated tasks to larger projects or to department or organization goals.
- Give employees the authority necessary to accomplish tasks.
- Allow employees access to all information, people, and departments necessary to perform delegated tasks.
- Provide training and guidance necessary for employees to complete delegated tasks satisfactorily.
- When possible, delegate tasks on the basis of employee interests.

Characteristics of the organization itself may also make delegation difficult. For example, a very small organization may present the supervisor with only a minimal number of activities to be delegated. In organizations where few job activities and little authority have been delegated in the past, an attempt to initiate the delegation process may make employees reluctant and apprehensive, for the supervisor would be introducing a significant change in procedure and change is often strongly resisted.[28]

Eliminating Obstacles to the Delegation Process

Because delegation has significant advantages for the organization, eliminating obstacles to the delegation process is important to managers. Among the advantages of delegation are enhanced employee confidence, improved subordinate involvement and interest, more free time for the supervisor to accomplish tasks, and, as the organization gets larger, assistance from subordinates in completing tasks the manager simply wouldn't have time for otherwise. True, there are potential disadvantages to delegation—such as the possibility that the manager will lose track of the progress of a delegated task—but the potential advantages of some degree of delegation generally outweigh the potential disadvantages.[29]

What can managers do to eliminate obstacles to the delegation process? First of all, they must continually strive to uncover any obstacles to delegation. Then they should approach taking action to eliminate these obstacles with the understanding that they may be deeply ingrained and therefore require much time and effort to overcome. Among the most effective managerial actions that can be taken to eliminate obstacles to delegation are building subordinate confidence in the use of delegated authority, minimizing the impact of delegated authority on established working relationships, and helping delegatees cope with problems whenever necessary.[30]

Koontz, O'Donnell, and Weihrich believe that overcoming the obstacles to delegation requires certain critical characteristics in managers. These characteristics include the willingness to consider the ideas of others seriously, the insight to allow subordinates the free rein necessary to carry out their responsibilities, trust in the abilities of subordinates, and the wisdom to allow people to learn from their mistakes without suffering unreasonable penalties for making them.[31]

class discussion highlight

MODERN RESEARCH AND RESPONSIBILITY AND DELEGATION SKILL

Authority and Trust[32]

Can you trust your manager? This important question has many implications for an employee's behavior. When employees trust their managers, they are likely to act in ways consistent with the desires of their managers. Conversely, when employees do not trust their managers, they may be less likely to engage in positive behaviors and more likely to engage in negative behaviors.

To examine the issue of trust in authority, David De Cremer and Tom Tyler ran a series of experiments examining how trust influences individuals' intentions to cooperate. Specifically, the authors asked subjects (i.e., students and employees) to rate their willingness to cooperate with a team led by a fictional leader. In one condition, the team leader could not be trusted, and in another condition the team leader could be trusted.

What do you think the authors found? Do you think that trust influenced subjects' intentions to cooperate with the leader? Why or why not? How might trust influence a manager's ability to delegate?

Centralization and Decentralization

Noticeable differences can be found from organization to organization in the relative number of job activities and the relative amount of authority delegated to subordinates. These differences are seldom a case of delegation existing in one organization and not existing in another. Rather, the differences come from degree of delegation.[33]

The terms **centralization** and **decentralization** describe the general degree to which delegation exists within an organization. They can be visualized as opposite ends of the delegation continuum depicted in Figure 12.4. It is apparent from this figure that centralization implies that a minimal number of job activities and a minimal amount of authority have been delegated to subordinates by management, whereas decentralization implies the opposite.

The issues practicing managers usually face are determining whether to further decentralize an organization and, if that course of action is advisable, deciding how to decentralize.[34] The section that follows presents practical suggestions on both issues.

Decentralizing an Organization: A Contingency Viewpoint The appropriate degree of decentralization for an organization depends on the unique situation of that organization. Some specific questions managers can use to determine the amount of decentralization appropriate for a situation are as follows:

1. **What is the present size of the organization?** As noted earlier, the larger the organization, the greater the likelihood that decentralization will be advantageous. As an organization increases in size, managers have to assume more and more responsibility and different types of tasks. Delegation is typically an effective means of helping them manage this increased workload.

   In some cases, however, top management will conclude that the organization is actually too large and decentralized. One signal that an organization is too large is labor costs that are high relative to other organizational expenses. In this instance, increased centralization of certain organizational activities could reduce the need for some workers and thereby lower labor costs to a more acceptable level.[35]

2. **Where are the organization's customers located?** As a general rule, the more physically separated the organization's customers are, the more viable a significant amount of decentralization is. Decentralization places appropriate management resources close to customers and thereby makes quick customer service possible. In **an example from the world of management,** retailer **JCPenney** decentralized its purchasing activities to give its managers the ability to buy merchandise best suited to the customers of its individual stores.[36]

3. **How homogeneous is the organization's product line?** Generally, as the product line becomes more heterogeneous, or diversified, the appropriateness of decentralization increases. Different kinds of decisions, talents, and resources are

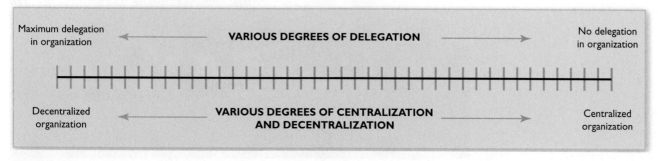

FIGURE 12.4 Centralized and decentralized organizations on delegation continuum

needed to manufacture different products. Decentralization usually minimizes the confusion that can result from diversification by separating organizational resources by product and keeping pertinent decision making close to the manufacturing process.[37]

4. **Where are organizational suppliers?** The location of raw materials needed to manufacture the organization's products is another important consideration. Time loss and high transportation costs associated with shipping raw materials over great distances from supplier to manufacturer could signal the need to decentralize certain functions.

   For example, the wood necessary to manufacture a certain type of bedroom set may be available only from tree growers in certain areas. If the bedroom set in question is an important product line for a furniture company and if the costs of transporting the lumber are substantial, a decision to decentralize may be a sound one. The effect of this decision would probably be building a plant that produces only bedroom sets in an area close to where the necessary wood is readily available. The advantages of such a costly decision, of course, would accrue to the organization only over the long term.

5. **Are quick decisions needed in the organization?** If speedy decision making is essential, a considerable amount of decentralization is probably in order. Decentralization cuts red tape and allows the subordinate to whom authority has been delegated to make on-the-spot decisions when necessary. It goes without saying that this delegation is advisable only if the potential delegatees have the ability to make sound decisions. If they don't, faster decision making results in no advantage for the organization. Quite the contrary, the organization may find itself saddled with the effects of unsound decisions.

6. **Is creativity a desirable feature of the organization?** If creativity is desirable, then some decentralization is advisable, for decentralization allows delegatees the freedom to find better ways of doing things. The mere existence of this freedom encourages the incorporation of new and more creative techniques within the task process.[38]

Decentralization at Massey-Ferguson: A Classic Example from the World of Management Positive decentralization is decentralization that is advantageous for the organization in which it is being implemented; negative decentralization is disadvantageous for the organization. To see how an organization should be

If an organization faces high costs associated with transporting raw materials over great distances, decentralization that puts facilities closer to resources might be an appropriate and cost-saving organization structure.

decentralized, it is worthwhile to study a classic example of an organization that achieved positive decentralization: Massey-Ferguson.[39]

GUIDELINES FOR DECENTRALIZATION Massey-Ferguson is a worldwide farm equipment manufacturer that has enjoyed noticeable success with decentralization over the past several years. The company has three guidelines for determining the degree of decentralization of decision making that is appropriate for a situation:

1. The competence to make decisions must be possessed by the person to whom authority is delegated. A derivative of this principle is that the superior must have confidence in the subordinate to whom authority is delegated.
2. Adequate and reliable information pertinent to the decision is required by the person making the decision. Decision-making authority therefore cannot be pushed below the point at which all information bearing on the decision is available.
3. If a decision affects more than one unit of the enterprise, the authority to make the decision must rest with the manager accountable for the most units affected by the decision.

DELEGATION AS A FRAME OF MIND Massey-Ferguson also encourages a definite attitude toward decentralization in its managers. The company's organization manual indicates that delegation is not delegation in name only but a frame of mind that includes both what a supervisor says to subordinates and the way the supervisor acts toward them. Managers at Massey-Ferguson are prodded to allow subordinates to make a reasonable number of mistakes and to help them learn from these mistakes.

COMPLEMENTING CENTRALIZATION Another feature of the positive decentralization at Massey-Ferguson is that decentralization is complemented by centralization:

> **The organization plan that best serves our total requirements is a blend of centralized and decentralized elements. Marketing and manufacturing responsibilities, together with supporting service functions, are located as close as possible to local markets. Activities that determine the long-range character of the company, such as the planning and control of the product line; the planning and control of facilities and money; and the planning of the strategy to react to changes in the patterns of international trade, are highly centralized.**

Thus, Massey-Ferguson management recognizes that decentralization is not necessarily an either/or decision and uses the strengths of both centralization and decentralization to its advantage.

MANAGEMENT RESPONSIBILITIES Not all activities at Massey-Ferguson are eligible for decentralization. Only management is allowed to follow through on the following responsibilities:

1. Responsibility for determining the overall objectives of the enterprise
2. Responsibility for formulating the policies that guide the enterprise
3. Final responsibility for control of the business within the total range of the objectives and policies, including control over any changes in the nature of the business
4. Responsibility for product design where a product decision affects more than one area of accountability
5. Responsibility for planning for achievement of overall objectives and for measuring actual performance against those plans
6. Final approval of corporate plans or budgets
7. Decisions pertaining to availability and application of general company funds
8. Responsibility for capital investment plans

CHALLENGE CASE SUMMARY

Chambers, the manager in the Challenge Case, is faced with the challenge of organizing the activities of an organization that is growing quickly. For example, Chambers must decide how to organize the activities of the company's salesforce—the tremendous growth means that the company has more customers. Organizing the sales department should help to ensure success if the activities directly reflect company objectives. Chambers's specific steps to organize should include the analysis of company sales objectives, the outlining of specific sales activities that must be performed to reach these objectives, the designing of sales jobs by the grouping of similar activities, and the assigning of these sales jobs to company personnel. To supplement these steps, Chambers must be careful not to create overlapping responsibilities, responsibility gaps, or responsibilities for sales activities that do not lead directly to the attainment of Hugger Mugger's goals.

In organizing the activities of employees in a growing organization like Hugger Mugger, Chambers must recognize, for example, that a manager's activities within the company, as well as those of subordinates, are a major factor in company success. Because the activity of a department manager can affect all personnel within that department, the activities of the department manager must be well defined. From the viewpoint of company divisions, one department manager's activities should be coordinated with those of other departments: For example, the activities in the sales department should be coordinated with activities in the company's marketing department.

Overall, for managers at Hugger Mugger to be responsible, they must perform the activities they are obligated to perform. Managers in the sales department, for example, are obligated to monitor the performance of all salespeople and to provide unbiased assessments.

Chambers must be sure that any individuals within Hugger Mugger who are delegated job activities are delegated a commensurate amount of authority to give orders and carry out those activities. Managers throughout Hugger Mugger must recognize, however, that authority must be accepted if obedience is to be exacted. To increase the probability of acceptance, care should be taken to ensure that individuals understand internal orders and see orders as being consistent with the objectives of both the department they work in and the company. Employees should perceive the orders they receive as being compatible with their individual interests, and they should see themselves as being mentally and physically able to follow those orders. Chambers must be careful to delegate jobs only to those organization members who are mentally and physically able to carry them out.

Assuming that a main objective of Hugger Mugger is to produce and sell the highest quality of yoga products possible, company personnel who are directly responsible for achieving this objective should possess line authority to perform their responsibilities. For example, individuals responsible for manufacturing yoga shorts must be given the right to do everything necessary to produce the highest-quality shorts possible.

As Hugger Mugger grows, the company will need individuals who are charged with the responsibility of assisting the line through a staff position. A new market research position in the company might be a good example of such a staff position. For example, a market researcher within Hugger Mugger might be given the responsibility of designing customer satisfaction surveys. Results of such surveys could be used for advising Hugger Mugger management on issues such as how to raise the perceived quality of Hugger Mugger's products in the eyes of the customers. Any individuals responsible for advising the line should be delegated appropriate staff authority.

As in all organizations, the potential for conflict between Hugger Mugger line and staff personnel could be significant. Chambers should be aware of this potential and encourage both line and staff personnel to minimize it.

Functional authority and accountability are two additional factors that Chambers must consider when organizing employee activities within Hugger Mugger. Some employees may have to be delegated functional authority to supplement the line or staff authority they already have. A Hugger Mugger human resource manager (staff person), for example, may need to gather information from the company's sales department in order to understand whether the company needs to hire additional salespeople. Functional authority would enable staff individuals to command that this information be channeled to them.

In organizing employee activity, Chambers should also stress the concept of accountability—that living up to assigned responsibilities brings rewards and not living up to them brings negative consequence.

To delegate activities effectively within Hugger Mugger, Chambers must assign specific duties to individuals, grant corresponding authority to these individuals, and make sure these individuals are aware that they are obligated to perform these activities.

In encouraging the use of delegation within Hugger Mugger, Chambers must be aware that obstacles to delegation may exist on the part of company managers, their subordinates, or the departments in which they work. She must be sure that managers can meet the delegation challenge by discovering which obstacles exist in their work environments and taking steps to eliminate them. If Chambers is to be a successful delegator, she also must be willing to consider the ideas of her subordinates, allow them the free rein necessary to perform their assigned tasks, trust them, and help them learn from their mistakes without suffering unreasonable penalties.

Centralization implies that few job activities and little authority have been delegated to subordinates; decentralization implies that many job activities and much authority have been delegated. Chambers will have to determine the best degree of delegation for her subordinates regarding all job activities. For guidelines, Chambers can rely on certain rules of thumb to determine that greater degrees of delegation will be appropriate for the company (1) as departments become larger, (2) as manufacturing facilities become more geographically dispersed and diversified, and (3) as the needs for quick decision making and creativity increase.

The Massey-Ferguson decentralization situation could provide Chambers with many valuable insights on what characteristics the decentralization process within the company should assume. First, managers should use definite guidelines to decide whether their situation warrants added decentralization. In general, additional delegation probably is warranted within the company as the competence of subordinates increases, as managers' confidence in their subordinates increases, and as more adequate and reliable decision-making information within the company becomes available to subordinates. For delegation to be advantageous for Hugger Mugger, company managers must help subordinates learn from their mistakes. Depending on their situations, individual Hugger Mugger managers may want to consider supplementing decentralization with centralization.

MANAGEMENT SKILL ACTIVITIES

This section is specially designed to help you develop responsibility and delegation skill. An individual's management skill is based upon an understanding of management concepts and the ability to apply those concepts in management situations. As a result, the following activities are designed both to heighten your understanding of responsibility and delegation concepts and to help you gain facility in applying these concepts in various management situations.

UNDERSTANDING RESPONSIBILITY AND DELEGATION CONCEPTS

This section is comprised of activities that will sharpen your understanding of responsibility and delegation concepts. Answer essay questions as completely as possible. Also, remember that many additional true/false and multiple choice questions appear online at MyManagementLab.com to help you further refine your understanding of concepts related to responsibility and delegation.

Essay Questions

1. Distinguish between responsibility and authority, and provide examples to support your distinctions.
2. Describe the three main types of authority that can exist within an organization.
3. Explain the three major steps in the delegation process.
4. Compare and contrast centralization versus decentralization. In your opinion, which is best for organizations?
5. What is acceptance of authority, and under which conditions will employees accept authority?

Developing Management Skill

Learning activities in this section are aimed at helping you to develop your responsibility and delegation skill. Learning activities include Exploring Your Management Skill: Part 2, Experiential Exercise, Cases, and a VideoNet exercise.

EXPLORING YOUR MANAGEMENT SKILL: PART 2

As you recall, you completed Exploring Your Management Skill before you started to study this chapter. Your responses gave you an idea of how much you initially knew about responsibility and delegation and helped you to focus on important points as you studied the chapter. Answer the Exploring Your Management Skill questions again now (p. 292) and compare your score to the first time you took it. This comparison will give you an idea of how much you have learned from studying this chapter and pinpoint areas for further clarification before you start studying the next chapter. Record your answers within the text or online at MymanagementLab.com. Completing the survey at MyManagementLab.com will allow you to grade and compare your test scores automatically. If you complete the test in the book, look up answers in the Exploring Your Management Skill section at the end of the book.

YOUR MANAGEMENT SKILLS PORTFOLIO

Your Management Learning Portfolio is a collection of activities especially designed to demonstrate your management knowledge and skill. By completing these activities online at MyManagementLab.com, you will be able to print, complete with cover sheet, as many activities as you choose. Be sure to save your work. Taking your printed portfolio to an employment interview could be helpful in obtaining a job.

The portfolio activity for this chapter is *Delegating Basketball Duties at Texas A&M.* Study the following information and complete the exercises that that follow.[40]

Delegating Basketball Duties at Texas A&M

Athletics programs are big business for universities, and the influence of athletics is no different at Texas A&M University. Recently, Texas A&M hired Mark Turgeon as the new men's basketball coach. Turgeon, who coached at Wichita State University before joining Texas A&M, has a great deal of work to complete. Some of Turgeon's responsibilities as the new head basketball coach include recruiting new players, designing offensive plays, designing defensive plays, and others.

As the new head coach at Texas A&M, Turgeon has asked you to help him perform his job both efficiently and effectively. Specifically, Turgeon believes that he needs to delegate effectively, but needs help in this process. In the following exercise, answer the questions related to the delegation process.

1. This exercise identified some of Turgeon's responsibilities as the new head basketball coach at Texas A&M University. List some of Turgeon's other responsibilities.

2. The first step in the delegation process is to assign specific duties to individuals. What do you think are Turgeon's primary duties, and to whom can he assign these duties? How would you state these duties in operational terms such that the employees understand them?

3. The second step in the delegation process involves granting authority to subordinates. How would Turgeon grant authority to others? How would he make sure that others accepted this new authority?

_____

_____

_____

4. The third step in the delegation process entails making sure the subordinate accepts responsibility for the delegated tasks. How would Turgeon ensure that subordinates accept responsibility?

_____

_____

_____

5. Finally, many obstacles could damage the effectiveness of Turgeon's delegation efforts. List the primary obstacles that Turgeon must overcome.

_____

_____

_____

EXPERIENTIAL EXERCISE: DEBATING CENTRALIZATION AT POTTERY BARN

Directions. Read the following scenario and then perform the listed activities. Your instructor may want you to perform the activities as an individual or within groups. Follow all of your instructor's directions carefully.

As discussed in the chapter, scholars have long debated the advantages and disadvantages of centralization and decentralization. Executives at the home furnishing store Pottery Barn have contacted your group to help them better understand whether the company should be either more centralized or more decentralized. Visit the Pottery Barn's Web site, and take note of the firm's size, locations, product line, and so on. After studying the company, revisit the discussion of centralization and decentralization in the chapter. How centralized or decentralized should Pottery Barn be? Use the guidelines presented in the text to frame and support your arguments.

CASES

ADOBE SYSTEMS REINVENTS ITSELF AGAIN AND AGAIN

Read the case and answer the questions that follow. Studying this case will help you better understand how concepts relating to organizational change and stress can be applied in a company such as Adobe Systems.

"One of my biggest challenges in taking over from two great founders has been trying to figure out how to change the company without destroying the culture that John [Warnock] and Chuck [Geschke] built," says Bruce Chizen, CEO of Adobe Systems. Founded in 1981 by two researchers with high-tech experience, Adobe has successfully introduced such innovations as Acrobat Reader document-viewing software, PostScript printer language, and Adobe PhotoShop imaging software. When Chizen became executive vice president in 1998 and again when he was named CEO in 2000, he initiated considerable organizational change at Adobe.

In 1998, the company was generating $850 million in annual revenues but had fallen behind schedule on a new software product and was suffering a sales slowdown due to economic woes in Asia. Moreover, it was so cash-rich (and debt-free) that it was a tempting takeover target, attracting an unwelcome acquisition bid from competitor Quark that Adobe successfully deflected. At that point, the only way to recapture growth was to initiate change, just as Adobe's technology had to continue changing to stay ahead of the curve. With a new executive team, the company refocused on specific customer needs and segments, thinned its employee ranks, and switched from a territory to a functional structure. It also centralized administration and control systems to give managers better and more timely information on which to base their decisions.

Adobe was soon back on track. However, by the time Chizen took over as CEO, he was convinced that the company could not sustain long-term growth without widening its scope beyond function-specific business software. This change was in keeping with the company's mission, which the CEO says has "always been about developing, designing, marketing, selling software to help people communicate better," as well as by Adobe's core competencies: "We know what we do well—we make software where 'good enough' is not acceptable."

To avoid being eclipsed by competitive technology, Adobe had to quickly develop cutting-edge software for organizations seeking to create, customize, exchange, and enhance all kinds of documents, not just images or graphics or text alone. In addition to a full internal program of software research and development, Chizen bought several smaller firms to gain their technical expertise in data capture and document management applications. Still, the CEO realized that his effort to widen Adobe's scope would be effective only with employee acceptance and support. He notes that "someone who left Adobe could get a job somewhere else with relatively little risk and a great deal of upside. So the people who chose to stay really saw the potential in this company. And because we had committed employees, the motivation to change was there. That was the biggest change."

These days, Adobe has grown to 2,460 employees and $1.2 billion in annual sales revenues, based on its broader array of software programs for enterprise-wide use. Its annual employee turnover rate has dropped from a high of 20 percent to a minimal 4 percent. Just as important, the company's Portable Document Format (PDF) has been adopted as the standard technology by a number of industries and government agencies seeking secure electronic documentation and interchange. Next on Chizen's list is software that will allow cell phone users to swap and read PDF documents on the fly.

The CEO acknowledges that change has not come easily, in part because the company is still relatively young and because "innovation is about the employees . . . it's what's in people's heads that makes a difference." With more rigorous processes for managing human resources and handling performance evaluation, Adobe has the tools to hire, motivate, and reward outstanding employees. The workforce has clearly embraced the changes, because the company has been named to *Fortune* magazine's "Best Places to Work" list more than once.

QUESTIONS

1. Using the model of stability and adaptation, explain what you think might happen to Adobe if Chizen continues to initiate major organizational changes every two years.

2. Which of the three kinds of changes did Adobe make in 1998, and how did it set the stage for the changes made in 2000 and later?

3. Would you recommend that Adobe allow all its employees to be fully mobile? Explain.

VIDEONET EXERCISE

Foundations of Behavior at TerraCycle

VIDEO HIGHLIGHTS

What do you need to know about human behavior when many of the people you hire are right out of college or previously unemployed? How can you tell if someone has the right attitude and personality for the company? How can you tell if someone has the right aptitude to do the job? Then, once you've made the hire, how do you ensure people are satisfied and will stick around? Small companies like TerraCycle move quickly and cannot afford to make bad hires or experience high turnover. So how do the managers at TerraCycle ensure their company continues to thrive by picking and retaining the right people?

Discussion Questions

1. Is there division of duties at TerraCycle? If so, how are they divided? Explain.
2. Which staff role does Milton, assistant production manager, describe in the video?
3. What are some of the possible obstacles to the delegation process faced by top management at TerraCycle? Explain.

Internet Activity

Go to TerraCycle's Web site at www.TerraCycle.net. Combining what you view on TerraCycle's history, story, and CEO with the information provided on the video clip, list three tasks that the chief executive officer might delegate to other top managers. To which managers would the tasks be delegated? Why?

13 Human Resource Management

OBJECTIVES

TO HELP BUILD MY HUMAN RESOURCE MANAGEMENT SKILL, WHEN STUDYING THIS CHAPTER, I WILL ATTEMPT TO ACQUIRE:

1. An overall understanding of how appropriate human resources can be provided for the organization

2. An appreciation for the relationship among recruitment efforts, an open position, sources of human resources, and the law

3. Insights into the use of tests and assessment centers in employee selection

4. An understanding of how the training process operates

5. A concept of what performance appraisals are and how they can best be conducted

TARGET SKILL

human resource management skill: the ability to take actions that increase the contributions of individuals within the organization

CHALLENGE CASE

CISCO RECRUITS THE BEST MINDS IN CHINA

John Chambers is the CEO of Cisco Systems, a company that manufactures and sells networking communications equipment to a wide array of customers in both the private and public sectors. In recent years, Cisco's success has been evidenced by its tremendous financial performance. Cisco's sales have been known to grow more than 50 percent annually over five-year periods—an astronomical rate for any corporation, especially for a company as large as Cisco.

To a large extent, Cisco's success has been the result of its human resource strategy. Often, Cisco has acquired other companies mainly to gain their bright engineers. As employees of acquired companies, people normally became Cisco's new employees. During a recent two-year period, Cisco averaged an acquisition every other week and doubled its employee base to 44,000 workers.

Complementing its acquisition strategy, Cisco used other tactics to recruit new employees during the technology boom in the late 1990s. For example, Cisco used focus groups to learn what type of movies and Web sites that the best and brightest potential employees favored. Then, Cisco programmed its Web site to recognize visitors from its chief rival 3Com and greeted these visitors with a special screen stating, "Welcome to Cisco; would you like a job?" Cisco figured that competitors bold enough to visit its Web site were just the type of employees it needed.

Cisco's human resources managers adapt their strategies to ensure the company recruits and retains the right people to meet its goals.

More recently, Cisco increased its focus on hiring employees in other countries. Specifically, Cisco concentrated intensely on recruiting and retaining employees in China. However, Cisco is not the only multinational company to recognize the importance of China's supply of human resources—Cisco competes with other companies such as Intel and IBM for these potential employees.

Despite China's enormous population, only a limited supply of qualified engineers there also speak English. As such, the competition for recruiting these employees remains fierce. In fact, Cisco has instituted several new tactics in hiring new employees. The company, for example, offers private shuttle buses from subways to the company's office. In addition, the company offers management development seminars to help the employees, who are young and focus largely on technology, improve their management skills. Relying on practices such as these has helped Cisco to hire some of the most talented engineers in Shanghai.

In short, Cisco is applying the human resource management practices perfected in the United States to other global markets. As market conditions change, though, John Chambers knows that Cisco's human resource strategy will also need to change its focus internationally if it wants to recruit and retain the best and brightest minds in the technology sector.[1]

"EXPLORE YOUR OWN MANAGEMENT SKILLS BY TAKING THE QUIZ ON THE NEXT PAGE"

Before studying this chapter, respond to the following questions regarding the type of advice that you would give to Cisco's John Chambers referenced in the Challenge Case. Then address the concerning human resource management challenges that he presently faces within the company. You are not expected to be a human resource management expert at this point. Answering the questions now can help you focus on important points when you study the chapter. Also, answering the questions again after you study the chapter will give you an idea of how much you have learned.

Record your answers here or go to MyManagementLab. com. Recording your answers in MyManagementLab will allow you to get immediate results and see how your score compares to your classmates. If you answer the questions in the book, the answers are located in the Exploring Your Management Skill Appendix at the end of the book.

FOR EACH STATEMENT CIRCLE:

- "Y" if you would give the advice to John Chambers.
- "N" if you would NOT give the advice to John Chambers.
- "NI" if you have no idea whether you would give the advice to John Chambers.

Mr. Chambers, in meeting your human resource management challenges at Cisco, you should . . .

Before Study	After Study

1. focus on hiring and retaining both appropriate and inappropriate human resources.

    Y, N, NI

2. recognize the three steps in the human resource management process: recruitment, selection, and training.

    Y, N, NI

3. focus primarily on hiring employees first and then work with the newly hired employees to define their jobs.

    Y, N, NI

4. understand that job openings may be filled by individuals who work within Cisco as well as other individuals who do not work at Cisco.

    Y, N, NI

5. rely on human resource inventory techniques such as the management inventory card, position replacement form, and management manpower replacement chart to monitor Cisco's human resources.

    Y, N, NI

6. understand that Cisco can choose potential employees based on race, color, religion, and gender for hiring, firing, and layoff policies.

    Y, N, NI

7. rely exclusively on personality tests—and not aptitude or achievement tests—in the selection process.

    Y, N, NI

8. focus on valid tests in the selection process and not worry as much about test reliability.

    Y, N, NI

9. understand that training is typically an ongoing activity, whereby individuals are trained multiple times throughout their careers at Cisco.

    Y, N, NI

10. employ both lectures and programmed learning as techniques for training Cisco employees.

    Y, N, NI

11. evaluate Cisco's training program periodically to assess its effectiveness.

    Y, N, NI

12. use performance appraisals to support salary increases but rely on other techniques for promotions, demotions, and terminations.

    Y, N, NI

13. performance appraisals should focus primarily upon the evaluator's impression of the employee's performance and not on objective measures of the employee's performance.

    Y, N, NI

14. performance appraisals should focus on both short-term and long-term measures of the employee's performance.

    Y, N, NI

15. individuals involved with the performance appraisal process should view the process as a punishment-reward situation.

    Y, N, NI

THE HUMAN RESOURCE MANAGEMENT CHALLENGE

The Challenge Case discusses tactics that management at Cisco Systems has used to hire and retain its brightest employees in China. The task of hiring and retaining not just people, but the *right* people is part of managing human resources in any organization. This chapter outlines the process of managing human resources within an organization and emphasizes how hiring and retaining the right people is part of this process for managers at a company such as Cisco. This chapter discusses this process by first defining appropriate human resources and then examining the steps to be followed in providing them.

DEFINING APPROPRIATE HUMAN RESOURCES

The phrase **appropriate human resources** refers to the individuals within the organization who make a valuable contribution to management system goal attainment. This contribution results from their productivity in the positions they hold. The phrase *inappropriate human resources* refers to organization members who do not make a valuable contribution to the attainment of management system objectives. For one reason or another, these individuals are ineffective in their jobs.

Productivity in all organizations is determined by how human resources interact and combine to use all other management system resources. Such factors as background, age, job-related experience, and level of formal education all play a role in determining how appropriate the individual is for the organization. Although the process of providing appropriate human resources for the organization is involved and somewhat subjective, the following section offers insights on how to increase the success of this process.

STEPS IN PROVIDING HUMAN RESOURCES

To provide appropriate human resources to fill both managerial and nonmanagerial openings, managers follow four sequential steps.[2]

1. Recruitment
2. Selection
3. Training
4. Performance appraisal

Figure 13.1 illustrates these steps.

Recruitment

Recruitment is the initial attraction and screening of the supply of prospective human resources available to fill a position. Its purpose is to narrow a large field of prospective employees to a relatively small group of individuals from which someone eventually will be hired. To be effective, recruiters must know the job they are trying to fill, where potential human resources can be located, and how the law influences recruiting efforts.

Knowing the Job Recruitment activities must begin with a thorough understanding of the position to be filled so the broad range of potential employees can be narrowed intelligently. The technique commonly used to gain that understanding is known as **job analysis.** Basically, job analysis is aimed at determining a **job description** (the activities a job entails) and a **job specification** (the characteristics of the individual who should be hired for the job).[3] Figure 13.2 shows the relationship of job analysis to job description and job specification.[4]

Most large companies have developed a procedure for performing a job analysis. As with all job analysis procedures, these procedures use information gathering as the primary means of determining what workers do and how and why they do it. Naturally, the quality of the job analysis depends on the accuracy of information gathered. This information is used to develop both a job description and a job specification.[5]

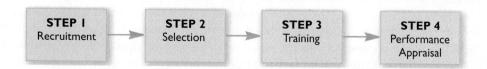

FIGURE 13.1 Four steps to providing appropriate human resources for an organization

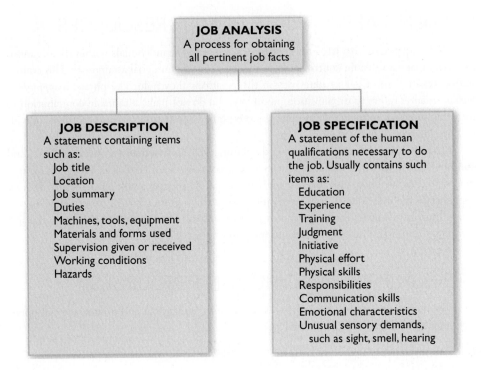

FIGURE 13.2
Relationship of job analysis, job description, and job specification

Knowing Sources of Human Resources Besides a thorough knowledge of the position the organization is trying to fill, recruiters must be able to pinpoint sources of human resources. The supply of individuals from which to recruit is continually changing, which means that at times, finding appropriate human resources will be much harder than at other times. Human resources specialists in organizations continually monitor the labor market so they will know where to recruit suitable people and what kind of strategies and tactics to use to attract job applicants in a competitive marketplace.[6]

Sources of human resources available to fill a position can be generally categorized in two ways: sources inside the organization and sources outside the organization.

Sources Inside the Organization The pool of employees within the organization is one source of human resources. Some individuals who already work for the organization may be well qualified for an open position. Although existing personnel are sometimes moved laterally within an organization, most internal movements are promotions. Promotion from within has the advantages of building employee morale, encouraging employees to work harder in hopes of being promoted, and enticing employees to stay with the organization because of the possibility of future promotions. Companies such as Exxon and General Electric find it especially rewarding to train their managers for advancement within the organization.[7]

HUMAN RESOURCE INVENTORY A **human resource inventory** consists of information about the characteristics of organization members. The focus is on past performance and future potential, and the objective is to keep management up to date about the possibilities for filling a position from within. This inventory should indicate which individuals in the organization would be appropriate for filling a position if it became available. In a classic article, Walter S. Wikstrom proposed that organizations keep three types of records that can be combined to maintain a useful human resource inventory.[8] Although Wikstrom focused on filling managerial positions, slight modifications to his inventory forms would make his records equally useful for filling nonmanagerial positions. Many organizations computerize records like the ones

NAME		AGE	EMPLOYED
Murray, Mel		47	1992

PRESENT POSITION	ON JOB
Manager, Sales (House Fans Division)	6 years

PRESENT PERFORMANCE
Outstanding—exceeded sales goal in spite of stiffer competition.

STRENGTHS
Good planner—motivates subordinates very well—excellent communication.

WEAKNESSES
Still does not always delegate as much as situation requires. Sometimes does not understand production problems.

EFFORTS TO IMPROVE
Has greatly improved in delegating in last two years; also has organized more effectively after taking a management course on own time and initiative.

COULD MOVE TO	WHEN
Vice President, Marketing	2010

TRAINING NEEDED
More exposure to problems of other divisions (attend top staff conference?). Perhaps university program stressing staff role of corporate marketing versus line sales.

COULD MOVE TO	WHEN
Manager, House or Industrial Fans Division	2011
	2012

TRAINING NEEDED
Course in production management; some project working with production people; perhaps a good business game somewhere.

FIGURE 13.3
Management inventory card

Wikstrom suggests to make their human resource inventory system more efficient and effective.

- The first of Wikstrom's three types of records for a human resource inventory is the **management inventory card.** The management inventory card in Figure 13.3 has been completed for a fictional manager named Mel Murray. It indicates Murray's age, year of employment, present position and the length of time he has held it, performance ratings, strengths and weaknesses, the positions to which he might move, when he would be ready to assume these positions, and additional training he would need to fill the positions. In short, this card contains both an organizational history of Murray and an indication of how he might be used in the future. Note that Figures 13.3, 13.4, and 13.5 depict a computerized version of Wikstrom's human resource inventory system.

- Figure 13.4 shows Wikstrom's second type of human resource inventory record—the **position replacement form.** This record focuses on position-centered information rather than the people-centered information maintained on the management inventory card. Note that the form in Figure 13.4 indicates little about Murray, but much about two individuals who could replace him. The position replacement form is helpful in determining what would happen to Murray's present position if Murray were selected to be moved within the organization or if he decided to leave the organization.

- Wikstrom's third human resource inventory record is the **management manpower replacement chart** (see Figure 13.5). This chart presents a composite view of the individuals management considers significant for human resource planning. Note in Figure 13.5 how Murray's performance rating and promotion potential can easily be compared with those of other employees when the company is trying to determine which individual would most appropriately fill a particular position.

POSITION	Manager, Sales (House Fans Division)		
PERFORMANCE Outstanding	**INCUMBENT** Mel Murray	**SALARY** $44,500	**MAY MOVE** I Year
REPLACEMENT I Chandra Singh		**SALARY** $39,500	**AGE** 39
PRESENT POSITION Field Sales Manager, House Fans		**EMPLOYED:** Present Job 3 years	Company 10 years
TRAINING NEEDED Special assignment to study market potential for air conditioners to provide forecasting experience.			**WHEN READY** Now
REPLACEMENT 2 Bernard Storey		**SALARY** $38,500	**AGE** 36
PRESENT POSITION Promotion Manager, House Fans		**EMPLOYED:** Present Job 4 years	Company 7 years
TRAINING NEEDED Rotation to field sales. Marketing conference in fall.			**WHEN READY** 2 years

FIGURE 13.4
Position replacement form

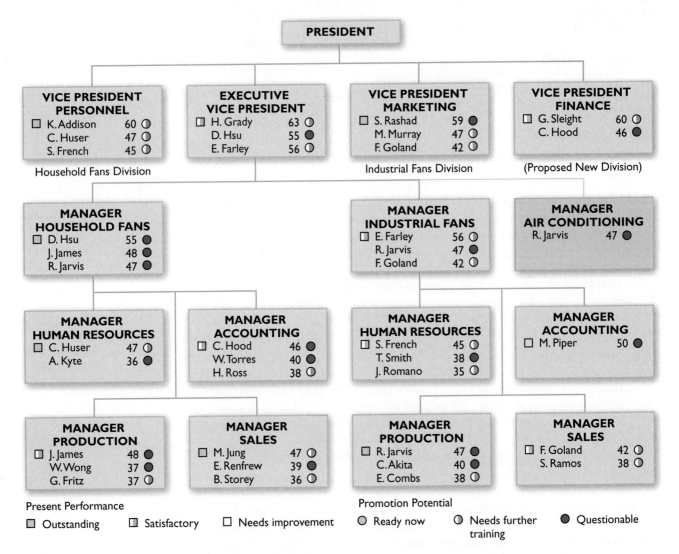

FIGURE 13.5 Management manpower replacement chart

The management inventory card, the position replacement form, and the management manpower replacement chart are three separate record-keeping devices for a human resource inventory. Each form furnishes different data on which to base a hiring-from-within decision. These forms help management to answer the following questions:

1. What is the organizational history of an individual, and what potential does that person possess (management inventory card)?
2. If a position becomes vacant, who might be eligible to fill it (position replacement form)?
3. What are the merits of one individual being considered for a position compared to those of another individual under consideration (management manpower replacement chart)?

Taken together, Wikstrom's human resource inventory system can serve as the foundation for succession planning in organizations. **Succession planning** is the process of outlining who will follow whom in various organizational positions. Michael Eisner, the chief executive officer at Walt Disney Company, has been strongly criticized for not developing a plan for who would succeed him. In 1994, moments before he underwent heart bypass surgery, Eisner summoned his wife and two sons to his hospital gurney. Eisner told them that if it becomes an issue, he thought that either Barry Diller or Michael Orvitz should succeed him. Criticism of Eisner several years later indicated that he still did not have a plan for who would succeed him. Conscientiously keeping a human resource inventory can help a manager such as Eisner to determine a plan not only for who would succeed him, but all other managers at Disney.[9] Computer software is available to aid managers in keeping track of the organization's complex human resource inventories and in making better decisions about how employees can best be deployed and developed.[10]

Sources Outside the Organization If a position cannot be filled by someone currently employed by the organization, management has available numerous sources of human resources outside the organization. These sources include the following:

1. **Competitors**—One often-tapped external source of human resources is competing organizations. Because of several advantages in luring human resources away from competitors, this type of piracy has become a common practice. Among the advantages are the following:
   - The individual knows the business.
   - The competitor will have paid for the individual's training up to the time of hire.
   - The competing organization will probably be weakened somewhat by the loss of the individual.
   - Once hired, the individual will be a valuable source of information about how to best compete with the other organization.
2. **Employment agencies**—Employment agencies help people find jobs and help organizations find job applicants. Such agencies can be either public or private. Public employment agencies do not charge fees, whereas private ones collect a fee from either the person hired or the organization doing the hiring, once the hire has been finalized.
3. **Readers of certain publications**—Perhaps the most widely used external source of human resources is the readership of certain publications. To tap this source, recruiters simply place an advertisement in a suitable publication. The advertisement describes the open position in detail and announces that the organization is accepting applications from qualified individuals. The type of position to be filled determines the type of publication in which the advertisement is placed. The objective is to advertise in a publication whose readers are likely to be interested in filling the position. An opening for a top-level executive might be advertised in the *Financial Times,* a training director opening might be advertised in the *Journal of Training and Development,* and an educational opening might be advertised in the *Chronicle of Higher Education.*
4. **Educational institutions**—Many recruiters go directly to schools to interview students close to graduation time. Liberal arts schools, business schools, engineering

Job applicants, like this woman seeking a job at Circuit City, an electronics retailer are an important source of human resources that companies can also attract through various recruitment strategies like job fairs.

schools, junior colleges, and community colleges all have somewhat different human resources to offer. Recruiting efforts should focus on the schools with the highest probability of providing human resources appropriate for the open position. In **an example from the world of management**, financial firms in Switzerland have changed their recruiting practices to focus more on college graduates. Although the company has typically recruited financial advisors without college degrees and inserted them in apprentice programs, the increased demand for financial advisors has caused financial firms such as **UBS** and **Citigroup** to change their recruiting practices.[11]

Knowing the Law Legislation has had a major impact on modern organizational recruitment practices. Managers need to be aware of the laws that govern recruitment efforts.In 2008, the European Commission adopted a proposal for a directive which provides for protection from discrimination on grounds of age, disability, sexual orientation, and religion or belief beyond the workplace. Laws such as this around the world can include provisions designed to prevent the discrimination of pregnant women, the elderly, those with disabilities, mental or physical, and so forth.

Equal opportunity legislation protects the right of a citizen to work and obtain a fair wage based primarily on merit and performance.

Affirmative Action In response to equal opportunity legislation, many organizations have established **affirmative action programs**.[13] Translated literally, *affirmative action* means positive movement: "In the area of equal employment opportunity, the basic purpose of positive movement or affirmative action is to eliminate barriers and increase opportunities for the purpose of increasing the utilization of underutilized and/or disadvantaged individuals."[14] An organization can judge how much progress it is making toward eliminating such barriers by taking the following steps:

1. Determining how many minority and disadvantaged individuals it presently employs
2. Determining how many minority and disadvantaged individuals it should be employing according to legal guidelines
3. Comparing the numbers obtained in steps 1 and 2

If the two numbers obtained in step 3 are nearly the same, the organization's employment practices probably should be maintained; if they are not nearly the same, the organization should modify its employment practices accordingly.

Modern management writers recommend that managers follow the guidelines of affirmative action, not merely because they are mandated by law, but because of the characteristics of today's labor supply.[15] As you are probably know, the world's workforce is diverse, and consists of many minorities, immigrants, and women. Because the overall workforce is so diverse, it follows that employees in today's organizations will also be more diverse than in the past. Thus today's managers face the challenge of forging a productive workforce out of an increasingly diverse labor pool, and this task is more formidable than simply complying with affirmative action laws.

Selection

The second major step involved in providing human resources for the organization is **selection**—choosing an individual to hire from all those who have been recruited.[16] Selection, obviously, is dependent on the first step, recruitment.

Selection is represented as a series of stages through which job applicants must pass in order to be hired.[17] Each stage reduces the total group of prospective employees until, finally, one individual is hired. Figure 13.6 lists the specific stages of the selection process, indicates reasons for eliminating applicants at each stage, and illustrates how the group of potential employees is narrowed to the individual who ultimately is hired. Two tools often used in the selection process are testing and assessment centers.

Testing Testing is examining human resources for qualities relevant to performing available jobs. Although many different kinds of tests are available for organizational use, they generally can be divided into the following four categories.[18]

1. **Aptitude tests**—Tests of aptitude measure the potential of an individual to perform a task. Some aptitude tests measure general intelligence, while others measure special abilities, such as mechanical, clerical, or visual skills.[19]
2. **Achievement tests**—Tests that measure the level of skill or knowledge an individual possesses in a certain area are called achievement tests. This skill or knowledge may have been acquired through various training activities or through experience in the area. Examples of skill tests are typing and keyboarding tests.
3. **Vocational interest tests**—Tests of vocational interest attempt to measure an individual's interest in performing various kinds of jobs. They are administered on the

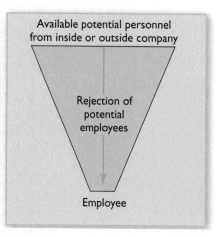

STAGES OF THE SELECTION PROCESS	REASONS FOR ELIMINATION	
Preliminary screening from records, data sheets, etc. Preliminary interview	Lack of adequate educational and performance record Obvious misfit from outward appearance and conduct	Available potential personnel from inside or outside company
Intelligence tests Aptitude tests	Failure to meet minimum standards Failure to have minimum necessary aptitude	Rejection of potential employees
Personality tests Performance references	Negative aspects of personality Unfavorable or negative reports on past performance	
Diagnostic interview	Lack of necessary innate ability, ambition, or other qualities	
Physical examination Personal judgment	Physically unfit for job Remaining candidate placed in available position	Employee

FIGURE 13.6 Summary of major factors in the selection process

assumption that certain people perform jobs well because they find the job activities stimulating. The basic purpose of this type of test is to select for an open position the individual who finds most aspects of that position interesting.

4. **Personality tests**—Personality tests attempt to describe an individual's personality dimensions in such areas as emotional maturity, subjectivity, honesty, and objectivity. These tests can be used advantageously if the personality characteristics needed to do well in a particular job are well defined and if individuals possessing those characteristics can be identified and selected. Managers must be careful, however, not to expose themselves to legal prosecution by basing employment decisions on personality tests that are invalid and unreliable.[20]

Testing Guidelines   Several guidelines should be observed when tests are used as part of the selection process. First, care must be taken to ensure that the test being used is both valid and reliable. A test is *valid* if it measures what it is designed to measure and *reliable* if it measures similarly time after time.[21] Second, test results should not be used as the sole determinant of a hiring decision. People change over time, and someone who doesn't score well on a particular test might still develop into a productive employee. Such factors as potential and desire to obtain a position should be assessed subjectively and used along with test scores in the final selection decision. Third, care should be taken to ensure that tests are nondiscriminatory.

Assessment Centers   Another tool often used in employee selection is the assessment center. Although the assessment center concept is discussed in this chapter primarily as an aid to selection, it is also used in such areas as human resource training and organization development. The first industrial use of the assessment center is usually credited to the telecommunications firm AT&T. Since AT&T's initial efforts, the assessment center concept has expanded greatly, and today it is used not only as a means for identifying individuals to be hired from outside an organization, but also for identifying individuals from inside the organization who should be promoted. Corporations that have used assessment centers extensively include the retailer JCPenney and IBM.[22]

An **assessment center** is a program (not a place) in which participants engage in a number of individual and group exercises constructed to simulate important activities at the organizational levels to which they aspire.[23] These exercises can include such activities as participating in leaderless discussions, giving oral presentations, and leading a group in solving some assigned problem.[24] The individuals performing the activities are observed by managers or trained observers who evaluate both their ability and their potential. In general, participants are assessed according to the following criteria:[25]

1. Leadership
2. Organizing and planning ability
3. Decision making
4. Oral and written communication skills
5. Initiative
6. Energy
7. Analytical ability
8. Resistance to stress
9. Use of delegation
10. Behavior flexibility
11. Human relations competence
12. Originality
13. Controlling
14. Self-direction
15. Overall potential

TABLE 13.1	Management Training Topics for Police Within the Alabama Department of Public Safety	
-Organization Theory		-Effective Communication
-Leadership		-Hiring Practices
-Organizational Goals		-Training Process
-Media Relations		-Measuring Productivity
-Problem Solving		-Employee Evaluations
-Decision Making		-Discipline
-Time Management		-Legal Aspects of Discipline and Termination
-Stress Management		-Motivation
-Ethics and Integrity		-Contingency Planning

Training

After recruitment and selection, the next step in providing appropriate human resources for the organization is training. **Training** is the process of developing qualities in human resources that will enable them to be more productive and thus to contribute more to organizational goal attainment. The purpose of training is to increase the productivity of employees by influencing their behavior. Table 13.1 provides an overview of the types and popularity of training being offered by organizations today.

The training of individuals is essentially a four-step process:

1. Determining training needs
2. Designing the training program
3. Administering the training program
4. Evaluating the training program

These steps are presented in Figure 13.7 and are described in the sections that follow.

Determining Training Needs The first step of the training process is determining the organization's training needs.[26] **Training needs** are the information or skill areas of an individual or group that require further development to increase the productivity of that individual or group. Only if training focuses on these needs can it be productive for the organization.

The training of organization members is typically a continuing activity. Even employees who have been with the organization for some time and who have undergone initial orientation and skills training need continued training to improve their skills.

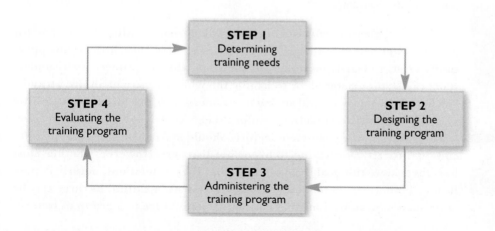

FIGURE 13.7
Steps of the training process

DETERMINING NEEDED SKILLS Several methods are available for determining which skills to focus on with established human resources. One method calls for evaluating the production process within the organization. Such factors as excessive rejected products, unmet deadlines, and high labor costs are clues to deficiencies in production-related expertise. Another method for determining training needs calls for getting direct feedback from employees on what they believe are the organization's training needs. Organization members are often able to verbalize clearly and accurately exactly what types of training they require to do a better job. A third way of determining training needs involves looking into the future. If the manufacture of new products or the use of newly purchased equipment is foreseen, some type of corresponding training almost certainly will be needed. In **an example from the world of management**, **Dell** recently designed a training program that helped employees understand the importance of diversity to the company. As the company grows globally, it is important for Dell's employees to understand that the company will hire employees with diverse backgrounds; this training program helps employees understand the benefits associated with diversity.[27]

Designing the Training Program
Once training needs have been determined, a training program aimed at meeting those needs must be designed. Basically, designing a program entails assembling various types of facts and activities that will meet the established training needs. Obviously, as training needs vary, so will the facts and activities designed to meet those needs.

Administering the Training Program
The next step in the training process is administering the training program—that is, actually training the individuals selected to participate in the program. Various techniques exist for both transmitting necessary information and developing needed skills in training programs, and several of these techniques are discussed in the sections that follow.

TECHNIQUES FOR TRANSMITTING INFORMATION Two techniques for transmitting information in training programs are lectures and programmed learning. Although it could be argued that these techniques develop some skills in individuals as well as transmit information to them, they are primarily devices for the dissemination of information.

In the offices of Wipro in Bangalore, India, employees receive a great deal of specialized training in order to provide software support services to the company's international clients.

1. **Lectures**—Perhaps the most widely used technique for transmitting information in training programs is the lecture. The **lecture** is primarily a one-way communication situation in which an instructor orally presents information to a group of listeners. The instructor typically does most of the talking, and trainees participate primarily through listening and note taking.

   An advantage of the lecture is that it allows the instructor to expose trainees to a maximum amount of information within a given time period. The lecture, however, has some serious disadvantages:[28]

   The lecture generally consists of a one-way communication: The instructor presents information to the group of passive listeners. Thus, little or no opportunity exists to clarify meanings, to check on whether trainees really understand the lecture material, or to handle the wide diversity of ability, attitude, and interest that may prevail among the trainees. Also, this format permits little or no opportunity for practice, reinforcement, knowledge of results, or overlearning. Ideally, the competent lecturer should make the material meaningful and intrinsically motivating to his or her listeners. However, whether most lectures achieve this goal is a moot question. These limitations, in turn, impose further limitations on the lecture's actual content. A skillful lecturer may be fairly successful in transmitting conceptual knowledge to a group of trainees who are ready to receive it; however, all the evidence available indicates that the nature of the lecture situation makes it of minimal value in promoting attitudinal or behavioral change.

2. **Programmed learning**—Another commonly used technique for transmitting information in training programs is called programmed learning. **Programmed learning** is a technique for instructing without the presence or intervention of a human instructor.[29] Small parts of information that require related responses are presented to individual trainees. The trainees can determine from checking their responses against provided answers whether their understanding of the information is accurate. The types of responses required of trainees vary from situation to situation but usually are multiple-choice, true-false, or fill-in-the-blank.

Like the lecture method, programmed learning has both advantages and disadvantages. Among the advantages are that it can be computerized and students can learn at their own pace, know immediately whether they are right or wrong, and participate actively in the learning process. The primary disadvantage of this method is that no one is present to answer a confused learner's questions.

Techniques for Developing Skills Techniques for developing skills in training programs can be divided into two broad categories: on-the-job and classroom. Techniques for developing skills on the job, referred to as **on-the-job training,** reflect a blend of job-related knowledge and experience. They include coaching, position rotation, and special project committees. *Coaching* is direct critiquing of how well an individual is performing a job.[30] *Position rotation* involves moving an individual from job to job to enable the person to gain an understanding of the organization as a whole. *Special project committees* are vehicles for assigning a particular task to an individual to furnish him or her with experience in a designated area.[31]

Classroom techniques for developing skills also reflect a blend of job-related knowledge and experience. The skills addressed through these techniques can range from technical, such as computer programming skills, to interpersonal, such as leadership skills. Specific classroom techniques aimed at developing skills include various types of management games and role-playing activities. The most common format for *management games* requires small groups of trainees to make and then evaluate various management decisions. The *role-playing format* typically involves acting out and then reflecting on some people-oriented problem that must be solved in the organization.

In contrast to the typical one-way communication of the lecturer, the skills instructor in the classroom encourages high levels of discussion and interaction among trainees, develops a climate in which trainees learn new behavior from carrying out various activities, clarifies related information, and facilitates learning by eliciting trainees' job-related knowledge and experience in applying that knowledge. The difference between the instructional role in information dissemination and the instructional role in skill development is dramatic.[32]

Evaluating the Training Program

After the training program has been completed, management should evaluate its effectiveness.[33] Because training programs represent an investment—costs include materials, trainer time, and production loss while employees are being trained rather than doing their jobs—a reasonable return is essential.

Basically, management should evaluate the training program to determine whether it meets the needs for which it was designed. Answers to questions such as the following help determine training program effectiveness:

1. Has the excessive reject rate of products declined?
2. Are deadlines being met more regularly?
3. Are labor costs per unit produced decreasing?

If the answer to such questions is yes, the training program can be judged as at least somewhat successful, though perhaps its effectiveness could be enhanced through certain selective changes. If the answer is no, significant modification to the training program is warranted.

In a noteworthy survey of businesspeople, 50 percent of respondents thought that their sales per year would be unaffected if training programs for experienced salespeople were halted.[34] Management needs to seek and scrutinize this kind of feedback to see whether present training programs should be discontinued, slightly modified, or drastically altered to make them more valuable to the organization. The results of the survey just mentioned indicate a need to make significant changes in sales training programs at the companies covered by the survey.

class discussion highlight

HUMAN RESOURCE MANAGEMENT SKILL AND YOUR CAREER

The beginning of the chapter distinguished between appropriate and inappropriate human resources and implied that employees should focus on demonstrating how they contribute to the organization's goals. The previous section suggests that training can help employees improve their job skills. How might training influence whether your employer (or future employer) considers you an "appropriate" human resource? How might your view of the training process affect your performance as an employee?

Performance Appraisal

Even after individuals have been recruited, selected, and trained, the task of making them maximally productive within the organization is not finished. The fourth step in the process of providing appropriate human resources for the organization is **performance appraisal**—the process of reviewing individuals' past productive activity to evaluate the contribution they have made toward attaining management system objectives. Like training, performance appraisal—which is also called *performance review* and *performance evaluation*—is a continuing activity that focuses on both established human resources within the organization and newcomers. Its main purpose is to furnish feedback to organization members about how they can become more productive and useful to the organization in its quest for quality.[35] Table 13.2 describes several methods of performance appraisal.

Performance appraisals provide feedback to organization members that can help them become more productive in their jobs. Managers who rely on day-to-day observation of employees, as this manager does, can accumulate needed evidence to back up their appraisals.

Why Use Performance Appraisals?   Many firms conduct performance appraisals. Douglas McGregor has suggested the following three reasons for using performance appraisals:[36]

1. They provide systematic judgments to support salary increases, promotions, transfers, and sometimes demotions or terminations.
2. They are a means of telling subordinates how they are doing and of suggesting needed changes in behavior, attitudes, skills, or job knowledge; they let subordinates know where they stand with the boss.
3. They furnish a useful basis for the coaching and counseling of individuals by superiors.

TABLE 13.2 Descriptions of Several Methods of Performance Appraisal

Appraisal Method	Description
Rating scale	Individuals appraising performance use a form containing several employee qualities and characteristics to be evaluated (e.g., dependability, initiative, leadership). Each evaluated factor is rated on a continuum or scale ranging, for example, from 1 to 7.
Employee comparisons	Appraisers rank employees according to such factors as job performance and value to organization. Only one employee can occupy a particular ranking.
Free-form essay	Appraisers simply write down their impressions of employees in paragraph form.
Critical-form essay	Appraisers write down particularly good or bad events involving employees as these events occur. Records of all documented events for any one employee are used to evaluate that person's performance.

class discussion highlight

MODERN RESEARCH AND HUMAN RESOURCES SKILL

Employee Performance and Vacations[37]

Understanding how to increase employee performance represents one of the chief responsibilities of management. Of course, many different mechanisms are available to help managers improve employee motivation. One such mechanism that might help to energize and refresh workers is the allocation of vacation time.

Professors Fritz and Sonnentag studied more than 200 university (non-academic) employees to better understand the role of vacations within the bigger picture employee performance. They asked study participants to complete a questionnaire four times: (1) one week before leaving for vacation, (2) during vacation, (3) within two days after vacation, and (4) two weeks after vacation. This questionnaire contained items regarding burnout, health complaints, job performance, effort expenditure, as well as items about the vacation itself.

Do you think the authors found that effort or performance changed after a vacation? Do you think that health complaints changed after a vacation? Why or why not?

Handling Performance Appraisals If performance appraisals are not handled well, their benefits to the organization will be minimal.[38] Several guidelines can assist management in increasing the appropriateness with which appraisals are conducted. The first guideline is that performance appraisals should stress both performance in the position the individual holds and the success with which the individual is attaining organizational objectives. Although conceptually separate, performance and objectives should be inseparable topics of discussion during performance appraisals. The second guideline is that appraisals should emphasize how well the individual is doing the job, not the evaluator's impression of the individual's work habits. In other words, the goal is an objective analysis of performance rather than a subjective evaluation of habits.

The third guideline is that the appraisal should be acceptable to both the evaluator and the subject—that is, both should agree that it has benefit for the organization and the worker. The fourth, and last, guideline is that performance appraisals should provide a base for improving individuals' productivity within the organization by making them better equipped to produce.[39]

Potential Weaknesses of Performance Appraisals

To maximize the payoff of performance appraisals to the organization, managers must avoid several potential weaknesses of the appraisal process, including the following pitfalls:[40]

1. Performance appraisals focus employees on short-term rewards rather than on issues that are important to the long-run success of the organization.
2. Individuals involved in performance appraisals view them as a reward–punishment situation.
3. The emphasis of performance appraisal is on completing paperwork rather than on critiquing individual performance.
4. Individuals being evaluated view the process as unfair or biased.
5. Subordinates react negatively when evaluators offer unfavorable comments.

To avoid these potential weaknesses, supervisors and employees should look on the performance appraisal process as an opportunity to increase the worth of the employee through constructive feedback, not as a means of rewarding or punishing the employee through positive or negative comments. Paperwork should be viewed only as an aid in providing this feedback, not as an end in itself. Also, care should be taken to make appraisal feedback as tactful and objective as possible to minimize negative reactions.

In **an example from the world of management**, executives at the insurer **Aetna** recently changed the company's performance appraisal system. The former system, which was paper-based, required a great deal of time to complete; as such, many managers did not have the time needed to appraise their employees. Aetna's new system, however, uses technology that constantly allows managers to assess their employees. At any time, managers can access a dashboard that allows managers to assess employee skills, assess career growth, and suggest training needs. The new plan seems to work. In a recent poll, 83 percent of Aetna's employees reported that they understood how they contribute to the company's goals. Just a few years earlier, less than 60 percent of the company's employees understood their contributions.[41]

{ CHALLENGE CASE SUMMARY

After training needs at Cisco have been determined and programs have been designed to meet those needs, the programs must be administered. Administering training programs at Cisco might involve the lecture technique as well as the programmed learning technique for transmitting information to trainees. For actually developing skills in trainees, Cisco could use on-the-job training methods, such as coaching, position rotation, or special project committees. For developing skills in a classroom setting, Cisco could use instructional techniques, such as role-playing activities. For example, salespeople could be asked to handle customers with various kinds of needs and budgets. These situations then could be analyzed from the viewpoint of how to improve salespeople–customer relationships.

Once a Cisco training program has been completed, it must be evaluated to determine whether it met the training need for which it was designed. Training programs aimed at specific skills such as computer programming would be much easier to evaluate than would training programs aimed at interpersonal skills such as developing customer relations. The evaluation of any training program at Cisco of course, should emphasize how to improve the program the next time it is implemented.

In hiring new employees for an operation like Cisco, management must be careful to emphasize not just hiring workers, but hiring the right workers. For Cisco, appropriate human resources are those people who will make a valuable contribution to the attainment of the company's organizational objectives. In hiring engineers, managers, salespeople, and administrative assistants, for example, management should consider hiring only those people who will best help the organization become successful. In finding appropriate human resources, management at Cisco has to follow four basic steps: (1) recruitment, (2) selection, (3) training, and (4) performance appraisal.

Basically, recruitment would entail the initial screening of individuals available to fill open positions at Cisco. For recruitment efforts to be successful, recruiters have to know the jobs they are trying to fill, where potential human resources can be located, and how the law influences recruiting efforts.

Recruiters could acquire an understanding of open positions at a company such as Cisco by performing a job analysis. The job analysis would force them to determine the job description of the open position—the activities of an engineer, programmer, salesperson, for example—and the job specification of the position, including the type of individual who should be hired to fill that position.

A successful recruitment effort at Cisco would require recruiters to know where to locate the available human resources to fill open positions at Cisco. These sources may be both within Cisco and outside it.

To ensure that Cisco maintains its position as one of the best technology companies in the world, management must plan for obtaining needed appropriate human resources along with other resources like equipment and real estate. To do this, management can keep current on the possibilities of filling positions from within by maintaining some type of human resource inventory. This inventory can help management to organize information about the organizational histories and potential of various Cisco employees as well as the relative abilities of various Cisco employees to fill the necessary openings. Some of the sources of potential human resources outside Cisco that management could be aware of are competitors, public and private employment agencies, the reader of industry-related publications, and various types of educational institutions. As mentioned in the case, Cisco went to great lengths to attract employees from 3Com, one of its main competitors.

Cisco management must also be aware of how the law influences its recruitment efforts. Basically, the law says that Cisco recruitment practices cannot discriminate on the basis of race, color, religion, sex, or national origin. If recruitment practices at Cisco are found to be discriminatory, the company is subject to prosecution.

After the initial screening of potential human resources, Cisco will be faced with the task of selecting the individuals to be hired from those who have been screened. Two tools that Cisco could suggest to help in this selection process are testing and assessment centers.

For example, after screening potential employees for positions at Cisco, management could use aptitude tests, achievement tests, vocational interest tests, or personality tests to see whether any of the individuals screened had the qualities necessary to work a specific job. In using these tests, however, management must make sure that the tests are both valid and reliable, that they were not the sole basis on which a selection decision is made, and that they are nondiscriminatory.

Cisco can also use assessment centers to simulate the tasks necessary to perform jobs that workers will be performing. Individuals who performed well on these tasks would probably be more appropriate for the positions than would those who did poorly. The use of assessment centers might be particularly appropriate in evaluating applicants for sales positions. Simulating this job would probably give management an excellent idea of how prospective salespeople would actually interact with customers during sales presentations.

After hiring, Cisco must train new employees, including those simply transferred to new locations within the company, to be productive organization members. To train effectively, Cisco must determine training needs, design a corresponding training program, and administer and evaluate the training program.

Designing a training program requires that Cisco assemble facts and activities that address specific company training needs. These needs are information or skill areas that must be further developed in Cisco employees in order to make them more productive. Over the long term, training at Cisco should focus on more established employees, employees transferred within the company, and employees hired outside the company.

As mentioned in the case, Cisco historically has used acquisitions to gain new employees. In these situations, management should probably try to learn as much as possible about the training programs that employees went through at the acquired companies. Knowing the strengths and weakness of training programs at such companies would probably help management at Cisco understand what further training, if any, these employees need to work effectively.

The last step in providing appropriate human resources at Cisco is performance appraisal through which the contributions that Cisco employees make toward the attainment of management system objectives must be evaluated. Because of Cisco's rapid expansion, employees will have various levels of experience at Cisco. As such, the performance appraisal process at Cisco should focus on newer as well as more established employees.

It would be difficult to visualize a Cisco employee who could not benefit from a properly conducted performance appraisal. Such an appraisal would stress activities on the job and effectiveness in accomplishing job objectives. An objective appraisal would provide Cisco employees with tactful, constructive criticism that should help to increase their productivity. Handled properly,

Cisco's appraisals would not be a reward or a punishment in themselves, but an opportunity to increase value to the company. Objective analysis of performance in a company such as Cisco should help employees to become more productive over time rather than being without guidance and perhaps moving toward the inevitable outcome of being fired. Overall, if these performance appraisal issues are addressed at Cisco as well as issues related to recruitment, selection and training discussed earlier, management should be successful in providing appropriate human resources for the company.

MANAGEMENT SKILL ACTIVITIES

This section is specially designed to help you develop human resource management skill. An individual's management skill is based upon an understanding of management concepts and the ability to apply those concepts in management situations. As a result, the following activities are designed both to heighten your understanding of human resource management concepts and to help you gain facility in applying these concepts in various management situations.

UNDERSTANDING HUMAN RESOURCE MANAGEMENT CONCEPTS

This section is comprised of activities that will sharpen your understanding of human resource management concepts. Answer essay questions as completely as possible. Also, remember that many additional true/false and multiple choice questions appear online at MyManagementLab.com to help you further refine your understanding of concepts related to human resource management.

Essay Questions

1. Describe the four steps in the human resource management process. In your opinion, which step is most important? Explain.
2. Compare and contrast the three types of records used to record an organization's human resource inventory.
3. Review and describe the different types of tests that organizations might use in the selection process.
4. Describe the four main steps in the training process. In your view, how important is the training process for organizations?
5. What are performance appraisals, and why are they important? Use an example from your life to illustrate either an effective or ineffective performance appraisal.

Developing Management Skill

Learning activities in this section are aimed at helping you to develop your human resource management skill. Learning activities include Exploring Your Management

Skill: Part 2, Experiential Exercises, Cases, and a VideoNet exercise.

EXPLORING YOUR MANAGEMENT SKILL: PART 2

As you recall, you completed Exploring Your Management Skill before you started to study this chapter. Your responses gave you an idea of how much you initially knew about human resource management and helped you to focus on important points as you studied the chapter. Answer the Exploring Your Management Skill questions again now (p. 314) and compare your score to the first time you took it. This comparison will give you an idea of how much you learned from studying this chapter and pinpoint areas for further clarification before you start studying the next chapter. Record your answers within the text or online at MyManagementLab.com. Completing the survey at MyManagementLab.com will allow you to grade and compare your test scores automatically. If you complete the test in the book, look up answers in the Exploring Your Management Skill section at the end of the book.

YOUR MANAGEMENT SKILLS PORTFOLIO

Your Management Learning Portfolio is a collection of activities especially designed to demonstrate your management knowledge and skill. By completing these activities online at MyManagementLab.com, you will be able to print, complete with cover sheet, as many activities as you choose. Be sure to save your work. Taking your printed portfolio to an employment interview could be helpful in obtaining a job.

The portfolio activity for this chapter is Designing a Human Resource Management Program at Room & Board. Study the information and complete the exercises that that follow.[42]

Designing a Human Resource Management Program at Room & Board

Room & Board is a furniture retailer based in Minneapolis. Although the company operates only a limited number of locations, customers have flocked to Room & Board stores to purchase sleek furniture. Resulting from customer demand, the company recently introduced an annual "cata-zine" and also introduced a Web site to fulfill online orders. As a result of its success, a number of investors are encouraging Room & Board's founder, John Gabbert, to expand its locations quickly.

Despite Room & Board's success, Gabbert is somewhat concerned that a rapid expansion of the company will damage the company's human resources policies and procedures. Currently, the organization's culture is positive, and the relatively flat organizational structure provides employees with high levels of authority and responsibility, which most find important. Moreover, the company encourages employees to work smarter—not harder—and encourages employees to only work 40 hours per week.

Gabbert has asked you to provide an analysis of the human resources policies at Room & Board. In particular, he is interested in learning more about how growth will influence a small company's human resource function. To help him better understand the situation, use the knowledge you have developed through this chapter to answer the questions.

1. How will growth influence a Room & Board's ***recruitment*** polices?

2. How will growth influence Room & Board's ***selection*** policies?

3. How will growth influence Room & Board's ***training*** policies?

4. How will growth influence Room & Board's ***performance*** appraisal system?

5. Write a job description for a sales associate position at Room & Board.

EXPERIENTIAL EXERCISE: DETERMINING TRAINING NEEDS AT WAL-MART

Directions. Read the following scenario and then perform the listed activities. Your instructor may want you to perform the activities as an individual or within groups. Follow all of your instructor's directions carefully.

Wal-Mart and Dell recently reached an agreement to sell Dell computers to customers in Wal-Mart stores. However, top executives at Wal-Mart and Dell are somewhat concerned, because most of Wal-Mart's sales associates do not have any experience selling computers.

As such, Wal-Mart has contacted your group to help design the training program that will be used in all Wal-Mart locations. Specifically, the executives want you to determine the training needs, which is the first step in the training process. Your group should describe the process you would use to determine these training needs. Assume that Wal-Mart and Dell will give you the resources necessary to implement your process (i.e., access to employees, managers, etc.). Also, rely on your own experiences with purchasing and using personal computers to describe some of the training needs from a customer's perspective.

CASES

CISCO RECRUITS THE BEST MINDS IN CHINA

"Cisco Recruits the Best Minds in China" (p. 313) and its related Challenge Case Summary were written to help you better understand the management concepts contained in this chapter. Answer the following discussion questions about the Challenge Case to better see how your understanding of managing human resources can be applied in a company such as Cisco.

1. How important is the training of employees to an organization such as Cisco? Explain.
2. What actions besides training must an organization such as Cisco take to make employees as productive as possible?
3. Based upon information in the case, what do you think will be the biggest challenge for Cisco management in successfully providing appropriate human resources for the organization? Explain.

PFIZER PUTS THE EMPHASIS ON PEOPLE

Read the case and answer the questions that follow. Studying this case will help you better see how your understanding of managing human resources can be applied in a company such as Pfizer.

Imagine spending billions on research and development yet being able to bring only 4 percent of all new product ideas to market. Now imagine that a few of the surviving products have the potential to become best-selling blockbusters. Welcome to the high-stakes world of pharmaceuticals, where a handful of successful prescription drugs can yield huge profits but the majority of ideas die in the concept stage. Meanwhile, the competitive landscape is always changing as rivals race to find new ways of treating diseases and send representatives out to show physicians how well their branded medicines work.

Hank McKinnell, the Ph.D. CEO of Pfizer, faces this environment every day. As the world's largest pharmaceutical firm, Pfizer annually sells $52 billion worth of

drugs and other health care products while investing $8 billion to search for new medicines. Among its best-selling drugs are Lipitor (for reducing cholesterol) and Zoloft (for fighting depression). Dr. McKinnell aims to double the percentage of new product ideas that get to market from 4 to 8 percent—lowering the failure rate from 96 to 92 percent—while maintaining profitable growth despite global competition. To make the most of the talented 91,000-person workforce, top management carefully plans for hiring, improving employee skills and knowledge, grooming future leaders, providing growth opportunities, and minimizing turnover.

Pfizer wants job applicants who are looking for more than a paycheck. "Pfizer employees must have a passion for health," says Stephen Leung, manager of Pfizer Hong Kong. "We take the slogan seriously: Life is our life's work. We don't just sell products, we spend our working lives saving lives, enhancing people's quality of life, prolonging life. We honestly believe that so when we hire, we look for people with the same passion."

The company invests a whopping 15 percent of its pharmaceuticals payroll in training, with 146 training experts on staff to provide 40 hours of training yearly for each Pfizer employee. Some of that training is delivered through lectures and some through distance learning, guided by employee input. The Support Staff Training Council, for example, consists of a group of staff members who discuss development needs, then create and promote support training programs. As another example, Pfizer uses satellite television to broadcast distance learning programs to more than 1,000 sales managers.

When Pfizer hires professionals to work in certain pharmaceutical specialties, such as diabetes, it arranges technical training and, in addition, sends the new hires to make the rounds with medical professionals for two days at a major New York hospital. "Getting them out with the medical community and engaging with healthcare professionals and patients helps them approach their jobs at Pfizer from more than an intellectual understanding," observes a senior company official. "When you see what our products have meant to patients in alleviating their suffering, it goes to that emotional impact and feeling you have about being a part of a special enterprise."

Retaining valuable employees is a critical challenge, as well. "Last year, Pfizer conducted a special intervention with the district managers about how to spot people at risk of turnover, how to engage them in conversations about what they are thinking and feeling, and what their opportunities with Pfizer are," says the senior vice president of global learning and development. This program reduced turnover by 2 percent in its first year alone; Pfizer spent $150,000 on retention but gained more than $3 million in higher productivity and lower training costs.

Dr. McKinnell recently established an internal Department of Measurement, Evaluation, and Strategic Analysis to examine the overall effect of Pfizer's training efforts. At the unit level, top managers keep training in mind when they review business plans and performance; they also receive feedback from physicians to check on the effectiveness of representatives' sales training. People will make the difference as McKinnell and his executive team keep Pfizer at the top of its industry in the coming years.

QUESTIONS

1. How would you suggest that Pfizer evaluate the performance of scientists who work on drugs that never make it to market?

2. Which of the four types of testing (if any) would you recommend that Pfizer use in selecting among applicants for research-and-development positions?

3. Do you agree with Pfizer's hefty investment of time, money, and effort in training? Explain.

VIDEONET EXERCISE

Human Resources at KPMG

VIDEO HIGHLIGHTS

Employees stick around when they see a bright future ahead of them. In order to amp up the perceived wattage for employees looking down the road, KPMG designed interactive software called Employee Career Architecture (ECA). Using this tool, someone in accounting who is beginning to doubt their passion for number-crunching can explore new functions and jobs within the company and choose to participate in a rotation, which allows them to sample their options firsthand. People can see where different tracks lead in terms of their earning potential, and they can see what kinds of skills they'll need to develop to continue moving upward.

Discussion Questions

1. What are some of the challenges faced by KPMG in trying to recruit employees from outside the organization? How do these impact the external recruiting sources?

2. How does the Employee Career Architecture program used by KPMG differ from a more traditional performance appraisal system?

3. How does KPMG use their Career program to help determine training needs?

Internet Activity

Go to the KPMG Web site at www.kpmg.com. How does KPMG use its company Web site as a recruiting tool? Which of the external recruiting sources would most likely be attracted to the information provided on the site?

14 Organizational Change

STRESS, CONFLICT, AND VIRTUALITY

OBJECTIVES

TO HELP BUILD MY ORGANIZATIONAL CHANGE SKILL, WHEN STUDYING THIS CHAPTER, I WILL ATTEMPT TO ACQUIRE:

1. A working definition of *changing an organization*

2. An understanding of the relative importance of change and stability to an organization

3. Some ability to recognize what kinds of changes should be made within an organization

4. An appreciation for why the people affected by a change should be considered when the change is being made

5. Some facility at evaluating change

6. An understanding of how organizational change and stress are related

7. Insights concerning how to handle conflict as a factor related to organizational change

8. Knowledge about virtuality as a vehicle for organizational change

TARGET SKILL organizational change skill: the ability to modify an organization in order to enhance its contribution to reaching company goals

CHALLENGE CASE

WRIGLEY CONTINUES TO CHANGE

The William Wrigley Jr. Company manufactures and markets chewing gum and other confectionary products to more than 150 countries and territories. The Wrigley Company's primary business involves chewing gum and other similar products. Wrigley Company began in 1891 as a soap and baking soda manufacturer that gave away chewing gum as a promotion.

In time, the company became publicly traded, but the Wrigley family has continued to own a large portion of the company's shares. In essence, then, the family has maintained tight control over the company since its inception. Over the years, the Wrigley Company and the Wrigley family have developed reputations as being both financially and strategically conservative.

In 1999, William Wrigley Jr. succeeded his father Bill Sr. as CEO of the Wrigley Company. After his arrival, Wrigley made a number of changes in the company that turned the conservative organization into more of a risk-taking company. One of his first moves involved changing the flavor formulations of the company's core brands such Juicy Fruit, Spearmint, Doublemint, and Winter Fresh. To publicize these new formulations, he also reintroduced the brands with edgier marketing campaigns.

Wrigley also focused more of the company's resources on attacking the sugar-free chewing gum market. When

Pictured are some of the popular products sold by Wrigley Company.

he became CEO in 1999, the company offered only one sugar-free gum. Extra, and controlled only about 30 percent of the sugar-free market. Since then, the Wrigley Company has introduced popular sugar-free gums such as Eclipse and Orbit—today the Wrigley Company controls more than 50 percent of the sugar-free market.

Not all of Wrigley's changes have provided such positive results. For example, he created a subsidiary devoted to developing chewing gums that released medication. One year later, the subsidiary released its first chewing gum, Surpass, which was formulated to fight antacid. Unfortunately, consumers did not respond well to Surpass, and Wrigley recently decided to stop its production.

At one of the Wrigley Company's recent annual meetings, Wrigley used a John F. Kennedy quote to demonstrate his position to shareholders: "There are risks and costs to any program of action, but they are far less than the long-range risks and costs of comfortable inaction." It seems as though Wrigley Company is committed to continual changing to improve operations and solve problems on the horizon. Recent examples of this change include improving organization structure[1] and dealing with impending competition.[2] Such change will normally cause uneasiness among many of the company's employees and shareholders. However, such change over time will undoubtedly be necessary if Wrigley Company is to survive.

"EXPLORE YOUR OWN MANAGEMENT SKILLS BY TAKING THE QUIZ ON THE NEXT PAGE"

Before studying this chapter, respond to the following questions regarding the type of advice that you would give to William Wrigley, Jr., the CEO referenced in the Case. Then address the concerning organizational change challenges that he faces within the company. You are not expected to be an organizational change expert at this point. Answering the questions now can help you focus on important points when you study the chapter. Also, answering the questions again after you study the chapter will give you an idea of how much you have learned.

Record your answers here or go to MyManagementLab. com. Recording your answers in MyManagementLab will allow you to get immediate results and see how your score compares to your classmates. If you answer the questions in the book, the answers are located in the Exploring Your Management Skill Appendix at the end of the book.

FOR EACH STATEMENT CIRCLE:

- "Y" if you would give the advice to Wrigley.
- "N" if you would NOT give the advice to Wrigley.
- "NI" if you have no idea whether you would give the advice to Wrigley.

Mr. Wrigley, in meeting your organizational change challenges at Wm Wrigley Jr. Company, you should . . .

Before Study   *After Study*

1. remember that most of the time changes should be aimed at helping the organization to better achieve its goals.

   Y, N, NI

2. also consider maintaining a desirable level of stability within the company.

   Y, N, NI

3. normally appoint yourself as change agent.

   Y, N, NI

4. generally focus more on structural change within the company rather than people or technology change.

   Y, N, NI

5. sometimes consider structural change from the viewpoint of decentralizing the organization to reduce the costs of coordination.

   Y, N, NI

6. normally view OD at Wrigley Company as a process for improving technology effectiveness.

   Y, N, NI

7. focus on avoiding surprises with employees as a tool for reducing resistance to changes to be made within Wrigley Company.

   Y, N, NI

8. keep in mind that a change being considered for implementation should probably be implemented if it creates more human work for Wrigley employees.

   Y, N, NI

9. evaluate potential change at Wrigley independent of the stress that the change might create for Wrigley employees.

   Y, N, NI

10. keep in mind that adverse effects of Wrigley employee stress will normally be evidenced in employee family life, but generally not employee work life because employees will not want to lose their jobs.

    Y, N, NI

11. be alert for continual employee fatigue because such fatigue could be a signal that change at Wrigley is causing too much employee stress.

    Y, N, NI

12. as a change agent, bully employees slightly to accept organizational change because small amounts of such bullying by change agents has been shown to speed employee acceptance of organizational changes.

    Y, N, NI

13. consider establishing virtual offices as a means of improving organizational effectiveness and efficiency.

    Y, N, NI

14. consider *hoteling* Wrigley employees as a program for establishing fully mobile Wrigley employees.

    Y, N, NI

15. probably establish some units at Wrigley Company as virtual work units because making such change normally lowers labor costs and generally does cause new or different change-related challenges.

    Y, N, NI

THE ORGANIZATIONAL CHANGE CHALLENGE

The Challenge Case illustrates organizational change challenges that William Wrigley Jr., the CEO of Wrigley Company, must meet. Wrigley must constantly assess the nature of his organization and make appropriate organizational changes that enhance goal attainment. Recent changes at the Wrigley Company have focused on adding new products. Wrigley knows, however, that the company will need to institute other types of change in the future to maintain the company's competitiveness. Managers such as Wrigley, who are faced with meeting organizational change challenges, would find the major topics in this chapter useful and practical. These topics are (1) fundamentals of changing an organization, (2) factors to consider when changing the organization, (3) change and stress, (4) change and conflict, and (5) virtuality.

FUNDAMENTALS OF CHANGING AN ORGANIZATION

Thus far, discussion in this "Organizing" section of the text has centered on the fundamentals of organizing, furnishing appropriate human resources for the organization, authority, delegation, and responsibility. This chapter focuses on changing the organization.

Defining Changing an Organization

Changing an organization is the process of modifying an existing organization to increase organizational effectiveness—that is, the extent to which an organization accomplishes its objectives. These modifications can involve virtually any organizational segment, but typically affect the lines of organizational authority, the levels of responsibility held by various organization members, and the established lines of organizational communication. Driven by new technology, expanding global opportunities, and the trend toward organizational streamlining, almost all modern organizations are changing in some way.[3]

The Importance of Change   Most managers agree that if an organization is to thrive, it must change continually in response to significant developments in the environment, such as changing customer needs, technological breakthroughs, and new government regulations. The study of organizational change is extremely important because managers at all organizational levels are faced throughout their careers with the task of changing their organization. Managers who can determine appropriate changes and then implement such changes successfully enable their organizations to be more flexible and innovative.[4] Because change is such a fundamental part of organizational existence, such managers are valuable to organizations of all kinds.[5]

Many managers consider change to be so critical to organizational success that they encourage employees to continually search for areas in which beneficial changes can be made. To take a classic example, General Motors provides employees with a "think list" to encourage them to develop ideas for organizational change and to remind them that change is vital to the continued success of GM. The think list contains the following questions:[6]

1. Can a machine be used to do a better or faster job?
2. Can the fixture now in use be improved?
3. Can handling of materials for the machine be improved?
4. Can a special tool be used to combine the operations?
5. Can the quality of the part being produced be improved by changing the sequence of the operation?
6. Can the material used be cut or trimmed differently for greater economy or efficiency?
7. Can the operation be made safer?
8. Can paperwork regarding this job be eliminated?
9. Can established procedures be simplified?

Change Versus Stability

In addition to organizational change, some degree of stability is a prerequisite for long-term organizational success. Figure 14.1 presents a model developed by Hellriegel and Slocum that shows the relative importance of change and stability to organizational survival. Although these authors use the word *adaptation* in their model rather than *change,* the two terms are essentially synonymous.

The model stresses that organizational survival and growth are most probable when both stability and adaptation are high within the organization (number 3 on the model depicted in Figure 14.1). The organization without enough stability to complement change is at a definite disadvantage. When stability is low, the probability of organizational survival and growth declines. Change after change without regard for the essential role of stability typically results in confusion and employee stress.[7]

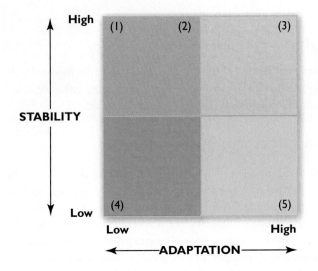

FIGURE 14.1
Adaptation, stability, and organizational survival

(1) High death probability (slow)
(2) High survival probability
(3) High survival and growth probability
(4) Certainty of death (quick)
(5) Certainty of death (quick)

FACTORS TO CONSIDER WHEN CHANGING AN ORGANIZATION

How managers deal with the major factors that need to be considered when an organizational change is being made will largely determine how successful that change will be. The following factors should be considered whenever change is being contemplated: (1) the change agent, (2) determining what should be changed, (3) the kind of change to make, (4) individuals affected by the change, and (5) evaluation of the change.

Although the following sections discuss each of these factors individually, Figure 14.2 makes the point that it is a collective influence that ultimately determines the success of a change.[8]

The Change Agent

Perhaps the most important factor managers need to consider when changing an organization is who will be the **change agent**—the individual inside or outside the organization who tries to modify the existing organizational situation.[9] The change agent might be a self-designated manager within the organization, or an outside consultant hired because of a special expertise in a particular area. This individual might be responsible for making broad changes, such as altering the culture of the whole organization; or more narrow ones, such as designing and implementing a new safety program or a new quality program.[10] Although

FIGURE 14.2
The collective influence of five major factors on the success of changing an organization

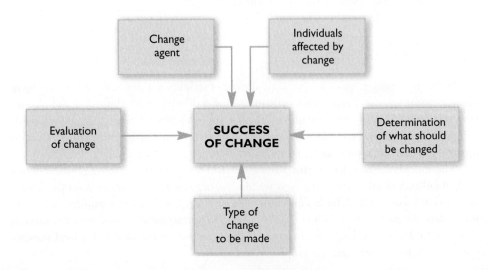

in some circumstances the change agent will not be a manager, the terms *manager* and *change agent* are used synonymously throughout this chapter.

Special skills are necessary for success as a change agent. Among them are the ability to determine how a change should be made, the skill to solve change-related problems, and facility in using behavioral science tools to influence people appropriately during the change process.[11] Perhaps the most overlooked skill of successful change agents, however, is the ability to determine how much change employees can withstand.[12]

Overall, managers should choose change agents who have the most expertise in all these areas. A potentially beneficial change might not result in any advantages for the organization if a person without expertise in these areas is designated as change agent.

Determining What Should Be Changed

Another major factor managers need to consider is exactly what should be changed within the organization. In general, managers should make only those changes that will increase organizational effectiveness.

It has been generally accepted for many years that organizational effectiveness depends primarily on activities centering around three classes of factors:

1. People
2. Structure
3. Technology

People factors are attitudes, leadership skills, communication skills, and all other characteristics of the human resources within the organization; **structural factors** are organizational controls, such as policies and procedures; and **technological factors** are any types of equipment or processes that assist organization members in the performance of their jobs.

As **an example from the world of management** concerning changing technological factors, consider recent changes in technology at **JPMorgan Chase & Co.**, a leading global financial services firm with assets of $1.8 trillion and operations in more than 60 countries.[13] In essence, the chief executive officer, Jamie Dimon, was forced into technological changes when he inherited an agglomeration of years of bank mergers. Today, the company is stuck with a patchwork of out-of-date technology systems that speak different computer languages and continue to be a huge drag on organizational efficiency. Dimon's fundamental goal is to eliminate this patchwork and in its place to establish a seamless, efficient technology system that can be used by all banking units. For Dimon, new technology enhancements are all about better serving the customer. His newly planned technology changes will enable the sprawling network of banks to better perform such simple tasks as efficiently serving a customer who moves to a new city.

For an organization to maximize its effectiveness, appropriate people must be matched with appropriate technology and appropriate structure. Thus, people factors, technological factors, and structural factors are not independent determinants of organizational effectiveness. Instead, as Figure 14.3 shows, organizational effectiveness is determined by the relationship among these three factors.

The Kind of Change to Make

The kind of change to make is the third major factor that managers need to consider when they set out to change an organization. Most changes can be categorized as technological, structural, or people. Note that these three kinds of change correspond to the three main determinants of organizational effectiveness—each change is named for the determinant it emphasizes.

For example, **technological change** emphasizes modifying the level of technology in the management system. Because this kind of change so often involves outside experts and highly technical language, it is more profitable to discuss structural change and people change in detail in this text.

FIGURE 14.3
Determination of organizational effectiveness by the relationship among people, technological, and structural factors

Fiat's CEO Sergio Marchionne has high hopes that the redesigned Fiat 500 will revive the automaker's fortunes. The plan to develop the new model was the result of many earlier decisions about what kind of changes the company needed to make in order to turn itself around.

Structural Change Structural change emphasizes increasing organizational effectiveness by changing controls that influence organization members during the performance of their jobs. The following section further describes this approach and provides managers with insights regarding how to deal with structural change issues.

Describing Structural Change **Structural change** is change aimed at increasing organizational effectiveness through modifications to the existing organizational structure. These modifications can take several forms:

1. Clarifying and defining jobs
2. Modifying organizational structure to fit the communication needs of the organization
3. Decentralizing the organization to reduce the cost of coordination, increase the controllability of subunits, increase motivation, and gain greater flexibility

Although structural change must take account of people and technology to be successful, its primary focus is obviously on changing organizational structure. In general, managers choose to make structural changes within an organization if information they have gathered indicates that the present structure is the main causes of organizational ineffectiveness. The precise structural changes they choose to make will vary from situation to situation, of course. After changes to organizational structure have been made, management should conduct periodic reviews to make sure the changes are accomplishing their intended purposes.[14]

People Change Although successfully changing people factors necessarily involves some consideration of structure and technology, the primary emphasis is on people. The following sections discuss people change and examine grid organization development, one commonly used means of changing organization members.

Describing People Change: Organization Development (OD) **People change** emphasizes increasing organizational effectiveness by changing certain aspects of organization members. The focus of this kind of change is on such factors as employees' attitudes and leadership skills. In general, managers should attempt to make this kind of change when human resources are shown to be the main cause of organizational ineffectiveness.

As **an example from the world of management** concerning people change, consider recent events at Caterpillar.[15] **Caterpillar, Inc.**, manufactures and sells heavy equipment related to construction and mining. Caterpillar recently endorsed trying to improve management attitudes and capabilities related to evaluating and improving the performance of employees. To focus on this people change, Caterpillar deployed a performance management training workshop to more than 20,000 managers. The workshop emphasized how managers were to improve the performance of their people and how employees were to take responsibility for their own development. The workshop also presented a new performance evaluation process that managers were expected to use and focused on building related management skills in the areas of coaching, goal setting, feedback, and communication. Management believes that the program successful in changing people in areas like getting employees to be better team players, to be more focus on company goals, and to be more consistent in rating performance of others.

The process of people change can be referred to as **organization development (OD).** Although OD focuses mainly on changing certain aspects of people, these changes are based on an overview of structure, technology, and all other organizational ingredients.

Grid OD One traditionally used OD technique for changing people in organizations is called **grid organization development,** or **grid OD.**[16] The **managerial grid,** a basic model describing various managerial styles, is used as the foundation for grid OD. The managerial grid is based on the premise that various managerial styles can be described by means of two primary attitudes of the manager: concern for people and concern for production. Within this model, each attitude is placed on an axis, which is scaled 1 through 9 and is used to generate five managerial styles. Figure 14.4 shows the managerial grid, its five managerial styles, and the factors that characterize each of these styles.

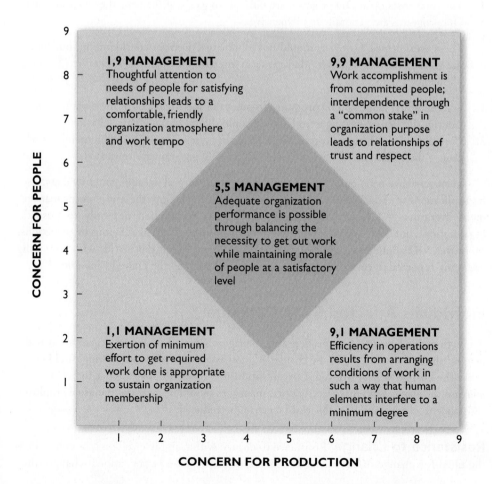

FIGURE 14.4
The managerial grid

CONCERN FOR PEOPLE

1,9 MANAGEMENT
Thoughtful attention to needs of people for satisfying relationships leads to a comfortable, friendly organization atmosphere and work tempo

9,9 MANAGEMENT
Work accomplishment is from committed people; interdependence through a "common stake" in organization purpose leads to relationships of trust and respect

5,5 MANAGEMENT
Adequate organization performance is possible through balancing the necessity to get out work while maintaining morale of people at a satisfactory level

1,1 MANAGEMENT
Exertion of minimum effort to get required work done is appropriate to sustain organization membership

9,1 MANAGEMENT
Efficiency in operations results from arranging conditions of work in such a way that human elements interfere to a minimum degree

CONCERN FOR PRODUCTION

THE IDEAL STYLE The central theme of this managerial grid is that 9,9 management (as shown on the grid in Figure 14.4) is the ideal managerial style. Managers using this style have a high concern for both people and production. Managers using any other style have lesser degrees of concern for people or production, and are thought to reduce organizational success accordingly. The purpose of grid OD is to change organization managers so they will use the 9,9 management style.

MAIN TRAINING PHASES How is a grid OD program conducted? The program has six main training phases that are used with all managers within the organization. The first two phases focus on acquainting managers with the managerial grid concept and assisting them in determining which managerial style they most commonly use. The last four phases of the grid OD program concentrate on encouraging managers to adopt the 9,9 management style and showing them how to use this style within their specific job situation. Emphasis throughout the program is on developing teamwork within the organization.

Some evidence suggests that grid OD is effective in enhancing profit, positively changing managerial behavior, and positively influencing managerial attitudes and values.[17] Grid OD will have to undergo more rigorous testing for an extended period of time, however, before conclusive statements can be made about it.

The Status of Organization Development If the entire OD area is taken into consideration, changes that emphasize both people and the organization as a whole seem to have inherent strength. However, several commonly voiced weaknesses in OD efforts include the following:[18]

1. The effectiveness of an OD program is difficult to evaluate.
2. OD programs are generally too time consuming.
3. OD objectives are commonly too vague.
4. The total costs of an OD program are difficult to gauge at the time the program starts.
5. OD programs are generally too expensive.

These weaknesses, however, should not eliminate OD from consideration, but should indicate areas to perfect within it. Managers can improve the quality of OD efforts by doing the following:[19]

1. Systematically tailoring OD programs to meet the specific needs of the organization
2. Continually demonstrating exactly how people should change their behavior
3. Conscientiously changing organizational reward systems so organization members who change their behavior in ways suggested by the OD program are rewarded

Managers have been employing OD techniques for several decades, and broad and useful applications of these techniques continue to be documented in the more recent management literature.[20] OD techniques are currently being applied not only to business organizations, but also to many other types of organizations, such as religious organizations. Moreover, OD applications are being documented throughout the world, with increasing use being reported in countries such as Hungary, Poland, and the United Kingdom.[21]

Individuals Affected By the Change

A fourth major factor to be considered by managers when changing an organization is the people who will be affected by the change. A good assessment of what to change and how to make the change will be wasted if organization members do not support the change. To increase the chances of employee support, managers should be aware of the usual employee resistance to change and how this resistance can be reduced.

Resistance to Change Resistance to change within an organization is as common as the need for change. After managers decide to make some organizational change, they typically meet with employee resistance aimed at preventing that change from occurring.[22] Behind this resistance by organization members lies the fear of some personal loss, such as a reduction in personal prestige, a disturbance of established social and working relationships, and personal failure because of inability to carry out new job responsibilities.[23]

Reducing Resistance to Change To ensure the success of needed modifications, managers must be able to reduce the effects of the resistance that typically accompanies proposed change.[24] Resistance can usually be lowered by following these guidelines:[25]

1. **Avoid surprises**—People need time to evaluate a proposed change before management implements it. Unless they are given time to evaluate and absorb how the change will affect them, employees are likely to be automatically opposed to it. Whenever possible, therefore, individuals who will be affected by a change should be informed of the kind of change being considered and the probability that it will be adopted.

2. **Promote real understanding**—When fear of personal loss related to a proposed change is reduced, opposition to the change is also reduced. Most managers find that ensuring that organization members thoroughly understand a proposed change is a major step in reducing this fear. Understanding may even generate enthusiastic support for the change if it focuses employees on individual gains that could materialize as a result of it. People should be given information that will help them answer the following change-related questions they invariably will have:
   * Will I lose my job?
   * Will my old skills become obsolete?
   * Am I capable of producing effectively under the new system?
   * Will my power and prestige decline?
   * Will I be given more responsibility than I care to assume?
   * Will I have to work longer hours?
   * Will it force me to betray or desert my good friends?

3. **Set the stage for change**—Perhaps the most powerful tool for reducing resistance to change is management's positive attitude toward the change. This attitude should be displayed openly by top and middle management as well as by lower management. In essence, management should convey that change is one of the basic prerequisites for a successful organization. Management should also strive to encourage change for increasing organizational effectiveness, rather than for the sake of trying something new. To reinforce this positive attitude toward change, some portion of organizational rewards should be earmarked for those organization members who are most instrumental in implementing constructive change.

4. **Make tentative change**—Resistance to change can also be reduced if the changes are made on a tentative basis. This approach establishes a trial period during which organization members spend some time working under a proposed change before voicing support or nonsupport of it. Tentative change is based on the assumption that a trial period during which organization members live under a change is the best way of reducing feared personal loss. Judson has summarized the benefits of using the tentative approach:
   * Employees affected by the change are able to test their reactions to the new situation before committing themselves irrevocably to it.
   * Those who will live under the change are able to acquire more facts on which to base their attitudes and behavior toward the change.
   * Those who had strong preconceptions about the change are in a better position to assess it with objectivity. Consequently, they may review and modify some of their preconceptions.
   * Those involved are less likely to regard the change as a threat.
   * Management is better able to evaluate the method of change and make any necessary modifications before carrying it out more fully.

class discussion highlight

MODERN RESEARCH AND ORGANIZATIONAL CHANGE SKILL

Employee Attitudes Toward Change in a Large Public Hospital[26]

Individuals can be affected by organizational change in various ways. This highlight focuses on a research study that explores the relationship between employee attitudes about change and various organizational levels at which the employees worked. Overall, the research tried to discover whether employee attitudes about change might be more positive for employees who worked at upper organizational levels than employees who worked at lower organizational levels.

The study was conducted in a large public hospital where employees were experiencing extensive organizational change. Changes focused on the downsizing of staff and the establishment of new multidisciplinary work teams. All hospital staff was mailed an anonymous survey focusing on their thoughts about organizational changes currently in progress and a postage-paid envelope for returning the survey once completed. A total of 1,500 surveys were sent to employees with 779 being returned for analysis. Of the surveys returned, 70 percent were women and 30 percent were men. Also, 62 percent were 20 to 40 years of age and 38 percent were 41 and over. The group of responding employees was representative of the composition of the organization's total workforce.

The purpose of the study was to test the prediction that upper-level staff would be more positive in their appraisals of change than lower-level staff. Do you think that results of the study were consistent with the prediction? Why? Why not?

Evaluation of the Change

As with all other managerial actions, managers should spend some time evaluating the changes they make. The purpose of this evaluation is not only to gain insight into how the change itself might be modified to further increase its organizational effectiveness, but to determine whether the steps taken to make the change should be modified to increase organizational effectiveness the next time they are used.

According to Margulies and Wallace, making this evaluation may be difficult because the data from individual change programs may be unreliable.[27] Nevertheless, managers must do their best to evaluate change in order to increase the organizational benefits from the change.[28]

Evaluation of change often involves watching for symptoms that indicate that further change is necessary. For example, if organization members continue to be oriented more to the past than the future, if they recognize the obligations of rituals more readily than they do the challenges of current problems, or if they pay greater allegiance to departmental goals than to overall company objectives, the probability is high that further change is necessary.

A word of caution is needed at this point. Although symptoms such as those listed in the preceding paragraph generally indicate that further change is warranted, the decision to make additional changes should not be made solely on that basis. More objective information should be considered. In general, additional change is justified if it will accomplish any of the following goals:[29]

1. Further improve the means for satisfying someone's economic wants
2. Increase profitability
3. Promote human work for human beings
4. Contribute to individual satisfaction and social well-being

The effects of change in an organization can be profound, as many autoworkers have found in recent years while the industry has suffered steadily declining sales and job losses.

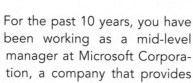

class discussion highlight

CHANGE AND YOUR CAREER

For the past 10 years, you have been working as a mid-level manager at Microsoft Corporation, a company that provides software products for various computing devices worldwide.[30] Your career has been progressing nicely given the company's traditional posture toward developing new, revolutionary software products. However, Microsoft's competition has now become much more formidable and you just heard that to continue its success, the company must now focus on developing software product groups, products that interact and work well together, rather than simply developing independent software products. You have also heard that such a strategy will demand that the company place higher value on managers with internal collaboration and customer services skills. The company is planning to reorganize by establishing departments aimed at developing the new product groups. The new departments will be held accountable for both developing and selling the new product groups via department profit and loss statements. The next upward move for your career would be to manage one of the newly formed departments in about two years. Would you modify your personal career plan given the recent plans for change at Microsoft? If not, why? If so, how?

CHANGE AND STRESS

Whenever managers implement changes, they should be concerned about the stress they may be creating. If the stress is significant enough, it may well cancel out the improvement that was anticipated from the change. In fact, stress could result in the organization being *less* effective than it was before the change was attempted. This section defines stress and discusses the importance of studying and managing it.

Defining Stress

The bodily strain that an individual experiences as a result of coping with some environmental factor is **stress**.[31] Hans Selye, an early authority on this subject, said that stress constitutes the factors affecting wear and tear on the body. In organizations, this wear and tear is caused primarily by the body's unconscious mobilization of energy when an individual is confronted with organizational or work demands.[32]

The Importance of Studying Stress

The study of stress is important for several reasons:[33]

- Stress can have damaging psychological and physiological effects on employees' health and on their contributions to organizational effectiveness. It can cause heart disease, and it can prevent employees from concentrating or making decisions. Increased levels of stress have also been associated with adverse effects on family relationships,[34] decreased productivity in the workplace, and increased psychiatric symptoms.[35]
- Stress is a major cause of employee absenteeism and turnover. Certainly, such factors severely limit the potential success of an organization.
- A stressed employee can affect the safety of other workers or even the public.
- Stress represents a significant cost to organizations. As examples of these costs, many modern organizations spend a great deal of money treating stress-related employee problems through medical programs, and they must absorb expensive legal fees when handling stress-related lawsuits.

Managing Stress in Organizations

Because stress is felt by virtually all employees in all organizations, insights about managing stress are valuable to all managers. This section is built on the assumption that in order to appropriately manage stress in organizations, managers must understand how stress influences worker performance, identify where unhealthy stress exists in organizations, and help employees handle stress.

Understanding How Stress Influences Worker Performance To deal with stress among employees, managers must understand the relationship between the amount of stress felt by a worker and the worker's performance. This relationship is shown in Figure 14.5. Note that extremely high and extremely low levels of stress tend to have negative effects on production. Additionally, while increasing stress tends to bolster performance up to some point (Point A in the figure), when the level of stress increases beyond this point, performance will begin to deteriorate.

In sum, a certain amount of stress among employees is generally considered to be advantageous for the organization because it tends to increase production. However, when

FIGURE 14.5
The relationship between worker stress and the level of worker performance

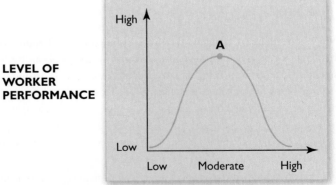

the fabric of organizational culture. Another management challenge to using virtual offices is that such offices make it more difficult for managers to control workers. An individual's presence in a traditional office can give a manager constant feedback throughout the day concerning worker commitment and performance, whereas in a virtual office situation, it is not as easy. Last, virtual offices make communication more difficult. Planned or unplanned face-to-face communication that takes place in a traditional office is essentially nonexistent in a virtual office. As a result, management may experience more difficulty in gathering information relevant to employee attitudes and work concerns.

{CHALLENGE CASE SUMMARY

The previous information furnishes several insights about how Bill Wrigley should make decisions such as whether to recommend a particular type of change in the company. Wrigley should evaluate such change in relation to the degree that it better enables the company to accomplish its objectives. Wrigley should understand that making such change is extremely important. If the company is to have continued success over the long run, such changes will probably have to be made a number of times. In fact, appropriate change is so important to a company that Wrigley might want to consider initiating some type of program that would encourage employees to submit their ideas on a continuing basis regarding new ideas that could increase company effectiveness. When considering possible changes, however, Wrigley must keep in mind that some level of stability is also necessary if his company is to survive and grow over the long term. To illustrate such stability, Wrigley Company has been manufacturing and selling Spearmint and Juicy Fruit for more than 100 years.

In the Challenge Case, it is clear that Wrigley is a change agent. Given his role as top management, he is probably the individual in the company best suited to evaluate the overall advantages and disadvantages of making changes such as offering one type of chewing gum as opposed to another or one type of candy as opposed to another. Because Wrigley has been involved with this business most of his life, he has the perspective necessary to evaluate such advantages and disadvantages. However, he would probably not be the person in the company best suited to change the training program for newly hired line workers.

In general, change agents such as Wrigley must have the ability to use behavioral science tools to influence organization members during the implementation of planned change. As examples, Wrigley must determine how much organizational change the company's employees can withstand and implement this change, perhaps gradually, so employees will not be overwhelmed. Changing the Wrigley Company's product line too dramatically, for example, would require Wrigley to transfer a large number of employees to different divisions, which may diminish employee morale. Overall, the ability to use behavioral science tools will help the change agent to be successful in implementing needed work situation changes at the company.

Wrigley can make many different types of changes. The preceding information indicates that change agents can change technological factors, people factors, and structural factors in order to increase organizational effectiveness. Wrigley's product line decisions discussed in the Challenge Case likely include change regarding all of these factors. For example, product line changes would likely precipitate changes to structural factors. That is, new departments might be created while others might be eliminated. In addition, the product line changes would probably include technological change. For example, the company might need new technology to develop new and better tasting sugar-free gums. Lastly, product line changes would probably include a focus on people and will be facilitated through action such as communicating with employees about product lines as well as motivating workers to achieve the objectives toward which product line change is aimed.

Technically, modifying the product line at the Wrigley Company would not be classified as people change. It is clear, however, that such modification changes will precipitate the need for people change. Wrigley is attempting to radically change the company's strategic position, and he will need to develop employees who will be able to help him make these modifications. As a result, he may find it useful to implement organization development (OD) to spur the people change that will be required to support his strategy. Alternatively, Wrigley may find it necessary to use grid OD in order to modify management styles. Of course, Wrigley may use both of these techniques to develop the managers that he will need to ensure that his organizational change succeeds.

Wrigley must realize that even though he may formulate structural change that would be beneficial to the company, any attempt to implement this change could prove unsuccessful if it does not appropriately consider the people affected by the change. For example, if the company introduces a new departmental structure, employees working under the old structure may fear that this change will diminish their opportunities for promotion within the company. As a result, they may subtly resist the change.

To overcome such resistance, Wrigley could use strategies such as giving employees enough time to fully evaluate and understand the change, presenting a positive attitude about the change, and, if resistance is strong, suggesting that the proposed change will be tentative until it is fully evaluated.

All changes at the Wrigley Company need to be evaluated after implementation to discover whether further organizational change is necessary and whether the change process used might be improved for future use. For example, concerning the establishment of a new departmental structure at the company, the evaluation process would include monitoring department activities to determine whether departments are functioning according to plan. If not, further changes to the departmental structure might be necessary.

Wrigley should be careful not to create too much stress on other organization members as a result of planned change. Such stress could be significant enough to eliminate any planned improvement at the company and eventually result in physical symptoms and the inability to make sound decisions.

Although some additional stress on organization members as a result of changes might improve the company's effectiveness, too much stress could have a negative impact on production. Signs to look for include constant fatigue, increased aggression, temper outbursts, and chronic worrying.

If Wrigley determines that undesirably high levels of stress have resulted from changes related to the company's new product line, he should try to reduce the stress. Wrigley may be able to do so through training programs aimed at better equipping organization members to execute new job demands resulting from the change. Alternatively, Wrigley may want simply to slow the rate of planned change.

It would probably be wise for Wrigley to take action that would prevent unwanted stressors from developing as a result of planned work-situation change. In this regard, he could ensure that the organizational climate at the Wrigley Company is supportive of individual needs and that jobs resulting from the planned change are as interesting as possible.

Wrigley should also keep in mind that conflict is a usual by-product of planning and implementing organizational changes. In handling this conflict, Wrigley can *compromise* (settle on a modified problem solution that reflects a change in the ideas of all conflicting parties, but which all parties find acceptable), *avoid* (pretend that no conflict exists), *force* (demand that a change be made), or *resolve* (confront the problem(s) causing the conflict and solve it).

Although Wrigley has focused on changes that improve the company's sales, he might also consider changes that improve the firm's cost structure. For example, he could consider establishing a virtual focus within the company. Such organizational change probably would not be as drastic as establishing the William Wrigley Jr. Company as a virtual corporation, but recommending some degree of virtuality that might begin by establishing virtual teams.

Wrigley could choose among various options that help to give the company a virtual dimension. For example, he could establish a virtual office that had workers in its market research group telecommute. Other options available for establishing a virtual office at the company could include workers "hoteling," tethered in the office, home-based with some mobility, or fully mobile. Wrigley's rationale for establishing this type of virtual office at the company probably should include cost savings due to rent savings and enhanced worker productivity. With such a virtual structure, the company would enable its market researchers to spend less time at work and more time on the road visiting with focus groups.

As with any type of change, establishing a virtual dimension at Wrigley Company will include a number of important challenges that must be met in order for newly established virtual components to be successful. Perhaps the most significant of these challenges is appropriately integrating virtual workers into the Wrigley Company's corporate culture. Building good communication among Wrigley's managers and virtual workers is an important step for integrating these workers into the culture and maintaining their continued presence. To build this communication, Wrigley's managers could take steps that include establishing regular communication times with virtual workers, publishing an online newsletter aimed at helping virtual workers deal with their unique problems, and having regular social events where virtual workers could meet and interact with other virtual workers as well as the company's employees in traditional work settings.

MANAGEMENT SKILL ACTIVITIES

This section is specially designed to help you develop organizational change skill. An individual's organizational change skill is based upon an understanding of organizational change concepts and the ability to apply those concepts in management situations. The following activities are designed both to heighten your understanding of organizational change fundamentals and to develop your ability to apply those concepts in various management situations.

UNDERSTANDING ORGANIZATIONAL CHANGE CONCEPTS

This section is comprised of activities that will sharpen your understanding of organizational change concepts. Answer essay questions as completely as possible. Complete Exploring Your Management Skill: Part 2 as directed. Also, remember that additional true/false and multiple choice questions appear online at My ManagementLab.com to help you further refine your understanding of organizational change.

Essay Questions

1. List and explain five reasons why organizations should undergo change.
2. What role should "organizational stability" play in the organizational change process?
3. Discuss an example of how you might use "freezing, unfreezing, and refreezing" in making a specific organizational change.
4. Discuss grid OD as a technique for changing people in organizations.
5. Why is handling conflict an important part of making organizational change?

Developing Management Skill

Learning activities in this section are aimed at helping you to develop organizational change skill. Learning activities include Exploring Your Management Skill: Part 2, Experiential Exercise, Cases, and a VideoNet exercise.

EXPLORING YOUR MANAGEMENT SKILL: PART 2

As you recall, you completed Exploring Your Management Skill before you started to study this chapter. Your responses gave you an idea of how much you initially knew about organizational change and helped you to focus on important points as you studied the chapter. Answer the Exploring Your Management Skill questions again now (p. 336) and compare your score to the first time you took it. This comparison will give you an idea of how much you have learned from studying this chapter

and pinpoint areas for further clarification before you start studying the next chapter. Record your answers within the text or go to MyManagementLab.com. Recording your answers in MyManagementLab will allow you to get immediate results and see how your score compares to your classmates. If you answer the questions in the book, the answers are located in the Exploring Your Management Skill section at the end of the book.

YOUR MANAGEMENT SKILLS PORTFOLIO

Your Management Learning Portfolio is a collection of activities especially designed to demonstrate your management knowledge and skill. By completing these activities online at MyManagementLab.com, you will be able to print, complete with cover sheet, as many activities as you choose. Be sure to save your work. Taking your printed portfolio to an employment interview could be helpful in obtaining a job.

The portfolio activity for this chapter is Managing Change-Related Stress. Read the highlight about the Ericson Manufacturing Company and answer the questions that follow.[54]

Managing Change-Related Stress at Ericson Manufacturing Company

For more than 80 years, the Ericson Manufacturing Company has been an industry leader in the manufacturing of temporary electrical power products. The company has built a reputation of manufacturing safe, high-quality products. Products the company manufactures are varied and include electrical plugs, extension cords, and hand lamps.

For most of its nearly nine decades in business, the management saw no need for extensive sales forecasting. Recently, however, Ericson's business world began to change. Rising costs of domestic materials used to make its products began to rise sharply. As a result of this price increase, the company began buying materials and parts from overseas vendors. Naturally, parts and materials purchased from overseas vendors took longer to arrive than the same goods purchased from domestic vendors. This delay in the delivery of materials and parts significantly disrupted Ericson's traditional production process and related work scheduling of employees. Manufacturing began to be delayed and customer complaints began to rise significantly. Management began to find that as predicted delivery times from overseas vendors became more unreliable, warehouse managers began to order more parts than necessary to keep extra on hand when needed. Too much money was being tied up in inventory and the company was becoming less profitable.

Assume that you are the president of Ericson Electric Company. You know that you must make some changes within the company and that you'll need a well-reasoned strategy for making the changes and minimizing the negative effects of employee stress related to the changes. Answering the following questions will help you develop this strategy.

What are four organizational changes you would like to make at Ericson?

1. _____

2. _____

3. _____

4. _____

Why would you like to make each change?

1. _____

2. _____

3. _____

4. _____

What is a stressor inherent in each of your proposed changes that could affect worker productivity at Ericson?

1. _____

2. _____

3. _____

4. _____

What will you do to try to eliminate the negative impact of each stressor?

1. _____

2. _____

3. _____

4. _____

EXPERIENTIAL EXERCISE: MANAGING FLORIDA'S QUARTERBACK[55]

Directions. Read the following scenario and then perform the listed activities. Your instructor may want you to perform the activities as an individual or within groups. Follow all of your instructor's directions carefully.

This year the University of Florida football team is defending its national championship title. Urban Meyer, the head coach at Florida, along with every Gator football fan, fully expects sophomore quarterback Tim Tebow to have an important role in this title defense. Tebow was a high school All American and proved last year that he can both throw and run the football.

Observing pre-season workouts, Meyer is starting to worry about Tebow. Tebow's arm is often sore, which prohibits him from throwing the football or forces him to sit out at practice. Meyer believes that Tebow's baseball style of throwing the football is causing this soreness. Meyer would like for Tebow to change his passing style from his present baseball passing style to a traditional shorter, more compact throwing style.

Questions

Your instructor will divide the class into small groups. Groups should answer the following questions.

1. Should Meyer attempt to change Tebow's throwing style? Why?
2. List three reasons why Tebow might not want to change his style.
3. List three reasons why Meyer might want to change Tebow's style.
4. Assuming that Meyer's attempts to change Tebow will result in conflict between Meyer and Tebow, which technique(s) for handling conflict discussed in the chapter would you advise Meyer to adopt? Why?

Role Play

Think about answers to the preceding questions and assume that Tebow is adamant about not wanting to change his style. Half of the groups assigned by the instructor should be prepared to play the role of Tebow and the other half prepared to play the role of Meyer. In the role play situation, Meyer is having a meeting with Tebow to introduce the idea of Tebow changing his passing style. Meyer definitely wants Tebow to change, Tebow definitely does not want to change. Meyer has invited Tebow to his office and starts the conversation. The conversation might be video taped by the instructor for instructional replay.

CASES

WRIGLEY CONTINUES TO CHANGE

"Wrigley Continues to Change" (p. 335) and its related Challenge Case Summary sections were written to help you better understand the management concepts contained in this chapter. Answer the following discussion questions about the Challenge Case to better understand how concepts relating to organizational change and stress can be applied in a company such as Wrigley.

1. How complicated would it be for other change agents who are not members of the Wrigley family to implement the product line changes in the company? Explain.
2. Do you think that certain employees at the Wrigley Company would subtly resist this change? Why or why not?
3. What elements of this change could cause organization members to experience stress, and what might the change agent do to help alleviate this stress? Be specific.

ADOBE SYSTEMS REINVENTS ITSELF AGAIN AND AGAIN

Read the case and answer the questions that follow. Studying this case will help you better understand how concepts relating to organizational change and stress can be applied in a company such as Adobe Systems.

"One of my biggest challenges in taking over from two great founders has been trying to figure out how to change the company without destroying the culture that John [Warnock] and Chuck [Geschke] built," says Bruce Chizen, CEO of Adobe Systems. Founded in 1981 by two researchers with high-tech experience, Adobe has successfully introduced such innovations as Acrobat Reader document-viewing software, PostScript printer language, and Adobe PhotoShop imaging software. When Chizen became executive vice president in 1998 and again when he was named CEO in 2000, he initiated considerable organizational change at Adobe.

In 1998, the company was generating $850 million in annual revenues but had fallen behind schedule on a new software product and was suffering a sales slowdown due to economic woes in Asia. Moreover, it was so cash-rich (and debt-free) that it was a tempting takeover target, attracting an unwelcome acquisition bid from competitor Quark that Adobe successfully deflected. At that point, the only way to recapture growth was to initiate change, just as Adobe's technology had to continue changing to stay ahead of the curve. With a new executive team, the company refocused on specific customer needs and segments, thinned its employee ranks, and switched from a territory to a functional structure. It also centralized administration and control systems to give managers better and more timely information on which to base their decisions.

Adobe was soon back on track. However, by the time Chizen took over as CEO, he was convinced that the company could not sustain long-term growth without widening its scope beyond function-specific business software. This change was in keeping with the company's mission, which the CEO says has "always been about developing, designing, marketing, selling software to help people communicate better," as well as by Adobe's core competencies: "We know what we do well—we make software where 'good enough' is not acceptable."

To avoid being eclipsed by competitive technology, Adobe had to quickly develop cutting-edge software for organizations seeking to create, customize, exchange, and enhance all kinds of documents, not just images or graphics or text alone. In addition to a full internal program of software research and development, Chizen bought several smaller firms to gain their technical expertise in data capture and document management applications. Still, the CEO realized that his effort to widen Adobe's scope would be effective only with employee acceptance and support. He notes that "someone who left Adobe could get a job somewhere else with relatively little risk and a great deal of upside. So the people who chose to stay really saw the potential in this company. And because we had committed employees, the motivation to change was there. That was the biggest change."

These days, Adobe has grown to 2,460 employees and $1.2 billion in annual sales revenues, based on its broader array of software programs for enterprise-wide use. Its annual employee turnover rate has dropped from a high of 20 percent to a minimal 4 percent. Just as important, the company's Portable Document Format (PDF) has been adopted as the standard technology by a number of industries and government agencies seeking secure electronic documentation and interchange. Next on Chizen's list is software that will allow cell phone users to swap and read PDF documents on the fly.

The CEO acknowledges that change has not come easily, in part because the company is still relatively young and because "innovation is about the employees . . . it's what's in people's heads that makes a difference." With more rigorous processes for managing human resources and handling performance evaluation, Adobe has the tools to hire, motivate, and reward outstanding employees. The workforce has clearly embraced the changes, because the company has been named to *Fortune* magazine's "Best Places to Work" list more than once.

QUESTIONS

1. Using the model of stability and adaptation, explain what you think might happen to Adobe if Chizen continues to initiate major organizational changes every two years.

2. Which of the three kinds of changes did Adobe make in 1998, and how did it set the stage for the changes made in 2000 and later?

3. Would you recommend that Adobe allow all its employees to be fully mobile? Explain.

VIDEONET EXERCISE

Organizational Change

VIDEO HIGHLIGHTS

Change is one of the challenges every manager can count on facing, as the employees and managers of Student Advantage attest to. Acquisition has been one of Student Advantage's most successful growth strategies, and the company's managers recognize the potential for corporate cultures to collide instead of meshing in the course of this kind of change. They discuss several strategies they have used to avoid conflict between cultures and other aspects of change that, for this firm, has so far been mostly top down.

Discussion Questions

1. List three factors that have led to the need for change at Student Advantage.

2. What methods has Student Advantage used to help reduce employee stress associated with all the changes taking place?

3. Why is important for managers of Student Advantage to continue to monitor the stress associated with the changes taking place now and in the future?

Internet Activity

Go to the Student Advantage Web site at www.student advantage.com. List three changes management might have to make in the future. How would you keep stress related to these changes from leading to dysfunction?

PART

5

INFLUENCING

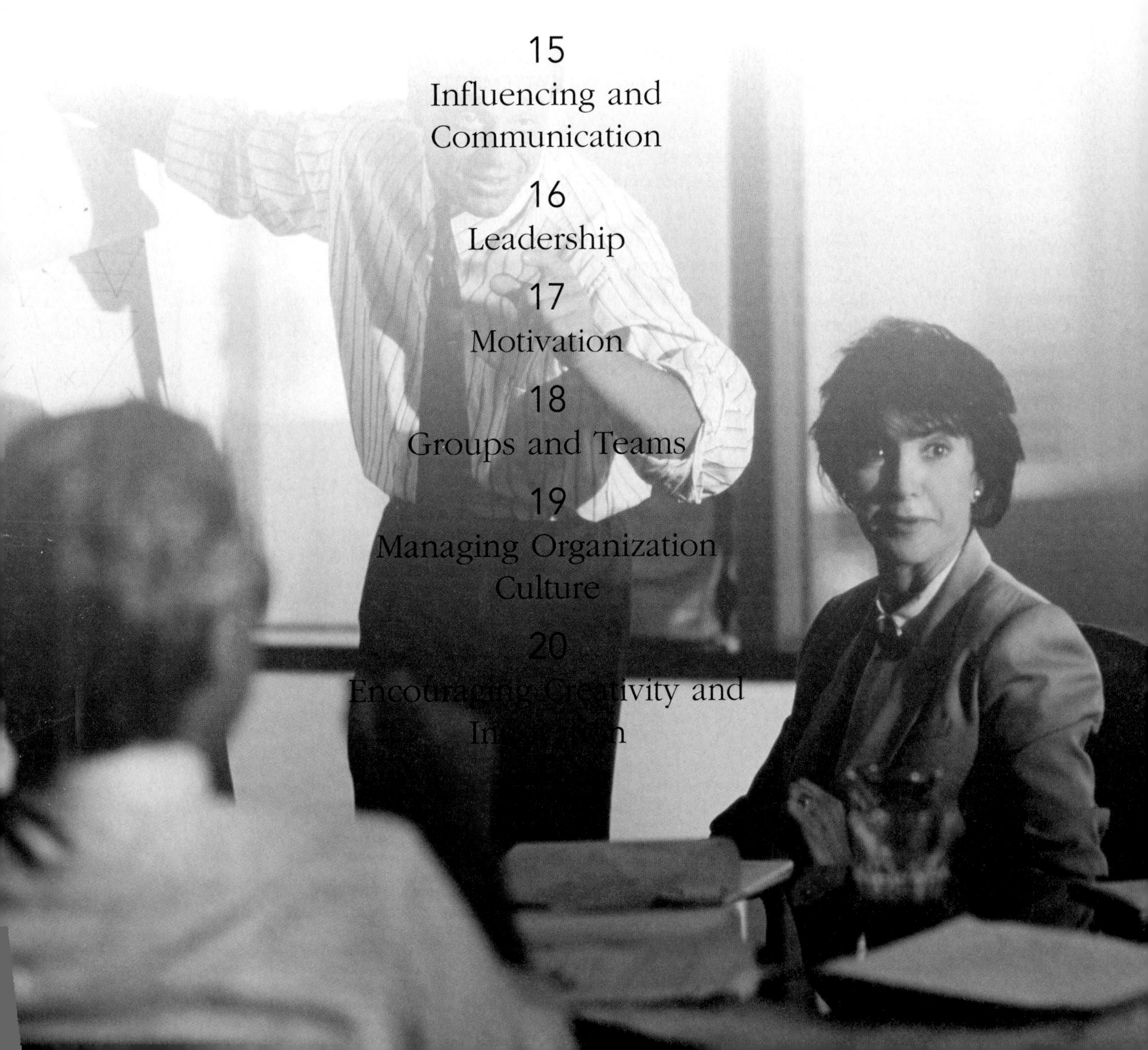

15 Influencing and Communication

OBJECTIVES

TO HELP BUILD MY COMMUNICATION SKILL, WHEN STUDYING THIS CHAPTER, I WILL ATTEMPT TO ACQUIRE:

1. An understanding of the relationship between influencing and emotional intelligence

2. An understanding of inter-personal communication

3. A knowledge of how to use feedback

4. An appreciation for the importance of nonverbal communication

5. Insights into formal orga-nizational communication

6. An appreciation for the importance of the grapevine

7. Some hints on how to encourage organizational communication

TARGET SKILL communication skill: the ability to share information with other individuals

LAFLEY'S COMMUNICATION SKILL CONTINUES TO PAY OFF AT PROCTER & GAMBLE

The Procter & Gamble Company (P&G) manufactures and markets more than 200 products to approximately 5 billion consumers. P&G's most popular products include Pampers disposable diapers, Crest toothpaste, and Tide laundry detergent. The company, which was formed in 1887, now sells its products in more than 100 countries. In 2002, P&G appointed A.G. Lafley, a mild-mannered Navy veteran, as its new chief executive officer.

Many credit Lafley's ability to communicate with P&G employees as the driving force behind the company's recent improved performance. In particular, Lafley focused on increasing communication with P&G's senior executives. On most Sunday nights, for example, Lafley meets with P&G's head of human resources to review the performance of the company's 200 most senior executives. After reviewing each manager's activities, Lafley communicates both positive and negative aspects of the manager's performance. This process helps P&G executives to understand clearly Lafley's expectations.

Lafley's communication style also helps to improve the flow of information within P&G. Many individuals, for example, note that he communicates primarily by asking questions. Lafley then uses employees' answers to these questions to shape the individual's future performance. He refers to this process as "peeling the onion." By relying on this communication technique, Lafley avoids

A.G. Lafley, CEO of Procter & Gamble. Many analysts believe Lafley owes much of his success to his special style of communicating with employees.

the appearance of a controlling boss who derives satisfaction from issuing orders. Instead, Lafley uses his smooth communication style to institute changes in P&G smoothly without upsetting top employees, who are sometimes referred to as "Proctoids" for their robotic decision-making styles.

Lafley also uses symbols to convey meaning to employees. For example, one of Lafley's first directives involved replacing the rectangular conference table used for meetings of the company's 12 top executives with a round table. With this round table, no single individual appears to control the conversation. Each of the top executives sitting around the round table enjoys the same view of and access to Lafley.

Lafley also uses simple phrases and slogans to ensure that everyone within the organization understands the company's main objectives. For example, he uses the slogan "The consumer is boss" to reiterate to employees that the company designs products to satisfy consumer needs. Additionally, he uses the phrase "The first moment of truth" to describe the importance of shelf space in retail outlets such as Carrefour and Wal-Mart as related to introducing new products to consumers.

Taken together, Lafley has employed a number of techniques to ensure that communication within P&G flows smoothly. Many believe Lafley's approach to organizational communication is one of the primary reasons that P&G stock has recently hit an all-time high.[1]

"EXPLORE YOUR OWN MANAGEMENT SKILLS BY TAKING THE QUIZ ON THE NEXT PAGE"

Before studying this chapter, respond to the following questions regarding the type of advice that you would give to A.G. Lafley, the CEO referenced in the Challenge Case. Then address the concerning communication challenges that he faces within Procter & Gamble. You are not expected to be a communication expert at this point. Answering the questions now can help you focus on important points when you study the chapter. Also, answering the questions again after you study the chapter will give you an idea of how much you have learned.

Record your answers here or go to MyManagementLab.com. Recording your answers in MyManagementLab will allow you to get immediate results and see how your score compares to your classmates. If you answer the questions in the book, the answers are located in the Exploring Your Management Skill section at the end of the book.

FOR EACH STATEMENT CIRCLE:

- "Y" if you would give the advice to Lafley.
- "N" if you would NOT give the advice to Lafley.
- "NI" if you have no idea whether you would give the advice to Lafley.

Mr. Lafley, in meeting your communication challenges at Procter & Gamble, you should . . .

Before   *After*
Study   *Study*

1. communicate as well as lead and plan to exercise the influencing management functions.
   Y, N, NI

2. be aware of your own emotions as well as the emotions of others in trying to influence people.
   Y, N, NI

3. keep in mind that sometimes the primary goal of your communication is simply to share information with other employees.
   Y, N, NI

4. decode a message and then send it to Procter & Gamble employees.
   Y, N, NI

5. think of yourself as a source/encoder who projects a message signal to a decoder destination.
   Y, N, NI

6. be careful not to overload Procter & Gamble employees with information that's too complex.
   Y, N, NI

7. ensure that you don't use words in your messages that have too many meanings.
   Y, N, NI

8. consider field of experience in attempting to communicate successfully.
   Y, N, NI

9. not be concerned that your view of the Procter & Gamble employee with whom you're communicating can affect your messages to that individual.
   Y, N, NI

10. keep in mind that interpersonal communication is essentially the same as organizational communication.
    Y, N, NI

11. use serial transmissions to avoid communication breakdowns.
    Y, N, NI

12. focus on eliminating the grapevine.
    Y, N, NI

13. construct communication networks to influence issues such as morale and accuracy of communication.
    Y, N, NI

14. remember that your communication effectiveness will probably be affected by your listening ability.
    Y, N, NI

15. keep in mind that your informal communication will usually be a detriment to attaining company goals.
    Y, N, NI

THE COMMUNICATION CHALLENGE

As described in the Challenge Case, A.G. Lafley, the CEO of Procter & Gamble, used his excellent communication skills to improve the flow of information within the organization. According to the case, Lafley wants to build P&G into a high-performing organization that processes information efficiently.

This chapter emphasizes the challenge of improving communication within organizations such as P&G and offers some insight into how this challenge can be accomplished. The chapter is divided into two main parts: fundamentals of influencing and communication.

FUNDAMENTALS OF INFLUENCING

The four basic managerial functions—planning, organizing, influencing, and controlling—were introduced in Chapter 1. *Planning* and *organizing* have already been discussed; *influencing* is the third of these basic functions covered in this text. A definition of *influencing* and a discussion of the influencing subsystem follow.

Defining Influencing

Influencing is the process of guiding the activities of organization members in appropriate directions. *Appropriate directions,* of course, are those that lead to the attainment of management system objectives. Influencing involves focusing on organization members as people and dealing with such issues as morale, arbitration of conflicts, and the development of good working relationships.[2] It is a critical part of a manager's job. In fact, the ability to influence others is a primary determinant of how successful a manager will be.[3]

The Influencing Subsystem

Like the planning and organizing functions, the influencing function can be viewed as a subsystem within the overall management system (see Figure 15.1). The primary purpose of the influencing subsystem, as already stated, is to enhance the attainment of management system objectives by guiding the activities of organization members in appropriate directions.[4]

Figure 15.2 shows the constituents of the influencing subsystem. The input of this subsystem is composed of a portion of the total resources of the overall management system, and its output is appropriate organization member behavior. The process of the influencing subsystem involves the performance of six primary management activities:

1. Leading
2. Motivating
3. Considering groups
4. Communicating
5. Encouraging creativity and innovation
6. Building corporate culture

Managers transform a portion of organizational resources into appropriate organization member behavior mainly by performing these activities.

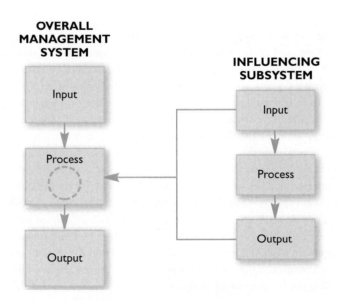

OVERALL MANAGEMENT SYSTEM

Input

Process

Output

INFLUENCING SUBSYSTEM

Input

Process

Output

FIGURE 15.1
Relationship between overall management system and influencing subsystem

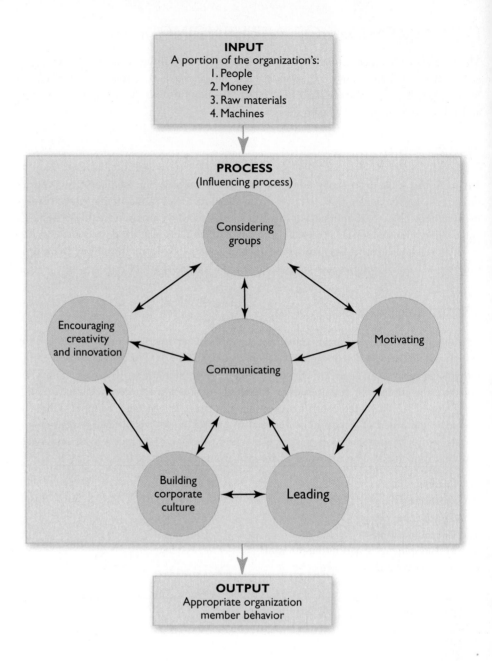

FIGURE 15.2
The influencing subsystem

As Figure 15.2 shows, leading, motivating, considering groups, building corporate culture, communicating, and encouraging creativity and innovation are interrelated. Managers accomplish each of these influencing activities, to some extent, by communicating with organization members. For example, managers can only decide what kind of leader they need to be after they analyze the characteristics of the various groups with which they will interact and determine how those groups can best be motivated. Then, regardless of the leadership strategy they adopt, their leading, motivating, and working with groups, for example, will be accomplished—at least partly—through communication with other organization members.

In fact, all management activities are accomplished at least partly through communication or communication-related endeavors. Because communication is used repeatedly by managers, the ability to communicate is often referred to as the fundamental management skill.

A recent survey of chief executives supports this notion that communication is the fundamental management skill. The results, which appear in Table 15.1, show that CEOs ranked oral and written communication skills first (along with interpersonal skills) among those that should be taught to management students.

TABLE 15.1	Chief Executives' Ranking of Skills They Believe Should Be Taught to Management Students	
Rank*	Key Learning Area	Frequency Indicated
1	Oral and written communication skills	25
1	Interpersonal skills	25
3	Financial/managerial accounting skills	22
4	Ability to think, be analytical, and make decisions	20
5	Strategic planning and goal setting—concern for long-term performance	13
6	Motivation and commitment to the firm—giving 110 percent	12
7	Understanding of economics	11
8	Management information systems and computer applications	9
8	Thorough knowledge of your business, culture, and overall environment	9
8	Marketing concept (the customer is king) and skills	9
11	Integrity	7
11	Knowledge of yourself: setting long- and short-term career objectives	7
13	Leadership skills	6
13	Understanding of the functional areas of the business	6
15	Time management: setting priorities—how to work smart, not long or hard	1

*1 is most important.

Emotional Intelligence

Earlier sections defined influencing and the influencing system. Overall, this influencing function of management focuses on guiding people to accomplish goals. Emotional intelligence, a concept developed by Daniel Goleman, is growing in popularity and prominence among both managers and management scholars. Overall, Goleman's concept enriches a discussion of influencing by focusing on specific skills that enable managers to become successful in guiding people toward goal accomplishment.[5]

Emotional intelligence is the capacity of people to recognize their own feelings and the feelings of others, to motivate themselves, and to manage their own emotions as well as the emotions in relationships with others. Overall, an individual's emotional intelligence is characterized by self-awareness, self-motivation, self-regulation, empathy for others, and adeptness in building relationships. Studies indicate many interesting points regarding emotional intelligence. First, research indicates that managers with higher levels of emotional intelligence are likely to be successful because they are likely to build organization culture characterized by trust, learning, information-sharing, and desirable risk taking. Research also indicates that managers with higher levels of emotional intelligence are more interpersonally effective when compared to managers with lower levels of emotional intelligence.[6] Also, research indicates that managers with higher levels of emotional intelligence are likely to be more satisfied in their jobs than other managers, and employees who work for managers with higher levels of emotional intelligence are more satisfied with their jobs than employees who work for managers with lower levels of emotional intelligence. Last, research indicates that managers with lower levels of emotional intelligence are likely to be relatively unsuccessful because they are less likely to produce a positive work culture.[7] Research seems to clearly indicate that demonstrating a high level of emotional intelligence positively affects not only managers, but also their employees.

At first glance, the close relationship between the traditional influencing function of management and Goleman's emotional intelligence may be hard to recognize. Upon inspecting the skills that Goleman outlines as being necessary to being an emotionally intelligent

Emotionally intelligent managers:

1. Motivate others
2. Focus on personal and organizational achievement
3. Understand others
4. Communicate efficiently and effectively
5. Lead others
6. Build successful teams
7. Handle conflict appropriately
8. Change organizations appropriately
9. Manage diversity
10. Manage creativity and innovation

FIGURE 15.3

Ten Skills possessed by emotionally intelligent managers

manager, however, the relationship becomes clearer. Figure 15.3 lists several of the skills of the emotionally intelligent manager. As you can see by inspecting Figure 15.3, the influencing section of this book and the concept of emotional intelligence both emphasize critical management concepts and skills in areas of motivation, communication, leadership, teamwork, creativity, and innovation.

Communication is discussed further in the rest of this chapter. Leading, motivating, and considering groups and teams, corporate culture, and creativity and innovation are discussed in Chapters 16, 17, 18, 19, and 20, respectively.

COMMUNICATION

Communication is the process of sharing information with other individuals. Information, as used here, is any thought or idea that managers want to share with others. In general, communication involves the process of one person projecting a message to one or more other people, which results in everyone arriving at a common understanding of the message. Because communication is a commonly used management skill and ability and is often cited as the skill most responsible for a manager's success, prospective managers must learn how to communicate.[8] To help managers become better interpersonal communicators, new training techniques are constantly being developed and evaluated.[9]

The communication activities of managers generally involve interpersonal communication—sharing information with other organization members.[10] The following sections feature both the general topic of interpersonal communication and the more specific topic of interpersonal communication in organizations.

Interpersonal Communication

To be a successful interpersonal communicator, a manager must understand the following:

1. How interpersonal communication works
2. The relationship between feedback and interpersonal communication
3. The importance of verbal versus nonverbal interpersonal communication

How Interpersonal Communication Works Interpersonal communication is the process of transmitting information to others.[11] To be complete, the process must have the following three basic elements:[12]

1. **The source/encoder**—The **source/encoder** is the person in the interpersonal communication situation who originates and encodes information to be shared with

Communication is the way we share thoughts and ideas with others.

others. Encoding is putting information into a form that can be received and understood by another individual. Putting one's thoughts into a letter is an example of encoding. Until information is encoded, it cannot be shared with others. (From here on, the *source/encoder* will be referred to simply as the *source.*)

2. **The signal**—Encoded information that the source intends to share constitutes a **message.** A message that has been transmitted from one person to another is called a **signal.**

3. **The decoder/destination**—The **decoder/destination** is the person or persons with whom the source is attempting to share information. This person receives the signal and decodes, or interprets, the message to determine its meaning. Decoding is the process of converting messages back into information. In all interpersonal communication situations, message meaning is a result of decoding. (From here on, the *decoder/destination* will be referred to simply as the *destination.*)

The classic work of Wilbur Schramm clarifies the role played by each of the three elements of the interpersonal communication process. As implied in Figure 15.4, the source determines what information to share, encodes this information in the form of a message, and then transmits the message as a signal to the destination. The destination decodes the transmitted message to determine its meaning and then responds accordingly.

A manager who desires to assign the performance of a certain task to a subordinate would use the communication process in the following way: First, the manager would determine exactly what task he or she wanted the subordinate to perform. Then the manager would encode and transmit a message to the subordinate that would accurately reflect this assignment. The message transmission itself could be as simple as the manager telling the subordinate what the new responsibilities include. Next, the subordinate would decode the message transmitted by the manager to ascertain its meaning and then respond to it appropriately.

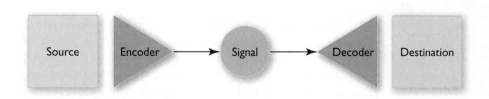

FIGURE 15.4 Role of the source, signal, and destination in the communication process

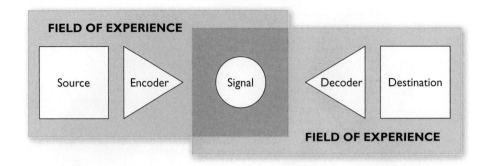

FIELD OF EXPERIENCE

Source Encoder Signal Decoder Destination

FIELD OF EXPERIENCE

FIGURE 15.5
Overlapping fields of experience that
ensure successful communication

Successful and Unsuccessful Interpersonal Communication Successful **communication** refers to an interpersonal communication situation in which the information the source intends to share with the destination and the meaning the destination derives from the transmitted message are the same. Conversely, **unsuccessful communication** is an interpersonal communication situation in which the information the source intends to share with the destination and the meaning the destination derives from the transmitted message are different.

To increase the probability that communication will be successful, the message must be encoded so that the source's experience of the way a signal should be decoded is equivalent to the destination's experience of the way it should be decoded. If these experiences match up, the probability is high that the destination will interpret the signal as intended by the source. Figure 15.5 illustrates these overlapping fields of experience that ensure successful communication.

Barriers to Successful Interpersonal Communication Factors that decrease the probability that communication will be successful are called *communication barriers*. A clear understanding of these barriers will help managers maximize their communication success. The following sections discuss both communication macrobarriers and communication microbarriers.

Nonverbal communication uses gestures, tone, and facial expression to convey information. What do you think this young woman is communicating?

MACROBARRIERS **Communication macrobarriers** are factors that hinder successful communication in a general communication situation.[13] These factors relate primarily to the communication environment and the larger world in which communication takes place. Some common macrobarriers are the following:[14]

1. **The increasing need for information**—Because society is changing constantly and rapidly, individuals have a greater and greater need for information. This growing need tends to overload communication networks, thereby distorting communication. To minimize the effects of this barrier, managers should take steps to ensure that organization members are not overloaded with information. Only information critical to the performance of their jobs should be transmitted to them.

   As **an example from the world of management**, illustrating how management can overload employees with information, consider a recent finding by management at **Genentech**, a bioresearch company. Management found that although efficient communication is a hallmark of a high-performing salesforce, company salespeople usually spend an average of 4.4 hours per week managing internal communications that are redundant, duplicative, or misdirected. Management discovered that sales staff productivity could be increased by more than 10 percent by eliminating unnecessary internal communications.[15]

2. **The need for increasingly complex information**—Because of today's rapid technological advances, most people are confronted with complex communication situations in their everyday lives. If managers take steps to emphasize simplicity in communication, the effects of this barrier can be lessened. Furnishing organization

members with adequate training to deal with more technical areas is another strategy for overcoming this barrier.

3. **The reality that people are increasingly coming into contact with people who use languages other than their own**—As business becomes more international in scope and as organization members travel more frequently, the need to know languages other than their own. The potential communication barrier of this multilanguage situation is obvious. Moreover, people who deal with foreigners need to be familiar not only with their languages, but also with their cultures. Formal knowledge of a foreign language is of little value unless the individual knows which words, phrases, and actions are culturally acceptable.[16]

4. **The constant need to learn new concepts cuts down on the time available for communication**—Many managers feel pressured to learn new and important concepts that they did not have to know in the past. Learning about the intricacies of international business or computer usage, for example, takes up significant amounts of managerial time. Many managers also find that the increased demands that training employees makes on their time leaves them with less time for communicating with other organization members.

MICROBARRIERS **Communication microbarriers** are factors that hinder successful communication in a specific communication situation.[17] These factors relate directly to such variables as the communication message, the source, and the destination. Among the microbarriers are the following:[18]

1. **The source's view of the destination**—The source in any communication situation has a tendency to view the destination in a specific way, and this view influences the messages sent. For example, individuals usually speak differently to people they think are informed about a subject than to those they believe are uninformed. The destination can sense the source's attitudes, which often block successful communication. Managers should keep an open mind about the people with whom they communicate and be careful not to imply negative attitudes through their communication behaviors. Figure 15.6 lists several examples of negative attitudes or stereotypes that managers in our modern society might possess regarding various types of employees. If managers possess such negative feelings about employees, the feelings will inevitably negatively impact the manner in which managers communicate to those employees and ultimately limit organizational success. Such negative attitudes or stereotypes have no place in the world of modern management.

2. **Message interference**—Stimuli that compete with the communication message for the attention of the destination are called **message interference,** or noise. An instance of message interference is a manager talking to an office worker while the worker is trying to input data into a word processor. The inputting of data is message interference here because it is competing with the manager's communication message. Managers should attempt to communicate only when they have the total attention of the individuals with whom they wish to share information.

FIGURE 15.6
Examples of managers' potentially negative attitudes toward employees

Employee Type	Possible Negative Attitude Held
Women	Women have weak math ability
Senior citizens	Older people have bad memory
Gay men	Gay men are dangerous to young children
Whites	Whites are racists
Men	Men are less capable than women in dealing with emotional issues
Black men	Black men are more coordinated than white man

Source: This figure is based on Loriann Roberson and Carol T. Kulik, "Stereotype Threat at Work," *Academy of Management Perspectives* 21, no. 2 (May 2007); 28–29.

3. **The destination's view of the source**—Certain attitudes of the destination toward the source can also hinder successful communication. If, for example, a destination believes that the source has little credibility in the area about which the source is communicating, the destination may filter out much of the source's message and pay only slight attention to that part of the message actually received. Managers should attempt to consider the worth of messages transmitted to them independently of their personal attitudes toward the source. Many valuable ideas will escape them if they allow their personal feelings toward others to influence which messages they attend to.

4. **Perception**—**Perception** is an individual's interpretation of a message. Different individuals may perceive the same message in different ways. The two primary factors that influence how a stimulus is perceived are the destination's education level and the destination's amount of experience. To minimize the negative effects of this perceptual factor on interpersonal communication, managers should try to send messages with precise meanings. Ambiguous words generally tend to magnify negative perceptions.

5. **Multimeaning words**—Because many words in the English language have several meanings, a destination may have difficulty deciding which meaning should be attached to the words of a message. A manager should not assume that a word means the same thing to all the people who use it.

A classic study by Lydia Strong substantiates this point. Strong concluded that for the 500 most common words in our language, there are 4,070 different dictionary definitions. On the average, each of these words has more than eight usages. The word *run* is an example:[19]

Baseball player Bert Blyleven scored a run.

Did you ever see track legend Kriss Akabusi run?

I have a run *in my stocking.*

There is a fine run *of salmon this year.*

Are you going to run *this company or am I?*

You have the run *of the place.*

What headline do you want to run?

There was a run *on the bank today.*

Did he run *the ship aground?*

I have to run *(drive the car) downtown.*

Who will run *for president this year?*

Joe flies the Paris-London run *twice a week.*

You know the kind of people they run *around with.*

The apples run *large this year.*

Please run *my bathwater.*

When encoding information, managers should be careful to define the terms they are using whenever possible, never use obscure meanings for words when designing messages, and strive to use words in the same way their destination uses them.

Feedback and Interpersonal Communication **Feedback** is the destination's reaction to a message. Feedback can be used by the source to ensure successful communication. For example, if the destination's message reaction is inappropriate, the source can conclude that communication was unsuccessful and that another message should be transmitted. If the destination's message reaction is appropriate, the source can conclude that communication was successful (assuming, of course, that the appropriate reaction did not happen merely by chance). Because of its potentially high value, managers should encourage feedback whenever possible and evaluate it carefully.[20]

Gathering and Using Feedback Feedback can be either verbal or nonverbal.[21] To gather verbal feedback, the source can simply ask the destination pertinent message-related questions; the destination's answers should indicate whether the message was perceived as intended. To gather nonverbal feedback, the source can observe the destination's nonverbal response to a message.[22] Say a manager has transmitted a message to a subordinate specifying new steps that must be taken in the normal performance of the subordinate's job. The subordinate's failure to follow the steps accurately constitutes nonverbal feedback telling the manager that the initial message needs to be clarified.

If managers discover that their communication effectiveness is relatively low over an extended period of time, they should assess the situation to determine how to improve their communication skills. It may be that their vocabulary is confusing to their destinations. For example, a study conducted by Group Attitudes Corporation found that when managers used certain words repeatedly in communicating with steelworkers, the steelworkers usually became confused.[23] Among the words causing confusion were *accrue, contemplate, designate, detriment, magnitude,* and *subsequently.*

Achieving Communication Effectiveness In general, managers can sharpen their communication skills by adhering to the following "10 commandments of good communication" as closely as possible:[24]

1. **Seek to clarify your ideas before communicating**—The more systematically you analyze the problem or idea to be communicated, the clearer it becomes. This is the first step toward effective communication. Many communications fail because of inadequate planning. Good planning must consider the goals and attitudes of those who will receive the communication and those who will be affected by it.

2. **Examine the true purpose of each communication**—Before you communicate, ask yourself what you really want to accomplish with your message—obtain information, initiate action, change another person's attitude? Identify your most important goal and then adapt your language, tone, and total approach to serve that specific objective. Don't try to accomplish too much with each communication. The sharper the focus of your message, the greater its chances of success.

3. **Consider the total physical and human setting whenever you communicate**—Meaning and intent are conveyed by more than words alone. Many other factors influence the overall impact of a communication, and managers must be sensitive to the total setting in which they communicate. Consider, for example, your sense of timing, or the circumstances under which you make an announcement or render a decision; the physical setting; whether you communicate in private or otherwise, for example, the social climate that pervades work relationships within your company or department and sets the tone of its communications; and custom and practice, or the degree to which your communication conforms to, or departs from, the expectations of your audience. Be constantly aware of the total setting in which you communicate. Like all living things, communication must be capable of adapting to its environment.

4. **Consult with others, when appropriate, in planning communications**—Frequently, it is desirable or necessary to seek the participation of others in planning a communication or in developing the facts on which to base the communication. Such consultation often lends additional insight and objectivity to your message. Moreover, those who have helped you plan your communication will give it their active support.

5. **Be mindful of the overtones while you communicate rather than merely the basic content of your message**—Your tone of voice, your expression, your apparent receptiveness to the responses of others—all have a significant effect on those you wish to reach. Frequently overlooked, these subtleties of communication often affect a listener's reaction to a message even more than its basic content. Similarly, your choice of language—particularly your awareness of the fine shades of meaning and emotion in the words you use—predetermines in large part the reactions of your listeners.

6. **Take the opportunity, when it arises, to convey something of help or value to the receiver**—Consideration of the other person's interests and needs—trying to look at things from the other person's point of view—frequently points out opportunities to convey something of immediate benefit or long-range value to the other person. Subordinates are most responsive to managers whose messages take the subordinates' interests into account.

7. **Follow up your communication**—Your best efforts at communication may be wasted, and you may never know whether you have succeeded in expressing your true meaning and intent, if you do not follow up and evaluate how well your message was received. You can do this by asking questions, by encouraging the receiver to express his or her reactions, by following up on contacts, and by subsequently reviewing performance. Make certain that you get feedback for every important communication so that complete understanding and appropriate action result.

8. **Communicate for tomorrow as well as today**—Even though communications may be aimed primarily at meeting the demands of an immediate situation, they must be planned with the past in mind if they are to be viewed as consistent by the receiver. Most importantly, however, communications must be consistent with long-range interests and goals. For example, it is not easy to communicate frankly on such matters as poor performance or the shortcomings of a loyal subordinate, but postponing disagreeable communications makes these matters more difficult in the long run and is actually unfair to your subordinates and your company.

9. **Be sure your actions support your communications**—In the final analysis, the most persuasive kind of communication is not what you say, but what you do. When your actions or attitudes contradict your words, others tend to discount what you have said. For every manager, good supervisory practices—such as clear assignment of responsibility and authority, fair rewards for effort, and sound policy enforcement—communicate more than all the gifts of oratory.

10. **Last, but by no means least: Seek not only to be understood, but also to understand—be a good listener**—When you start talking, you often cease to listen, or at least to be attuned to the other person's unspoken reactions and attitudes. Even more serious is the occasional inattentiveness you may be guilty of when others are attempting to communicate with you. Listening is one of the most important, most difficult, and most neglected skills in communication. It demands that you concentrate, not only on the explicit meanings another person is expressing, but also on the implicit meanings, unspoken words, and undertones that may be far more significant.

Verbal and Nonverbal Interpersonal Communication Interpersonal communication is generally divided into two types: verbal and nonverbal. Up to this point, the chapter has emphasized **verbal communication**—communication that uses either spoken or written words to share information with others.

Nonverbal communication is the sharing of information without using words to encode thoughts. Factors commonly used to encode thoughts in nonverbal communication are gestures, vocal tones, and facial expressions.[25] In most interpersonal communication, verbal and nonverbal communications are not mutually exclusive. Instead, the destination's interpretation of a message is generally based both on the words contained in the message and on such nonverbal factors as the source's gestures and facial expressions.

The Importance of Nonverbal Communication In an interpersonal communication situation in which both verbal and nonverbal factors are present, nonverbal factors may have more influence on the total effect of the message.[26] Over two decades ago, Albert Mehrabian developed the following formula to show the relative contributions of verbal and nonverbal factors to the total effect of a message: Total message impact = .07 words + .38 vocal tones + .55 facial expressions. Other nonverbal factors besides vocal tones that can influence the effect of a verbal message are facial expressions, gestures, gender, and dress. Managers who are aware of this great potential influence of nonverbal factors on the effect of their communications will use nonverbal message ingredients to complement their verbal message ingredients whenever possible.[27]

Nonverbal messages can also be used to add content to verbal messages. For instance, a head might be nodded or a voice toned to show either agreement or disagreement.

Managers must be especially careful when they are communicating that verbal and non-verbal factors do not present contradictory messages. For example, if the words of a message express approval while the nonverbal factors express disapproval, the result will be message ambiguity that leaves the destination frustrated.

Managers who are able to communicate successfully through a blend of verbal and non-verbal communication are critical to the success of virtually every organization. In fact, a recent survey of corporate recruiters revealed that the skill organizations most seek in prospective employees is facility at verbal and nonverbal communication.

Interpersonal Communication in Organizations

To be effective communicators, managers must understand not only general interpersonal communication concepts, but also the characteristics of interpersonal communication within organizations, or **organizational communication.** Organizational communication directly relates to the goals, functions, and structure of human organizations.[28] To a major extent, organizational success is determined by the effectiveness of organizational communication.[29]

Although organizational communication was frequently referred to by early management writers, the topic did not receive systematic study and attention until after World War II. From World War II through the 1950s, the discipline of organizational communication made significant advances in such areas as mathematical communication theory and behavioral communication theory, and the emphasis on organizational communication has grown stronger in colleges of business since the 1970s.[30] The following sections focus on three fundamental organizational communication topics: (1) formal organizational communication, (2) informal organizational communication, and (3) the encouragement of formal organizational communication.

Formal Organizational Communication In general, organizational communication that follows the lines of the organization chart is called **formal organizational communication.**[31] As discussed in Chapter 11, the organization chart depicts relationships of people and jobs and shows the formal channels of communication among them.

Types of Formal Organizational Communication The three basic types of formal organizational communication are downward, upward, and lateral.

1. **Downward organizational communication** is communication that flows from any point on an organization chart downward to another point on the organization chart. This type of formal organizational communication relates primarily to the direction and control of employees. Job-related information that focuses on what activities are required, when they should be performed, and how they should be coordinated with other activities within the organization must be transmitted to employees. This downward communication typically includes a statement of organizational philosophy, management system objectives, position descriptions, and other written information relating to the importance, rationale, and interrelationships of various departments.

2. **Upward organizational communication** is communication that flows from any point on an organization chart upward to another point on the organization chart.[32] This type of organizational communication contains primarily the information managers need to evaluate the organizational area for which they are responsible and to determine whether something is going wrong within it. Techniques that managers commonly use to encourage upward organizational communication are informal discussions with employees, attitude

surveys, the development and use of grievance procedures, suggestion systems, and an "open door" policy that invites employees to come in whenever they would like to talk to management.[33] Organizational modifications based on the feedback provided by upward organizational communication will enable a company to be more successful in the future.

3. **Lateral organizational communication** is communication that flows from any point on an organization chart horizontally to another point on the organization chart. Communication that flows across the organization usually focuses on coordinating the activities of various departments and developing new plans for future operating periods. Within the organization, all departments are related to all other departments. Only through lateral communication can these departmental relationships be coordinated well enough to enhance the attainment of management system objectives.

Patterns of Formal Organizational Communication By its very nature, organizational communication creates patterns of communication among organization members. These patterns evolve from the repeated occurrence of various serial transmissions of information. According to Haney, a **serial transmission** involves passing information from one individual to another in a series. It occurs under the following circumstances:[34]

> A communicates a message to B; B then communicates A's message (or rather his or her interpretation of A's message) to C; C then communicates his or her interpretation of B's interpretation of A's message to D; and so on. The originator and the ultimate recipient of the message are separated by middle people.

One obvious weakness of a serial transmission is that messages tend to become distorted as the length of the series increases. Research has shown that message details may be omitted, altered, or added in a serial transmission.

The potential inaccuracy of transmitted messages is not the only weakness of serial transmissions. A classic article by Alex Bavelas and Dermot Barrett[35] makes the case that serial transmissions can also influence morale, the emergence of a leader, the degree to which individuals involved in the transmissions are organized, and their efficiency. Three basic organizational communication patterns and the corresponding effects on the variables just mentioned are shown in Figure 15.7.

FIGURE 15.7

Comparison of three patterns of organizational communication based on the variables of speed, accuracy, organization, emergence of leader, and morale

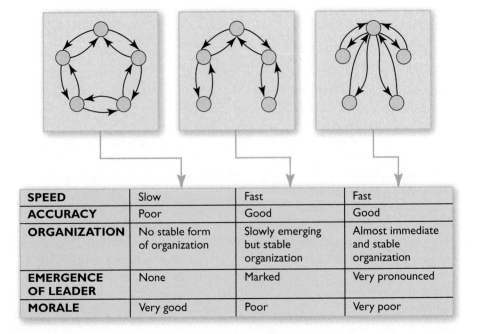

SPEED	Slow	Fast	Fast
ACCURACY	Poor	Good	Good
ORGANIZATION	No stable form of organization	Slowly emerging but stable organization	Almost immediate and stable organization
EMERGENCE OF LEADER	None	Marked	Very pronounced
MORALE	Very good	Poor	Very poor

class discussion highlight

COMMUNICATION AND YOUR CAREER[36]

Linnea Haakenson is a production supervisor in a low-tech toy company that produces wooden cars and boats for children 2–4 years of age. Linnea supervises 25 employees and has been performing well in this same job for five years. In personal reflection, Linnea wants to be promoted, but doesn't think she'll be offered promotion in the foreseeable future. Linnea doesn't really understand why, however. Linnea has 24/7 e-mail access and is "always on" via her wireless technology. In fact, Linnea is somewhat of a legend at the company for always being on her BlackBerry. Linnea not only has conversations through her BlackBerry, but does quite a bit of message texting. Linnea has always believed that because of the efficiency involved, electronic means of communication are better than face-to-face communication.

Can Linnea's personal philosophy about communication affect her career? If yes, why? If no, why not? If you were Linnea, what personal philosophy about communication would you have in order to maximize not only your job success, but also the success of your career?

Informal Organizational Communication Informal organizational communication is organizational communication that does not follow the lines of the organization chart.[37] Instead, this type of communication typically follows the pattern of personal relationships among organization members: One friend communicates with another friend, regardless of their relative positions on the organization chart. Informal organizational communication networks generally exist because organization members have a desire for information that is not furnished through formal organizational communication.[38]

In order to manage informal organizational communication appropriately, managers must strive to understand how this informal network operates in their organizations. As **an example from the world of management,** consider action taken to better understand informal organizational communication by management at **Steelcase,** the global leader in office furniture manufacturing. Steelcase management actually conducted a special study to better understand informal organization communication within the company. The study yielded valuable information: for instance, at Steelcase the days of standing around the water cooler to exchange the latest organizational gossip or company news may be over. Only 1 percent of Steelcase employees go to the cooler for more than water. At Steelcase, informal communication conversations are more likely to take place in the office kitchen, at a coworker's desk, or through e-mail.[39]

class discussion highlight

MODERN RESEARCH AND COMMUNICATION SKILL

The Impact of Diversity on Organizational Communication in Foreign Subsidiaries[40]

Various attributes of people can affect the interpersonal communication process in organizations. This highlight focuses on a research study by Vesa Peltokorpi that explores the relationship between employee diversity and interpersonal communication in organizations.

The study focused on nine different sales subsidiaries in Japan owned by different Nordic companies. Nordic refers to the northwestern European countries of Norway, Sweden, Denmark, Iceland, and Finland.

For the study, a survey was specially designed to see whether individuals from diverse cultural backgrounds within a company were reluctant to communicate with one another. Employees in all subsidiaries, including Nordic expatriates, were analyzed together. Overall, 110 employees from the nine subsidiaries participated in the study. All subjects were engaged in sales activities, but the industries in which they operated varied.

The researchers wanted to see whether diversity variables—such as differences in employee ages, gender, race, education, and work values—would encourage or discourage communication among the employees in organizations. The researcher predicted that differences in characteristics would actually discourage people from communicating with one another. Do you think that results of the study were consistent with the prediction? Why? Why not? How would you use your expected findings to increase your communication skill as a manager?

Patterns of Informal Organizational Communication The informal organizational communication network, or **grapevine,** has three main characteristics:

1. It springs up and is used irregularly within the organization.
2. It is not controlled by top executives, who may not even be able to influence it.
3. It exists largely to serve the self-interests of the people within it.

Understanding the grapevine is a prerequisite for a complete understanding of organizational communication. It has been estimated that 70 percent of all communication in organizations flows along the organizational grapevine. Not only do grapevines carry great amounts of communication, but they carry it at rapid speeds. Employees commonly cite the company grapevine as the most reliable and credible source of information about company events.[41]

Like formal organizational communication, informal organizational communication uses serial transmissions. The difference is that it is more difficult for managers to identify organization members involved in these transmissions than members of the formal communication network. A classic article by Keith Davis has been a significant help to managers in understanding how organizational grapevines spring up and operate. Figure 15.8 sketches the four most common grapevine patterns as outlined by Davis. They are as follows:[42]

1. **The single-strand grapevine**—*A* tells *B*, who tells *C*, who tells *D*, and so on. This type of grapevine tends to distort messages more than any other.
2. **The gossip grapevine**—*A* informs everyone else on the grapevine.
3. **The probability grapevine**—*A* communicates randomly—for example, to *F* and *D*. *F* and *D* then continue to inform other grapevine members in the same way.
4. **The cluster grapevine**—*A* selects and tells *C, D,* and *F. F* selects and tells *I* and *B*, and *B* selects and tells *J*. Information in this grapevine travels only to selected individuals.

DEALING WITH GRAPEVINES Clearly, grapevines are a factor managers must deal with because they can, and often do, generate rumors that are detrimental to organizational success. Exactly how individual managers should deal with the grapevine, of course, depends on the specific organizational situation in which they find themselves. Managers can use grapevines advantageously to maximize information flow to employees. When employees have what they view as sufficient organizational information, it seems to build their sense of belonging to the organization and their level of productivity. Some writers even argue that managers should encourage the development of grapevines and strive to

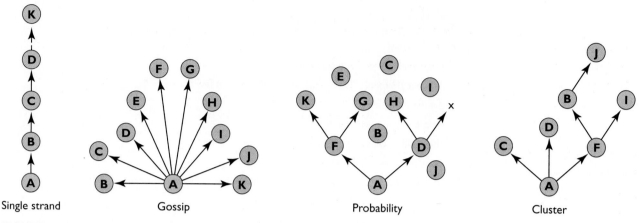

FIGURE 15.8 Four types of organizational grapevines

become grapevine members in order to gain feedback that could be valuable in improving the organization.[43]

Encouraging Formal Organizational Communication
Because the organization acts only in the way that its organizational communication directs it to act, organizational communication is often called the nervous system of the organization. Formal organizational communication is generally the more important type of communication within an organization, so managers should encourage its free flow.

One strategy for promoting formal organizational communication is to listen attentively to messages that come through formal channels. Listening shows organization members that the manager is interested in what subordinates have to say and encourages them to use formal communication channels in subsequent situations. Table 15.2 presents some general guidelines for listening well.

As **an example from the world of management** concerning the importance of listening, consider recent events within the United Kingdom segment of **McDonald's**, a worldwide fast-food retailer. When faced with meeting a number of daunting organizational challenges, United Kingdom CEO Peter Beresford decided to institute a program called *Listening Campaign*. This campaign entailed Beresford and his staff getting out and having face-to-face meetings with various stakeholder groups including staff, customers, and investors. The purpose of the meetings was to listen to stakeholders to gather input regarding how to meet the challenges that Beresford faced. According to Beresford, the success of *Listening Campaign* was undeniable. Through listening, Beresford was able to achieve benefits that included building more effective work teams, identifying organizational problems and their solutions, and implementing sound problem solutions.[44]

Some other strategies to encourage the flow of formal organizational communication are as follows:

- Support the flow of clear and concise statements through formal communication channels. Receiving an ambiguous message through a formal organizational communication channel can discourage employees from using that channel again.

- Take care to ensure that all organization members have free access to formal communication channels. Obviously, organization members cannot communicate formally within the organization if they don't have access to the formal communication network.

- Assign specific communication responsibilities to staff personnel who could be of enormous help to line personnel in spreading important information throughout the organization.

1. *Stop talking!*

You cannot listen if you are talking.

Polonius (*Hamlet*): "Give every man thine ear, but few thy voice."

2. *Put the talker at ease.*

Help the talker feel free to talk.

This is often called establishing a permissive environment.

3. *Show the talker that you want to listen.*

Look and act interested. Do not read your mail while he or she talks.

Listen to understand rather than to oppose.

4. *Remove distractions.*

Do not scribble on, tap, or shuffle papers.

Will it be quieter if you shut the door?

5. *Empathize with the talker.*

Try to put yourself in the talker's place so that you can see his or her point of view.

6. *Be patient.*

Allow plenty of time. Do not interrupt the talker.

Do not start for the door to walk away.

7. *Hold your temper.*

An angry person gets the wrong meaning from words.

8. *Go easy on argument and criticism.*

This puts the talker on the defensive. He or she may "clam up" or get angry.

Do not argue: even if you win, you *lose*.

9. *Ask questions.*

This encourages the talker and shows you are listening.

It helps to develop points further.

10. *Stop talking!*

This is the first and last commandment, because all other commandments depend on it. You just can't do a good listening job while you are talking. Nature gave us two ears but only one tongue, which is a gentle hint that we should listen more than we talk.

CHALLENGE CASE SUMMARY

One of the primary functions of P&G's A.G. Lafley is *influencing*—guiding the activities of P&G employees to enhance the accomplishment of organizational objectives. Lafley could perform this function by *leading* such individuals as division managers or perhaps corporate market research staff, by *motivating* them to do better jobs, by working well with various *groups* of employees, *encouraging creativity and innovation*, and by *communicating* successfully with employees.

Of all of these influencing activities, however, communication should be especially important to Lafley. Communication is the main tool through which Lafley should, at least to some extent, accomplish his duties as P&G CEO. As an example in the Challenge Case, through communication Lafley spreads the message that P&G needs to focus on customer needs when designing new products. Almost any impact that Lafley plans to exert on P&G (planning, organizing, or controlling) will require him to communicate with other P&G employees. In essence, Lafley must be a good communicator if he is to be a successful manager at P&G.

In discussing A.G. Lafley's ability to communicate, we are actually discussing his ability to share ideas with other Procter & Gamble employees. For Lafley to be a successful communicator, he must concentrate on the three essential elements of the communication process. The first element is the source—the individual who wishes to share information with another. In this case, the source is Lafley. The second element is the signal—the message transmitted by Lafley. The third element is the destination—the Procter & Gamble employee with whom Lafley wishes to share information. Lafley should communicate with Procter & Gamble employees by determining what information he wants to share, encoding the information, and then transmitting the message. The subordinates would then interpret the message and respond accordingly. Lafley's communication would be successful if subordinates interpreted messages as he intended.

If Lafley is to be a successful communicator, he must minimize the impact of numerous communication barriers. These barriers include:

1. P&G employees need to have more information and more complex information to do their jobs
2. Message interference
3. Lafley's view of the destination as well as the destination's view of Lafley
4. The perceptual process of the people involved in the communication attempt
5. Multimeaning words

The employees' reactions to Lafley's messages can provide Lafley with perhaps his most useful tool in making communication successful—feedback. When feedback does not seem appropriate, Lafley should transmit another message to clarify the meaning of his first message. He must be alert to both verbal and nonverbal feedback. Over time, if feedback indicates that Lafley is a relatively unsuccessful communicator, he should analyze his situation carefully to improve his communication effectiveness. He might find, for instance, that he is using a vocabulary that is generally inappropriate for certain employees or that he is not following one or more of the 10 commandments of good communication.

In addition, Lafley must remember that he can communicate to others without using words. His facial expressions, gestures, and even the tone of his voice say things to people. Most of Lafley's communication situations involve both verbal and nonverbal messages to Procter & Gamble employees. Because the impact of a message may be generated mostly by its nonverbal components, Lafley must be certain that his nonverbal messages complement his verbal messages. By installing the round conference table mentioned in the Challenge Case, for example, Lafley nonverbally conveyed the importance of each one of P&G's senior executives.

As chairman at Procter & Gamble, A.G. Lafley must strive to understand the intricacies of organizational communication—interpersonal communication as it takes place within the organization. The success of organizational communication at P&G is an important factor in determining the company's level of success. Lafley can communicate with his people in two basic ways: formally and informally.

In general, Lafley's formal communication should follow the lines on the organization chart. Lafley can communicate downward to, for example, divisional managers or upward to, for example, P&G's board of directors. Lafley's downward communication will commonly focus on the activities subordinates are performing. His upward communication will usually illustrate how the company is performing. Because Lafley is CEO and has no one at the same level within the organization, he would not communicate laterally. He should, however, take steps to ensure that lateral communication does occur at other organizational levels to enhance planning and coordination at Procter & Gamble.

It is certain that an extensive grapevine exists at Procter & Gamble. Although the company grapevine must be dealt with, Lafley may not be able to influence it significantly. Procter & Gamble employees, as well as employees for any company, typically are involved in grapevines for self-interest and because the formal organization has not furnished them with the information they believe they need.

By developing various social relationships, Lafley could conceivably become part of the grapevine and obtain valuable feedback from it. Also, because grapevines generate rumors that could have a detrimental effect on Procter & Gamble's success, Lafley should try to ensure that personnel are given all the information they need to do their jobs well through formal organizational communication, thereby reducing the need for a grapevine.

Because formal organizational communication is vitally important to P&G, Lafley should try to encourage its flow as much as possible. By listening intently to messages that come to him over formal channels, supporting the flow of clear messages, and making sure that all P&G employees have access to these channels, Lafley can make sure P&G's communication is the best it can be.

MANAGEMENT SKILL ACTIVITIES

This section is specially designed to help you develop communication skill. An individual's communication skill is based upon an understanding of communication concepts and the ability to apply those concepts in management situations. The following activities are designed both to heighten your understanding of communication fundamentals and to develop your ability to apply those concepts in various management situations.

UNDERSTANDING COMMUNICATION CONCEPTS

This section is comprised of activities that will sharpen your understanding of communication concepts. Answer essay questions as completely as possible. Complete Exploring Your Management Skill: Part 2 as directed. Also, remember that additional true/false and multiple choice questions appear online at MyManagementLab.com to help you further refine your understanding of communication.

Essay Questions

1. Discuss the significance of "field of experience" in communication.
2. What is feedback and how should managers use it when communicating?
3. How can managers encourage the flow of formal communication in organizations?
4. What is "emotional intelligence" and how does it relate to influencing people in organizations?
5. Draw three types of organizational grapevines and explain how communication effectiveness might be impacted by each type.

Developing Management Skill

Learning activities in this section are aimed at helping you to develop communication skill. Learning activities include Exploring Your Management Skill: Part 2, Experiential Exercises, Cases, and a VideoNet exercise.

EXPLORING YOUR MANAGEMENT SKILL: PART 2

As you recall, you completed Exploring Your Management Skill before you started to study this chapter. Your responses gave you an idea of how much you initially knew about communication and helped you to focus on important points as you studied the chapter. Answer the Exploring Your Management Skill questions again now (p. 362) and compare your score to the first time you took it. This comparison will give you an idea of how much you have learned from studying this chapter and pinpoint areas for further clarification before you start studying the next chapter. Record your answers within the text or go to MyManagementLab.com. Recording your answers in MyManagementLab will allow you to get immediate results and see how your score compares to your classmates. If you answer the questions in the book, the answers are located in the Exploring Your Management Skill section at the end of the book.

YOUR MANAGEMENT SKILLS PORTFOLIO

Your Management Learning Portfolio is a collection of activities especially designed to demonstrate your management knowledge and skill. By completing these activities online at MyManagementLab.com, you will be able to print, complete with cover sheet, as many activities as you choose. Be sure to save your work. Taking your printed portfolio to an employment interview could be helpful in obtaining a job.

The portfolio activity for this chapter is Developing a New Communication Environment.[45] Read the highlight about Ericsson and answer the questions that follow.

Developing a New Communication Environment

Ericsson, headquartered in Stockholm, Sweden, is a world-leading provider of telecommunications equipment with more than 1,000 networks in 140 countries. Forty percent of all mobile calls are made through Ericsson's systems. Ericsson has about 63,000 employees and is one of a few companies that offers worldwide solutions for all major mobile communication networks. A recent joint venture with Sony enabled Ericsson to offer a wide range of mobile devices, including cell phones and related equipment. The company's portfolio containing more than 20,000 patents is evidence of successful research efforts and its goal to be on the cutting edge of technology.

Over the years, Ericsson has invested heavily in maintaining its internal communication. Traditionally, the majority of this investment has been in the area of print and electronic publishing devices. Recently, management indicated that this historical investment approach for maintaining internal communications is no longer appropriate because it no longer meets Ericsson's ambitions for global best practice in all areas of the business. As part of rebuilding internal communications, all the publishing activities were outsourced to an external agency. A new area for significant investment in management's program was to improve internal communications by improving managers' interpersonal communication skills. Further, management wants the company's communication environment to change from an environment where internal communication was more focused on news flow, to an environment where the communication focuses on helping management achieve organizational goals.

Assuming that you have the primary responsibility at Ericsson for building this new communication environment, answer the following questions.

What four goals would you set for building the new communication environment at Ericsson?

1. _____

2. _____

3. _____

4. _____

Explain what each goal contributes toward establishing the new environment that supports reaching organizational goals.

1. _____

2. _____

3. _____

4. _____

List a primary step that you would take in trying to achieve each goal.

1. _____

2. _____

3. _____

4. _____

How long do you think it would take to establish the new communication environment at Ericsson? Why? Explain fully.

_____

_____

_____

EXPERIENTIAL EXERCISE: DEVELOPING NONVERBAL COMMUNICATION SKILLS

Directions. Read the following scenario and then perform the listed activities. Your instructor may want you to perform the activities as an individual or within groups. Follow all of your instructor's directions carefully.

The purpose of this exercise is to help you develop your nonverbal communication skills. Apply yourself as much as possible. The more you focus on the exercise, the greater your chance of developing your skill.

Procedure

1. Your instructor will divide the class into groups of approximately four members.
2. Each group will have about 10 minutes to complete the following task through a group discussion:

   List as many advantages and disadvantages as you can to allowing illegal aliens or undocumented workers to remain in your country.

3. Before discussion begins, each group will be given approximately 5 minutes so that *members can work individually* to (a) list two feelings that they would like to project during the group discussion, and (b) list corresponding nonverbal actions that they will use to express those feelings. For example, one feeling might be anger and the related nonverbal action could be yelling words. Individual should *NOT* share their work with other group members.

4. Once members have finished their individual work in part 3, the instructor will signal for group discussion to begin.

5. After the discussion, the instructor will allow each group about 5 minutes so that individuals can tell what feelings they think other individuals were trying to communicate. All should keep track of how many times their nonverbal messages were successful in communicating their target feelings.

6. The instructor will open discussion about the exercise by asking questions such as the following:
   a. Were you successful in communicating nonverbally? Why?
   b. Is it easy for you to communicate nonverbally? Why?
   c. What did *you* learn from this exercise about increasing your managerial skill to communicate nonverbally?

CASES

NEW PROCTER & GAMBLE CHIEF USES SPECIAL STYLE OF COMMUNICATION

"Lafley's Communication Skill Continues to Pay Off at Procter & Gamble" (p. 361) and its related Challenge Case Summary were written to help you better understand the management concepts contained in this chapter. Answer the following discussion questions about the Challenge Case to better see how your understanding of influencing and communication can be applied in a company like P&G.

1. List three problems that could be caused at Procter & Gamble if Lafley happened to be a poor communicator.
2. Explain *how* the problems you listed in number 1 can be caused by Lafley's inability to communicate.
3. Assuming that Lafley is a good communicator, discuss three ways that he is positively affecting Procter & Gamble as a result of this communication expertise.

HOW EBAY STAYS CONNECTED TO ITS COMMUNITY

Read the case and answer the questions that follow. Studying this case will help you better see how your understanding of influencing and communication can be applied in a company such as eBay.

Staying in touch with a worldwide community of 114 million buyers and sellers is all in a day's work for eBay CEO Meg Whitman. When she joined eBay in 1998, it employed fewer than 100 people; today, the company employs 6,300 people and auctions $24 billion worth of merchandise annually. From clothing to cars to computers, eBay auctions a diverse mix of 29 million items daily on its sites in Europe, the Americas, and Asia. In this fast-paced environment, far-flung employees, managers, buyers, and sellers routinely communicate using their keyboards rather than by talking things over in person.

Fresh from management jobs at Walt Disney, Hasbro, Stride-Rite, and other big corporations, Whitman was both amazed and impressed by the reaction of eBay users she met soon after becoming CEO. "Their passion for eBay [good and bad] was nothing I'd ever seen in 20 years of business," she remembers. This vivid introduction to the eBay community helped shape her approach to influencing and communication.

First, Whitman listens carefully and respectfully before responding. Each morning, she chats with staff members in the cubicles surrounding her own before she logs on to read and then answer e-mail from traders. Every few hours, she checks eBay's message boards to get a sense of what's going on in the community. And after auctioning furniture and other possessions on her company's site, she insists that other eBay executives auction items to gain firsthand knowledge of the experience and learn to appreciate the user's perspective.

Second, the CEO and her colleagues pay close attention to feedback. For example, only after surveying 50,000 users and finding that 80 percent approved did management move ahead with a proposed change to the customizable features of its My eBay page. Although sellers in particular are quick to criticize changes that might impair auction activity or confuse buyers, "most of these sellers know more about eBay than most [eBay] employees," acknowledges Whitman. "They use it every single day. They're the experts." Still, she and her team can't always predict how a particular change will strike the community. Not long ago, Whitman heard from thousands of users complaining about a new enhancement to the eBay site. "That week, I probably got a total of 3,000 or 4,000 e-mails from pottery and glass sellers saying, 'My business is down. You've done the wrong thing,'" she says. Her response? "We fixed it. We rolled back the changes."

Third, Whitman proves through her actions that she understands what eBay really means to its users. In 1999, when technical glitches crashed the site for 22 hours and then caused intermittent problems for several weeks afterward, the CEO drove to the office at 4 A.M. on the first morning trouble erupted. She knew little about hardware and software, yet she stayed and brainstormed solutions day and night with employees and vendors. Whitman explains: "I did the only thing I knew how to do—be there. If I was there, then the best people from the vendors would be there." Looking back, the CEO of Sun Microsystems (which supplies eBay with servers) observed that Whitman "has an amazing velvet-glove touch. Instead of making me angry, she made me want to do just about anything we could to solve her problem. And that's what we did."

Once this crisis was resolved, the CEO shuffled tech management and set tough new standards to prevent similar problems in the future. Now eBay is known around the world for the reliability of its operations, with the site unavailable for just a few seconds during an average month. Small wonder that Whitman receives loud applause when she appears at the company's annual member conference. "It's this unique blend of commerce and community. The community of users is endlessly interesting and endlessly surprising. That's what I love the most."

QUESTIONS

1. What macrobarriers and microbarriers might hinder successful communication between Meg Whitman and eBay users? What do you suggest she do to address these potential barriers?

2. Do you think the channels of communication in an online business such as eBay differ from those in a traditional business? Explain.

3. How would you recommend that new managers at eBay establish rapport with buyers and sellers?

VIDEONET EXERCISE

Communication and IT at Kluster

VIDEO HIGHLIGHTS

Ben Kaufman's new venture, Kluster (previously named Illuminator Project), is changing the way products are developed. His company has created a Web site where companies can involve their employees, customers, or anyone else in the product design process. It is the ultimate feedback loop. Inventors and designers can bring their ideas to market as well and see if anyone bites. The Kluster site allows people to communicate in whatever way they like to express their ideas. If video is your thing, you can post a video to the site. Those prone to doodling can submit drawings. Verbal types who don't want to go on-camera can upload an audio file. Will these high-tech, virtual modes of communication allow for more honest and meaningful dialog? Word on the street is "yes." Watch out focus groups; your days are numbered.

Discussion Questions

1. Would the communication on the Kluster Web site be considered formal or informal communication?

2. Why do companies post ideas on Kluster's site? How does this relate to the communication process?

3. Discuss some of the possible communication microbarriers that might hinder the effectiveness of this Web site.

Internet Activity

Go to the Kluster home page at www.kluster.com. Learn more about this company. Click on the "name this" link and join in some of the discussions. What is your impression of the communication process encouraged by this site? Is it an effective form of communication? Explain.

16 Leadership

TO HELP BUILD MY LEADERSHIP SKILL, WHEN STUDYING THIS CHAPTER, I WILL ATTEMPT TO ACQUIRE:

1. A working definition of *leadership*

2. An understanding of the relationship between leading and managing

3. An appreciation for the trait and situational approaches to leadership

4. Insights into using leadership theories that emphasize decision-making situations

5. Insights into using leadership theories that emphasize more general organizational situations

6. An understanding of alternatives to leader flexibility

7. An appreciation of emerging leadership styles and leadership issues of today

TARGET SKILL leadership skill: the ability to direct the behavior of others toward the accomplishment of objectives

CHALLENGE CASE

CARLY FIORINA: HIRED AND FIRED AT HEWLETT-PACKARD

Hewlett-Packard Company (HP) is a leading provider of technology products and services to both individual and corporate consumers. HP's popular products include personal computers, printers, and printer accessories like inkjet refill cartridges.

HP's CEO, Carleton "Carly" Fiorina, and the company's other top executives recently decided that HP should pay $19 billion to acquire Compaq, another personal computer manufacturer. According to Fiorina, acquiring Compaq would help HP sell more products while simultaneously reducing the company's cost structure. Regardless of these benefits, the decision to acquire Compaq provided Carly Fiorina, HP's CEO, with an enormous leadership challenge.

In the process of planning for HP's acquisition of Compaq, HP's external advisors warned of the difficulties associated with acquiring a large company such as Compaq. In the two weeks following the announcement of the Compaq acquisition, HP's stock price plummeted nearly 40 percent. This suggested that some people thought HP would face significant challenges in successfully acquiring Compaq. Scott McNealy, CEO of HP's rival Sun Microsystems, summed up the views of many by describing the proposed acquisition as "a slow-motion collision of two rubbish trucks."

At first, Fiorina had a difficult time explaining the benefits of the Compaq acquisition. Through effective communication and leadership, however, she convinced a number of skeptics, and the acquisition was finalized. Since the deal's completion, Fiorina has used her leadership skills to integrate the operations of both companies. She developed a team of 30 executives to oversee the integration of the two companies. With her support, the team talked to other executives and consultants to develop tactics that would ease the integration of the two companies. For example, the team decided to give acquired employees (i.e., former Compaq employees) bonuses and salary increases in an effort to keep them as employees.

Over time, though, the prospects of the Compaq acquisition that Fiorina fought for declined. To convince investors of the acquisition's merits, Fiorina proposed several profitability goals for the company. As the acquisition progressed, HP began to miss these specific goals due to intense competition from Dell and IBM. On one occasion, after the company missed its profit targets, Fiorina told executives on a conference call that "You've let HP down, you've let the board down and you've let me down." Perhaps unsurprisingly, key executives within HP began to leave the company to join competitors.

After almost six years as HP's CEO, the board of directors fired Fiorina. Mark V. Hurd was named as Fiorina's replacement. After being in his new position for approximately two years, HP's market value doubled.[1]

Carly Fiorina was a sometimes controversial leader at Hewlett-Packard before she was fired by the board of directors.

"EXPLORE YOUR OWN MANAGEMENT SKILLS BY TAKING THE QUIZ ON THE NEXT PAGE"

Before studying this chapter, respond to the following questions regarding the type of advice that you would give to Carly Fiorina, the former Hewlett-Packard CEO referenced in the Challenge Case. Then address improving her success as a leader in her next job. You are not expected to be a leadership expert at this point. Answering the questions now can help you focus on important points when you study the chapter. Also, answering the questions again after you study the chapter will give you an idea of how much you have learned.

Record your answers here or go to MyManagementLab.com. Recording your answers in MyManagementLab will allow you to get immediate results and see how your score compares to your classmates. If you answer the questions in the book, the answers are located in the Exploring Your Management Skill section at the end of the book.

FOR EACH STATEMENT CIRCLE:

- "Y" if you would give the advice to Fiorina.
- "N" if you would NOT give the advice to Fiorina.
- "NI" if you have no idea whether you would give the advice to Fiorina.

Ms. Fiorina, in meeting your leadership challenges in your next job, you should . . .

Before Study   After Study

1. remember that managing and leading are synonyms.

   Y, N, NI

2. realize that you'll be successful as a leader because, given your traits, it's obvious that you were born to be a leader.

   Y, N, NI

3. use subordinate-centered leadership to make and announce your decisions to your subordinates.

   Y, N, NI

4. understand that the profitability of your organization is a force influencing your leadership decisions.

   Y, N, NI

5. make decisions alone even if your subordinates are capable of helping you to make those decisions.

   Y, N, NI

6. work to constantly improve your leadership style, your view of what you should be as a leader.

   Y, N, NI

7. focus on matching your low task and low relationship leadership style with followers who are of average job maturity.

   Y, N, NI

8. use chronological follower maturity as the main factor to determine your leadership style.

   Y, N, NI

9. use position power to influence follower behavior.

   Y, N, NI

10. use the path–goal theory of leadership as your rationale to clarify follower behavior necessary to earn organizational rewards.

    Y, N, NI

11. be flexible, changing leadership style as dictated by circumstances.

    Y, N, NI

12. always tell followers what they must do in their jobs.

    Y, N, NI

13. sometimes act entrepreneurially, functioning as if you're self-employed.

    Y, N, NI

14. probably sometimes think of yourself as a steward, following the concept of servant leadership.

    Y, N, NI

15. think about integrating concepts from theories such as transformational leadership, servant leadership, and superleadership in order to develop the best leadership style for you personally.

    Y, N, NI

THE LEADERSHIP CHALLENGE

Carleton "Carly" Fiorina is the former Chief Executive Officer of Hewlett-Packard Company (HP). The Challenge Case reviews how Fiorina led HP to acquire Compaq and ends by noting that the acquisition failed and that Fiorina was fired. The information in the chapter would be helpful to an individual such as Fiorina as the basis for developing a useful leadership strategy to achieve success. Often, leaders can learn as much, if not more, from their mistakes as from their successes. The chapter discusses (1) how to define leadership, (2) the difference between a leader and a manager, (3) the trait approach to leadership, (4) the situational approach to leadership, (5) leadership today, and (6) current topics in leadership.

DEFINING LEADERSHIP

Leadership is the process of directing the behavior of others toward the accomplishment of some objective. Directing, in this sense, means causing individuals to act in a certain way or to follow a particular course. Ideally, this course is perfectly consistent with such factors as established organizational policies, procedures, and job descriptions. The central theme of leadership is getting things accomplished through people.[2]

As indicated in Chapter 15, leadership is one of the four main interdependent activities of the influencing subsystem and is accomplished, at least to some extent, by communicating with others. It is extremely important that managers have a thorough understanding of what leadership entails. Leadership has always been considered a prerequisite for organizational success. Today, given the increased capability afforded by enhanced communication technology and the rise of international business, leadership is more important than ever before.[3]

Leader Versus Manager

Leading is not the same as managing. Many executives fail to grasp the difference between the two and therefore labor under a misapprehension about how to carry out their organizational duties. Although some managers are leaders and some leaders are managers, leading and managing are not identical activities.[4] According to Theodore Levitt, management consists of

> the rational assessment of a situation and the systematic selection of goals and purposes (what is to be done); the systematic development of strategies to achieve these goals; the marshalling of the required resources; the rational design, organization, direction, and control of the activities required to attain the selected purposes; and, finally, the motivating and rewarding of people to do the work.[5]

Leadership, as one of the four primary activities of the influencing function, is a subset of management. Managing is much broader in scope than leading and focuses on nonbehavioral as well as behavioral issues. Leading emphasizes mainly behavioral issues. Figure 16.1 makes the point that although not all managers are leaders, the most effective managers over the long term are leaders.

Merely possessing management skills is no longer sufficient for success as an executive in the business world. Modern executives need to understand the difference between managing and leading and know how to combine the two roles to achieve organizational success. A manager makes sure that a job gets done, and a leader cares about and focuses on the people who do the job. To combine management and leadership, therefore, requires demonstrating a calculated and logical focus on organizational processes (management) along with a genuine concern for workers as people (leadership).[6]

FIGURE 16.1
The most effective managers over the long term are also leaders

THE TRAIT APPROACH TO LEADERSHIP

The **trait approach to leadership** is based on early leadership research that assumed a good leader is born, not made. The mainstream of this research attempted to describe successful leaders as precisely as possible. The reasoning was that if a complete profile of the traits of a successful leader could be drawn, it would be fairly easy to identify the individuals who should and should not be placed in leadership positions.[7]

Many of the early studies that attempted to summarize the traits of successful leaders were documented. One of these summaries concludes that successful leaders tend to possess the following characteristics:[8]

1. Intelligence, including judgment and verbal ability
2. Past achievement in scholarship and athletics
3. Emotional maturity and stability
4. Dependability, persistence, and a drive for continuing achievement
5. The skill to participate socially and adapt to various groups
6. A desire for status and socioeconomic position

Traits that mark the leadership style of Bill Gates, CEO of Microsoft, include high intelligence and a strong drive to succeed.

Evaluations of these trait studies, however, have concluded that their findings are inconsistent. One researcher says that 50 years of study have failed to produce one personality trait or set of qualities that can be used consistently to differentiate leaders from nonleaders.[9] It follows, then, that no trait or combination of traits guarantees that someone will be a successful leader. Leadership is apparently a much more complex issue.

Contemporary management writers and practitioners generally agree that leadership ability cannot be explained by an individual's traits or inherited characteristics. They believe, rather, that individuals can be trained to be good leaders. In other words, leaders are made, not born.[10] That is why thousands of employees each year are sent through leadership training programs.[11]

As **an example from the world of management** illustrating how companies focus on training leaders, consider events at **General Electric**.[12] For its outstanding efforts in developing leaders, General Electric was recently cited as the company that does the best job of developing leaders. One way to determine the effectiveness of how General Electric develops leaders is to see what happens to leaders who leave the company. As examples, leaders who have left General Electric often go on to run other Fortune 500 companies. At General Electric, a beautiful 52-acre leadership development campus an hour north of New York City is obviously expensive to maintain, not to mention the costs of running thousands of managers through programs at the site every year. Companies such as General Electric are finding that the benefits of building leadership talent include not only enhancing company success, but also gaining an advantage in attracting the best college graduates as new hires.

THE SITUATIONAL APPROACH TO LEADERSHIP: A FOCUS ON LEADER BEHAVIOR

Leadership studies have shifted their emphasis from the trait approach to the situational approach, which suggests that leadership style must be appropriately matched to the situation the leader faces. The more modern **situational approach to leadership** is based on the assumption that each instance of leadership is different and therefore requires a unique combination of leaders, followers, and leadership situations.[13]

This interaction is commonly expressed in formula form: $SL = f(L,F,S)$, where SL is *successful leadership;* f stands for *function of;* and L, F, and S are, respectively, the *leader,* the *follower,* and the *situation.*[14] Translated, this formula says that successful leadership is a function of a leader, follower, and situation that are appropriate for one another.

Leadership Situations and Decisions

The Tannenbaum and Schmidt Leadership Continuum Because one of the most important tasks of a leader is making sound decisions, all practical and legitimate

BOSS-CENTERED LEADERSHIP

SUBORDINATE-CENTERED LEADERSHIP

Use of authority
by the manager

Area of freedom
for subordinates

| Manager makes decision and announces it | Manager "sells" decision | Manager presents ideas and invites questions | Manager presents tentative decision subject to change | Manager presents problem, gets suggestions, makes decision | Manager defines limits; asks group to make decision | Manager permits subordinates to function within limits defined by superior |

FIGURE 16.2 Continuum of leadership behavior that emphasizes decision making

leadership thinking emphasizes decision making. Tannenbaum and Schmidt, who wrote one of the first and perhaps most often quoted articles on the situational approach to leadership, stress situations in which a leader makes decisions.[15] Figure 16.2 presents their model of leadership behavior.

This model is actually a continuum, or range, of leadership behavior available to managers when they are making decisions. Note that each type of decision-making behavior depicted in the figure has both a corresponding degree of authority used by the manager and a related amount of freedom available to subordinates. Management behavior, at the extreme left of the model, characterizes the leader who makes decisions by maintaining high control and allowing subordinates little freedom. Behavior at the extreme right characterizes the leader who makes decisions by exercising little control and allowing subordinates much freedom and self-direction. Behavior in between the extremes reflects graduations in leadership from autocratic to democratic.

Managers displaying leadership behavior toward the right of the model are more democratic, and are called *subordinate-centered* leaders. Those displaying leadership behavior toward the left of the model are more autocratic, and are called *boss-centered* leaders.

Each type of leadership behavior in this model is explained in more detail in the following list:

1. **The manager makes the decision and announces it**—This behavior is characterized by the manager (a) identifying a problem, (b) analyzing various alternatives available to solve it, (c) choosing the alternative that will be used to solve it, and (d) requiring followers to implement the chosen alternative. The manager may or may not use coercion, but the followers have no opportunity to participate directly in the decision-making process.

2. **The manager "sells" the decision**—The manager identifies the problem and independently arrives at a decision. Rather than announce the decision to subordinates for implementation, however, the manager tries to persuade subordinates to accept the decision.

3. **The manager presents ideas and invites questions**—Here, the manager makes the decision and attempts to gain acceptance through persuasion. One additional step is taken, however: Subordinates are invited to ask questions about the decision.

4. **The manager presents a tentative decision that is subject to change**—The manager allows subordinates to have some part in the decision-making process but retains the responsibility for identifying and diagnosing the problem. The manager then arrives at a tentative decision that is subject to change on the basis of subordinate input. The final decision is made by the manager.

5. **The manager presents the problem, gets suggestions, and then makes the decision**—This leadership activity is the first of those described thus far that allows subordinates the opportunity to offer problem solutions before the manager does. The manager, however, is still the one who identifies the problem.

6. **The manager defines the limits and asks the group to make a decision**—In this type of leadership behavior, the manager first defines the problem and sets the boundaries within which a decision must be made. The manager then enters into partnership with subordinates to arrive at an appropriate decision. The danger here is that if the group of subordinates does not perceive that the manager genuinely desires a serious group decision-making effort, it will tend to arrive at conclusions that reflect what it thinks the manager wants rather than what the group actually wants and believes is feasible.

7. **The manager permits the group to make decisions within prescribed limits**—Here the manager becomes an equal member of a problem-solving group. The entire group identifies and assesses the problem, develops possible solutions, and chooses an alternative to be implemented. Everyone within the group understands that the group's decision will be implemented.

Determining How to Make Decisions as a Leader The true value of the model developed by Tannenbaum and Schmidt lies in its use in making practical and desirable decisions. According to these authors, the three primary factors, or forces, that influence a manager's determination of which leadership behavior to use in making decisions are as follows:

1. **Forces in the Manager**—Managers should be aware of four forces within themselves that influence their determination of how to make decisions as a leader. The first force is the manager's values, such as the relative importance to the manager of organizational efficiency, personal growth, the growth of subordinates, and company profits. For example, a manager who values subordinate growth highly will probably want to give group members the valuable experience of making a decision, even though he or she could make the decision much more quickly and efficiently alone.

   The second influencing force is level of confidence in subordinates. In general, the more confidence a manager has in his or her subordinates, the more likely it is that the manager's decision-making style will be democratic, or subordinate-centered. The reverse is also true: The less confidence a manager has in subordinates,

The degree to which managers allow subordinates freedom and seek their input to decision making is what differentiates boss-centered and subordinate-centered leadership. Which type of leadership do you think is being used in this case?

the more likely it is that the manager's decision-making style will be autocratic, or boss-centered.

The third influencing force within the manager is personal leadership strengths. Some managers are more effective in issuing orders than in leading group discussions, and vice versa. Managers must be able to recognize their own leadership strengths and capitalize on them.

The fourth influencing force within the manager is tolerance for ambiguity. The move from a boss-centered style to a subordinate-centered style means some loss of certainty about how problems should be solved. A manager who is disturbed by this loss of certainty will find it extremely difficult to be successful as a subordinate-centered leader.

2. **Forces in Subordinates**—A manager also should be aware of forces within subordinates that influence the manager's determination of how to make decisions as a leader.[16] To lead successfully, the manager needs to keep in mind that subordinates are both somewhat different and somewhat alike and that any cookbook approach to leading all subordinates is therefore impossible. Generally speaking, however, managers can increase their leadership success by allowing subordinates more freedom in making decisions when:

   - The subordinates have a relatively high need for independence (people differ greatly in the amount of direction they desire).
   - They have a readiness to assume responsibility for decision making (some see additional responsibility as a tribute to their ability; others see it as someone above them "passing the buck").
   - They have a relatively high tolerance for ambiguity (some employees prefer to be given clear-cut directives; others crave a greater degree of freedom).
   - They are interested in the problem and believe it is important to solve it.
   - They understand and identify with the organization's goals.
   - They have the necessary knowledge and experience to deal with the problem.
   - They have learned to expect to share in decision making (people who have come to expect strong leadership and then are suddenly told to participate more fully in decision making are often upset by this new experience; conversely, people who have enjoyed a considerable amount of freedom usually resent the boss who assumes full decision-making powers).

   If subordinates do not have these characteristics, the manager should probably assume a more autocratic, or boss-centered, approach to making decisions.

3. **Forces in the Situation**—The last group of forces that influence a manager's determination of how to make decisions as a leader are forces in the leadership situation. The first such situational force is the type of organization in which the leader works. Organizational factors, including the size of working groups and their geographic distribution, are especially important influences on leadership style. Extremely large work groups or wide geographic separations of work groups, for example, could make a subordinate-centered leadership style impractical.

   The second situational force is the effectiveness of a group. To gauge this force, managers should evaluate such issues as the experience of group members in working together and the degree of confidence they have in their ability to solve problems as a group. As a general rule, managers should assign decision-making responsibilities only to effective work groups.

   The third situational force is the problem to be solved. Before deciding to act as a subordinate-centered leader, a manager should be sure that the group has the expertise necessary to make a decision about the problem in question. If it does not, the manager should move toward more boss-centered leadership.

   The fourth situational force is the time available to make a decision. As a general guideline, the less time available, the more impractical it is to assign decision making to a group because a group typically takes more time than an individual to reach a decision.

As the situational approach to leadership implies, managers will be successful decision makers only if the method they use to make decisions appropriately reflects the leader, the followers, and the situation.

Determining How to Make Decisions as a Leader: An Update

Tannenbaum and Schmidt's 1957 article on leadership decision making was so widely accepted that the two authors were invited by the *Harvard Business Review* to update their original work in the 1970s.[17] In this update, they warned that in modern organizations, the relationship among forces within the manager, subordinates, and situation had become more complex and more interrelated since the 1950s, which obviously made it harder for managers to determine how to lead.

The update also pointed out that new organizational environments had to be considered in determining how to lead. For example, such factors as affirmative action and pollution control—which hardly figured in the decision making of managers in the 1950s—have become significant influences on the decision making of leaders since the 1970s.

The Vroom–Yetton–Jago Model

Another major decision-focused theory of leadership that has gained widespread attention was first developed in 1973 and refined and expanded in 1988.[18] This theory, which we will call the **Vroom–Yetton–Jago (VYJ) model of leadership** after its three major contributors, focuses on how much participation to allow subordinates in the decision-making process. The VYJ model is built on two important premises:

1. Organizational decisions should be of high quality (should have a beneficial impact on performance).
2. Subordinates should accept and be committed to organizational decisions that are made.

Decision Styles

The VYJ model suggests five different decision styles or ways that leaders make decisions. These styles range from autocratic (the leader makes the decision) to consultative (the leader makes the decision after interacting with the followers) to group-focused (the manager meets with the group, and the group makes the decision). All five decision styles within the VYJ model are described in Figure 16.3.

Using the Model

The VYJ model, presented in Figure 16.4, is a method for determining when a leader should use which decision style. As you can see, the model is a type of decision tree. To determine which decision style to use in a particular situation, the leader starts at the left of the decision tree by stating the organizational problem being addressed. Then

FIGURE 16.3

The five decision styles available to a leader according to the Vroom–Yetton–Jago Model

DECISION STYLE	DEFINITION
AI	Manager makes the decision alone.
AII	Manager asks for information from subordinates but makes the decision alone. Subordinates may or may not be informed about what the situation is.
CI	Manager shares the situation with individual subordinates and asks for information and evaluation. Subordinates do not meet as a group, and the manager alone makes the decision.
CII	Manager and subordinates meet as a group to discuss the situation, but the manager makes the decision.
GII	Manager and subordinates meet as a group to discuss the situation, and the group makes the decision.
A = autocratic; C = consultative; G = group	

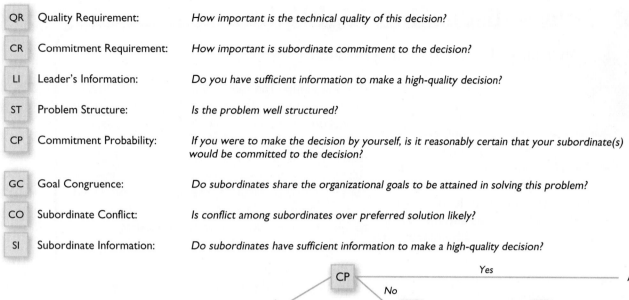

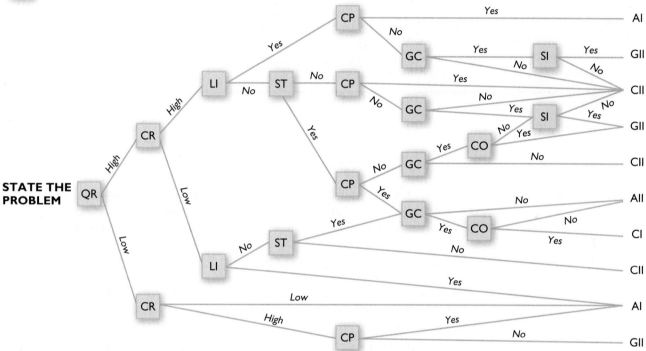

FIGURE 16.4 The Vroom–Yetton–Jago model

the leader asks a series of questions about the problem as determined by the structure of the decision tree until he or she arrives at a decision style appropriate for the situation at the far right side of the model.

Consider, for example, the bottom path of the decision tree. After stating an organizational problem, the leader determines that a decision related to that problem has a low quality requirement, that it is important that subordinates be committed to the decision, and it is uncertain whether a decision made solely by the leader will be committed to by subordinates. In this situation, the model suggests that the leader use the GII decision—that is, the leader should meet with the group to discuss the situation, and then allow the group to make the decision.

The VYJ model seems promising. Research on an earlier version of this model yielded some evidence that managerial decisions consistent with the model are more successful than are managerial decisions inconsistent with the model.[19] The model is rather complex, however, and therefore difficult for practicing managers to apply.[20]

class discussion highlight

MODERN RESEARCH AND LEADERSHIP SKILL

Leaders and Encouraging Creativity[21]

Various attributes of leaders affect how they relate to subordinates. This highlight focuses on a research study by Karen Yuan Wang and Gian Casimir exploring the relationship between leader beliefs about the reliability of subordinates and the extent to which leaders encourage those subordinates to be creative.

The study focused on 219 leaders from 31 privately owned enterprises in Northern and Southern China. The enterprises were from a variety of industries including textiles, real estate, and equipment manufacturing. The majority of individuals studied were males under 40 years old. Most had a college education, were lower or middle level managers, and had less than 10 years of experience. For the study, reliability was defined as a leader's belief that a subordinate can be relied on to act in ways that are consistent and predictable. The researcher predicted that the more reliable leaders saw their subordinates to be, the more leaders would encourage those subordinates to be creative.

Do you think that results of the study were consistent with the prediction? Why? Why not? How would you use your expected findings to increase your leadership skill as a manager?

Leadership Behaviors

The failure to identify predictive leadership traits led researchers in this area to turn to other variables to explain leadership success. Rather than looking at traits leaders should possess, the behavioral approach looked at what good leaders do. Are they concerned with getting a task done, for instance, or do they concentrate on keeping their followers happy and maintaining high morale?

Two major studies series were conducted to identify leadership behavior, one by the Bureau of Business Research at Ohio State University (referred to as the OSU studies), and another by the University of Michigan (referred to as the Michigan studies).

The OSU Studies The OSU studies concluded that leaders exhibit two main types of behavior:

- **Structure behavior** is any leadership activity that delineates the relationship between the leader and the leader's followers or establishes well-defined procedures that followers should adhere to in performing their jobs. Overall, structure behavior limits the self-guidance of followers in the performance of their tasks, but while it can be relatively firm, it is never rude or malicious.

  Structure behavior can be useful to leaders as a means of minimizing follower activity that does not significantly contribute to organizational goal attainment. Leaders must be careful, however, not to go overboard and discourage follower activity that *will* contribute to organizational goal attainment.

- **Consideration behavior** is leadership behavior that reflects friendship, mutual trust, respect, and warmth in the relationship between leader and followers. This type of behavior generally aims to develop and maintain a good human relationship between the leader and the followers.

As **an example from the world of management**, illustrating how management can destroy trust between itself and workers, consider recent findings by **Lore International Institute**, a consulting firm. The company found that to succeed in the workplace, it's important for leaders to demonstrate trustworthiness, honesty, and an ability to collaborate. According to the findings, leaders can "kill" trust between themselves and workers by being (1) *credit hogs* who take credit for the good ideas of others, (2) *lone rangers* who work mostly by themselves and not closely with other workers, (3) *egomaniacs* who believe that success will only come through the efforts of management as opposed to workers, or (4) *mules* who are stubborn and inflexible.[22]

Leadership Style The OSU studies resulted in a model that depicts four fundamental leadership styles. A **leadership style** is the behavior a leader exhibits while guiding organization members in appropriate directions.[23] Each of the four leadership styles depicted in Figure 16.5 is a different combination of structure behavior and consideration behavior. For example, the high structure/low consideration leadership style emphasizes structure behavior and deemphasizes consideration behavior.

The OSU studies made a significant contribution to our understanding of leadership, and the central ideas generated by these studies still serve as the basis for modern leadership thought and research.[24]

The Michigan Studies About the same time the OSU leadership studies were being carried out, researchers at the University of Michigan, led by Rensis Likert, were also conducting a series of historically significant leadership studies.[25] After analyzing information based on interviews with both leaders and followers (managers and subordinates), the Michigan studies pinpointed two basic types of leader behavior: job-centered behavior and employee-centered behavior.

JOB-CENTERED BEHAVIOR **Job-centered behavior** is leader behavior that focuses primarily on the work a subordinate is doing. The job-centered leader is interested in the job the subordinate is doing and in how well the subordinate is performing at that job.

EMPLOYEE-CENTERED BEHAVIOR **Employee-centered behavior** is leader behavior that focuses primarily on subordinates as people. The employee-centered leader is attentive to the personal needs of subordinates and is interested in building cooperative work teams that are satisfying to subordinates and advantageous for the organization.

The results of the OSU studies and the Michigan studies are similar. Both research efforts indicated two primary dimensions of leader behavior: a work dimension (structure behavior/job-centered behavior) and a people dimension (consideration behavior/employee-centered behavior). The following section focuses on determining

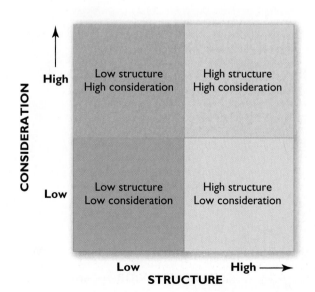

FIGURE 16.5
Four fundamental leadership styles based on structure behavior and consideration behavior

which of these two primary dimensions of leader behavior is more advisable for a manager to adopt.

Effectiveness of Various Leadership Styles An early investigation of high school superintendents concluded that desirable leadership behavior is associated with high leader emphasis on both structure and consideration and that undesirable leadership behavior is associated with low leader emphasis on both dimensions. Similarly, the managerial grid described in Chapter 14 implies that the most effective leadership style is characterized by high consideration and high structure. Results of a more recent study indicate that high consideration is always preferred by subordinates.[26]

Comparing Styles One should be cautious, however, about concluding that any single leadership style is more effective than any other. Leadership situations are so varied that pronouncing one leadership style as the most effective is an oversimplification. In fact, a successful leadership style for managers in one situation may prove ineffective in another situation. Recognizing the need to link leadership styles to appropriate situations, A. K. Korman notes, in a classic article, that a worthwhile contribution to leadership literature would be a rationale for systematically linking appropriate styles with various situations so as to ensure effective leadership.[27] The life cycle theory of leadership, which is covered in the next section, provides such a rationale.

The Hersey–Blanchard Life Cycle Theory of Leadership The **life cycle theory of leadership** is a rationale for linking leadership styles with various situations so as to ensure effective leadership. This theory posits essentially the same two types of leadership behavior as the OSU leadership studies, but it calls them "task" and "relationships" rather than "structure" and "consideration."

Maturity The life cycle theory is based on the relationship among follower maturity, leader task behavior, and leader relationship behavior. In general terms, according to this theory, leadership style should reflect the maturity level of the followers. Maturity is defined as the ability of followers to perform their job independently, to assume additional responsibility, and to desire to achieve success. The more of each of these characteristics that followers possess, the more mature they are said to be. (Maturity here is not necessarily linked to chronological age.)

The Life Cycle Model Figure 16.6 illustrates the life cycle theory of leadership model. The curved line indicates the maturity level of the followers: Maturity level

FIGURE 16.6
The life cycle theory of leadership model

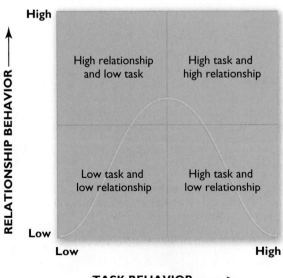

increases as the maturity curve runs from right to left. In more specific terms, the theory indicates that effective leadership behavior should shift as follows:[28] (1) high-task/low-relationships behavior to (2) high-task/high-relationships behavior to (3) high-relationships/low-task behavior to (4) low-task/low-relationships behavior, as one's followers progress from immaturity to maturity. In sum, a manager's leadership style will be effective only if it is appropriate for the maturity level of the followers.

Exceptions to the Model Some exceptions apply to the general philosophy of the life cycle theory. For example, if there is a short-term deadline to meet, a leader may find it necessary to accelerate production through a high-task/low-relationships style rather than use a low-task/low-relationships style, even if the followers are mature. A high-task/low-relationships leadership style carried out over the long term with such followers, though, would typically result in a poor working relationship between leader and subordinates.

Applying Life Cycle Theory Following is an example of how the life cycle theory applies to a leadership situation:

- A man has just been hired as a salesperson in a men's clothing store. At first, this individual is extremely immature—that is, unable to solve task-related problems independently. According to the life cycle theory, the appropriate style for leading this salesperson at his level of maturity is high-task/low-relationships—that is, the leader should tell the salesperson exactly what should be done and how to do it. The salesperson should be shown how to make cash and charge sales and how to handle merchandise returns. The leader should also begin laying the groundwork for developing a personal relationship with the salesperson. Too much relationship behavior at this point, however, should be avoided, because it can easily be misinterpreted as permissiveness.

- As time passes and the salesperson gains somewhat in job-related maturity, the appropriate style for leading him would be high-task/high-relationships. Although the salesperson's maturity has increased somewhat, the leader still needs to watch him closely because he requires guidance and direction at times. The main difference between this leadership style and the first one is the amount of relationship behavior displayed by the leader. Building on the groundwork laid during the period of the first leadership style, the leader can now start to encourage an atmosphere of mutual trust, respect, and friendliness between herself and the salesperson.

- As more time passes and the salesperson's maturity level increases still further, the appropriate style for leading this individual will become high-relationships/low-task. The leader can now deemphasize task behavior because the salesperson is of above-average maturity in his job and is capable of solving most job-related problems independently. The leader would continue to develop a human relationship with her follower.

- Once the salesperson's maturity level reaches its maximum, the appropriate style for leading him is low-task/low-relationships. Again, the leader deemphasizes task behavior because the follower is thoroughly familiar with the job. Now, however, the leader can also deemphasize relationship behavior because she has fully established a good working relationship with the follower. At this point, task behavior is seldom needed, and relationship behavior is used primarily to nurture the good working rapport that has developed between the leader and the follower. The salesperson, then, is left to do his job without close supervision, knowing that he has a positive working relationship with a leader who can be approached for guidance whenever necessary.

The life cycle approach more than likely owes its acceptance to its intuitive appeal. Although at first glance it appears to be a useful leadership concept, managers should bear in mind that little scientific investigation has been conducted to verify its worth, and therefore it should be applied with caution.[29]

Fiedler's Contingency Theory Situational theories of leadership such as the life cycle theory are based on the concept of **leader flexibility**—the idea that successful leaders must change their leadership styles as they encounter different situations. Can any leader be so flexible as to span all major leadership styles? The answer to this question is that some leaders can be that flexible, and some cannot. Unfortunately, numerous obstacles get in the way of leader flexibility. One is that a leadership style is sometimes so ingrained in a leader that it takes years to even approach flexibility. Another is that some leaders have experienced such success in a basically static situation that they believe developing a flexible style is unnecessary.

Changing the Organization to Fit the Leader One strategy, proposed by Fred Fiedler, for overcoming these obstacles is changing the organizational situation to fit the leader's style, rather than changing the leader style to fit the organizational situation.[30] Applying this idea to the life cycle theory of leadership, an organization may find it easier to shift leaders to situations appropriate for their leadership styles than to expect those leaders to change styles as situations change. After all, it would probably take three to five years to train a manager to use a concept such as life cycle theory effectively, while changing the situation that the leader faces can be done quickly simply by exercising organizational authority.

According to Fiedler's **contingency theory of leadership,** leader–member relations,[31] task structure, and the position power of the leader are the three primary factors that should be considered when moving leaders into situations appropriate for their leadership styles:

- **Leader–member relations** is the degree to which the leader feels accepted by the followers.

- **Task structure** is the degree to which the goals—the work to be done—and other situational factors are outlined clearly.

- **Position power** is determined by the extent to which the leader has control over the rewards and punishments followers receive.

How these three factors can be arranged in eight different combinations, called *octants,* is presented in Table 16.1.

Figure 16.7 shows how effective leadership varies among the eight octants. From an organizational viewpoint, this figure implies that management should attempt to match permissive, passive, and considerate leaders with situations reflecting the middle of the continuum containing the octants. It also implies that management should try to match controlling, active, and structuring leaders with the extremes of this continuum.

TABLE 16.1 Eight Combinations, or Octants, of Three Factors: Leader–Member Relations, Task Structure, and Leader Position Power

Octant	Leader–Member Relations	Task Structure	Leader Position Power
I	Good	High	Strong
II	Good	High	Weak
III	Good	Weak	Strong
IV	Good	Weak	Weak
V	Moderately poor	High	Strong
VI	Moderately poor	High	Weak
VII	Moderately poor	Weak	Strong
VIII	Moderately poor	Weak	Weak

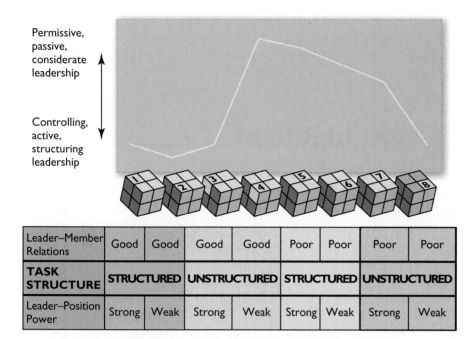

Leader–Member Relations	Good	Good	Good	Good	Poor	Poor	Poor	Poor
TASK STRUCTURE	STRUCTURED		UNSTRUCTURED		STRUCTURED		UNSTRUCTURED	
Leader–Position Power	Strong	Weak	Strong	Weak	Strong	Weak	Strong	Weak

FIGURE 16.7
How effective leadership style varies with Fiedler's eight octants

Fiedler suggests some actions that can be taken to modify the leadership situation. They are as follows:[32]

1. In some organizations, we can change the individual's task assignment. We may assign to one leader the structured tasks that have implicit or explicit instructions telling him what to do and how to do it, and we may assign to another the tasks that are nebulous and vague. The former are the typical production tasks; the latter are exemplified by committee work, by the development of policy, and by tasks that require creativity.

2. We can change the leader's position power. We not only can give him a higher rank and corresponding recognition, we also can modify his position power by giving him subordinates who are equal to him in rank and prestige or subordinates who are two or three ranks below him. We can give him subordinates who are experts in their specialties or subordinates who depend on the leader for guidance and instruction. We can give the leader the final say in all decisions affecting his group, or we can require that he make decisions in consultation with his subordinates, or even that he obtain their concurrence. We can channel all directives, communications, and information about organizational plans through the leader alone, giving him expert power, or we can provide these communications concurrently to all his subordinates.

3. We can change the leader–member relations in this group. We can have the leader work with groups whose members are very similar to him in attitude, opinion, technical background, race, and cultural background, or we can assign him subordinates with whom he differs in any one or several of these important aspects. Finally, we can assign the leader to a group in which the members have a tradition of getting along well with their supervisors or to a group that has a history and tradition of conflict.

Fiedler's work certainly helps destroy the myths about one best leadership style and that leaders are born, not made. Further, his work supports the theory that almost every manager in an organization can be a successful leader if placed in a situation appropriate to that person's leadership style. This matching of leadership style to the situation, of course, assumes that someone in the organization has the ability to assess the characteristics of the organization's leaders and of other important organizational variables and then to bring the two together accordingly.

Fiedler's model, like all theoretical models, has its limitations; even though it may not provide concrete answers, it does emphasize the importance of situational variables in determining leadership effectiveness. As said earlier, it may actually be easier to change the leadership situation or move the leader to a more favorable situation than to try to change a leader's style.[33]

class discussion highlight

LEADERSHIP AND YOUR CAREER[34]

You have just graduated from college and are interested in a career in government. In looking for your first job, you have found out that the city manager's office has recently begun to recognize the significant retirement projections among its baby boomer employees. According to the city manager, to deal with the impending retirements, the city government will start designing and offering leadership development programs to its employees. According to the city manager, the programs will focus on helping younger leaders to understand how various parts of city government operate as well as helping them to develop a broad network of relationships within city government as a whole.

Would this information you've found out about the city's government raise or lower your interest in working there? Explain. How would you find out if other potential employers offer similar programs? Name another topic that you would like to see covered in the city's leadership development program and explain its significance.

The Path–Goal Theory of Leadership The **path–goal theory of leadership** suggests that the primary activities of a leader are to make desirable and achievable rewards available to organization members who attain organizational goals and to clarify the kinds of behavior that must be performed to earn those rewards.[35] The leader outlines the goals that followers should aim for and clarifies the path that followers should take to achieve those goals and earn the rewards contingent on doing so.[36] Overall, the path–goal theory maintains that managers can facilitate job performance by showing employees how their performance directly affects their reception of desired rewards.

Leadership Behavior According to the path–goal theory of leadership, leaders exhibit four primary types of behavior:

1. **Directive behavior**—Directive behavior is aimed at telling followers what to do and how to do it. The leader indicates what performance goals exist and precisely what must be done to achieve them.
2. **Supportive behavior**—Supportive behavior is aimed at being friendly with followers and showing interest in them as human beings. Through supportive behavior, the leader demonstrates sensitivity to the personal needs of followers.
3. **Participative behavior**—Participative behavior is aimed at seeking suggestions from followers regarding business operations to the extent that followers are involved in making important organizational decisions. Followers often help to determine the rewards that will be available to them in organizations and what they must do to earn those rewards.
4. **Achievement behavior**—Achievement behavior is aimed at setting challenging goals for followers to reach and expressing and demonstrating confidence that they will measure up to the challenge. This leader behavior focuses on making goals difficult enough that employees will find achieving them challenging, but not so difficult that they will view them as impossible and give up trying to achieve them.

Although it isn't appropriate for every management situation, directive leadership—in which the leader tells followers exactly what to do—is highly appropriate for emergencies like this one, where quick decisions and unambiguous action are critical.

Adapting Behavior to Situations As with other situational theories of leadership, the path–goal theory proposes that leaders will be successful if they appropriately match these four types of behavior to situations that they face. For example, if inexperienced followers do not have a thorough understanding of a job, a manager may appropriately use more directive behavior to develop this understanding and to ensure that serious job-related problems are avoided. For more experienced followers, who have a more complete understanding of a job, directive behavior would probably be inappropriate and might create interpersonal problems between leader and followers.

If jobs are highly structured, with little room for employee interpretation of how the work should be done, directive behavior is less appropriate than when much room is provided for employees to determine how the work gets done. When followers are deriving much personal satisfaction and encouragement from work and enjoy the support of other members of their work group, supportive behavior by the leader is not as important as when followers are gaining little or no satisfaction from their work or from personal relationships in the work group.

The primary focus of the path–goal theory of leadership is on how leaders can increase employee effort and productivity by clarifying performance goals and the path to be taken to achieve those goals. This theory of leadership has gained increasing acceptance in recent years. In fact, research suggests that the path–goal theory is highly promising for enhancing employee commitment to achieving organizational goals and thereby increasing the probability that organizations will be successful. It should be pointed out, however, that the research done on this model has been conducted mostly on its parts rather than on the complete model.[37]

LEADERSHIP TODAY

Leaders in modern organizations have been confronting many situations rarely encountered by organizational leaders of the past.[38] Today's leaders are often called upon to make massive personnel cuts in order to eliminate unnecessary levels of organizations and thereby lower labor expenses, to introduce work teams in order to enhance organizational decision making and work flow, to reengineer work so that organization members will be more efficient and effective, and to initiate programs designed to improve the overall quality of organizational functioning.

LEADER	MANAGER
SOUL	**MIND**
Visionary	Rational
Passionate	Consultative
Creative	Persistent
Flexible	Problem-solving
Inspirational	Tough-minded
Innovative	Analytical
Courageous	Structured
Imaginative	Deliberate
Experimental	Authoritative
Independent	Stabilizing

FIGURE 16.8
Characteristics of the emerging leader versus characteristics of the manager

In reaction to these new situations, organizations are emphasizing leadership styles that concentrate on getting employees involved in the organization and giving them the freedom to use their abilities as they think best. This type of leadership is dramatically different from that known in organizations of the past, which largely concentrated on controlling people and work processes. Figure 16.8 contrasts the "soul" of the new leader with the "mind" of the manager.

The information in this section of the text points out the trend among today's leaders to get employees involved in their organizations and to give them the freedom to make and carry out decisions.

Five leadership styles have emerged in recent years to suit these new situations: transformational leadership, coaching, "superleadership," servant leadership, and entrepreneurial leadership.[39] Each of these new styles is discussed in the following sections.

Transformational Leadership

Transformational leadership is leadership that inspires organizational success by profoundly affecting followers' beliefs in what an organization should be, as well as their values, such as justice and integrity.[40] This style of leadership creates a sense of duty within an organization, encourages new ways of handling problems, and promotes learning for all organization members.[41] Transformational leadership is closely related to concepts such as charismatic leadership and inspirational leadership.

Perhaps transformational leadership is receiving more attention nowadays because of the dramatic changes that many organizations are going through and the critical importance of transformational leadership in "transforming" or changing organizations successfully. Lee Iacocca is often cited as an exemplar of transformational leadership because of his success in transforming Chrysler Corporation from a company on the verge of going under into a successful company.[42]

The Tasks of Transformational Leaders Transformational leaders perform several important tasks. First, they raise followers' awareness of organizational issues and their consequences. Organization members must understand an organization's high-priority issues and what will happen if these issues are not successfully resolved. Second, transformational leaders create a vision of what the organization should be, build commitment to that vision throughout the organization, and facilitate organizational changes that support the vision. In sum, transformational leadership is consistent with strategy developed through an organization's strategic management process.[43]

Managers of the future will continue to face the challenge of significantly changing their organizations, primarily because of the accelerating trend to position organizations to be more competitive in a global business environment. Therefore, transformational leadership will probably get increasing attention in the leadership literature. Although the practical appeal and interest in this style of leadership are high, more research is needed to develop insights into how managers can become successful transformational leaders.

Coaching

Coaching is leadership that instructs followers on how to meet the special organizational challenges they face.[44] Operating like an athletic coach, the coaching leader identifies inappropriate behavior in followers and suggests how they might correct that behavior.[45] The increasing use of teams has elevated the importance of coaching in today's organizations. Characteristics of an effective coach are presented in Table 16.2.

Coaching Behavior A successful coaching leader is characterized by many different kinds of behavior. Among these behaviors are the following:

- **Listens closely**—The coaching leader tries to gather both the facts in what is said and the feelings and emotions behind what is said. Such a leader is careful to really listen and not fall into the trap of immediately rebutting statements made by followers.

TABLE 16.2 Characteristics of an Effective Coach

Trait, Attitude, or Behavior	Action Plan for Improvement
1. Empathy (putting self in other person's shoes)	*Sample:* Will listen and understand person's point of view. Your own:
2. Listening skill	*Sample:* Will concentrate extra-hard on listening. Your own:
3. Insight into people (ability to size them up)	*Sample:* Will write down observations about people on first meeting, then verify in the future. Your own:
4. Diplomacy and tact	*Sample:* Will study book of etiquette. Your own:
5. Patience toward people	*Sample:* Will practice staying calm when someone makes a mistake. Your own:
6. Concern for welfare of people	*Sample:* When interacting with another person, will ask myself, "How can this person's interests best be served?" Your own:
7. Minimum hostility toward people	*Sample:* Will often ask myself, "Why am I angry at this person?" Your own:
8. Self-confidence and emotional stability	*Sample:* Will attempt to have at least one personal success each week. Your own:
9. Noncompetitiveness with team members	*Sample:* Will keep reminding myself that all boats rise with the same tide. Your own:
10. Enthusiasm for people	*Sample:* Will search for the good in each person. Your own:

A manager who uses the coaching style demonstrates many characteristics of an athletic coach, including listening to followers, showing by example, and offering emotional support to members of the team.

- **Gives emotional support**—The coaching leader gives followers personal encouragement.[46] Such encouragement should constantly be aimed at motivating them to do their best to meet the high demands of successful organizations.
- **Shows by example what constitutes appropriate behavior**—The coaching leader shows followers, for instance, how to handle an employee problem or a production glitch. By demonstrating expertise, the coaching leader builds the trust and respect of followers.

Superleadership

Superleadership is leading by showing others how to lead themselves. If superleaders are successful, they develop followers who are productive, work independently, and need only minimal attention from the superleader.

In essence, superleaders teach followers how to think on their own and act constructively and independently.[47] They encourage people to eliminate negative thoughts and beliefs about the company and coworkers and to replace them with more positive and constructive beliefs. An important aspect of superleadership is building the self-confidence of followers by convincing them that they are competent, have a significant reservoir of potential, and are capable of meeting the difficult challenges of the work situation.

The objective of superleaders is to develop followers who require very little leadership. This objective is important in the typical organization of today, where structure is flatter than that of organizations of the past and therefore has fewer leader–managers. Organizations cannot be successful in such a situation unless their members become proficient at leading themselves.

Servant Leadership

Servant leadership is an approach to leading in which leaders view their primary role as helping followers in their quests to satisfy personal needs, aspirations, and interests.[48] Servant leaders see their pursuit of their own personal needs, aspirations, and interests as secondary to the followers' pursuit of these factors.[49] Overall, servant leaders place high value on service to others over self-interests[50] and see their main responsibility as the care of human resources of the organizations.[51] Servant leaders maintain that human resources are the most valuable resources in organizations and constantly strive to transform their followers into wiser and more autonomous individuals. Logically, the result of wiser and more autonomous followers is more successful organizations.

Servant leaders possess several distinctive characteristics which, when taken together, better enable servant leaders to better help followers pursue their needs, aspirations, and interests.[52] As a few of the more notable of these characteristics, servant leaders are[53]

. . . good listeners. Listening is a critical characteristic of servant leaders. The ability to listen carefully to follower comments, for example, helps the servant leader to more accurately define the critical factors of follower needs, aspirations, and interests and thereby more effectively assist followers in their quest to achieve them. Without such accurate definition, the servant leader's task of helping followers to achieve these factors would virtually be hopeless. Overall, listening provides servant leaders with feedback that they can use better to serve their followers.

. . . persuasive. Seldom do servant leaders use authority to mandate action to be taken by followers. Instead, servant leaders focus on convincing followers of activity that should be performed. Such persuasive ability enables servant leaders to ensure that followers act appropriately without creating the resentment between leader and followers that typically appears when a leader mandates activity without follower input.

. . . aware of their surroundings. Servant leaders are keenly aware of organizational surroundings. As such, servant leaders know what factors might create barriers to followers in their quest to pursue needs, interests, and aspirations and take action to eliminate those barriers. Servant leaders help followers handle such barriers by furnishing followers with critical ideas and information regarding formidable organizational challenges.[54]

. . . empathetic. Empathy is the intellectual identification with the feelings, thoughts, or attitudes of another. Being empathetic helps servant leaders to better relate to followers in helping them to solve problems. Servant leaders appreciate the situations in which followers find themselves and are thereby better equipped to assist them in their pursuit of interests, aspirations, and needs.

. . . stewards. A **steward** is defined as an individual who is entrusted with managing the affairs of another. Overall, servant leaders see themselves as being entrusted with managing the human assets of an organization and are responsible for helping organization members to maximize their potential. Servant leaders are committed to building human assets that are more instrumental in achieving organizational success.

Undeniably, servant leadership has gained increasing and significant popularity in recent decades. The notion of servant leadership, however, is not new. Servant leadership was first introduced by Christianity's founder, Jesus Christ, and has been practiced by ancient monarchs for more than 1,000 years.[55] Some of the growing popularity of the servant leadership concept is probably attributable to the intuitive attractiveness of the concept.[56] For example, some management theorists believe that servant leadership's focus on empowerment, sense of community, and sharing of authority suggest that servant leadership is likely a theory with significant potential for enhancing organizational success.[57]

Recent research has analyzed the relationship between servant leadership and personality characteristics.[58] For example, one study assessed whether[59] whether a relationship between one's ability to be a servant leader and personality traits such as agreeableness could be identified. Agreeableness has been defined in this context to describe someone who is altruistic, generous, and eager to help others. The results of this study indicated that managers who were rated by their employees as servant leaders were also highly agreeable people. Also, servant leaders demonstrated high values of empathy, integrity, and competence. Although some research has been done in this area, additional research aimed at more precisely defining the worth of servant leadership theory to practicing managers is advisable.

Entrepreneurial Leadership

Entrepreneurial leadership is leadership that is based on the attitude that the leader is self-employed.[60] Leaders of this type act as if they are playing a critical role in the organization rather than a mostly unimportant one. In addition, they behave as if they are taking the

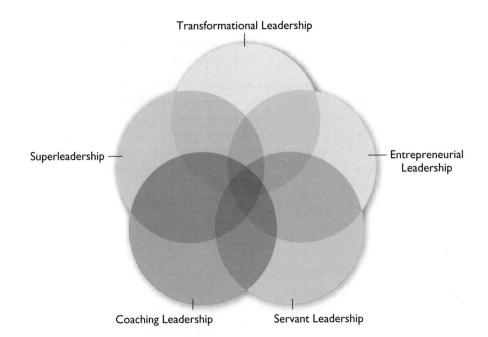

FIGURE 16.9
Various combinations of transformational, coaching, superleader, servant, and entrepreneurial leadership styles

risk of losing money but will receive the profit if one is made. They approach each mistake as if it were a significant error rather than a smaller error that will be neutralized by the normal functioning of the organization.[61]

As **an example from the world of management** about developing the skill of entrepreneurial leaders, consider recent events at **Walt Disney Company in Asia Pacific**. The company instituted an *action learning* program aimed at developing skills of entrepreneurial leaders. Action learning is defined as a means of developing people by having them actually be involved in solving real, complex business issues. The program had about five teams of six to eight people working as groups to solve a real and complex business problem. The problem that participants focused on was to create a new business opportunity for Disney that actually could be launched within six months after the program ended. To be a valid problem solution, the proposed opportunity had to be able to positively affect Disney's level of profitability. According to managers who designed this action learning program, program activities helped to hone systems thinking of participants, a fundamental skill of an entrepreneurial leader.[62]

Each of these contemporary leadership styles has received notable attention in recent management literature. Managers should realize that these five styles are not mutually exclusive; they can be combined in various ways to generate a unique style. For example, a leader can assume both a coaching and an entrepreneurial role. Figure 16.9 shows the various combinations of these five leadership styles that a leader can adopt. The shaded portion of the figure represents a leader whose style comprises all five.

{CHALLENGE CASE SUMMARY

As noted in the preceding material, managers such as Carly Fiorina, the former CEO of HP in the Challenge Case, should understand that leadership activities involve directing the behavior of organization members so that the company will achieve its success. Managers also should understand that leading and managing are not the same thing. Managing involves planning, organizing, influencing, and controlling, while leading is performing an activity that is part of the influencing function of management. To maximize long-term success, managers should strive to be both a manager and a leader.

In assessing leadership, managers such as Fiorina should not fall into the trap of trying to increase leadership success by changing personal traits or attitudes to mirror those of successful leaders that they might know. Studies based on the trait approach to leadership indicate to managers that merely changing their characteristics will not guarantee leadership success.

The situational approach to leadership affords more insights on how managers can help their companies achieve success than does the trait approach. The situational approach would suggest that successful leadership is determined by the appropriateness of a combination of three factors: (1) the manager as a leader, (2) the manager's employees as followers, and (3) the situation(s) within the company that the manager faces. Each of these factors plays a significant role in determining whether managers are successful leaders.

One of the most important activities that managers perform as leaders is making decisions. They can make decisions in any number of ways, ranging from authoritarian to democratic. As described in the Challenge Case, Fiorina led HP to acquire Compaq because she felt the acquisition was vital for HP's future. Fiorina could have authoritatively made the decision to acquire Compaq without consulting any of her employees. Alternatively, Fiorina could have used more subordinate-centered leadership by defining broad limits regarding HP's future and allowing employees to make the proper decision regarding HP's future. Most likely, however, Fiorina was less extreme in her decision making, in that her leadership behavior probably fell in the middle of the continuum. For example, she most likely suggested to appropriate HP personnel the type of company HP was to be and asked them to develop ideas for the types of businesses that HP needed to acquire in order to become that type of company. She then most likely made the decision on the basis of her own ideas and those of the staff.

Based upon the preceding information, in trying to decide exactly how to make decisions as leaders, managers should consider forces in themselves as managers, forces in the manager's subordinates, and forces in the specific organizational situations they face. Forces within managers include their own ideas about how to lead and their level of confidence in the employees that they are leading. If managers believe that they are more knowledgeable about achieving acquisition success, for example, than their staff is, they will likely make boss-centered decisions about what steps to take to create acquisition success. Forces within subordinates, such as the need for independence, the readiness to assume responsibility, and the knowledge of and interest in the issues to be decided, also affect managers' decisions as leaders. If a manager's staff is relatively independent and responsible and its members feel strongly about acquisition success means and how it should be achieved, then a manager should be more inclined to allow his or her employees more freedom in deciding how to achieve that acquisition success.

Forces within the company include the number of people making decisions and the problem to be solved. For example, if the manager's staff is small, he or she will be more likely to use a democratic decision-making style, allowing his or her employees to become involved in such decisions as how to best achieve acquisition success. Managers will also be likely to use a subordinate-centered leadership style if their employees are knowledgeable about what makes a company successful. The VYJ model suggests that managers should try to make decisions in such a fashion that the quality of decisions is enhanced and followers are committed to the decisions. Managers can try to ensure that such decisions are made by matching their decision style (autocratic, consultative, or group) to the particular situation they face.

The OSU leadership studies should furnish a manager with insights on leadership behavior in general situations. According to these studies, managers can exhibit two general types of leadership behavior: structure and consideration. Managers will be using structure behavior if they tell personnel what to do—for example, exactly how to design new ink jet cartridges for HP printers. In contrast, they will be using consideration behavior if they attempt to develop a more human rapport with their employees by discussing their concerns and developing friendships with them.

Of course, depending on how managers emphasize these two behaviors, their leadership styles can reflect a combination of structure and consideration ranging from high structure/low consideration to low structure/high consideration. For example, if managers stress giving orders to employees and deemphasize developing relationships, they will be exhibiting high structure/low consideration. If they emphasize a good rapport with their employees and allow their members to function mostly independently, their leadership styles will be termed low structure/high consideration.

Although no single leadership style is more effective than any other in all situations, the life cycle theory of leadership provides managers with a strategy for using various styles in various situations. According to the theory, managers should make their style consistent primarily with the maturity level of the organization members that they are leading. As managers' followers progress from immaturity to maturity, their leadership style should shift systematically from (1) high task/low relationships behavior to (2) high task/high relationships behavior to (3) high relationships/low task behavior to (4) low task/low relationships behavior.

The life cycle theory suggests that managers should be flexible enough to behave as required by situations at their organizations. If managers find it extremely difficult to be flexible, however, they should attempt to structure their situation so as to make it appropriate for their style. As suggested by Fiedler, if a manager's leadership style is high task in nature, he or she generally will be a more successful leader in situations best described by octants 1, 2, 3, and 8 in Table 16.1 and Figure 16.7. If, however, a manager's leadership style is more relationship oriented, he or she will probably be a more successful leader in situations representative of octants 4, 5, 6, and 7. Overall, Fiedler's work provides managers with insights on how to engineer situations so they will be appropriate for their own leadership styles.

The path–goal theory of leadership suggests that in leading, managers should emphasize clarifying what rewards are available to followers in the organization, how those rewards can be earned, and eliminating barriers that could prohibit followers from earning the rewards. Managers can use directive behavior, supportive behavior, participative behavior, and achievement behavior in implementing the path–goal theory.

Based upon the preceding information, during her tenure at HP, Fiorina could have focused on being a transformational leader, a leader who inspires followers to seriously focus on achieving organizational objectives. As a transformational leader, she would have strived to encourage new ideas, created a sense of duty, and encouraged employees to learn and grow. As HP experienced more and more significant change, the importance of its leader being a transformational leader increased.

Three other popular leadership styles also offer managers such as Fiorina insights about how to lead. As coaching leaders, managers can focus on instructing followers to meet special challenges they face such as expansion through global acquisition. In the role of coaching leaders, they would listen closely, give emotional support, and show by example what should be done. As superleaders, managers would teach followers how to think on their own and act constructively and independently. As entrepreneurial leaders, managers would act much like a self-employed owner of the company. They would act, for example, like an individual personally incurring the risk of acquiring another computer company, but also benefiting from the profit if it is made.

Overall, managers must keep in mind that these leadership styles are aimed at getting people involved in an organization and giving them the freedom to use their abilities as they think best. Such leaders must always keep in mind that regardless of the type of leader they may be, they must earn and maintain the trust of their followers if they are to be successful in the long run.

MANAGEMENT SKILL ACTIVITIES

This section is specially designed to help you develop leadership skill. An individual's leadership skill is based upon an understanding of leadership concepts and the ability to apply those concepts in management situations. The following activities are designed both to heighten your understanding of leadership fundamentals and to develop your ability to apply those concepts in various management situations.

UNDERSTANDING LEADERSHIP CONCEPTS

This section is comprised of activities that will sharpen your understanding of leadership concepts. Answer essay questions as completely as possible. Complete Exploring Your Management Skill: Part 2 as directed. Also, remember that additional true/false and multiple choice questions appear online at MyManagementLab.com to help you further refine your understanding of leadership.

Essay Questions

1. Is it important for you as a manager to understand the difference between leadership and management? Explain fully.
2. What is the difference between the "situational approach" and the "trait approach" to leadership? Which approach seems to have more relevance to you as a manager? Explain.
3. Draw and explain the life cycle model of leadership. Would this model be useful to you as a manager? Why?
4. Would it be easy for you to be a "servant leader"? Why?

5. Given all that you've learned in this chapter, what kind of leader will you try to be as a manager? Explain.

Developing Management Skill

Learning activities in this section are aimed at helping you to develop leadership skill. Learning activities include Exploring Your Management Skill: Part 2, Experiential Exercises, Cases, and a VideoNet exercise.

EXPLORING YOUR MANAGEMENT SKILL: PART 2

As you recall, you completed Exploring Your Management Skill before you started to study this chapter. Your responses gave you an idea of how much you initially knew about leadership and helped you to focus on important points as you studied the chapter. Answer the Exploring Your Management Skill questions again now (p. 386) and compare your score to the first time you took it. This comparison will give you an idea of how much you have learned from studying this chapter and pinpoint areas for further clarification before you start studying the next chapter. Record your answers within the text or go to MyManagementLab.com. Recording your answers in MyManagementLab will allow you to get immediate results and see how your score compares to your classmates. If you answer the questions in the book, the answers are located in the Exploring Your Management Skill Appendix at the end of the book.

YOUR MANAGEMENT SKILLS PORTFOLIO

Your Management Learning Portfolio is a collection of activities especially designed to demonstrate your management knowledge and skill. By completing these activities online at MyManagementLab.com, you will be able to print, complete with cover sheet, as many activities as you choose. Be sure to save your work. Taking your printed portfolio to an employment interview could be helpful in obtaining a job.

The portfolio activity for this chapter is Leadership Skill in a Special Situation.[63] Read the highlight about Martha Stewart and answer the questions that follow.

Leadership Skill in a Special Situation

Homemaking icon Martha Stewart strolled outdoors with her dog and fed her horses, hours after returning from prison to the lavish estate. Stewart's release came one day shy of the one-year anniversary of her conviction on charges stemming from her 2001 sale of nearly 4,000 shares of the biotechnology company ImClone Systems Inc. She was convicted of obstructing justice and lying to the government.

For the next five months, Stewart had to wear an electronic anklet so authorities could track her every move. But she was allowed to receive her $900,000 salary again and could leave home for up to 48 hours a week to work, shop, or run other approved errands.

Leaving the women's prison in Alderson, West Virginia, shortly after midnight Friday, Stewart flew in a private jet to Westchester County airport and then was driven to the 61-hectare (153-acre) estate in Katonah, 65 kilometers north of midtown Manhattan.

Stewart hopes to turn around the fortunes of her company, Martha Stewart Living, which produces everything from television shows and magazines to bed sheets and bakeware. In 2004, the company suffered a loss and its revenues sagged, but the stock price rose considerably during her prison stint as investors bet on a Stewart comeback. Stewart's contract with her company says her salary, which was suspended while she was behind bars, will be reinstated during home detention. While in home confinement, Stewart will be free to entertain colleagues, neighbors, friends, and relatives as long as they're not criminals. Convicted felons aren't allowed to consort with other convicted felons.

Activity 1

Circle the option that best reflects your opinion about Martha Stewart's leadership situation at Martha Stewart Living: Martha Stewart's background as a convicted felon will present special leadership challenges that Martha will have to overcome.

1. Definitely

2. Probably Will

3. Maybe

4. Probably Won't

5. Definitely Not

Activity 2

Now that you have expressed your opinion about Martha Stewart's possible new leadership challenges, in the following space explain this opinion in 50 words or less.

Activity 3

In the first few months after returning as top manager at Martha Stewart Living, should Stewart portray a leadership style that focuses more on low task/low relationships, low task/high relationships, high task/high relationships, or low relationships/high task? Why?

_____

_____

_____

_____

_____

Activity 4

Using the life cycle theory of leadership's four main leadership styles, how should Stewart change her leadership style over time, if at all? Explain fully.

_____

_____

_____

_____

_____

EXPERIENTIAL EXERCISE: MAKE A DECISION AT WENDY'S[64]

Directions. Read the following scenario and then perform the listed activities. Your instructor may want you to perform the activities as an individual or within groups. Follow all of your instructor's directions carefully.

According to Jack Schuessler, Wendy's CEO, management is considering whether to begin offering a breakfast menu that was discontinued about 20 years ago. Schuessler did indicate, however, that if offered, Wendy's breakfast menu would need to be significantly different from the sausage-and-biscuits or egg-on-an-English-muffin approach offered by competitors.

Some individuals support Schuessler's new breakfast menu idea. Some believe that the best opportunity for Wendy's to improve profitability is to introduce breakfast. In addition, Wendy's owns Tim Horton's, a chain dominant in Canada that knows the breakfast business. Wendy's should be able to use the knowledge and experience at Tim Horton's as help in introducing a new successful breakfast menu.

The competition in the fast-food breakfast segment is heavy. McDonald's began offering breakfast in the 1970s and is the market leader of the morning sales period. Burger King reportedly is testing new breakfast sandwiches and platters. In addition, the fast-food restaurant Carl's Jr. recently introduced a breakfast burger topped with a fried egg at its 1,000 restaurants.

Although offering breakfast at Wendy's could improve sales by making use of the store during hours it is empty, the company has found that breakfast can be disastrous if not done correctly. According to Schuessler, when Wendy's offered breakfast between 1983 and 1985, it operated inappropriately and as a result breakfast was not a profitable activity. The breakfast offered was expensive, it wasn't portable, service was too slow, and offering breakfast took away some of the focus on the company's burger business.

Learning Activity

Your instructor will divide the class into small groups and ask each group to arrive at a consensus in answering the answering the following questions.

1. Assume that you are Jack Schuessler. As a leader at Wendy's, how would you make the decision regarding whether to introduce serving breakfast?

   a. Simply make the decision and announce it.

   b. Make the decision but try to convince others it's best.

   c. Present a tentative decision subject to change based upon input.

   d. Present the dilemma and ask for input before making the decision.

   e. Allow a group to make the decision.

2. Explain your answer to question 1. Be sure to focus on why you chose the option you did as well as why you did not choose other options.

3. As a leader, would you find making this decision at Wendy's challenging? Why?

<h1 style="text-align:center">C A S E S</h1>

CARLY FIORINA: HIRED AND FIRED AT HEWLETT-PACKARD

"Carly Fiorina: Hired and Fired at Hewlett-Packard" (p. 385) and its related Challenge Case Summary were written to help you better understand the management concepts contained in this chapter. Answer the following discussion questions about the Challenge Case to further enrich your understanding of chapter content.

1. List and define five activities that Fiorina might have performed as a manager while integrating her company with Compaq, as defined in the Challenge Case.

2. Do you feel that Fiorina should have used more of a boss-centered or subordinate-centered leadership style in making decisions about achieving acquisition success? Why?

3. If you were Fiorina, would understanding the transformational and the entrepreneurial leadership styles have been valuable to you in leading HP employees to acquisition success? Explain fully.

TOYOTA'S DRIVE FOR GLOBAL LEADERSHIP

Read the case and answer the questions that follow. Studying this case will help you better understand how concepts relating to leadership can be applied in a company such as Toyota.

Steering toward its goal of capturing 15 percent of the global car market by 2010, Toyota Motor Corp. has already achieved impressive results. The company doubled its revenue in the past decade and recently announced a net annual income of $10.5 billion, the highest ever reported by a Japanese company. If Toyota continues at this pace, it will overtake General Motors—currently the world's largest auto manufacturer—by the end of the decade.

Nonetheless, outgoing Toyota president Fujio Cho sees a number of challenges that must be addressed to stay on course. One priority is raising product quality without sacrificing efficiency. Since the 1980s, the Toyota Production System (TPS) has been synonymous with high quality, minimal waste, continuous improvement, and employee involvement. Cho recently admitted, however, that "Toyota quality isn't improving as fast as it should." In fact, the Camry's initial quality standing among premium midsize cars slipped from number 1 in 2000 to number 8 in 2004 in an important annual survey.

In response, Cho and his executives have enlisted managers at all levels in the fight to reinvigorate quality. He insists that middle managers from factories outside Japan experience TPS first-hand by rotating through the company's state-of-the-art Global Production Center southwest of Tokyo. He also sends TPS specialists to troubleshoot problems and coach the workforce in different factories. Sometimes TPS experts aren't immediately available, prompting local plant managers to get creative. Gary Convis, who heads the factory in the United States (which Cho opened and managed in 1988), arranged for his line managers to sharpen their quality improvement skills by working on projects for plant suppliers. In addition, Convis was involved in establishing an Organization Development Group to educate shop-floor managers as the plant leaders of the future.

Another priority is reinforcing employee commitment and involvement. Yoshi Inaba, once the top sales executive in Toyota's U.S. division and now one of the corporation's 14 senior managing directors, is particularly concerned about instilling a bottom-line orientation. "When I came [to the U.S. division], I thought we weren't making enough money," he says. He took the unprecedented step of releasing profit and expense data to all U.S. sales personnel so they can understand how their activities affect financial performance. In his role as managing director, Inaba helps Toyota managers grapple with decisions about balancing market share and profitability. Not long ago, an official from the U.S. division described competitive price cuts, warning that sales and profits could suffer if Toyota didn't discount to rental car companies buying in volume. Inaba suggested investigating other, higher-profit opportunities for selling to businesses that buy in volume, instead of focusing on rental cars. "Maybe we lose in terms of total volume," he explained, but that's acceptable because "it's all about return."

Finally, Cho knows that Toyota must have a global outlook. This is where Akio Toyoda, great-grandson of Toyota's founder and a senior managing director, is proving himself. Toyoda was appointed head of the China business in 2001, when it had a joint venture with a financially troubled firm controlled by the city of Tianjin. Impatient for faster results, Toyoda worked for a year to complete a merger with a larger, more aggressive local firm by convincing Toyota's top management and government officials to approve the deal.

With the merger a reality, Toyoda's next step was to revamp the management structure. The country's department heads were accountable only to headquarters executives, which isolated the managers and complicated coordination. With Toyoda's change, department heads work more closely with each other and report to an executive vice president who can make decisions for the China business instead of waiting for corporate approvals. "We're creating a new and more aggressive way of business that is necessary to boost our chances of becoming the number one auto maker in the world," he states. "We're building a new Toyota." Based on their leadership capabilities, Toyoda and Inaba are in the running to become president when Fujio Cho retires.

QUESTIONS

1. How would you describe Akio Toyoda's leadership style? Explain.
2. Where on the continuum of leadership behavior would you place Yoshi Inaba, and why?
3. Do you think position power, task structure, or leader–member relations was the most important aspect of Gary Convis's leadership at the U.S. Georgetown plant?

VIDEONET EXERCISE

Leadership at Kluster

VIDEO HIGHLIGHT

What kind of leader demotes himself? Ben Kaufman, that's who. His parents re-mortgaged their house so he could start a company focused on creating innovative iPod accessories. After launching a bunch of great products, Ben's plan is to now revolutionize the way consumer products are developed via his latest entrepreneurial venture, Kluster (formerly known as the Illuminator Project). He's fearless, charismatic, and prone to having visions. Will he rock the world the same way the founders of YouTube, FaceBook, and Google have? Hear the 20-year-old's thoughts on leadership and find out if his colleagues think he's the real thing.

Discussion Questions

1. Is there evidence in the video clip that Kaufman is both a leader and a manager? Explain.
2. Describe Kaufman using the trait approach to leadership.
3. Using the Vroom–Yetton–Jago model, explain how Kaufman makes decisions for Kluster.

Internet Activity

Go to the Kluster home page at www.kluster.com. Watch the video presented under the link "What Happened Here." Based on Ben Kaufman's dialogue, which leadership style do you think best applies to his way of doing business? Explain.

17 Motivation

OBJECTIVES

TO HELP BUILD MY MOTIVATION SKILL, WHEN STUDYING
THIS CHAPTER, I WILL ATTEMPT TO ACQUIRE:

1. A basic understanding of
human motivation

2. Insights into various
human needs

3. An appreciation for the
importance of motivating
organization members

4. An understanding of various motivation strategies

TARGET SKILL

motivation skill: the ability to create organizational situations in which individuals performing organizational activities are simultaneously satisfying personal needs and helping the organization attain its goals

be determined by two major factors: her perception of the value of $600 and her perception of the probability that she can actually paint the houses satisfactorily and receive the $600. As the student's perceived value of the $600 reward and perceived probability that she can paint the houses increase, the student's motivation strength to paint the houses will also increase.

Equity Theory of Motivation **Equity theory,** the work of J. Stacy Adams, looks at an individual's perceived fairness of an employment situation and finds that perceived inequities can lead to changes in behavior. Adams found that when individuals believe they have been treated unfairly in comparison with their coworkers, they will react in one of the following ways to try to right the inequity:[8]

1. Some will change their work outputs to better match the rewards they are receiving. If they believe they are being paid too little, they will decrease their work outputs; if they believe they are being paid more than their coworkers, they will increase their work outputs to match their rewards.
2. Some will try to change the compensation they receive for their work by asking for a raise or by taking legal action.
3. If attempts to change the actual inequality are unsuccessful, some will try to change their own perception of the inequality. They may do this by distorting the status of their jobs or by rationalizing away the inequity.
4. Some will leave the situation rather than try to change it. People who feel they are being treated unfairly on the job may decide to quit that job rather than endure the inequity.

Perceptions of inequities can arise in any number of management situations—among them, work assignments, promotions, ratings reports, and office assignments—but they occur most often in the area of pay. All of these issues are emotionally charged, however, because they pertain to people's feelings of self-worth. What is a minor inequity in the mind of a manager can loom as extremely important in the mind of an employee. Effective managers strive to deal with equity issues because the steps that workers are prone to take to balance the scales are often far from good for the organization.

As **an example from the world of management** regarding equity theory, consider events at **American Airlines**.[9] Representatives of the Transport Workers Union recently presented the chairman and chief executive of America Airlines, Gerard J. Arpey, with an online petition bearing 17,000 signatures that protested the company's executive compensation practices. Company employees and unions have taken pay cuts and made other concessions worth $1.62 billion a year through 2008. Last month, the company's top executives received $21 million in bonuses, a figure that generated more than 500,000 e-mail messages in protest. Union members feel little pay equity between the concessions made by nonmanagers and the bonuses received by managers. Such a perceived lack of pay equity could lead to an employee strike to remedy the situation.

The Porter–Lawler Theory of Motivation Porter and Lawler developed a motivation theory that provides a more complete description of the motivation process than either the needs-goal theory or the Vroom expectancy theory.[10] Still, the **Porter–Lawler theory** of motivation (see Figure 17.3) is consistent with those two theories in that it accepts the premises that felt needs cause human behavior and that effort expended to accomplish a task is determined by the perceived value of rewards that will result from finishing the task and the probability that those rewards will materialize.

The Motivation Process In addition, the Porter–Lawler motivation theory stresses three other characteristics of the motivation process:

1. The perceived value of a reward is determined by both intrinsic and extrinsic rewards that result in need satisfaction when a task is accomplished. **Intrinsic rewards** come

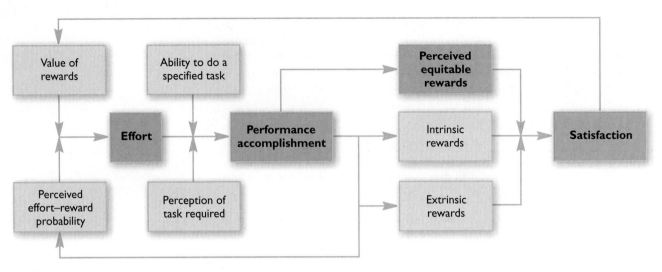

FIGURE 17.3   The Porter–Lawler theory of motivation

directly from performing the task, while **extrinsic rewards** are extraneous to the task.[11] For example, when a manager counsels a subordinate about a personal problem, the manager may get some intrinsic reward in the form of personal satisfaction at helping another individual. In addition to this intrinsic reward, however, the manager also receives an extrinsic reward in the form of the overall salary the manager is paid.[12]

As **an example from the world of management** concerning extrinsic rewards, consider recent events at **Bank of America**.[13] Management has decided that some Bank of America employees will receive $3,000 cash if they buy one of the fuel-efficient hybrid vehicles available in the marketplace. In essence, the rebate is an extrinsic reward for working at Bank of America. Management decided that about 21,000 employees would be eligible for the program. The company is offering employees a $3,000 rebate that matches a $3,000 tax credit for buying a hybrid. Like Anne Finucane, global marketing and corporate affairs executive for Bank of America, many employees seem excited about the new program. According to Finucane, the program should improve the quality of the local environment, help keep employees motivated, improve the bank's ability to recruit new employees, and draw new customers who appreciate environmental improvement.

2. The extent to which an individual effectively accomplishes a task is determined primarily by two variables: the individual's perception of what is required to perform the task and the individual's ability to perform the task. Effectiveness at accomplishing a task increases as the perception of what is required to perform the task becomes more accurate and the ability to perform the task increases.

3. The perceived fairness of rewards influences the amount of satisfaction produced by those rewards. The more equitable an individual perceives the rewards to be, the greater the satisfaction that individual will experience as a result of receiving them.

Content Theories of Motivation: Human Needs

The motivation theories discussed thus far imply that an understanding of motivation is based on an understanding of human needs. Some evidence indicates that most people have strong needs for self-respect, respect from others, promotion, and psychological growth.[14] Although identifying all human needs is impossible, several theories have been developed to

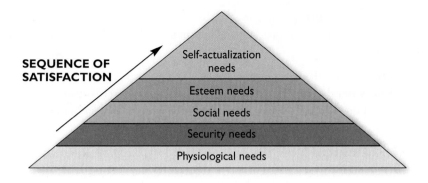

SEQUENCE OF SATISFACTION

Self-actualization needs

Esteem needs

Social needs

Security needs

Physiological needs

FIGURE 17.4
Maslow's hierarchy of needs

help managers better understand these needs:

1. Maslow's hierarchy of needs
2. Alderfer's ERG theory
3. Argyris's maturity-immaturity continuum
4. McClelland's acquired needs theory

Maslow's Hierarchy of Needs Perhaps the most widely accepted description of human needs is the hierarchy of needs concept developed by Abraham Maslow.[15] Maslow states that human beings possess the five basic needs described here and theorizes that these five basic needs can be arranged in a hierarchy of importance—the order in which individuals generally strive to satisfy them.[16] The needs and their relative positions in the hierarchy of importance are shown in Figure 17.4.

- **Physiological needs** relate to the normal functioning of the body. They include the needs for water, food, rest, sex, and air. Until these needs are met, a significant portion of an individual's behavior will be aimed at satisfying them. Once the needs are satisfied, however, behavior is aimed at satisfying the needs on the next level of Maslow's hierarchy.

- **Security**, or **safety, needs** relate to the individual's desire to be free from harm, including both bodily and economic disaster.

    Traditionally, management has best helped employees satisfy their physiological and security needs through adequate wages or salaries, which employees use to purchase such things as food and housing.

- **Social needs** include the desire for love, companionship, and friendship. These needs reflect a person's desire to be accepted by others. As they are satisfied, behavior shifts to satisfying esteem needs.

- **Esteem needs** are concerned with the desire for respect. They are generally divided into two categories: self-respect and respect from others. Once esteem needs are satisfied, the individual moves to the pinnacle of the hierarchy and emphasizes satisfying self-actualization needs.

- **Self-actualization needs** refer to the desire to maximize whatever potential an individual possesses. For example, in the nonprofit public setting of a high school, a principal who seeks to satisfy self-actualization needs would strive to become the best principal possible. Self-actualization needs occupy the highest level of Maslow's hierarchy.[17]

The traditional concerns about Maslow's hierarchy are that it has no research base, that it may not accurately pinpoint basic human needs, and that it is questionable whether human needs can be neatly arranged in such a hierarchy. Nevertheless, Maslow's hierarchy is probably the most popular conceptualization of human needs to date, and it continues to be positively discussed in management literature.[18] Still, the concerns expressed about it should remind managers to look upon Maslow's hierarchy more as a subjective statement than an objective description of human needs.[19]

Members of the AFL-CIO Amalgamated Transit Union striking in Los Angeles. An employee strike usually indicates unmet human needs.

Alderfer's ERG Theory Clayton Alderfer responded to some of the criticisms of Maslow's work by conducting his own study of human needs.[20] He identified three basic categories of needs:

1. **Existence needs**—the need for physical well-being
2. **Relatedness needs**—the need for satisfying interpersonal relationships
3. **Growth needs**—the need for continuing personal growth and development

The first letters of these needs form the acronym ERG, by which the theory is now known.

Alderfer's ERG theory is similar to Maslow's theory except in three major respects. First, Alderfer identified only three orders of human needs, compared to Maslow's five orders. Second, in contrast to Maslow, Alderfer found that people sometimes activate their higher-level needs before they have completely satisfied all of their lower-level needs. Third, Alderfer concluded that movement in his hierarchy of human needs is not always upward. For instance—and this is reflected in his frustration-regression principle—he found that a worker frustrated by his failure to satisfy an upper-level need might regress by trying to fulfill an already satisfied lower-level need.

Alderfer's work, in conjunction with Maslow's, has implications for management. Employees frustrated by work that fails to provide opportunities for growth or development on the job might concentrate their energy on trying to make more money, thus regressing to a lower level of needs. To counteract such regression, management might use job enrichment strategies designed to help people meet their higher-order needs.

Argyris's Maturity-Immaturity Continuum

Argyris's maturity-immaturity continuum also furnishes insights into human needs.[21] This continuum concept focuses on the personal and natural development of people to explain human needs. According to Argyris, as people naturally progress from immaturity to maturity, they move:

1. From a state of passivity as an infant to a state of increasing activity as an adult
2. From a state of dependence on others as an infant to a state of relative independence as an adult
3. From being capable of behaving only in a few ways as an infant to being capable of behaving in many different ways as an adult
4. From having erratic, casual, shallow, and quickly dropped interests as an infant to having deeper, more lasting interests as an adult
5. From having a short time perspective as an infant to having a much longer time perspective as an adult
6. From being in a subordinate position as an infant to aspiring to occupy an equal or superordinate position as an adult
7. From a lack of self-awareness as an infant to awareness and control over self as an adult

According to Argyris's continuum, then, as individuals mature, they have increasing needs for more activity, enjoy a state of relative independence, behave in many different ways, have deeper and more lasting interests, are capable of considering a relatively long time perspective, occupy an equal position vis-à-vis other mature individuals, and have more awareness of themselves and control over their own destiny. Note that, unlike Maslow's needs, Argyris's needs are not arranged in a hierarchy. Like Maslow's hierarchy, however, Argyris's continuum is a primarily subjective explanation of human needs.

McClelland's Acquired Needs Theory

Another theory about human needs, called **McClelland's acquired needs theory,** focuses on the needs that people acquire through their life experiences. This theory, formulated by David C. McClelland in the 1960s, emphasizes three of the many needs human beings develop in their lifetimes:

1. **Need for achievement (nAch)**—the desire to do something better or more efficiently than it has ever been done before

2. **Need for power (nPower)**—the desire to control, influence, or be responsible for others

3. **Need for affiliation (nAff)**—the desire to maintain close, friendly, personal relationships

The individual's early life experiences determine which of these needs will be highly developed and therefore dominate the personality.

McClelland's studies of these three acquired human needs have significant implications for management.

NEED FOR ACHIEVEMENT McClelland claims that in some businesspeople, the need to achieve is so strong that it is more motivating than the quest for profits. To maximize their satisfaction, individuals with high achievement needs set goals for themselves that are challenging, yet achievable. Although such people are willing to assume risk, they assess it carefully because they do not want to fail. Therefore, they will avoid tasks that involve too much risk. People with a low need for achievement, on the other hand, generally avoid challenges, responsibilities, and risk.

NEED FOR POWER People with a high need for power are greatly motivated to influence others and to assume responsibility for subordinates' behavior. They are likely to seek advancement and to take on increasingly responsible work activities to earn that advancement. Power-oriented managers are comfortable in competitive situations and enjoy their decision-making role.

NEED FOR AFFILIATION Managers with a high need for affiliation have a cooperative, team-centered managerial style. They prefer to influence subordinates to complete tasks through team efforts. The danger is that managers with a high need for affiliation can lose their effectiveness if their need for social approval and friendship interferes with their willingness to make managerial decisions.[22]

MOTIVATING ORGANIZATION MEMBERS

People are motivated to perform behavior that satisfies their personal needs. Therefore, from a managerial viewpoint, motivation is the process of furnishing organization members with the opportunity to satisfy their needs by performing productive behavior within the organization. In reality, managers do not motivate people. Rather, they create environments in which organization members motivate themselves.[23]

As discussed in Chapter 15, motivation is one of the four primary interrelated activities of the influencing function performed by managers to guide the behavior of organization members toward the attainment of organizational objectives. The following sections discuss the importance of motivating organization members and present some strategies for doing so.

The Importance of Motivating Organization Members

Figure 17.5 makes the point that unsatisfied needs can lead organization members to perform either appropriate or inappropriate behavior. Successful managers minimize inappropriate behavior and maximize appropriate behavior among subordinates, thus raising the probability that productivity will increase and lowering the probability that it will decrease.

Strategies for Motivating Organization Members

Managers have various strategies at their disposal for motivating organization members. Each strategy is aimed at satisfying subordinates' needs (consistent with the descriptions of human needs in Maslow's hierarchy, Alderfer's ERG theory, Argyris's maturity-immaturity

Generous company benefits and a congenial work environment that encourages employees to pursue their love of the outdoors are among the motivating strategies employed by Patagonia's founder and CEO, Yvon Chouinard.

continuum, and McClelland's acquired needs theory) through appropriate organizational behavior. These managerial motivation strategies are as follows:

1. Managerial communication
2. Theory X–Theory Y
3. Job design
4. Behavior modification
5. Likert's management systems
6. Monetary incentives
7. Nonmonetary incentives

The strategies are discussed in the sections that follow.

Throughout the discussion, it is important to remember that no single strategy will always be more effective for a manager than any other. Most managers find that some combination of these strategies is most effective in the organization setting.

FIGURE 17.5
Unsatisfied needs of organization members resulting in either appropriate or inappropriate behavior

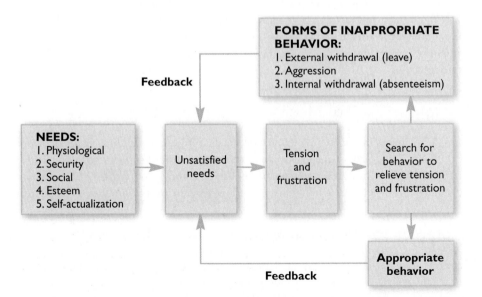

Managerial Communication Perhaps the most basic motivation strategy for managers is to communicate well with organization members. Effective manager–subordinate communication can satisfy such basic human needs as recognition, a sense of belonging, and security. For example, such a simple managerial action as attempting to become better acquainted with subordinates can contribute substantially to the satisfaction of each of these three needs. For another example, a message praising a subordinate for a job well done can help satisfy the subordinate's recognition and security needs.

As a general rule, managers should strive to communicate often with other organization members, not only because communication is the primary means of conducting organizational activities, but also because it is a basic tool for satisfying the human needs of organization members.[24]

Theory X–Theory Y Another motivation strategy involves managers' assumptions about human nature. Douglas McGregor identified two sets of assumptions: **Theory X** involves negative assumptions about people that McGregor believes managers often use as the basis for dealing with their subordinates (e.g., the average person has an inherent dislike of work and will avoid it whenever he or she can). **Theory Y** represents positive assumptions about people that McGregor believes managers should strive to use (e.g., people will exercise self-direction and self-control in meeting their objectives).[25]

McGregor implies that managers who use Theory X assumptions are "bad" and that those who use Theory Y assumptions are "good."[26] Reddin, however, argues that production might be increased by using *either* Theory X or Theory Y assumptions, depending on the situation the manager faces: "Is there not a strong argument for the position that any theory may have desirable outcomes if appropriately used?" The difficulty is that McGregor considered only the ineffective application of Theory X and the effective application of Theory Y. Reddin proposes a **Theory Z**—an effectiveness dimension that implies that managers who use either Theory X or Theory Y assumptions when dealing with people can be successful, depending on their situation.[27]

The basic rationale for using Theory Y rather than Theory X in most situations is that managerial activities that reflect Theory Y assumptions generally are more successful in satisfying the human needs of most organization members than are managerial activities that reflect Theory X assumptions. Therefore, activities based on Theory Y assumptions are more apt to motivate organization members than are activities based on Theory X assumptions.[28]

Job Design A third strategy managers can use to motivate organization members involves designing jobs that organization members perform. The following two sections discuss earlier and more recent job design strategies.

Earlier Job Design Strategies A movement has long existed in American business to make jobs simpler and more specialized in order to increase worker productivity. The idea behind this movement is to make workers more productive by enabling them to be more efficient. Perhaps the best example of a job design inspired by this movement is the automobile assembly line. The negative result of work simplification and specialization, however, is job boredom. As jobs become simpler and more specialized, they typically become more boring and less satisfying to workers, and, consequently, productivity suffers.

JOB ROTATION The first major attempt to overcome job boredom was **job rotation**—moving workers from job to job rather than requiring them to perform only one simple and specialized job over the long term.[29] For example, a gardener would do more than just mow lawns; he might also trim bushes, rake grass, and sweep sidewalks.

Although job rotation programs have been known to increase organizational profitability, most of them are ineffective as motivation strategies because, over time, people become bored with all the jobs they are rotated into.[30] Job rotation programs, however, are often effective for achieving other organizational objectives, such as training, because they give individuals an overview of how the various units of the organization function.

JOB ENLARGEMENT Another strategy developed to overcome the boredom of doing very simple and specialized jobs is **job enlargement,** or increasing the number of operations an individual performs in order to enhance the individual's satisfaction in work. According to the job enlargement concept, the gardener's job would become more satisfying as such activities as trimming bushes, raking grass, and sweeping sidewalks were added to his initial activity of mowing grass. Some research supports the contention that job enlargement does make jobs more satisfying, and some does not.[31] Still, job enlargement programs are more successful at increasing job satisfaction than job rotation programs.

A number of other job design strategies have evolved since the development of job rotation and job enlargement programs. Two of these more recent strategies are job enrichment and flextime.

Job Enrichment
Frederick Herzberg concluded from his research that the degrees of satisfaction and dissatisfaction organization members feel as a result of performing a job are two different variables determined by two different sets of items.[32] The items that influence the degree of job dissatisfaction are called **hygiene, or maintenance, factors,** while those that influence the degree of job satisfaction are called **motivating factors, or motivators.** Hygiene factors relate to the work environment, and motivating factors to the work itself. The items that make up Herzberg's hygiene and motivating factors are presented in Table 17.1.

Herzberg believes that when the hygiene factors of a particular job situation are undesirable, organization members will become dissatisfied. Making these factors more desirable—for example, by increasing salary—will rarely motivate people to do a better job, but it will keep them from becoming dissatisfied. In contrast, when the motivating factors of a particular job situation are high, employees usually are motivated to do a better job. People tend to be more motivated and productive as more motivators are built into their job situation.

The process of incorporating motivators into a job situation is called **job enrichment.**[33] Early reports indicated that companies such as Texas Instruments and Volvo had notable success in motivating organization members through job enrichment programs. More recent reports, even though they continue to support the value of job enrichment, indicate that for a job enrichment program to be successful, it must be carefully designed and administered.[34]

JOB ENRICHMENT AND PRODUCTIVITY Herzberg's overall conclusions are that the most productive organization members are those involved in work situations that have both desirable hygiene and motivating factors. The needs in Maslow's hierarchy that desirable hygiene factors and motivating factors generally satisfy are shown in Figure 17.6. Esteem needs can be satisfied by both types of factors. An example of esteem needs satisfied by a hygiene factor is a private parking space—a status symbol and a working condition evidencing the employee's importance to the organization. An example of esteem needs satisfied by a motivating factor

TABLE 17.1 Herzberg's Hygiene Factors and Motivators	
Dissatisfaction: Hygiene or Maintenance Factors	**Satisfaction: Motivating Factors**
1. Company policy and administration	1. Opportunity for achievement
2. Supervision	2. Opportunity for recognition
3. Relationship with supervisor	3. Work itself
4. Relationship with peers	4. Responsibility
5. Working conditions	5. Advancement
6. Salary	6. Personal growth
7. Relationship with subordinates	

Self-actualization
needs

Esteem needs

Social needs

Security needs

Physiological needs

☐ Needs that hygiene factors generally satisfy

☐ Needs that motivating factors generally satisfy

FIGURE 17.6
Needs in Maslow's hierarchy of needs that desirable hygiene and motivating factors generally satisfy

is an award given for outstanding performance—a public recognition of a job well done that displays the employee's value to the organization.

Flextime   Another more recent job design strategy for motivating organization members is based on a concept called *flextime*.[35] In many countries a set number of working hours per day is the norm. This tradition has been challenged. Faced with motivation problems and excessive absenteeism, many managers have turned to scheduling innovations as a possible solution.[36]

The main purpose of these scheduling innovations is not to reduce the total number of work hours, but rather to give workers greater flexibility in scheduling their work hours. The main thrust of **flextime,** or a flexible working hours program, is that it allows workers to complete their jobs within a workweek of a normal number of hours that they arrange themselves.[37] The choices of starting and finishing times can be as flexible as the organizational situation allows. To ensure that flexibility does not become counterproductive within the organization, however, many flextime programs stipulate a core period during which all employees must be on the job.

ADVANTAGES OF FLEXTIME Various kinds of organizational studies have indicated that flextime programs have some positive organizational effects. Douglas Fleuter, for example, reported that flextime contributes to greater job satisfaction, which typically results in greater productivity. Other researchers conclude that flextime programs can result in higher

Flextime can be highly motivating to some workers, giving them greater control over their work day and often leading to higher productivity and job satisfaction. If flextime allowed you to avoid rush hour, for instance, would you be more productive?

TABLE 17.2	Advantages and Disadvantages of Using Flextime Programs	
Advantages	**Disadvantages**	
Improved employee attitude and morale	Lack of supervision during some hours of work	
Accommodation of working parents	Key people unavailable at certain times	
Decreased tardiness	Understaffing at times	
Fewer commuting problems—workers can avoid congested streets and highways	Problem of accommodating employees whose output is the input for other employees	
Accommodation of those who wish to arrive at work before normal workday interruptions begin	Employee abuse of flextime program	
Increased production	Difficulty in planning work schedules	
Facilitation of employees scheduling of medical, dental, and other types of appointments	Problem of keeping track of hours worked or accumulated	
Accommodation of leisure-time activities of employees	Inability to schedule meetings at convenient times	
Decreased absenteeism	Inability to coordinate projects	
Decreased turnover		

motivation levels of workers. Because organization members generally consider flextime programs desirable, organizations that have such programs can usually better compete with other organizations in recruiting qualified new employees. (A listing of the advantages and disadvantages of flextime programs appears in Table 17.2.) Although many well-known companies have adopted flextime programs,[38] more research is needed before flextime's true worth can be conclusively assessed.

Behavior Modification A fourth strategy that managers can use to motivate organization members is based on a concept known as behavior modification. As stated by B. F. Skinner, the Harvard psychologist considered by many to be the father of behavioral psychology, **behavior modification** focuses on encouraging appropriate behavior by controlling the consequences of that behavior.[39] According to the law of effect, behavior that is rewarded tends to be repeated, while that which is punished tends to be eliminated.

Although behavior modification programs typically involve the administration of both rewards and punishments, it is rewards that are generally emphasized because they are more effective than punishments in influencing behavior. Obviously, the main theme of behavior modification is not new.

REINFORCEMENT Behavior modification theory asserts that if managers want to modify subordinates' behavior, they must ensure that appropriate consequences occur as a result of that behavior. **Positive reinforcement** is a reward that consists of a desirable consequence of behavior, and **negative reinforcement** is a reward that consists of the elimination of an undesirable consequence of behavior.[40]

If arriving at work on time is positively reinforced, or rewarded, the probability increases that a worker will arrive on time more often.[41] If arriving late for work causes a worker to experience some undesirable outcome, such as a verbal reprimand, that worker will be negatively reinforced when this outcome is eliminated by on-time arrival. According to behavior modification theory, positive reinforcement and negative reinforcement are both rewards that increase the likelihood that a behavior will continue.

PUNISHMENT **Punishment** is the presentation of an undesirable behavior consequence or the removal of a desirable behavior consequence that decreases the likelihood that the behavior will continue. To use our earlier example, a manager could punish employees for arriving late for work by exposing them to some undesirable consequence, such as verbal reprimand, or by removing a desirable consequence, such as their wages for the amount of time they are late.[42] Although punishment would probably quickly convince most workers to come to work on time, it might have undesirable side effects, such as high absenteeism and turnover, if it is emphasized over the long term.[43]

class discussion highlight

PUNISHMENT AND YOUR CAREER

The above information implies that punishment can be an effective tool in managing employee behavior. Eric Mangini, the manager of the New York Jets football team, has a team that commits few mistakes in games.[44] As evidence, the Jets recently ranked No. 3 in the league in fewest penalties and No. 2 in lowest penalty yardage assessed. How has the coach accomplished this feat? Mangini reinforces his message of playing smart by having players run extra penalty laps for practice infractions that fall under the category of penalties. One player, Rashad Washington, believes that the punishment laps have a lot to do with the penalty free nature of the team. According to Washington, "Those things get tiring, especially after you've been practicing twice a day and you end up having to run a lap in the middle of practice, then come back and jump right back in. You try your best in practice not to make dumb penalties so you don't have to run, and it carries over to the game."

Would you want a manager to help build your career by using such punishment tactics on you? Explain.

As a manager, would you use punishment to help build the careers of your employees? Explain.

List two advantages and two disadvantages of punishment to build the careers of others.

Applying Behavior Modification Behavior modification programs have been applied both successfully and unsuccessfully in a number of organizations. Management at Emery Worldwide, for example, found that an effective feedback system is crucial to making a behavior modification program successful.[45] This feedback system should be aimed at keeping employees informed of the relationship between various behaviors and their consequences.

Other ingredients of successful behavior modification programs are the following:[46]

1. Giving different levels of rewards to different workers according to the quality of their performances
2. Telling workers what they are doing wrong
3. Punishing workers privately in order not to embarrass them in front of others
4. Always giving out rewards and punishments that are earned to emphasize that management is serious about its behavior modification efforts

The behavior modification concept is also being applied to cost control in organizations, with the objective of encouraging employees to be more cost conscious. Under this type of behavior modification program, employees are compensated in a manner that rewards cost control and cost reduction and penalizes cost acceleration.[47]

Recently, managers have added another component to the behavior modification process that identifies the role of cognitions in workplace behavior.[48] More specifically, when tackling problems such as inappropriate corporate culture, managers may recognize a need to change the way that employees think about corporate culture in addition to the way that they behave. Cognitive behavior modification programs are best implemented by an expert outside consultant who can identify negative cognitive and behavioral processes. Even though these programs have demonstrated much promise, further empirical analysis is necessary to solidify their place in the corporate environment.

Likert's Management Systems Another strategy that managers can use to motivate organization members is based on the work of Rensis Likert, a noted management scholar.[49] After studying several types and sizes of organizations, Likert concluded that management styles in organizations can be categorized into the following systems:

- **System 1**—This style of management is characterized by a lack of confidence or trust in subordinates. Subordinates do not feel free to discuss their jobs with superiors and are motivated by fear, threats, punishments, and occasional rewards. Information flow in the organization is directed primarily downward; upward communication is viewed with great suspicion. The bulk of all decision making is done at the top of the organization.

- **System 2**—This style of management is characterized by a condescending master-to-servant–style confidence and trust in subordinates. Subordinates do not feel free to discuss their jobs with superiors and are motivated by rewards and actual or potential punishments. Information flows mostly downward; upward communication may or may not be viewed with suspicion. Although policies are made primarily at the top of the organization, decisions within a prescribed framework are made at lower levels.

- **System 3**—This style of management is characterized by substantial, though not complete, confidence in subordinates. Subordinates feel fairly free to discuss their jobs with superiors and are motivated by rewards, occasional punishments, and some involvement. Information flows both upward and downward in the organization. Upward communication is often accepted, though at times, it may be viewed with suspicion. Although broad policies and general decisions are made at the top of the organization, more specific decisions are made at lower levels.

- **System 4**—This style of management is characterized by complete trust and confidence in subordinates. Subordinates feel completely free to discuss their jobs with superiors and are motivated by such factors as economic rewards based on a compensation system developed through employee participation and involvement in goal setting. Information flows upward, downward, and horizontally. Upward communication is generally accepted—but even where it is not, employees' questions are answered candidly. Decision making is spread widely throughout the organization and is well coordinated.

Styles, Systems, and Productivity Likert has suggested that as management style moves from system 1 to system 4, the human needs of individuals within the organization tend to be more effectively satisfied over the long term. Thus, an organization that moves toward system 4 tends to become more productive over the long term.

Figure 17.7 illustrates the comparative long- and short-term effects of both system 1 and system 4 on organizational production. Managers may increase production in the short term by using a system 1 management style, because motivation by fear, threat, and punishment is generally effective in the short run. Over the long run, however, this style usually causes production to decrease, primarily because of the long-term nonsatisfaction of organization members' needs and the poor working relationships between managers and subordinates.

Conversely, managers who initiate a system 4 management style will probably face some decline in production initially but will see an increase in production over the long term. The short-term decline occurs because organization members must adapt to the new system management is implementing. The production increase over the long term materializes as a result of organization members' adjustment to the new system, greater satisfaction of their needs, and good working relationships that develop between managers and subordinates.

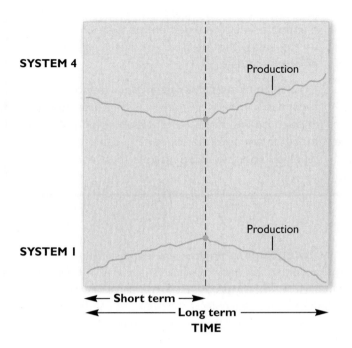

SYSTEM 4

Production

SYSTEM I

Production

← **Short term** →

← **Long term** →

TIME

FIGURE 17.7
Comparative long-term and short-term effects of system 1 and system 4 on organizational production

This long-term production increase under system 4 can also be related to decision-making differences in the two management systems. Because decisions reached in system 4 are more likely to be thoroughly understood by organization members than decisions reached in system 1, decision implementation is more likely to be efficient and effective in system 4 than in system 1.

Monetary Incentives A number of firms make a wide range of money-based compensation programs available to their employees as a form of motivation. For instance, employee stock ownership plans (ESOPs) motivate employees to boost production by offering them shares of company stock as a benefit. Managers are commonly given stock bonuses as an incentive to think more like an owner and ultimately do a better job of building a successful organization. Other incentive plans include lump-sum bonuses—one-time cash payments— and gain-sharing, a plan under which members of a team receive a bonus when their team exceeds a goal. All of these plans link pay closely to performance.[50] Many organizations have found that by putting more of their employees' pay at risk, they can peg more of their total wage costs to sales, which makes expenses more controllable in a downturn.[51]

class discussion highlight

MODERN RESEARCH AND MOTIVATION SKILL

Responses to Monetary Incentives: Men vs. Women

A recent study by Harry J. Paarsch and Bruce S. Shearer investigated the impact of monetary incentives on the behavior of men versus women.[52] The researchers studied the behavior of workers of a tree-planting firm in British Columbia, Canada. The firm actually replants or reforests areas where pine trees have been harvested. The mechanics of reforestation are straightforward. Prior to harvesting of any tract of pine timber, pine cones are taken from the trees on the tract, and seedlings are grown from the seeds contained in these cones. This process ensures that the seedlings to be replanted on the tract are compatible with the local climate and soil. The tree planting itself is simple, yet physically demanding. Planting involves digging a hole with a special shovel, placing a seedling in this hole, and then covering its roots with soil. When planting, workers must ensure that the tree is upright and that the roots are fully covered. The effort required to plant seedlings depends on the terrain on which the planting is done.

In the study, an incentive was established to be paid for each tree planted by a worker. Men and women workers were paid the same incentive for planting a tree. Management paid the incentive to try to raise the number of seedlings workers planted in a day.

Do you think that the researchers found that the incentive's impact on men was different from the impact on women? Why? Assuming that your thoughts are accurate, what hints can this research give you about developing your motivation skill?

Nonmonetary Incentives A firm can also keep its employees committed and motivated by nonmonetary means. For instance, some companies have a policy of promoting from within. They go through an elaborate process of advertising jobs internally before going outside to fill vacancies. Another nonmonetary incentive emphasizes quality, on the theory that most workers are unhappy when they know their work goes to producing a shoddy product.[53]

{CHALLENGE CASE SUMMARY

Motivation is an inner state that causes individuals to act in certain ways that ensure the accomplishment of some goal. Jack Cooper in the Challenge Case seems to have an accurate understanding of the motivation process. He is focusing on influencing the behavior of his employees to enhance the success of his digital strategy program at Bristol-Myers Squibb. Cooper encourages employees within the company to be creative and efficient in implementing digital strategy. Cooper's focus on motivation should be a valuable tool in making his Internet strategy implementation efforts effective.

To motivate employees at Bristol-Myers Squibb, Cooper must keep five specific principles of human motivation clearly in mind: (1) felt needs cause behavior aimed at reducing those needs, (2) the degree of desire to perform a particular behavior is determined by an individual's perceived value of the result of performing the behavior and the perceived probability that the behavior will cause the result to materialize, (3) the perceived value of a reward for a particular behavior is determined by both intrinsic and extrinsic rewards that result in need satisfaction when the behavior is accomplished, (4) individuals can effectively accomplish a task only if they understand what the task requires and have the ability to perform the task, and (5) the perceived fairness of a reward influences the degree of satisfaction generated when the reward is received.

Jack Cooper undoubtedly understands the basic motivation principle that felt needs cause behavior. Before managers can have maximum impact on motivating their organization members, they must meet the more complex challenge of being thoroughly familiar with various individual human needs of their employees.

According to Maslow, people generally possess physiological needs, security needs, social needs, esteem needs, and self-actualization needs arranged in a hierarchy of importance. Argyris suggests that as people mature, they have increasing needs for activity, independence, flexibility, deeper interests, analyses of longer time perspectives, a position of equality with other mature individuals, and control over personal destiny. McClelland believes that the need for achievement—the desire to do something better or more efficiently than it has ever been done before—is a strong human need.

By guaranteeing every worker a position with no pay cuts as part of the Internet strategy implementation program, Cooper could focus on satisfying employee physiological and safety needs. Other possible features of Cooper's implementation program to further motivate employees could be "Best Implementer of the Month" or "Best Implementation Idea of the Week" to focus on other needs that employees might have.

Once a manager understands that felt needs cause behavior and is aware of people's different types of needs, he is ready to apply this information to motivating his workforce. From Cooper's viewpoint, motivating employees means furnishing them with the opportunity to satisfy their human needs by performing their jobs. This notion is especially important because successful motivation tends to increase employee productivity. If Cooper does not furnish his employees with an opportunity to satisfy their human needs while working, low morale within the company will eventually develop. Signs of this low morale might be only a few employees initiating new ideas, people avoiding the confrontation of tough situations, and employees resisting innovation.

What does the preceding information recommend that Cooper actually do to motivate employees involved in his digital strategy implementation efforts? One strategy he might follow is taking time to communicate with his employees. Manager–employee communication can help satisfy employee needs for recognition, belonging, and security. Another of Cooper's strategies might be based on McGregor's Theory X–Theory Y concept. In following this concept when dealing with employees, Cooper should assume that work is as natural as play; that employees can be self-directed in goal accomplishment; that the granting of rewards encourages the achievement of implementation objectives; that employees seek and accept responsibility; and that most employees are creative, ingenious, and imaginative. The adoption of such assumptions by Cooper can lead to satisfying many of the needs defined by Maslow, Argyris, and McClelland.

Jack Cooper could use two major job design strategies to motivate his employees at Bristol-Myers Squibb. With job enrichment, Cooper can incorporate into employee jobs such motivating factors as opportunities for achievement, recognition, and personal growth. Cooper's allowing workers to transfer back and forth among work teams and not work on just one product can be viewed as a type of job enrichment allowing workers opportunities for personal growth. However, for maximum success, hygiene factors at Bristol-Myers Squibb—company policy and administration, supervision, salary,

and working conditions, for example—also should be perceived as desirable by employees.

The second major job design strategy that Cooper can use to motivate his employees is flextime. With flextime, his employees could have some freedom in scheduling the beginning and ending of workdays. This freedom could be somewhat limited by organizational factors such as the urgency of Internet strategy implementation or the availability of skilled employees to perform implementation jobs.

Jack Cooper can apply behavior modification to his situation at Bristol-Myers Squibb by rewarding appropriate employee behavior and punishing inappropriate employee behavior. Punishment has to be used carefully, however. If used continually, the working relationship between Cooper and his employees can be destroyed. For the behavior modification program to be successful, Cooper has to furnish employees with feedback on which behaviors are appropriate and inappropriate, to give workers different rewards depending on the quality of their performance, to tell workers what they were doing wrong, to punish workers privately, and to consistently give rewards and punishments when earned.

To use Likert's system 4 management style to motivate employees over the long term, Cooper has to demonstrate complete confidence in his workers and to encourage workers to feel completely free to discuss problems with him. In addition, communication among those involved in digital strategy implementation at Bristol-Myers Squibb has to flow freely in all directions within the organization structure, with upward communication discussed candidly. Cooper's decision-making process under system 4 has to involve many employees. Cooper can use the principle of supportive relationships as the basis for his system 4 management style. No single strategy mentioned in this chapter for motivating organization members would necessarily be more valuable to managers such as Cooper than any of the other strategies. In reality, Cooper will probably find that some combination of all of these strategies is most useful in motivating Internet strategy implementation workers at Bristol-Myers Squibb.

MANAGEMENT SKILL ACTIVITIES

This section is specially designed to help you develop motivation skill. An individual's motivation skill is based upon an understanding of motivation concepts and the ability to apply those concepts in management situations. The following activities are designed both to heighten your understanding of motivation fundamentals and to develop your ability to apply those concepts in various management situations.

UNDERSTANDING MOTIVATION CONCEPTS

This section is comprised of activities that will sharpen your understanding of motivation concepts. Answer essay questions as completely as possible. Complete Exploring Your Management Skill: Part 2 as directed. Also, remember that additional true/false and multiple choice questions appear online at MyManagementLab.com to help you further refine your understanding of motivation.

Essay Questions

1. Write out the equation for the expectancy theory of motivation. How can you use this equation to improve your motivation skill? Be specific.

2. Is Maslow's hierarchy of needs useful to managers? Why?

3. Describe your maturity level according to Argyris's maturity-immaturity continuum. What insights about your human needs does this description give you?

4. Which strategy for motivating organization members presented in the chapter would you find easiest to implement? Why? Which would you find most difficult to use? Why?

5. Discuss your personal opinion about how to use positive reinforcement, negative reinforcement, and punishment in motivating organization members. Which of the three do you think is the most important ingredient of behavior modification? Explain.

Developing Management Skill

Learning activities in this section are aimed at helping you to develop motivation skill. Learning activities include Exploring Your Management Skill: Part 2, Experiential Exercise, Cases, and a VideoNet exercise.

EXPLORING YOUR MANAGEMENT SKILL: PART 2

As you recall, you completed Exploring Your Management Skill: Part 1 before you started to study this chart. Your responses gave you an idea of how much you initially knew about motivation and helped you to focus on important points as you studied the chapter. Answer the Exploring Your Management Skill questions again now (p. 416) and compare your score to the first time you took it. This comparison will give you an idea of how much you have learned from studying this chapter and pinpoint areas for further clarification before you start studying the next chapter. Record your answers within the text or go to MyManagementLab.com. Recording your answers in MyManagementLab will allow you to get immediate results and see how your score compares to your classmates. If you answer the questions in the book, the answers are located in the Exploring Your Management Skill Appendix at the end of the book.

YOUR MANAGEMENT SKILLS PORTFOLIO

Your Management Learning Portfolio is a collection of activities especially designed to demonstrate your management knowledge and skill. By completing these activities online at MyManagementLab.com, you will be able to print, complete with cover sheet, as many activities as you choose. Be sure to save your work. Taking your printed portfolio to an employment interview could be helpful in obtaining a job.

The portfolio activity for this chapter is Motivating Workers at Honda of America. Read the highlight about Honda of America and answer the questions that follow.

Motivating Workers at Honda of America

In 1977 Honda, a Japanese company, announced plans to build a motorcycle manufacturing plant in the United States, and in 1980 announced plans to build an automobile manufacturing facility in the same area. Since these announcements, Honda's history has been nothing but impressive. To highlight this success, the Marysville Auto Plant now produces the Accord Coupe for export to Japan, Honda of America has become a leading auto exporter in the United States, and the motorcycle plant produced its one-millionth unit of the Gold Wing motorcycle. Many maintain that the following belief statement, which appears prominently on the Honda of America Web site, is a primary reason for the company's success:

Activities

You have just been contacted to interview for the top management position at Honda of America. You would be responsible for both automobile and motorcycle manufacturing. Before you visit the Marysville facility for a series of face-to-face interviews, however, you have been asked to answer the following questions related to your own beliefs about how managers should handle people. Answer the following questions in preparation for your trip to Marysville.

1. What role do you think that individual needs of people play in building a successful company?

2. What insights do you have about building employee commitment to the success of Honda of America?

_____

_____

_____

3. Do you believe that maintaining fair pay in Honda's Maryville plants is important? Why?

_____

_____

_____

4. What is your personal philosophy about using "job design" as a tool for motivating Honda of America employees?

_____

_____

_____

5. What management style would you use at Honda of America? Discuss its short- and long-term implications on production levels.

_____

_____

_____

EXPERIENTIAL EXERCISE: ANALYZING STUDY RESULTS

Directions. Read the following scenario and then perform the listed activities. Your instructor may want you to perform the activities as an individual or within groups. Follow all of your instructor's directions carefully.

You are part of a special task force established by the human resources department of a farm equipment manufacturing company. The company has 2,200 employees, 405 of which are managers at various organizational levels. The assignment of your task force is to analyze the results of a survey recently completed by managers within the company and to recommend

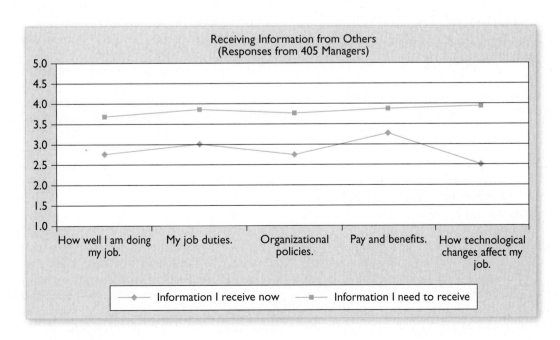

whatever action might be necessary, if any, given your opinions about survey results.

The following chart summarizes survey results concerning manager beliefs about the amount of information they receive from others in the company regarding how well their job is being done, their job duties, organizational policies, pay and benefits, and how technology changes within the company affect their jobs. According to survey results, managers believe that they need more information in all areas in order to do their job properly.

Activity

Your instructor will divide your class into small groups and appoint a discussion leader for each group. Assuming the role of the task force and answer the following questions.

After discussion has been completed, your instructor will lead the class in a discussion regarding the opinions of all groups.

1. Do you believe that the results are having a negative effect within the company on the level of managers' commitment to attaining organizational success? Explain.
2. Given survey results and Maslow's hierarchy of needs, discuss the extent to which you believe managers' personal needs are being met within the organization. Explain.
3. Given your thoughts in #1 & #2, what action would you recommend (if any) should be taken to improve the level of organizational success? Explain. Be as specific as possible.

CASES

MOTIVATION SAVVY MANAGEMENT AT BRISTOL-MYERS SQUIBB ENSURES CUTTING-EDGE INTERNET PRESENCE

"Motivation Savvy Management at Bristol-Myers Squibb Ensures Cutting-Edge Internet Presence" (p. 415) and its related Challenge Case Summary were written to help you better understand the management concepts contained in this chapter. Answer the following discussions about the Challenge Case to better understand how motivation concepts can be applied in a company such as Bristol-Myers Squibb.

1. Do you think it would be unusual for a manager such as Jack Cooper to spend a significant portion of his time motivating his workforce? Explain.
2. Which of the needs on Maslow's hierarchy of needs could implementing Internet strategy at Bristol-Myers Squibb help satisfy? Why? If you have omitted one or more of the needs, explain why the implementation would not satisfy those needs.
3. Is it possible for Cooper's efforts to be successful in motivating workers yet detrimental to organizational success? Explain.

THE CONTAINER STORE'S MOTIVATING EXPERIENCE

Read the case and answer the questions that follow. Studying this case will help you better understand how motivation concepts can be applied in a company such as The Container Store.

Being cited on *Fortune* magazine's annual list of "100 Best Companies to Work For" is quite an honor—but only a special firm can place among the top three for five consecutive years. That company is The Container Store, a 30-store chain selling storage products to help customers organize homes and offices. In an industry where the employee turnover rate can exceed 100 percent per year, The Container Store stands out for the stability and commitment of its workforce. Its annual turnover in full-time employees is just 8 percent; for part-timers, the annual turnover is 20 percent, far below that of a typical retail firm. Yet even as The Container Store approaches its thirtieth year in business, it continues to emphasize recruiting, training, and retaining exceptional employees as it opens new stores in an aggressive growth strategy.

Retailers usually say that the key to a store's success is "location, location, location." Location is certainly important, but The Container Store's main claim to fame is personalized customer service with a smile. Its store personnel are always ready, willing, and able to help customers select just the right components to solve any storage problem. Money may be part of the reason: On average, salaries at the Container Store are 50 to 100 percent higher than salaries at most other retail establishments, and the benefits are more generous, as well. "People wonder how we can afford to do that," explains CEO and co-founder Kip Tindell, "but we respond that in a service-oriented business, how can you afford not to?"

Chairman and co-founder Garrett Boone believes that his store employees work for more than money: "You have to work for a common cause," he says. Tindell goes even further, saying, "We think the employer has a huge moral obligation to make employees want to get out of bed and come to work in the morning." How does The Container Store do this?

Tindell points to his company's focus on "the basic people side of our business, educating and empowering [employees], giving them the tools they need to service our customers to the fullest." Each new full-time salesperson receives 235 hours of training during the first year; each new part-timer receives more than 100 hours of training in the first year. Kevin Fuller, director of training and recruiting, remembers feeling proud, respected, and confident after undergoing this intensive training. "It makes you do a better job and give back 110 percent to the company," he notes.

Communication is another key factor. "The way to retain employees, to make them care, is to communicate everything to them," CEO Tindell says. By "everything," he means not just product information but also chain-wide goals, daily sales results, and many facts and figures usually available only to the most senior managers. There are risks, he acknowledges, "but we decided a long time ago that the advantages of communicating information that empowers our employees and strengthens their development and loyalty far outweighs the disadvantages of that information falling into the hands of competitors."

Finally, The Container Store believes in saying "thank you" for a job well done. After closing time, store employees gather and recognize those who made a special effort that day. Some of these stories make their way to the "celebration mailbox," a voicemail system where employees and managers can record compliments to be heard by anyone in the company. Employees who have been with

The Container Store for five years receive a tiny wooden box, a smaller version of the cash box that Tindell and Boone used when they launched their first store. For their 10-year anniversary, employees (and their spouses) receive a trip to Dallas and are feted by the co-founders at dinner in their honor. Working at The Container Store is not just about making a living, Boone says: "The people here give an effort that goes far beyond the economic rewards, because they love it here."

QUESTIONS

1. How does The Container Store use behavior modification to motivate its employees?
2. Do you think The Container Store would be as successful if its managers applied Theory X assumptions? Why?
3. Use the Porter–Lawler theory of motivation to explain the effect of the intrinsic and extrinsic rewards that The Container Store's employees receive from their work.

VIDEONET EXERCISE

Motivating Employees at KPMG

VIDEO HIGHLIGHTS

When Bruce Pfau was hired as vice-chair of Human Resources at KPMG, the company was in trouble: Employee satisfaction was at an all-time low, and turnover was high. He had to turn the place around. A transformation this big could only happen with the full support of senior management. Bruce used employee surveys to find out what employees really wanted, and he delivered. While compensation matters, many folks develop a loyalty to KPMG because of other benefits. Working mom Liz Harper has a new lease on life thanks to her alternative work arrangement involving a flexible schedule and a shorter work week. (Liz had left KPMG 12 years ago because she wasn't able to juggle the demands of her

job and her new family.) Other employees chime in about what makes them tick.

Discussion Questions

1. Which of the process theories of motivation explains the choice of benefits used by KPMG?
2. Using the job enrichment concept, does the benefit package offered by KPMG motivate people to work harder? Explain.
3. Does top management at KPMG hold Theory X or Theory Y assumptions about the nature of man? Explain.

Internet Activity

Go to the KPMG Web site at www.kpmg.com. Combining what you learned at the Web site with what you learned via the video, would you be a motivated worker at KPMG? Why?

18 Groups and Teams

OBJECTIVES

TO HELP BUILD MY TEAM SKILL, WHEN STUDYING THIS
CHAPTER, I WILL ATTEMPT TO ACQUIRE:

1. A definition of the term *group* as used in the context of management

2. A thorough understanding of the difference between formal and informal groups

3. Knowledge of the types of formal groups that exist in organizations

4. An understanding of how managers can determine which groups exist in an organization

5. An appreciation for what teams are and how to manage them

TARGET SKILL

team skill: the ability to manage a collection of people so that they influence one another toward the accomplishment of an organizational objective(s)

CHALLENGE CASE

TEAMWORK SPREADS AT XEROX

Xerox Corporation is a global leader in providing document solutions that enhance business productivity. Company focus is on developing, manufacturing, marketing, servicing, and financing a complete range of document-processing products designed to make organizations more productive. The company's digital output includes color copiers and printers with production speeds ranging from 20 to 65 pages per minute.

Xerox manages an extremely complex logistics system that focuses on asset management, which entails tracking and coordinating thousands of pieces of equipment at hundreds of customer work locations. The company must keep track of the specific equipment requirements involving issues such as space, electricity, cooling, network connectivity, supplies, and maintenance. Solutions also have to be developed for helping customer organizations coordinate equipment service, related training, and ordering of supplies from almost anywhere in the world.

Asset management at Xerox also involves the proper billing of customers. Customers must be billed for every single piece of equipment based on its specific usage, and they need invoices that clearly delineate equipment usage costs but don't overwhelm with too much information.

Another component of Xerox's asset management includes providing outstanding service and support to customers who can call a toll-free number with questions, problems, and requests related to thousands of equipment assets. At Xerox, after equipment is sold or leased, the formidable challenge of technical support begins.

Many of Xerox's most successful initiatives in asset management depend on the work of teams that cooperate closely to keep customers' document-processing products working effectively.

According to company officials, asset management at Xerox is a challenging and labor-intensive job. Alan Asher, one of the managers, believes that successful asset management requires a tremendous amount of coordination and is exceedingly difficult to pull off, because you must have processes in place that are really detailed and really tight, or things can fall through the cracks.

One of the firm's American offices has had some success because of a small, tightly knit work team, but it has had to confront a serious problem in operations: managing fleets of office equipment at multiple sites from a remote location. Evelyn Grubb, the customer account manager of the office explains: "We've got a group of people here that truly works together. It's really a family. Everyone works together. If we didn't have that spirit here, none of this would have happened."

Learning from the success of this team in Houston, Xerox management is encouraging the spread of teamwork into a number of different organizational areas. The company's recent use of teams to design successful new products for the marketplace has been particularly impressive.[1]

> "EXPLORE YOUR OWN MANAGEMENT SKILLS BY TAKING THE QUIZ ON THE NEXT PAGE"

Before studying this chapter, respond to the following questions regarding the type of advice that you would give to Xerox's Alan Asher, referenced in the Challenge Case. Then address the concerning team challenges that managers face within the company. You are not expected to be a team expert at this point. Answering the questions now can help you focus on important points when you study the chapter. Also, answering the questions again after you study the chapter will give you an idea of how much you have learned.

Record your answers here or go to MyManagement Lab.com. Recording your answers in MyManagementLab will allow you to get immediate results and see how your score compares to your classmates. If you answer the questions in the book, the answers are located in the Exploring Your Management Skill section at the end of the book.

FOR EACH STATEMENT CIRCLE:

- "Y" if you would give the advice to Asher.
- "N" if you would NOT give the advice to Asher.
- "NI" if you have no idea whether you would give the advice to Asher.

Mr. Asher, in meeting your team challenges at Xerox, you should . . .

Before Study   *After Study*

1. try to eliminate informal groups whenever possible.
   Y, N, NI

2. incorporate "groupthink" into your team process to increase the accuracy of team decisions.
   Y, N, NI

3. know that the acceptance stage of formal group development is characterized by group members communicating frankly to one another.
   Y, N, NI

4. try to increase the overall desirability of the work environment by encouraging the development of informal groups.
   Y, N, NI

5. try to apply the basic concepts of sociometry in attempting to determine the members of informal groups.
   Y, N, NI

6. remember that informal groups commonly develop to provide safety and growth for their members, which is more difficult to obtain through formal group membership.
   Y, N, NI

7. know that *groups* and *teams* are synonymous concepts.
   Y, N, NI

8. understand that teams you establish can be self-managed as well as cross-functional.
   Y, N, NI

9. help developing teams to work though "norming" before "performing."
   Y, N, NI

10. try to bypass "storming" in the team development process.
    Y, N, NI

11. sometimes enhance organizational stability and job security to enhance team effectiveness.
    Y, N, NI

12. try to build effective work teams by developing clear objectives and deemphasizing technical direction.
    Y, N, NI

13. build trust a team has for you by being predictable.
    Y, N, NI

14. sometimes demonstrate your competence to build trust a team has for you.
    Y, N, NI

15. focus on building trust as opposed to open communication in building team effectiveness.
    Y, N, NI

THE TEAM CHALLENGE

The Challenge Case highlights the important role that teams play in the success of operations at Xerox. The material in this chapter should help managers such as those at Xerox to gain insights about how to successfully manage teams. This chapter (1) defines groups, (2) discusses the kinds of groups that exist in organizations, (3) explains what steps managers should take to manage groups appropriately, and (4) explains team management.

The previous chapters in Part 5 dealt with three primary activities of the influencing function: communication, leadership, and motivation. This chapter focuses on managing teams, the last major influencing activity to be discussed in this text. As with the other three activities, managing teams requires guiding the behavior of organization members in ways that increase the probability of reaching organizational objectives.

GROUPS

To deal with groups appropriately, managers must have a thorough understanding of the nature of groups in organizations.[2] As used in management-related discussions, a **group** is not simply a gathering of people. Rather, it is "any number of people who (1) interact with one another, (2) are psychologically aware of one another, and (3) perceive themselves to be a group."[3] Groups are characterized by frequent communication among members over time and a size small enough to permit each member to communicate with all other members on a face-to-face basis. As a result of this communication, each group member influences and is influenced by all other group members.

The study of groups is important to managers because the most common ingredient of all organizations is people and the most common technique for accomplishing work through these people is dividing them into work groups. In a classic article, Cartwright and Lippitt list four additional reasons why managers should study groups:[4]

1. Groups exist in all kinds of organizations.
2. Groups inevitably form in all facets of organizational existence.
3. Groups can cause either desirable or undesirable consequences within the organization.
4. An understanding of groups can help managers raise the probability that the groups with which they work will cause desirable consequences within the organization.[5]

KINDS OF GROUPS IN ORGANIZATIONS

Organizational groups are typically divided into two basic types: formal and informal.

Formal Groups

A **formal group** is a group that exists within an organization by virtue of management decree to perform tasks that enhance the attainment of organizational objectives.[6] Figure 18.1 is an organization chart showing a formal group. The placements of organization

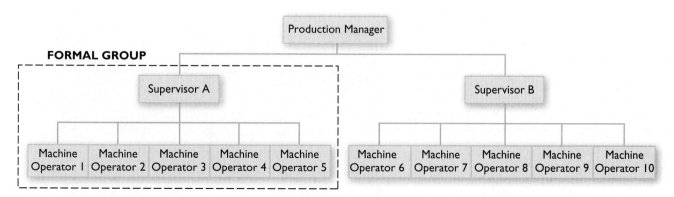

FIGURE 18.1 A formal group

members in such areas as marketing departments, personnel departments, and production departments are examples of establishing formal groups.

Actually, organizations are made up of a number of formal groups that exist at various organizational levels. The coordination of and communication among these groups is the responsibility of managers, or supervisors, commonly called "linking pins."

Formal groups are clearly defined and structured. The next sections discuss the basic kinds of formal groups, examples of formal groups as they exist in organizations, and the four stages of formal group development.

Kinds of Formal Groups

Formal groups are commonly divided into command groups and task groups. **Command groups** are formal groups that are outlined in the chain of command on an organization chart. They typically handle routine organizational activities.

Task groups are formal groups of organization members who interact with one another to accomplish most of the organization's nonroutine tasks. Although task groups are usually made up of members on the same organizational level, they can consist of people from different levels in the organizational hierarchy.[7] For example, a manager might establish a task group to consider the feasibility of manufacturing some new product and include representatives from various levels of such organizational areas as production, market research, and sales.[8]

Examples of Formal Groups

Two formal groups that are often established in organizations are committees and work teams. Committees are the more traditional formal group; work teams have only recently become more prevalent organizations. The part of this text dealing with the managerial function of organizing emphasized command groups; however, the examples here emphasize task groups.

Committees

A **committee** is a group of individuals charged with performing some type of specific activity and is usually classified as a task group. From a managerial viewpoint, committees are established for four major reasons:[9]

1. To allow organization members to exchange ideas
2. To generate suggestions and recommendations that can be offered to other organizational units
3. To develop new ideas for solving existing organizational problems
4. To assist in the development of organizational policies

Committees exist in virtually all organizations and at all organizational levels. As Figure 18.2 suggests, however, the larger the organization, the greater the probability that it will use committees on a regular basis. The following two sections discuss why managers should use committees and what makes a committee successful.

FIGURE 18.2

Percent of companies that have committees, by size of company

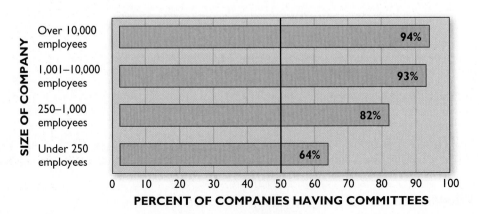

WHY MANAGERS SHOULD USE COMMITTEES Managers generally agree that committees have several uses in organizations.

- Committees can improve the quality of decision making. As more people become involved in making a decision, the strengths and weaknesses of various alternatives tend to be discussed in greater detail and the chances of reaching a higher-quality decision increase.

- Committees encourage the expression of honest opinions. Committee members feel protected enough to say what they really think because the group output of a committee cannot be associated with any one member of that group.

- Committees also tend to increase organization members' participation in decision making and thereby enhance the chances of widespread support of decisions. Another result of this increased participation is that committee members satisfy their social or self-esteem needs through committee work.

- Finally, committees ensure the representation of important groups in the decision-making process. Managers must choose committee members wisely, however, to achieve appropriate representation, for if a committee does not adequately represent various interest groups, any decision it comes to may well be counter to the interests of some important organizational group.[10]

Although executives vary somewhat in their enthusiasm about using committees in organizations, a study reported by McLeod and Jones concludes that most executives favor using committees. The executives who took part in this study said they got significantly more information from organizational sources other than committees, but found the information from committees more valuable than the information from any other source. Nevertheless, some top executives express only qualified support for using committees as work groups, and others had negative feelings toward committees. Still, the executives who feel positively about committees or who display qualified acceptance of them in general outnumber those who look upon committees negatively.

WHAT MAKES COMMITTEES SUCCESSFUL Although committees have become an accepted management tool, managerial action taken to establish and run them is a major variable in determining their degree of success.

A committee is a team charged with a specific task. It is most successful when that task is clearly defined and the committee is given appropriate authority for decision making.

Procedural Steps Several procedural steps can be taken to increase the probability that a committee will be successful:[11]

- The committee's goals should be clearly defined, preferably in writing, in order to focus the committee's activities and reduce the time members devote to discussing just what it is the committee is supposed to be doing.

- The committee's authority should be specified. Is it merely to investigate, advise, and recommend, or is it authorized to implement decisions?

- The optimum size of the committee should be determined. With fewer than 5 members, the advantages of group work may be diminished. With more than 10 or 15 members, the committee may become unwieldy. Although optimal size varies with the circumstances, the ideal number of committee members for most tasks seems to be from 5 to 10.

- A chairperson should be selected on the basis of ability to run an efficient meeting—that is, the ability to keep committee members from getting bogged down in irrelevancies and to see to it that the necessary paperwork gets done.

- Appointing a permanent secretary to handle communications is often useful.

- The agenda and all supporting material for the meeting should be distributed before the meeting takes place. When members have a chance to study each item beforehand, they are likely to stick to the point and be prepared to make informed contributions.

- Meetings should start on time, and their ending time should be announced at the outset.

People-Oriented Guidelines In addition to these procedural steps, managers can follow a number of more people-oriented guidelines to increase the probability that a committee will succeed. In particular, a manager can raise the quality of committee discussions by doing the following:[12]

- **Rephrasing ideas already expressed**—This rephrasing ensures that the manager as well as other people on the committee clearly understand what has been said.

- **Bringing all members into active participation**—Every committee member is a potential source of useful information, so the manager should serve as a catalyst to spark individual participation whenever appropriate.

- **Stimulating further thought by members**—The manager should encourage committee members to think ideas through carefully and thoroughly, for only this type of analysis will generate high-quality committee output.

Groupthink Managers should also help the committee avoid a phenomenon called "groupthink." **Groupthink** is the mode of thinking that group members engage in when the desire for agreement so dominates the group that it overrides the need to realistically appraise alternative problem solutions.[13] Groups tend to slip into groupthink when their members become overly concerned about being too harsh in judging one another's ideas and lose their objectivity.[14] Such groups tend to seek complete support on every issue to avoid conflicts that might endanger the "we-feeling" atmosphere.[15]

Groupthink, a term initially established by Irving Janis, occurs in five stages. The first stage, antecedents, describes what precursors are associated with the development of groupthink. For example, a group with a high level of cohesiveness is likely to be susceptible to groupthink. The second stage, concurrence seeking, occurs when a group member agrees with the entire group's position, even when the group member might privately oppose the entire group's position. The third stage, symptoms of groupthink, occurs as group members feel pressure to conform and censor their own ideas. The fourth stage, decision-making defects, occurs when group members fail to make effective decisions. An example of decision-making defects occurs when a group does not collect the needed information in order to make an effective decision. The fifth stage, poor decision outcomes, occurs when the group performs poorly. It is important to recognize the different stages of groupthink so that they can be identified and rectified quickly in the workplace.

Work Teams **Work teams** are another example of task groups used in organizations. Contemporary work teams in the United States evolved out of the problem-solving teams—based on Japanese-style quality circles—that were widely adopted in the 1970s.[16] Problem-solving teams consist of 5 to 12 volunteer members from different areas of the department who meet weekly to discuss ways to improve quality and efficiency.

SPECIAL-PURPOSE AND SELF-MANAGED TEAMS Special-purpose teams evolved in the early to middle 1980s out of problem-solving teams. The typical special-purpose team consists of workers and union representatives meeting together to collaborate on operational decisions at all levels. The aim is to create an atmosphere conducive to quality and productivity improvements.

Special-purpose teams laid the foundation for the self-managed work teams that arose in the 1990s, and it is these teams that appear to be the wave of the future. Self-managed teams consist of 5 to 15 employees who work together to produce an entire product. Members learn all the tasks required to produce the product and rotate from job to job. Self-managed teams even take over such managerial duties as scheduling work and vacations and ordering materials. Because these work teams give employees so much control over their jobs, they represent a fundamental change in how work is organized. (Self-managed teams will be discussed in some detail later in this chapter.)

Employing work teams allows a firm to draw on the talent and creativity of all its employees, not just a few maverick inventors or top executives, to make important decisions. As product quality becomes more and more important in the business world, companies will need to rely more and more on the team approach in order to stay competitive. Consider a recent situation at Yellow Freight Systems, a shipping company whose management was intent on giving its customers excellent service. To address this concern, management established a work team made up of employees from many different parts of the company, including marketing, sales, operations, and human resources. The overall task of the work team was to run an excellence-in-service campaign that management had initiated.[17]

Stages of Formal Group Development Another requirement for successfully managing formal groups is understanding the stages of formal group development. In a classic book, Bernard Bass suggested that group development is a four-stage process that unfolds as the group learns how to use its resources.[18] Although these stages may not occur sequentially, for the purpose of clarity, the discussion that follows will assume that they do.

The Acceptance Stage It is common for members of a new group to mistrust one another somewhat initially. The acceptance stage occurs only after this initial mistrust melts and the group has been transformed into one characterized by mutual trust and acceptance.

The Communication and Decision-Making Stage Once they have passed through the acceptance stage, group members are better able to communicate frankly with one another. This frank communication provides the basis for establishing and using an effective group decision-making mechanism.

The Group Solidarity Stage Group solidarity comes naturally as the mutual acceptance of group members increases and communication and decision making continue within the group. At this stage, members become more involved in group activities and cooperate, rather than compete, with one another. Members find belonging to the group extremely satisfying and are committed to enhancing the group's overall success.

The Group Control Stage A natural result of group solidarity is group control. In this stage, group members attempt to maximize the group's success by matching individual abilities with group activities and by assisting one another. Flexibility and informality usually characterize this stage.

As a group passes through each of these four stages, it generally becomes more mature and effective—and therefore more productive. The group that reaches maximum maturity and effectiveness is characterized by the following traits in its members:

- **Members function as a unit**—The group works as a team. Members do not disturb one another to the point of interfering with their collaboration.

- **Members participate effectively in group effort**—Members work hard when there is something to do. They seldom loaf, even if they have the opportunity to do so.

- **Members are oriented toward a single goal**—Group members work for the common purpose; they do not waste group resources by moving in different directions.

- **Members have the equipment, tools, and skills necessary to attain the group's goals**—Members are taught the various parts of their jobs by experts and strive to acquire whatever resources they need to attain group objectives.

- **Members ask and receive suggestions, opinions, and information from one another**—A member who is uncertain about something stops working and asks another member for information. Group members generally talk to one another openly and frequently.

Informal Groups

Informal groups, the second major kind of group that can exist within an organization, are groups that develop naturally as people interact. An **informal group** is defined as a collection of individuals whose common work experiences result in the development of a system of interpersonal relations that extend beyond those established by management.[19]

As Figure 18.3 shows, informal group structures can deviate significantly from formal group structures. As is true of Supervisor A in the figure, an organization member can belong to more than one informal group at the same time. In contrast to formal groups, informal groups are not highly structured in procedure and are not formally recognized by management.

The next sections discuss the following subjects:

1. Various kinds of informal groups that exist in organizations
2. The benefits people usually reap from belonging to informal groups

Kinds of Informal Groups Informal groups are divided into two general types: interest groups and friendship groups. **Interest groups** are informal groups that gain and

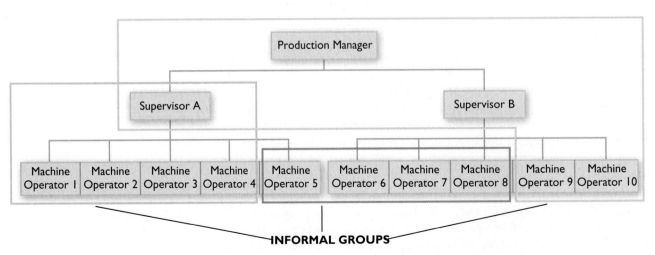

FIGURE 18.3 Three informal groups that deviate significantly from formal groups within the organization

maintain membership primarily because of a common concern members have about a specific issue. An example is a group of workers pressing management for better pay or working conditions. Once the interest or concern that instigated the formation of the informal group has been eliminated, the group will probably disband.

As its name implies, **friendship groups** are informal groups that form in organizations because of the personal affiliation members have with one another. Such personal factors as recreational interests, race, gender, and religion serve as foundations for friendship groups. As with interest groups, the membership of friendship groups tends to change over time. Here, however, membership changes as friendships dissolve or new friendships are made.

Benefits of Informal Group Membership

Benefits of Informal Group Membership Informal groups tend to develop in organizations because of various benefits that group members obtain:[20]

1. Perpetuation of social and cultural values that group members consider important
2. Status and social satisfaction that people might not enjoy without group membership
3. Increased ease of communication among group members
4. Increased desirability of the overall work environment

These benefits may be one reason that employees who are on fixed shifts or who continually work with the same groups tend to be more satisfied with their work than employees whose shifts are continually changing.

MANAGING WORK GROUPS

To manage work groups effectively, managers must simultaneously consider the effects of both formal and informal group factors on organizational productivity. This consideration requires two steps:

1. Determining group existence
2. Understanding the evolution of informal groups

Determining Group Existence

The most important step that managers need to take in managing work groups is to determine what informal groups exist within the organization and who their members are. **Sociometry** is an analytical tool managers can use for this purpose. They can also use sociometry to get information on the internal workings of an informal group, including the identity of the group leader, the relative status of group members, and the group's communication networks.[21] This information on informal groups, combined with an understanding of the established formal groups shown on the organization chart, will give managers a complete picture of the organization's group structure.

Sociometric Analysis The procedure for performing a sociometric analysis in an organization is quite basic. Various organization members simply are asked, through either an interview or a questionnaire, to name several other organization members with whom they would like to spend free time. A sociogram is then constructed to summarize the informal relationships among group members. **Sociograms** are diagrams that visually link individuals within the population queried according to the number of times they were chosen and whether the choice was reciprocated.

Applying the Sociogram Model Figure 18.4 shows two sample sociograms based on a classic study of two groups of boys in a summer camp—the Bulldogs and the Red Devils. An analysis of these sociograms leads to several interesting conclusions. First,

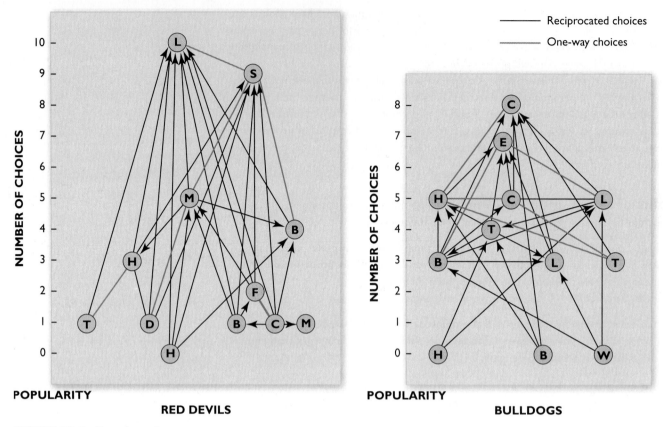

FIGURE 18.4 Sample sociograms

more boys within the Bulldogs than within the Red Devils were chosen as being desirable to spend time with. The implication is that the Bulldogs are a closer-knit informal group than the Red Devils. Second, the greater the number of times an individual was chosen, the more likely it was that the individual would be the group leader. Thus, individuals C and E in Figure 18.4 are probably Bulldog leaders, while L and S are probably Red Devil leaders. Third, communication between L and most other Red Devils members is likely to occur directly, whereas communication between C and other Bulldogs is likely to pass through other group members.

Sociometric analysis can give managers many useful insights concerning the informal groups within their organization. Managers who do not want to perform a formal sociometric analysis can at least casually gather information on what form a sociogram might take in a particular situation. They can pick up this information through normal conversations with other organization members as well as through observations of how various organization members relate to one another.

Understanding the Evolution of Informal Groups

As we have seen, the first prerequisite for managing groups effectively is knowing what groups exist within an organization and what characterizes the membership of those groups. The second prerequisite is understanding how informal groups evolve. This understanding will give managers some insights on how to encourage the development of appropriate informal groups, that is, groups that support the attainment of organizational objectives and whose members maintain good relationships with formal work groups.

Informal groups like this one provide status, social satisfaction, and ease of communication among members, as well as other personal and organizational benefits.

Homans Model   Perhaps the most widely accepted framework for explaining the evolution of informal groups was developed by George Homans.[22] Figure 18.5 broadly summarizes his theory. According to Homans, the informal group is established to provide satisfaction and growth for its members. At the same time, the sentiments, interactions, and activities that emerge within an informal group result from the sentiments, interactions, and activities that already exist within a formal group. Given these two premises, it follows that feedback on the functioning of the informal group can give managers ideas about how to modify the formal group so as to increase the probability that informal group members will achieve the satisfaction and growth they desire. The ultimate consequence will be to reinforce the solidarity and productiveness of the formal group—to the advantage of the organization.

Applying the Homans Model   To see what Homans's concept involves, suppose that 12 factory workers are members of a formal work group that manufactures toasters. According to Homans, as these workers interact to assemble toasters, they might discover common personal interests that encourage the evolution of one or more informal groups that would maximize the satisfaction and growth of their members. Once established, these informal groups will probably resist changes in the formal work group that threaten the satisfaction and growth of the informal group's members. On the other hand, modifications in the formal work group that enhance the satisfaction and growth of the informal group's members will tend to be welcomed.

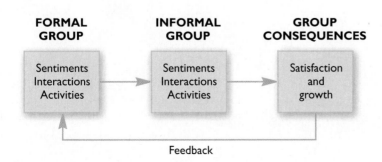

FORMAL GROUP → **INFORMAL GROUP** → **GROUP CONSEQUENCES**

Sentiments Interactions Activities → Sentiments Interactions Activities → Satisfaction and growth

Feedback

FIGURE 18.5
Homans's ideas on how informal groups develop

TEAMS

The preceding sections of this chapter discussed groups—what they are, what kinds exist in organizations, and how such groups should be managed. This section focuses on a special type of group: teams. It covers the following topics:

1. Difference between groups and teams
2. Types of teams that exist in organizations
3. Stages of development that teams go through
4. What constitutes an effective team
5. Relationship between trust and team effectiveness

Groups Versus Teams

The terms *group* and *team* are not synonymous. As we have seen, a group consists of any number of people who interact with one another, are psychologically aware of one another, and think of themselves as a group. A **team** is a group whose members influence one another toward the accomplishment of an organizational objective(s).

Not all groups in organizations are teams, but all teams are groups. A group qualifies as a team only if its members focus on helping one another to accomplish organizational objectives.[23] In today's quickly changing business environment, teams have emerged as a requirement for success.[24] Therefore, good managers constantly try to help groups become teams. This part of the chapter provides insights on how managers can facilitate the evolution of groups into teams.

Types of Teams in Organizations

Organizational teams take many different forms. The following sections discuss three types of teams commonly found in today's organizations: problem-solving teams, self-managed teams, and cross-functional teams.

Problem-Solving Teams Management confronts many different organizational problems daily. Examples are production systems that are not manufacturing products at the desired levels of quality, workers who appear to be listless and uninvolved, and managers who are basing their decisions on inaccurate information.

Teams operate in all kinds of situations. The members of race-car pit crew must depend on one another to get the job done, with each contributing expertise in a particular task.

For assistance in solving such formidable problems, management commonly establishes special teams. A team set up to help eliminate a specified problem within the organization is called a **problem-solving team.**[25] The typical problem-solving team has 5 to 12 members and is formed to discuss ways to improve quality in all phases of the organization, to make organizational processes more efficient, or to improve the overall work environment.[26]

After the problem-solving team reaches a consensus, it makes recommendations to management about how to deal with the specified problem. Management may respond to the team's recommendations by implementing them in their entirety, by modifying and then implementing them, or by requesting further information to assess them. Once the problem that management asked the problem-solving team to address has been solved, the team is generally disbanded.

Self-Managed Teams The **self-managed team,** sometimes called a *self-managed work group* or *self-directed team,* is a team that plans, organizes, influences, and controls its own work situation with only minimal intervention and direction from management.[27] This creative team design involves a highly integrated group of several skilled individuals who are cross-trained and have the responsibility and authority to perform some specified activity.

Activities typically carried out by management in a traditional work setting—creating work schedules, establishing work pace and breaks, developing vacation schedules, evaluating performance, determining the level of salary increases and rewards received by individual workers, and ordering materials to be used in the production process—are instead carried out by members of the self-managed team. Generally responsible for whole tasks as opposed to "parts" of a job,[28] the self-managed team is an important new way of structuring, managing, and rewarding work. Because these teams require only minimum management attention, they free managers to pursue other management activities such as strategic planning.

Reports of successful self-managed work teams are plentiful.[29] These teams are growing in popularity because today's business environment seems to require such work teams to solve complex problems independently, because American workers have come to expect more freedom in the workplace, and because the speed of technological change demands that employees be able to adapt quickly. Not all self-managed teams are successful. To ensure the success of a self-managed team, the manager should carefully select and properly train its members.[30]

class discussion highlight

MODERN RESEARCH AND TEAM SKILL

Predicting the Attributes of Effective Self-Managed Teams[31]

A recent study by Duimering and Robinson investigated the behavioral characteristics of a self-managed team. More specifically, the study investigated a self-directed team in a large manufacturing firm over a period of six months. The firm produced industrial electronics products at several international locations and the study was conducted in its largest North American factory. The plant employed approximately 200 management and support staff and 450 unionized production workers in four departments: Circuit Pack Assembly, Frame Assembly, Final Assembly, and System Test. Corporate management had directed local factory managers to implement self-directed teams as part of an improvement program called "Team Directed Work Force." Training materials and courses were provided for production employees and managers. The study began approximately four months after the launch of the Team Directed Work Force program.

A primary purpose of the research was to describe how a self-managed effective team behaved. Management wished to understand the characteristics of successfully implemented self-managed teams and hoped to duplicate them in other parts of the factory.

List five specific behaviors that you predict the researchers found that characterize the behaviors of an effective self-managed team. Would it be difficult for managers to duplicate such characteristics in other work teams? Explain.

Cross-Functional Teams A **cross-functional team** is a work team composed of people from different functional areas of the organization—marketing, finance, human resources, and operations, for example—who are all focused on a specified objective.[32] Cross-functional teams may or may not be self-managed, though self-managed teams are generally cross-functional. Because cross-functional team members are from different departments within the organization, the team possesses the expertise to coordinate all the department activities within the organization that affect its own work.[33]

Some examples of cross-functional teams are teams established to choose and implement new technologies throughout the organization, teams formed to improve marketing effectiveness within the organization, and teams established to control product costs.[34]

This section discussed three types of teams that exist in organizations: problem-solving, self-directed, and cross-functional. It should be noted here that managers can establish various combinations of these three types of teams. Figure 18.6 illustrates some possible combinations that managers could create. For example, *a* in the figure represents a team that is problem-solving, self-directed, and cross-functional, while *b* represents one that is problem-solving, but neither cross-functional nor self-directed. Before establishing a team, managers should carefully study their own unique organizational situation and set up the type of team that best suits that situation.

STAGES OF TEAM DEVELOPMENT

More and more modern managers are using work teams to accomplish organizational tasks. Simply establishing such a team, however, does not guarantee it will be productive. In fact, managers should be patient when an established work team is not initially productive, for teams generally need to pass through several developmental stages before they become productive. Managers must understand this developmental process so they can facilitate it. The following sections discuss the various stages a team usually must pass through before it becomes fully productive.[35]

FIGURE 18.6

Possible team types based on various combinations of self-directed, problem-solving, and cross-functional teams

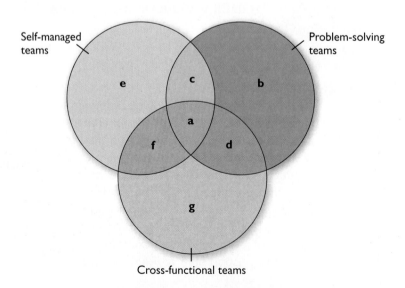

Forming **Forming** is the first stage of the team development process. During this stage, members of the newly formed team become oriented to the team and acquainted with one another. This period is characterized by exploring issues related to the members' new job situation, such as what is expected of them, who has what kind of authority within the team, what kind of people are team members, and what skills team members possess.

The forming stage of team development is usually characterized by uncertainty and stress. Recognizing that team members are struggling to adjust to their new work situations and to one another, managers should be tolerant of lengthy, informal discussions exploring team specifics and not regard them as time wasters. The newly formed team must be allowed an exploratory period if it is to become truly productive.

Storming After a team has formed, it begins to storm. **Storming,** the second stage of the team development process, is characterized by conflict and disagreement as team members become more assertive in clarifying their individual roles. During this stage, the team seems to lack unity because members are continually challenging the way the team functions.

To help the team progress beyond storming, managers should encourage team members to feel free to disagree with any team issues and to discuss their own views fully and honestly. Most of all, managers should urge team members to arrive at agreements that will help the team reach its objective(s).

Norming When the storming stage ends, norming begins. **Norming,** the third stage of the team development process, is characterized by agreement among team members on roles, rules, and acceptable behavior while working on the team. Conflicts generated during the storming stage are resolved in this stage.

Managers should encourage teams that have entered the norming stage to progress toward developing team norms and values that will be instrumental in building a successful organization. The process of determining what behavior is and is not acceptable within the team is critical to the work team's future productivity.

Performing The fourth stage of the team development process is **performing.** At this stage, the team fully focuses on solving organizational problems and on meeting assigned challenges. The team is now productive: After successfully passing through the earlier stages of team development, it knows itself and has settled on team roles, expectations, and norms.

During this stage, managers should recognize the team's accomplishments regularly, for productive team behavior must be reinforced to enhance the probability that it will continue in the future.

Adjourning The fifth, and last, stage of the team development process is known as **adjourning.** Now the team is finishing its job and preparing to disband. This stage normally occurs only in teams established for some special purpose to be accomplished in a limited time period. Special committees and task groups are examples of such teams. During the adjourning stage, team members generally feel disappointment that their team is being broken up because disbandment means the loss of personally satisfying relationships or an enjoyable work situation.

During this phase of team development, managers should recognize team members' disappointment and sense of loss as normal and assure them that other challenging and exciting organizational opportunities await them. It is important that management then do everything necessary to integrate these people into new teams or other areas of the organization.

Although some work teams do not pass through every one of the development stages just described, understanding the stages of forming, storming, norming, performing, and adjourning will give managers many useful insights on how to build productive work teams. Above all, managers must realize that new teams are different from mature teams and that their challenge is to build whatever team they are in charge of into a mature, productive work team.[36]

Team Effectiveness

Earlier in this chapter, teams were defined as groups of people who influence one another to reach organizational targets. It is easy to see why effective teams are critical to organizational success. Effective teams are those that come up with innovative ideas, accomplish their goals, and adapt to change when necessary.[37] Their individual members are highly committed to both the team and organizational goals. Such teams are highly valued by upper management and recognized and rewarded for their accomplishments.[38]

Figure 18.7 sketches the characteristics of an effective team. Note the figure's implications for the steps managers need to take to build effective work teams in organizations. *People-related steps* include the following:[39]

1. Trying to make the team's work satisfying
2. Developing mutual trust among team members and between the team and management
3. Building good communication—from management to the team as well as within the team
4. Minimizing unresolved conflicts and power struggles within the team
5. Dealing effectively with threats toward and within the team
6. Building the perception that the jobs of team members are secure

Organization-related steps managers can take to build effective work teams include:

1. Building a stable overall organization or company structure that team members view as secure
2. Becoming involved in team events and demonstrating interest in team progress and functioning
3. Properly rewarding and recognizing teams for their accomplishments
4. Setting stable goals and priorities for the team

Finally, Figure 18.7 implies that managers can build effective work teams by taking six *task-related steps:*

1. Developing clear objectives, directions, and project plans for the team
2. Providing proper technical direction and leadership for the team
3. Establishing autonomy for the team and challenging work within the team

FIGURE 18.7
Factors contributing to team effectiveness

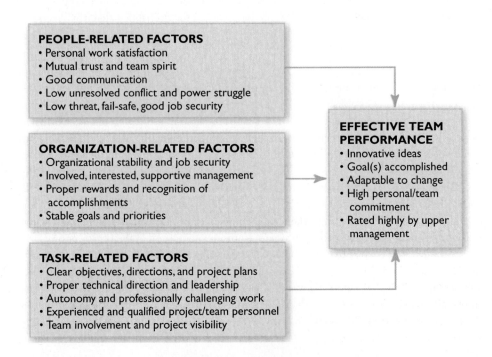

4. Appointing experienced and qualified team personnel
5. Encouraging team involvement
6. Building visibility within the organization for the team's work

Modern managers must focus on building the effectiveness of not only domestic teams, but global teams. Consider the following **example from the world of management** concerning the building of the effectiveness of global teams.[40] In the past, the effectiveness of global teams was mainly reached by simply having bodies and factories on the ground in various countries with the activities of these global teams being carefully and methodically coordinated by headquarters. Today, however, the challenge is much different. Globally dispersed teams must be built into highly effective, sometimes even self-managed teams. Because of the ever-changing and fast-moving nature of the competition, workers spread across the globe must be able to communicate and collaborate instantly. Fortunately for modern managers, the Internet is available to enable such collaboration. Managers must remember, however, that the availability of the Internet in itself does not guarantee that global teams will be effective. The appropriate use of the Internet by global teams, however, can be a significant contributor to their effectiveness.

Trust and Effective Teams

Probably the most fundamental ingredient of effective teams is trust. Trust is belief in the reliance, ability, and integrity of another. Unless team members trust one another, the team leader, and management, managers may well find that building an effective work team is impossible.[41]

Today the concern is that management is not inspiring the kind of trust that is essential to team effectiveness. In fact, subordinates' trust in their managers is critically low, and employee opinion polls indicate that it may well decline even further in the future.

Management urgently needs to focus on reversing this trend.[42] Managers can use a number of different strategies to build trust within groups.[43]

* **Communicate often to team members**—This is a fundamental strategy. Keeping team members informed of organizational news, explaining why certain decisions have been made, and sharing information about organizational operations are examples of how managers should communicate to team members.

    As **an example from the world of management** concerning communicating often with team members to build trust, consider a profile of Burberry's president Angela Ahrendts. Burberry is considered the quintessential British fashion house offering British fashion elegance throughout the world. Ahrendts has become known as a people-oriented manager, communicating often with members of her team. According to Stacey Cartwright, the company's chief financial officer, Ahrendts is collaborative, likes to gather her team around her, and seems energized by the debates within the team. Ahrendts knows that such communication with her team will almost certainly help to build trust within the team, which should significantly contribute to team success.[44]

* **Show respect for team members**—Managers need to show team members that they are highly valued. They can demonstrate their respect for team members by delegating tasks to them, listening intently to feedback from the group, and acting on it appropriately.

* **Be fair to team members**—Team members must receive the rewards they have earned. Managers must therefore conduct fair performance appraisals and objectively allocate and distribute rewards. It should go without saying that showing favoritism in this area sows mistrust and resentment.

* **Be predictable**—Managers must be consistent in their actions. Team members should usually be able to forecast what decisions management will make before those decisions

Effective teamwork is built on trust. When conductor Michael Tilson-Thomas works with an orchestra, he trusts the musicians to know their parts thoroughly, while they trust his vision of the music they are to perform.

are made. Moreover, managers must live up to commitments made to team members. Managers who make inconsistent decisions and fail to live up to commitments will not be trusted by teams.

- **Demonstrate competence**—To build team trust, managers must show team members that they are able to diagnose organizational problems and have the skill to implement solutions to those problems. Team members tend to trust managers they perceive as competent and distrust those they perceive as incompetent.

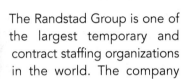

class discussion highlight

TWO-PERSON TEAMS AND YOUR CAREER[45]

The Randstad Group is one of the largest temporary and contract staffing organizations in the world. The company has subsidiaries in Europe, North America, and Asia with about 13,000 employees. On average, the company places about of 250,000 people in other companies every day. The company is trying to win the loyalty of its own young employees by pairing them in two-person teams with older, more experienced employees. Every new sales agent is assigned a partner to work with until their business

has grown to a certain size, which usually takes a few years. Neither person is "the boss." Each employee is expected to teach the other. Then they both start over again with someone who has just joined the company. The company's motto is "Nobody should be alone."

Would you like to start your career in this program? Why? As an experienced hand, would you like to be involved in this program about mid-career? Why? Why do you think the company instituted this program?

{CHALLENGE CASE SUMMARY

In order for managers to be able to manage work they need to understand the definition of the term *group*, and they need to understand that several types of groups exist in organizations. A group at Xerox or any other organization is any number of people who interact, who are psychologically aware of each other, and who perceive themselves as a group. A company such as Xerox is made up of formal groups, the groups that appear on the company's organization charts, such as the marketing department. Managers of groups act as the "linking pins" among departments. The ability of Xerox managers to coordinate and communicate with these groups and their success in dealing with their own departments are certainly important factors in the future success of the company as a whole.

At times, managers at Xerox can form new groups to handle some of the more nonroutine challenges. For example, management could form a task group by choosing two people from each of several different departments and

getting them together on developing a new and more efficient system for improving company asset management procedures. Then, as with any other organization, Xerox also has informal groups (those that do not appear on the organization chart) to consider. More discussion on informal groups will follow later in this Challenge Case Summary.

Xerox management could decide to form a committee to achieve some specific goal. For example, a committee might be formed on how to enhance the quality of copiers offered by Xerox, which could allow various departments to exchange quality improvement ideas and generate related suggestions to management. Such a committee could improve Xerox decision making in general by encouraging honest feedback from employees about quality issues in the organization. It could also be used to get fresh ideas about enhancing product quality, and to encourage Xerox employees to participate more seriously in improving the quality of equipment offered by the company. This approach would help to ensure that all appropriate departments are represented in important quality decisions, so when Xerox takes action to improve the quality of its copiers, for example, every important angle would be considered, including design, production, marketing, sales, and so on.

In managing such a quality committee at Xerox, management should encourage the members to take certain steps that can help the committee to be successful, because a poorly run committee wastes a lot of time. For example, the committee should develop a clear definition of its goals and the limits of its authority: Is it just going to come up with quality improvement ideas, or should it also take the initial steps toward implementing its ideas?

In addition, the quality committee should not have too few or too many members. Issues such as appointing a secretary to handle communications and appointing a chairperson who is people-oriented must be addressed. Such a quality committee needs someone who can rephrase ideas clearly to ensure that everyone understands; and someone who can get members to participate and think about the issues while avoiding "groupthink": Original ideas should be generated by the committee, not by a unanimous opinion because everyone is trying to avoid conflict.

Managers in companies such as Xerox must be patient and understand that it will take some time for a new group to develop into a productive working unit. The members in any new work group must start by trusting and accepting one another and then begin communicating and exchanging ideas. Once this acceptance and communication increases, group solidarity and control come naturally. The group members get involved, cooperate, and try to maximize the group's success.

With the quality committee that is being used as an example, Xerox management must be patient and let it mature before maximum effectiveness and productivity can be expected. If given time to grow, the group will function as a unit, members will participate willingly and effectively, and the group will reach valuable decisions about what needs to be done to improve the quality of equipment that Xerox offers.

Other issues regarding informal groups could affect the success of work groups at Xerox. Employee groups get together at times because of certain issues. For example, certain minority employees could get together as a group to increase the opportunities for their professional growth at Xerox; and employees form friendship groups, which ease communication and provide feelings of satisfaction in a company. In general, such informal groups can improve the work environment for everyone involved, so it can be advantageous for management to encourage their development.

Perhaps Xerox management could accelerate the development of a quality committee into a productive unit by including individuals who already know and trust one another through membership in one or more informal groups at Xerox. For example, some members of the newly formed quality committee might know and trust one another immediately as a result of membership on a company bowling or softball team. Under such circumstances, a trust developed among employees through past informal group affiliations could help the formal quality committee to develop into a productive group more quickly.

In order for a company such as Xerox to be successful, managers must be able to consider how both formal and informal groups affect organizational productivity, and they need to determine what informal groups exist, know who the group members are, and understand how these groups form. Armed with this information, Xerox management can strive to make their work groups more effective.

One way management can get information about the groups at Xerox is to use sociometry. A questionnaire can be designed asking their employees with whom they spend time and a sociogram can be constructed to summarize this information. Managers could also do a more casual analysis by just talking to their employees and observing how they interact with one another.

Managers in a company such as Xerox should try to understand how informal groups evolve and should be aware that an organization's formal structure influences how the informal groups develop within it. For example, assume that in one department at Xerox, 30 people work on copier design. Many of them are interested in sports, have become friends because of this common interest, and work well together as a result. If a manager needed to make some changes in such a department, he or she should try to accommodate such informal friendship groups to keep employees satisfied. Only with very good reason should a manager of such a department damage the existence of the productive friendship group by transferring any informal group members out of the design department.

Managers in a company such as Xerox should consider the four major factors that influence work-group effectiveness. First, the size of the work group can be important to its productivity. A 20-person quality committee would probably be somewhat large and would hamper the group's effectiveness. Remember also, however, that managers should consider informal groups before making changes in group size. The quality committee could end up being less productive without one or more of its respected members than it would be if it were slightly too large.

Another important factor that influences work group effectiveness is group cohesiveness, because a more cohesive group will tend to be more effective. The Challenge Case mentions that the cohesiveness of the asset management work group at Xerox's Houston office was instrumental in its success. Evelyn Grubb increased the cohesiveness of her formal asset management group by doing such things as allowing members to take breaks together or rewarding informal group members for a job well done.

Group norms, or appropriate behaviors required within the informal group, are a third factor that affects the productivity of formal group behavior. Because these norms affect profitability, managers must be aware of them and understand how to influence them within the formal group structure. For example, assume that a smaller informal group of workers within Xerox's asset management department normally maintains the quality of asset management by focusing mainly on tracking the durability of Xerox equipment. Unfortunately, because of this quality norm, the informal group members are taking too much time tracking durability and too little time servicing customer requests via e-mail feedback. Management could try to improve this situation by giving bonuses to group members who best service e-mail requests while tracking equipment durability. This reward would probably increase the formal group productivity while encouraging a positive norm within the informal group.

Status within the informal groups also affects work group productivity. For example, if Xerox managers want to increase productivity for a group, management should try to encourage the informal group's leaders, as well as the group's formal supervisor. Chances are that a targeted group will become more productive if its informal, high-status members support that objective.

Overall, if the company wants to maximize work group effectiveness, management must remember both the formal and informal dimensions of its work groups while considering the four main factors that influence work group productivity.

MANAGEMENT SKILL ACTIVITIES

This section is specially designed to help you develop team skill. An individual's team skill is based upon an understanding of team concepts and the ability to apply those concepts in management situations. The following activities are designed to both heighten your understanding of team concepts and to develop the ability to apply those concepts in a variety of management situations.

UNDERSTANDING TEAM CONCEPTS

This section is comprised of activities that will sharpen your understanding of team concepts. Answer essay questions as completely as possible. Also, remember that many additional true/false and multiple choice questions appear online at MyManagementLab.com to help you further refine your understanding of team concepts.

Essay Questions

1. What is the difference between formal and informal groups? Explain how you would manage each type of group in helping an organization achieve success.

2. What is the difference between a group and a team?

3. As a manager, would you ever create a team that is both problem-solving and cross-functional? Explain.

4. What signs would you look for as a manager to indicate that a team in your organization is "storming"? What would you do if the team was indeed "storming"? Why?

5. What is the role of trust in building effective teams? As a manager, how would you build trust within a team?

Developing Management Skill

Learning activities in this section are aimed at helping you to develop management skill. Learning activities include Exploring Your Management Skill: Part 2, Your Management Skill Portfolio, Experiential Exercise, Cases, and a VideoNet exercise.

EXPLORING YOUR MANAGEMENT SKILL: PART 2

As you recall, you completed Exploring Your Management Skill before you started to study this chapter. Your responses gave you an idea of how much you initially knew about teams and helped you to focus on important points as you studied the chapter. Answer the Exploring Your Management Skill questions again now (p. 440) and compare your score to the first time you took it. This comparison will give you an idea of how much you have learned from studying this chapter and pinpoint areas for further clarification before you start studying the next chapter. Record your answers within the text or go to MyManagementLab.com. Recording your answers in MyManagementLab will allow you to get immediate results and see how your score compares to your classmates. If you answer the questions in the book, the answers are located in the Exploring Your Management Skill Appendix at the end of the book.

YOUR MANAGEMENT SKILLS PORTFOLIO

Your Management Learning Portfolio is a collection of activities especially designed to demonstrate your management knowledge and skill. By completing these activities online at MyManagementLab.com, you will be able to print, complete with cover sheet, as many activities as you choose. Be sure to save your work. Taking your printed portfolio to an employment interview could be helpful in obtaining a job.

The portfolio activity for this chapter is *Using Committees and Teams in Accomplishing Florida Hospital's Mission.*

Read the following highlight about Florida Hospital and answer the questions that follow.[46]

Using Committees and Teams in Accomplishing Florida Hospital's Mission

Florida Hospital, a Christian-based Adventist Health System hospital, is an acute-care health care system with 3,025 beds throughout Central Florida. Florida Hospital treats more than one million patient visits each year. In fact, the Florida Hospital system is the busiest system in the country. For the last six years, *U.S. News & World Report* has recognized Florida Hospital as one of "America's Best Hospitals."

Florida Hospital offers a wide range of health services for the entire family, including many nationally and internationally recognized programs in cardiology, cancer, diabetes, and digestive health. Because Florida Hospital performs more complex cardiac procedures than any other facility in the country, MSNBC selected Florida Hospital as the premier focus of their hour long special—"Heart Hospital."

Florida Hospital's mission statement appears in Exhibit 1.

EXHIBIT 1   Florida Hospital Mission Statement

To Our Patients

Our first responsibility as a Christian hospital is to extend the healing ministry of Christ to all patients who come to us. We endeavor to deliver high-quality service, showing concern for patients' emotional and spiritual needs, as well as their physical condition. It is our desire to serve patients promptly, with consideration and dignity.

To Our Employees

We are responsible to our employees and depend upon their teamwork. We show concern for the whole person, respecting each worker's individuality and listening to each one's concerns and suggestions. We pay fair wages and offer clean and safe working conditions. We provide opportunities for our employees' professional growth and development.

To Our Medical Staff

We are responsible to the doctors who are the leaders of the medical team. We provide them with a professional environment, state-of-the-art medical facilities and equipment, and trained support staff. We strive to process their requests for patient care accurately and in a timely manner.

To Our Community

We are responsible to our community both as an organization and as individuals. We must be a strong corporate citizen with interests in the total community welfare, not just those aspects in which we have a business interest. We maintain and use our buildings and grounds to enhance the interest of the community.

To Our Future

We are responsible for the future success and security of our institution's resources. We protect our financial investments through responsible fiscal management, strategic planning and effective marketing. We cultivate and protect the preferred patronage of patients, doctors and businesses.

To Our Religious Heritage

In response to the Seventh-day Adventist faith and heritage upon which Florida Hospital is built, we celebrate the healing ministry of our Lord, encourage preventive health care practices, respect the seventh-day Sabbath, and observe high moral and ethical standards.

To Our God

We are responsible to communicate through caring service that God is a loving, gracious and protecting Father who places infinite value on every individual and is worthy of our admiration, affection and willing commitment.

Learning Activity

Assume that you are the president of Florida Hospital and have decided to establish a hospital-wide committee to monitor and ensure the accomplishment of the hospital's mission. Answer the following questions to outline how you would form this committee and mold it into an effective work team.

1. What reason(s) could you use to explain to your employees why you are instituting this committee at Florida Hospital?

_____

_____

_____

2. List four procedures that you will have the committee follow as it does its work. Be sure to explain the value of each procedure.

Procedure 1:

_____

_____

_____

Value of Procedure 1:

_____

_____

_____

Procedure 2:

_____

_____

_____

Value of Procedure 2:

_____

_____

_____

Procedure 3:

_____

_____

_____

Value of Procedure 3:

_____

_____

_____

Procedure 4:

_____

_____

_____

Value of Procedure 4:

_____

_____

_____

3. Outline what you would say to the committee to encourage it to function as a team as opposed to a group.

_____

_____

_____

4. Would you make the committee aware of the stages of team development? Explain.

_____

_____

_____

5. How would you help the committee members to develop trust for one another? Be as specific as possible.

_____

_____

_____

EXPERIENTIAL EXERCISE: PLANNING YOUR TEAM DEVELOPMENT PROGRAM

Directions. Your instructor will divide your class into small groups of about five and appoint a discussion leader for each group. Each group is to evaluate the Mountain Top Game that appears here as a team-building activity. Decide whether you would use the activity as a real manager trying to build a real team in your organization. You would be the instructor or the one actually administering the game. Be sure to explain why the group does or does not believe that the exercise would be useful. After all groups have finished discussion, the instructor will lead a discussion of the entire class focused on conclusion of the small groups.

Mountain Top Game[47]

Objective:

For group members to work together for the good of the group

Group Size:

8 to 15 is ideal

Materials:

- A rope hanging from the ceiling (i.e., gym climbing rope)
- Rope or other boundary marker
- 2 coffee cans or similar height blocks or cans
- 1 pole, stick, or piece of pipe about 1" in diameter

Procedure for Administering the Game:

Set up the two coffee cans with a pole set horizontally across them about three or four feet to one side of the rope. On the other side of the rope, use a different piece of rope to make a circle that the whole group can stand in. For added challenge make the circle small so the group must work together to stand in it without falling out of the boundary. This circle should be about three to four feet from the rope as well.

(continued)

Mountain Top Game[47] (Continued)

Set this activity up by telling a story that requires the group to get from a cliff to a mountaintop some distance away. Starting behind the "cliff" (pole) they must get hold of the climbing rope without stepping off the "cliff." Once they have the rope, they must swing across to the other side and land on the "mountain" (the rope circle). Only one person may go across at once at a time. If anyone steps out of the boundary, knocks the pole off of the cans, or touches the ground, the group must start over. For safety reasons, the leader should stand near the climbing rope to catch anyone who falls.

Possible Questions for Leading Discussion After the Game:

1. How did the group come up with a plan?

2. How did the order that you were in factor in to the plan?

3. How did you ensure that your teammates were safe during this activity?

4. How would this activity have been different if there was a real cliff and a real mountaintop?

5. Would you trust your teammates if it were real? Why or why not?

6. How can you build trust as a team?

Variations:

• Give group members things to carry with them to the mountain for an added challenge.

• Set up a low platform for the group to stand on in place of the circle.

C A S E S

TEAMWORK SPREADS AT XEROX

"Teamwork Spreads at Xerox" (p. 439) and its related Challenge Case Summary were written to help you better understand the management concepts contained in this chapter. Answer the following discussions about the Challenge Case to better understand how concepts relating to groups and teams can be applied in a company such as Xerox.

1. Describe the characteristics of an effective work team at Xerox.

2. As a manager at Xerox, what steps would you take to turn a work group into an effective team? Explain the importance of each step.

GOOGLE'S MOTTO OF "DON'T BE EVIL"

Read the case and answer the questions that follow. Studying this case will help you better understand how concepts relating to groups and teams can be applied in a company such as Google.

Sergey Brin and Larry Page are well aware that size matters. As graduate students at Stanford, the two envisioned a new technology for ranking Web search results based on relevance and the number of links to each site. By 1998, they had translated their ideas into action with the launch of a search site they called Google—now one of the most influential Internet firms on the planet. From its beginnings as a tiny Silicon Valley start-up, the company grew to 500 employees by 2002. By 2004, it was earning $350 million in profits, employed 3,000 people, and was hiring 3 new employees per day.

Even today, Google's growth spurt is far from over. With millions of dollars raised by selling stock to the public, the company is aggressively investing in new technology and pursuing new avenues for generating revenue. Meanwhile, it must fend off strong competition from Microsoft, Yahoo!, and other longer-established firms. In this pressured environment, the top management trio—consisting of CEO Eric Schmidt and the two co-founders—must grow Google in ways that are consistent with its traditions and strengths.

"Don't be evil," even if it means making less money, is Google's basic corporate tenet. "We believe strongly that in the long term, we will be better served—as shareholders and in all other ways—by a company that does good things for the world even if we forgo some short-term gains," Page and Brin wrote in a recent letter to prospective shareholders. "This is an important aspect of our company philosophy and is broadly shared within the company."

Yet because of Google's huge popularity, its executives are inevitably drawn into controversies that test their commitment to doing good. What should Google do about searches that turn up hate Web sites, for example? In countries where these sites are illegal, local Google versions omit them from search results. Where hate sites are not illegal, however, Google aims to remain neutral. After receiving complaints that a hate Web site topped the results for searches on a particular phrase, management posted a message alongside the listing to say "We're disturbed about these results as well"—but refused to make changes.

Top management maintains Google's creative strength by allowing all employees to spend one out of five working days on projects of their own devising. The most promising of these ideas ultimately become official projects and, if feasible, are developed into innovative features. This is how Google News, a search feature that enables users to scour the latest headlines, got its start. The co-founders observe: "Talented people are attracted to Google because we empower them to change the world; Google has large computational resources and distribution that enables individuals to make a difference. Our main benefit is a workplace with important projects, where employees can contribute and grow."

Brin, Page, and Schmidt facilitate collaboration by minimizing bureaucracy wherever possible. This is why Google lacks layers of middle management; it's also why meetings don't always start or end on time. Instead of isolating its 100-plus Ph.D.s in a separate research department, the company spreads them throughout the organization. Even if Internet technology is not exactly rocket science or brain surgery, Google employs both—a former rocket scientist and a former brain surgeon—as well as many computer science specialists. This eclectic workforce, which the *New York Times* calls an "unorthodox portfolio of human capital," sparks dynamic teamwork and yields breakthroughs that keep the company competitive and user-responsive.

Preserving Google's unique work environment will not be easy as the company matures and moves in new business directions. However, Page and Brin insist that "Google is not a conventional company. We do not intend to become one." With lava lamps in the lobby, free gourmet meals, free massages, even on-site washers and dryers so employees who work odd hours can do their laundry, Google has an internal climate all its own.

QUESTIONS

1. Which of the factors that contribute to team effectiveness seem to have been the most important to Google's success to date?

2. How does Google's management create opportunities for informal group structures to develop, and why?

3. What would you recommend that Schmidt, Brin, and Page do to perpetuate Google's unique work environment?

VIDEONET EXERCISE

Groups and Teams at Kluster

VIDEO HIGHLIGHTS

Teamwork is integral to Kluster. Back when Ben Kaufman was making iPod accessories, before Mophie morphed into Kluster, product development was a team effort. When Ben Kaufman's company shifted its focus to creating a new process, replete with sophisticated software and a Web site for involving a company's external communities in product development, the complicated task required a dream team. Meet some of the people who made the cut, and hear how their crazy team operates. What are the challenges of working with a bunch of young, high-energy, creative people who might not be the most focused or structured people in the world?

Discussion Questions

1. Would you describe the groups used at Kluster as formal or informal? Explain.

2. In the video clip, employees referred to their work arrangement by both the terms "group" and "team." Which do you think best applies?

3. Based on the evidence presented, which type of team is being used at Kluster? Which stage of development is this team in?

Internet Activity

Go to Kluster's home page at http://kluster.com. Discuss how the basic concepts of groups are at the core of their product and services offered.

19 Managing Organization Culture

OBJECTIVES

TO HELP BUILD MY ORGANIZATION CULTURE SKILL, WHEN STUDYING THIS CHAPTER, I WILL ATTEMPT TO ACQUIRE:

1. A definition of organization culture

2. An understanding of the importance of organization culture in building organizational success

3. Insights regarding the functions of organization culture

4. An appreciation for various types of cultures that can exist in organizations

5. Thoughts about how to build a high-performance organization culture

6. Tactics for keeping an organization culture alive and well

TARGET SKILL

organization culture skill: the ability to establish a set of shared values of organization members regarding the functioning and existence of their organization to enhance the probability of organizational success

CHALLENGE CASE

ESTABLISHING A SAFETY CULTURE AT BP[1]

BP, the world's second largest oil and gas company, produces about 3 percent of the oil and gas consumed in the world through operations in 100 countries. The company employs more than 104,000 employees around the world.[2] A chemical safety board's recent report on an explosion at BP a refinery, in the U.S. state of Texas, resulted in 15 deaths and 170 injuries, concluded that the company failed to establish a "corporate safety culture."

The board's report suggested that "BP should involve the relevant stakeholders to develop a positive, trusting and open safety culture within each U.S. refinery." Due to increased public scrutiny and media attention, companies around the world are becoming more savvy about the importance of creating a corporate culture around safety.

To create a culture of safety, companies need to make someone accountable for the effort. They need to put in place incentives to encourage safety and communicate the goals of the program to all employees. Even though BP had a code of conduct that it shared with employees, the code was generic and didn't provide specifics on what workers should be doing.

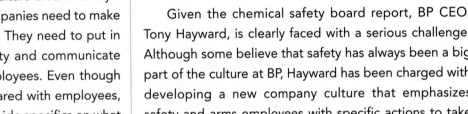

BP faces the challenge of reshaping its culture to restore a focus on safety first.

The chemical safety board report also reprimanded BP for being too focused on personal injuries as a metric for success. Instead, companies should focus on "process safety metrics," which include the company's goals, the report said. For example, instead of measuring injuries, companies should set goals on how many safety meetings each plant has in a quarter, then measure how well each plant meets that goal. Managers should measure the drivers within organizations that actually create a change in the culture. In addition, companies need to create incentives so employees feel comfortable reporting accidents or the potential for accidents. According to the report, BP did not have a trusting and open environment to facilitate these kinds of discussions.

Given the chemical safety board report, BP CEO, Tony Hayward, is clearly faced with a serious challenge. Although some believe that safety has always been a big part of the culture at BP, Hayward has been charged with developing a new company culture that emphasizes safety and arms employees with specific actions to take in safety crisis situations.

"EXPLORE YOUR OWN MANAGEMENT SKILLS BY TAKING THE QUIZ ON THE NEXT PAGE"

EXPLORING YOUR MANAGEMENT SKILL: PART 1

Before studying this chapter, respond to the following questions regarding the type of advice that you would give to BP's CEO Tony Hayward, referenced in the Challenge Case. Then address the concerning organization culture challenges that he presently faces within the company. You are not expected to be an organization culture expert at this point. Answering the questions now can help you focus on important points when you study the chapter. Also, answering the questions again after you study the chapter will give you an idea of how much you have learned.

Record your answers here or go to MyManagementLab.com. Recording your answers in MyManagementLab will allow you to get immediate results and see how your score compares to your classmates. If you answer the questions in the book, the answers are located in the Exploring Your Management Skill section at the end of the book.

FOR EACH STATEMENT CIRCLE:

- "Y" if you would give the advice to Hayward.
- "N" if you would NOT give the advice to Hayward.
- "NI" if you have no idea whether you would give the advice to Hayward.

Mr. Hayward, in meeting your organization culture challenges at BP, you should . . .

Before Study	After Study

1. aim at building shared values in organization members that will lead to organizational success.

   Y, N, NI

2. proceed with caution because the real value of establishing organization culture is still being debated vigorously.

   Y, N, NI

3. expect that once the culture is established, organization members will follow cultural artifacts like a code of conduct.

   Y, N, NI

4. strive to establish a clan culture if you want to focus on having a more regimented, stable organization.

   Y, N, NI

5. establish an adhocracy culture if you need an organization that is flexible, where people exercise discretion, and has an external focus.

   Y, N, NI

6. champion whatever culture you'd like to establish.

   Y, N, NI

7. use a hierarchy of objectives to help you encourage organization member performance.

   Y, N, NI

8. deemphasize building values because values often influence organization members to make somewhat emotional decisions.

   Y, N, NI

9. use sagas to emphasize historical issues of the past that can influence company success in the present.

   Y, N, NI

10. deemphasize using organizational symbols because they are too simplistic for building more complicated organizational values.

    Y, N, NI

11. reward organization members who perform behavior that reflects organization culture, beliefs, and values.

    Y, N, NI

12. consider applying organizational socialization concepts mainly for individuals who have been with the organization for more than five years.

    Y, N, NI

13. from time to time evaluate the cultural fit of new recruits.

    Y, N, NI

14. focus on monitoring and improving the health of organization culture.

    Y, N, NI

15. probably not consider emphasizing special dimensions of organization culture such as innovation or quality.

    Y, N, NI

THE ORGANIZATION CULTURE CHALLENGE

The Challenger Case illustrates corporate culture challenges that BP must meet. The remaining material in this chapter explains corporate culture concepts and helps to develop the corresponding corporate culture skill that you will need to meet such challenges throughout your career. After studying chapter concepts, read the Challenge Case Summary at the end of the chapter to help you to relate chapter content to meeting corporate culture challenges at BP.

FUNDAMENTALS OF ORGANIZATION CULTURE

This first chapter section is an introduction to the concept of organization culture. Major topics in this section focus on discussing both a definition of organization culture and the importance of organization culture. Overall, this section explains what organization culture is and tells why managing organization culture is a critical component of a manager's job.

Defining Organization Culture

Organization culture is a set of shared values that organization members have regarding the functioning and existence of their organization. Organization culture is not established at once by a manager, but evolves slowly over time. Basically, organization culture can be thought of as the personality of the organization, a description of how the organization functions. As such, organization culture has dimensions such as organizational rituals, special language, norms, and habits. Organization culture can be characterized in an organization by describing such dimensions. Management that understands the significance of all such dimensions can use them to develop an organization culture that is beneficial to the firm.[3]

At times, organization culture may seem to include an almost endless list of considerations, and managers can become frustrated trying to accurately define their cultures. As help to define a culture, research suggests that managers ask a few basic questions:[4]

1. Do people innovate and take risks?
2. Are people attentive to detail?
3. Are people focused on outcomes of what they do?
4. Is the organization sensitive to people?
5. Do people function as a team?
6. Are people in the organization aggressive?
7. Are people focused on maintaining the status quo?

Although discussions regarding organization culture seem to assume that only one culture exists within an organization, in fact, many subcultures can exist within an organization. An **organization subculture** is a mini-culture within an organization that can reflect the values and beliefs of a specific segment of an organization formed along lines such as established departments or geographic regions. Managers must be aware of subcultures that exist and how to manage them because subcultures can negatively or positively affect management efforts such as organizational planning.[5] In managing organization culture, managers sometimes have a tendency to manage only the **dominant organization culture,** the shared values about organizational functioning held by the majority of organization members.[6] In managing organization culture, it's normally advisable for managers to consider the characteristics and potential influence of an organization's dominant organization culture as well as organization subcultures.

The Importance of Organization Culture

Understanding and managing organization culture have become extremely important issues for modern managers in achieving organizational success. According to Michael Porter, a professor at Harvard Business School, organization culture is such an important issue that managers should not merely be taking it seriously as a sound idea, but embedding it into organizational strategy to help build a competitive advantage.[7] Many management writers believe an important prerequisite to organizational success is a manager's thorough understanding of organization culture concepts. Only through such an understanding can a manager begin to have impact on encouraging behavior of organization members that will lead to organizational success.[8]

FUNCTIONS OF ORGANIZATION CULTURE

What purpose does organization culture play in an organization? In general terms, organization culture influences the behavior of everyone within an organization and, if carefully crafted, can have a significant positive impact on organizational success.[9] Organization culture influences the way people carry out organizational processes and can create immense pressure for organization members to act in ways consistent with the culture. As a result, organization culture should reflect values that are conducive to organizational goal attainment.

In more specific terms, organization culture has a variety of functions within an organization. First, organization culture can enhance organizational productivity. Organization members often become more productive as organization culture increases focus on such factors as rewarding performance and setting goals.[10] Second, organization culture can serve as a component of organizational strategy.[11] Following this line of reasoning, competitive advantage arises from complex combinations of tangible as well as intangible resources. One such intangible resource is a culture that enhances organizational success. Third, organization culture provides a rationale for staffing.[12] Management must make sure that new hires fit the organization's culture. The employment interview is a prime opportunity for managers to see whether applicants might fit within the organization culture and for applicants to assess whether the organization culture is a good fit for their personal needs and aspirations. Within the interview, employers are looking for clues to issues such as an applicant's work ethic and personality while job seekers want to learn more about company culture issues, including the allocation of rewards and promotions. Last, organization culture can act as a guideline for making operational decisions. Given an explicit organization culture, organization members tend to make decisions that are consistent with the values embedded in that culture.

Overall, organization culture functions to influence organization members to act in ways that are consistent with the accepted values of the organization. To assist organization members in identifying these beliefs and values, many organizations establish a code of conduct. A **code of conduct** is a document that reflects the core values of an organization and suggests how organization members should act in relation to them.

Managers must remember, however, that simply possessing a code of conduct does not guarantee for the organization that its members will follow the code. As **an example from the world of management** concerning organization members not following a code of conduct, consider recent events at **The Australian Wheat Board**, a private company that is involved in all Australian wheat exports.[13] This organization was recently under investigation for $290 million in kickbacks given to the former Iraqi regime headed by Saddam Hussein. The investigation yielded conclusions that although the company followed the letter of the law, it violated its own code of corporate conduct. One explanation for these violations to the code of conduct is that the organization had an incentive system that inadvertently rewarded unethical behavior.[14] Overall, management must not only work to establish a code of conduct within an organization, but take steps to ensure that behavior that follows the code is rewarded.

TYPES OF ORGANIZATION CULTURE

Based on the preceding discussion, we see that organization culture is made up of several different factors. Needless to say, putting all of these factors together into a meaningful rationale for describing a culture can be difficult and frustrating for managers.

Fortunately, a model developed by Cameron and Quinn called the Competing Values Framework presents a rationale that managers can use to categorize organization cultures.[15] The Competing Values Framework appears in Figure 19.1. According to the model, cultures differ with respect to two sets of opposite values. The first set of opposite values is organizational flexibility and discretion versus organizational stability, order, and control. The second set of opposite values is an internal organizational focus versus an external organizational

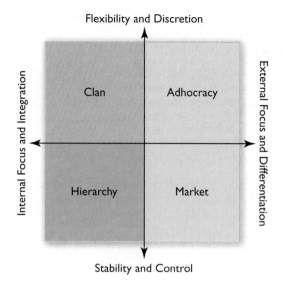

FIGURE 19.1
The Competing Values Framework model depicts four different kinds of organization culture
Source: Kim S. Cameron and Robert E.Quinn, *Diagnosing and Changing Organizational Culture* (Reading, MA:Addison Wesley 1999), 32.

focus. Depending on how a culture contains various combinations of the competing values represented by these two dimensions, cultures are divided into four types:

1. *Clan Culture.* As shown in Figure 19.1, **clan culture** is an organization culture characterized by a strong internal focus with a high degree of flexibility and discretion. The *clan culture* derives its name from the fact that this organization culture seems much like a family. In a clan culture, leaders are seen more as mentors and perhaps even parent figures. This culture includes activities that reflect shared values and goals, cohesion among organization members, teamwork, and organization commitment to employees.

   The culture at Southwest Airlines is often used as an example of a clan culture. The following excerpt of a recent Thanksgiving Day message by Southwest Airlines president Colleen Barrett shows the emphasis of the Southwest culture on internal focus, flexibility, shared values and goals, and a high commitment to employees:

   As a Company, we are blessed to have 33,000-plus Employees who continually amaze me with their ability to Live the Southwest Way. In an industry where change doesn't happen gradually, it happens overnight—if you are lucky to have that much advance notice—our People adapt to change faster than a chameleon. Unlike chameleons, when Southwest Employees adapt, they never change their true colors. Their Warrior Spirit, Servant's Heart, and Fun-LUVing attitude are part of my Thanksgiving blessings.[16]

2. *Adhocracy Culture.* **Adhocracy culture** is an organization culture characterized by flexibility and discretion along with an external focus. As illustrated in Figure 19.1, an adhocracy is a culture reflecting an organization with a simple structure or lack of structure. In essence, adhocracy is the opposite of bureaucracy. Within the adhocracy culture one will find few rules or procedures. This culture is characterized by a creative workplace where people are entrepreneurial, taking risks to achieve success.

   Google's organization culture has often been used as an example of an adhocracy culture. The following quote depicts the Google corporate culture as reflecting adhocracy characteristics:

   Though growing rapidly, Google still maintains a small company feel. At the Googleplex headquarters almost everyone eats in the Google café (known as "Charlie's Place"), sitting at whatever table has an opening and enjoying conversations with Googlers from all different departments. Topics range from the trivial to the technical, and whether the discussion is about computer games or encryption

or ad serving software, it's not surprising to hear someone say, "That's a product I helped develop before I came to Google."

Google's emphasis on innovation and commitment to cost containment means each employee is a hands-on contributor. There's little in the way of corporate hierarchy and everyone wears several hats. The international webmaster who creates Google's holiday logos spent a week translating the entire site into Korean. The chief operations engineer is also a licensed neurosurgeon. Because everyone realizes they are an equally important part of Google's success, no one hesitates to skate over a corporate officer during roller hockey.[17]

3. *Hierarchy Culture.* Figure 19.1 shows that **hierarchy culture** is an organization culture characterized by an internal focus along with an emphasis on stability and control. The workplace within this type of culture is formal and structured. Leaders tend to focus on coordination and organization. Individuals within the workplace are concerned about efficiency and formal rules and policies govern how people operate.

McDonald's restaurants are commonly given as an example of a hierarchy culture. The typical McDonald's restaurant has younger employees with little significant experience and produces standardized products for customers. Restaurant success is built upon efficient and fast food production. French fries are cooked for an established period and hamburgers are topped with exact amounts of toppings like mustard and ketchup. Employees are thoroughly trained in production rules covering all facets of restaurant operations and management closely monitors employee behavior to make sure that rules are precisely executed.

4. *Market Culture.* As indicated in Figure 19.1, **market culture** is an organization culture that reflects values that emphasize stability and control along with an external focus. An organization with a market culture is oriented toward all stakeholders in the market, not just customers. As such, this culture emphasizes relationships with all constituencies including customers, suppliers, contractors, government regulators, and unions. Leaders in this culture tend to be hard-driving. The organization is focused on winning and emphasizes achieving stretch goals and outpacing the competition.

General Electric is often used as an example of a company with a market culture. The company operates under the premise that if any of its subsidiaries were not number one or two in market sales, the subsidiaries would be sold. As a result of this premise, the company has sold more than 300 businesses over the last few decades. The organization culture is highly competitive with a "results or else" mentality.

Research tells us that competent managers in each of these four organization cultures tend to act in different ways.[18] Figure 19.2 lists each type of culture and shows corresponding activities that competent managers within each of these cultures tend to emphasize. Studying this figure carefully will provide insight concerning how managers operating in each culture might act in order to increase the effectiveness of that culture.

BUILDING A HIGH-PERFORMANCE ORGANIZATION CULTURE

The development of culture within an organization is inevitable. In all organizations, culture can develop naturally over time as organization members interact with one another. Under these circumstances, the culture that develops may or may not facilitate or enhance organizational performance. On the other hand, the establishment and growth of culture within an organization can be influenced by specific actions taken by management. Under these circumstances, the culture that develops will generally have a higher probability of encouraging high performance within an organization than if left to developing naturally over time as organization members interact.

CULTURE TYPE	ACTIVITIES MANAGERS TEND TO PERFORM
The Hierarchy Culture	... Make sure employees know exactly what is expected of them. ... Standardize policies and procedures so employees know exactly how to get work accomplished. ... Include in employee orientation a focus on tradition, values, and vision of the organization. ... Give employees regular feedback on how well they are performing jobs. ... Establish a monitoring system that shows how well employees are performing jobs.
The Market Culture	... Make sure everyone can name their three most critical customers. ... Accept only world-class quality in products and services. ... Give customers what they want the first time. ... Track how competitors are performing. ... Understand the keys to your competitors' success.
The Clan Culture	... Establish a clear goal for the work team. ... Establish specific work targets with deadlines that the team can accomplish. ... Empower others to perform. ... Coach and counsel employees. ... Celebrate the successes of work teams and individuals.
The Adhocracy Culture	... Hold people accountable for generating innovative ideas. ... Talk to people about their new ideas and what they expect the results of ideas could be. ... Reward those who come up with new ways to perform work. ... Establish vehicles for trying out new ideas. ... Make continuous improvement a feature of the workplace.

FIGURE 19.2
Four types of culture and corresponding activities managers can take to make them successful

Figure 19.3 summarizes the steps that managers can take to help build an organization culture that yields high performance.[19] Each of the steps is discussed here:

1. *Lead as Champion.* Leaders in organizations must champion organization climate. As such, leaders throughout the organization must explain repeatedly why the practices that help to build organization culture are necessary and how such practices will benefit the organization. If the practices represent new practices, leaders must convince organization members that change is necessary.

General Electric's hard-driving market culture is highly competitive and focused on getting results. The parent company has sold 300 subsidiary units that failed to measure up.

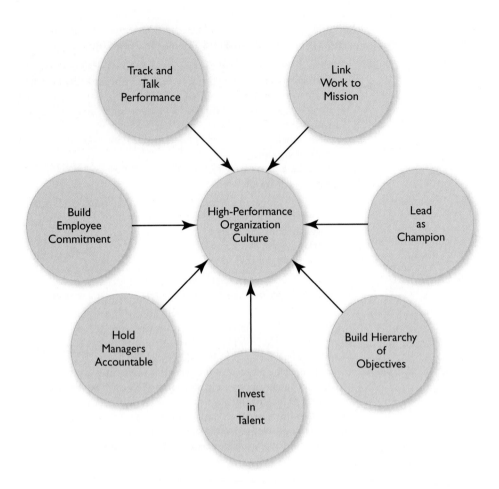

FIGURE 19.3
Steps managers can take to build a high-performance organization culture

2. *Link Work to Organizational Mission.* The purpose of organizational mission is to clarify the purpose(s) of the organization. The mission statement helps employees to understand why their organization exists. Helping employees understand how their work contributes to accomplishing organizational mission is critical. Such understanding emphasizes the great importance of employee efforts to the success of the organization and helps to build a sense of pride in their jobs and the work they do. If employees understand how their efforts result in the accomplishment of organizational mission, commitment to working hard so that the mission can be accomplished will normally grow.

3. *Track and Talk About Performance.* All organization members should always be thinking about their individual performance. What is excellent performance? How can performance be improved? Why is excellent performance necessary? Why should organization members strive to be excellent performers? Performance, by managers and nonmanagers alike, should be defined and tracked to monitor how appropriately individuals are performing. As performance is tracked, corrective action should be taken, if necessary, to foster performance improvement. Also, employees generally like to know how well their organization as a whole is performing. When organization members receive regular communication regarding the performance of the entire organization, they tend to stay focused on contributing to that performance.

4. *Build a Hierarchy of Objectives.* As discussed earlier, a hierarchy of objectives is a set of objectives wherein the overall objectives of the organization are divided into subobjectives for all sections and levels of the organization. As objectives at lower levels of the organization are accomplished, they contribute to the attainment of objectives at the next higher level. Although defining objectives at lower levels may be difficult, the effort used to develop the hierarchy is well spent. Even employees at the lowest organizational levels will generally be more focused on performance when they see the cascading set of objectives in the hierarchy of objectives. Throughout the organization, objectives should be challenging and have clear rewards to be earned when reached.

5. *Invest in Talent.* Certain employees tend to have more talent to perform a job than others. As such, these talented individuals have a greater capacity for performance. Talented employees generally demand higher wages in the labor market than others. Management must recognize that although talented employees may be more expensive to hire and retain, such employees are normally an effective means to better organizational performance. In addition, managers must do whatever they can to retain talented employees once they are hired.

   In addition to hiring individuals with better talent to improve organizational performance, management can also invest in developing the talents of present employees. Through training, for example, management can focus on developing organization member abilities in order to improve organizational performance. Organizations that invest in and maintain employee work abilities send the message to all organization members that excellent performance is a top priority.

6. *Recognize and Reward.* Management needs to help employees *learn* to be high performers. As such, appropriate performance behavior needs to be reinforced or rewarded. Because research tells us that reinforced behavior tends to be repeated, as management reinforces appropriate performance, appropriate performance will tend to be repeated. Reinforcement can be monetary or nonmonetary. In certain instances a simple, nonmonetary certificate of high performance can be as powerful a reinforcement as a monetary cash bonus. Periodically, recognition and reward practices within any organization should be evaluated for possible improvement.

7. *Hold Managers Accountable.* The performance of managers should be tracked with job-related progress being communicated to them both formally and informally. Maintaining this performance contributes to ensuring the success of a manager's area of responsibility, which in turn contributes to the performance and success of the organization as a whole. Managers should understand what it takes for employees to be high performers and advise, coach, and counsel them in ways to improve performance and reach performance goals. Given the critical contribution that employee performance makes to organizational success, managers should be held accountable for managing that performance.

8. *Build Organizational Commitment.* **Organizational commitment** can be defined as the dedication of organization members to uphold the values of the organization and to make worthwhile contributions to fulfilling organizational purpose. Research indicates that one way to build organizational commitment is to maintain an organizational focus on providing excellent customer service. Such a focus seems to result in higher job satisfaction which, in turn, seems to help build stronger organizational commitment.[20] Overall, this increased commitment to the organization seems to raise the desire of employees to remain in the organization and focus on providing quality goods and services. Foundation studies in this area indicate that organizational commitment serves as a "psychological bond" that influences individuals to act in ways that are consistent with the interests of the organization.[21]

class discussion highlight

MODERN RESEARCH AND ORGANIZATION CULTURE SKILL

Building Organizational Commitment through Psychological Safety in Small Mexican Firms

A recent study by De Clercq and Rius investigated the effects that various organization components can have on employee commitment to the organization.[22] The researchers surveyed 863 small Mexican firms. The average firm had 25 employees, 60 percent were family businesses, 26 percent were manufacturing firms, and 74 percent were service or commercial businesses. All firms were based in Mexico, and none were subsidiaries of other companies.

Specifically, the researchers investigated relationship between organization member perception of "psychological safety" within an organization and their commitment to the organization. Psychology safety was defined as an organization characterized by supportive management, clear roles for organization members to perform, and the possibility for self-expression. The researchers hypothesized that the greater an employee's feeling of psychological safety within an organization, the higher the level of commitment that employee has for the organization.

Do you think that study results supported the study hypothesis that the greater an employee's feeling of psychological safety within the culture of an organization, the higher the level commitment that employee has for the organization? Why? Would you get the same results in large Mexican firms? Explain. Assuming that your thoughts are accurate, what hints can this research give you about developing your organization culture skill?

KEEPING ORGANIZATION CULTURE ALIVE AND WELL

Given the critical contribution that organization culture makes to organizational success, managers must keep organization culture alive and well in their organizations. Important steps in this process include establishing a vision for organization culture, building and maintaining organization culture through artifacts, integrating new employees within organization culture, and maintaining the health of organization culture. Each of these steps is discussed in the following sections.

Establishing a Vision of Organization Culture

Managing organization culture normally begins by establishing a vision of what the culture of an organization should be. In essence, this vision becomes a target at which management aims. Without such a target management will not have a benchmark for modifying and improving organization culture over time.

Management should reflect on what type of culture would be appropriate given specific organizational circumstances. Given the complexity of circumstances for most modern organizations, most modern organization cultures tend to be multidimensional. Managers should strive to establish various dimensions in their own cultures that will best contribute to accomplishing organizational mission. Dimensions commonly observed in modern organization cultures include a focus on quality, ethics, innovation, spirituality, diversity, and customer. Not all organization cultures contain all of these dimensions. Instead, managers tend to decide which dimension(s) will best help to enhance organizational success and then take steps to include that dimension as a major feature of organization culture. Each of these dimensions is discussed here.

Quality Dimension The **quality dimension of organization culture** is an element of organization culture that focuses on making sure that a product, in the opinion of the customer, does what it is supposed to do. Organizations with such cultures tend to focus on communicating their focus on quality to customers and explaining how quality processes operate within the organization. Management generally hopes to benefit from such cultural emphasis by winning customer loyalty and repeat purchases through customer satisfaction with products or services. An example of an organization with a strong quality dimension of organization culture is KB Home, a U.S. home builder. KB Home uses its Web site to communicate its focus on quality to customers. At KB Home, the quality of houses produced is especially important to the company.

At KB home, quality is so important to organizational culture that on its web site the homebuilding company promises 100% customer satisfaction on 10 construction checkpoints.

The company has a "100% Satisfied Pledge," which offers homebuyers 10 quality construction checkpoints.

Ethics Dimension The **ethics dimension of organization culture** is a facet of organization culture that focuses on making sure that an organization emphasizes not only what is good for the organization, but what is good for other human beings. Until recently, an ethics dimension has been dangerously ignored. The debate about the ethics dimension now needs to move from whether it should exist in organizations to how to build it.[23]

Ethics training is arguably the most commonly used vehicle for developing the ethics dimension of organization culture.[24] Ethics training normally focuses on developing a common understanding throughout the organization of the role that ethics plays in organizational operations. Ethics training will not guarantee that employees will choose the desired ethical behavior in every situation. Such training will, however, start useful dialogue about right and wrong behavior in various organizational situations. In essence, ethics training strives to give employees a worthwhile framework for ethical reasoning that will help them to make ethical choices in various organizational situations after training ends.

What can managers do to increase the probability that ethics training influences organization members to act ethically over time? First, after ethics training concludes, management can provide employees with a vehicle for making ethical queries anonymously. Some organizations provide a hotline that employees can call to get advice about ethical dilemmas. Management can also try to make sure that organization members act ethically after ethics training concludes by establishing methods for the resurfacing of topics covered in ethics training. For example, a company can use its intranet, publish brochures, and even use screensavers to keep reminding employees about issues covered in ethics training. As another tactic that management can use to try to ensure that organization members act ethically after ethics training, management can promote employees who behave ethically. Rewarding ethical behavior of the past is a powerful vehicle for increasing the probability that organization members will act ethically in the future.

Innovation Dimension The **innovation dimension of organization culture** is an aspect of organization culture that encourages the application of new ideas to the improvement of organizational processes, products, or services. Innovation is a major source of organizational change and improvement. Once an innovation dimension is established, management cannot assume that it will continue to exist over time. An innovation dimension of organization culture can become significantly weakened or even extinct if not properly nurtured.

As **an example from the world of management** illustrating how an innovation dimension of organization culture can become weakened or extinct, consider recent events at **3M**. The 3M Company is known for producing thousands of imaginative products. Long known for having an organization culture that focused on innovation and creativity, management recently realized that this focus was being destroyed.[25] The culture was being changed to emphasize efficiency and as an unpredicted by-product, innovation was being squeezed out.

Because invention, by its nature, is commonly a disorderly and inefficient process, changes to culture aimed at imposing efficiency seemed to reduce employee focus on innovation. Historically, 3M allowed researchers to spend years testing products with little regard for the efficiency of the process. Consider 3M's invention of the Post-It note. The inventor of the Post-It note, Art Fry, fiddled with the idea for several years before the product went into full production in 1980. The company is now somewhat deemphasizing its focus on efficiency and spending more on research and development in an effort to reinvigorate its culture of innovation, long considered to be the lifeblood of the company.

Spirituality Dimension

The **spirituality dimension of organization culture** is an aspect of organization culture that encourages organization members to integrate spiritual life and work life. A spiritual awakening seems to be occurring in the American workplace. Many managers are encouraging the development of this new trend.[26] Managers seem to be encouraging this trend because of their belief that a spiritually humanistic work environment is beneficial for both employees and the organization. According to the logic of such managers, a spiritually reflective work environment will be personally satisfying to organization members who will thereby become more productive and creative. On the other hand, such managers tend to believe that a workplace without a spiritual dimension will normally result in unsatisfied organization members who will become frustrated and thereby consistently absent from the workplace.[27] Organization cultures that have a spiritual emphasis typically do not focus on one specific type of spiritual belief or religion, but emphasize the acceptance of whatever spiritual focus organization member might possess. In emphasizing a spiritual focus, organizations create opportunities for spiritually based activities such as prayer, meditation, reading sacred texts, listening to worship music, and having objects in the workplace as reminders of spiritual beliefs.

Diversity Dimension

The **diversity dimension of organization culture** is a component of organization culture that encourages the existence of basic human differences among organization members. Such differences can relate to ethnicity, religion, physical ability, or sexual orientation. The diversity dimension is a mainstay of modern organization culture mainly because managers are anxious to reap diversity-related advantages such as increased perspectives on how to solve problems and how to better relate to diverse customers.

The CEO of the German company Siemens recently concluded that its corporate culture lacked diversity.[28] Organization members as a group were thought to be too homogeneous, thereby depriving management of the benefits of a diverse workforce. To solve this problem, Siemens is trying to make organization members as a whole more diverse by hiring more people from around the world who better represent its client base.

Customer Dimension

The **customer dimension of organization culture** is a facet of organization culture that focuses on catering to the needs of those individuals who buy goods or services produced. One recent survey indicates that 80 percent of executives believe that they are doing an excellent job of serving customers yet only 8 percent of their customers agree.[29] Perhaps because of such survey results along with the calamity that such results could cause in organizations, many managers are strengthening their organization culture focus on customers.

Some organizations, however, are well known for an enduring commitment to customer satisfaction, have achieved much success because of it, and are expected to continue benefiting from it in the future. For example, many believe that Apple's success over the years is primarily due to its enduring commitment to know what customers want even before customers know it. At General Electric, as another example, CEO Immelt has initiated "dreaming sessions" to brainstorm with key customers in order to have a forward-looking view of customer needs.

Building and Maintaining Organization Culture Through Artifacts

A **cultural artifact** is a dimension of an organization that helps to describe and reinforce the culture, or beliefs, values, and norms, in which an artifact exists. Cultural artifacts can change over time as organization culture changes, because what the artifacts represent, how they appear, how they are used, and why they are used are no longer pertinent given the new culture. Several cultural artifacts commonly used by modern managers are discussed here.[30]

Values At the heart of any organization's culture, by definition, are its values. From a societal viewpoint, **values** are the beliefs of a person or social group in which they have an emotional investment. In society, values can be "for" something, such as excellent health care for all society, or "against" something, such as violence among society members. In organizations, values can also be for things such as hiring talented workers, rewarding excellent performance, and developing leadership skills, or against things such as polluting the environment, discrimination in hiring practices, and maintaining the status quo.

Organizational values are reflected in organizational ingredients, including strategy, structure, and processes. Values are also reflected in the way leaders lead as well as in organizational rules, reward systems, policies, and procedures. More and more, modern managers are crafting value statements to clearly communicate held cultural values throughout the organization. A **values statement** is a formally drafted document that summarizes the primary values within the culture of a specific organization. A values statement gives managers the opportunity to communicate effectively and efficiently the values that drive an organization and thereby help to increase the probability that appropriate values will influence organization member behavior. Figure 19.4 contains a partial statement of values for the organic grocery chain the Whole Foods Market.

Organizational Myths An **organizational myth** is a popular belief or story that has become associated with a person or institution that is considered to illustrate an organization culture ideal. Myths are used to explain organizational beginnings or events that are of great significance to the organization. Myths stimulate organization members to do well and provide the logic for action taken. The events contained in myths never actually happened, but act as an inspirational foundation for behavior. Organizational myths are commonly perpetuated in organizations to enhance organization member pride in belonging and overall commitment to the organization. In addition, myths are commonly perpetuated in order to build employee commitment reflected by the myth.

One of the most famous myths in business history centers on CEO Lee Iacocca and how he "saved" Chrysler Corporation from bankruptcy.[31] Iacocca took over as chairman of Chrysler Corporation in 1979. At that time, Chrysler was in deep crisis. The company was losing money, had acquired unprofitable companies, and was producing low-quality products necessitating huge, expensive product recalls. Iacocca took bold, nontraditional action to save the company. He negotiated government backing of the company, took charismatic personal ads to the marketplace asking for customer support, and negotiated significant concessions with the United Auto Workers Union in order to dodge bankruptcy. Word began to quickly

Selling the Highest Quality Natural and Organic Products Available

Passion For Food
We appreciate and celebrate the difference natural and organic products can make in the quality of one's life.

Quality Standards
We have high standards and our goal is to sell the highest quality products we possibly can. We define quality by evaluating the ingredients, freshness, safety, taste, nutritive value and appearance of all of the products we carry. We are buying agents for our customers and not the selling agents for the manufacturers.

Satisfying and Delighting Our Customers

Our Customers
They are our most important stakeholders in our business and the lifeblood of our business. Only by satisfying our customers first do we have the opportunity to satisfy the needs of our other stakeholders.

Extraordinary Customer Service
We go to extraordinary lengths to satisfy and delight our customers. We want to meet or exceed their expectations on every shopping trip. We know that by doing so we turn customers into advocates for our business. Advocates do more than shop with us, they talk about Whole Foods to their friends and others. We want to serve our customers competently, efficiently, knowledgeably and with flair.

Education
We can generate greater appreciation and loyalty from all of our stakeholders by educating them about natural and organic foods, health, nutrition and the environment.

Meaningful Value
We offer value to our customers by providing them with high quality products, extraordinary service and a competitive price. We are constantly challenged to improve the value proposition to our customers.

Retail Innovation
We value retail experiments. Friendly competition within the company helps us to continually improve our stores. We constantly innovate and raise our retail standards and are not afraid to try new ideas and concepts.

Inviting Store Environments
We create store environments that are inviting and fun, and reflect the communities they serve. We want our stores to become community meeting places where our customers meet their friends and make new ones.

FIGURE 19.4
Statement of Values for the Whole Foods Market

spread that Iacocca had single-handedly saved the company, which of course was not true. Many people were involved in saving Chrysler. The myth of Iacocca saving the company single-handedly, however, helped to build the Chrysler cultural value of trust and support for Chrysler leadership.

Organizational Sagas An **organizational saga** is a narrative describing the adventures of a heroic individual or family significantly linked to an organization's past or present. In general, the purpose of a saga is to identify and perpetuate the organization's shared values. Organizational sagas usually reveal important historical facts about an organization relating to issues such as early organizational pioneers and products, past triumphs and failures of the organization, and the leaders who founded or transformed the company.

Mary Kay Ash is the founder of Mary Kay Cosmetics and one of the most successful women entrepreneurs in modern history. Information on the Web site of the company she founded outlines a saga related to Mary Kay Ash's company history. This information serves as an inspirational saga to all organization members that significant success is available to all within the company through hard work, dedication, and self-confidence.

Managers at all levels can become involved in **organizational storytelling,** the act of passing organizational myths and sagas to other organization members. Obviously, given the example about Mary Kay Ash, modern managers can tell stories not only via word of mouth, but also via the Internet.

Organizational Language

The language used in organizations often points to the organization's shared values. Some companies reveal how they feel about the competition through repeatedly using phrases such as "let's be #1 in the marketplace," or how they feel about technology by repeatedly using phrases such as "win through technology." Still other organizations repeatedly use the phrase "customer is king" to emphasize how they feel about dealing with customer satisfaction. Language used at Walt Disney Companies reflects organizational values that are particularly interesting. At Walt Disney, rather than being called an employee, everyone is called a "member of the cast." This language emphasizes that rather than simply working, organization members should think of themselves as always being *on stage*, and always giving the best *performance* possible for customers. Many companies use slogans internally and externally through advertising to convey important organizational values. Figure 19.5 contains several well-known slogans and the companies that use them to convey important organizational values.

Organizational Symbols

Organizational symbols are objects that have meanings beyond their intrinsic content. Symbols provide a roadmap for what is important in a particular organization. Some companies use impressive buildings to convey company strength. Other companies use logos, flags, and coats of arms to convey the importance they place on certain ideas or events. As examples, the financial services firm UBS uses a logo that resembles a set of keys. The logo suggests to investors that using UBS's services is the key to unlocking wealth, and McDonald's uses the clown Ronald McDonald as a symbol of child-friendliness and fun within McDonald's restaurants.

Organizational Ceremonies

Organizational ceremonies are formal activities conducted on important organizational occasions. Such occasions could include openings of new stores, anniversary dates for hiring of employees, and employee promotions. Perhaps one of the most well-known organizational ceremonies is the ceremony celebrating successful sales campaigns at Mary Kay Cosmetics. At Mary Kay Cosmetics sales celebrations, everything has a purpose—not just the decorations, but sales prizes, including the automobiles awarded.

Organizational Rewards

Rewards tailor behavior in some way in most organizations.[32] Some rewards come from sources within the organization and can include compensation, satisfying work, and verbal recognition. Rewards can also come from outside the organization and can include comments from customers, competitors, and suppliers.

COMPANY	SLOGAN	VALUE REFLECTED
Audi	"Advancement through Technology."	Audi's technology races it ahead.
Petland	"Petland Pets Make Life Better!"	Petland pets improve lives.
L'Oréal	"Because I'm worth it."	L'Oréal makes products worth paying more for.
HSBC	"The world's local bank."	HBSC personally cares for its customers.
Wal-Mart	"Always low prices. Always."	Wal-Mart has low prices every day.

FIGURE 19.5
Well-known companies, their slogans, and the values these slogans reflect

Mary Kay Cosmetics builds its company culture through inspirational stories, including that of founder Mary Kay Ash, organizational ceremonies, and rewards, including autos for topselling representatives.

Management should continually be involved with identifying and rewarding those individuals who uphold the values of the organization. Rewarding people for engaging in behavior that reflects important organization culture values is critical in increasing the probability of organizational success.

class discussion highlight

ORGANIZATION CULTURE SKILL AND YOUR CAREER

You are looking for a job and see a position opening that piques your interest. You like the position and qualify for it. In preparing for your employment interview, you decide to ask three questions about culture within the organization that would be vital in assessing the likelihood of your career flourishing within the company. List the three questions that you believe would help you assess the degree of career success you would expect within the company. Explain why you would ask each question.

Integrating New Employees into the Organization Culture

The previous section discussed how to keep organization culture alive and well through the use of cultural artifacts. This section focuses on how to keep organization culture alive and well by appropriately integrating newly hired organization members within an existing organization culture.

Organizational socialization is the process by which management can appropriately integrate new employees within an organization's culture.[33] Figure 19.6 is visual scheme showing recommended steps for a socialization process and how the steps relate to one another. The following material discusses the process as a whole as well as each step in more detail.

As shown in Figure 19.6, the organizational socialization process can begin by carefully planning the organization's recruitment process. As part of this planning, management should determine what type of individual characteristics would best fit within the organization

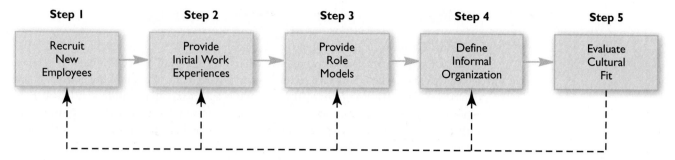

FIGURE 19.6   Possible steps of a socialization process

culture. Such characteristics might include an individual's determination to be successful in a job, commitment to personal ethics, and level of self-confidence and competitiveness. After such best-fit characteristics have been determined, management should use the recruitment process to identify individuals possessing those characteristics. Naturally, after management has identified individuals who possesses the characteristics, serious steps should be taken to hire the individuals.

Once individuals possessing the best-fit characteristics are hired, management should continue their socialization process (step 2) by carefully crafting meaningful experiences for them within the first four to six weeks of new recruits' lives within the organization. In this situation, experiences are meaningful if they expose new hires to important organization culture values and emphasize the importance of new individuals' commitment to them. Such values might include the importance of tackling challenging work, openness to training for handling new situations, and the importance of functioning as a team member. Such initial experiences can also involve new recruits observing and practicing new jobs with input from established organization members.

Once individuals with appropriate personal characteristics have been hired and have experienced meaningful activities within the first four to six weeks, management should continue with the socialization of these individuals by exposing the new recruits to appropriate role models (step 3). Management should be focused on connecting new recruits to role models who possess vital characteristics that would be valuable for new recruits. The role models should illustrate cultural values such as being productive, highly motivated, loyal to the organization, and having high trust in management.

As the next step of the organizational socialization process, management can help new recruits to understand various facets of the organization's informal structure and how it complements the formal structure. Helping new recruits to infiltrate and become members of informal groups that uphold important organizational values can be especially important to management. On the other hand, ignoring this informal focus in the organizational socialization process could allow new recruits to unknowingly align with less productive facets of an organization's informal structure and thereby limit the contribution of the new recruits to organizational success.

As a final step in the organizational socialization process, management must control the cultural fit of new recruits. New recruits are generally considered new for about one year. During this first year within the organization, management must keep in mind that new recruits will be making mistakes and struggling to appropriately fit within organization culture. This struggle to acquire organizational fit can be frustrating to new recruits and lead to premature turnover if not handled sensitively by management. New recruits must be able to practice new jobs, at times employing trial and error, without fear of punishment or failure.

Management must also remember that not all recruits are ideal fits for organization culture and that some recruits my need to be weeded out to make room for other new recruits who may be a better fit. This weeding out can take place by either moving poor performers out of the organization or to jobs comprised of less critical roles. As this weeding out process occurs, management should reflect on any possible mistakes made during the organizational socialization process of the recruits and thereby come up with ideas on how to improve the process so that such mistakes will not be made in the future.

Maintaining the Health of Organization Culture

Arguably, the most important step that management takes to maximize the success of an organization is to create a healthy culture within that organization. *Health* is defined in terms of the extent to which a culture facilitates the achievement of organizational mission and objectives. A **healthy organization culture** is an organization culture that facilities the achievement of the organization's mission and objectives. An **unhealthy organization culture** is an organization culture that does not facilitate the accomplishment of the organization's mission and objectives.

Managers must always be analyzing symptoms or signs related to the health of an organization and take action to build and maintain a healthy organization culture. *Healthy organization culture* is usually people oriented and contains the characteristics listed in Figure 19.7. A manager should keep the characteristics of a healthy organization climate in mind and focus on maintaining and building organization culture health whenever possible. For example, if managers believe that organization culture is healthy, they should take steps to improve this health wherever possible. Even though an organization culture might be considered healthy, increasing a cultural focus on risk-taking or excellence in job performance might make it even healthier. On the other hand, a manager might believe that his or her organization culture is unhealthy. In such a case, the manager must determine what factors are making the organization climate unhealthy, take steps to eliminate these factors, and introduce ingredients into the culture that will make it healthy.

As **an example from the world of management** concerning turning an unhealthy organization culture into a healthy one, consider recent events at **Uchumi Supermarkets** in Kenya, Africa.[34] A new CEO, Jonathan Ciano, upon entering Uchumi Supermarkets, saw obvious signs that organization culture was unhealthy. Staff theft and unregulated procurement systems led to record debts and uncertainty regarding the sustainability of the company. To change the unhealthy culture into a healthy one, besides confronting the issues of

FIGURE 19.7
Eight characteristics of a healthy organization culture

Source: Developed by the Institute for Business, Technology, and Ethics (IBTE); www.customerfocusconsult.com/articles/articles_template.asp?ID=36.

1. **Openness and humility from top to bottom of the organization**
   Arrogance kills off learning and growth by blinding us to our own weaknesses. Strength comes out of receptivity and the willingness to learn from others

2. **An environment of accountability and personal responsibility**
   Denial, blame, and excuses harden relationships and intensify conflict. Successful teams hold each other accountable and willingly accept personal responsibility.

3. **Freedom for risk-taking within appropriate limits**
   Both extremes—an excessive, reckless risk-taking and a stifling, fearful control—threaten any organization. Freedom to risk new ideas flourishes best within appropriate limits.

4. **A fierce commitment to "do it right"**
   Mediocrity is easy; excellence is hard work, and there are many temptations for shortcuts. A search for excellence always inspires both inside and outside an organization.

5. **A willingness to tolerate and learn from mistakes**
   Punishing honest mistakes stifles creativity. Learning from mistakes encourages healthy experimentation and converts negatives into positives.

6. **Unquestioned integrity and consistency**
   Dishonesty and inconsistency undermine trust. Organizations and relationships thrive on clarity, transparency, honesty, and reliable follow-through.

7. **A pursuit of collaboration, integration, and holistic thinking**
   Turf wars and narrow thinking are deadly. Drawing together the best ideas and practices, integrating the best people into collaborative teams, multiplies organizational strength.

8. **Courage and persistence in the face of difficulty**
   The playing field is not always level, or life fair, but healthy cultures remain both realistic about the challenges they face and unintimidated and undeterred by difficulty.

theft and uncontrolled procurement, the new CEO initiated a culture in which employees were able to think for themselves on behalf of the company. Employees started making independent judgments and decisions. If Ciano's steps to make organization culture healthier are successful, he will start to see signs such as organization members fixing mistakes rather than rationalizing them, and new ideas and information will start to flow freely within the company. On the other hand, if the organization culture is not becoming healthier, the CEO will see signs that include employees blaming others when mistakes occur.

{ CHALLENGE CASE SUMMARY

In order for Tony Hayward, the BP chief executive officer mentioned in the Challenge Case, to build a culture emphasizing safety within his organization, he must understand the fundamental concepts of organization culture. He must know that in building this safety focus, he is actually attempting to build shared values within BP so that organization members view safety as a critical organizational activity. Ultimately, building such a safety culture at BP could help the company to avoid dealing with future explosions and other catastrophes and thereby contribute to greater organizational success. This safety-focused culture can serve such useful and valuable functions at BP as enhancing company productivity, becoming a part of the company's strategy for success, and providing a rationale for adding new staff.

In all likelihood, Hayward's organization culture challenges will extend beyond the issue of safety. It would probably be worthwhile for Hayward to determine what type of overall organization culture he would like to see at BP. He might consider establishing a clan culture, an adhocracy culture, a hierarchy culture, or a market culture. In making this determination, Hayward should consider the challenges facing BP and anticipate which culture or combination of cultures would best help BP to meet these challenges.

Given information presented in the case, safety is one of the challenges that BP is facing. In facing the task of establishing a safety focus to BP's organization culture, Hayward should also plan for establishing a broader organization culture that encourages high performance. To create a high-performance culture, Hayward must lead as a champion. That is, he must explain repeatedly why organization culture values such as safety are critical for BP and take steps to encourage organization members to act in ways that are consistent with such cultural values. To create this high-performance culture, Hayward can also focus on linking work to BP's mission and recognize and reward those individuals whose actions are consistent

with accomplishing BP's mission. In helping to build a high-performance culture, Hayward can also take actions that include investing in outstanding talent, holding managers accountable for their actions, and building the commitment of organization members to BP.

In planning to establish a safety dimension to BP's organization culture, Hayward should plan on keeping the culture alive and well once established. Keeping the culture alive and well actually starts with Hayward envisioning exactly what the culture should be. Without such a vision, Hayward will be unable to tweak the culture over time to make it consistent with this vision. In addition to a safety dimension, Hayward's vision of the culture could include a combination of dimensions focusing on areas such as quality, ethics, innovation, spirituality, diversity, or customer.

Once the vision for the BP culture is complete in Hayward's mind, the process of keeping BP's culture alive and well should probably focus on Hayward choosing the artifacts that he would like to use to establish and maintain BP's organization culture. Such artifacts might include a values statement outlining BP's key organization culture values, the development of organizational myths and sagas that can be used to perpetuate cultural values, special language and ceremonies to bring key ingredients of BP's cultural values to life, and organization rewards that reinforce and encourage behavior that is consistent with organization culture.

Bringing new organization members into BP's culture is a serious matter. Socializing new individuals into the culture will help to ensure that the culture stays alive and well over the long run. Steps that Hayward can take to appropriately socialize new organization members into BP's culture include carefully planning BP's recruitment process, providing significant experiences at BP once individuals are hired, exposing newcomers to appropriate BP role models, and changing organization members when individuals do not seem to be fitting well within the BP culture. Overall, Hayward must focus on establishing a healthy organization culture at BP, a culture that facilitates the achievement of BP's goals.

MANAGEMENT SKILL ACTIVITIES

This section is specially designed to help you develop organization culture skills. An individual's organization culture skill is based upon an understanding of organization culture concepts and the ability to apply those concepts in management situations. The following activities are designed to both heighten your understanding of organization culture concepts and to develop the ability to apply those concepts in a variety of management situations.

UNDERSTANDING ORGANIZATION CULTURE CONCEPTS

This section is comprised of activities that will sharpen your understanding of organization culture concepts. Answer essay questions as completely as possible. Also, remember that many additional true/false and multiple choice questions appear online at My Management Lab.com to help you further refine your understanding of social responsibility concepts.

Essay Questions

1. Define *organization culture* and explain why organization culture skill is valuable to managers.

2. Explain the advantages and disadvantages of having a *clan culture* within an organization. As a manager, would this culture be hard for you to establish? Why?

3. Assume that you are a professor teaching a management course. What vision would you have for the course culture? List three artifacts that you would use to establish and maintain this vision. Be sure to explain why you chose each artifact.

4. List three challenges that a manager might face in appropriately socializing new employees into an organization culture. What advice would you give managers for how to meet these challenges?

5. How would you turn an unhealthy organization culture into a healthy one? Be as specific as possible.

Developing Management Skill

Learning activities in this section are aimed at helping you to develop organization culture skill. Learning activities include Exploring Your Management Skill: Part 2, Your Management Skill Portfolio exercise, an Experiential Exercise, Cases, and a VideoNet exercise.

EXPLORING YOUR MANAGEMENT SKILL: PART 2

As you recall, you completed Exploring Your Management Skill before you started to study this chapter. Your responses gave you an idea of how much you initially knew about organization culture and helped you to focus on important points as you studied the chapter. Answer the Exploring Your Management Skill questions again now (p. 466) and compare your score to the first time you took it. This comparison will give you an idea of how much you have learned from studying this chapter and pinpoint areas for further clarification before you start studying the next chapter. Record your answers within the text or go to MyManagementLab.com. Recording your answers in MyManagementLab will allow you to get immediate results and see how your score compares to your classmates. If you answer the questions in the book, the answers are located in the Exploring Your Management Skill Appendix at the end of the book.

YOUR MANAGEMENT SKILLS PORTFOLIO

Your Management Learning Portfolio is a collection of activities especially designed to demonstrate your management knowledge and skill. By completing these activities online at MyManagementLab.com, you will be able to print, complete with cover sheet, as many activities as you choose. Be sure to save your work. Taking your printed portfolio to an employment interview could be helpful in obtaining a job.

The portfolio activity for this chapter is Establishing Organization Culture at Eden's Fresh Company. Read the highlight about Eden's Fresh Company and perform the skills activities that follow.

Establishing Organization Culture at Eden's Fresh Company

Brian Certo had just graduated from college with an MBA. Rather than entering the job market, he decided to open Eden's Fresh Company, a fast casual restaurant specializing in salads and wraps in a town in the U.S. state of Florida.

Brian began planning for the opening of Eden's by producing a spreadsheet reflecting all projected costs and revenues anticipated. Having developing a spreadsheet business model that seemed workable, Brian began taking steps to start his restaurant. His first step was to recruit a partner, Colin Knight, who had just graduated from the University of Florida. Together, Brian and Colin acquired funding, selected and renovated a site, interviewed and chose suppliers, designed the restaurant's décor, and purchased appropriate equipment and furnishings. As one of the last steps, they hired eight employees and began training.

Skills Activities

Assume that you are opening Eden's. The last part of your planning is to plan for and implement the organization culture that you would like to exist within the restaurant. Perform the organization culture planning tasks that follow:

1. Write a paragraph describing the type of organization culture that you would like to establish at Eden's. Be sure to emphasize all of the values that you would like to exist.

_____

_____

_____

_____

_____

_____

_____

2. List and discuss in detail five cultural artifacts that you would use to implement and maintain the values contained in your organization culture vision.

Artifact 1:

_____

_____

_____

What organization culture value does this artifact emphasize and how?

_____

_____

_____

Artifact 2:

_____

_____

What organization culture value does this artifact emphasize and how?

_____

_____

_____

_____

Artifact 3:

_____

_____

_____

_____

What organization culture value does this artifact emphasize and how?

_____

_____

_____

_____

Artifact 4:

_____

_____

_____

_____

What organization culture value does this artifact emphasize and how?

_____

_____

_____

_____

Artifact 5:

_____

_____

_____

_____

What organization culture value does this artifact emphasize and how?

_____

_____

_____

_____

EXPERIENTIAL EXERCISE: EXPLORING THE VALUES OF NEW RECRUITS

Directions. Read the following scenario and then perform the listed activities. Your instructor may want you to perform the activities as an individual or within groups. Follow all of your instructor's directions carefully.

You are the head of the human resources department of a major real estate investment company involved in buying and selling commercial real estate property around the world. You have a new position opening and next week you will be going to the Kelly School of Business at Indiana University to interview prospective graduating students who might fill this position. Today you are meeting with a small group of human resource personnel to develop a plan for uncovering during a job interview the personal values that prospective job applicants might have. You and your team understand how important it is to discover such values as part of the organizational socialization process.

Directions. Your instructor will divide your class into small groups and designate who will be the head of human resources. This individual will lead the group in developing its plan. Later in the class your instructor might ask someone from each group to *actually conduct* the planned employment interview with someone outside the group. This interview might be video taped and replayed in class for special discussion and learning opportunities.

Sales Executive Opening

Opening: Chicago Sales Executive	
Company: Real Estate Sales Worldwide, 215 employees	
Salary: USD 50,000/year, Benefits: Medical, Dental, Vision, 401(k), and Vacation	
Industry: Real Estate	
Location: Chicago, IL	
Status: Full Time, Employee	
Career: No Experience Necessary	
Education Required: Bachelor's Degree	
Expectation of Employee: Team-oriented individual, will be successful in direct sales, possesses time management skills, will contribute to overall marketing plan, will provide innovative ideas, and will increase sales volume in slow periods.	
Essential Job Duties Include: Solicit new real estate buyers in the local market, follow furnished sales leads, design and execute strategies to meet sales goals, analyze market trends, attend networking events, attend trade shows, schedule property tours with customers, make sales presentations, and schedule customer meetings.	

C A S E S

ESTABLISHING A SAFETY CULTURE AT BP

"Establishing a Safety Culture at BP" (p. 465) and its related Challenge Case Summary were written to help you better understand the management concepts contained in this chapter. Answer the following discussion questions about the Challenge Case to better understand how concepts relating to organization culture be applied in a company such as BP.

1. What first step would you advise Hayward to take in establishing the new safety focus in the organization culture at BP? Why would this be the first step that you recommend?

2. Assuming that you're Hayward, would you choose to establish a clan, market, hierarchy, or adhocracy culture at BP? Why?

3. Discuss how you would ensure that BP's organization culture is a high-performance culture.

ONE CULTURAL BRICK AT A TIME AT LEGO[35]

Read the case and answer the questions that follow. Studying this case will help you better understand how concepts relating to organization culture can be applied in a company like LEGO.

Brick by plastic brick, the world of LEGO is built on fantasy. Whether it's Viking ships and model houses for kids or high-tech toys for adults that can be plugged into a computer and designed via the Internet, following instructions has always been optional when it comes to arranging the 8,000 different interlocking pieces that form the LEGO universe . . .

Unfortunately, what makes for a great toy doesn't always make for a great toy company. And by the 1990s, with children turning away from traditional toys in favor of videogames and PCs, LEGO had lost its way. Privately held and still majority-controlled by Christiansen's heirs, LEGO tried and failed to expand into everything from clothes and computer games to LEGO theme parks in Europe and the United States. By 2004, LEGO was losing hundreds of millions a year, and the company looked as if it might go the way of a once-beloved game now consigned to the attic.

Enter Jorgen Vig Knudstorp, a boyish 37-year-old Dane who combines modesty with bluntness about the importance of making money and surviving in a world dominated by PlayStations and iPods. Since taking over as CEO a year and a half ago, the former McKinsey consultant has done more than cut jobs (1,000 in Billund alone) and outsource manufacturing to cheaper locales such as the Czech Republic.

LEGO's first leader to come from outside the founding family, Knudstorp has also upended LEGO's corporate culture, replacing "nurturing the child" as the top priority in LEGO's employee mission statement with "I am here to make money for the company." That might sound obvious to most people, but in sleepy Billund, with a population of 6,500 who have long looked to LEGO as both their chief employer and paterfamilias, it has been a shock. "The company was very focused on doing good—that's fine," says Knudstorp, sitting in a glass-enclosed office surrounded by LEGO toys, from big block Duplos for the toddler set to Bionicles, futuristic creations that scarcely resemble the LEGOs most of us remember. "But the attitude was 'We're doing great stuff for kids—don't bother us with financial goals.' It was a culture where delivering what was promised wasn't critical."

Knudstorp's cultural revolution also reached into the cultlike quarters of LEGO's design team. Development time for new toys has been sliced in half, with the goal of going from idea to box in 12 months. To save on manufacturing costs, LEGO has cut the number of pieces, or "elements," as they are known—for example, eliminating different versions of a little chef, some with a mustache, some without. "People had personal relationships with elements," says design director Dorthe Kjaerulff, describing how her staff fought to keep favorites alive but in the end created a memorial to the discontinued pieces, complete with little black crosses.

More serious cuts were also made; they included selling off LEGO's theme parks division for nearly $500 million last summer and reducing LEGO's worldwide employment from 7,300 in 2004 to 5,300 today. LEGO still employs 1,000 blue-collar workers churning out elements in Billund, and while Knudstorp says he wants to preserve as many of those jobs as possible, the company is scouting out new factories in Eastern Europe.

Knudstorp says LEGO still has a ways to go, but his efforts appear to be paying off. The company eked out an $87 million net profit last year, after losing more than $300 million in 2004, while revenues rose 12 percent to $1.2 billion. And new games built around Batman comics, Star Wars movies, and Ferrari race cars seem to be connecting with the children of parents who grew up on simple red, white, and yellow LEGO bricks.

QUESTIONS

1. Upon Knudstorp's arrival at LEGO, was the organization culture healthy or unhealthy? Explain.

2. Describe Knudstorp's vision for the new culture at LEGO. What were the primary dimensions of the new culture?

3. Assuming that you are Knudstorp, list three artifacts you would use to reinforce behavior within the new culture. Explain why you would use each artifact.

VIDEONET EXERCISE

Organizational Culture at Terracycle

VIDEO HIGHLIGHTS

Picture the following and you begin to get a sense of the culture at TerraCycle. Most the employees are 25 and younger, and they're willing to work insane hours for minimal pay because they believe in the company. All of the desks, chairs, phones, and computers in the office are recycled or made out of recycled materials. The outside of the building is covered in graffiti. Every year, they have a graffiti jam in which they paint all the walls black again so new graffiti artists from all over the world can give the place a new look. In honor of their graffiti-rich workplace, they are launching a new line of pots covered in original graffiti as well. Culture can be hard to discern at a large corporation, but at TerraCycle, you can't miss it.

Discussion Questions

1. How does TerraCycle's use of graffiti support their organizational culture?
2. Which of the primary mechanisms for reinforcing culture is used most by Tom Szaky, CEO and founder of TerraCycle?
3. How does the organizational culture of TerraCycle contribute to the organization's success?

Internet Activity

Go to TerraCycle's home page at www.TerraCycle.net. How have they used their company products to build their corporate culture? Explain.

20 Encouraging Creativity and Innovation

TO HELP BUILD MY CREATIVITY AND INNOVATION
SKILL, WHEN STUDYING THIS CHAPTER, I WILL
ATTEMPT TO ACQUIRE:

1. A definition of creativity
   and an awareness of its
   importance in
   organizations

2. Insights about the three
   components that comprise
   creativity in individuals

3. Guidelines for how to
   increase creativity in
   organizations

4. A definition of innovation
   and an understanding of

   the relationship between
   creativity and innovation

5. An awareness of the
   innovation process

6. An understanding of total
   quality as a base for
   spawning creative ideas

7. Insights about achieving
   quality and the quality
   improvement process

TARGET SKILL

creativity and innovation skill: the ability to
generate original ideas or new perspectives
on existing ideas and to take steps to
implement these new ideas

FOSTERING CREATIVITY AND INNOVATION AT HORMEL FOODS

Jeffrey Ettinger is the chief executive officer of Hormel Foods Corporation, a multinational manufacturer of meat and food products. The company has more than 19,000 employees.

Hormel Foods has long enjoyed a strong reputation for innovation. As an example, George A. Hormel, the founder of the company, encouraged his employees to "Originate, don't imitate." This philosophy, which continues today, is largely responsible for Hormel's products, which are highly regarded for quality, taste, nutrition, and value. Products include hams, bacon, sausages, franks, and canned luncheon meats. Perhaps the most easily recognized company label names are Fast 'n Easy, Always Tender, and Jennie-o-Turkey Store.

Probably the best known Hormel product is Spam. Developed in the 1930s by Jay C. Hormel, founder of the company, Spam was initiated as the result of a creative way to use pork shoulder meat left over from pork processing. The leftover pork shoulder was actually thrown away until Hormel came up with the idea for this product. Spam gained national attention during World War II, when it was served to U.S. troops morning, noon, and night. On the home front during the war, Spam became a popular standby when fresh meat was scarce.

Horme s   meat pouch s 'oven-ready' for anyth ng

Hormel's new standup pouch packs a punch for meats and roasts under its own Oven Ready label and under the Sutton & Dodge brand being unveiled at Target Super Stores.

Lauren R. Hartman, Senior Editor   Packaging Digest, 5/1/2007

Hormel Foods known for its Dinty Moore(R) canned stews chili and Spam luncheon meat, has adopted a generously sized package for refrigerated fresh meats and roasts. Called the Showpack(R) standup pouch from P ntpack (www.printpack.com), the handy package with a "no-goof" inner oven bag is being used for five different stockkeeping nits One of them is being sold at Super Target stores nder

Hormel Foods has performed well over its long history by developing creative new products.

Despite the company's long history, Hormel continues to innovate and produce new products. Recently, Hormel introduced a new line of meats that contain proprietary cook-in bags. These bags allow consumers to put the meat in the oven without actually touching the meat; this new packaging helps consumers to keep their hands clean during the cooking process. This new packaging is a first for the meat category, and Hormel reports that initial sales have exceeded expectations.

In addition to the new products introduced by the company, Hormel has also used innovative techniques to improve the processes used in its manufacturing facilities. For example, engineers at Hormel recently began using personal digital assistants (PDAs) to monitor the performance of each manufacturing facility. Specifically, these engineers use their PDAs to record statistics about the quality of the company's products and employees. In addition, they use their PDAs to take pictures inside the plants if problems arise; these pictures help them to communicate these issues to engineers in other plants.

Hormel Foods management remains committed to providing consumers with high-quality, high-value products that are flavorful, nutritional, and convenient. The company's century-old tradition of product excellence is valued today by management as much as ever before.[1]

"EXPLORE YOUR OWN MANAGEMENT SKILLS BY TAKING THE QUIZ ON THE NEXT PAGE"

Before studying this chapter, respond to the following questions regarding the type of advice that you would give to Hormel Food's Jeffrey Ettinger, referenced in the Challenge Case. Then address the concerning creativity and innovation challenges that he presently faces within the company. You are not expected to be a creativity and innovation expert at this point. Answering the questions now can help you focus on important points when you study the chapter. Also, answering the questions again after you study the chapter will give you an idea of how much you have learned.

Record your answers here or go to MyManagementLab.com. Recording your answers in MyManagementLab will allow you to get immediate results and see how your score compares to your classmates. If you answer the questions in the book, the answers are located in the Exploring Your Management Skill section at the end of the book.

FOR EACH STATEMENT CIRCLE:

- "Y" if you would give the advice to Ettinger.
- "N" if you would NOT give the advice to Ettinger.
- "NI" if you have no idea whether you would give the advice to Ettinger.

Mr. Ettinger, in meeting your creativity and innovation challenges at Hormel Foods, you should . . .

Before Study	After Study

1. reward Hormel's employees for extending old ideas and discourage them from producing new ideas. _____
   Y, N, NI

2. increase employee creativity by encouraging employees to ignore organizational goals. _____
   Y, N, NI

3. understand that creativity and motivation are distinct concepts that bear little relationship. _____
   Y, N, NI

4. establish and encourage worker autonomy to promote creativity within Hormel. _____
   Y, N, NI

5. establish support systems within Hormel that encourage creativity. _____
   Y, N, NI

6. limit diversity within work groups to encourage creativity.
   _____
   Y, N, NI

7. reinforce to Hormel's employees that creativity and innovation are interchangeable terms that have the same meaning. _____
   Y, N, NI

8. understand that the first step in Hormel's innovation process is monitoring. _____
   Y, N, NI

9. recognize that one of the important steps in the innovation process is integrating, which entails establishing a new product or process as a permanent part of Hormel. _____
   Y, N, NI

10. promote total quality management within Hormel as a technique that complements creativity and innovation. _____
    Y, N, NI

11. encourage innovation at Hormel, as innovation turns sound ideas into tangible benefit. _____
    Y, N, NI

12. understand that total quality management will address the quality of Hormel's products but will not address the quality of the firm's processes. _____
    Y, N, NI

13. recognize that total quality management is particularly important in the United States, because the principles of TQM were initially developed in the United States. _____
    Y, N, NI

14. promote total quality management within Hormel, because it has the ability to simultaneously increase market share and lower costs. _____
    Y, N, NI

15. view TQM as a quick fix to remedy any production processes at Hormel. _____
    Y, N, NI

THE CREATIVITY AND INNOVATION CHALLENGE

The Challenge Case discusses how Hormel Foods is experiencing declining revenue caused by both decreasing product demand and lower prices being charged customers. The case emphasizes that company management is faced with the challenge of generating creative ways for dealing with this declining revenue environment. This chapter covers concepts to help managers such as those at Hormel to find creative ways to meet such organizational challenges. Topics covered are (1) creativity, (2) innovation, and (3) total quality management as a catalyst for creativity and innovation.

CREATIVITY

This chapter begins with a focus on *creativity*. Defining creativity, the importance of creativity in organizations, creativity in individuals, and increasing creativity in organizations are discussed in the following sections.

Defining Creativity

Creativity is the ability to generate original ideas or new perspectives on existing ideas.[2] In our modern society, the term *creativity* often sparks thoughts related to the arts or literature and highly original contributions such as those of Michelangelo and his work on the figure of *David*, or Lu Xun's and his writing of *A Madman's Diary*.

Although how best to define creativity from a management viewpoint may be somewhat controversial,[3] creativity in organizations does indeed relate to generating original ideas or new perspectives on existing ideas. Originality or newness, however, is not enough when analyzing creativity from an organizational perspective. An idea must be useful and actionable. Overall, an idea must have a desirable impact on how organizational goals are accomplished. That is, an idea must be evaluated for positive impact on critical organizational factors such as productivity, communication, coordination, or product quality.

Importance of Creativity in Organizations

Creativity involves seeing issues from different angles and breaking away from old rules and norms that bind us to traditional methods of accomplishing tasks. Creativity allows us to be different and helps us find new answers and solutions to problems, both old and new.[4]

The relationship between breaking away from old rules and norms for accomplishing tasks and meeting critical organizational challenges is clear. For example, many managers face the daily challenge of motivating organization members and, as a result, are constantly searching for new ways to encourage employees to be more committed to their work. Additionally, managers often face the challenge of dealing more effectively with competitors and, as a result, commonly search for new ways to increase the quality of their products or develop new and more competitive products. Overall, meeting the challenges of motivating organization members or dealing more effectively with competitors is necessary for ensuring organizational success. Because creativity is the source of new ideas on how to meet such challenges, managers should view creativity as a vital element for ensuring organizational success.

Creativity in Individuals

Within each individual, creativity is a function of three components. These components are expertise, creative thinking skills, and motivation. Figure 20.1 illustrates these three components and depicts how, when overlapping, they result in creativity.

Expertise, as depicted in Figure 20.1, is everything an individual knows and can do in the broad domain of his or her work. This knowledge pertains to work-related techniques and procedures as well as a thorough understanding of overall work circumstances. Take, for example, a produce worker in a hypermarket. Her expertise includes basic abilities in trimming and cleaning fresh fruits and vegetables, building appealing displays that encourage customers to buy products, and building customer relations. As with all organization members, the abilities of this produce worker can be acquired through formal education, experience, and interaction with peers and other professionals.

Creative thinking is the capacity to put existing ideas together in new combinations. Overall, creative thinking determines how flexibly and imaginatively individuals approach problems. For example, the produce worker will tend to be more creative if she feels comfortable disagreeing with people about how the produce department

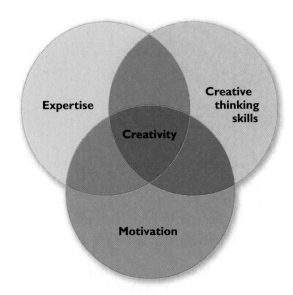

FIGURE 20.1
The three components of creativity

presently functions. Such disagreement will often result in new thoughts about how to improve the department, such as keeping produce fresher for longer periods. In addition, she will tend to have more creative success if she keeps plodding along to face and solve department problems, such as buying new technology to keep produce cool and not necessarily always looking for quick problem solutions. This enduring attention to problems will afford the produce worker the attention necessary to generate creative solutions to complex organizational problems.

Motivation, as depicted in Figure 20.1, refers to an individual's need or passion to be creative. If an individual feels a need to be creative, that individual is more likely to do so. Expertise and creative thinking are the individual's raw materials for being creative, but motivation determines whether an individual will actually be creative. An individual can be driven to be creative either extrinsically through organizational rewards and punishments, or intrinsically through personal interest and passion related to a situation. Normally, people will be most creative when motivated by personal interest, satisfaction, and the challenge of the work. Continuing with our hypermarket example, the produce worker could have the expertise and critical thinking necessary to be creative, but unless she is motivated, she probably will not be creative. Generally, the produce worker will be more motivated to be creative if she is personally interested in hypermarket problems, tends to be personally satisfied by solving these problems, and sees solving the problems as challenging.

class discussion highlight

CREATIVITY AND INNOVATION SKILL AND YOUR CAREER

The previous sections have highlighted the importance of creativity for organizational success. As such, organizations will continue to search for creative employees. How would you rate your own creativity skills? What evidence do you have to support your rating? Think about an interview with a potential employer who is searching for creative employees. How would you use examples from your life to demonstrate your creative skills? In addition to helping you obtain a job, your creative skills might help you advance in an organization. If you currently hold a job, how might you demonstrate your creative skills to your manager?

Increasing Creativity in Organizations

As discussed, creativity is a critical ingredient for meeting challenges in organizations of all types. Accordingly, managers should conscientiously take specific action aimed at building creativity in organizations. To encourage creativity in organizations, managers can take the steps discussed next.[5]

Challenge Workers Of all of the steps that managers can take to stimulate creativity, perhaps the most effective is providing organization members with an appropriate level of job-related challenge. When people feel appropriately challenged, they seem almost naturally to search for new creative ideas to help perform a job in an improved way. People should not be placed in jobs that are too simple or too difficult. If organization members have jobs that stretch their abilities too little, they can easily become bored on the job and distracted from being creative. If a job stretches worker abilities too much, workers can feel overwhelmed and therefore not inclined to generate creative solutions to job-related problems. Managers must struggle to understand both organization members and their jobs to make sure that workers are challenged at a level that encourages creative solutions for meeting job challenges.

Establish Worker Autonomy People tend to be more creative in their jobs if they have some freedom to influence the process used to perform their jobs. Providing this freedom, of course, assumes that organization members have a clear understanding of work goals to be accomplished. Without such understanding, organization member creativity will lack the consistent direction needed to promote organizational success. Overall, creativity is promoted to the best advantage of organizations when members are clear on work goals to accomplish and can exercise some freedom in determining better ways of accomplishing these goals.

Afford Time for Accomplishing Work Appropriate time is commonly discussed as a critical resource that fuels creativity in organization members. Without enough time in which to perform a job appropriately, organization members can be so engaged with simply performing a job that generating creative solutions to job-related problems is curbed. Managers who use unnecessarily tight deadlines to push organization members to reach higher levels of production can simultaneously cause employees to feel overly controlled and helpless in terms of being creative.

In addition to providing plenty of challenging tasks and worker autonomy, Google also allows its employees sufficient time to accomplish their jobs. That includes down time that helps refresh their creative juices. Here two Google employees use some down time to engage in a light saber duel at the office.

In the past, many managers believed that organization members normally generated their best creative ideas when operating under tight time constraints. Based upon this belief, managers imposed tight deadlines as a tactic for encouraging creativity in organizations. A recent stream of research, however, suggests that time pressures can actually affect creativity in different ways, depending on various other organizational conditions.[6]

The time-pressure/creativity matrix presented in Figure 20.2 illustrates how managers can either encourage or discourage the likelihood of creative thinking in organizations depending upon how high and low time pressures are combined with various organizational factors. According to this matrix, given the condition of low time pressure, the likelihood of creativity in an organization could be low if workers feel they're *on autopilot* and get little encouragement to be creative from management. Under the same low time pressure condition, however, the likelihood of creativity in an organization could be high if people feel they're *on an expedition* and thereby are characterized by creativity slanted more towards exploring ideas.

High time pressure is examined in Figure 20.2. Given the high time pressure condition, the likelihood of creativity in an organization could be high if people feel they're

Time Pressure

	Low	High
High	Creative thinking under low time pressure is more likely when people feel as if they are on an expedition. They: • show creative thinking that is more oriented toward generating or exploring ideas than identifying problems. • tend to collaborate with one person rather than with a group.	Creative thinking under extreme time pressure is more likely when people feel as if they are on a mission. They: • can focus on one activity for a significant part of the day because they are undisturbed or protected. • believe that they are doing important work and report feeling positively challenged by and involved in the work. • show creative thinking that is equally oriented toward identifying problems and generating or exploring ideas.
Low	Creative thinking under low time pressure is unlikely when people feel as if they are on autopilot. They: • receive little encouragement from senior management to be creative. • tend to have more meetings and discussions with groups rather than with individuals. • engage in less collaborative work overall.	Creative thinking under extreme time pressure is unlikely when people feel as if they are on a treadmill. They: • feel distracted. • experience a highly fragmented workday, with many different activities. • don't get the sense that the work they are doing is important. • feel more pressed for time than when they are "on a mission" even though they work the same number of hours. • tend to have more meetings and discussions with groups rather than with individuals. • experience lots of last-minute changes in their plans and schedules.

Likelihood of Creative Thinking

FIGURE 20.2   Time-pressure/creativity matrix

on a mission to discover solutions to job-related problems. Under the same high pressure condition, however, the likelihood of creativity in an organization could be low if people feel they're *on a treadmill* and commonly experience extensive last-minute changes to schedules and plans.

Establish Diverse Work Groups

Work groups that are characterized by members with a diversity of perspectives and backgrounds tend to be more creative than groups characterized by members who have similar backgrounds and perspectives. Diversity by itself, however, is simply not enough. To complement this diversity in generating creativity, members of a work group should share excitement for accomplishing the group's work goal(s), be willing to help each other through difficult periods and setbacks, and recognize and respect the differences of unique knowledge and perspective that each group member possesses.

Personally Encourage Workers

As with any other desirable behavior in organizations, managers should personally encourage organization members to be creative. Such encouragement may take many different forms and range from a simple, verbal "thank you," to awarding a Creative Achievement Certificate of Appreciation, to holding a creativity appreciation luncheon.

Because managers are extremely busy and under constant pressure for achieving results, they can be easily distracted from personally encouraging creativity. Organization members often find their work challenging and interesting and can display creativity in the shorter run without much personal encouragement from management. To sustain creativity in organization members over the longer run, however, encouragement from management is vital. Such encouragement assures organization members that creativity is important to the organization and that management values creative efforts, even those that at times may be unsuccessful.

Establish Systems Support

To complement the personal encouragement discussed, organizational systems and procedures should clearly support organization member creativity. Such organizational support clearly identifies organization member creativity as a highly valued endeavor. Organizational procedures that promote information sharing and collaboration as related to solving organizational problems are examples of such a procedure. Additionally, research suggests that managers who are trustworthy and provide employees with developmental feedback help to increase employee creativity.[7]

In **an example from the world of management, Coca-Cola Company** has often been cited for creating organizational systems that clearly support organization member creativity. At Coca-Cola, being creative is considered an everyday activity, not an activity initiated by some new program or an activity focused on only from time to time. Instead, at Coca-Cola creativity is a constant theme supported throughout the very fabric of the company, including the way organization members interact through meetings and problem-solving collaboration.[8]

Hire and Retain Creative People

As one last tactic for increasing creativity in organizations, managers can attempt to hire and retain organization members who are creative. Although this tactic may sound simple, it can be difficult to implement. Identifying people who are creative can be a formidable challenge. Retaining creative employees is particularly important given research suggesting that individuals' social structures can influence their creativity.[9] In other words, it may help to surround creative employees with other creative employees. To help managers identify creative people, Figure 20.3 contains a list of characteristics that creative people tend to possess.

Creative people tend to be...	
...free spirited	...open to new opportunities
...unorthodox	...flexible decision makers
...quiet	...open to taking risk
...introverted	...persistent
...emotional	...tolerant of ambiguity
...challenging reality	...perceptive
...outrageous	...willing to grow
...intuitive	...willing to change
...playful	...tolerant of criticism
...humorous	...moderately concerned with failure
...different	...trying new things

FIGURE 20.3
Characteristics of creative people

INNOVATION

This second major chapter segment builds upon the topic of creativity by discussing *innovation*. The discussion focuses on defining innovation, linking innovation and creativity, and the innovation process.

Defining Innovation

The term *innovation* can be defined in several different ways.[10] From a management viewpoint, **innovation** is the process of applying a new idea to the improvement of organizational processes, products, or services. Innovation is critical to the long-run success of virtually any organization. Without innovation, organizations tend to become less competitive and less desirable to customers as well as organization members. Overall, organizations that do not innovate tend to fail.[11] Many management theorists believe that innovation is so critical that it not only can fuel the prosperity of organizations, but of nations.[12] To be sure, though, innovation starts with employees. In **an example from the world of management**, Arthur Levinson, chairman and chief executive officer of **Genentech**, which is one of the leading biotechnology companies in the world, said "If you want an innovative environment, hire innovative people, listen to them tell you what they want, and do it."[13] Table 20.1 displays a list of some of the most innovative companies in the world.

Linking Innovation and Creativity

Confusion often exists in organizations over the relationship between innovation and creativity.[14] Basically, innovation involves turning a new idea into new or improved processes, products, or services that promote the attainment of organizational goals. The ideas upon which innovation is based come from creativity in the organization. Innovation is the process of turning those ideas into something tangible that benefits the organization. An organization that is creative but not innovative is characterized by a fertile source of good ideas, but lacking in the ability to make the ideas tangible. An organization that is innovative but not creative is characterized by the ability to turn ideas into tangible benefit, but lacking good ideas to make tangible. Figure 20.4 illustrates that organizations can be either creative or innovative, and makes the point that managers should strive to build organizations that are both a source of sound ideas and capable of turning the ideas into tangible benefits for the organization.

TABLE 20.1	The World's Most Innovative Companies
1. Apple	
2. Google	
3. Toyota	
4. General Electric	
5. Microsoft	
6. Procter & Gamble	
7. 3M	
8. Walt Disney	
9. IBM	
10. Sony	

Source: Based on Jena McGregor, "25 Most Innovative Companies," *BusinessWeek*, May 14, 2007, 52–60.

The Innovation Process

Innovation process is defined as the steps that managers take to implement creative ideas. In reality, the number of steps that specific implementations require may be debatable. Such steps can range from straightforward steps, such as issuing specific orders to production supervisors, to complicated steps that might include determining the potential value of a planned innovation under consideration. To make managing the innovation process more practical, however, managers can visualize the process as having five main steps: inventing, developing, diffusing, integrating, and monitoring. Each step is discussed here.[15]

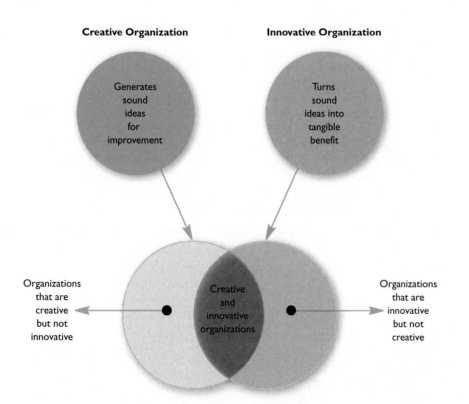

FIGURE 20.4
Managers should strive to build organizations that are both creative and innovative

class discussion highlight

MODERN RESEARCH AND CREATIVITY AND INNOVATION SKILL

Creativity and Incentives

How can companies encourage employees to come up with creative ideas? Managers struggle with this important question on a routine basis. Olivier Toubia attempts to shed light on this issue through his study of incentives and creativity.[16]

In Toubia's experimental study, subjects were asked to provide creative ideas to solve a fictional problem. Even though all subjects studied the same problem, they received different incentives. In the "Flat" incentive, subjects received a flat monetary reward ($10) for participation. In the "Impact" condition, each subject was rewarded based on the impact of his or her ideas. The ideas were then judged by a panel of experts in terms of uniqueness, length, breadth, and depth.

Do you think that incentives influenced the subjects' creative ideas? If so, how?

STEP 1 **Inventing. Inventing** is defined as that step of the innovation process that establishes a new idea that could help the organization to be more successful. The innovation process begins with the determination of some new idea. Consistent with the previous section of this chapter, creativity provides such ideas within organizations. Such ideas naturally vary from organization to organization but usually fall into one of the following categories: technology, product, process, and management.[17]

- **Technology ideas** are ideas that focus on invention that enhances the use of technology within organizations. Technology ideas can cover a broad array of topics and could include ideas such as employing bar coding to better manage inventory or using videoconferencing to help organization members across the globe communicate more effectively.

- **Product ideas** are ideas that focus on invention that develops new products or services, or enhances existing products or services. Such ideas can include issues related to product pricing, promoting products in the marketplace, distributing products, packaging products, and advertising products.

- **Process ideas** are ideas that focus on inventions for improving a manufacturing process. Examples of process ideas could include adopting robotics to make a manufacturing process more efficient, or redesigning work stations to make workers more productive.

- **Management ideas** are ideas that focus on invention relating to the way in which the organization is managed. These ideas involve management as a whole and center on improving human resource management, redesigning organizational structure, changing organizational leadership, or refining competitive strategy.

One interesting example of inventing in organizations involves a new idea in the photography equipment industry.[18] Eastman Kodak, a major company in this industry, has for decades successfully sold traditional photography products. Over the years, Kodak has been especially successfully manufacturing and selling disposable cameras employing traditional film. To better deal with the new wave of digital photography being pushed by competitors, Kodak developed the idea of manufacturing and selling disposable digital cameras. This idea would probably be categorized as a product idea, since the new disposable digital camera is actually a modification of the existing disposable camera employing traditional film.

STEP 2 **Developing. Developing** is defined as that step of the innovation process that makes a new idea practical. After being established in step 1, an idea must next be

The giant Airbus A380 passenger aircraft represents an innovative manufacturing process, in which parts are made in a number of different countries and then assembled at plants in France.

developed, or made practical as a vehicle for enhancing organizational success. Some creative ideas defy practicality and should never be pursued.[19] On the other hand, some ideas are practical and can focus on diverse areas such as improving cell phone service to attract more customers,[20] adding attractions to a theme park to make it more competitive,[21] or better training to conquer the hurdle of getting professionals both comfortable and effective with operating newly purchased equipment.[22]

3M Company has become world famous for developing new ideas. Perhaps the most well-known 3M innovation is the Post-It note. 3M may have achieved this fame through a formal, simple, and well-established company policy that helps to assure that every idea that deserves to be developed is indeed developed. This policy encourages employees to see if managers in other parts of the company will help to develop a new idea after the employee's immediate boss has rejected it.[23]

Eastman Kodak's new idea for establishing a new disposable digital camera illustrates step 1 of the innovation process. Step 2 of the innovation process indicates that this new camera idea must now be made practical. In essence, management must now determine feasible methods for manufacturing and selling the new camera. Such a determination would include where the camera will be manufactured, what suppliers will be involved in manufacturing the camera, and how the camera will be sold.

STEP 3 Diffusing. **Diffusing** is defined as that step of the innovation process that puts a new idea to use by end users or customers. Step 3 of the innovation process takes place after an idea has been established (step 1) and developed (step 2). If the idea is for an improvement to an organizational process, organization members who would be affected by the idea would explore using the idea to test its utility and worth. If the idea is for establishing a new product, perhaps certain customers would be given a prototype product to test the ultimate utility and worth of the product.

In the Eastman Kodak example the idea for manufacturing and selling a disposable digital camera was established and the new product was made practical in innovation process steps 1 and 2, respectively. In step 3, customers would actually be given prototype disposable digital cameras to enable Kodak to determine camera utility and worth to customers. If customer feedback is negative at this point, Kodak may wish to discontinue the disposable digital camera project or take additional time to improve the proposed product. If customer feedback is positive at this point, Kodak would probably proceed to the next step of the innovation process.

STEP 4 Integrating. **Integrating** is defined as that step of the innovation process that establishes an invention as a permanent part of the organization. If the invention focuses

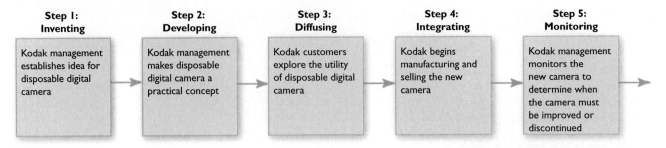

FIGURE 20.5 How steps of the innovation process relate to Eastman Kodak's disposable digital camera innovation

on a new organizational process, for example, management takes steps to make the new process standard operating procedure within the organization. If the invention focuses on a new product, management takes steps to start manufacturing and selling the new product to the marketplace.

In the example of relating Kodak's proposed disposable digital camera to the innovation process, the idea for the camera has been established, developed or made practical, and customers have verified the desirable value and worth of the product. Now, in step 4, Kodak management integrates the new idea or makes the new disposable digital camera an established component of the company's product line. In essence, management takes appropriate steps to start manufacturing and selling the new camera.

STEP 5 Monitoring. Monitoring is that step of the innovation process in which a newly implemented idea is tracked to determine if and when the idea should be improved or terminated. Management monitors newly implemented ideas to make sure contributions to organizational success generated by the ideas continues to accrue. As long as implemented ideas continue to make a contribution to organizational success, the useful lives of those ideas continue. When new ideas cease to make a contribution to organizational success, however, the ideas should be improved or terminated.

At this stage of the innovation process in the Kodak example, the idea for the camera was established, was made practical for use, customers endorsed the idea, and the camera is being built and sold. Now Kodak must monitor the contribution that the new disposable digital camera makes to organizational success and be improved or discontinued when the contribution becomes unacceptable. Figure 20.5 summarizes the major steps of the innovation process discussed here and shows how the Eastman Kodak disposable digital camera example relates to each step.

CATALYST FOR CREATIVITY AND INNOVATION: TOTAL QUALITY MANAGEMENT

As discussed earlier, creativity spawns new ideas to promote organizational success and innovation makes those ideas a reality. As also discussed earlier, organization member expertise is normally a significant catalyst in spawning new creative ideas.

This section presents critical insights into building expertise in total quality management for both managers and nonmanagers in organizations. This expertise is intended as a wellspring for generating new creative, quality-oriented ideas to promote organizational success. Major topics discussed are the essentials of total quality management and creative ideas based upon TQM expertise.

Essentials of Total Quality Management (TQM)

This chapter section outlines the fundamental principles of total quality management. Topics include defining total quality management, the importance of quality in organizations, established quality awards, and the quality improvement process.

Defining Total Quality Management Quality is defined as how well a product does what it is supposed to do—how closely and reliably it satisfies the specifications to which it is built. Quality is presented as the degree of excellence on which products or services can be ranked on the basis of selected features.

Total quality management (TQM) is the continuous process of involving all organization members in ensuring that every activity related to the production of goods or services has an appropriate role in establishing product quality.[24] In other words, all organization members emphasize the appropriate performance of activities throughout the company in order to maintain the quality of products offered by the company. Under the TQM concept, organization members work both individually and collectively to maintain the quality of products offered to the marketplace.

Although the TQM movement actually began in the United States, its establishment, development, and growth throughout the world are largely credited to the Japanese. The Japanese believe that a TQM program should be companywide and must include the cooperation of all people within a company. Top managers, middle managers, supervisors, and workers throughout the company must strive together to ensure that all phases of company operations appropriately affect product quality. The company operations referred to include areas such as market research, research and development, product planning, design, production, purchasing, vendor management, manufacturing, inspection, sales, after-sales customer care, financial control, personnel administration, and company training and education.

The Importance of Quality Many managers and management theorists warn that organizations without high-quality products will soon be unable to compete in the world marketplace. A 1990 book by Armand V. Feigenbaum put the problem succinctly:

> **Quality. Remember it? American manufacturing has slumped a long way from the glory days of the 1950s and 1960s when "Made in the U.S.A." proudly stood for the best that industry could turn out. . . . While the Japanese were developing remarkably higher standards for a whole host of products, from consumer electronics to cars and machine tools, many U.S. managers were smugly dozing at the switch. Now, aside from aerospace and agriculture, there are few markets left where the U.S. carries its own weight in international trade. For American industry, the message is simple: Get Better or Get Beat.[25]**

Total Quality Management is a robust quality process whose development is largely credited to Japanese managers. Here Motorola employees participate in a Total Quality Management training course.

Producing high-quality products is not an end in itself. Rather, successfully offering high-quality goods and services to the marketplace typically results in three important ends for the organization: a positive company image, lower costs and higher market share, and decreased product liability costs.

POSITIVE COMPANY IMAGE A reputation for high-quality products creates a positive image for an organization, and organizations gain many advantages from having such an image. A positive image helps a firm recruit valuable new employees, accelerate sales of its new products, and obtain needed loans from financial institutions. To summarize, high-quality products generally result in a positive company image, which leads to numerous organizational benefits.[26]

LOWER COSTS AND HIGHER MARKET SHARE Activities that support product quality benefit the organization by yielding lower costs and greater market share. Figure 20.6 illustrates this point. As shown in the top half of this figure, greater market share or gain in product sales is a direct result of customer perception of improved product quality. As shown in the bottom half of the figure, organizational activities that contribute to product quality result in such benefits as increased productivity, lower rework and scrap costs, and lower warranty costs, which, in turn, result in lower manufacturing costs and lower costs of servicing products after they are sold. Figure 20.6 also makes the important point that both greater market share and lower costs attributed to high quality normally result in greater organizational profits.

DECREASED PRODUCT LIABILITY COSTS Product manufacturers are increasingly facing costly legal suits over damages caused by faulty products. More and more frequently, organizations

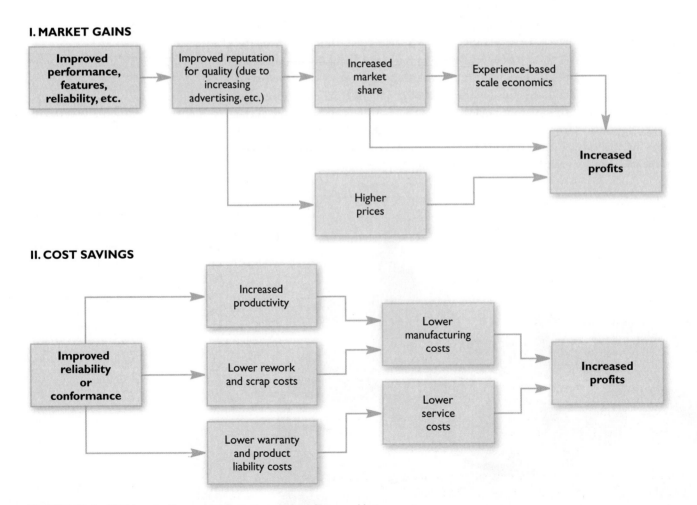

FIGURE 20.6 TQM typically results in greater market share and lower costs

that design and produce faulty products are being held liable in the courts for damages resulting from the use of such products. To take one dramatic example, Pfizer, a company that develops mechanical heart valves, recently settled an estimated 180 lawsuits by heart-implant patients claiming that the valves used in their implants were faulty.[27] Successful TQM efforts typically result in improved products and product performance, and the normal result of improved products and product performance is lower product liability costs.

Established Quality Awards Recognizing all these benefits of quality, U.S. companies have placed significant emphasis on manufacturing high-quality products. Several major awards have been established in the United States and abroad to recognize those organizations that produce exceptionally high-quality products and services. The most prestigious international award is the Deming Award, established in Japan in honor of W. Edwards Deming, who introduced Japanese firms to statistical quality control and quality improvement techniques after World War II. The Malcolm Baldrige National Quality Award, awarded by the American Society of Quality and Control, was established in 1988.[28]

As these examples suggest, quality is an increasingly important element in an organization's ability to compete in today's global marketplace.

The Quality Improvement Process Two approaches may be taken to improve quality. The first is the one advocated by most of the quality experts. This process can be described as "incremental improvement"—or improve one thing at a time. Actually, many incremental improvements may be undertaken simultaneously throughout an organization; recall Toyota's average of instituting 5,000 improvements per day in 1982.

The second approach, advocated by Michael Hammer, consists of completely reengineering a process.[29] This approach requires starting with a clean slate. Management looks at operations and asks, "If we were to start over today, how would we do this?"

Each approach is discussed in detail in the following sections.

THE INCREMENTAL IMPROVEMENT PROCESS Researchers and consultants have advocated a variety of incremental approaches to achieving excellent quality in products and processes. Despite their differences, almost all of these plans bear some remarkable similarities. Although a specific improvement process may not precisely follow the outline in Figure 20.7, most such processes at least approximate it.

- **Step 1: An area of improvement is chosen, which often is called the improvement "theme"**—Either management or an improvement team may choose the theme. Examples are:
  - Reduction in production cycle time
  - Increase in the percentage of nondefective units produced
  - Reduction in the variability of raw material going into production
  - Increase in on-time deliveries
  - Reduction in machine downtime
  - Reduction in employee absenteeism

  Many other examples are possible, of course, but these suffice to make the point that an improvement objective must be chosen.

  Consider a pizza company whose delivery business is lagging behind that of its competitors, chiefly because of slow deliveries. The improvement theme in this case may be a reduction in delivery time (i.e., cycle time).

- **Step 2: If a quality improvement team has not already been organized, one is organized**—Members of this team might include:
  - One or more associates directly responsible for the work being done

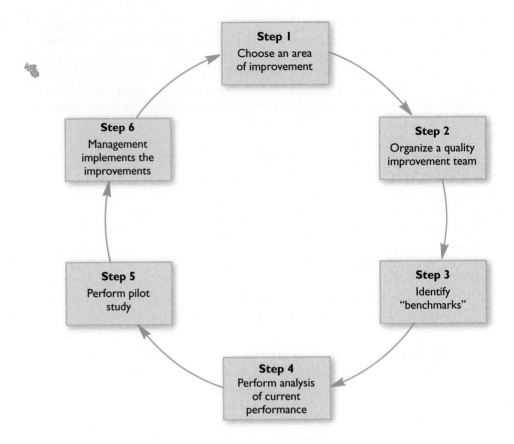

FIGURE 20.7
The incremental approach to improving quality

- • One or more customers receiving the benefits of the work
- • One or more suppliers providing input into the work
- • A member of management
- • Perhaps one or more experts in areas particularly relevant to solving the problem and making the improvement

  For the pizza delivery company, the team might include two pizza builders, a driver, a university student customer, a local resident customer, and a store manager.

- • **Step 3: The team "benchmarks" the best performers—that is, identifies how much improvement is required in order to match the best performance—** For example, the pizza company may discover in this step that the benchmark (i.e., the fastest average time between the moment an order is taken until the moment of front-door delivery) established by a competitor is 20 minutes.

  Suppose the company's current average delivery performance is 35 minutes. That leaves a minimum possible improvement of 15 minutes on the average.

- • **Step 4: The team performs an analysis to find out how current performance can be improved to meet, or beat, the benchmark—**Factors to be analyzed here include potential problems related to equipment, materials, work methods, people, and the environment, such as legal constraints, physical conditions, and weather. To return to the pizza delivery company, suppose the team discovered that the pizza-building process could be shortened by 4 minutes. Also suppose they found an average lag of 5 minutes between the time the pizza is ready and the time the delivery van picks it up. Finally, suppose the team discovered that a different oven could shorten cooking time by 7 minutes. Total potential savings in delivery time, then, would be 16 minutes—which would beat the benchmark by 1 minute.

- • **Step 5: The team performs a pilot study to test the selected remedies to the problem—**In the pizza case, suppose the team conducted a pilot program for a month, during which the new pizza-building process was implemented, a new driver and van were added, and a new oven was rented. At the end of the month, suppose actual improvement was 17 minutes on average.

The question then becomes, "Is the improvement worth the cost?" In this case, the improved pizza-building process is improving other customer service as well, thereby increasing the company's overall sales capacity. By beating the benchmark, the company can establish a new delivery system standard—a significant marketing advantage. Suppose, then, that a cost–benefit study favors the changes.

- **Step 6: Management implements the improvements**—Making many such incremental improvements can greatly enhance a company's competitiveness. Of course, as more and more companies achieve better and better quality, the market will become more and more demanding. The key, therefore, is to continually improve both product and process.

REENGINEERING IMPROVEMENTS Hammer argues that significant improvement requires "breaking away from . . . outdated rules and . . . assumptions." It demands a complete rethinking of operations. He, too, recommends that management organize a team representing the functional units involved in the process to be reengineered, as well as other units that depend on the process.

One important reason for reengineering instead of attempting incremental improvements is the need to integrate computerized production and information systems. This change is expensive and one that is difficult to accomplish piecemeal through an incremental approach.

Hammer outlines seven principles of reengineering:

- **Principle 1: Organize around outcomes, not tasks**—Traditionally, work has been organized around different tasks, such as sawing, typing, assembling, and supervising. This first principle of reengineering would, instead, have one person or team performing all the steps in an identified process. The person or team would be responsible for the outcome of the total process.

- **Principle 2: Have those who use the output of the process perform the process**—For example, a production department may do its own purchasing, and even its own cost accounting. This principle would require a broader range of expertise from individuals and teams, and a greater integration of activities.

- **Principle 3: Subsume information-processing work into the real work that produces the information**—Modern computer technology now makes it possible for a work process to process information simultaneously. For example, scanners at checkout counters in stores both process customer purchases and update accounting and inventory records at the same time.

- **Principle 4: Treat geographically dispersed resources as though they were centralized**—Hammer uses Hewlett-Packard as an example of how this principle works. Each of the company's 50 manufacturing units had its own purchasing department, which prevented the company from achieving the benefits of scale discounts. Rather than centralize purchasing, which would have reduced responsiveness to local manufacturing needs, Hewlett-Packard introduced a corporate unit to coordinate local purchases, so that scale discounts could be achieved. That way, local purchasing units retained their decentralized authority and preserved their local responsiveness.

- **Principle 5: Link parallel activities instead of integrating their results**—Several processes are often required to produce products and services. Too often, though, companies segregate these processes so that the product comes together only at the final stage. Meanwhile, problems may occur in one or more processes, and those problems may not become apparent until too late, at the final step. It is better, Hammer says, to coordinate the various processes so that such problems are avoided.

- **Principle 6: Put the decision point where the work is performed and build control into the process**—Even though traditional bureaucracies separate decision authority from the work, this principle suggests that the people doing the work are the ones who should make the decisions about that work. The salesperson should have the authority and responsibility to approve credit, for example. This principle saves time and allows the organization to respond more effectively and efficiently to customer needs.

Some managers worry that this principle will reduce control over the process. However, control can be built into the process. In the example cited, criteria for credit approval can be built into a computer program, so the salesperson has guidance for every credit decision.

- **Principle 7: Capture information once and at the source**—Computerized online databases help make this principle achievable. It is now easy to collect information when it originates, store it, and send it to those who need it.

Reengineering allows major improvements to be made all at once. Although reengineering can be an expensive way to improve quality, today's rapidly changing markets sometimes demand such a drastic response.

Creative Ideas Based on TQM Expertise

Expertise in TQM, understanding TQM principles, can serve as a foundation for generating creative ideas in organizations. Indeed, the number of creative ideas that can be spawned by TQM expertise seems limitless. Keep in mind, however, that an idea that may seem new and creative in one organization may not seem new and creative in another because it has already been considered. The following sections discuss several possible new ideas for organizations based on the work of Phillip B. Crosby and W. Edwards Deming, two internationally acclaimed quality experts.[30]

Possible Creative Ideas Based on Crosby's Work
Philip B. Crosby is known throughout the world as an expert in the area of quality.[31] His work provides managers with valuable insights on how to achieve product quality. According to Crosby, organizational integrity, systems, communications, operations, and policies must all be consistent with achieving product quality before significant progress in reaching product quality can be reached and maintained. Several possible creative ideas based upon Crosby's work for how to achieve quality in organizations are listed in Figure 20.8.

FIGURE 20.8
Possible creative ideas for enhancing organizational success based upon Crosby's thoughts about TQM

1. Dedicate the quality management function to measuring conformance to requirements and reporting and differences accurately.

2. Continually inform all employees about the progress of quality improvement and related successes.

3. Begin each management meeting with a factual and financial review of quality.

4. Create relevant policies on quality management that are clear and unambiguous.

5. Educate suppliers to ensure that they will deliver quality materials in a dependable fashion.

6. Dedicate top management to having customers receive products as promised.

7. Dedicate all managers to getting jobs done correctly the first time.

8. Develop communication systems that allow employees to inform management immediately about any observed deviations from quality.

9. Develop communications systems that allow managers to respond immediately to quality issues.

10. Establish an organizational bias toward handling quality issues immediately.

1. Publish quality goals for all workers so they know exactly what they are expected to do.

2. Use product inspections to improve the manufacturing process and to reduce costs.

3. Choose your suppliers on the basis of how they can support your quality goals.

4. Train for maintaining quality.

5. Drive out fear of reporting mistakes.

6. Build teams (not just individuals) that focus on quality.

7. Eliminate production processes based simply on producing a quota.

8. Create production processes based upon learning how to improve the processes.

9. Build pride for maintaining quality.

10. Encourage self-development of workers as more useful players in maintaining quality.

FIGURE 20.9
Possible creative ideas for enhancing organizational success based upon Deming's thoughts about TQM

Possible Creative Ideas Based on Deming's Work W. Edwards Deming, who originally trained as a statistician and began teaching statistical quality control in Japan shortly after World War II, is recognized internationally as a primary contributor to Japanese quality improvement programs. Deming advocated that the way to achieve product quality is continuously to improve the design of a product and the process used to manufacture it.[32] According to Deming, management has the primary responsibility for achieving product quality. Several possible creative ideas based upon Deming's work for how to achieve quality in organizations are listed in Figure 20.9.

{CHALLENGE CASE SUMMARY

The Challenge Case points out that Hormel Foods management is faced with finding creative ways to deal with declining revenue. In essence, Hormel management must seek original ideas or ideas based upon existing conditions at Hormel that will help management to meet this challenge. The ideas must not only be original, but be useful and actionable. That is, the ideas must help Hormel as a company to become more productive, communicate more effectively, achieve better coordination, and enhance product quality. Such ideas are important because they will help Hormel to break away from old rules and norms about accomplishing tasks. At Hormel, the expertise, motivation level, and creative thinking skills of organization members will be the foundation upon which creative ideas will be conceived.

Earlier information provides insights to managers such as those at Hormel regarding how to encourage creativity within the company. For example, managers at Hormel can encourage creativity by making sure that workers are challenged just enough. Worker abilities should be stretched, but not so overwhelmed that they give up on being creative. As another example, Hormel managers should make sure that workers have an appropriate level of freedom in their jobs. Workers with such freedom are prone to experiment somewhat in order to find creative solutions to job challenges.

One of the most important steps Hormel managers can take to encourage creativity in organization members is to manage time pressure carefully. Depending upon whether Hormel organization members feel they're on autopilot, on an expedition, on a mission, or on a treadmill, time pressure can either encourage or discourage creativity. Hormel managers must find the right combination of time pressure and other organizational conditions to make sure that creativity is encouraged within the company.

Hormel management should focus not only on searching for creative ideas, but on innovation, or putting those ideas into action. As an example, assume that to meet its low revenue trend challenge, the company has generated the creative idea of establishing a whole new class of fast-cooking pork loin products with various flavoring, including spicy Western barbecue and teriyaki.

Based upon the earlier discussion of the innovation process, this concept of a new class of pork loin products would indeed be an invention, a new idea. Additionally, the idea would be a *product idea,* or invention that focuses on developing new products. After generating this new product idea, Hormel management must develop the idea, or make it practical. Management must focus on where the new product will be manufactured, who will sell the product, and how the best product flavors will be developed. Once the idea is made practical, it must be diffused, or market tested. Management must assess the true potential of the new product. After the new pork loin product has been market tested with favorable results, the new product must be integrated, or made available to the marketplace. Once integrated, the new pork loin product must be monitored to make sure that its contribution to organizational success continues.

Based upon earlier information, Hormel management must realize that expertise in total quality management can serve as a stimulus for generating creative ideas within the company. As such, Hormel management should take steps to educate itself as well as other organization members about what TQM entails. All Hormel organization members should know that product quality, adherence to specifications, must be maintained throughout the product lines. The new pork loin products being offered as a new idea must have specifications regarding issues such as weight, thickness, and freshness that must be constantly maintained. Hormel organization members should realize that TQM within the company should be a continuous process involving everyone within the company, from management to salespeople to meat cutters.

Hormel has much to gain from maintaining product quality. Through product quality, Hormel will gain a positive image both inside and outside the organization. Such an image can be especially valuable when trying to recruit new and talented management. High product quality can also help Hormel to lower costs and gain market share. Gaining market share would be particularly valuable in Hormel's present declining revenue environment. Last, Hormel's high product quality can decrease liability costs. Consumers' legal suits over tainted meat, for example, can be minimized. To maximize the benefit of high product quality, Hormel management may opt to apply for the Malcolm Baldrige Award.

Hormel management can deliberate on improving quality either incrementally or through reengineering. Incremental improvement would focus on improving Hormel quality slowly and over time. Reengineering improvement would focus on improving Hormel quality through more drastic improvement in the nearer term.

Assume that Hormel management has decided to focus on improving quality at Hormel incrementally. Improving quality incrementally would involve steps such as targeting an area at Hormel for quality improvement, establishing a quality improvement team to effect desired improvements, identifying benchmarks or standards for quality, comparing current Hormel operations with the benchmarks, and performing a pilot study to see that formulated improvement activities are effective and efficient. Naturally, if the activities actually work, management would opt to adopt the activities as normal operating procedure.

Hormel management can study the work of both Crosby and Deming to gain possible new ideas for implementing and maintaining the company quality improvement process. Such ideas could include building an organization culture that has a bias for handling quality issues quickly and emphatically, dedicating top management to having customers receive all products as promised, and training organization members in how to build product quality.

MANAGEMENT SKILL ACTIVITIES

This section is specially designed to help you develop creativity and innovation skill. An individual's creativity and innovation skill is based upon an understanding of creativity and innovation concepts and the ability to apply those concepts in management situations. As a result, the following activities are designed both to heighten your understanding of creativity and innovation concepts and to help you gain facility in applying these concepts in various management situations.

UNDERSTANDING CREATIVITY AND INNOVATION CONCEPTS

This section is comprised of activities that will sharpen your understanding of creativity and innovation concepts. Answer essay questions as completely as possible. Also, remember that many additional true/false and multiple choice questions appear online at MyManagement.com to help you further refine your understanding of concepts related to responsibility and delegation.

Essay Questions

1. Define and describe the relationships between expertise, creative thinking skills, motivation, and creativity.
2. Explain the differences between creativity and innovation.
3. Describe five ways that organizations might increase creativity.
4. Describe the five steps of the innovation process.
5. Define total quality management (TQM), and describe the relationship between TQM and innovation.

Developing Management Skill

Learning activities in this section are aimed at helping you to develop your creativity and innovation skill. Learning activities include Exploring Your Management Skill: Part 2, Experiential Exercises, Cases, and a VideoNet exercise.

EXPLORING YOUR MANAGEMENT SKILL: PART 2

As you recall, you completed Exploring Your Management Skill before you started to study this chapter. Your responses gave you an idea of how much you initially knew about creativity and innovation and helped you to focus on important points as you studied the chapter. Answer the Exploring Your Management Skill questions again now (p. 492) and compare your score to the first time you took it. This comparison will give you

an idea of how much you have learned from studying this chapter and pinpoint areas for further clarification before you start studying the next chapter. Record your answers within the text or go to MyManagementLab.com. Recording your answers in MyManagementLab will allow you to get immediate results and see how your score compares to your classmates. If you answer the questions in the book, the answers are located in the Exploring Your Management Skill Appendix at the end of the book.

YOUR MANAGEMENT SKILLS PORTFOLIO

Your Management Learning Portfolio is a collection of activities especially designed to demonstrate your management knowledge and skill. By completing these online at MyManagement.com, you will be able to print, complete with cover sheet, as many activities as you choose. Be sure to save your work. Taking your printed portfolio to an employment interview could be helpful in obtaining a job.

The portfolio activity for this chapter is Innovating at Electronic Arts. Study the information and complete the exercises that that follow.[33]

Innovating at Electronic Arts

Although creativity and innovation are important for all companies, these terms are the essence of many companies. An example of such a company is Electronic Arts (EA), a company based in California, that develops, produces, markets, and distributes video games such as Tiger Woods PGA Golf, Medal of Honor, and Madden NFL.

EA is currently interested in diversifying its product line to include more video games for younger children. EA's management team views this age group as a prime target market for new video games. Specifically, EA wants you to develop a game that helps preschool through elementary school-aged children further develop their math skills. In other words, your mission is to develop a new product idea.

In the following sections, record your answers as you walk through the five steps of the innovation process.

1. *Inventing:* Describe the main characteristics of your new video game (i.e., What will the children do in the new game? How will it help them develop their math skills?).

2. *Developing:* Describe how you can make the new video game practical for EA.

_____

_____

3. *Diffusing:* How would you test the new video game's utility and worth?

_____

_____

4. *Integrating:* How would you make the new video game a permanent part of the organization?

_____

_____

5. *Monitoring:* Describe how you monitor the new video game and determine the extent to which the new game is helping EA.

_____

_____

EXPERIENTIAL EXERCISE

Creativity and innovation are important for organizational success. The BBC has contacted your group to help create a new comedy series that will consist of five-minute episodes that they will broadcast on the company's Web site. The BBC's executives want this comedy series to appeal to college-aged individuals. To be clear, NBC does not want your group to create this new series—NBC has the employees necessary to approach this project. Instead, The BBC's executives want your group to outline the most important techniques they can use to foster the creativity and innovation that they need within their company. In your group, create five different recommendations (and provide examples) to help The BBC foster creativity within the organization. Be prepared to present these recommendations in class.

C A S E S

CREATIVE SOLUTIONS AT HORMEL FOODS

"Fostering Creativity and Innovation at Hormel Foods" (p. 491) and its related Challenge Case Summary sections were written to help you better understand the management concepts contained in this chapter. Answer the following discussions about the Challenge Case to better understand how the concepts of creativity and innovation can be applied in a company such as Hormel.

1. Is creativity or innovation more important to Hormel management in facing declining revenue environment? Explain fully.
2. If you were the top manager at Hormel, name two organizational systems that you would establish to encourage organization member creativity. Be as specific as possible. Why are these systems important to the future success of Hormel?
3. List three creative ideas based upon your TQM expertise that, if implemented, would ensure Hormel's future success. Be sure to explain how each idea would contribute to that success.

THE CORE OF INNOVATION AT APPLE COMPUTER

Read the case and answer the questions that follow. Studying this case will help you better understand how the concepts of creativity and innovation can be applied in a company such as Apple Computer.

Co-founder and CEO Steve Jobs describes the work of Apple Computer with one word: "Innovate," he says. "That's what we do." His company has long been known as one of the most innovative high-tech firms on the planet. It introduced the novel Apple II personal computer in the 1970s, the user-friendly Macintosh personal computer in the 1980s, and the colorful iMac personal computer in the 1990s. Moving beyond computers, it launched the trend-setting iPod digital music player in 2001, followed by the online iTunes Music Store in 2003. The company has received more than 1,300 patents in the past decade, far outstripping the number of patents received by rival Dell, for example. And its customers are famously loyal, thanks to management's dedication to top-notch functionality and cutting-edge style.

Consider the process that Jobs and his managers used to create the iPod. Other digital music players were already on store shelves when Apple's development team came up with new software for playing songs, which they dubbed iTunes. At this point, company executives realized that existing players were selling slowly because, in the words of an Apple vice president, "the products stank." Apple hired an engineer to head an intensive development effort aimed at putting a new digital music player on the market in only nine months. The new player would have to be capable of blazing-fast Internet connections to minimize music download time. It would also have to be compatible with iTunes software, be intuitive to use, and look elegant. "From early on we wanted a product that would seem so natural and so inevitable and so simple you almost wouldn't think of it as having been designed," remembers the project's industrial designer.

The development team collected ideas from all over the Apple organization. For instance, one of the company's vice presidents contributed the idea of including a handy scroll wheel to control the iPod's operational menus. By October 2001, the first model was ready for sale, a sleek white player priced at $399. Jobs had the iPod updated often, starting with a larger-capacity version at a lower price than the original model, followed by versions ready for Windows or Macintosh operating systems, tinier cases in new fashion colors, improved battery life, and imaginative new features.

Once Apple opened its Web-based iTunes Music Store, the iPod's popularity soared even higher. Industry-wide sales of all digital players are expected to surpass 15 million units within a couple of years, which is good news for Apple, because its iPod holds a commanding market lead. Whether Jobs can maintain that healthy lead over the long term is another story. Even as Apple adds an unending series of bells and whistles to its iPod, competitors such as Dell are aiming for the mass market by selling digital music players at lower prices.

Not every Apple product has been as successful as the iPod. Look at the Newton, introduced in 1993, which was one of the first handheld computers. The Newtown never really caught on and eventually it disappeared, eclipsed by lighter, easy-to-use models from Palm that emerged as top sellers. These days, Apple's annual revenues have shot past the $6 billion level, powered mainly by sales of computers. However, the hugely popular iPod players return lower profit margins, one reason why Apple's overall profit margin is one-fifth of the industry average—and well below the company's heftier profit margins of the 1980s.

Moreover, despite a steady stream of new products and new technology, Apple's share of the global personal computer market has been shrinking. In 1989, it held 10 percent of this lucrative market; today, it holds less than 2 percent. Now the challenge for Steve Jobs and his managers is to balance Apple's appetite and aptitude for tech innovation with the ongoing need to build sales and profits.

QUESTIONS

1. How has Apple Computer relied on the three components of creativity to drive innovation?
2. Consultant Howard Anderson states: "Companies that rely too heavily on creativity flame out." Do you think this statement applies to Apple Computer? Explain.
3. If you headed Apple Computer, what would you do to help the iPod hold onto its lead in the marketplace?

VIDEONET EXERCISE

Change and Innovation at Terracycle

VIDEO HIGHLIGHTS

TerraCycle is coming out with several new products, one of which is a new fire log—a more earth-friendly pressed log made out of shredded wax cardboard (aka, recycled milk and juice containers), scrap wood chips from furniture manufacturers, and recycled glycerin. It will be wrapped in recycled newspaper ,and the only "new" part of this product will be its sticker. Tom gets orders for products that are still in development and often only has a few months to deliver. What's the method behind the madness, or is there one? Why is innovation so critical to the company's success? How does a small company like TerraCycle have an edge over many larger companies when it comes to product development cycles?

Discussion Questions

1. How does TerraCycle encourage creativity in their organization?
2. How does TerraCycle manage to successfully link innovation and creativity?
3. How important is creativity in achieving success at TerraCycle? Why?

Internet Activity

Go to TerraCycle's home page at www.TerraCycle.net. Learn more about the different products offered by this company. Can the innovation process discussed in the chapter be applied to the development of the different types of products offered by this firm? Explain.

21 Controlling, Information, and Technology

OBJECTIVES

TO HELP BUILD MY CONTROLLING SKILL, WHEN
STUDYING THIS CHAPTER, I WILL ATTEMPT TO ACQUIRE:

1. A definition of control

2. A thorough understanding of the controlling subsystem

3. Insights into the relationship between power and control

4. An understanding of the steps required to increase the quality of a controlling subsystem

5. An understanding of the relationship between data and information

6. Insights regarding the main factors that influence the value of information

7. An understanding of the importance of an information system (IS) to an organization

8. Insights regarding how to manage an IS effectively

TARGET SKILL controlling skill: the ability to use information and technology to ensure that an event occurs as it was planned to occur

CHALLENGE CASE

IMPLEMENTING CONTROLS AND TECHNOLOGY AT COCA-COLA[1]

The Coca-Cola Company manufactures and sells soft drinks and noncarbonated beverages around the globe. In addition to its major brands such as Coke, Diet Coke, and Sprite, Coca-Cola also sells juice drinks such as Minute Maid juices, water products such as Dasani, and fitness drinks such as POWERade. Although Coca-Cola is an American icon, the company faces a new environment as consumers flock to noncarbonated drinks such as coffee and tea. Moreover, the company is facing intense pressure from its most prominent competitor, PepsiCo.

Despite these problems, Coca-Cola continues to grow around the globe. Although this continued global growth provides the company with a number of benefits, it also presents the company with some challenges. One major challenge involves controlling the daily operations of a company selling approximately 1.4 billion servings of Coke per day in more than 45 countries.

Muhtar Kent, Coca-Cola's CEO, is currently attempting to overcome these controlling challenges with technology. In addition to focusing on his own company, Kent also has to manage relationships with 53 Coca-Cola bottlers around the world. Coca-Cola sells its concentrate to the bottlers, and then these bottlers distribute Coca-Cola products throughout the world. This bottler network includes more than 1,000 production facilities and a delivery fleet five times larger than that of the giant delivery service United Parcel Service.

Coca-Cola is now in the process of establishing software systems that allow Coca-Cola and its bottlers to share real-time information regarding finances, human resources, and manufacturing. Although executives at Coca-Cola do not anticipate that all of these entities will operate the same software program, they do expect these organizations to use common processes.

By sharing common processes across organizations, Coca-Cola expects to increase the quality of information used during key decision-making processes. Such information, for example, might

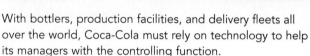

With bottlers, production facilities, and delivery fleets all over the world, Coca-Cola must rely on technology to help its managers with the controlling function.

help Coca-Cola executives to assess quickly the extent to which different markets around the world react differently to the company's new products. In addition, the company might use this information to better understand how Coca-Cola employees are responding to new human resource policies. In other words, this information will help Coca-Cola to improve its control function.

Going forward, Coca-Cola will face an increasingly competitive market. How well the company uses information to effectively control its operations will play a large role in determining whether Coca-Cola will continue to be an American icon in the future.

"EXPLORE YOUR OWN MANAGEMENT SKILLS BY TAKING THE QUIZ ON THE NEXT PAGE"

Before studying this chapter, respond to the following questions regarding the type of advice that you would give to Coca-Cola's Muhtar Kent, referenced in the Challenge Case. Then address the concerning controlling challenges that he presently faces within the company. You are not expected to be a controlling expert at this point. Answering the questions now can help you focus on important points when you study the chapter. Also, answering the questions again after you study the chapter will give you an idea of how much you have learned.

Record your answers here or go to MyManagementLab.com. Recording your answers in MyManagementLab will allow you to get immediate results and see how your score compares to your classmates. If you answer the questions in the book, the answers are located in the Exploring Your Management Skill section at the end of the book.

FOR EACH STATEMENT CIRCLE:

- "Y" if you would give the advice to Kent.
- "N" if you would NOT give the advice to Kent.
- "NI" if you have no idea whether you would give the advice to Kent.

Mr. Kent, in meeting your controlling challenges at Coca-Cola, you should . . .

*Before   After
Study   Study*

1. understand that the planning and controlling functions at Coca-Cola are clearly separate.

    Y, N, NI

2. recognize that controlling is primarily an organization-level concept and is not particularly relevant for lower-level employees.

    Y, N, NI

3. realize that the first step in the controlling process is measuring performance.

    Y, N, NI

4. understand that Coca-Cola must develop its own standards, which may or may not be the same standards as its competitors such as PepsiCo.

    Y, N, NI

5. emphasize to Coca-Cola's employees that problems and symptoms are often the same thing.

    Y, N, NI

6. understand that managerial power is a function of an individual's position and personal relationships with others.

    Y, N, NI

7. understand that conveying a high level of expertise will increase the level of power that Coca-Cola employees will associate with managers who demonstrate such expertise.

    Y, N, NI

8. understand that information has value that depends on the appropriateness, quality, timeliness, and quantity of the information.

    Y, N, NI

9. use the terms *data* and *information* interchangeably, because they are virtually the same.

    Y, N, NI

10. update information systems as needed to ensure that Coca-Cola's managers have access to the information they need to make quality decisions.

    Y, N, NI

11. recognize that the first step needed to operate an IS effectively entails summarizing data.

    Y, N, NI

12. distribute all important information to all of Coca-Cola's managers, because these managers all need access to the same information.

    Y, N, NI

13. not worry about an information system's ease of use; evidence suggests that users will learn to use even difficult systems if such use is necessary for their job performance.

    Y, N, NI

14. recognize that the world is filled with IS professionals, and as such traditional human resource management techniques are unnecessary for Coca-Cola's IS employees.

    Y, N, NI

15. understand that information security continues to represent an important factor for companies such as Coca-Cola to consider as they maintain their information systems.

    Y, N, NI

THE CONTROLLING CHALLENGE

According to the Challenge Case, issues at Coca-Cola involve maintaining and improving production costs, internal communication, communication with suppliers, and customer relations. The management function called *control* can help managers such as those at Coca-Cola improve such issues, and the material in this chapter explains why these activities would be considered controlling. The following material also elaborates on the control function as a whole. Major topics in this chapter are (1) fundamentals of controlling, (2) power and control, (3) information, and (4) information systems.

THE FUNDAMENTALS OF CONTROLLING

As the scale and complexity of modern organizations grow, so does the problem of control in organizations. Prospective managers, therefore, need a working knowledge of the essentials of the controlling function.[2] To this end, the following sections provide a definition of control, a definition of the process of controlling, and a discussion of the various types of control that can be used in organizations.

Defining Control

Stated simply, **control** entails ensuring that an event occurs as it was planned to occur.[3] As implied by this definition, planning and control are virtually inseparable functions.[4] In fact, these two functions have been called the Siamese twins of management. According to Robert L. Dewelt:

> The importance of the planning process is quite obvious. Unless we have a soundly charted course of action, we will never quite know what actions are necessary to meet our objectives. We need a map to identify the timing and scope of all intended actions. This map is provided through the planning process.
>
> But simply making a map is not enough. If we don't follow it or if we make a wrong turn along the way, chances are we will never achieve the desired results. A plan is only as good as our ability to make it happen. We must develop methods of measurement and control to signal when deviations from the plan are occurring so that corrective action can be taken.[5]

"Murphy's Law" is a lighthearted adage making the serious point that managers should continually control—that is, check to see that organizational activities and processes are going as planned. According to Murphy's Law, anything that can go wrong will go wrong.[6] This adage reminds managers to remain alert for possible problems, because even if a management system appears to be operating well, it might be eroding under the surface. Managers must always seek feedback on how the system is performing and make corrective changes whenever warranted.

Defining Controlling

Controlling is the process managers go through to control. According to Roberto Mockler, controlling is

> a systematic effort by business management to compare performance to predetermined standards, plans, or objectives to determine whether performance is in line with these standards and presumably to take any remedial action required to see that human and other corporate resources are being used in the most effective and efficient way possible in achieving corporate objectives.[7]

For example, production workers generally have daily production goals. At the end of each working day, the number of units produced by each worker is recorded so weekly production levels can be determined. If these weekly totals are significantly below weekly goals, the supervisor must take corrective action to ensure that actual production levels equal planned ones. If, on the other hand, production goals are being met, the supervisor should allow work to continue as it has in the past.[8]

The following sections discuss the controlling subsystem and provide more details about the control process itself.

Objectives
The controller (or comptroller) is responsible for all accounting activities within the organization.

Functions
1. *General accounting*—Maintain the company's accounting books, accounting records, and forms.
   a. Preparing balance sheets, income statements, and other statements and reports
   b. Giving the president interim reports on operations for the recent quarter and fiscal year to date
   c. Supervising the preparation and filing of reports to the government
2. *Budgeting*—Prepare a budget outlining the company's future operations and cash requirements.
3. *Cost accounting*—Determine the cost to manufacture a product and prepare internal reports for management of the processing divisions.
   a. Developing standard costs
   b. Accumulating actual cost data
   c. Preparing reports that compare standard costs to actual costs and highlight unfavorable differences
4. *Performance reporting*—Identify individuals in the organization who control activities and prepare reports to show how well or how poorly they perform.
5. *Data processing*—Assist in the analysis and design of a computer-based information system. Frequently, the data-processing department is under the controller, and the controller is involved in management of that department as well as other communications equipment.
6. *Other duties*—Other duties that may be assigned to the controller by the president or by corporate bylaws include:
   a. Tax planning and reporting
   b. Service departments such as mailing, telephone, janitors, and filing
   c. Forecasting
   d. Corporate social relations and obligations

FIGURE 21.1 Specific components of the controlling subsystem

The Controlling Subsystem As with the planning, organizing, and influencing functions described in earlier chapters, controlling can be viewed as a subsystem of the overall management system. The purpose of this subsystem is to help managers enhance the success of the overall management system through effective controlling. Figure 21.1 shows the specific components of the controlling subsystem.

The Controlling Process As Figure 21.2 illustrates, there are three main steps in the controlling process:

1. Measuring performance
2. Comparing measured performance to standards
3. Taking corrective action

MEASURING PERFORMANCE Before managers can determine what must be done to make an organization more effective and efficient, they must measure current organizational performance.[9] However, before they can take such a measurement, they must establish some unit of measure that gauges performance and observe the quantity of this unit as generated by the item whose performance is being measured.[10]

- *How to Measure.* A manager who wants to measure the performance of five janitors, for example, first must establish units of measure that represent janitorial performance—such as the number of floors swept, the number of windows washed,

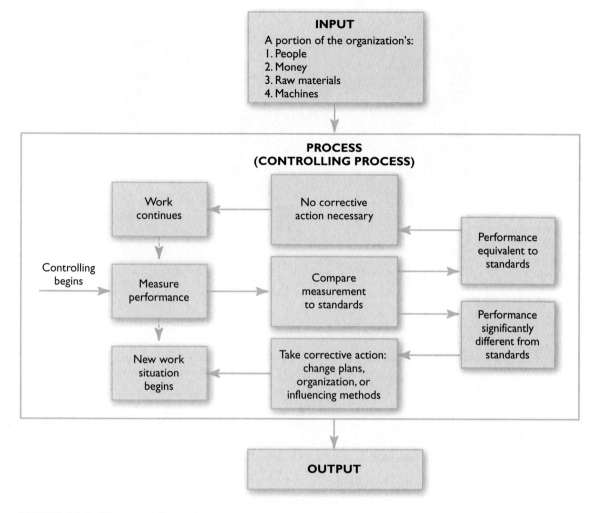

FIGURE 21.2 The controlling subsystem

or the number of light bulbs changed. After designating these units of measure, the manager has to determine the number of each of these units accomplished by each janitor. The process of determining both the units of measure and the number of units associated with each janitor furnishes the manager with a measure of janitorial performance.

- *What to Measure.* Managers must always keep in mind that a wide range of organizational activities can be measured as part of the control process. For example, the amounts and types of inventory on hand are commonly measured to control inventory, while the quality of goods and services being produced is commonly measured to control product quality. Performance measurements can relate as well to various effects of production, such as the degree to which a particular manufacturing process pollutes the atmosphere.

The degree of difficulty in measuring various types of organizational performance, of course, is determined primarily by the activity being measured. For example, it is far more difficult to measure the performance of a highway maintenance worker than to measure the performance of a student enrolled in a college-level management course.

COMPARING MEASURED PERFORMANCE TO STANDARDS Once managers have taken a measure of organizational performance, their next step in controlling is to compare this measure against some standard. A **standard** is the level of activity established to serve as a model for

This pharmacist studies an inventory list in the pharmacy store room. Understanding what to measure in inventory is a critical step in the control process.

evaluating organizational performance.[11] The performance evaluated can be for the organization as a whole or for some individuals working within the organization.[12] In essence, standards are the yardsticks that determine whether organizational performance is adequate or inadequate.[13]

In **an example from the world of management**, studying operations at **General Electric (GE)** will give us some insights into the different kinds of standards managers can establish. GE has established the following standards:

1. **Profitability standards**—In general, these standards indicate how much money GE would like to make as profit over a given period—that is, its return on investment. More and more, GE is using computerized preventive maintenance on its equipment to help maintain profitability standards. Such maintenance programs have reduced labor costs and equipment downtime and thereby have helped raise company profits.

2. **Market position standards**—These standards indicate the share of total sales in a particular market that GE would like to have relative to its competitors. GE market position standards were set by company chairman John F. Welch, Jr., in 1988, when he announced that henceforth any product his company offers must achieve the highest or second-highest market share compared to similar products offered by competitors or it would be eliminated or sold to another firm.

3. **Productivity standards**—How much various segments of the organization should produce is the focus of these standards. Management at GE has found that one of the best ways to convince organization members to commit themselves to increasing company productivity is simply to treat them with dignity and make them feel they are part of the GE team.

4. **Product leadership standards**—GE intends to assume a leading position in product innovation in its field. Product leadership standards indicate what must be done to attain such a position. Reflecting this interest in innovation, GE has pioneered the development of synthetic diamonds for industrial use. In fact, GE is considered the leader in this area, having recently discovered a method for making synthetic diamonds at a purity of 99.9 percent. In all probability, such diamonds will eventually be used as a component of super-high-speed computers.

5. **Personnel development standards**—Standards in this area indicate the type of training programs GE personnel should undergo to develop properly. GE's commitment to sophisticated training technology is an indication of the seriousness with which the company takes personnel development standards. Company training sessions are

commonly supported by sophisticated technology such as large-screen projection systems, computer-generated visual aids, combined video and computer presentations, and laser videos.

6. **Employee attitudes standards**—These standards indicate what types of attitudes GE managers should strive to inculcate in GE employees. Like many other companies today, GE is trying to build positive attitudes toward product quality in its employees.

7. **Social responsibility standards**—GE recognizes its responsibility to make a contribution to society. Standards in this area outline the level and types of contributions management believes GE should make. One recent activity that reflects social responsibility standards at GE is the renovation of a center for the homeless in the U.S. state of California, accomplished by work teams made up of GE employees. These teams painted, cleaned, and remodeled a building to create a better facility for some of San Diego's disadvantaged citizens.

8. **Standards reflecting the relative balance between short- and long-range goals**—These standards express the relative emphasis that should be placed on attaining various short- and long-range goals. GE recognizes that short-range goals exist to enhance the probability that long-range goals will be attained.

Successful managers pinpoint all important areas of organizational performance and establish corresponding standards in each area.[14] In **an example from the world of management**, **American Airlines** has set two specific standards for appropriate performance of its airport ticket offices: (1) at least 95 percent of the flight arrival times posted should be accurate, meaning that actual arrival times do not deviate more than 15 minutes from posted times, and (2) at least 85 percent of customers coming to the airport ticket counter should not have to wait more than 5 minutes to be serviced.

TAKING CORRECTIVE ACTION After actual performance has been measured and compared with established performance standards, the next step in the controlling process is to take corrective action if necessary. **Corrective action** is managerial activity aimed at bringing organizational performance up to the level of performance standards.[15] In other words, corrective action focuses on correcting organizational mistakes that are hindering organizational performance. Before taking any corrective action, however, managers should make sure that the standards they are using were properly established and that their measurements of organizational performance are valid and reliable.[16]

• *Recognizing Problems.* At first glance, it seems a fairly simple proposition that managers should take corrective action to eliminate **problems**—factors within an organization that are barriers to organizational goal attainment.[17] In practice, however, it often proves difficult to pinpoint the problem causing some undesirable organizational effect. Let us suppose that a performance measurement indicates a certain worker is not adequately passing on critical information to fellow workers. If the manager is satisfied that the communication standards are appropriate and that the performance measurement information is both valid and reliable, the manager should take corrective action to eliminate the problem causing this substandard performance.

• *Recognizing Symptoms.* What exactly is the problem causing substandard communication in this situation? Is it that the worker is not communicating adequately simply because he or she doesn't want to communicate? Is it that the job makes communication difficult? Is it that the worker does not have the necessary training to communicate in an appropriate manner? Before attempting to take corrective action, the manager must determine whether the worker's failure to communicate is a problem in itself or a **symptom**—a sign that a problem exists.[18] For example, the worker's failure to communicate adequately could be a symptom of inappropriate job design or a cumbersome organizational structure.

Once the problem has been properly identified, corrective action can focus on one or more of the three primary management functions of planning, organizing, and influencing.

That is, corrective action can include such activities as modifying past plans to make them more suitable for future organizational endeavors, making an existing organizational structure more suitable for existing plans and objectives, or restructuring an incentive program to ensure that high producers are rewarded more than low producers. Note that because planning, organizing, and influencing are closely related, it is likely that corrective action taken in one area will necessitate some corresponding action in one or both of the other two areas.

class discussion highlight

CONTROLLING SKILL AND YOUR CAREER

In the previous sections we provided an overview of the controlling process, which involves measuring performance, comparing performance to standards, and taking corrective action if necessary. During your career in both management and nonmanagement roles, you will deal with performance standards. How have standards played a role in your life so far? Examples might include your academic career, your current or previous employer, or even extracurricular activities such as participation in sports. Until now, who has defined the standards that apply to you, and what role have you played in this process? How might your familiarity with strandards influence your career in the future?

POWER AND CONTROL

To control successfully, managers must understand not only the control process, but also how organization members relate to it. Up to this point, the chapter has emphasized the nonhuman variables of controlling. This section focuses on power, perhaps the most important human-related variable in the control process. The following sections present a definition of power, elaborate on the total power of managers, and list the steps managers can take to increase their power over other organization members.

A Definition of Power

Perhaps the two most often confused terms in management are *power* and *authority*. Authority was defined in Chapter 12 as the right to command or give orders. The extent to which an individual is able to influence others so that they respond to orders is called **power.**[19] The greater this ability, the more power an individual is said to have.

Obviously, power and control are closely related. To illustrate, after comparing actual performance with planned performance and determining that corrective action is necessary, a manager usually gives orders to implement this action. Although the orders are issued by virtue of the manager's organizational authority, they may or may not be followed precisely, depending on how much power the manager has over the individuals to whom the orders are addressed.

Total Power of a Manager

The **total power** a manager possesses is made up of two different kinds of power: position power and personal power. **Position power** is power derived from the organizational position a manager holds.[20] In general, a manager moving from lower-level management to upper-level management accrues more position power. **Personal power** is power derived from a manager's relationships with others.[21]

Steps for Increasing Total Power

Managers can increase their total power by enhancing either their position power or their personal power or both. Position power is generally enhanced by a move to a higher organizational position, but most managers have little personal control over when they will move up in an organization. Managers do, however, have substantial control over the amount of personal power they hold over other organization members. John P. Kotter stresses the importance of developing personal power:

> To be able to plan, organize, budget, staff, control, and evaluate, managers need some control over the many people on whom they are dependent. Trying to control others solely by directing them and on the basis of the power associated with one's position simply will not work—first, because managers are always dependent on some people over whom they have no formal authority, and second, because virtually no one in modern organizations will passively accept and completely obey a constant stream of orders from someone just because he or she is the "boss."[22]

To increase personal power, a manager should attempt to develop the following attitudes and beliefs in other organization members:[23]

1. **A sense of obligation toward the manager**—If a manager succeeds in developing this sense of obligation, other organization members will allow the manager to influence them within certain limits. The basic strategy suggested for creating this sense of obligation is to do personal favors for people.
2. **A belief that the manager possesses a high level of expertise within the organization**—In general, a manager's personal power increases as organization members perceive that the manager's level of expertise is increasing. To raise perceptions of their expertise, managers must quietly make their significant achievements visible to others and build up a successful track record and a solid professional reputation.
3. **A sense of identification with the manager**—The manager can strive to develop this identification by behaving in ways that other organization members respect and by espousing goals, values, and ideals commonly held by them. The following description

Steve Jobs, Apple's CEO, gains a large part of his management power from his acknowledged technological expertise. Here he unveils the new MacBook Air.

illustrates how a certain sales manager took steps to increase the degree to which his subordinates identified with him:

> One vice president of sales in a moderate-sized manufacturing company was reputed to be so much in control of his sales force that he could get them to respond to new and different marketing programs in a third of the time taken by the company's best competitors. His power over his employees was based primarily on their strong identification with him and what he stood for. Immigrating to the United States at age seventeen, this person worked his way up "from nothing." When made a sales manager in 1965, he began recruiting other young immigrants and sons of immigrants from his former country. When made vice president of sales in 1970, he continued to do so. In 1975, 85 percent of his sales force was made up of people whom he hired directly or who were hired by others he brought.[24]

4. **The perception that they are dependent on the manager**—The main strategy here is to clearly convey the amount of authority the manager has over organizational resources—not only those necessary for organization members to do their jobs, but also those organization members personally receive in such forms as salaries and bonuses. This strategy is aptly reflected in the managerial version of the Golden Rule: "He who has the gold makes the rules."

Making Controlling Successful

In addition to avoiding the potential barriers to successful controlling mentioned in the previous section, managers can perform certain activities to make the control process more effective. To increase the quality of the controlling subsystem, managers should make sure that controlling activities take all the following factors into account.

Specific Organizational Activities Being Focused On Managers should make sure the various facets of the control process are appropriate to the control activity under consideration. For example, standards and measurements concerning a line worker's productivity are much different from standards and measurements concerning a vice president's productivity. Controlling ingredients related to the productivity of these individuals, therefore, must be different if the control process is to be applied successfully.

Different Kinds of Organizational Goals According to Jerome, control can be used for such different purposes as standardizing performance, protecting organizational assets from theft and waste, and standardizing product quality.[25] Managers should remember that the control process can be applied to many different facets of organizational life and that, if the organization is to receive maximum benefit from controlling, each of these facets must be emphasized.

Timely Corrective Action Some time will necessarily elapse as managers gather control-related information, develop necessary reports based on this information, and decide what corrective action should be taken to eliminate a problem. However, managers should take the corrective action as promptly as possible to ensure that the situation depicted by the information gathered has not changed. Unless corrective actions are timely, the organizational advantage of taking them may not materialize.

Communication of the Mechanics of the Control Process Managers should take steps to ensure that people know exactly what information is required for a particular control process, how that information is to be gathered and used to compile various reports, what the purposes of the various reports actually are, and what corrective actions are appropriate given those reports. The lesson here is simple: For control to be successful, all individuals involved in controlling must have a working knowledge of how the control process operates.[26]

ESSENTIALS OF INFORMATION

As mentioned in the previous sections, *controlling* is the process of making things happen as planned. Of course, managers cannot make things happen as planned if they lack information on the manner in which various events in the organization occur. The remainder of this chapter discusses the fundamental principles of handling information in an organization by first presenting the essentials of information and then examining both information technology and information systems (IS).

The process of developing information begins with gathering some type of facts or statistics, called **data.** Once gathered, data typically are analyzed in some manner. In general terms, **information** is the set of conclusions derived from data analysis. In management terms, information is the set of conclusions derived from the analysis of data that relate to the operation of an organization. As examples to illustrate the relationship between data and information, managers gather data regarding pay rates that individuals are receiving within industries in order to collect information about how to develop competitive pay rates, data regarding hazardous-materials accidents in order to gain information about how to improve worker safety, and data regarding customer demographics in order to gain information about product demand in the future.[27]

The information that managers receive heavily influences managerial decision making, which, in turn, determines the activities that will be performed within the organization, which, in turn, dictates the eventual success or failure of the organization. Some management writers consider information to be of such fundamental importance to the management process that they define *management* as the process of converting information into action through decision making.[28] The next sections discuss the factors that influence the value of information and how to evaluate information.

Factors Influencing the Value of Information

Some information is more valuable than other information.[29] The value of information is defined in terms of the benefit that can accrue to the organization through its use.[30] The greater this benefit, the more valuable the information.

Four primary factors determine the value of information:

1. Information appropriateness
2. Information quality
3. Information timeliness
4. Information quantity

In general, management should encourage generation, distribution, and use of organizational information that is appropriate, of high quality, timely, and of sufficient quantity. Following this guideline will not necessarily guarantee sound decisions, but it will ensure that important resources necessary to make such decisions are available.[31] Each of the factors that determines information value is discussed in more detail in the paragraphs that follow.

Information Appropriateness **Information appropriateness** is defined in terms of how relevant the information is to the decision-making situation the manager faces. If the information is quite relevant, then it is said to be appropriate. Generally, as the appropriateness of information increases, so does the value of that information.

Figure 21.3 shows the characteristics of information appropriate for the following common decision-making situations:[32]

1. Operational control
2. Management control
3. Strategic planning

CHARACTERISTICS OF INFORMATION	OPERATIONAL CONTROL	MANAGEMENT CONTROL	STRATEGIC PLANNING
Source	Largely internal	⟶	External
Scope	Well defined, narrow	⟶	Very wide
Level of aggregation	Detailed	⟶	Aggregate
Time horizon	Historical	⟶	Future
Currency	Highly current	⟶	Quite old/historical
Required accuracy	High	⟶	Low
Frequency of use	Very frequent	⟶	Infrequent

FIGURE 21.3

Characteristics of information appropriate for decisions related to operational control, management control, and strategic planning

Operational Control, Management Control, and Strategic Planning Decisions *Operational control decisions* relate to ensuring that specific organizational tasks are carried out effectively and efficiently. *Management control decisions* relate to obtaining and effectively and efficiently using the organizational resources necessary to reach organizational objectives. *Strategic planning decisions* relate to determining organizational objectives and designating the corresponding action necessary to reach them.

As Figure 21.3 shows, characteristics of appropriate information change as managers shift from making operational control decisions to making management control decisions to making strategic planning decisions. Strategic planning decision makers need information that focuses on the relationship of the organization to its external environment, emphasizes the future, is wide in scope, and presents a broad view. Appropriate information for this type of decision is generally not completely current, but more historical in nature. In addition, this information does not need to be completely accurate because strategic decisions tend to be characterized by some subjectivity and focus on areas that are difficult to measure, such as customer satisfaction.

Information appropriate for making operational control decisions has dramatically different characteristics from information appropriate for making strategic planning decisions. Operational control decision makers need information that focuses for the most part on the internal organizational environment, emphasizes the performance history of the organization, and is well-defined, narrow in scope, and detailed. In addition, appropriate information for this type of decision is both highly current and highly accurate.

Information appropriate for making management control decisions generally has characteristics that fall somewhere between the extreme of appropriate operational control information and appropriate strategic planning information.

Information Quality The second primary factor that determines the value of information is **information quality**—the degree to which information represents reality. The more closely information represents reality, the higher the quality and the greater the value of that information. In general, the higher the quality of information available to managers, the better equipped managers are to make appropriate decisions and the greater the probability that the organization will be successful over the long term.

Perhaps the most significant factor in producing poor-quality information is *data contamination*. Inaccurate data gathering can result in information that is of low quality—a poor representation of reality.[33]

Information Timeliness **Information timeliness,** the third primary factor that determines the value of information, is the extent to which the receipt of information allows decisions to be made and action to be taken so the organization can gain some benefit from possessing the information. Information received by managers at a point when it can be used to the organization's advantage is said to be timely.

For example, a product may be selling poorly because its established market price is significantly higher than the price of competitive products. If this information is received by management after the product has been discontinued, the information will be untimely. If, however, it is received soon enough to adjust the selling price of the product and thereby significantly increase sales, it will be timely.

Information Quantity The fourth and final determinant of the value of information is **information quantity**—the amount of decision-related information managers possess. Before making a decision, managers should assess the quantity of information they possess that relates to the decision being made. If this quantity is judged to be insufficient, more information should be gathered before the decision is made. If the amount of information is judged to be as complete as necessary, managers can feel justified in making the decision.

There is such a thing as *too* much information. Information overload—too much information to consider properly—can make managers afraid to make decisions and result in important decisions going unmade. Information overload is generally considered to be the major cause of indecision in organizations—commonly referred to as "paralysis by analysis."[34]

Evaluating Information

Evaluating information is the process of determining whether the acquisition of specified information is justified. As with all evaluations of this kind, the primary concern of management is to weigh the dollar value of benefit gained from using some quantity of information against the cost of generating that information.

Identifying and Evaluating Data According to the flowchart in Figure 21.4, the first major step in evaluating organizational information is to ascertain the value of that information by pinpointing the data to be analyzed, and then determine the expected value or return to be received from obtaining perfect information based on these data. Then this expected value is reduced by the amount of benefit that will not be realized because of deficiencies and inaccuracies expected to appear in the information.

L.L.Bean retail operations have grown from its original catalog business to include a Web site and a few retail stores like this one. Managers of each retail arm require different kinds of information. For instance, data about shoppers' access to technology and their privacy concerns are important to the company's Web site manager, while the demographics of the local labor supply matter to managers of the telephone centers and retail outlets.

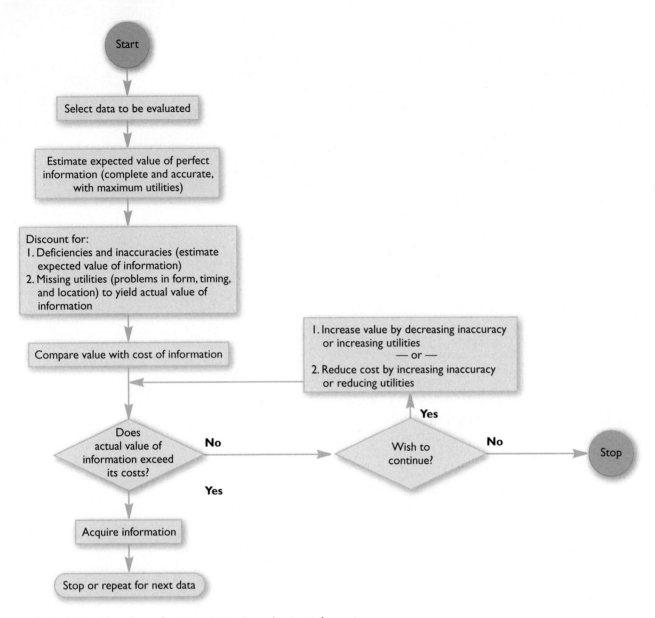

FIGURE 21.4 Flowchart of main activities in evaluating information

Evaluating the Cost of Data Next, the expected value of organizational information is compared with the expected cost of obtaining that information. If the expected cost does not exceed the expected value, the information should be gathered. If it does exceed the expected value, managers either must increase the information's expected value or decrease its expected cost before the information gathering can be justified. If neither of these objectives is possible, management cannot justify gathering the information.

INFORMATION TECHNOLOGY

Technology consists of any type of equipment or process that organization members use in the performance of their work. This definition includes tools as old as a black-smith's anvil and tools as new and innovative as virtual reality. This section discusses one segment of technology, **information technology (IT),** which is technology such as computers and telecommunication devices that focus on the use of information in the performance of work.

THE INFORMATION SYSTEM (IS)

In simple terms, an **information system (IS)** is a network of applications established within an organization to provide managers with information that will assist them in decision making.[35] The following, more complete definition of an IS was developed by the Management Information System Committee of the Financial Executives Institute:

> **A system designed to provide selected decision-oriented information needed by management to plan, control, and evaluate the activities of the corporation. It is designed within a framework that emphasizes profit planning, performance planning, and control at all levels. It contemplates the ultimate integration of required business information subsystems, both financial and nonfinancial, within the company.[36]**

The typical IS is a formally established organizational network that gives managers continual access to vital information. For example, the IS normally provides managers with ongoing reports relevant to significant organizational activities such as sales, worker productivity, and labor turnover. Based on information they gain via an IS, managers make decisions that are aimed at improving organizational performance. Because the typical IS is characterized by computer usage, managers can use an IS to gain online access to company records and condensed information in the form of summaries and reports. Overall, the IS is a planned, systematic mechanism for providing managers with relevant information in a systematic fashion.[37]

The title of the specific organization member responsible for developing and maintaining an IS varies from organization to organization. In smaller organizations, a president or vice president may have this responsibility. In larger organizations, an individual with a title such as "director of information systems" or "chief information officer (CIO)" may be solely responsible for appropriately managing an entire IS department. The term *IS manager* is used in the sections that follow to indicate the person within the organization who has the primary responsibility for managing the IS. The term *IS personnel* is used to designate the nonmanagement individuals within the organization who possess the primary responsibility for actually operating the IS. Examples of nonmanagement individuals are computer operators and computer programmers. The sections that follow describe an IS more fully and outline the steps managers take to establish an IS.

Describing the IS

The IS is perhaps best described by a summary of the steps necessary to properly operate it,[38] and by a discussion of the different kinds of information various managers need to make job-related decisions.

Operating the IS IS personnel generally need to perform six sequential steps to properly operate an IS.[39] Figure 21.5 summarizes the steps and indicates the order in which they are performed. The first step is to determine what information is needed within the organization, when it will be needed, and in what form it will be needed. Because the basic purpose of the IS is to assist management in making decisions, one way to begin determining management information needs is to analyze the following:

1. Decision areas in which management makes decisions
2. Specific decisions within these decision areas that management must actually make
3. Alternatives that must be evaluated to make these specific decisions

For example, insights regarding what information management needs in a particular organization can be gleaned by understanding that management makes decisions in the area of plant and equipment, that a specific decision related to this area involves acquiring new equipment, and that two alternatives that must be evaluated relating to this decision are

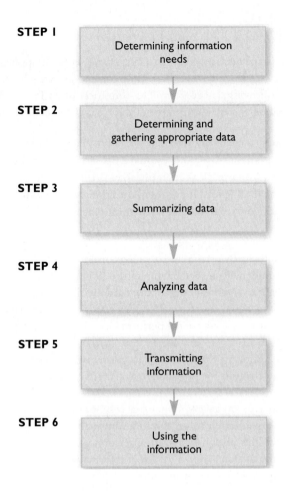

STEP 1 — Determining information needs

STEP 2 — Determining and gathering appropriate data

STEP 3 — Summarizing data

STEP 4 — Analyzing data

STEP 5 — Transmitting information

STEP 6 — Using the information

FIGURE 21.5
The six steps necessary to operate an IS properly in order of their performance

buying newly developed, high-technology equipment versus buying more standard equipment that has been around for some time in the industry.

The second major step in operating the IS is pinpointing and collecting data that will yield needed organizational information. This step is just as important as determining information needs of the organization. If collected data do not relate properly to information needs, it will be impossible to generate needed information.

After information needs of the organization have been determined and appropriate data have been pinpointed and gathered, summarizing the data and analyzing the data are, respectively, the third and fourth steps IS personnel generally should take to properly operate an IS. It is in the performance of these steps that IS personnel find computer assistance of great benefit.

The fifth and sixth steps are transmitting the information generated by data analysis to appropriate managers and getting the managers to actually use the information. The performance of these last two steps results in managerial decision making. Although each of the six steps is necessary if an IS is to run properly, the time spent on performing each step will naturally vary from organization to organization.

Different Managers Need Different Kinds of Information For maximum benefit, an IS must collect relevant data, transform that data into appropriate information, and transmit that information to the appropriate managers. Appropriate information for one manager within an organization, however, may not be appropriate information for another. Robert G. Murdick suggests that the degree of appropriateness of IS information for a manager depends on the activities for which the manager will use the information, the organizational objectives assigned to the manager, and the level of management at which the manager functions.[40] All of these factors are closely related.

Organizational Level	Type of Management	Manager's Organizational Objectives	Appropriate Information from IS	How IS Information Is Used
1. Top management	CEO, president, vice president	Survival of the firm, profit growth, accumulation and efficient use of resources	Environmental data and trends, summary reports of operations, exception reports of problems, forecasts	Corporate objectives, policies, constraints, decisions on strategic plans, decisions on control of the total company
2. Middle management	Middle managers in such areas as marketing, production, and finance	Allocation of resources to assigned tasks, establishment of plans to meet operating objectives, control of operations	Summaries and exception reports of operating results, corporate objectives, policies, constraints, decisions on strategic plans, relevant actions and decisions of other middle managers	Operating plans and policies, exception reports, operating summaries, control procedures, decisions on resource allocations, actions and decisions related to other middle managers
3. First-line management	First-line managers whose work is closely related	Production of goods to meet marketing needs, supplying budgets, estimates of resource requirements, movement and storage of materials	Summary reports of transactions, detailed reports of problems, operating plans and policies, control procedures, actions and decisions of related first-line managers	Exception reports, progress reports, resource requests, dispatch orders, cross-functional reports

FIGURE 21.6 Appropriate IS information under various sets of organizational circumstances

Murdick's thoughts on this matter are best summarized in Figure 21.6. As you can see from this figure, because the overall job situations of top managers, middle managers, and first-line managers are significantly different, the kinds of information these managers need to satisfactorily perform their jobs are also significantly different.

Managing Information Systems

The effectiveness of an organization's IS depends largely on the ability of individuals within the organization to properly manage the IS. Three activities that improve IS effectiveness are managing user satisfaction, managing the IS workforce, and managing IS security. To the extent that employees are able to manage these activities, organizations will reap rewards in the form of IS effectiveness.

Managing User Satisfaction[41] One of the most important determinants of IS effectiveness is the degree to which employees, or users, are satisfied with the IS. User satisfaction, which denotes the degree of user satisfaction with the IS, is determined by two main factors: (1) the quality of the IS and (2) information quality. The quality of the IS refers to its ease of use. If a company's employees consider an IS easy to use, that IS would be labeled a high-quality IS. Information quality, on the other hand, measures the degree to which the information produced by the IS is accurate and in a format required by the user. Taken together, then, users are satisfied with the IS when the IS is of high quality and provides high-quality information.

User satisfaction is important because of its direct influence on IS effectiveness. When users are satisfied with the IS, the IS will be more integrated in the user's work routine, and the user will become more dependent on the IS. Stated differently, when employees are satisfied with the IS, they will use the IS in their work routines. As users become dependent on the IS and integrate the IS into their routines, the IS becomes effective. These relationships are depicted in Figure 21.7.

In **an example from the world of management**, the relationships in Figure 21.7 may be reinforced through better understanding **Armstrong Industries**, a designer and manufacturer of floors and ceilings that recently designed an implemented a new information system. Managers at Armstrong will attempt to increase both IS quality and information quality, because both of these factors influence the satisfaction of Armstrong employees in terms of using the IS. If Armstrong's employees are not satisfied with the IS, they will not use it in their everyday routines, which would make it much more difficult for Armstrong's managers to coordinate globally. By improving IS quality and information quality, though, Armstrong's managers will ensure that employees will use the IS in appropriate circumstances. When Armstrong's employees use the IS, Armstrong's managers are likely to enjoy the global coordination for which the IS was designed.

Managing the IS Workforce In recent years, executives have faced different obstacles in managing the IS workforce. During the economic and technological boom of the late 1990s, executives faced tremendous hurdles in terms of hiring and retaining IS employees.[42] During that period, as compared to other professionals, IS professionals were considered more difficult to hire and retain because the economic and technological boom created a multitude of job prospects for IS professionals. Moreover, executives found it quite expensive to replace IS professionals who left; some estimates suggest that the cost of replacing an IS employee is 1 to 2.5 times their annual salary.[43]

In more recent years, however, companies have started to use workers in other countries such as India to staff IS departments—and many expect this trend to continue.[44] A recent survey indicated that almost half of firms outsource work to workers in other countries to reap cost advantages.[45] Specifically, the cost of IS employees in developing countries is much less than for IS employees in developed countries

FIGURE 21.7
A model of IS effectiveness

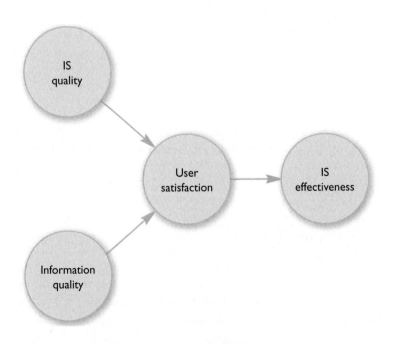

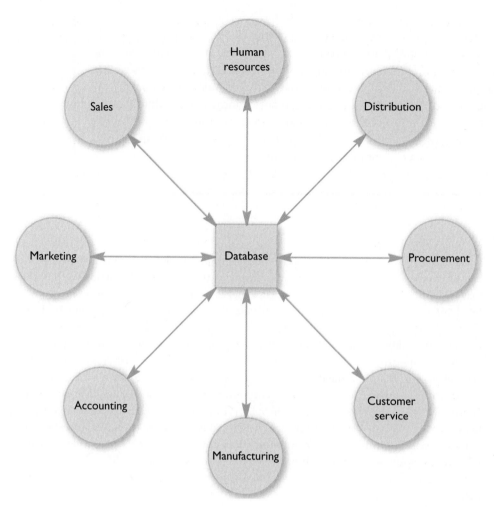

FIGURE 21.8
Centralized databases: An illustration

(see Figure 21.8). This issue of lower costs partly explains why EDS, a U.S. firm that offers its clients IT-based solutions, employs about 1,000 IS workers in India but expects this number to increase to nearly 20,000 in the near future.

Despite the cost advantages associated with these international workers, this practice creates other problems such as integrating domestic and nondomestic workforces, managing international languages and cultures, and defining global work expectations. In addition, domestic firms could face a backlash from their domestic customers for outsourcing IS work to other countries, as some customers could view the practice as being unpatriotic.

class discussion highlight

MODERN RESEARCH AND CONTROLLING SKILL

Managing IS Road Warriors[46]

Organizations must find ways to stay current with the most recent technological advances. Due to this need, the IS consulting industry has continued to develop in recent years. These consulting companies will send to a given organization an individual or team of consultants to help the organization implement the most advanced information systems. These consultants will often travel to new cities and stay for days, weeks, or months at a time.

Although this practice of employing IS consultants continues to grow, little is known about the consultants who travel to work with other organizations. To better understand these individuals, Professor Ahuha and colleagues examined a sample of 171 "road warriors." According to their framework, road warriors are consultants who spend most of the week in a different city working with another organization and then return home for the weekend.

The researchers were particularly interested in the factors that influence the road warriors' commitment to their home organizations as well as their general levels of exhaustion. As you think about this unique set of individuals, which factors might influence their overall level of work exhaustion? Which factors might influence their commitment to their home organization (i.e., the consulting firms)? Why?

Managing IS Security As corporations rely more heavily on information systems, they become more susceptible to security issues involving these systems. In particular, companies may lose valuable financial, employee, or customer data due to security breaches involving IS. In addition, companies become increasingly vulnerable to viruses, worms, and trojan horses designed to paralyze information systems. As technology continues to change rapidly, it becomes more difficult for IS employees to prevent and eliminate these security threats.

In response to the increasing threat of security issues to information systems, private and public organizations around the world came together in 1992 to form the International Information Security Foundation. This committee produced a document known as the Generally Accepted System Security Principles (GASSP), which included a set of best practices for IS managers.[47] The best practices listed within the GASSP provide a good starting point for managers when they are attempting to prevent security threats. Table 21.1 provides an overview of some of the broad principles outlined in the GASSP.

TABLE 21.1	GASSP's Key Principles for Maintaining Information Security
Accountability principle	Organizations must clearly define and acknowledge information security accountability and responsibility.
Ethics principle	Organizations should use information and execute information security in an ethical manner.
Timeliness principle	Organizations should act in a timely manner to prevent or respond to breaches of and threats to information systems.
Assessment principle	Organizations should periodically assess the risks to information and information systems.
Equity principle	Management shall respect the rights of all employees when setting policy regarding security measures.

CHALLENGE CASE SUMMARY

The information in this chapter supports the notion that high production costs (as well as the other issues mentioned in the Challenge Case) at Coca-Cola actually should be categorized as a control problem. Control is making things happen at Coca-Cola in a way they were planned to happen. Going one step further, the process of controlling is the action that management takes in order to control. Ideally, this process at Coca-Cola, as within any company, would include a determination of company plans, standards, and objectives for manufacturing products such as Diet Coke, so steps can be taken to eliminate company characteristics that caused deviation from these factors.

In theory, Coca-Cola management should view controlling activities within the company as a subsystem of the organization's overall management system. For management to achieve organizational control, the controlling subsystem requires a portion of the people, money, raw materials, and machines available within the company.

The process portion of the controlling subsystem at Coca-Cola involves three steps:

1. Measuring the performance levels of various productive units
2. Comparing these performance levels to predetermined performance standards for these units
3. Taking any corrective action necessary to make sure that planned performance levels are consistent with actual performance levels

Based on information in the Challenge Case, one area in which management should emphasize standards is in the arena of desired profitability. According to the case, high production costs are a primary reason that the company is not as profitable as management would like it to be. To ensure that the company continues to earn a desirable level of profits, management is initiating a new set of processes to ensure that Coca-Cola and its bottlers are working with the same information.

As the company gathers more information and considers potential corrective actions, management must be certain that the action is aimed at organizational problems rather than at symptoms of problems. For example, if production costs are too high because workers are not trained well enough to operate their equipment properly, the symptom will disappear as a result of improved training of production workers.

Inevitably, corrective action at Coca-Cola, such as improved worker training, must focus on further planning, organizing, or influencing efforts. As examples: How must Coca-Cola's scheduling of workers change if production workers are being more carefully trained? Does the company still need the same number of production supervisors if workers become more competent as a result of improved training?

For Coca-Cola's management to be successful in controlling, they have to be aware not only of the intricacies of the control process itself, but also of how to deal with people as they relate to the control process. With regard to people and control, managers must consider the amount of power they hold over organization members—that is, their ability to encourage workers to follow orders. Based on the Challenge Case, many of these orders would probably be related to implementing new and better production methods as well as improved communication with stakeholders, including suppliers and customers.

The total amount of power that Coca-Cola management possesses comes from the positions they hold and from their personal relationships with other organization members. For example, the top managers already have more position power than any other managers in the organization. Therefore, to increase their total power, they would have to develop their personal power. Top management might attempt to expand personal power by developing:

1. A sense of obligation in other organization members toward top managers
2. The belief in other organization members that top management has a high level of task-related expertise
3. A sense of identification that other organization members have with top management
4. The perception in organization members that they are dependent on top management

Information at Coca-Cola can be defined as conclusions derived from the analysis of data relating to the way in which the company operates. The case implies that managers at Coca-Cola will be better able to make sound decisions, including better control decisions, because of the successful data handling achieved by its information system. One important factor in evaluating the overall worth of Coca-Cola's information handling system would be the overall impact of the system on the value of information that company managers would receive. A manager such as Kent must see that investing in computers, satellites, and other data-handling devices at a reasonable cost can enhance the value of information that he receives and improve the appropriateness of downsizing decisions. That is, investments in improving information system components can enhance the appropriateness, quality, timeliness, and quantity of information that Kent can use to make downsizing decisions. Kent must believe and act on the notion that the benefits of making investments in computers and information systems will outweigh the costs of the equipment by significantly improving his decisions.

In order for a company such as Coca-Cola to get maximum benefit from computer assistance, management must appropriately build each main ingredient of its IS. The IS the organizational network established to provide managers with information that helps them make job-related decisions. Such a system would normally necessitate the use of several IS personnel who would help determine information needs at the company, help determine and collect appropriate Coca-Cola data, summarize and analyze these data, transmit analyzed data to appropriate Coca-Cola managers, and generally help managers in interpreting received IS information.

To make sure that managers get appropriate information, Coca-Cola's IS personnel must appreciate how different managers need different kinds of information. As an example, a top manager would normally need information that summarizes trends in consumer tastes, competitor moves, and perhaps most important for downsizing, summary reports for productivity and costs related to various organizational units. Middle managers would need information that focuses more on specific operating divisions or units within the company, such as all specifics regarding home appliance production. More lower-level managers, perhaps production supervisors, would normally need information about daily production rates, regular versus overtime labor costs, and the status of meeting production goals.

Assume that Kent has just decided to establish a new IS within Coca-Cola that interfaces with the company's bottler network. Coca-Cola, like any other company, would probably gain significantly by carefully planning the way in which its IS would be established. For example, perhaps the answers to the following questions, such as those that arise during the planning stage of Coca-Cola's IS, would be useful: Is an appropriate computer-based system being acquired and integrated? Does the company need new IS personnel, or will present personnel require further training in order to operate the new IS? Will managers need additional training in order to operate the new IS?

About the design and implementation stages of Coca-Cola's new IS, Kent should seek answers to such questions as: How do we design the new IS based upon managerial decision making? How can we ensure that the new IS as designed and implemented will actually exist and be functional?

Kent as well as IS personnel should continually try to improve the new IS. All users of the IS should be aware of the symptoms of an inadequate IS and should constantly attempt to pinpoint and eliminate corresponding weaknesses. Suggestions for improving the new IS could include (1) building additional cooperation between IS managers, IS personnel, and line managers; (2) stressing that the purpose of the IS is to provide managers with decision-related information; (3) using cost-benefit analysis to evaluate IS activities; and (4) ensuring that the IS operates in a people-conscious manner.

MANAGEMENT SKILL ACTIVITIES

This section is specially designed to help you develop controlling skill. An individual's controlling skill is based upon an understanding of controlling concepts and the ability to apply those concepts in management situations. As a result, the following activities are designed both to heighten your understanding of controlling concepts and to help you gain facility in applying these concepts in various management situations.

UNDERSTANDING CONTROLLING CONCEPTS

This section is comprised of activities that will sharpen your understanding of controlling concepts. Answer essay questions as completely as possible. Also, remember that many additional true/false and multiple choice questions appear online at MyManagement.com to help you further refine your understanding of concepts related to controlling.

Essay Questions

1. Describe the three main steps in the controlling process.
2. Define power and describe the determinants of an individual's power within an organization.
3. What is the difference between a problem and a symptom? Use an example to support your response.
4. Describe the six steps involved with information system performance.
5. What are the determinants of information system effectiveness?

Developing Management Skill

Learning activities in this section are aimed at helping you to develop your controlling skill. Learning activities include Exploring Your Management Skill: Part 2, Experiential Exercise, Cases, and a VideoNet exercise.

EXPLORING YOUR MANAGEMENT SKILL: PART 2

As you recall, you completed Exploring Your Management Skill before you started to study this chapter. Your responses gave you an idea of how much you initially knew about controlling and helped you to focus on important points as you studied the chapter. Answer the Exploring Your Management Skill questions again now (p. 518) and compare your score to the first time you took it. This comparison will give you an idea of how much you have learned from studying this chapter and pinpoint areas for further clarification before you start studying the next chapter. Record your answers within the text or go to MyManagementLab.com. Recording your answers in MyManagementLab will allow you to get immediate results and see how your score compares to your classmates. If you answer the questions in the book, the answers are located in the Exploring Your Management Skill section at the end of the book.

YOUR MANAGEMENT SKILLS PORTFOLIO

Your Management Learning Portfolio is a collection of activities especially designed to demonstrate your management knowledge and skill. By completing these online at MyManagement.com, you will be able to print, complete with cover sheet, as many activities as you choose. Be sure to save your work. Taking your printed portfolio to an employment interview could be helpful in obtaining a job.

The portfolio activity for this chapter is Controlling at Merrill Lynch. Study the information and complete the exercises that that follow.[48]

Controlling at Merrill Lynch

The firm Merrill Lynch provides a number of financial services to both corporations and individuals. One of Merrill Lynch's primary activities involves providing advisory services to individual investors. To provide these services, financial planners work with clients and provide advice regarding potential investment decisions. In exchange for this advice, the financial planners earn money for the company based on commissions and other fees. Financial planners at Merrill Lynch work with different numbers of clients, and these clients vary dramatically in terms of their total assets.

Greg Fleming, Merrill Lynch's president, has contacted you to help him think of ways to improve the performance of the many financial planners working for the company. His specific task for you involves making the controlling process relevant to the financial planners. In the following sections, answer the various questions as they pertain to Merrill Lynch. Visiting the company's Web site (*www.ml. com*) might help you as you think about this process.

1. The first step in the controlling process involves measuring performance. If you were Greg Fleming, how would you measure the performance of the financial planners? Be specific.

2. The second step in the controlling process entails comparing measured performance to standards.

   a. What types of standards would you develop to help assess performance of these financial planners?

   b. What information sources would you use for developing these standards?

3. The final step in the controlling process involves taking corrective actions if necessary.

a. What types of corrective actions would you take to help control the performance of financial planners?

_____

_____

_____

b. How would you determine whether corrective actions were necessary?

_____

_____

_____

EXPERIENTIAL EXERCISE: WORKING WITH INFORMATION

Directions. Read the following scenario and then perform the listed activities. Your instructor may want you to perform the activities as an individual or within groups. Follow all of your instructor's directions carefully.

Perhaps the most critical aspect of an information system is determining what information a given organization needs to operate effectively. When an organization understands what information is needed, leaders can design an information system that will allow them to collect this information efficiently. In this exercise, your group should choose a local restaurant and then assume that you are the top management team for this restaurant. With this restaurant in mind, determine the primary pieces of information that you need to ensure that the restaurant operates effectively. If possible, group these different pieces of information into logical categories.

CASES

IMPLEMENTING CONTROLS AND TECHNOLOGY AT COCA-COLA

"Implementing Controls and Technology at Coca-Cola" (p. 517) and its related Challenge Case Summary sections were written to help you better understand the management concepts contained in this chapter. Answer the following discussion questions about this Challenge Case to further enrich your understanding of chapter content:

1. List three decisions that an improved IS could help Kent to make. For each decision, describe the data that must be in the database in order to provide such help.
2. The main steps of the controlling process are measuring performance, comparing performance to standards, and taking corrective action. Discuss the possible role of an IS at Coca-Cola in each of these steps.
3. In addition to soft drinks, PepsiCo, Coca-Cola's chief competitor, manufactures and distributes snack products. Because of these additional products, do you think that PepsiCo's IS should differ from Coca-Cola's? Why?

TECHNOLOGY HELPS NIKE RACE TOWARD HIGHER PERFORMANCE

Read the case and answer the questions that follow. Studying this case will help you better see how your understanding of information technology can be applied in a company such as Nike.

Nike takes a step forward in its race for sales and profits every time it sells a pair of sneakers. The Oregon-based company has a commanding lead over Adidas and other rivals because of its 32 percent share of the global athletic shoe market. Still, CEO Mark Parker and his executive team know they must sell a lot of shoes and sports apparel to expand beyond the current $12 billion in yearly sales and hike the gross profit margin above 43 percent (the highest margin in company history). They have to estimate how well each product will sell, allow enough time to manufacture the right quantities, get the products to the right place at the right time at the right cost, and reach out to the right customers. The unpredictability of fashion trends makes their decisions even more challenging.

So how does Nike do it? With technology, a healthy dose of human expertise, and patience. The company was using 27 different information systems to handle sales forecasting, factory orders, and deliveries to retailers worldwide when management began planning for a single, integrated IS. One goal was to slash, from nine months to six months, the time needed to get shoes and other items from the design stage to store shelves. Another goal was closer coordination with the Asian factories that manufacture Nike's shoes as a way to minimize inventory. This coordination would help the company avoid some of the financial risks of catering to fashion-conscious customers whose tastes can change overnight. Finally, management wanted a single, centralized system for forecasting and ordering that managers and employees could learn to use efficiently and effectively.

Months of preparation went into the project, as company managers worked with specialists to customize software to Nike's unique situation and then implemented the system before a new corporate-wide IT project took effect. At first, the forecasting/ordering system struggled to handle the more than 10 million stock numbers needed to track all product variations; it also operated more slowly than expected when tied to the existing IT network. Then the system issued factory orders for too many of some models and too few of others, causing Nike to lose an estimated $100 million worth of sales.

The project managers created workarounds to make data available for planning purposes while they analyzed what had happened, revamped the system design, and got ready to implement it more gradually. "Once we got into this, we quickly realized that what we originally thought was going to be a two-to-three-year effort would be more like five to seven [years]," observes Roland Wolfram, Nike's vice president of global operations and technology. In fact, the new system was phased in, area

by area, over the next two years, and users received intensive training in advance. As a double-check, Nike managers carefully scrutinize system output "to make sure it makes sense," says Wolfram; they also ask retailers for input when forecasting demand for new items. Now, six years after the original project began, the system is working so well that Nike managers have set a new goal of reducing the lead time for orders even further.

The Internet plays a major role in Nike's plans for communicating with customers to build brand loyalty and stimulate demand. For example, Nike keeps its trademark "swoosh" symbol in front of soccer fans by inviting them to log onto the company's Web site and participate in multiplayer games such as Football Olé. It has teamed up with MSN Europe to create an Instant Messenger version of the same game that can be played by people across the continent. In addition, Nike has developed a series of Web sites tailored to the interests of specific customer groups, such as *www.nikegoddess.com* for women, *www.nikerunning.com* for runners, and *www.nikebasketball.com* for basketball fans. Watch for more technological innovation as Nike continues its never-ending race for higher sales and higher profits.

QUESTIONS

1. Why are information quality and timeliness particularly important to Nike's success?
2. What security issues do you think Nike management should take into account when planning, designing, and implementing a system for sales forecasting and factory orders? Why?
3. What else should Nike do to use the World Wide Web for communicating with customers?

VIDEONET EXERCISE

Foundations of Control at Terracycle

VIDEO HIGHLIGHTS

Sure, TerraCycle is a cool company filled with ingenious young entrepreneurs and eager beavers, but it takes more than great eco-friendly products to run a company. After things started to take off, Tom Szaky, TerraCycle's CEO, knew he needed help getting his company under control, so he hired some more experienced people to help him create some order from the chaos. When CFO Betsy Cotton came on board, TerraCycle had bad credit and no financial controls to speak of. Find out how she and other key staff whipped TerraCycle into shape.

Discussion Questions

1. What type of control standards have been implemented at TerraCycle by Betsy Cotton?
2. What types of control should Szaky be emphasizing at TerraCycle? Why?
3. What are some of the barriers to controlling at TerraCycle?

Internet Activity

Go to the TerraCycle home page at www.TerraCycle.net. Using the criteria discussed in the chapter, is this Web site well-designed? Be specific.

22 Production and Control

OBJECTIVES

TO HELP BUILD MY PRODUCTION SKILL, WHEN STUDYING THIS CHAPTER, I WILL ATTEMPT TO ACQUIRE:

1. Definitions of production, productivity, and quality

2. An understanding of the importance of operations and production strategies, systems, and processes

3. Insights into the role of operations management concepts in the workplace

4. An understanding of how operations control procedures can be used to control production

5. Insights into operations control tools and how they evolve into a continual improvement approach to production management and control

TARGET SKILL : production skill: the ability to transform organizational resources into products

CHALLENGE CASE

DELTA ATTEMPTS TO BOOST PRODUCTIVITY[1]

Delta Air Lines provides air transportation for travelers and cargo throughout the world, flying to more than 30 foreign countries. Despite these many markets, the company has struggled in recent years to maintain profitability. To help remedy Delta's troubles, the board of directors recently named Richard Anderson as the company's new chief executive officer.

Improving Delta's performance will entail increasing customer satisfaction. Recent Delta surveys of passengers revealed that they had grown tired of the time required to board Delta's planes. In addition, industry surveys suggest that travelers can tolerate about 17 minutes of waiting, but after that mark satisfaction declines substantially for every 5 additional minutes of standing in line.

In response to this survey, Delta invested approximately $200 million to speed up the check-in process. A large portion of this $200 million will support Delta's new strategy of using self-service kiosks that help passengers check in more quickly. With these kiosks, which Delta has already installed in more than 80 airports, passengers can check in by themselves. After inserting either credit cards or Delta frequent flier cards as identification, passengers can use the kiosks to identify their flights and choose their seats. At the end of the process, the kiosks print out boarding passes, and baggage labels are printed out at nearby locations where Delta employees attach the labels to the luggage.

Management at Delta Air Lines is focusing on eliminating waiting lines for passenger check-in.

Delta has also made other changes to speed up the check-in process. For example, Delta is now installing telephones in airports under banners entitled "Delta Direct." When passengers need to make changes to their itineraries, they simply pick up one of the telephones. These telephones, in turn, will connect them to service agents who specialize in making such itinerary changes. Delta processes about 500,000 such requests per month through this important function. With these phone banks, Delta reduces the number of employees needed at airport counters to respond to these passenger requests.

Delta has enjoyed some early success with these changes. According to the company, the check-in process at the kiosks usually takes about two minutes. In addition, this self-service process requires fewer employees, which means the kiosk-system improves Delta's productivity. This new process may help to explain why Cordell believes that soon 80 percent of Delta's passengers will check in someplace other than the traditional ticket counter.

Delta needs the productivity increases from these changes desperately if it wants to survive. Since the terrorist attacks on September 11, 2001, numerous airlines have undergone bankruptcy restructuring. By continuing to increase productivity, however, Delta might regain its position as a leader in the airline industry.

> "EXPLORE YOUR OWN MANAGEMENT SKILLS BY TAKING THE QUIZ ON THE NEXT PAGE"

Before studying this chapter, respond to the following questions regarding the type of advice that you would give to Delta's Richard Anderson, referenced in the Challenge Case. Then address the concerning production and control challenges that he presently faces within the company. You are not expected to be a production expert at this point. Answering the questions now can help you focus on important points when you study the chapter. Also, answering the questions again after you study the chapter will give you an idea of how much you have learned.

Record your answers here or go to MyManagementLab. com. Recording your answers in MyManagementLab will allow you to get immediate results and see how your score compares to your classmates. If you answer the questions in the book, the answers are located in the Exploring Your Management Skill section at the end of the book.

FOR EACH STATEMENT CIRCLE:

- "Y" if you would give the advice to Anderson.
- "N" if you would NOT give the advice to Anderson.
- "NI" if you have no idea whether you would give the advice to Anderson.

Mr. Anderson, in meeting your production management challenges at Delta Air Lines, you should . . .

Before Study	*After Study*

1. understand that the production process involves all those activities needed to transform organizational resources into products. _____

   Y, N, NI

2. encourage Delta's employees to increase productivity by maximizing the inputs necessary to create a given output (product). _____

   Y, N, NI

3. focus more on productivity and less on quality, because quality efforts undermine productivity.

   _____

   Y, N, NI

4. use quality circles as a mechanism to gain insights from Delta's employees regarding ways to improve productivity. _____

   Y, N, NI

5. realize that Delta's operations management is mostly quantitative and does not require managerial decision making. _____

   Y, N, NI

6. realize that when formulating Delta's capacity strategy, it's better to error on the side of having excess capacity, because having excess capacity imposes no costs on the company. _____

   Y, N, NI

7. ignore just-in-time strategies, because such techniques to not apply to Delta. _____

   Y, N, NI

8. understand that if Delta does choose to pursue just-in-time strategies, the company will need to work closely with its suppliers. _____

   Y, N, NI

9. realize that pure-preventive maintenance and pure-breakdown maintenance control policies would have similar effects on Delta's operations. _____

   Y, N, NI

10. understand that budgetary controls have virtually no pitfalls and are the safest operations controls. _____

    Y, N, NI

11. recognize that relying on budgetary controls limits potential human relations problems, because such controls are purely quantitative in nature. _____

    Y, N, NI

12. realize that when using ratio analysis, the different ratios communicate information regarding different components of Delta's operations. _____

    Y, N, NI

13. encourage employees to continuously inspect all aspects of Delta's operations to improve productivity. _____

    Y, N, NI

14. rely on break-even analysis to understand those aspects of Delta's operations that do not involve profit or loss. _____

    Y, N, NI

15. consider only transportation and communication costs when reviewing Delta's location strategy. _____

    Y, N, NI

THE PRODUCTION CHALLENGE

The Challenge Case describes the changes that Delta is implementing to improve productivity. Specifically, it explains how Delta is making changes in airports in an effort to reduce the time it takes passengers to board their flights. This chapter is designed to help managers in companies such as Delta increase productivity.

This chapter emphasizes the fundamentals of **production control**—ensuring that an organization produces goods and services as planned. The primary discussion topics in the chapter are (1) production, (2) operations management, (3) operations control, and (4) selected operations control tools.

PRODUCTION

To reach organizational goals, all managers must plan, organize, influence, and control to produce some type of goods or services. Naturally, these goods and services vary significantly from organization to organization. This section of the chapter defines production and productivity and discusses the relationship between quality and productivity and automation.

Defining Production

Production is the transformation of organizational resources into products.[2] In this definition, *organizational resources* are all assets available to a manager to generate products, *transformation* is the set of steps necessary to change these resources into products, and *products* are various goods or services aimed at meeting human needs. Inputs at a manufacturing firm, for example, would include raw materials, purchased parts, production workers, and even schedules. The transformation process would encompass the preparation of customer orders, the design of various products, the procurement of raw materials, and the production, assembly, and (perhaps) warehousing of products. Outputs, of course, would consist of products fit for customer use.

"Production" occurs at service organizations as well. Inputs at a hospital, for instance, would include ambulances, rooms, employees (doctors, nurses, administrators, receptionists), supplies (medicines, bandages, food), and (as at a manufacturer) funds, schedules, and records. The transformation process might begin with transporting patients to the facility and end with discharging them. In between, the hospital would attend to patients' needs (nursing and feeding them, administering their medication, recording their progress). The output here is health care.

Productivity

Productivity is an important consideration in designing, evaluating, and improving modern production systems.[3] We can define **productivity** as the relationship between the total amount of goods or services being produced (output) and the organizational resources needed to produce them (input). This relationship is usually expressed by the following equation:[4]

$$\text{productivity} = \frac{\text{outputs}}{\text{inputs}}$$

The higher the value of the ratio of outputs to inputs, the higher the productivity of the operation.

Managers should continually strive to make their production processes as productive as possible.[5] It is no secret that over the past 20 years, the rate of productivity growth related to production management and innovation in U.S. manufacturing, for example, has lagged significantly behind that of countries such as Japan, West Germany, and France.[6] Some of the more traditional strategies for increasing productivity are as follows:[7]

1. Improving the effectiveness of the organizational workforce through training
2. Improving the production process through automation
3. Improving product design to make products easier to assemble
4. Improving the production facility by purchasing more modern equipment
5. Improving the quality of workers hired to fill open positions

In **an example from the world of management**, several companies such as **Intel** and **Cisco** are changing the way they design offices in an attempt to improve worker productivity.[8] Although many have credited Intel with the popularization of cubicles, executives at the company are reconsidering the costs and benefits of cubicle arrangements, which block worker visibility while failing to reduce noise. Intel is now testing alternative office arrangements in several locations. One such arrangement involves using large tables that employees can sit around in groups with notebook computers. Intel is hopeful that this new arrangement will help to boost both morale and productivity.

Quality and Productivity

Quality can be defined as how well a product does what it is intended to do—how closely it satisfies the specifications to which it was built.[9] In a broad sense, quality is the degree of excellence on which products or services can be ranked on the basis of selected features or characteristics. It is customers who determine this ranking, and customers define quality in terms of appearance, performance, availability, flexibility, and reliability.[10] Product quality determines an organization's reputation.

During the last decade or so, managerial thinking about the relationship between quality and productivity has changed drastically. Many earlier managers chose to achieve higher levels of productivity simply by producing a greater number of products given some fixed level of available resources. They saw no relationship between improving quality and increasing productivity. Quite the contrary: They viewed quality improvement as a controlling activity that took place toward the end of the production process and largely consisted of rejecting a number of finished products that were too obviously flawed to be offered to customers. Under this approach, quality improvement efforts were generally believed to *lower* productivity.

Focus on Continual Improvement Management theorists have more recently discovered that concentrating on improving product quality throughout all phases of a production process actually improves the productivity of the manufacturing system.[11] U.S. companies were far behind the Japanese in making this discovery. As early as 1948, Japanese companies observed that continual improvements in product quality throughout the production process normally resulted in improved productivity. How does this improvement happen? According to Dr. W. Edwards Deming, a world-renowned quality expert, a serious and consistent quality focus normally reduces nonproductive variables such as the reworking of products, production mistakes, delays and production snags, and inefficient use of time and materials.

Deming believed that for continual improvement to become a way of life in an organization, managers need to understand their company and its operations. Most managers feel they do know their company and its operations, but when they begin drawing flowcharts,

Printed circuits are made to exacting standards, so production quality is a primary concern of these technicians, who are checking over their work.

they discover that their understanding of strategy, systems, and processes is far from complete. Deming recommended that managers question every aspect of an operation and involve workers in discussion before they take action to improve operations. He maintained that a manager who seriously focuses on improving product quality throughout all phases of a production process will initiate a set of chain reactions that benefits not only the organization, but also the society in which the organization exists.

Focus on Quality and Integrated Operations Deming's flow diagram for improving product quality (see Figure 22.1) contains a complete set of organizational variables. It establishes the customer as part of the operations process and introduces the idea of continually refining knowledge, design, and inputs into the process in order to constantly increase customer satisfaction. The diagram shows the operations process as an integrated whole, from the first input to actual use of the finished product; a problem at the beginning of the process will affect the whole process and the end product. Deming's scheme eliminates barriers between the company and the customer, between the customer and suppliers, or between the company and its employees. Because the process is unified, the greater the harmony among all its components, the better the results will be.

An organization's interpretation of quality is expressed in its strategies. If a company does not incorporate quality into its strategic plan, customers may look for other solutions. In **an example from the world of management**, **Wal-Mart**'s continuous focus on low-price has led some consumers to equate the company with low quality.[12] Because of these perceptions, Wal-Mart's sales growth has decreased as many Wal-Mart customers have started shopping at other big-box stores associated with higher quality. The following sections elaborate on the relationship between quality and production by discussing quality assurance and quality circles as part of organizational strategy.

Quality Assurance **Quality assurance** is an operations process involving a broad group of activities aimed at achieving the organization's quality objectives.[13] Quality assurance is a continuum of activities that starts when quality standards are set and ends when quality goods and services are delivered to the customer. Although the precise activities involved in quality assurance vary from organization to organization, activities such as determining the

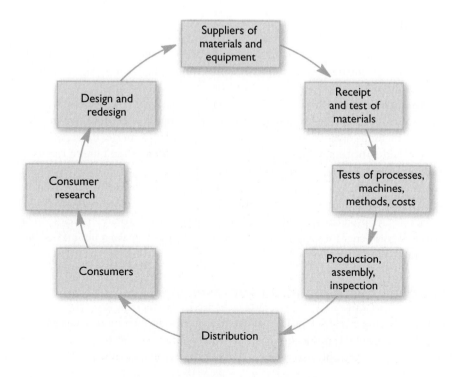

FIGURE 22.1
Deming's flow diagram for improving product quality

safest system for delivering goods to customers and maintaining the quality of parts or materials purchased from suppliers are part of most quality assurance efforts.[14]

Statistical Quality Control   Statistical quality control is a much narrower concept than quality assurance. **Statistical quality control** is the process used to determine how many products should be inspected to calculate a probability that the total number of products will meet organizational quality standards. An effective quality assurance strategy reduces the need for quality control and subsequent corrective actions.

"No Rejects" Philosophy   Quality assurance works best when management adopts a "no rejects" philosophy. Unfortunately, such a philosophy is not economically feasible for most mass-produced products. What is possible is training employees to approach production with a "do not make the same mistake once" mind-set. Mistakes are costly, and detecting defective products in the final quality control inspection is expensive. Emphasizing quality in the early stages—during product and process design—will reduce rejects and production costs.

Quality Circles   Another practice is to involve all company employees in quality control by soliciting their ideas for judging and maintaining product quality. This trend developed out of a successful Japanese control system known as *quality circles*. Although many corporations are now moving beyond the concept of the quality circle to that of the work team, as discussed in Chapter 18, many ideas generated from quality circles continue to be valid.[15]

Quality circles are small groups of workers that meet to discuss quality assurance of a particular project and to communicate their solutions to these problems to management directly at a formal presentation session.[16] Figure 22.2 shows the quality circle problem-solving process.

Most quality circles operate in a similar manner. The circle usually has fewer than eight members, and the circle leader is not necessarily the members' supervisor. Members may be workers on the project and/or outsiders. The focus is on operational problems rather than interpersonal ones. The problems discussed in the quality circle may be ones assigned by management or ones uncovered by the group itself.

Automation

The preceding section discussed the relationship between quality and productivity organizations. This section introduces the topic of automation, which shows signs of increasing organizational productivity in a revolutionary way.[17]

Automation is defined as the replacement of human effort by electromechanical devices in such operations as welding, materials handling, design, drafting, and decision making. It includes robots—mechanical devices built to perform repetitive tasks efficiently—and **robotics,** which is the study of the development and use of robots.

Over the past 20 years, a host of advanced manufacturing systems have been developed and implemented to support operations. Most of these automated systems combine hardware-industrial robots and computers—and software. The goals of new automation include reduced inventories, higher productivity, and faster billing and product distribution cycles. So far, the industrialized Asian countries appear to be doing the best job of making optimal use of company resources through automation.

Strategies, Systems, and Processes

According to Kemper and Yehudai, an effective and efficient operations manager is skilled not only in management, production, and productivity, but also in strategies, systems, and processes. A *strategy* is a plan of action. A *system* is a particular linking of organizational

FIGURE 22.2 The quality circle problem-solving process

components that facilitates carrying out a process. A *process* is a flow of interrelated events toward a goal, purpose, or end. Strategies create interlocking systems and processes when they are comprehensive, functional, and dynamic—when they designate responsibility and provide criteria for measuring output.[18]

OPERATIONS MANAGEMENT

Operations management deals with managing the production of goods and services in organizations. The sections that follow define *operations management* and discuss various strategies that managers can use to make production activities more effective and efficient.

Automation replaces human effort with electromechanical devices, like this police department robot.

Defining Operations Management

According to Chase and Aquilano, **operations management** is the performance of managerial activities entailed in selecting, designing, operating, controlling, and updating production systems.[19] Figure 22.3 describes these activities and categorizes them as either periodic or continual. The distinction between periodic and continual activities is one of relative frequency of performance: Periodic activities are performed from time to time, while continual activities are performed essentially without interruption.

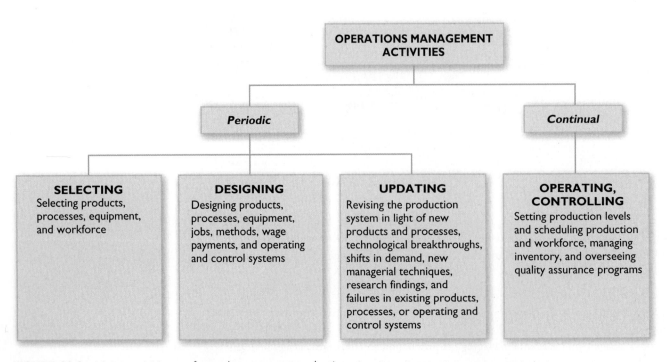

FIGURE 22.3 Major activities performed to manage production

Operations Management Considerations

Overall, *operations management* is the systematic direction and control of operations processes that transform resources into finished goods and services.[20] The concept conveys three key notions:

- Operations management involves managers—people who get things done by working with or through other people.
- Operations management takes place within the context of objectives and policies that drive the organization's strategic plans.
- The criteria for judging the actions taken as a result of operations management are standards for effectiveness and efficiency.

Effectiveness is the degree to which managers attain organizational objectives: "doing the right things." **Efficiency** is the degree to which organizational resources contribute to productivity: "doing things right." A review of organizational performance based on these standards is essential to enhancing the success of any organization.

Operations strategies—capacity, location, product, process, layout, and human resources—are specific plans of action designed to ensure that resources are obtained and used effectively and efficiently. An operational strategy is implemented by people who get things done with and through people. It is achieved in the context of objectives and policies derived from the organization's strategic plan.

Capacity Strategy

Capacity strategy is a plan of action aimed at providing the organization with the right facilities to produce the needed output at the right time. The output capacity of the organization determines its ability to meet future demands for goods and services. *Insufficient capacity* results in loss of sales that, in turn, affects profits. *Excess capacity* results in higher production costs. A strategy that aims for *optimal capacity*, where quantity and timing are in balance, provides an excellent basis for minimizing operating costs and maximizing profits.

Capacity flexibility enables the company to deliver its goods and services to its customers in a shorter time than its competitors. This component of capacity strategy involves having flexible plants and processes, broadly trained employees, and easy and economical access to external capacity, such as suppliers.

Managers use capacity strategy to balance the costs of overcapacity and undercapacity. The difficulty of accurately forecasting long-term demand makes this balancing task risky. Modifying long-range capacity decisions while in production is both hard and costly. In a highly competitive environment, construction of a new high-tech facility might take longer than the life cycle of the product. Correcting overcapacity by closing a plant saddles management with high economic costs and even higher social costs—such as lost jobs that devastate both employees and the community in which the plant operates—that will have a long-term adverse effect on the firm.

The traditional concept of economies of scale led management to construct large plants that tried to do everything. The more modern concept of the focused facility has shown management that better performance can be achieved in more specialized plants that concentrate on fewer tasks and are therefore smaller.

Five Steps in Capacity Decisions

Managers are more likely to make sound strategic capacity decisions if they adhere to the following five-step process:

1. Measure the capacity of currently available facilities.
2. Estimate future capacity needs on the basis of demand forecasts.
3. Compare future capacity needs and available capacity to determine whether capacity must be increased or decreased.
4. Identify ways to accommodate long-range capacity changes (expansion or reduction).
5. Select the best alternative based on a quantitative and qualitative evaluation.

Location Strategy **Location strategy** is a plan of action that provides the organization with a competitive location for its headquarters, manufacturing, services, and distribution activities. A competitive location results in lower transportation and communication costs among the various facilities. These costs—which run as high as 20 to 30 percent of a product's selling price—greatly affect the volume of sales and amount of profit generated by a particular product. Many other quantitative and qualitative factors are important when formulating location strategy.

Factors in a Good Location A successful location strategy requires a company to consider the following major factors in its location study:

* Nearness to market and distribution centers
* Nearness to vendors and resources
* Requirements of governments
* The character of direct competition
* The degree of interaction with the rest of the corporation
* The quality and quantity of labor pools
* The environmental attractiveness of the area
* Taxes and financing requirements
* Existing and potential transportation
* The quality of utilities and services

The dynamic nature of these factors could make what is a competitive location today an undesirable location in five years.

Product Strategy **Product strategy** is an operational plan of action outlining which goods and services an organization will produce and market.[21] Product strategy is a main component of an organization's operations strategy—in fact, it is the link between the operations strategy and the other functional strategies, especially marketing and research and development. In essence, product, marketing, and research and development strategies must fit together if management is to be able to build an effective overall operations strategy. A business's product and operations strategies should take into account the strengths and weaknesses of operations, which are primarily internal, as well as those of other functional areas concerned more with external opportunities and threats.

Cooperation and coordination among its marketing, operations, and research and development departments from the inception of a new product are strongly beneficial to a company. At the very least, it ensures a smooth transition from research and development to production, because operations people will be able to contribute to the quality of the total product, rather than merely attempt to improve the quality of the components. Even the most sophisticated product can be designed so that it is relatively simple to produce, thus reducing the number of units that must be scrapped or reworked during production, as well as the need for highly trained and highly paid employees. All of these strategies lower production costs and hence increase the product's price competitiveness or profits or both.

Process Strategy **Process strategy** is a plan of action outlining the means and methods the organization will use to transform resources into goods and services. Materials, labor, information, equipment, and managerial skills are resources that must be transformed. A competitive process strategy will ensure the most efficient and effective use of these organizational resources.

Types of Processes All manufacturing processes may be grouped into three different types. The first is the *continuous process,* a product-oriented, high-volume, low-variety process used, for example, in producing chemicals, beer, and petroleum products. The second is the *repetitive process,* a product-oriented production process that uses modules to produce items in large lots. This mass-production or assembly-line process is characteristic of the auto and appliance industries.

The third type of manufacturing process is used to produce small lots of custom-designed products such as furniture. This high-variety, low-volume system, commonly known as the *job-shop process,* includes the production of one-of-a-kind items as well as unit production. Spaceship and weapons systems production are considered job-shop activities.

Organizations commonly employ more than one type of manufacturing process at the same time and in the same facility.

Process strategy is directly linked to product strategy. The decision to select a particular process strategy is often the result of external market opportunities or threats. The corporation decides what it wants to produce, then selects a process strategy to produce it. The product takes center stage and the process becomes a function of the product.

The function of process strategy is to determine what equipment will be used, what maintenance will be necessary, and what level of automation will be most effective and efficient. The type of employees and the level of employee skills needed are dependent on the process strategy chosen.

Layout Strategy
Layout strategy is a plan of action that outlines the location and flow of all organizational resources around, into, and within production and service facilities. A cost-effective and cost-efficient layout strategy is one that minimizes the expenses of processing, transporting, and storing materials throughout the production and service cycle.

Layout strategy—which is usually the last part of operations strategy to be formulated—is closely linked, either directly or indirectly, with all other components of operations strategy: capacity, location, product, process, and human resources. It must target capacity and process requirements. It must satisfy the organization's product design, quality, and quantity requirements. It must target facility and location requirements. Finally, to be effective, the layout strategy must be compatible with the organization's established quality of work life.

A **layout** is the overall arrangement of equipment, work areas, service areas, and storage areas within a facility that produces goods or provides services.[22] Three basic types of layouts are used for manufacturing facilities:

1. A **product layout** is designed to accommodate high production volumes, highly specialized equipment, and narrow employee skills. It is appropriate for organizations that produce and service a limited number of different products. It is not appropriate for an organization that experiences constant or frequent changes of products.
2. A **process (functional) layout** is a layout pattern that groups together similar types of equipment. It is appropriate for organizations involved in a large number of different tasks. It best serves companies whose production volumes are low, whose equipment is multipurpose, and whose employees' skills are broad.
3. The **fixed-position layout** is one in which the product is stationary while resources flow. It is appropriate for organizations involved in a large number of different tasks that require low volumes, multipurpose equipment, and broad employee skills. A *group technology layout* is a product layout cell within a larger process layout. It benefits organizations that require both types of layout.

Figure 22.4 illustrates the three basic layout patterns. Actually, most manufacturing facilities are a combination of two or more different types of layouts. Various techniques are available to assist management in designing an efficient and effective layout that meets the required specifications.

The right facilities layout strategy can help streamline the work of this candymaker, who is pouring melted fudge at a chocolate factory. The design of his workplace must take into account the distance the fudge travels between the cooking area and the marble table shown here, the weight of the vats, the temperature and humidity of the work area, the next step in the manufacturing process, and many other factors.

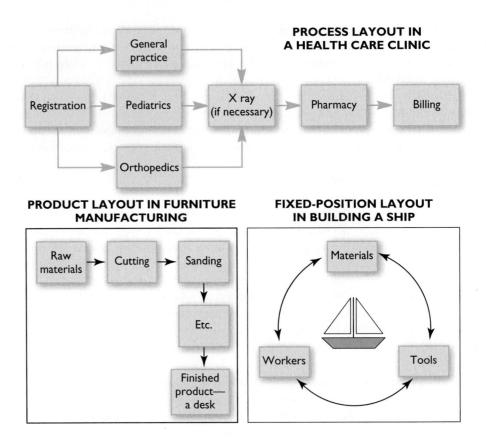

FIGURE 22.4
Three basic layout patterns

Human Resources Strategy *Human resources* is the term used for individuals engaged in any of the organization's activities. Two human resource imperatives are as follows:

1. It is essential to optimize individual, group, and organizational effectiveness.
2. It is essential to enhance the quality of organizational life.

A **human resources strategy** is an operational plan to use the organization's human resources effectively and efficiently while maintaining or improving the quality of work life.[23]

Hiring the right people for every job and training them to be productive is a human resources strategy with implications for management control.

As discussed in Chapter 13, human resource management is about employees—who are the best means of enhancing organizational effectiveness. Whereas financial management attempts to increase organizational effectiveness through the allocation and conservation of financial resources, human resource management (personnel management) attempts to increase organizational effectiveness through such factors as the establishment of personnel policies, education and training, and procedures.

Operational Tools in Human Resources Strategy Operations management attempts to increase organizational effectiveness by employing the methods used in the manufacturing and service processes. Human resources, one important factor of operations, must be compatible with operations tasks.

Labor force planning is the primary focus of the operations human resources strategy. It is an operational plan for hiring the right employees for a job and training them to be productive. This process is lengthy and costly. A human resources strategy must be founded on fair treatment and trust. The employee, not operations, must take center stage.

Job design is an operational plan that determines who will do a specific job and how and where the job will be done. The goal of job design is to facilitate productivity. Successful job design takes efficiency and behavior into account. It also guarantees that working conditions are safe and that the health of employees will not be jeopardized in the short or the long run.[24]

Work methods analysis is an operational tool used to improve productivity and ensure the safety of workers. It can be performed for new or existing jobs. **Motion-study techniques** are another set of operational tools used to improve productivity.

Work measurement methods are operational tools used to establish labor standards. These standards are useful for planning, control, productivity improvements, costing and pricing, bidding, compensation, motivation, and financial incentives.

OPERATIONS CONTROL

Once a decision has been made to design an operational plan of action, resource allocations are considered. After management has decided on a functional operations strategy, using marketing and financial plans of action, it determines what specific tasks are necessary to accomplish functional objectives. This process is known as *operations control*.

Operations control is defined as making sure that operations activities are carried out as planned. The major components of operations control are just-in-time inventory control, maintenance control, cost control, budgetary control, ratio analysis, and materials control. Each of these components is discussed in detail in the following sections.

Just-in-Time Inventory Control

Just-in-time (JIT) inventory control is a technique for reducing inventories to a minimum by arranging for production components to be delivered to the production facility "just in time" to be used.[25] The concept, developed primarily by the Toyota Motor Company of Japan, is also called "zero inventory" or *kanban*—the latter a Japanese term referring to purchasing raw materials by using a special ordering form.[26]

JIT is based on the management philosophy that products should be manufactured only when customers need them and only in the quantities customers require in order to minimize the amounts of raw materials and finished goods inventories manufacturers keep on hand. It emphasizes maintaining organizational operations by using only the resources that are absolutely necessary to meet customer demand.

Best Conditions for JIT JIT works best in companies that manufacture relatively standardized products that experience consistent demand. Such companies can comfortably order materials from suppliers and assemble products in small, continuous batches. The result is a smooth, consistent flow of purchased materials and assembled products, with little inventory buildup. Companies that manufacture nonstandardized products that experience sporadic or seasonal demand, however, generally face more irregular purchases of raw materials from suppliers, more uneven production cycles, and greater accumulations of inventory.

Advantages of JIT   When successfully implemented, JIT enhances organizational performance in several important ways. First, it reduces the unnecessary labor expenses generated by manufacturing products that are not sold. Second, it minimizes the tying up of monetary resources in purchases of production-related materials that do not result in timely sales. Third, it helps management hold down inventory expenses—particularly storage and handling costs. Better inventory management and control of labor costs, in fact, are the two most commonly cited benefits of JIT.

Characteristics of JIT   Experience indicates that successful JIT programs have certain common characteristics:[27]

1. **Closeness of suppliers**—Manufacturers using JIT find it beneficial to use raw materials suppliers who are based only a short distance from them. When a company is ordering smaller quantities of raw materials at a time, suppliers must sometimes be asked to make one or more deliveries per day. Short distances make multiple deliveries per day feasible. Nonetheless, relying on one large supplier may present disadvantages as well. In **an example from the world of management**, **Toyota** recently encountered problems when an earthquake caused one of its suppliers of pistons, Riken Corp., to temporarily suspend operations in one of its manufacturing facilities. Because Toyota relies on JIT, this delay at Riken caused Toyota to delay its delivery of approximately 55,000 vehicles.[28]

2. **High quality of materials purchased from suppliers**—Manufacturers using JIT find it especially difficult to overcome problems caused by defective materials. Because they keep their materials inventory small, defective materials purchased from a supplier may force them to discontinue the production process until another delivery from the supplier can be arranged. Such production slowdowns can be disadvantageous, causing late delivery to customers or lost sales.

3. **Well-organized receiving and handling of materials purchased from suppliers**—Companies using JIT must be able to receive and handle raw materials effectively and efficiently. Materials must be available for the production process where and when they are needed, because if they are not, extra costs will be built into the production process.

4. **Strong management commitment**—Management must be strongly committed to the concept of JIT. The system takes time and effort to plan, install, and improve—and is therefore expensive to implement. Management must be willing to commit funds to initiate the JIT system and to support it once it is functioning.

Maintenance Control

Maintenance control is aimed at keeping the organization's facility and equipment functioning at predetermined work levels. In the planning stage, managers must select a strategy that will direct personnel to fix equipment either before it malfunctions or after it malfunctions. The first strategy is referred to as a **pure-preventive maintenance policy**—machine adjustments, lubrication, cleaning, parts replacement, painting, and needed repairs and overhauls are done regularly, before facilities or machines malfunction. At the other end of the maintenance control continuum is the **pure-breakdown (repair) policy,** which decrees that facilities and equipment be fixed only after they malfunction.

Most organizations implement a maintenance strategy somewhere in the middle of the maintenance continuum. Management usually tries to select a level and a frequency of maintenance that minimize the cost of both preventive maintenance and breakdowns (repair). Because no level of preventive maintenance can eliminate breakdowns altogether, repair will always be an important activity.

Whether management decides on a pure-preventive or pure-breakdown policy, or on something in between, the prerequisite for a successful maintenance program is the availability of maintenance parts and supplies or replacement (standby) equipment. Some organizations choose to keep standby machines to protect themselves against the consequences of breakdowns. Plants that use special-purpose equipment are more likely to invest in standby equipment than those that use general-purpose equipment.

Cost Control

Cost control is broad control aimed at keeping organizational costs at planned levels.[29] Because cost control relates to all organizational costs, it emphasizes activities in all organizational areas, such as research and development, operations, marketing, and finance. If an organization is to be successful, costs in all organizational areas must be controlled. Cost control is therefore an important responsibility of all managers in an organization.

Operations activities are cost-intensive—perhaps the most cost-intensive of all organizational activities—so when significant cost savings are realized in organizations, they are generally realized at the operations level.

Operations managers are responsible for the overall control of the cost of goods or services sold. Producing goods and services at or below planned cost levels is their principal objective, so operations managers are commonly evaluated primarily on their cost control activities. When operations costs are consistently above planned levels, the organization may need to change its operations management.

Stages in Cost Control The general cost control process has four stages:

1. Establishing standard or planned cost amounts
2. Measuring actual costs incurred
3. Comparing planned costs to incurred costs
4. Making changes to reduce actual costs to planned costs when necessary

Following these stages for specific operations cost control, the operations manager must first establish planned costs or cost standards for operations activities such as labor, materials, and overhead. Next, the operations manager must actually measure or calculate the costs incurred for these activities. Third, the operations manager must compare actual operations costs to planned operations costs, and fourth, take steps to reduce actual operations costs to planned levels if necessary.

Budgetary Control

As described in Chapter 10, a budget is a single-use financial plan that covers a specified length of time. An organization's **budget** is its financial plan outlining how funds in a given period will be obtained and spent.

In addition to being a financial plan, however, a budget can be the basis for *budgetary control*—that is, for ensuring that income and expenses occur as planned. As managers gather information on actual receipts and expenditures within an operating period, they may uncover significant deviations from budgeted amounts. If so, they should develop and implement a control strategy aimed at bringing actual performance in line with planned performance. This effort, of course, assumes that the plan contained in the budget is appropriate for the organization. The following sections discuss some potential pitfalls of budgets and human relations considerations that may make a budget inappropriate.

Potential Pitfalls of Budgets To maximize the benefits of using budgets, managers must avoid several potential pitfalls. Among these pitfalls are the following:

1. **Placing too much emphasis on relatively insignificant organizational expenses**—In preparing and implementing a budget, managers should allocate more time for dealing with significant organizational expenses and less time for relatively insignificant organizational expenses. For example, the amount of time managers spend on developing and implementing a budget for labor costs typically should be much more than the amount of time they spend on developing and implementing a budget for office supplies.

2. **Increasing budgeted expenses year after year without adequate information**—It does not necessarily follow that items contained in last year's budget should be increased this year. Perhaps the best-known method for overcoming this potential pitfall is zero-base budgeting.[30] **Zero-base budgeting** is a planning and budgeting process that requires managers to justify their entire budget request in detail rather than simply referring to budget amounts established in previous years.

    Some management theorists believe that zero-base budgeting is a better management tool than traditional budgeting—which simply starts with the budget amount established in the prior year—because it emphasizes focused identification and control of each budget item. It is unlikely, however, that this tool will be implemented successfully unless management adequately explains what zero-base budgeting is and how it is to be used in the organization. One of the earliest and most commonly cited successes in implementing a zero-base budgeting program took place in the Department of Agriculture's Office of Budget and Finance.

3. **Ignoring the fact that budgets must be changed periodically**—Managers should recognize that such factors as costs of materials, newly developed technology, and product demand change constantly and that budgets must be reviewed and modified periodically in response to these changes.

A special type of budget called a *variable budget* is sometimes used to determine automatically when such changes in budgets are needed. A **variable budget,** also known as a *flexible budget,* outlines the levels of resources to be allocated for each organizational activity according to the level of production within the organization. It follows, then, that a variable budget automatically indicates an increase in the amount of resources allocated for various organizational activities when production levels go up and a decrease when production goes down.

Human Relations Considerations in Using Budgets Many managers believe that although budgets are valuable planning and control tools, they can result in major human relations problems in an organization. A classic article by Chris Argyris, for example, shows how budgets can build pressures that unite workers against management, cause harmful conflict between management and factory workers, and create tensions that result in worker inefficiency and worker aggression against management.[31] If such problems are severe enough, a budget may result in more harm than good to the organization.

Reducing Human Relations Problems Several strategies have been suggested to minimize the human relations problems caused by budgets. The most often recommended strategy is to design and implement appropriate human relations training programs for finance personnel, accounting personnel, production supervisors, and all other key people involved in the formulation and use of budgets. These training programs should emphasize both the advantages and disadvantages of applying pressure on people through budgets and the possible results of using budgets to imply that an organization member is a success or a failure at his or her job.

Ratio Analysis

Another type of control uses ratio analysis.[32] A *ratio* is a relationship between two numbers that is calculated by dividing one number into the other. **Ratio analysis** is the process of generating information that summarizes the financial position of an organization through the calculation of ratios based on various financial measures that appear on the organization's balance sheet and income statements.

The ratios available to managers for controlling organizations, shown in Table 22.1, can be divided into four categories:

1. Profitability ratios
2. Liquidity ratios
3. Activity ratios
4. Leverage ratios

Using Ratios to Control Organizations Managers should use ratio analysis in three ways to control an organization:[33]

- **Managers should evaluate all ratios simultaneously.** This strategy ensures that they will develop and implement a control strategy appropriate for the organization as a whole rather than one that suits only one phase or segment of the organization.

- **Managers should compare computed values for ratios in a specific organization with the values of industry averages for those ratios.** (The values of industry averages for the ratios can be obtained from private information providers such as Dun & Bradstreet, the European Commission, and the U.S. Securities and Exchange Commission, for example). Managers increase the probability of formulating and implementing appropriate control strategies when they compare their financial situation to that of competitors in this way.

- **Managers' use of ratios should incorporate trend analysis.** Managers must remember that any set of ratio values is actually only a determination of relationships that existed in a specified time period (often a year). To employ ratio analysis to maximum advantage, they need to accumulate ratio values for several successive time periods to uncover specific organizational trends. Once these trends are revealed, managers can formulate and implement appropriate strategies for dealing with them.

Materials Control

Materials control is an operations control activity that determines the flow of materials from vendors through an operations system to customers. The achievement of desired levels of product cost, quality, availability, dependability, and flexibility heavily depends on the

TABLE 22.1 Four Categories of Ratios

Type	Example	Calculation	Interpretation
Profitability	Return on investment (ROI)	$\frac{\text{Profit after taxes}}{\text{Total assets}}$	Productivity of assets
Liquidity	Current ratio	$\frac{\text{Current assets}}{\text{Current liabilities}}$	Short-term solvency
Activity	Inventory turnover	$\frac{\text{Sales}}{\text{Inventory}}$	Efficiency of inventory management
Leverage	Debt ratio	$\frac{\text{Total debt}}{\text{Total assets}}$	How a company finances itself

effective and efficient flow of materials. Materials management activities can be broadly organized into six groups or functions: purchasing, receiving, inventorying, floor controlling, trafficking, and shipping and distributing.

Procurement of Materials

More than 50 percent of the expenditures of a typical manufacturing company are for the procurement of materials, including raw materials, parts, subassemblies, and supplies. This procurement is the responsibility of the purchasing department. Actually, purchases of production materials are largely automated and linked to a resources requirement planning system. Purchases of all other materials, however, are based on requisitions from users. The purchasing department's job does not end with the placement of an order; order follow-up is just as crucial.

Receiving, Shipping, and Trafficking

Receiving activities include unloading, identifying, inspecting, reporting, and storing inbound shipments. Shipping and distribution activities are similar and may include preparing documents, packaging, labeling, loading, and directing outbound shipments to customers and to distribution centers. Shipping and receiving are sometimes organized as one unit.

A traffic manager's main responsibilities are selection of the transportation mode, coordination of the arrival and departure of shipments, and auditing freight bills.

Inventory and Shop-Floor Control

Inventory control activities ensure the continuous availability of purchased materials. Work-in-process and finished-goods inventory are inventory control subsystems. Inventory control specifies what, when, and how much to buy. Held inventories buffer the organization against a variety of uncertainties that can disrupt supply, but since holding inventory is costly, an optimal inventory control policy provides a predetermined level of certainty of supply at the lowest possible cost.

Shop-floor control activities include input/output control, scheduling, sequencing, routing, dispatching, and expediting.

Although many materials management activities can be programmed, the human factor is the key to a competitive performance. Skilled and motivated employees are therefore crucial to successful materials control.

class discussion highlight

DOES QUALITY CONTROL MATTER?[34]

This chapter highlights how a company's operations management is important, but do these management techniques ultimately help managers to improve the performance of their firms? To answer this question, Professors Tan, Kannan, and Narasimhans examined the influence of quality control and just-in-time strategies on firm performance.

The researchers designed a survey to better understand how operations management techniques influence firm performance, and they received more than 500 responses from operations management professionals. Do you think that the authors found support for relationships between quality control and just-in-time strategies and firm performance? Why or why not? If managers share your beliefs, what are the implications for organizations and their budgets?

SELECTED OPERATIONS CONTROL TOOLS

In addition to understanding production, operations management, and operations control, managers also need to be aware of various operations control tools that are useful in an operations facility. A **control tool** is a specific procedure or technique that presents pertinent organizational information in a way that helps managers and workers develop and implement an appropriate control strategy. That is, a control tool aids managers and workers in pinpointing the organizational strengths and weaknesses on which a useful control strategy must focus. This section discusses specific control tools for day-to-day operations as well as for longer-run operations.

Using Control Tools to Control Organizations

Continual improvement of operations is a practical, not a theoretical, managerial concern. It is, essentially, the development and use of better methods. Different types of organizations have different goals and strategies, but all organizations struggle daily to find better ways of doing things. This goal of continual improvement applies not just to money-making enterprises, but to those with other missions as well. Because organizational leaders are continually changing systems and personal styles of management, everyone within the organization is continually learning to live with change.

Inspection

Traditionally, managers believed that if you wanted good quality, you hired many inspectors to make sure an operation was producing at the desired quality level. These inspectors examined and graded finished products or components, parts, or services at any stage of operation by measuring, tasting, touching, weighing, disassembling, destroying, and testing. The goal of inspection was to detect unacceptable quality levels before a bad product or service reached a customer. Whenever a lot of defects were found, management blamed the workers and hired more inspectors.

To Inspect or Not to Inspect Today, managers know that inspection cannot catch problems built into the system. The traditional inspection process does not result in improvement and does not guarantee quality. In fact, according to Deming, inspection is a limited, grossly overused, and often misused tool. He recommended that management stop relying on mass inspection to achieve quality, and advocated instead either 100 percent inspection in those cases where defect-free work is impossible or no inspection at all where the level of defects is acceptably small.

Management by Exception

Management by exception is a control technique that allows only significant deviations between planned and actual performance to be brought to a manager's attention. Management by exception is based on the *exception principle,* a management principle that appears in early management literature.[35] This principle recommends that subordinates handle all routine organizational matters, leaving managers free to deal with nonroutine, or exceptional, organizational issues.

Establishing Rules Some organizations rely on subordinates or managers themselves to detect the significant deviations between standards and performance that signal exceptional issues. Other organizations establish rules to ensure that exceptional issues surface as a matter of normal operating procedure. Setting rules must be done carefully to ensure that all true deviations are brought to the manager's attention.

Two examples of rules based on the exception principle are the following:[36]

1. A department manager must immediately inform the plant manager if actual weekly labor costs exceed estimated weekly labor costs by more than 15 percent.
2. A department manager must immediately inform the plant manager if actual money spent plus estimated money to be spent on a special project exceed the funds approved for the project by more than 10 percent.

Although these two rules happen to focus on production-related expenditures, detecting and reporting significant rules deviations can be established in virtually any organizational area.

If appropriately administered, the management-by-exception control technique ensures the best use of managers' time. Because only significant issues are brought to managers' attention, the possibility that managers will spend their valuable time working on relatively insignificant issues is automatically eliminated.

Of course, the significant issues brought to managers' attention could be organizational strengths as well as organizational weaknesses. Obviously, managers should try to reinforce the first and eliminate the second.

Management by Objectives

In management by objectives, which was discussed in Chapter 7, the manager assigns a specialized set of objectives and action plans to workers and then rewards those workers on the basis of how close they come to reaching their goals. This control technique has been implemented in corporations intent on using an employee-participative means to improve productivity.

Break-Even Analysis

Another production-related control tool commonly used by managers is break-even analysis. **Break-even analysis** is the process of generating information that summarizes various levels of profit or loss associated with various levels of production. The next sections discuss three facets of this control tool: basic ingredients of break-even analysis, types of break-even analysis available to managers, and the relationship between break-even analysis and controlling.

Basic Ingredients of Break-Even Analysis Break-even analysis typically involves reflection, discussion, reasoning, and decision making relative to the following seven major aspects of production:

1. **Fixed costs**—**Fixed costs** are expenses incurred by the organization regardless of the number of products produced. Some examples are real estate taxes, upkeep to the exterior of a business building, and interest expenses on money borrowed to finance the purchase of equipment.
2. **Variable costs**—Expenses that fluctuate with the number of products produced are called **variable costs.** Examples are costs of packaging a product, costs of materials needed to make the product, and costs associated with packing products to prepare them for shipping.
3. **Total costs**—**Total costs** are simply the sum of the fixed and variable costs associated with production.
4. **Total revenue**—**Total revenue** is all sales money accumulated from selling manufactured products or services. Naturally, total revenue increases as more products are sold.
5. **Profits**—**Profits** are defined as the amount of total revenue that exceeds the total costs of producing the products sold.

6. **Loss**—**Loss** is the amount of the total costs of producing a product that exceeds the total revenue gained from selling the product.
7. **Break-even point**—The **break-even point** is the level of production at which the total revenue of an organization equals its total costs—that is, the point at which the organization is generating only enough revenue to cover its costs. The company is neither gaining a profit nor incurring a loss.

Types of Break-Even Analysis Two somewhat different procedures can be used to determine the same break-even point for an organization: algebraic break-even analysis and graphic break-even analysis.

Algebraic Break-Even Analysis The following simple formula is commonly used to determine the level of production at which an organization breaks even:

$$BE = \frac{FC}{P - VC}$$

where

BE = the level of production at which the firm breaks even
FC = total fixed costs of production
P = price at which each individual unit is sold to customers
VC = variable costs associated with each product manufactured and sold

In using this formula to calculate a break-even point, two sequential steps must be followed. First, the variable costs associated with producing each unit must be subtracted from the price at which each unit will sell. The purpose of this calculation is to determine how much of the selling price of each unit sold can go toward covering total fixed costs incurred from producing all products. Second, the remainder calculated in the first step must be divided into total fixed costs. The purpose of this calculation is to determine how many units must be produced and sold to cover fixed costs. This number of units is the break-even point for the organization.

Say a book publisher faces the fixed and variable costs per paperback book presented in Table 22.2. If the publisher wants to sell each book for $12, the break-even point could be calculated as follows:

$$BE = \frac{\$88,800}{\$12 - \$6}$$

$$BE = \frac{\$88,800}{\$6}$$

$$BE = 14,800 \text{ copies}$$

TABLE 22.2 Fixed Costs and Variable Costs for a Book Publisher

Fixed Costs (Yearly Basis)		Variable Costs per Book Sold	
1. Real estate taxes on property	$1,000	1. Printing	$2.00
2. Interest on loan to purchase equipment	5,000	2. Artwork	1.00
3. Building maintenance	2,000	3. Sales commission	.50
4. Insurance	800	4. Author royalties	1.50
5. Salaried labor	80,000	5. Binding	1.00
Total fixed costs	$88,800	Total variable costs per book	$6.00

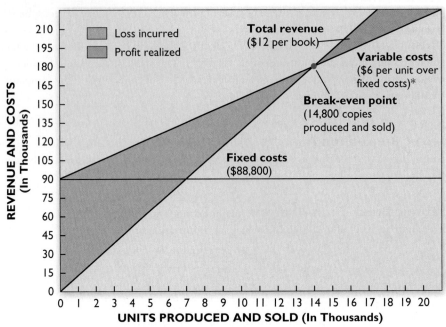

FIGURE 22.5
Break-even analysis for a book publisher

* Note that drawing the variable costs line on top of the fixed costs line means that variable costs have been added to fixed costs. Therefore, the variable costs line also represents total costs.

This calculation indicates that if expenses and selling price remain stable, the book publisher will incur a loss if book sales are fewer than 14,800 copies, will break even if book sales equal 14,800 copies, and will make a profit if book sales exceed 14,800 copies.

Graphic Break-Even Analysis Graphic break-even analysis entails the construction of a graph showing all the critical elements in a break-even analysis. Figure 22.5 is such a graph for the book publisher. Note that in a break-even graph, the total revenue line starts at zero.

Advantages of Using the Algebraic and Graphic Break-Even Methods
Both the algebraic and the graphic methods of break-even analysis for the book publisher result in the same break-even point—14,800 books produced and sold—but the processes used to arrive at this point are quite different.

Which break-even method managers should use is usually determined by the situation they face. For a manager who desires a quick yet accurate determination of a break-even point, the algebraic method generally suffices. For a manager who wants a more complete picture of the cumulative relationships between the break-even point, fixed costs, and escalating variable costs, the graphic break-even method is more useful. For example, the book publisher could quickly and easily see from Figure 22.5 the cumulative relationships of fixed costs, escalating variable costs, and potential profit and loss associated with various levels of production.

Control and Break-Even Analysis Break-even analysis is a useful control tool because it helps managers understand the relationships between fixed costs, variable costs, total costs, and profit and loss within an organization. Once these relationships are understood, managers can take steps to modify one or more of the variables to reduce deviation between planned and actual profit levels.[37]

Increasing costs or decreasing selling prices has the overall effect of increasing the number of units an organization must produce and sell to break even. Conversely, the managerial strategy for decreasing the number of products an organization must produce and sell to break even entails lowering or stabilizing fixed and variables costs or increasing the selling price of each unit. The exact break-even control strategy a particular manager should develop and implement is dictated primarily by that manager's unique organizational situation.

Other Broad Operations Control Tools

Some of the best-known and most commonly used operations control tools are discussed in the following sections. The primary purpose of these tools is to control the production of organizational goods and services.[38]

Decision Tree Analysis **Decision tree analysis,** as you recall from Chapter 8, is a statistical and graphical multiphased decision-making technique that contains a series of steps showing the sequence and interdependence of decisions. Decision trees allow a decision maker to deal with uncertain events by determining the relative expected value of each alternative course of action. The probabilities of different possible events are known, as are the monetary payoffs that result from a particular alternative and a particular event. Decision trees are best suited to situations in which capacity decisions involve several capacity expansion alternatives and the selection of the alternative with the highest expected profit or the lowest expected cost is necessary.

Process Control Statistical process control, known as **process control,** is a technique that assists in monitoring production processes. Production processes must be monitored continually to ensure that the quality of their output is acceptable. The earlier the detection of a faulty production process can occur, the better. If detection occurs late in the production process, the company may find parts that do not meet quality standards, and scrapping or reworking these units is a costly proposition. If a production process results in unstable performance or is downright out of control, corrective action must be taken. Process control can be implemented with the aid of graphical charts known as control charts.

Value Analysis **Value analysis** is a cost control and cost reduction technique that helps managers control operations by focusing primarily on material costs. The goal of this analysis, which is performed by examining all the parts and materials and their functions, is to reduce costs by using cheaper components and materials in such a way that product quality or appeal is not affected. Simplification of parts—which lowers production costs—is also a goal of value analysis. Value analysis can result not only in cost savings, but in an improved product.

Value analysis requires a team effort. The team, if not companywide, should at least include personnel from operations, purchasing, engineering, and marketing.

Computer-Aided Design **Computer-aided design (CAD)** systems include several automated design technologies. *Computer graphics* is used to design geometric specifications for parts, while *computer-aided engineering (CAE)* is employed to evaluate and perform engineering analyses on a part. CAD also includes technologies used in process design. CAD functions to ensure the quality of a product by guaranteeing not only the quality of parts in the product, but also the appropriateness of the product's design.

Computer-Aided Manufacturing **Computer-aided manufacturing (CAM)** employs computers to plan and program equipment used in the production and inspection of manufactured items. Linking CAM and CAD processes through a computer is especially beneficial when production processes must be altered, because when CAD and CAM systems can share information easily, design changes can be implemented in a short period of time.

CHALLENGE CASE SUMMARY

Increasing productivity at Delta, as described in the Challenge Case, is mainly a matter of integrating resources such as people, equipment, and materials to provide better customer service.

Although the level of productivity at Delta was far from disastrous, management decided it was necessary to lower operating costs through improved productivity in order to stay competitive in the increasingly combative airline carrier business. One of Delta's first moves involved installing self-service kiosks that help passengers move through the airports more quickly. To increase productivity at Delta even further, managers might also take such actions as implementing more effective training programs for employees and being more selective in hiring people.

To maintain and improve the quality of customer service, Delta management could establish a quality assurance program that continually monitors services to ensure that they are at acceptable levels. Quality circles could be established to involve employees in the effort to improve customer service both in the specific area of reducing check-in times and in more general terms.

In attempting to reduce the time it takes its passengers to reach their planes, Delta's management is involved in operations management. Most of the issues mentioned in the Challenge Case pertain to the "periodic updating" segment of operations management activities—revising systems to provide better customer service. Delta's periodic updating should focus on the appropriate use of company resources such as ticket agents, caterers, fuel trucks, and ramp agents. Once established, the new operations procedure must be continually monitored by Delta's management for both effectiveness—"doing the right things"—and efficiency—"doing things right."

Factors that Delta's management must consider in making operations decisions include *capacity strategy*, making sure that the airline has appropriate resources to perform needed functions at appropriate times; *location strategy*, making sure that airline resources are appropriately postured for work when the work must be performed; *product strategy*, making sure appropriate customer services are targeted and provided; *process strategy*, making sure that Delta is employing appropriate steps in providing various customer services; *layout strategy*, making sure that the flow of Delta's resources in the process of providing customer services is desirable; and *human resources strategy*, making sure that Delta has appropriate people providing services to customers.

Operations control activities help Delta's management make certain that customer services are carried out as planned. *Just-in-time inventory control*, for example, would ensure that enough self-service kiosks are in place and available just when customers need them. Putting money into large surpluses of these kiosks, however, would needlessly tie up company resources and reduce company profitability. *Maintenance control* would ensure that equipment (e.g., baggage conveyors) needed to provide customer services is operating at a desirable level. *Cost control* would ensure that Delta is not providing services to customers too expensively. *Budgetary control* would focus on acquiring company resources and using them to provide customer services as stipulated by Delta's financial plan.

Operations control at Delta can also include ratio analysis, or determining relationships between various factors on Delta's income statement and balance sheet to arrive at a good indication of the company's financial position. Through ratio analysis, Delta's management could monitor issues such as customer services to determine their overall impact on company profitability, liquidity, and leverage. To assess the impact of providing various customer services on the financial condition of Delta, management would track ratios over time to discern trends.

Finally, operations control at Delta would need to include materials control to ensure that materials purchased from suppliers are flowing appropriately from vendors to customers in the form of customer services. For example, the goal of monitoring the drinks, snacks, and meals that caterers are providing to Delta's passengers would be to improve the quality of such items in terms of temperature, freshness, and nutritional value.

Several useful production control tools are available to Delta's management to ensure that various services are provided to customers as planned. First, management can have customer services inspected to determine which, if any, services should be improved and how to improve them. Second, Delta can use management by exception to control customer services. In this case, Delta's workers would handle all routine customer service issues and bring only exceptional matters to management's attention. To successfully use management by exception at Delta, it would be necessary to implement a number of carefully designed rules. One such rule might be that when 5 percent or more of passengers are late for a given flight, a customer service representative must report this fact to a supervisor. The supervisor would then carefully inspect the check-in process to see why so many passengers are late—perhaps because the airport does not offer enough self-service kiosks—and management would take steps to correct the situation.

Delta might prefer to use management by objectives to control customer service issues. For example, management could set such customer service objectives as answering a ticket counter phone within three rings or ticketing a passenger within five minutes. If such objectives are deemed both worthwhile and realistic, yet Delta's employees are not reaching them consistently, management would take steps to ensure that they are met.

Another control tool Delta's management might find highly useful is break-even analysis. Break-even analysis would furnish management with information about the various levels of profit or loss associated with various levels of revenue. To use this tool, Delta would have to determine the total fixed costs necessary to operate the airline, the price at which flights are sold, and the variable costs associated with various flights.

For example, if management wanted to determine how many tickets had to be sold before the company would break even on a particular flight, it could arrive at this break-even point algebraically by following three steps. First, all fixed costs attributable to operating the flight—for example, airport facility rent—would be totaled. Second, all the variable costs of furnishing a flight to a passenger would be totaled, and from this total, management would subtract the revenue that a ticket will generate. Variable costs include such expenses as meal costs, fuel costs, and labor needed to furnish the flight. Finally, the answer calculated in step 2 would be divided into the answer derived in

step 1, and this figure would tell management how many tickets must be sold at the projected revenue level to break even.

Delta's management also could choose to determine the break-even point by constructing a graph showing fixed costs, variable costs, and revenue per flight. Such a graph would probably give managers a more useful picture for formulating profit-oriented flight plans.

Decision tree analysis, process control, value analysis, computer-aided design, and computer-aided manufacturing were presented in the text as broader operations tools that are highly useful to managers exercising the control function. Of all these tools, value analysis would have the most application to Delta's service-oriented operation. Delta's management could use this cost control and cost reduction technique to examine the cost and worth of every component of customer service. To gain a complete picture of customer service components and their usefulness, Delta might establish a team comprising members from different customer service areas.

For instance, a team composed of a ticket agent, a flight attendant, a maintenance supervisor, and a baggage handler might explore different options for establishing comfortable cabin temperature while a plane is being loaded but before it taxis to the runway to await takeoff. If this team concludes, for example, that expediting the baggage-handling process would expose passengers to uncomfortable temperatures for shorter periods of time, management could take steps to speed up the process. Implementation of more efficient ways of handling baggage would result not only in better customer service, but in lower airline operating costs.

MANAGEMENT SKILL ACTIVITIES

This section is specially designed to help you develop production and control skill. An individual's production and control skill is based upon an understanding of production and control concepts and the ability to apply those concepts in management situations. The following activities are designed to both heighten your understanding of production and control concepts and to develop the ability to apply those concepts in a variety of management situations.

UNDERSTANDING PRODUCTION AND CONTROL CONCEPTS

This section is comprised of activities that will sharpen your understanding of production and control concepts. Answer essay questions as completely as possible. Also, remember that many additional true/false and multiple

choice questions appear online at MyManagement.com to help you further refine your understanding of concepts related to production and control.

Essay Questions

1. Describe the relationship between quality and productivity.

2. Define capacity strategy and describe the five steps involved with making capacity decisions.

3. Describe the advantages and disadvantages associated with just-in-time inventory control.

4. Compare and contrast the following operations controls: maintenance control, cost control, budgetary control, and ratio analysis.

5. What is operations management?

Developing Management Skill

Learning activities in this section are aimed at helping you to develop your production and control skill. Learning activities include Exploring Your Management Skill: Part 2, Experiential Exercises, Cases, and a VideoNet exercise.

EXPLORING YOUR MANAGEMENT SKILL: PART 2

As you recall, you completed Exploring Your Management Skill before you started to study this chapter. Your responses gave you an idea of how much you initially knew about production and control and helped you to focus on important points as you studied the chapter. Answer the Exploring Your Management Skill questions again now (p. 544) and compare your score to the first time you took it. This comparison will give you an idea of how much you have learned from studying this chapter and pinpoint areas for further clarification before you start studying the next chapter. Record your answers within the text or go to My ManagementLab.com. Recording your answers in MyManagementLab will allow you to get immediate results and see how your score compares to your classmates. If you answer the questions in the book, the answers are located in the Exploring Your Management Skill Appendix at the end of the book.

YOUR MANAGEMENT SKILLS PORTFOLIO

Your Management Learning Portfolio is a collection of activities especially designed to demonstrate your management knowledge and skill. By completing these online at MyManagement.com, you will be able to print, complete with cover sheet, as many activities as you choose. Be sure to save your work. Taking your printed portfolio to an employment interview could be helpful in obtaining a job.

The portfolio activity for this chapter is Improving Production and Control at Nissan. Study the information and complete the exercises that follow.

Improving Production and Control at Nissan

In recent years, Nissan—a car manufacturer based in Japan—has established a positive reputation with respect to the quality of its cars. Much of this reputation is based on the company's CEO, Carlos Ghosn, and the strategies and tactics he has employed as the CEO of Nissan. Ghosn is largely responsible for an increased reputation for both Nissan and Infiniti, which is one of Nissan's subsidiaries.

Ghosn believes strongly that a large driver of the company's success is derived from its production and control processes. In fact, he believes so strongly in this notion that he plans to distribute a 500-word memo to all new employees highlighting the benefits of production and control processes. As Ghosn's personal assistant, your task is to prepare a first draft of this memo. This memo should include an overview of the importance of productivity, quality, and the relationship between these two concepts. In addition, the memo should also contain brief descriptions of some techniques that Nissan might use to increase quality.

Remember that the audience for this memo—new employees—knows little about production and control. Your task requires you to communicate these ideas in a way that this audience will understand.

EXPERIENTIAL EXERCISE

Directions. Read the following scenario and then perform the listed activities. Your instructor may want you to perform the activities as an individual or within groups. Follow all of your instructor's directions carefully.

The owner of a small business in your community has contacted your group to help him with his organization. The owner recently encountered the term *management by exception* in a magazine article, but he is not clear about what it means or how organizations implement this practice. Your assignment involves searching the Internet for examples of how companies implement management by exception. Prepare a five-minute presentation that defines this term and then includes examples of how organizations use management by exception.

CASES

DELTA ATTEMPTS TO BOOST PRODUCTIVITY

"Delta Attempts to Boost Productivity" (p. 543) and its related Challenge Case Summary were written to help you better understand the management concepts contained in this chapter. Answer the following discussion questions about the Challenge Case to better see how your understanding of production and control can be applied in a company such as Delta.

1. Why is Delta attempting to raise productivity? From your personal experience with airlines, in what other ways do you think the company could increase productivity?

2. List three concepts discussed in this chapter that could help Delta's management increase productivity. Be sure to explain how each concept could help.

3. Which concept listed in question 2 do you think would have the most positive impact on increasing productivity? Explain fully.

ST. JOSEPH HEALTH CENTER'S QUEST FOR QUALITY

Read the case and answer the questions that follow. Studying this case will help you better see how your understanding of production and control can be applied in a company such as St. Joseph Health Center.

St. Joseph Health Center a hospital in the U.S. state of Missouri, is on a quest to improve quality. Although good quality is important in any organization, it is especially vital (and urgent) in a medical setting. St. Joseph is one of 20 hospitals in four states that are operated by SSM Health Care Corp., which is sponsored by the Franciscan Sisters of Mary. In any given year, SSM hospitals admit about 150,000 patients and treat more than 1 million people on an outpatient basis. SSM was the first health care organization to win the Malcolm Baldrige National Quality Award, which recognizes the outstanding quality performance of businesses and nonprofits.

Managers at the 364-bed St. Joseph facility have pursued continual improvement for more than 15 years. Early on, Dr. Filippo Ferrigni, head of the intensive-care unit, found that staff members used slightly different methods for measuring the blood pressure of different patients. He quickly standardized measurements for blood pressure, temperature, and other vital signs. Later, he read research showing that high blood-sugar levels are linked to higher infection risks. Knowing that patients sometimes become infected while in the hospital, he suggested the goal of lowering the blood-sugar levels of intensive-care patients.

Because his colleagues were concerned about possible adverse reactions to such treatment, Dr. Ferrigni initially sought gradual improvements. The results were quite impressive: overall mortality among intensive-care patients dropped by 40 percent. To make this new process work, the nurses had to check each patient's blood-sugar level 12 times per day instead of 4 times per day; however, the results convinced them that the extra effort and additional tests were worthwhile. Building on the intensive-care unit's success, hospital management then set a quality goal of lowering the blood-sugar levels of all patients—a decision that cut the facility's overall mortality rate by 28 percent within three years. Treating a serious infection can cost $35,000 per patient, so reducing incidences of infection not only saved patients' lives, it saved the hospital many thousands of dollars.

The 30/30 program, another of St. Joseph's quality improvement initiatives, requires emergency room staff to evaluate seriously ill patients within 30 seconds and complete the patient admission process for in-hospital treatment in 30 minutes or less. When the 30/30 program began, the facility was achieving its emergency room objectives only 65 percent of the time. After two years, it was meeting its objectives 94 percent of the time. Management had to hire more staff members to achieve this improvement, which raised the cost of providing emergency room care by $200,000 annually. The higher cost was more than offset by increases in admissions as St. Joseph gained a higher share of the local market for emergency medical treatment.

Quality improvements have led to financial improvements for St. Joseph and its parent company, SSM. Although SSM had no profits in 1999, it was reporting a net profit of $17 million by 2002, the year it was honored with the Baldrige Award. Winning was wonderful, but as Bill Thompson, SSM's senior vice president for strategic planning, says, "It's not the award, it's the process that shows how to improve quality." In the course of applying for the award and having its results reviewed by examiners, SSM's management refined the processes for analyzing patient care operations, setting quality improvement standards, and assessing performance from internal and external perspectives.

St. Joseph's executives, like the top managers of all SSM institutions, are responsible for formulating the hospital's strategy for serving the community and making decisions about which medical specialties will be offered. As in other SSM hospitals, senior managers evaluate results in terms of the number of procedures completed, market share, patient and staff satisfaction, revenue, and other measures. Patients benefit, staff members benefit, and the community benefits from SSM's focus on performance: "If the activity's not getting the results we want, then we change the activity. It's the result that's important."

QUESTIONS

1. Would you recommend that St. Joseph's top managers put more emphasis on efficiency or on effectiveness? Explain.

2. How have St. Joseph's quality improvement initiatives affected capacity strategy and product strategy?

3. Do you think that St. Joseph's executives should use management by exception for controlling emergency room activities? Explain.

VIDEONET EXERCISE

Body Glove

VIDEO HIGHLIGHTS

As avid surfers and divers, the two brothers who founded Body Glove began manufacturing wetsuits in the 1950s after discovering neoprene kept them warmer than the rubber wetsuits of the time. The high costs of neoprene and labor in the United States forced the company to outsource its manufacturing to Thailand. After 40 years of providing customers with the highest quality of professional-grade surfing and diving apparel, Body Glove decided to focus on international branding, lending its name to a wide range of goods and services that includes neoprene cell phone covers, resort hotels, and diving cruises. Today, Body

Glove's management team no longer worries about inventory and production costs.

Discussion Questions

1. What is the product strategy for Body Glove?
2. What operation control issues are of greatest concern to Body Glove? In what way does the company benefit from these control issues?
3. Is the management team of Body Glove using management by exception?

Internet Activity

Go to the Body Glove home page at www.bodyglove.com. How does Body Glove's image increase the productivity and profitability of their partner companies?

EXPLORING YOUR MANAGEMENT SKILL ANSWERS

CHAPTER 1
1. Y
2. N
3. N
4. N
5. Y
6. Y
7. Y
8. N
9. Y
10. N
11. Y
12. N
13. N
14. N

CHAPTER 2
1. Y
2. N
3. Y
4. N
5. Y
6. N
7. Y
8. Y
9. N
10. N
11. N
12. Y
13. Y
14. N
15. Y

CHAPTER 3
1. Y
2. N
3. N
4. N
5. Y
6. Y
7. Y
8. N
9. Y
10. N
11. Y
12. N
13. Y
14. Y
15. N

CHAPTER 4
1. Y
2. N
3. N
4. Y

5. Y
6. N
7. Y
8. N
9. N
10. N
11. Y
12. N
13. Y
14. N
15. N

CHAPTER 5
1. N
2. N
3. Y
4. N
5. Y
6. N
7. Y
8. Y
9. Y
10. N
11. N
12. Y
13. Y
14. Y
15. N

CHAPTER 6
1. N
2. Y
3. N
4. Y
5. Y
6. N
7. Y
8. Y
9. N
10. N
11. N
12. Y
13. N
14. N
15. Y

CHAPTER 7
1. N
2. N
3. N
4. Y
5. Y
6. N
7. N
8. N

9. Y
10. N
11. Y
12. N
13. Y
14. Y
15. N

CHAPTER 8
1. N
2. Y
3. N
4. N
5. N
6. N
7. Y
8. N
9. Y
10. N
11. Y
12. N
13. N
14. Y
15. N

CHAPTER 9
1. N
2. N
3. Y
4. N
5. N
6. Y
7. Y
8. Y
9. N
10. N
11. Y
12. N
13. Y
14. N
15. Y

CHAPTER 10
1. Y
2. N
3. N
4. N
5. Y
6. N
7. Y
8. N
9. Y
10. N
11. N
12. NI

13. N
14. N
15. Y

CHAPTER 11
1. N
2. Y
3. N
4. Y
5. N
6. N
7. N
8. Y
9. N
10. N
11. Y
12. N
13. N
14. Y
15. N

CHAPTER 12
1. Y
2. N
3. Y
4. N
5. Y
6. Y
7. N
8. N
9. N
10. Y
11. Y
12. N
13. Y
14. N
15. Y

CHAPTER 13
1. N
2. N
3. N
4. Y
5. Y
6. N
7. N
8. N
9. Y
10. Y
11. Y
12. N
13. N
14. Y
15. N

CHAPTER 14
1. N
2. Y
3. N
4. N
5. Y
6. N
7. Y
8. Y
9. N
10. N
11. Y
12. N
13. Y
14. N
15. N

CHAPTER 15
1. N
2. Y
3. N
4. N
5. Y
6. Y
7. Y
8. Y
9. N
10. N
11. N
12. N
13. Y
14. Y
15. N

CHAPTER 16
1. N
2. N
3. N

4. Y
5. N
6. N
7. N
8. N
9. Y
10. Y
11. Y
12. N
13. Y
14. Y
15. Y

CHAPTER 17
1. N
2. N
3. N
4. Y
5. Y
6. Y
7. N
8. Y
9. N
10. N
11. N
12. N
13. N
14. Y
15. N

CHAPTER 18
1. N
2. N
3. N
4. Y
5. Y
6. Y
7. N

8. Y
9. Y
10. N
11. Y
12. N
13. Y
14. Y
15. N

CHAPTER 19
1. Y
2. N
3. N
4. N
5. Y
6. Y
7. Y
8. N
9. Y
10. N
11. Y
12. N
13. Y
14. Y
15. N

CHAPTER 20
1. N
2. N
3. N
4. Y
5. Y
6. N
7. N
8. N
9. Y
10. Y
11. Y

12. N
13. N
14. Y
15. N

CHAPTER 21
1. N
2. N
3. Y
4. Y
5. N
6. Y
7. Y
8. Y
9. Y
10. Y
11. N
12. N
13. N
14. N
15. Y

CHAPTER 22
1. Y
2. N
3. N
4. Y
5. N
6. N
7. N
8. Y
9. N
10. N
11. N
12. Y
13. N
14. N
15. N

GLOSSARY

Accountability refers to the management philosophy whereby individuals are held liable, or accountable, for how well they use their authority or live up to their responsibility of performing predetermined activities. *p. 300*

Activities are specified sets of behavior within a project. *p. 260*

Adhocracy culture is an organization culture characterized by flexibility and discretion along with an external focus. *p. 469*

Adjourning the fifth and last stage of the team development process, is the stage in which the team finishes its job and prepares to disband. *p. 453*

Affirmative action programs are organizational programs whose basic purpose is to eliminate barriers against and increase employment opportunities for underutilized or disadvantaged individuals. *p. 320*

Alderfer's ERG theory is an explanation of human needs that divides them into three basic types: existence needs, relatedness needs, and growth needs. *p. 422*

Angel investor is a wealthy individual who provides capital to new companies. *p. 169*

Appropriate human resources are the individuals in the organization who make a valuable contribution to management system goal attainment. *p. 315*

Argyris's maturity-immaturity continuum is a concept that furnishes insights into human needs by focusing on an individual's natural progress from immaturity to maturity. *p. 422*

Assessment center is a program in which participants engage in, and are evaluated on, a number of individual and group exercises constructed to simulate important activities at the organizational levels to which they aspire. *p. 322*

Authority is the right to perform or command. *p. 296*

Automation is the replacement of human effort by electromechanical devices. *p. 548*

Avoiding is a conflict management technique whereby managers simply ignore the conflict. *p. 349*

Bank financing occurs when an entrepreneur obtains financing from a financial institution in the form of a loan. *p. 170*

Behavior modification is a program that focuses on encouraging appropriate behavior by controlling the consequences of that behavior. *p. 428*

Behavioral approach to management is a management approach that emphasizes increasing production through an understanding of people. *p. 61*

Bias refers to departures from rational theory that produce suboptimal decisions. *p. 212*

Bicultural stress is stress resulting from having to cope with membership in two cultures simultaneously. *p. 113*

Bounded rationality refers to the fact that managers are bounded in terms of time, computational power, and knowledge when making decisions. *p. 212*

Brainstorming is a group decision-making process in which negative feedback on any suggested alternative to any group member is forbidden until all group members have presented alternatives that they perceive as valuable. *p. 217*

Break-even analysis is the process of generating information that summarizes various levels of profit or loss associated with various levels of production. *p. 562*

Break-even point is that level of production where the total revenue of an organization equals its total costs. *p. 563*

Budget is a control tool that outlines how funds in a given period will be spent, as well as how they will be obtained. *p. 252, 557*

Bureaucracy is the term Max Weber used to describe a management system characterized by detailed procedures and rules, a clearly outlined organizational hierarchy, and impersonal relationships among organization members. *p. 273*

Business portfolio analysis is an organizational strategy formulation technique that is based on the philosophy that organizations should develop strategy much as they handle investment portfolios. *p. 235*

Buyer power refers to the power that customers have over the firms operating in an industry; as buyer power increases, the attractiveness of an industry decreases. *p. 231*

Capacity strategy is an operational plan of action aimed at providing the organization with the right facilities to produce the needed output at the right time. *p. 541*

Career is a sequence of work-related positions occupied by a person over the course of a lifetime. *p. 42*

Career plateauing is a period of little or no apparent progress in the growth of a career. *p. 43*

Centralization refers to the situation in which a minimal number of job activities and a minimal amount of authority are delegated to subordinates. *p. 303*

Change agent is an individual inside or outside the organization who tries to modify an existing organizational situation. *p. 338*

Change-related activities are management efforts aimed at modifying organizational components. *p. 38*

Changing an organization is the process of modifying an existing organization to increase organizational effectiveness. *p. 337*

Clan culture is an organization culture characterized by a strong internal focus with a high degree of flexibility and discretion. *p. 469*

Classical approach to management is a management approach that emphasizes organizational efficiency to increase organizational success. *p. 55*

Closed system is one that is not influenced by, and does not interact with, its environment. *p. 66*

Coaching is a leadership that instructs followers on how to meet the special organizational challenges they face. *p. 403*

Code of conduct is a document that reflects the core values of an organization and suggests how organization members should act in relation to them. *p. 468*

Code of ethics is a formal statement that acts as a guide for making decisions and acting within an organization. *p. 94*

Command group is a formal group that is outlined in the chain of command on an organization chart. Command groups handle routine activities. *p. 442*

Commercial entrepreneurship involves individuals or corporations that pursue entrepreneurial opportunities for the purposes of generating sales and profits, *p. 171*

Commitment principle is a management guideline that advises managers to commit funds for planning only if they can anticipate, in the foreseeable future, a return on planning expenses as a result of long-range planning analysis. *p. 227*

Committee is a task group that is charged with performing some type of specific activity. *p. 442*

Communication is the process of sharing information with other individuals. *p. 366*

Communication macrobarriers are factors hindering successful communication that relate primarily to the communication environment and the larger world in which communication takes place. *p. 368*

Communication microbarriers are factors hindering successful communication that relate primarily to such variables as the communication message, the source, and the destination. *p. 369*

Communication skill is the ability to direct the behavior of others toward the accomplishment of objectives. *p. 360*

Comprehensive management skill is the ability to collectively apply concepts from various major management approaches to performaing a manager's job. *p. 52*

Compromise means the parties to the conflict settle on a solution that gives both of them *part* of what they wanted. *p. 349*

Computer-aided design (CAD) is a computerized technique for designing new products or modifying existing ones. *p. 565*

Computer-aided manufacturing (CAM) is a technique that employs computers to plan and program equipment used in the production and inspection of manufactured items. *p. 565*

Conceptual skills are skills involving the ability to see the organization as a whole. *p. 38*

Conflict is defined as a struggle that results from opposing needs or feelings between two or more people. *p. 348*

Consensus is an agreement on a decision by all the individuals involved in making that decision. *p. 206*

Consideration behavior is leadership behavior that reflects friendship, mutual trust, respect, and warmth in the relationship between leader and followers. *p. 294*

Content theories of motivation are explanations of motivation that emphasize people's internal characteristics. *p. 417*

Contingency approach to management is a management approach emphasizing that what managers do in practice depends on a given set of circumstances—a situation. *p. 65*

Contingency theory of leadership is a leadership concept that hypothesizes that, in any given leadership situation, success is determined primarily by (1) the degree to which the task being performed by the followers is structured, (2) the degree of position power possessed by the leader, and (3) the type of relationship that exists between the leader and the followers. *p. 398*

Control entails ensuring that an event occurs as it was planned to occur. *p. 519*

Control tool is a specific procedure or technique that presents pertinent organizational information in a way that helps managers to develop and implement an appropriate control strategy. *p. 561*

Controlling is the process managers go through to control. It is a systematic effort to compare performance to predetermined standards, plans, or objectives to determine whether performance is in line with those standards or needs to be corrected. *p. 519*

Coordination is the orderly arrangement of group effort to provide unity of action in the pursuit of a common purpose. It involves encouraging the completion of individual portions of a task in an appropriate, synchronized order. *p. 274*

Coordination skill is the ability to use information and technology to ensure that an event occurs as it was planned to occur. *p. 516*

Corporate entrepreneurship is the process in which an individual or group of individuals in an existing corporation create a new organization or instigate renewal or innovation within that corporation. *p. 170*

Corporate social responsibility is the managerial obligation to take action that protects and improves both the welfare of society as a whole and the interests of the organization. *p. 79*

Corporate social responsibility skill is the ability to take action that protects and improves both the welfare of society and the interests of the organization. *p. 76*

Corrective action is managerial activity aimed at bringing organizational performance up to the level of performance standards. *p. 523*

Cost leadership is a strategy that focuses on making an organization more competitive by producing products more cheaply than competitors can. *p. 237*

Creativity is the ability to generate original ideas or new perspectives on existing ideas. *p. 493*

Creativity and innovation skill is the ability to generate original ideas or new perspectives on existing ideas and to take steps to implement these new ideas. *p. 490*

Critical path is the sequence of events and activities within a program evaluation and review technique (PERT) network that requires the longest period of time to complete. *p. 261*

Critical question analysis is a strategy development tool that consists of answering basic questions about the present purposes and objectives of the organization, its present direction and environment, and actions that can be taken to achieve organizational objectives in the future. *p. 234*

Cross-functional team is an organizational team composed of people from different functional areas of the organization who are all focused on a specified objective. *p. 451*

Cultural artifact is a dimension of an organization that helps to describe and reinforce the culture, or beliefs, values, and norms in which an artifact exists. *p. 477*

Culture is the set of characteristics of a given group of people and their environment. *p. 149*

Customer dimension of organization culture is a facet of organization culture that focuses on catering to the needs of those individuals who buy goods or services produced. *p. 476*

Data are facts or statistics. *p. 527*

Decentralization refers to the situation in which a significant number of job activities and a maximum amount of authority are delegated to subordinates. *p. 303*

Decision is a choice made between two or more available alternatives. *p. 205*

Decision-making skill is the ability to choose alternatives that increase the likelihood of accomplishing objectives. *p. 202*

Decision tree is a graphic decision-making tool typically used to evaluate decisions involving a series of steps. *p. 215*

Decision tree analysis is a statistical and graphical multiphased decision-making technique that contains a series of steps showing the sequence and interdependence of decisions. *p. 565*

Decline stage is the fourth and last stage in career evolution; it occurs near retirement age, when individuals of about 65 years of age show declining productivity. *p. 43*

Decoder/destination is the person or persons in the interpersonal communication situation with whom the source is attempting to share information. *p. 267*

Delegation is the process of assigning job activities and related authority to specific individuals within the organization. *p. 300*

Delphi technique is a group decision-making process that involves circulating questionnaires on a specific problem among group members, sharing the questionnaire results with them, and then continuing to recirculate and refine individual responses until a consensus regarding the problem is reached. *p. 217*

Demographics are statistical characteristics of a population. *p. 110, 230*

Department is a unique group of resources established by management to perform some organizational task. *p. 278*

Deparmentalizing is the process of establishing departments within the management system. *p. 278*

Developing is that step of the innovation process that makes a new idea practical. *p. 500*

Differentiation is a strategy that focuses on making an organization more competitive by developing a product or products that customers perceive as being different from products offered by competitors. *p. 237*

Diffusing is that step of the innovation process that puts a new idea to use by end users or customers. *p. 501*

Direct investing is using the assets of one company to purchase the operating assets of another company. *p. 144*

Discrimination is the act of treating an issue, person, or behavior unjustly or inequitably on the basis of stereotypes or prejudices. *p. 112*

Diversity refers to characteristics of individuals that shape their identities and the experiences they have in society. Major areas of diversity are gender, race, ethnicity, religion, social class, physical ability, sexual orientation, and age. *p. 107*

Diversity dimension of organization culture is a component of organization culture that encourages the existence of basic human differences among organization members. *p. 476*

Diversity skill is the ability to establish and maintain an organizational workforce that represents a combination of assorted human characteristics appropriate for achieving organizational success. *p. 104*

Diversity training is a learning process designed to raise managers' awareness and develop their competencies to deal with the issues endemic to managing a diverse workforce. *p. 123*

Divestiture is a strategy adopted to eliminate a strategic business unit that is not generating a satisfactory amount of business and has little hope of doing so in the near future. *p. 238*

Division of labor is the assignment of various portions of a particular task among a number of organization members. Division of labor calls for specialization. *p. 274*

Domain definition occurs when a firm proactively seeks to create a new product market position that competitors have not recognized. *p. 171*

Domestic organization is an organization that essentially operates within a single country. *p. 137*

Dominant organization culture is the shared values about organizational functioning held by the majority of organization members. *p. 467*

Downside loss refers to the resources (i.e., money, relationships, etc.) that the entrepreneur could lose if the opportunity does not succeed. *p. 167*

Downward organizational communication is communication that flows from any point on an organization chart downward to another point on the organization chart. *p. 373*

Economics is the science that focuses on understanding how people of a particular community or nation produce, distribute, and use various goods and services. *p. 229*

Effectiveness is the degree to which managers attain organizational objectives; it is doing the right things. *p. 551*

Efficiency is the degree to which organizational resources contribute to production; it is doing things right. *p. 365*

Emotional intelligence is the capacity of people to recognize their own feelings and the feelings of others, to motivate themselves, and to manage their own emotions as well as the emotions in relationships with others. *p. 365*

Empathy is the intellectual identification with the feelings, thoughts, or attitudes of another. *p. 405*

Employee-centered behavior is leader behavior that focuses primarily on subordinates as people. *p. 395*

Entrepreneur is an individual who identifies, evaluates, and exploits opportunities. *p. 163*

Entrepreneurial alertness refers to an individual's ability to notice and be sensitive to new information about objects, incidents, and patterns of behavior in the environment. *p. 166*

Entrepreneurial leadership is leadership that is based on the attitude that the leader is self-employed. *p. 406*

Entrepreneurial opportunities are occasions to bring into existence new products and services that allow outputs to be sold at a price greater than their cost of production. *p. 163*

Entrepreneurial risk is the likelihood and magnitude of the opportunity's downside loss. *p. 167*

Entrepreneurship refers to the identification, evaluation, and exploitation of opportunities. *p. 163*

Entrepreneurship skill involves the identification, evaluation, and exploitation of opportunities. *p. 160*

Environmental analysis is the study of the organizational environment to pinpoint environmental factors that can significantly influence organizational operations. *p. 228*

Equal Employment Opportunity Commission (EEOC) is an agency established to enforce federal laws prohibiting discrimination on the basis of race, color, religion, sex, and national origin in recruitment, hiring, firing, layoffs, and all other employment practices. *p. 320*

Equity theory is an explanation of motivation that emphasizes the individual's perceived fairness of an employment situation and how perceived inequities can cause certain behaviors. *p. 419*

Establishment stage is the second stage in career evolution; individuals of about 25 to 45 years of age typically start to become more productive, or higher performers. *p. 43*

Esteem needs are Maslow's fourth set of human needs—including the desires for self-respect and respect from others. *p. 421*

Ethics is the capacity to reflect on values in the corporate decision-making process, to determine how these values and decisions affect various stakeholder groups, and to establish how managers can use these observations in day-to-day company management. *p. 93*

Ethics dimension of organization culture is a facet of organization culture that focuses on making sure that an organization emphasizes not only what is good for the organization, but what is good for other human beings. *p. 475*

Ethnocentric attitude reflects the belief that multinational corporations should regard home-country management practices as superior to foreign-country management practices. *p. 149*

Ethnocentrism is the belief that one's own group, culture, country, or customs are superior to others'. *p. 112*

Events are the completions of major project tasks. *p. 260*

Expatriate is an organization member who lives and works in a country where he or she does not have citizenship. *p. 141*

Expected value (EV) is the measurement of the anticipated value of some event, determined by multiplying the income an event would produce by its probability of producing that income (EV = I × P). *p. 214*

Exploitation refers to the activities and investments committed to gain returns from the new product or service arising from the opportunity. *p. 168*

Exploration stage is the first stage in career evolution; it occurs at the beginning of a career, when the individual is typically 15 to 25 years of age, and it is characterized by self-analysis and the exploration of different types of available jobs. *p. 42*

Exporting is selling goods or services to another country. *p. 144*

Extrinsic rewards are rewards that are extraneous to the task accomplished. *p. 420*

Feasibility analysis is analysis that helps entrepreneurs understand whether an idea is practical. *p. 167*

Feedback is, in the interpersonal communication situation, the destination's reaction to a message. *p. 270*

Fixed costs are expenses incurred by the organization regardless of the number of products produced. *p. 562*

Fixed-position layout is a layout plan in which the product is stationary while

resources flow. It is appropriate for organizations involved in a large number of different tasks that require low volumes, multipurpose equipment, and broad employee skills. *p. 553*

Flextime is a program that allows workers to complete their jobs within a workweek of a normal number of hours that they schedule themselves. *p. 427*

Focus is a strategy that emphasizes making an organization more competitive by targeting a particular customer. *p. 237*

Forcing is a technique for managing conflict in which managers use authority to declare that conflict is ended. *p. 350*

Forecasting is a planning tool used to predict future environmental happenings that will influence the operation of the organization. *p. 255*

Formal group is a group that exists within an organization by virtue of management decree to perform tasks that enhance the attainment of organizational objectives. *p. 441*

Formal organizational communication is organizational communication that follows the lines of the organization chart. *p. 373*

Formal structure is defined as the relationships among organizational resources as outlined by management. *p. 275*

Forming is the first stage of the team development process, during which members of the newly formed team become oriented to the team and acquainted with one another as they explore issues related to their new job situation. *p. 453*

Friendship group is an informal group that forms in organizations because of the personal affiliation members have with one another. *p. 447*

Functional authority consists of the right to give orders within a segment of the management system in which the right is normally nonexistent. *p. 299*

Functional similarity method is a method for dividing job activities in the organization. *p. 293*

Gangplank is a communication channel extending from one organizational division to another but not shown in the lines of communication outlined on an organization chart. Use of Fayol's gangplank may be quicker, but could prove costly in the long run. *p. 285*

Gantt chart is a scheduling tool composed of a bar chart with time on the horizontal

axis and the resource to be scheduled on the vertical axis. It is used for scheduling resources. *p. 259*

Gender-role stereotypes are perceptions about people based on what our society believes are appropriate behaviors for men and women. *p. 113*

General environment is the level of an organization's external environment that contains components normally having broad long-term implications for managing the organization; its components are economic, social, political, legal, and technological. *p. 228*

Geocentric attitude reflects the belief that the overall quality of management recommendations, rather than the location of managers, should determine the acceptability of management practices used to guide multinational corporations. *p. 149*

Global management skill is the ability to manage global factors as components of organizational operations. *p. 132*

Graciunas's formula is a formula that makes the span-of-management point that as the number of a manager's subordinates increases arithmetically, the number of possible relationships between the manager and the subordinates increases geometrically. *p. 277*

Grapevine is the network of informal organizational communication. *p. 376*

Grid organization development (grid OD) is a commonly used organization development technique based on a theoretical model called the managerial grid. *p. 341*

Group is any number of people who (1) interact with one another, (2) are psychologically aware of one another, and (3) perceive themselves to be a group. *p. 441*

Groupthink is the mode of thinking that group members engage in when the desire for agreement so dominates the group that it overrides the need to realistically appraise alternative problem solutions. *p. 444*

Growth is a strategy adopted by management to increase the amount of business that a strategic business unit is currently generating. *p. 238*

Healthy organization culture is an organization culture that facilities the achievement of the organization's mission and objectives. *p. 482*

Heuristics are simple rules of thumb used to make decisions. *p. 212*

Hierarchy culture is an organization culture characterized by an internal focus along with an emphasis on with stability and control. *p. 470*

Horizontal dimensioning of an organization refers to the extent to which firms use lateral subdivisions or specialties within an organization. *p. 278*

Host country is the country in which an investment is made by a foreign company. *p. 139*

Host-country national is an organization member who is a citizen of the country in which the facility of a foreign-based organization is located. *p. 141*

Human relations movement is a people-oriented approach to management in which the interaction of people in organizations is studied to judge its impact on organizational success. *p. 62*

Human relations skill is the ability to work with people in a way that enhances organizational success. *p. 62*

Human resource inventory is information about the characteristics of organization members; the focus is on past performance and future potential, and the objective is to keep management up to date about the possibilities for filling a position from within. *p. 316*

Human resource management skill is the ability to take action in the form of recruitment, selection, training, and performance appraisal that increases the contributions of individuals within the organization toward the organization's goal attainment. *p. 312*

Human resource planning involves reflecting on organizational objectives to determine overall human resource needs; comparing these needs to the existing human resource inventory to determine net human resource needs; and, finally, seeking appropriate organization members to meet the net human resource needs. *p. 254*

Human resources strategy is an operational plan to use the organization's human resources effectively and efficiently while maintaining or improving the quality of work life. *p. 554*

Human skills are skills involving the ability to build cooperation within the team being led. *p. 37*

Hygiene, or maintenance, factors are items that influence the degree of job dissatisfaction. *p. 426*

Illusion of control exists when entrepreneurs overestimate the extent to which they can control the outcome of an opportunity. *p. 168*

Importing is buying goods or services from another country. *p. 144*

Industry environment is the level of an organization's external environment that contains components normally having relatively specific and immediate implications for managing the organization. *p. 230*

Influencing is the process of guiding the activities of organization members in appropriate directions. *p. 363*

Informal group is a collection of individuals whose common work experiences result in the development of a system of interpersonal relations that extend beyond those established by management. *p. 466*

Informal organizational communication is organizational communication that does not follow the lines of the organization chart. *p. 375*

Informal structure is defined as the patterns of relationships that develop because of the informal activities of organization members. *p. 275*

Information is the set of conclusions derived from data analysis. *p. 527*

Information appropriateness is the degree to which information is relevant to the decision-making situation the manager faces. *p. 527*

Information asymmetry refers to the fact that individuals vary in terms of the information to which they have access. *p. 166*

Information quality is the degree to which information represents reality. *p. 528*

Information quantity is the amount of decision-related information a manager possesses. *p. 529*

Information system (IS) is a network of applications established within an organization to provide managers with information that will assist them in decision making. An IS gets information to where it is needed. *p. 531*

Information technology is technology that focuses on the use of information in the performance of work. *p. 530*

Information timeliness is the extent to which the receipt of information allows decisions to be made and action to be taken so the organization can gain some benefit from possessing the information. *p. 528*

Innovation is the process of applying a new idea to the improvement of organizational processes, products, or services. *p. 498*

Innovation dimension of organization culture is an aspect of organization culture that encourages the application of new ideas to the improvement of organization processes, products, or services. *p. 475*

Innovation process is defined as the steps that managers take to implement creative ideas. *p. 499*

Input planning is the development of proposed action that will furnish sufficient and appropriate organizational resources for reaching established organizational objectives. *p. 252*

Integrating is that step of the innovation process which establishes an invention as a permanent part of the organization. *p. 501*

Intensity of rivalry refers to the intensity of competition among the organizations in an industry; as the intensity of rivalry increases, the attractiveness of an industry decreases. *p. 231*

Interest group is an informal group that gains and maintains membership primarily because of a common concern members have about a specific issue. *p. 446*

Intermediate-term objectives are targets to be achieved in one to five years. *p. 189*

Internal environment is the level of an organization's environment that exists inside the organization and normally has immediate and specific implications for managing the organization. *p. 232*

International joint venture is a partnership formed by a company in one country with a company in another country for the purpose of pursuing some mutually desirable business undertaking. *p. 145*

International management is the performance of management activities across national borders. *p. 132*

International market agreement is an arrangement among a cluster of countries that facilitates a high level of trade among these countries. *p. 145*

International organization is an organization based primarily within a single country but having continuing, meaningful transactions in other countries. *p. 138*

Intrinsic rewards are rewards that come directly from performing a task. *p. 419*

Intuition refers to an individual's inborn ability to synthesize information quickly and effectively. *p. 212*

Inventing is that step of the innovation process that establishes a new idea that could help the organization to be more successful. *p. 500*

Job analysis is a technique commonly used to gain an understanding of what a task entails and the type of individual who should be hired to perform that task. *p. 315*

Job-centered behavior is leader behavior that focuses primarily on the work a subordinate is doing. *p. 395*

Job description is a list of specific activities that must be performed to accomplish some task or job. *p. 293, 315*

Job design is an operational plan that determines who will do a specific job and how and where the job will be done. *p. 555*

Job enlargement is the process of increasing the number of operations an individual performs in order to enhance the individual's satisfaction in work. *p. 425*

Job enrichment is the process of incorporating motivators into a job situation. *p. 426*

Job rotation is the process of moving workers from one job to another rather than requiring them to perform only one simple and specialized job over the long term. *p. 425*

Job specification the characteristics of the individual who should be hired to perform a specific task or job. *p. 315*

Jury of executive opinion method is a method of predicting future sales levels primarily by asking appropriate managers to give their opinions on what will happen to sales in the future. *p. 256*

Just-in-time (JIT) inventory control is a technique for reducing inventories to a minimum by arranging for production components to be delivered to the production facility "just in time" to be used. *p. 555*

Labor force planning is an operational plan for hiring the right employees for a job and training them to be productive. *p. 555*

Lateral organizational communication is communication that flows from any point on an organization chart horizontally to another point on the organization chart. *p. 374*

Law of small numbers occurs when individuals rely on a small sample of information to inform their decisions. *p. 167*

Layout is the overall arrangement of equipment, work areas, service areas, and storage areas within a facility that produces goods or provides services. *p. 553*

Layout strategy is an operational plan that determines the location and flow of organizational resources around, into, and within production and service facilities. *p. 553*

Leader flexibility is the idea that successful leaders must change their leadership styles as they encounter different situations. *p. 398*

Leadership is the process of directing the behavior of others toward the accomplishment of objectives. *p. 387*

Leadership skill is the ability to direct the behavior of others toward the accomplishment of objectives. *p. 384*

Leadership style is the behavior a leader exhibits while guiding organization members in appropriate directions. *p. 395*

Learning organization is an organization that does well in creating, acquiring, and transferring knowledge, and in modifying behavior to reflect new knowledge. *p. 68*

Lecture is primarily a one-way communication situation in which an instructor trains an individual or group by orally presenting information. *p. 324*

Level dimension of a plan is the level of the organization at which the plan is aimed. *p. 249*

License agreement is a right granted by one company to another to use its brand name, technology, product specifications, and so on in the manufacture or sale of goods and services. *p. 144*

Life cycle theory of leadership is a leadership concept that hypothesizes that leadership styles should reflect primarily the maturity level of the followers. *p. 396*

Line authority consists of the right to make decisions and to give orders concerning the production-, sales-, or finance-related behavior of subordinates. *p. 298*

Location strategy is an operational plan of action that provides the organization with a competitive location for its headquarters, manufacturing, services, and distribution activities. *p. 552*

Long-term objectives are targets to be achieved within five to seven years. *p. 189*

Loss is the amount of the total costs of producing a product that exceeds the total revenue gained from selling the product. *p. 563*

Maintenance stage is the third stage in career evolution; individuals of about 45 to 65 years of age show either increased performance (career growth), stabilized performance (career maintenance), or decreased performance (career stagnation). *p. 43*

Majority group refers to that group of people in the organization who hold most of the positions that command decision-making power, control of resources and information, and access to system rewards. *p. 107*

Management is the process of reaching organizational goals by working with and through people and other organizational resources. *p. 32*

Management by exception is a control tool that allows only significant deviations between planned and actual performance to be brought to a manager's attention. *p. 561*

Management functions are activities that make up the management process. The four basic management activities are planning, organizing, influencing, and controlling. *p. 32*

Management ideas are ideas that focus on invention relating to the way in which the organization is managed. *p. 500*

Management inventory card is a form used in compiling a human resource inventory. It contains the organizational history of an individual and indicates how that individual might be used in the organization in the future. *p. 317*

Management manpower replacement chart is a form used in compiling a human resource inventory. It is people oriented and presents a composite view of individuals management considers significant to human resource planning. *p. 317*

Management responsibility guide is a tool that is used to clarify the responsibilities of various managers in the organization. *p. 295*

Management science approach is a management approach that emphasizes the use of the scientific method and mathematical techniques to solve operational problems. *p. 64*

Management skill is the ability to carry out the process of reaching organizational goals by working with and through people and other organizational resources. *p. 27 36*

Management system is composed of a number of parts that function interdependently to achieve a purpose; its main parts are organizational input, organizational process, and organizational output. *p. 66*

Managerial effectiveness refers to management's use of organizational resources in meeting organizational goals. *p. 24*

Managerial efficiency is the proportion of total organizational resources used during the production process. *p. 35*

Managerial grid is a theoretical model based on the premise that concern for people and concern for production are the two primary attitudes that influence management style. *p. 341*

Market culture is an organization culture that reflects values that emphasize stability and control along with an external focus. *p. 470*

Materials control is an operational activity that determines the flow of materials from vendors through an operations system to customers. *p. 559*

McClelland's acquired needs theory is an explanation of human needs that focuses on the desires for achievement, power, and affiliation that people develop as a result of their life experiences. *p. 422*

Mechanistic structures are formal organizational structures. *p. 284*

Message is encoded information that the source intends to share with others. *p. 367*

Message interference refers to stimuli that compete with the communication message for the attention of the destination. *p. 369*

Minority group refers to that group of people in the organization who are fewer in number than the majority group or who lack critical power, resources, acceptance, or social status. *p. 107*

Mission statement is a written document developed by management, normally based on input by managers as well as nonmanagers, that describes and explains what the mission of an organization actual is. *p. 233*

Monitoring is that step of the innovation process in which a newly implemented idea is tracked to determine if and when the idea should be improved or terminated. *p. 502*

Motion study finds the best way to accomplish a task by reducing each job to the most basic movements possible. *p. 57*

Motion-study techniques are operational tools that are used to improve productivity. *p. 555*

Motivating factors, or **motivators,** are items that influence the degree of job satisfaction. *p. 426*

Motivation is the inner state that causes an individual to behave in a way that ensures the accomplishment of some goal. *p. 417*

Motivation skill is the ability to create organizational situations in which individuals performing organizational activities are simultaneously satisfying personal needs and helping the organization attain its goals. *p. 414*

Motivation strength is an individual's degree of desire to perform a behavior. *p. 417*

Moving average method utilizes historical data to predict future sales levels. *p. 257*

Multinational corporation is a company that has significant operations in more than one country. *p. 138*

Needs-goal theory is a motivation model that hypothesizes that felt needs cause human behavior. *p. 417*

Negative reinforcement is a reward that consists of the elimination of an undesirable consequence of behavior. *p. 428*

Nominal group technique is a group decision-making process in which every group member is assured of equal participation in making the group decision. After each member writes down individual ideas and presents them orally to the group, the entire group discusses all the ideas and then votes for the best idea in a secret ballot. *p. 217*

Nonprogrammed decisions are typically one-shot decisions that are usually less structured than programmed decisions. *p. 205*

Nonverbal communication is the sharing of information without using words. *p. 372*

Norming the third stage of the team development process, is characterized by agreement among team members on roles, rules, and acceptable behavior while working on the team. *p. 453*

On-the-job training is a training technique that blends job-related knowledge with experience in using that knowledge on the job. *p. 325*

Open system is one that is influenced by, and is continually interacting with, its environment. *p. 66*

Operations control is making sure that operations activities are carried out as planned. *p. 555*

Operations management is performance of managerial activities entailed in selecting, designing, operating, controlling, and updating production systems. *p. 550*

Organic structures are less formal organizational structures and represent loosely coupled networks of workers. *p. 284*

Organization chart is a graphic illustration of organizational structure. *p. 275*

Organization culture is a set of shared values that organization members have regarding the functioning and existence of their organization. *p. 467*

Organization culture skill is the ability to establish a set of shared values of organization members regarding the functioning and existence of their organization to enhande the probability of organizational success. *p. 464*

Organization development (OD) is the process that emphasizes changing an organization by changing organization members and bases these changes on an overview of structure, technology, and all other organizational ingredients. *p. 341*

Organization subculture is a mini-culture within an organization that can reflect the values and beliefs of a specific segment of an organization formed along lines such as established departments or geographic regions. *p. 467*

Organizational ceremonies are formal activities conducted on important organizational occasions. *p. 479*

Organizational change skill is the ability to modify an organization in order to enhance its contribution to reaching company goals. *p. 334*

Organizational commitment can be defined as the dedication of organization members to uphold the values of the organization and to make worthwhile contributions to fulfilling organizational purpose. *p. 473*

Organizational communication is interpersonal communication within organizations that directly relates to the goals, functions, and structure of human organizations. *p. 373*

Organizational mission is the purpose for which, or the reason why, an organization exists. *p. 233*

Organizational myth is a popular belief or story that has become associated with a person or institution that is considered to illustrate an organization culture ideal. *p. 477*

Organizational objectives are the targets toward which the open management system is directed. They flow from the organization's mission. *p. 187*

Organizational purpose is what the organization exists to do, given a particular group of customers and customer needs. *p. 187*

Organizational resources are all assets available for activation during the production process; they include human resources, monetary resources, raw materials resources, and capital resources. *p. 34*

Organizational saga is a narrative describing the adventures of a heroic individual or family significantly linked to an organization's past or present. *p. 478*

Organizational socialization is the process by which management can appropriately integrate new employees within an organization's culture. *p. 480*

Organizational storytelling is the act of passing organizational myths and sagas to other organization members. *p. 479*

Organizational symbols are objects that have meanings beyond their intrinsic content. *p. 479*

Organized rejuvenation involves improving the firm's ability to execute strategies and focuses on new processes instead of new products. *p. 170*

Organizing is the process of establishing orderly uses for resources within the management system. *p. 271*

Organizing skill is the ability to establish orderly uses for resources within the management system. *p. 268, 271*

Overlapping responsibility refers to a situation in which more than one individual is responsible for the same activity. *p. 294*

Parent company is the company investing in international operations. *p. 139*

Path–goal theory of leadership is a theory of leadership that suggests that the primary activities of a leader are to make desirable and achievable rewards available to organization members who attain organizational goals and to clarify the kinds of behavior that must be performed to earn those rewards. *p. 400*

People change is a type of organizational change that emphasizes increasing organizational effectiveness by changing certain aspects of organization members. *p. 340*

People factors are attitudes, leadership skills, communication skills, and all other characteristics of the organization's employees. *p. 339*

People-related activities are management efforts aimed at managing people in organizations. *p. 38*

Perception is an individual's interpretation of a message. *p. 370*

Performance appraisal is the process of reviewing individuals' past productive activity to evaluate the contribution they have made toward attaining management system objectives. *p. 326*

Performing, the fourth stage of the team development process, is characterized by a focus on solving organizational problems and meeting assigned challenges. *p. 443*

Personal power is the power derived from a manager's relationships with others. *p. 524*

Physiological needs are Maslow's first set of human needs—for the normal functioning of the body, including the desires for water, food, rest, sex, and air. *p. 421*

Plan is a specific action proposed to help the organization achieve its objectives. *p. 249*

Planning is the process of determining how the organization can get where it wants to go, and what it will do to accomplish its objectives. *p. 183*

Planning skill is the ability to take action to determine the objectives of the organization as well as what is necessary to accomplish those objectives. *p. 180*

Planning tools are techniques managers can use to help develop plans. *p. 255*

Planning tools skill is the ability to employ the qualitative and quantitative techniques necessary to help develop plans. *p. 246*

Plant facilities planning involves determining the type of buildings and equipment an organization needs to reach its objectives. *p. 252*

Pluralism refers to an environment in which differences are acknowledged, accepted, and viewed as significant contributors to the entirety. *p. 119*

Policy is a standing plan that furnishes broad guidelines for taking action consistent with reaching organizational objectives. *p. 250*

Polycentric attitude reflects the belief that because foreign managers are closer to foreign organizational units, they probably understand them better, and therefore foreign management practices should generally be viewed as more insightful than home-country management practices. *p. 149*

Porter–Lawler theory is a motivation theory that hypothesizes that felt needs cause human behavior and that motivation strength is determined primarily by the perceived value of the result of performing the behavior and the perceived probability that the behavior performed will cause the result to materialize. *p. 419*

Position power is power derived from the organizational position a manager holds. *p. 524*

Position replacement form is used in compiling a human resource inventory. It summarizes information about organization members who could fill a position should it open up. *p. 317*

Positive reinforcement is a reward that consists of a desirable consequence of behavior. *p. 428*

Power is the extent to which an individual is able to influence others so that they respond to orders. *p. 524*

Prejudice is a preconceived judgment, opinion, or assumption about an issue, behavior, or group of people. *p. 112*

Probability theory is a decision-making tool used in risk situations—situations in which decision makers are not completely sure of the outcome of an implemented alternative. *p. 214*

Problem-solving team is an organizational team set up to help eliminate a specified problem within the organization. *p. 451*

Problems are factors within an organization that are barriers to organizational goal attainment. *p. 523*

Procedure is a standing plan that outlines a series of related actions that must be taken to accomplish a particular task. *p. 251*

Process control is a technique that assists in monitoring production processes. *p. 565*

Process (functional) layout is a layout pattern based primarily on grouping together similar types of equipment. *p. 553*

Process ideas are ideas that focus on inventions for improving a manufacturing process. *p. 500*

Process strategy is an operational plan of action outlining the means and methods the organization will use to transform resources into goods and services. *p. 552*

Process theories of motivation are explanations of motivation that emphasize how individuals are motivated. *p. 417*

Product ideas are ideas that focus on invention that develops new products or services, or enhances existing products or services. *p. 500*

Product layout is a layout designed to accommodate a limited number of different products that require high volumes, highly specialized equipment, and narrow employee skills. *p. 553*

Product life cycle is the five stages through which most products and services pass: introduction, growth, maturity, saturation, and decline. *p. 258*

Product stages method predicts future sales by using the product life cycle to better understand the history and future of the product. *p. 258*

Product strategy is an operational plan of action outlining which goods and services an organization will produce and market. *p. 552*

Production is the transformation of organizational resources into products. *p. 545*

Production skill is the ability to transform organizational resources into products. *p. 532*

Productivity is the relationship between the total amount of goods or services being produced (output) and the organizational resources needed to produce them (input). *p. 545*

Profits are the amount of total revenue that exceeds the total costs of producing the products sold. *p. 562*

Program is a single-use plan designed to carry out a special project in an organization that, if accomplished, will contribute to the organization's long-term success. *p. 252*

Program evaluation and review technique (PERT) is a scheduling tool that is essentially a network of project activities showing estimates of time necessary to complete each activity and the sequence of activities that must be followed to complete the project. *p. 260*

Programmed decisions are decisions that are routine and repetitive and that typically require specific handling methods. *p. 205*

Programmed learning is a technique for instructing without the presence or intervention of a human instructor. Small pieces of information requiring responses are presented to individual trainees, and the trainees determine from checking their responses against provided answers whether their understanding of the information is accurate. *p. 325*

Punishment is the presentation of an undesirable behavior consequence or the removal of a desirable one that decreases the likelihood that the behavior will continue. *p. 428*

Pure-breakdown (repair) policy is a maintenance control policy that decrees that machine adjustments, lubrication, cleaning, parts replacement, painting, and needed repairs and overhaul will be performed only after facilities or machines malfunction. *p. 556*

Pure-preventive maintenance policy is a maintenance control policy that tries to ensure that machine adjustments, lubrication, cleaning, parts replacement, painting, and needed repairs and overhauls will be performed before facilities or machines malfunction. *p. 556*

Quality is the extent to which a product reliably does what it is intended to do. *p. 503, 546*

Quality assurance is an operations process involving a broad group of activities aimed at achieving the organization's quality objectives. *p. 546*

Quality circles are small groups of workers that meet to discuss quality-related problems on a particular project and to communicate their solutions to these problems to management at a formal presentation session. *p. 548*

Quality dimension of organization culture is an element of organization culture that focuses on making sure that a product, in the opinion of the customer, does what it is supposed to do. *p. 474*

Ratio analysis is a control tool that summarizes the financial position of an organization by calculating ratios based on various financial measures that appear on the organization's balance sheet and income statements. *p. 559*

Rational decision-making process comprises the steps the decision maker takes to arrive at a choice. *p. 206*

Recruitment is the initial attraction and screening of the supply of prospective human resources available to fill a position. *p. 315*

Regression method predicts future sales by analyzing the historical relationship between sales and time. *p. 257*

Relevant alternative is an alternative that is considered feasible for solving an existing problem and for implementation. *p. 206*

Repatriation is the process of bringing individuals who have been working abroad back to their home country and reintegrating them into the organization's home-country operations. *p. 143*

Repetitiveness dimension of a plan is the extent to which the plan is to be used over and over again. *p. 249*

Resolving a technique for managing conflict by working out the difference(s) between managers and employees. *p. 350*

Responsibility is the obligation to perform assigned activities. *p. 293*

Responsibility and delegation skill is the ability to understand one's obligation to perform assigned activities and to enlist the help of others to complete these activities. *p. 290*

Responsibility gap exists when certain organizational tasks are not included in the responsibility area of any individual organization member. *p. 294*

Retrenchment is a strategy adopted by management to strengthen or protect the amount of business a strategic business unit is currently generating. *p. 338*

Reverse discrimination is the term used to describe inequities affecting members of the majority group as an outcome of programs designed to help underrepresented groups. *p. 117*

Risk refers to situations in which statistical probabilities can be attributed to alternative potential outcomes. *p. 213*

Robotics is the study of the development and use of robots. *p. 548*

Role conflict is the conflict that results when a person has to fill competing roles because of membership in two cultures. *p. 113*

Role overload refers to having too many expectations to comfortably fulfill. *p. 114*

Rule is a standing plan that designates specific required action. *p. 251*

Salesforce estimation method predicts future sales levels primarily by asking appropriate salespeople for their opinions of what will happen to sales in the future. *p. 257*

Satisfice occurs when an individual makes a decision that is not optimal but is "good enough." *p. 212*

Scalar relationships refer to the chain-of-command positioning of individuals on an organization chart. *p. 275*

Scheduling is the process of formulating a detailed listing of activities that must be accomplished to attain an objective, allocating the resources necessary to attain the objective, and setting up and following timetables for completing the objective. *p. 259*

Scientific management emphasizes the "one best way" to perform a task. *p. 56*

Scope dimension of a plan is the portion of the total management system at which the plan is aimed. *p. 249*

Scope of the decision is the proportion of the total management system that a particular decision will affect. The broader the scope of a decision, the higher the level of the manager responsible for making that decision. *p. 206*

Security, or safety, needs are Maslow's second set of human needs—reflecting the human desire to keep free from physical harm. *p. 421*

Selection is choosing an individual to hire from all those who have been recruited. *p. 321*

Self-actualization needs are Maslow's fifth, and final, set of human needs—reflecting the human desire to maximize personal potential. *p. 421*

Self-managed team is an organizational team that plans, organizes, influences, and controls its own work situation with only minimal intervention and direction from management. *p. 451*

Serial transmission involves the passing of information from one individual to another in a series. *p. 374*

Servant leadership is an approach to leading in which leaders view their primary role as helping followers in their quests to satisfy personal needs, aspirations, and interests. *p. 404*

Short-term objectives are targets to be achieved in one year or less. *p. 189*

Signal is a message that has been transmitted from one person to another. *p. 367*

Single-use plans are plans used only once—or, at most, several times—because they focus on unique or rare situations within the organization. *p. 249*

Site selection involves determining where a plant facility should be located. It may use a weighting process to compare site differences. *p. 252*

Situational approach to leadership is a relatively modern view of leadership that suggests that successful leadership requires a unique combination of leaders, followers, and leadership situations. *p. 388*

Social audit is the process of measuring the present social responsibility activities of an organization. It monitors, measures, and appraises all aspects of an organization's social responsibility performance. *p. 91*

Social entrepreneurship involves the recognition, evaluation, and exploitation of opportunities that create social value as opposed to personal or shareholder wealth. *p. 171*

Social needs are Maslow's third set of human needs—reflecting the human desire to belong, including longings for friendship, companionship, and love. *p. 421*

Social networks represent individuals' patterns of social relationships. *p. 166*

Social obligation approach is an approach to meeting social obligations that considers business as have primarily economic purposes and confines social responsibility activity mainly to existing legislation. *p. 87*

Social responsibility approach is an approach to meeting social obligations that considers business as having both and economic and societal goals. *p. 87*

Social responsiveness is the degree of effectiveness and efficiency an organization displays in pursuing its social responsibilities. *p. 85*

Social responsiveness approach is an approach to meeting social obligations that considers business as having both societal and economic goals as well as the obligation to anticipate potential social problems and work actively toward preventing their occurrence. *p. 87*

Social value refers to the basic long-standing needs of society and has little to do with profits. *p. 171*

Social values are the relative degrees of worth society places on the manner in which it exists and functions. *p. 230*

Sociogram is a sociometric diagram that summarizes the personal feelings of organization members about the people in the organization with whom they would like to spend free time. *p. 447*

Sociometry is an analytical tool that can be used to determine what informal groups exist in an organization and who the leaders and members of those groups are. *p. 447*

Source/encoder is the person in the interpersonal communication situation who originates and encodes information to be shared with others. *p. 366*

Span of management is the number of individuals a manager supervises. *p. 275*

Spirituality dimension of organization culture is an aspect of organization culture that encourages organization members to integrate spiritual life and work life. *p. 476*

Stability is a strategy adopted by management to maintain or slightly improve the amount of business that a strategic business unit is generating. *p. 238*

Staff authority consists of the right to advise or assist those who possess line authority as well as other staff personnel. *p. 298*

Stakeholders are all those individuals and groups that are directly or indirectly affected by an organization's decisions. *p. 85*

Standard is the level of activity established to serve as a model for evaluating organizational performance. *p. 521*

Standing plans are plans that are used over and over because they focus on organizational situations that occur repeatedly. *p. 249*

Statistical quality control is the process used to determine how many products should be inspected to calculate a probability that the total number of products will meet organizational quality standards. *p. 548*

Stereotype is a positive or negative assessment of members of a group or their perceived attributes. *p. 112*

Steward is an individual who is entrusted with managing the affairs of another. *p. 405*

Storming, the second stage of the team development process, is characterized by conflict and disagreement as team members try to clarify their individual roles and challenge the way the team functions. *p. 453*

Strategic business unit (SBU) is, in business portfolio analysis, a significant organizational segment that is analyzed to develop organizational strategy aimed at generating future business or revenue. SBUs vary in form, but all are a single business (or collection of businesses), have their own competitors and a manager accountable for operations, and can be independently planned for. *p. 235*

Strategic control is the last step of the strategy management process, consists of monitoring and evaluating the strategy management process as a whole to ensure that it is operating properly. *p. 239*

Strategic management is the process of ensuring that an organization possesses and benefits from the use of an appropriate organizational strategy. *p. 228*

Strategic planning is long-range planning that focuses on the organization as a whole. *p. 227*

Strategic planning skill is the ability to engage in long-range planning that focuses on the organization as a whole. *p. 224*

Strategic renewal occurs when a firm attempts to alter its own competitive strategy. *p. 170*

Strategy is a broad and general plan developed to reach long-term objectives; it is the end result of strategic planning. *p. 227*

Strategy formulation is the process of determining appropriate courses of action for achieving organizational objectives and thereby accomplishing organizational purpose. Strategy development tools include critical question analysis, SWOT analysis, business portfolio analysis, and Porter's Model for Industry Analysis. *p. 233*

Strategy implementation is the fourth step of the strategy management process, is putting formulated strategy into action. *p. 238*

Stress is the bodily strain that an individual experiences as a result of coping with some environmental factor. *p. 345*

Stressor is an environmental demand that causes people to feel stress. *p. 347*

Structural change is a change aimed at increasing organizational effectiveness through modifications to the existing organizational structure. *p. 340*

Structural factors are organizational controls, such as policies and procedures. *p. 339*

Structure refers to the designated relationships among resources of the management system. *p. 275*

Structure behavior is leadership activity that (1) delineates the relationship between the leader and the leader's followers or (2) establishes well-defined procedures that the followers should adhere to in performing their jobs. *p. 394*

Suboptimization is a condition wherein subobjectives are conflicting or not directly aimed at accomplishing the overall organizational objectives. *p. 190*

Successful communication refers to an interpersonal communication situation in which the information the source intends to share with the destination and the meaning the destination derives from the transmitted message are the same. *p. 368*

Succession planning is the process of outlining who will follow whom in various organizational positions. *p. 319*

Superleadership is leading by showing others how to lead themselves. *p. 404*

Supplier power denotes the power that suppliers have over the firms operating in an industry; as supplier power increases, industry attractiveness decreases. *p. 231*

Sustained regeneration occurs when firms develop new cultures, processes, or structures to support new product innovations in current markets as well as with existing products into new markets. *p. 170*

SWOT analysis is a strategic development tool that matches internal organizational strengths and weaknesses with external opportunities and threats. *p. 234*

Symptom is a sign that a problem exists. *p. 523*

System is a number of interdependent parts functioning as a whole for some purpose. *p. 66*

System approach to management is a management approach based on general system theory—the theory that to understand fully the operation of an entity, the entity must be viewed as a system. *p. 66*

Tactical planning is short-range planning that emphasizes the current operations of various parts of the organization. *p. 239*

Task group is a formal group of organization members who interact with one another to accomplish nonroutine organizational tasks. Members of any one task group can come from various levels in the organizational hierarchy. *p. 442*

Task-related activities are management efforts aimed at carrying out critical management-related duties in organizations. *p. 38*

Team is a group whose members influence one another toward the accomplishment of an organizational objective(s). *p. 450*

Team skill is the ability to manage a collection of people so that they influence one another toward the accomplishment of an organizational objective(s). *p. 438*

Technical skills are skills involving the ability to apply specialized knowledge and expertise to work-related techniques and procedures. *p. 37*

Technological change is a type of organizational change that emphasizes modifying the level of technology in the management system. *p. 339*

Technological factors are any types of equipment or processes that assist organization members in the performance of their jobs. *p. 339*

Technology consists of any type of equipment or process that organization members use in the performance of their work. *p. 530*

Technology ideas are ideas that focus on invention that enhances the use of technology within organizations. *p. 500*

Testing is examining human resources for qualities relevant to performing available jobs. *p. 321*

Theory X is a set of essentially negative assumptions about human nature. *p. 425*

Theory Y is a set of essentially positive assumptions about human nature. *p. 425*

Theory Z is the effectiveness dimension that implies that managers who use either Theory X or Theory Y assumptions when dealing with people can be successful, depending on their situation. *p. 425*

Third-country national is an organization member who is a citizen of one country and who works in another country for an organization headquartered in still another country. *p. 141*

Threat of new entrants refers to the ability of new firms to enter an industry; as the threat of new entrants increases, the attractiveness of an industry decreases. *p. 231*

Threat of substitute products refers to the extent to which customers may use products or services from another industry instead of the focal industry. As the threat of substitutes increases, which implies that customers have more choices, the attractiveness of an industry decreases. *p. 231*

Time dimension of a plan is the length of time the plan covers. *p. 249*

Tokenism refers to being one of few members of your group in the organization. *p. 112*

Total costs are the sum of fixed costs and variable costs. *p. 562*

Total power is the entire amount of power an individual in an organization possesses. It is made up of position power and personal power. *p. 524*

Total quality management (TQM) is the continuous process of involving all organization members in ensuring that every activity related to the production of goods or services has an appropriate role in establishing product quality. *p. 503*

Total revenue is all sales dollars accumulated from selling manufactured products or services. *p. 562*

Training is the process of developing qualities in human resources that will enable them to be more productive and thus to contribute more to organizational goal attainment. *p. 323*

Training needs are the information or skill areas of an individual or group that require further development to increase the productivity of that individual or group. *p. 323*

Trait approach to leadership is an outdated view of leadership that sees the personal characteristics of an individual as the main determinants of how successful that individual could be as a leader. *p. 388*

Transformational leadership is leadership that inspires organizational success by profoundly affecting followers' beliefs in what an organization should be, as well as their values, such as justice and integrity. *p. 402*

Transnational organization also called global organization, takes the entire world as its business arena. *p. 151*

Triangular management is a management approach that emphasizes using information from the classical, behavioral, and management science schools of thought to manage the open management system. *p. 67*

Uncertainty refers to situations where the probability that a particular outcome will occur is not known in advance. *p. 213*

Unhealthy organization culture is an organization culture that does not facilitate the accomplishment of the organization's mission and objectives. *p. 482*

Unity of command is the management principle that recommends that an individual have only one boss. *p. 275*

Universal means that the principles of management are applicable to all types of organizations and organizational levels. *p. 36*

Unsuccessful communication refers to an interpersonal communication situation in which the information the source intends to share with the destination and the meaning the destination derives from the transmitted message are different. *p. 368*

Upward organizational communication is communication that flows from any point on an organization chart upward to another point on the organization chart. *p. 373*

Value analysis is a cost control and cost reduction technique that examines all the parts, materials, and functions of an operation to help managers control operations. *p. 565*

Values are the beliefs of a person or social group in which they have an emotional investment. *p. 477*

Values statement is a formally drafted document that summarizes the primary values within the culture of a specific organization. *p. 477*

Variable budget (also known as a flexible budget) is one that outlines the levels of resources to be allocated for each organizational activity according to the level of production within the organization. *p. 578*

Variable costs are expenses that fluctuate with the number of products produced. *p. 562*

Verbal communication is the sharing of information through words, either written or spoken. *p. 372*

Venture capitalist is a firm that raises money from investors and then uses this money to make investments in new firms. *p. 169*

Vertical dimensioning refers to the extent to which an organization uses vertical levels to separate job responsibilities. *p. 275*

Virtual corporation is an organization that goes significantly beyond the boundaries and structure of a traditional organization by comprehensively "tying together" a company's stakeholders—employees, suppliers, and customers—via an elaborate system of e-mail, the World Wide Web, and other Internet-related vehicles such as videoconferencing. *p. 351*

Virtual office is a work arrangement that extends beyond the structure and boundaries of the traditional office arrangement. *p. 351*

Virtual organization is an organization having the essence of a traditional organization, but without some aspect(s) of traditional boundaries and structure. *p. 351*

Virtual teams are groups of employees formed by managers that go beyond the boundaries and structure of traditional teams by having members in geographi-

cally dispersed locations meeting via real-time messaging on an intranet or the Internet to discuss special or unanticipated organizational problems. *p. 351*

Virtual training is a training process that goes beyond the boundaries and structure of traditional training. *p. 351*

Vroom expectancy theory is a motivation theory that hypothesizes that felt needs cause human behavior and that motivation strength depends on an individual's degree of desire to perform a behavior. *p. 418*

Vroom-Yetton-Jago (VYJ) Model of leadership is a modern view of leadership that suggests that successful leadership requires determining, through a decision tree, what style of leadership will produce decisions that are beneficial to the organization and will be accepted and committed to by subordinates. *p. 392*

Whistle-blower is the employee who reports the alleged activities of suspected misconduct or corruption within an organization. *p. 98*

Whistle-blowing is the act of an employee reporting suspected misconduct or corruption believed to exist within an organization. *p. 98*

Work measurement methods are operational tools that are used to establish labor standards. *p. 555*

Work methods analysis is an operational tool used to improve productivity and ensure the safety of workers. *p. 555*

Work team is a task group used in organizations to achieve greater organizational flexibility or to cope with rapid growth. *p. 445*

Workplace bullying refers to individuals being isolated or excluded socially and having work efforts devalued. *p. 347*

Zero-base budgeting requires managers to justify their entire budget request in detail rather than simply referring to budget amounts established in previous years. *p. 558*

ENDNOTES

CHAPTER 1

1. Jim Ellis, "Harry Potter theme park slated for 2009," *Dallas Morning News,* www.dallasnews.com, June 4, 2007.
2. Beth Kassab, "Universal to spend up to $265 million in building Harry Potter 'Wizarding World,' " *Orlando Sentinel*, June 1, 2007.
3. James Luxford, "Harry Potter vs. Mickey Mouse," Entertainmentwise.com, June 4, 2007.
4. For an interesting discussion of how the World Bank is launching a pilot program to address the scarcity of well-trained managers in developing and transition countries, see "Improving Management in Developing Countries," *Finance & Development* 40, no.2 (June 2003): 5.
5. "For Women, Equal Pay? No Way," *Time* 169, no. 19 (May 7, 2007).
6. "Shareholders Win One at Home Depot: An Arrogant CEO's Exorbitant Pay Had No Relation to Sagging Stock Price," *Knight Ridder Tribune Business News,* January 15, 2007, 1.
7. Alan Murray, "A Gathering Consensus on CEO Pay," *Wall Street Journal,* March 15, 2006, A2.
8. Marcy Gordon, "Lawmakers Take Up Issue of Excessive Executive Pay," *The Orlando Sentinel,* May 21, 2003, C3.
9. John R. Schermerhorn Jr., *Management* (New York: John Wiley & Sons, Inc., 2005): 19.
10. Jacqueline McLean, "Making Things Happen," *The British Journal of Administrative Management,* October/November 2006, 16.
11. Gary Hamel and C. K. Prahalad, "Seeing the Future First," *Fortune,* September 5, 1994, 64–70; Paul J. Di Stefano, "Strategic Planning—Both Short Term and Long Term," *Rough Notes* 149, no. 8 (August 2006): 26.
12. T. L. Stanley, "Management: A Journey in Progress," *SuperVision* 67, no. 12 (December 2006): 15–18.
13. Jared Sandberg, "Office Democracies: How Many Bosses Can One Person Have?" *Wall Street Journal,* November 22, 2005, B1.
14. For an example of tactics taken by Chase Manhattan Corporation to enhance its efficiency, see Matt Murray, "Chase Combines International Units in Efficiency Move," *Wall Street Journal,* February 19, 1998, C17.
15. William Wiggenhorn, "Motorola U: When Training Becomes an Education," *Harvard Business Review* (July/August 1990): 71–83.
16. Wyatt Wells, "Concept of the Corporation," *Business History Review* 81, no. 1 (Spring 2007): 142.
17. Henri Fayol, *General and Industrial Management* (London: Sir Isaac Pitman & Sons, 1949).
18. B. C. Forbes, *Forbes,* March 15, 1976, 128.
19. Les Worrall and Cary Cooper, "Management Skills Development: A Perspective on Current Issues and Setting the Future Agenda," *Leadership & Organization Development Journal* 22, no. 1 (2001): 34–39.
20. Based upon current information at PSA Peugeot Citroen www.psa-peugeot-citroen.com; and Elaine Priestly, "Developing Management Skills at PSA Peugeot Citroen" *Training & Management Development Methods* 18, no. 1 (2004): 401–404.
21. Robert L. Katz, "Skills of an Effective Administrator," *Harvard Business Review* (January/February 1955): 33–41.
22. Ruth Davidhizar, "The Two-Minute Manager," *Health Supervisor* 7 (April 1989): 25–29; for an article that demonstrates how important human skills are for middle managers, see also Philip A. Rudolph and Brian H. Kleiner, "The Art of Motivating Employees," *Journal of Managerial Psychology* 4 (1989): i–iv.
23. Gary Yukl, Angela Gordon, and Tom Taber, "A Hierarchical Taxonomy of Leadership Behavior: Integrating a Half Century of Behavior Research," *Journal of Leadership & Organizational Studies* 9, no. 1 (Summer 2002): 15–32.
24. Tim O. Peterson and David D. Van Fleet, "The Ongoing Legacy of R. L. Katz: An Updated Typology of Management Skills," *Management Decision* 42, no. 10 (2004): 1297–1308.
25. Kent E. Neupert, C. Christopher Baughn, and Thi Thanh Lam Dao, "International Management Skills for Success in Asia: A Needs-Based Determination of Skills for Foreign Managers and Local Managers," *Journal of European Industrial Training* 29, nos. 2/3 (2005); 165–180.
26. Don Hellriegel, John W. Slocum Jr., and Richard W. Woodman, *Organizational Behavior,* 6th ed. (St. Paul: West Publishing Company, 1992), 681.
27. Perri Capell, "Why Increased Pay Isn't Always Best Reason to Accept Another Job," *Wall Street Journal,* December 19, 2006, B8.
28. John Ivancevich and Michael T. Matteson, *Organizational Behavior and Management* (Homewood, IL: BPJ/Irwin, 1990), 593–95.
29. Patrick J. Purcell, "Older Workers: Employment and Retirement Trends," *Monthly Labor Review* 123, no. 10 (October 2000): 19–30.
30. John W. Slocum Jr., William L. Cron, and Linda C. Yows, "Whose Career Is Likely to Plateau?" *Business Horizons* (March/April 1987): 31–38.
31. Joseph E. McKendrick Jr., "What Are You Doing the Rest of Your Life?" *Management World* (September/October 1987): 2; Carl Anderson, *Management: Skills, Functions, and Organizational Performance,* 2d ed. (Boston: Allyn and Bacon, 1988).
32. Paul H. Thompson, Robin Zenger Baker, and Norman Smallwood, "Improving Personal Development by Applying the Four-Stage Career Model," *Organizational Dynamics* (Autumn 1986): 49–62.
33. Kenneth Labich, "Take Control of Your Career," *Fortune,* November 18, 1991, 87–90; Buck Blessing, "Career Planning: Five Fatal Assumptions," *Training and Development Journal* (September 1986): 49–51.
34. Thomas J. Peters Jr., "The Best New Managers Will Listen, Motivate, Support," *Working Woman,* September 1990, 142–143, 216–217.
35. Ann Pomeroy, "Peak Performances," *HR Magazine* 52, no. 4 (April 2007): 48–53.
36. Jan Torrisi-Mokwa, "The Seven Questions Firm Leaders Need to Ask to Advance Professional Women More Effectively" *CPA Practice Management Forum* 2, no. 12 (December 2006): 13–14.
37. For an interesting discussion of challenges of dual-career versus single-career couples, see David F. Elloy and Catherine R Smith, "Patterns of Stress, Work-Family Conflict, Role Conflict, Role Ambiguity, and Overload Among Dual-Career and Single-Career Couples: An Australian Study," *Cross-Cultural Management* 10, no. 1 (2003): 55.
38. For additional information, see Sue Shellenbarger, "For the Burseks, Best Parent Regimen Is Back-to-Back Shifts," *Wall Street Journal,* February 25, 1998, B1; Jacqueline B. Stanfield, "Couples Coping with Dual Careers: A Description of Flexible and Rigid Coping Styles," *Social Science Journal* 35, no. 1 (1998): 53–64; R. S. Hall and T. D. Hall, "Dual Careers—How Do Couples and Companies Cope with the Problems?" *Organizational Dynamics* 6 (1978): 57–77.
39. Information for this portfolio exercise is based upon www.theblindpig.com.

CHAPTER 2

1. Andrew Martin, "Burger King Shifts Policy on Animals," *New York Times,* March 28, 2007, 1.
2. Thomas J. Lueck, "City May Ask Restaurants to List Calories," *New York Times,* October 30, 2006, B1.
3. Charlie LeDuff, "Dreams in the Dark at the Drive-Through Window," *New York Times,* November 27, 2006, A12.
4. James H. Donnelly, Jr., James L. Gibson, and John M. Ivancevich, *Fundamentals of Management* (Plano, TX: Business Publications, 1987), 6–8; Harold Koontz, Cyril O'Donnell, and Heinz Weihrich, *Management,* 8th ed. (New York: McGraw-Hill, 1984), 52–69; W. Warren Haynes and Joseph L. Massie, *Management,* 2d ed. (Upper Saddle River, NJ: Prentice Hall, 1969), 4–13.
5. David W. Hays, "Quality Improvement and Its Origin in Scientific Management," *Quality Progress,* May 5, 1994, 89–90.
6. For an article describing how Taylor's work has given rise to other types of modern production research, see Betsi Harris Ehrlich, "Service with a Smile," *Industrial Engineer* 38, no. 8 (August 2006): 40–44.
7. Frederick W. Taylor, *The Principles of Scientific Management* (New York: Harper & Bros., 1947), 66–71.

8. For more information on the work of Frederick Taylor, see Edward Rimer, "Organization Theory and Frederick Taylor," *Public Administration Review* 53 (May/June 1993): 270–272; Alan Farnham, "The Man Who Changed Work Forever," *Fortune,* July 21, 1997, 114; Hans Picard, "Quit Following Marx's Advice," *ENR* 246, no. 12 (March 26, 2001): 99.

9. Franz T. Lohrke, "Motion Study for the Blinded: A Review of the Gilbreths' Work with the Visually Handicapped," *International Journal of Public Administration* 16 (1993): 667–68. For information illustrating how the career of Lillian Gilbreth is an inspiration for modern women managers, see Thomas R. Miller and Mary A. Lemons, "Breaking the Glass Ceiling: Lessons from a Management Pioneer," *S.A.M. Advanced Management Journal* 63, no. 1 (Winter 1998): 4–9.

10. Edward A. Michaels, "Work Measurement," *Small Business Reports* 14 (March 1989): 55–63. For information regarding the application of time studies in nursing home, see Greg Arling, Robert L. Kane, Christine Mueller, and Teresa Lewis, "Explaining Direct Care Resource Use of Nursing Home Residents: Findings from Time Studies in Four States," *Health Services Research,* 42, no. 2 (April 2007): 827.

11. Dennis Karwatka, "Frank Gilbreth and Production Efficiency," *Tech Directions*, 65, no. 6 (January 2006): 10.

12. This exercise based on Edward V. Morandi, Jr., "On the Job, Time Study Supervisor," *Telegram & Gazette*, November 13, 2006, E1.

13. Henry L. Gantt, *Industrial Leadership* (New Haven, CT: Yale University Press, 1916), 57.

14. For more information on the Gantt chart, see Jeff Angus, "Software Speeds Up Project Management," *Informationweek,* September 8, 1997, 85–88; Mel Lofurno, "The Gantt Chart," *Compoundings* 52 (2002): 35.

15. Marc Puich, "The Critical Path," *Biopharm International*, 20, no. 3 (March 2007): 28, 30.

16. Doug Green and Denise Green, "MacSchedule Has Rich Features at Low Price," *InfoWorld,* July 12, 1993, 88.

17. Gantt, *Industrial Leadership*, 85.

18. Chester I. Barnard, *Organization and Management* (Cambridge, MA: Harvard University Press, 1952).

19. Alvin Brown, *Organization of Industry* (Upper Saddle River, NJ: Prentice Hall, 1947); Henry S. Dennison, *Organization Engineering* (New York: McGraw-Hill, 1931); Luther Gulick and Lyndall Urwick, eds., *Papers on the Science of Administration* (New York: Institute of Public Administration, 1937); J. D. Mooney and A. C. Reiley, *Onward Industry!* (New York: Harper & Bros., 1931); Oliver Sheldon, *The Philosophy of Management* (London: Sir Isaac Pitman and Sons, 1923).

20. Henri Fayol, *General and Industrial Management* (London: Sir Isaac Pitman and Sons, 1949). See also David Frederick, "Making Sense of Management I," *Credit Management,* December 2000, 34–35.

21. Charles A. Mowll, "Successful Management Based on Key Principles," *Healthcare Financial Management* 43 (June 1989): 122, 124; Carl A. Rodrigues, "Fayol's 14 Principles of Management Then and Now: A Framework for Managing Today's Organizations Effectively," *Management Decision* 39 (2001): 880–889.

22. Fayol, *General and Industrial Management,* 19–42. For an excellent discussion of the role of accountability and organization structure, see Elliott Jaques, "In Praise of Hierarchy," *Harvard Business Review* 68 (January/February 1990): 127–133.

23. For an interesting discussion on how "chain of command" helps to minimize the negative impact of oil spills, see James Hunt, Bruce Carter, and Frank Kelly, "Clearly Defined Chain-of-Command Helps Mobilize Oil Spill," *Occupational Health & Safety,* June 1993, 40–45. For a discussion of the impact of remuneration on an organization, see Jeffrey Bradt, "Pay for Impact," *Personnel Journal* (January 1992): 76–79.

24. Lee D. Parker and Philip Ritson, "Fads, Stereotypes, and Management Gurus: Fayol and Follett Today" *Management Decision* 43, no. 10 (2005): 1335–1357.

25. For detailed summaries of these studies, see *Industrial Worker,* 2 vols. (Cambridge, MA: Harvard University Press, 1938); and F. J. Roethlisberger and W. J. Dickson, *Management and the Worker* (Cambridge, MA: Harvard University Press, 1939).

26. Stephen Jones, "Worker Interdependence and Output: The Hawthorne Studies Reevaluated," *American Sociological Review* (April 1990): 176–190.

27. Jennifer Laabs, "Corporate Anthropologists," *Personnel Journal* (January 1992): 81–91; Samuel C. Certo, *Human Relations Today: Concepts and Skills* (Burr Ridge, IL: Irwin, 1995), 4; Scott Highhouse, "Well-Being: The Foundations of Hedonic Psychology," *Personnel Psychology* 54, no. 1 (Spring 2001): 204–206.

28. Michael Wilson, "The Psychology of Motivation and Employee Retention," *Maintenance Supplies* 50, no. 5 (July 2005): 48–49.

29. A. H. Reylito Elbo, "In the Workplace," *BusinessWorld* (2002): 1.

30. Evelyn Ai Lin Teo, Florence Yean Yng Ling, and Derrick Sern Yau Ong, "Fostering Safe Work Behavior in Workers at Construction Sites," *Engineering, Construction, and Architectural Management* 12, no. 4 (2005): 410–422.

31. C. West Churchman, Russell L. Ackoff, and E. Leonard Arnoff, *Introduction to Operations Research* (New York: Wiley, 1957), 18.

32. Hamdy A. Taha, *Operations Research: An Introduction* (New York: Macmillan, 1988), 1–2; see also Scott Shane and Karl Ulrich, "Technological Innovation, Product Development, and Entrepreneurship in Management Science," *Management Science* 2 (2004): 133–145.

33. Kalyan Singhal, Jaya Singhal, and Martin K Starr, "The Domain of Production and Operations Management and the Role of Elwood Buffa in its Delineation," *Journal of Operations Management* 25, no. 2 (March 2007): 310.

34. James R. Emshoff, *Analysis of Behavioral Systems* (New York: Macmillan, 1971), 10.

35. Catherine L. Morgan, "A Survey of MS/OR Surveys," *Interfaces* 19 (November/December 1989): 95–103; H. J. Zimmermann, "Some Observations on Practicing Successful Operational Research," *The Journal of the Operational Research Society* 49, no. 4 (April 1998): 413–419.

36. The discussion concerning these characteristics is adapted from Donnelly, Gibson, and Ivancevich, *Fundamentals of Management,* 302–303; Efraim Turban and Jack R. Meredith, *Fundamentals of Management Science* (Plano, TX: Business Publications, 1981), 15–23.

37. Harold Koontz, "The Management Theory Jungle Revisited," *Academy of Management Review* 5 (1980): 175–187. For a practical application of the contingency approach to management, see Henri Barki, Suzanne Rivard, and Jean Talbot, "An Integrative Contingency Model of Software Project Risk Management," *Journal of Management Information Systems* 17, no. 4 (Spring 2001): 37–69.

38. For an application of the contingency approach to management in an information systems organization, see Narayan S. Umanath, "The Concept of Contingency Beyond 'It Depends': Illustrations from IS Research Stream," *Information & Management* 40 (2003): 551–562.

39. Don Hellriegel, John W. Slocum, and Richard W. Woodman, *Organizational Behavior* (St. Paul, MN: West Publishing, 1986), 22.

40. J. W. Lorsch, "Organization Design: A Situational Perspective," *Organizational Dynamics* 6 (1977): 2–4; Louis W. Fry and Deborah A. Smith, "Congruence, Contingency, and Theory Building," *Academy of Management Review* (January 1987): 117–132.

41. For a more detailed development of von Bertalanffy's ideas, see "General System Theory: A New Approach to Unity of Science," *Human Biology* (December 1951): 302–361.

42. L. Thomas Hopkins, *Integration: Its Meaning and Application* (New York: Appleton-Century-Crofts, 1937), 36–49. For an interesting illustration of how wholeness applies to managed care, see Jill Wechsler, "Managed Care Firms Are Kicking Butts!" *Managed Healthcare* 8, no. 4 (April 1998): 32–36.

43. Joe Schwartz, "Why They Buy," *American Demographics* 11 (March 1989): 40–41.

44. Ken Starkey, "What Can We Learn from the Learning Organization?" *Human Relations* 51, no. 4. (April 1998): 531–46.

45. David A. Garvin, "Building a Learning Organization," *Harvard Business Review* 74, no. 4. (July 1993): 78. For more recent discussion of learning organizations, see Bente Elkjaer, "The Dance of Change: The Challenges of Sustaining Momentum in Learning Organizations," *Management Learning* 32, no. 1 (March 2000): 153–156.

46. For a study on the effectiveness of the learning organization approach, see Ashok Jashapara, "Cognition, Culture, and Competition: An Empirical Test of the Learning Organization," *The Learning Organization* 10 (2003): 31–50.

47. Peter Senge, *The Fifth Discipline, The Art & Practice of the Learning Organization* (New York: Doubleday/Currency, 1990). Used by permission of Doubleday, a division of Random House, Inc. For more background regarding learning organizations and innovation, see Li-Fen Liao, "A Learning Organization Perspective on Knowledge-Sharing Behavior and Firm Innovation," *Human Systems Management* 25, no. 4 (2006): 227.

CHAPTER 3

1. Al Bawaba, "Launch of KidSmart Program in Egypt," London: November 23, 2005, 1.

2. For a good discussion of many factors involved in the modern meanings of social responsibility, see Frederick D. Sturdivant and Heidi Vernon-Wortzel, *Business and Society: A Managerial Approach,* 4th ed. (Homewood, IL: Irwin, 1990), 3–24. The definition of corporate social responsibility is adapted

from Keith Davis and Robert L. Blomstrom, *Business and Society: Environment and Responsibility,* 3rd ed. (New York: McGraw-Hill, 1975), 6. For illustrations of how social responsibility makes good economic sense, see Ernest Beck, "Body Shop Founder Roddick Steps Aside as CEO," *Wall Street Journal,* May 13, 1998, B14; Gerard J. J. M. Zwetsloot, "From Management Systems to Corporate Social Responsibility," *Journal of Business Ethics* 44 (2003): 201–208; see also Christine Hemingway and Patrick Maclagan, "Managers' Personal Values as Drivers of Corporate Social Responsibility," *Journal of Business Ethics* 50 (2004): 33.

3. Patricia L. Short, "Keeping It Clean," *Chemical & Engineering News* 85, no. 17 (April 23, 2007): 13.

4. Peter L. Berger, "New Attack on the Legitimacy of Business," *Harvard Business Review* (September/October 1981): 82–89.

5. Keith Davis, "Five Propositions for Social Responsibility," *Business Horizons* (June 1975): 9–24. For additional comments supporting social responsibility activities, see Lois A. Mohr, Deborah J. Webb, and Katherine E. Harris, "Do Consumers Expect Companies to Be Socially Responsible? The Impact of Corporate Social Responsibility on Buying Behavior," *Journal of Consumer Affairs* 35, no. 1 (Summer 2001): 45–72.

6. Virginia Gewin, "Industry Lured by the Gains of Going Green," *Nature,* July 14, 2005, 173.

7. ———— "Mohawk Going Green in Bath Rugs," *Home Textiles Today* 28, no. 7 (February 26, 2007): 12.

8. Kate Arthur, "Going Green: Simple Changes Make Vast Improvements on the Environment," *Knight Ridder Tribune Business News,* Washington: March 2, 2007, 1.

9. Dick de Gilder, Theo N. M. Schuyt, and Melissa Breedijk "Effects of an Employee Volunteering Program on the Work Force: The ABN-AMRO Case," *Journal of Business Ethics* 61 (2005): 143–152.

10. For extended discussion of arguments for and against social responsibility, see William C. Frederick, Keith Davis, and James E. Post, *Business and Society: Corporate Strategy, Public Policy, Ethics,* 6th ed. (New York: McGraw-Hill, 1988), 36–43.

11. For discussion in favor of corporate social responsibility, see Jane Fuller, "Banking on a Good Reputation: Companies Should Look at Corporate Social Responsibility on a Cost–Benefit Approach, Not by Whatever Campaign Is in the News," *Financial Times* (2003): 6.

12. For comments on a new way of exploring the relationship between the financial performance of an organization and its social responsibility activities, see Sandra A. Waddock and Samuel B. Graves, "Finding the Link Between Stakeholder Relations and Quality of Management," *Journal of Investing* 6, no. 4 (Winter 1997): 20–24.

13. J. B. McGuire, A. Sundgren, and T. Schneeweis, "Corporate Social Responsibility and Firm Financial Performance," *Academy of Management Journal* (December 1988): 854–872; Vogel, "Ethics and Profits Don't Always Go Hand in Hand," *Los Angeles Times,* December 28, 1988, 7.

14. For Friedman's view, see "Freedom and Philanthropy: An Interview with Milton Friedman," *Business and Society Review* (Fall 1989): 11–18.

15. Milton Friedman, "Does Business Have Social Responsibility?" *Bank Administration* (April 1971): 13–14.

16. Eric J. Savitz, "The Vision Thing: Control Data Abandons It for the Bottom Line," *Barron's,* May 7, 1990, 10–11, 22.

17. For a discussion of radical environmentalism, see Jeffrey Salmon, "We're All 'Corporate Polluters' Now," *Wall Street Journal,* July 2, 1997, A14.

18. Joan E. Rigdon, "The Wrist Watch: How a Plant Handles Occupational Hazard with Common Sense," *Wall Street Journal,* September 28, 1992, 1.

19. Sandra L. Holmes, "Executive Perceptions of Corporate Social Responsibility," *Business Horizons* (June 1976): 34–40.

20. For insights regarding SC Johnson Wax's position on social responsibility involvement, see Reva A. Holmes, "At SC Johnson Wax Philanthropy Is an Investment," *Management Accounting* (August 1994): 42–45.

21. Bill Richards, "Nike Hires an Executive from Microsoft for New Post Focusing on Labor Policies," *Wall Street Journal,* January 15, 1998, B14.

22. Samuel C. Certo and J. Paul Peter, *The Strategic Management Process,* 3rd ed. (Chicago: Irwin, 1995), 219; Marianne M. Jennings, "Manager's Journal: Trendy Causes Are No Substitute for Ethics," *Wall Street Journal,* December 1, 1997, A22.

23. Carlo Wolff, "Living with the New Amenity," *Lodging Hospitality* (December 1994): 66–68; for an article demonstrating the importance of stakeholders' opinions in social responsibility, see David Wheeler, Barry Colbert, and Edward Freeman, "Focusing on Value: Reconciling Corporate Social Responsibility, Sustainability and a Stakeholder Approach in a Network World," *Journal of General Management* 28 (2003): 1.

24. Harry A. Lipson, "Do Corporate Executives Plan for Social Responsibility?" *Business and Society Review* (Winter 1974–75): 80–81.

25. S. Prakash Sethi, "Dimensions of Corporate Social Performance: An Analytical Framework," *California Management Review* (Spring 1975): 58–64.

26. For information on the growing trend for business to make contributions to support education, see Joel Keehn, "How Business Helps the Schools," *Fortune,* October 21, 1991, 161–171.

27. Frank H. Cassell, "The Social Cost of Doing Business," *MSU Business Topics* (Autumn 1974): 19–26.

28. Donald W. Garner, "The Cigarette Industry's Escape from Liability," *Business and Society Review* 33 (Spring 1980): 22.

29. Meinolf Dierkes and Ariane Berthoin Antal, "Whither Corporate Social Reporting: Is It Time to Legislate?" *California Management Review* (Spring 1986): 106–121.

30. Condensed from Jerry McAfee, "How Society Can Help Business," *Newsweek,* July 3, 1978, 15. Copyright 1978 by Newsweek, Inc. All rights reserved. Reprinted by permission.

31. "Borden Chemicals Lashes Back at EPA," *Chemical Marketing Reporter,* November 7, 1994, 5, 19.

32. Leonard J. Brooks Jr., "Corporate Codes of Ethics," *Journal of Business Ethics* (February/March 1989): 117–129.

33. For an interesting discussion of the ethical dilemma of fairly allocating an individual's time between work and personal life, see Paul B. Hoffmann, "Balancing Professional and Personal Priorities," *Healthcare Executive* (May/June 1994): 42.

34. Archie B. Carroll, "In Search of the Moral Manager," *Business Horizons* (March/April 1987): 7–15.

35. For an article outlining the relationship between ethics and management, see Elliott Jaques, "Ethics for Management," *Management Communication Quarterly* 17 (2003): 136.

36. Sundeep Waslekar, "Good Citizens and Reap Rewards," *Asian Business* (January 1994): 52. See also Genine Babakian, "Who Will Control Russian Advertising?" *Adweek* [Eastern Edit.] August 1, 1994, 16.

37. Natalie M. Green, "Creating an Ethical Workplace," *Employment Relations Today* 24, no. 2 (Summer 1997): 33–44.

38. "Helping Workers Helps Bottom Line," *Employee Benefit Plan Review,* July 1990.

39. Sandy Lutz, "Psych Hospitals Fight for Survival," *Modern Healthcare,* May 8, 1995, 62–65.

40. Patrick E. Murphy, "Creating Ethical Corporate Structures," *Sloan Management Review* (Winter 1989): 81–87; Louis J. D'Amore, "A Code of Ethics and Guidelines for Socially and Environmentally Responsible Tourism," *Journal of Travel Research* (Winter 1993): 64–66.

41. James B. Treece, "Nissan Rattles Japan with Tough Ethics Code," *Automotive News,* May 4, 1998, 1, 49.

42. Richard A. Spinell, "Lessons from the Salomon Scandal," *America,* December 28, 1991, 476–477; Touche Ross, *Ethics in American Business* (New York: Touche Ross & Co., January 1988). For a view on developing a code of ethics for the workplace, see O. C. Ferrell, "An Assessment of the Proposed Academy of Marketing Science Code of Ethics for Marketing Educators," *Journal of Business Ethics,* 19, no. 2 (April 1999): 225–228.

43. For additional insights on how and why to create an ethical workplace, see Curt Smith, "The Ethical Workplace," *Association Management* 52, no. 6 (June 2000): 70–73.

44. For an interesting study of ethics codes, see Lawrence Chonko, Thomas Wotruba, and Terry Loe, "Ethics Code Familiarity and Usefulness: Views on Idealist and Relativist Managers Under Varying Conditions of Turbulence," *Journal of Business Ethics* 42 (2003): 237.

45. Alan L. Otten, "Ethics on the Job: Companies Alert Employees to Potential Dilemmas," *Wall Street Journal,* July 14, 1986, 25.

46. Gene R. Laczniak, "Framework for Analyzing Marketing Ethics," *Journal of Macromarketing* (Spring 1983): 7–18. See also Patricia Haddock and Marilyn Manning, "Ethically Speaking," *Sky* (March 1990): 128–31.

47. Saul W. Gellerman, "Managing Ethics from the Top Down," *Sloan Management Review* (Winter 1989): 73–79. For an interesting discussion of what management should do when charged with unethical actions see John A. Byrne, "Here's What to Do Next, Dow Corning," *BusinessWeek,* February 24, 1992, 33.

48. Samar Srivastava, "Sprint Drops Clients Over Excessive Inquiries," *Wall Street Journal,* July 7, 2007, A3.

49. "Special Report: SEC Follows Up on Sarbanes–Oxley Reform Standards," *Directors & Trustees Digest* 62, no. 3 (March 2003): 1.

50. John Schwartz, "Playing Know and Tell," *New York Times,* June 9, 2002, 4.2.

51. ———— "Enron Ruling to Stand" *New York Times,* November 22, 2006, 6.

CHAPTER 4

1. Ben Werner, "Restaurateur Was Once Struggling Under Racism, Lawsuits, Weak Sales" *Tribune Business News,* July 1, 2006, 1.

2. Sonia Alleyne Nicole Marie Richardson, "The 40 Best Companies for Diversity," *Black Enterprise* 36, no. 12 (July 2006): 100.

3. For a discussion of diversity issues in the United Kingdom, see Ian Dodds, "Differences Can Be Strengths," *People Management* (April 20, 1995): 40–43. For a list of companies well-known for their positive work in the area of diversity, see Roy S. Johnson, "The 50 Best Companies for Asians, Blacks and Hispanics," *Fortune* 138, no. 3 (August 3, 1998): 94–96.

4. Liz Winfeld and Susan Spielman, "Making Sexual Orientation Part of Diversity," *Training & Development* (April 1995): 50–51.

5. For an article describing the benefits of diversity management, see Mary Salomon and Joah Schork, "Turn Diversity to Your Advantage," *Research Technology Management* 46 (2003): 37.

6. Judith C. Giordan, "Valuing Diversity," *Chemical & Engineering News,* February 20, 1995, 40.

7. Ann M. Morrison, "Leadership Diversity as Strategy," in *The New Leaders: Guidelines on Leadership Diversity in America* (San Francisco: Jossey-Bass, 1992), 11–28.

8. Prem Benimadh, "Adding Value through Diversity," *Canadian Business Review* (Spring 1995): 6–11; Tara Parker-Pope, "Inside P&G, a Pitch to Keep Women Employees," *Wall Street Journal,* September 9,1998, B1.

9. Ann Pomeroy, "Cultivating Female Leaders," *HR Magazine* 52, no. 2 (February 2007): 44–51.

10. Frans Johansson, "Masters of the Multicultural" *Harvard Business Review* 83, no. 10 (October 2005): 18–19.

11. Jonathan Moules, "Benefits of Ethnic Diversity Doubted" *Financial Times* February 20, 2007, 4.

12. For a detailed look at the potential pitfalls of diversity management, see C. Von Bergen, Barlow Soper, and Teresa Foster, "Unintended Negative Effects of Diversity Management," *Public Personnel Management* 31 (2002): 239–252.

13. William B. Johnston and Arnold E. Packer, "Executive Summary," *Workforce 2000: Work and Workers for the Twenty-First Century* (Indianapolis: Hudson Institute, June 1987), xiii–xiv.

14. Roosevelt Thomas, "Affirmative Action or Affirming Diversity," *Harvard Business Review* (1990): 110.

15. ———, "Stereotyping Muslims? Know Your Facts," *Knight Ridder Tribune Business News,* June 17, 2006, p. 1.

16. Michele Himmelberg, "Age Discrimination Alleged," *Knight Ridder Tribune Business News* April 14, 2007.

17. Rosabeth Moss Kanter, *Men and Women of the Corporation* (New York: Basic Books, 1977).

18. Rosabeth Moss Kanter, "Numbers: Minorities and Majorities," in *Men and Women of the Corporation* (New York: Basic Books, 1977), 206–244. For a closer look at the effects of gender-role stereotypes, see N. Lane and N. Piercy, "The Ethics of Discrimination: Organizational Mindsets and Female Employment Disadvantage," *Journal of Business Ethics* 44 (2003): 313.

19. Ann M. Morrison, *Breaking the Glass Ceiling: Can Women Reach the Top of America's Largest Corporations?* (Reading, MA: Addison Wesley, 1992).

20. Annelies van Vianen and Agneta Fischer, "Illuminating the Glass Ceiling: The Role of Organizational Culture Preferences," *Journal of Occupational and Organizational Psychology* 75 (2002): 315.

21. Susan Webb, *Step Forward: Sexual Harassment in the Workplace* (New York: MasterMedia, 1991); Susan B. Garland, "Finally, a Corporate Tip Sheet on Sexual Harassment," *BusinessWeek,* July 13, 1998, 39; see also Maureen O'Connor, Barbara Gutek, Margaret Stockdale, Tracey Geer, and Renee Melancon, "Explaining Sexual Harassment Judgments: Looking Beyond Gender of the Rater," *Law and Human Behavior* 28 (2004): 69.

22. Charles B. Eldridge, Paula Park, Abbee Phillips, and Ellen Williams, "Execute Women in Finance," *The CPA Journal* 77, no. 1 (January 2007): 58–60.

23. Ella Bell, "The Bicultural Life Experience of Career Oriented Black Women," *Journal of Organizational Behavior* 11 (November 1990): 459–478.

24. For insights on how to manage older employees, see Carol Hymowitz, "Young Managers Learn How to Bridge the Gap with Older Employees," *Wall Street Journal,* July 21, 1998, B1.

25. Department of Labor Statistics, "Civilian Labor Force by Age, Sex, Race, and Hispanic Origin—1992, 2002, and Projected 2012," February 11, 2004.

26. Anonymous, "Time to Start Focusing on Attracting Older Workers," *HR Focus* 81, no. 2 (February 2004):13–14.

27. ———, "Companies May Lose Older Workers with Shortsighted Policies," *PR Newswire,* May 29, 2007.

28. Jeffrey Sonnenfeld, "Dealing with the Aging Workforce," *Harvard Business Review* 56 (1978): 81–92.

29. Frederick, Jim "Walgreen's New DC Breakthrough for Disabled" *Drug Store News* 29, no. 8 (June 25, 2007): 150.

30. William B. Johnston and Arnold E. Packer, "Executive Summary," *Workforce 2000: Work and Workers for the Twenty-First Century* (Indianapolis: Hudson Institute, June 1987): xii–xiv.

31. Patrick F. McKay, Derek R Avery, Scott Tonidandel, Mark A Morris, et al., "Racial Differences in Employee Retention: Are Diversity Climate Perceptions the Key?" *Personnel Psychology* 60, no.1 (Spring 2007): 35–62.

32. Jean Kim, "Issues in Workforce Diversity," Panel Presentation at the First Annual National Diversity Conference (San Francisco, May 1991).

33. *The Holy Bible,* Authorized King James Version (Nashville: Holman Bible Publishers, 1984).

34. J. Stewart Black and Hal B. Gregersen, "Serving Two Masters: Managing the Dual Allegiance of Expatriate Employees," *Sloan Management Review* (Summer 1992): 61–71.

35. Gwendolyn Combs, "Meeting the Leadership Challenge of a Diverse and Pluralistic Workplace: Implications of Self-Efficacy for Diversity Training," *Journal of Leadership and Organizational Studies* 8 (2002): 1.

36. Richard Lowther, "Embracing and Managing Diversity at Dell" *Strategic HR Review* 5, no. 6 (September/October 2006): 16–19.

37. Les Donaldson and Edward E. Scannell, *Human Resource Development: The New Trainer's Guide,* 2nd ed. (Reading, MA: Addison-Wesley, 1986), 8–9.

CHAPTER 5

1. Jonathan Birchall, "International sales lift Wal-Mart," *Financial Times,* November 15, 2006, 30.

2. William Hoffman, "Wal-Mart Losses Mount in Japan," *Traffic World,* August 22, 2006, 1.

3. For additional information on this topic, see Samuel C. Certo, *Human Relations Today: Concepts and Skills* (Chicago: Austen Press/Irwin, 1995), 352–375.

4. "Dossier: Telecommunications in Asia, Malaysia, Thailand," *International Business Newsletter,* June 1993, 12.

5. Jean J. Boddewyn, Brian Toyne, and Zaida L Martinez, "The Meanings of International Management," *Management International Review* 44, no. 2 (Second Quarter 2004): 195–212.

6. For a summary of recent developments in international management, see Steve Werner, "Recent Developments in International Management Research: A Review of 20 Top Management Journals," *Journal of Management* 28 (2002): 277.

7. Robert N. Lussier, Robert W. Baeder, and Joel Corman, "Measuring Global Practices: Global Strategic Planning Through Company Situational Analysis," *Business Horizons* 37 (September/October 1994): 56–63. For a detailed look at a successful internationally managed company, Hitachi Maxell, see Ray Moorcroft, "International Management in Action," *British Journal of Administrative Management* (March/April 2001): 12–13.

8. Alyssa A. Lappen, "Worldwide Connections," *Forbes,* June 27, 1988, 78–82.

9. Gale Eisenstodt, " 'We Are Happy,'" *Forbes,* May 8, 1995, 44–45.

10. Ben J. Wattenberg, "Their Deepest Concerns," *Business Month* (January 1988): 27–33; American Assembly of Collegiate Schools of Business, *Accreditation Council Policies, Procedures, and Standards* (St. Louis, MO: Assembly Collegiate School of America, 1990–92).

11. For additional information regarding various forms of organization based on international involvement, see Arvind Phatak, *International Dimensions of Management* (Boston: Kent, 1993).

12. "Nu Horizons Electronics," *Fortune,* June 13, 1994, 121. For an empirical study assessing the mobility of knowledge within a multinational corporation, see Anil K. Gupta and Vijay Govindarajan, "Knowledge Flows within Multinational Corporations," *Strategic Management Journal* 21, no. 4 (April 2000): 473–496.

13. U.S. Department of Commerce, *The Multinational Corporation: Studies on U.S. Foreign Investment* (Washington, DC: Government Printing Office).

14. Benjamin Gomes-Casseres, "Group versus Group: How Alliance Networks Compete," *Harvard Business Review* 72 (July/August 1994), 62–74.

15. Grover Starling, *The Changing Environment of Business* (Boston: Kent, 1980), 140.

16. This section is based primarily on Richard D. Robinson, *International Management* (New York: Holt, Rinehart & Winston, 1967), 3–5. For a focus on complexity related to differing ethical values of various societies, see Paul F. Buller, John J. Kohls, and Kenneth S. Anderson, "When Ethics Collide: Managing Conflicts Across Cultures," *Organizational Dynamics* 28, no. 4 (Spring 2000): 52–65.

17. 1971 Survey of National Foreign Trade Council, cited in Frederick D. Sturdivant, *Business and Society: A Managerial Approach* (Homewood, IL: Richard D. Irwin, 1977), 425.

18. Barrie James, "Reducing the Risks of Globalization," *Long Range Planning* 23 (February 1990): 80–88.

19. "NCR's Standard Contract Clause," *Harvard Business Review* 72 (May/June 1994): 125.

20. For a discussion of family adjustments as a major factor in expatriate failure, see Sandra L. Fisher, Michael E. Wasserman, and Jennifer Palthe, "Management Practices for On-Site Consultants: Lessons Learned from the Expatriate Experience," *Consulting Psychology Journal: Practice and Research* 59, no. 1 (March 2007): 17.

21. For an interesting article discussing the work relationship between expatriates and host-country nationals, see Charles M. Vance and Yongsun Paik, "Forms of Host-Country National Learning for Enhanced MNC Absorptive Capacity," *Journal of Managerial Psychology* 20, no. 7 (2005): 590–606.

22. Jan Selmer, "Cross-Cultural Training and Expatriate Adjustment in China: Western Joint Venture Managers," *Personnel Review* 34, no 1 (2005): 68–84.

23. For a look at challenges facing women expatriates, see Babita Mathur-Helm, "Expatriate Women Managers: At the Crossroads of Success, Challenges and Career Goals," *Women in Management Journal* 17 (2002): 18.

24. Brenda Paik Sunoo, "Loosening Up in Brazil," *Workforce* 3 (May 1998): 8–9.

25. Sergio Matviuk, "Cross-Cultural Leadership Behavior Expectations: A Comparison Between United States Managers and Mexican Managers," *Journal of American Academy of Business* 11, no. 1 (March 2007): 253–260.

26. For a review of the possible effects of repatriation, see Jobert E. Abueva, "Many Repatriations Fail, at Huge Cost to Companies," *New York Times,* May 17, 2000, E1; Margaret Linehan and Hugh Scullion, "The Repatriation of Female International Managers: An Empirical Study," *International Journal of Manpower* 23 (2002): 649.

27. David C. Martin and John J Anthony, "The Repatriation and Retention of Employees: Factors Leading to Successful Programs," *International Journal of Management* 23, no. 3 (September 2006): 620–631.

28. Roberta Maynard, "Importing Can Help a Firm Expand and Diversify," *Nation's Business* (January 1995): 11.

29. Karen Paul, "Fading Images at Eastman Kodak," *Business and Society Review* 48 (Winter 1984): 56.

30. G. Sam Samdani, "Mobil Develops a Way to Extract Hg from Gas Streams," *Chemical Engineering* 102 (April 1995): 17.

31. Leonard Berkowitz, "Supreme Court Says You Can License and Sue," *Research Technology Management* 50, no. 2 (March/April 2007): 9.

32. Robert Neff, "The Japanese Are Back—But There's a Difference," *BusinessWeek,* Industrial/Technology Edition, October 31, 1994, 58–59.

33. For insights on adding organizational value through international joint ventures, see Iris Berdrow and Henry Lane, "International Joint Ventures: Creating Value through Successful Knowledge Management," *Journal of World Business* 38 (2003): 15; see also Lifeng Geng, "Ownership and International Joint Ventures' Level of Expatriate Managers," *Journal of American Academy of Business* 4 (2004): 75.

34. Ken Korane, "Geo Metro: Economy Is Key," *Machine Design* 67 (April 6, 1995): 146–48.

35. Shyam Sunder, "Uniform Financial Reporting Standards," *The CPA Journal* 77, no. 4 (April 2007): 6, 8–9.

36. Francisco Granell, "The European Union's Enlargement Negotiations with Austria, Finland, Norway, and Sweden," *Journal of Common Market Studies* 33 (March 1995): 117–141; Jim Rollo, "EC Enlargement and the World Trade System," *European Economic Review* 39 (April 1995): 467–473. For a history surrounding the formation of NAFTA, see Richard N. Cooper, "The Making of NAFTA: How the Deal Was Done," *Foreign Affairs* 80, no. 3 (May/June 2001): 136.

37. For an interesting article discussing how NAFTA countries settle disputes among themselves, see John H. Knox, "The 2005 Activity of the NAFTA Tribunals," *The American Journal of International Law* 100, no. 2 (April 2006): 429–442.

38. Jim Mele, "Mexico in '95: From Good to Better," *Fleet Owner,* January 1995, 56–60; William C. Symonds, "Meanwhile, to the North, NAFTA Is a Smash," *BusinessWeek,* February 27, 1995, 66; Robert Selwitz, "NAFTA Expansion Possibilities," *Global Trade & Transportation,* October 1994, 17.

39. For an interesting account of organizing to go global, see Regina Fazio Maruca, "The Right Way to Go Global: An Interview with Whirlpool CEO David Whitwam," *Harvard Business Review* 72 (March/April 1994): 134–145.

40. Howard V. Perlmutter, "The Tortuous Evolution of the Multinational Corporation," *Columbia Journal of World Business* (January/February 1969): 9–18;

Rose Knotts, "Cross-Cultural Management: Transformations and Adaptations," *Business Horizons* (January/February 1989): 29–33.

41. Yan Tian, "Communicating with Local Publics: A Case Study of Coca-Cola's Chinese Web Site" *Corporate Communications* 11, no.1 (2006): 13–22.

42. Geert Hotstede, "Motivation, Leadership, and Organization: Do American Theories Apply Abroad?" *Organizational Dynamics* 9 (Summer 1980): 42–63.

43. Min-Huei Chien, "A Study of Cross Culture Human Resource Management in China," *The Business Review* 6, no. 2 (December 2006): 231–237.

44. Walter Sweet, "International Firms Strive for Uniform Nets Abroad," *Network World,* May 28, 1990, 35–36.

45. For further information about developing global organizations, see Philip Harris, "European Challenge: Developing Global Organizations," *European Business Review* 14 (2002): 416; see Jonathon Cummings, "Work Groups, Structural Diversity, and Knowledge Sharing in a Global Organization," *Management Science* 50 (2004): 352.

46. To gain a feel for the broad range of activities occurring at a transnational company such as Nestlé, see Joel Chernoff, "Advancing Corporate Governance in Europe," *Pensions & Investments,* June 12, 1995, 3, 37; E. Guthrie McTigue and Andy Sears, "The Safety 80," *Global Finance,* May 1995, 62–65; Robert W. Lear, "Whatever Happened to the Old-Fashioned Boss?" *Chief Executive,* April 1995, 71; Claudio Loderer and Andreas Jacobs, "The Nestlé Crash," *Journal of Financial Economics* 37 (March 1995): 315–339.

47. Byeong-Seon Yoon, "Who Is Threatening Our Dinner Table? The Power of Transnational Agribusiness," *Monthly Review* 58, no. 6 (November 2006): 56–64.

48. This section is mainly based on Thomas Donaldson, "Values in Tension: Ethics Away from Home," *Harvard Business Review* 74, no. 5 (September/October 1996): 48–62.

49. Anabelle Perez, "Sports Apparel Goes to Washington: New Sweatshop," *Sporting Goods Business* 30, no. 7 (May 12, 1997): 24.

50. Edward M. Mervosh and John S. McClenahen, "The Care and Feeding of Expats," *Industry Week* 246, no. 22 (December 1, 1977): 68–72.

51. Valerie Frazee, "Research Points to Weaknesses in Expat Policy," *Workforce* 3, no. 1 (January 1998): 9.

CHAPTER 6

1. This challenge case was based on Ed Welles, "Maggie Overfelt," *Fortune Small Business* 12, no. 7 (September 2002): 24–32; "Inside the Googleplex," *The Economist,* September, 1, 2007, 53.

2. Scott Shane and S. Venkataraman, "The Promise of Entrepreneurship as a Field of Research," *Journal of Management* 25, no. 1(2000): 217–226.

3. *Webster's College Dictionary* (New York: Random House, 1996).

4. Scott Shane, "Prior Knowledge and the Discovery of Entrepreneurial Opportunities," *Organization Science* 11, no 4 (2000): 448–469.

5. Robert Fairlie, "Kaufman Index of Entrepreneurial Activity," Ewing Marion Kauffman Foundation, 2005.

6. Scott Shane and S. Venkataraman, "The Promise of Entrepreneurship as a Field of Research," *Journal of Management* 25, no. 1(2000): 217–226.

7. Matt Hayward, Dean Shepherd, and Dale Griffin, "A Hubris Theory of Entrepreneurship," *Management Science* 52, no. 2 (2006): 160–172.

8. A. C. Cooper and C. M. Daily, "Entrepreneurial Teams," in D. L. Sexton and R. W. Smilor (Eds.), *Entrepreneurship* (Chicago: Upstart Publishing Company, 2000), 127–150.

9. G. N. Chandler and S. H. Hanks, "An Examination of the Substitutability of the Founds' Human and Financial Capital in Emerging Business Ventures," *Journal of Business Venturing* 13 (1998): 353–369.

10. D. Ucbasaran, A. Lockett, M. Wright, and P. Westhead, "Entrepreneurial Founder Teams: Factors Associated with Member Entry and Exit," *Entrepreneurship Theory & Practice,* 2003, 107–128.

11. C. M. Beckman, M. D. Burton, and C. O'Reilly, "Early Teams: The Impact of Team Demography on VC Financing and Going Public," *Journal of Business Venturing* 22 (2007): 147–173.

12. This discussion is based on J. Schumpeter, *Capitalism, Socialism, and Democracy* (New York: Harper & Row, 1934).

13. A. Weintraub, "Heart Trouble," *BusinessWeek,* October 29, 2007, 54.

14. Jonathan Eckhardt and Scott Shane, "Opportunities and Entrepreneurship," *Journal of Management* 29, no. 3 (2003): 333–349.

15. Scott Shane, "Prior Knowledge and the Discovery of Entrepreneurial Opportunities," *Organization Science* 11, no 4 (2000): 448–469; S. Venkataraman, "The Distinctive Domain of Entrepreneurship Research: An Editor's Perspective," in. J. Katz and R. Brockhaus (eds.), *Advances in*

Entrepreneurship, Firm Emergence, and Growth (Greenwich, CT: JAI Press, 1999).

16. Alexander Ardichvili, Richard Cardozo, and Sourav Ray, "A Theory of Entrepreneurial Identification and Development," *Journal of Business Venturing* 18 (2003): 105–123.

17. Alexander Ardichvili, Richard Cardozo, and Sourav Ray, "A Theory of Entrepreneurial Identification and Development," *Journal of Business Venturing* 18 (2003): 105–123; Scott Shane and S. Venkataraman, "The Promise of Entrepreneurship as a Field of Research," *Journal of Management* 25, no. 1(2000): 217–226.

18. G. Hills, G. T. Lumpkin, and R. P. Singh, "Opportunity Recognition: Perceptions and Behaviors of Entrepreneurs," *Frontiers of Entrepreneurship Research* (Wellesley, MA: Babson College, 1997), 203–218.

19. Alexander Ardichvili, Richard Cardozo, & Sourav Ray, "A Theory of Entrepreneurial Identification and Development," *Journal of Business Venturing* 18 (2003): 105–123.

20. Scott Shane, "Selling University Technology: Patterns from MIT," *Management Science* 48, no. 1 (2002): 122–137.

21. Andrew Corbett, "Experiential Learning Within the Process of Opportunity Identification and Exploitation," *Entrepreneurship Theory & Practice*, 2005, 473–491.

22. M. Csikszentmihalyi, *Creativity* (New York: HarperCollins, 1996).

23. For more information on feasibility analysis, see R. G. Wyckham and W. C. Wedley, "Factors Related to Venture Feasibility Analysis and Business Plan Preparation," *Journal of Small Business Management* 28 (1990): 48–59.

24. This section based on H. T. Keh, M. D. Foo, and B. C. Lim, "Opportunity Evaluation Under Risky Conditions: The Cognitive Processes of Entrepreneurs," *Entrepreneurship Theory & Practice*, 2002, 125–148.

25. For an exception, see L. W. Busenitz and J. B. Barney, "Differences Between Entrepreneurs and Managers in Large Organizations: Biases and Heuristics in Strategic Decision Making," *Journal of Business Venturing* 12, no. 1 (1997): 9–30.

26. E. J. Langer, "The Illusion of Control," *Journal of Personality and Social Psychology* 32, no. 2 (1975): 311–328.

27. Young Rok Choi and Dean Shepherd, "Entrepreneurs' Decisions to Exploit Opportunities," *Journal of Management* 30, no. 3 (2004): 377–395.

28. This discussion is based on Young Rok Choi and Dean Shepherd, "Entrepreneurs' Decisions to Exploit Opportunities," *Journal of Management* 30, no. 3 (2004): 377–395.

29. For a review of top management teams, see S. T. Certo, R. H. Lester, C. M. Dalton, and D. R. Dalton, "Top Management Team Demographics, Strategy, and Financial Performance: A Meta-Analytic Review," *Journal of Management Studies* 43 (2003): 813–839.

30. Stephen G. Morrissette, "A Profile of Angel Investors," *Journal of Private Equity* 10, no. 3 (2007): 52–66.

31. R. J. Gaston, *Finding Private Venture Capital for Your Firm: A Complete Guide* (New York: John Wiley, 1989).

32. Andrew Zacharakis, Jeffery McMullen, and Dean Shepherd, "Venture Capitalists' Decision Policies Across Three Countries: An Institutional Theory Perspective," *Journal of International Business Studies*, 38, 691–708.

33. Stephen G. Morrissette, "A Profile of Angel Investors," *Journal of Private Equity* 10, no. 3 (2007): 52–66.

34. P. Sharma and J. J. Chrisman. "Toward a Reconciliation of the Definitional Issues in the Field of Corporate Entrepreneurship," *Entrepreneurship Theory & Practice*, 1999, 23 no. 3 (1999): 11–27.

35. R. C. Wolcott and M. J. Lippitz, "The Four Models of Corporate Entrepreneurship," *MIT Sloan Management Review*, 2007, 75–82.

36. R. C. Wolcott and M. J. Lippitz, "The Four Models of Corporate Entrepreneurship," *MIT Sloan Management Review*, 2007, 75–82.

37. The discussion of these forms of corporate entrepreneurship are based on J. G. Covin and M. P. Miles, "Corporate Entrepreneurship and the Pursuit of Competitive Advantage," *Entrepreneurship Theory & Practice* 23, no. 3 (1999): 47–63; G. D. Dess, R. D. Ireland, S. A Zahra, S. W. Floyd, J. J Janney, and P. J. Lane, "Emerging Issues in Corporate Entrepreneurship," *Journal of Management* 29, no. 3 (2003): 351–378.

38. M. Troy, "Wal-Mart Tries on Fashionable New Look," *DSN Retailing Today* 45, no. 7 (April 10, 2006): 3–4.

39. J. Austin, H. Stevenson, and J. Wei-Skillern, "Social and Commercial Entrepreneurship: Same, Different, or Both?" *Entrepreneurship Theory & Practice*, 2006, 1–22.

40. J. Austin, H. Stevenson, and J. Wei-Skillern, "Social and Commercial Entrepreneurship: Same, Different, or Both?" *Entrepreneurship Theory & Practice*, 2006, 1–22.

41. P. Smith and E. Thurman, *A Billion Bootstraps* (New York: McGraw Hill, 2007).

42. A. M. Peredo and M. McLean, "Social Entrepreneurship: A Critical Review of the Concept," *Journal of World Business* 41 (2006): 56–65.

43. M. Sharir and M. Lerner, "Gauging the Success of Social Ventures Initiated by Individual Social Entrepreneurs," *Journal of World Business* 41 (2006): 6–20.

44. M. Sharir and M. Lerner, "Gauging the Success of Social Ventures Initiated by Individual Social Entrepreneurs," *Journal of World Business* 41 (2006): 6–20.

45. www.burgerking.com; and Jena McGregor, "Room & Board Plays Impossible to Get," *BusinessWeek*, October 1, 2007, 80.

CHAPTER 7

1. Bernard Simon, "VW 'returns to its roots' in US Automotive," *Financial Times*, February 13, 2007, 22; Stephen Power and Singer, Jason. "VW CEO's exit raises doubts on restructuring." *Wall Street Journal*, November 8, 2006, A3.

2. Harry Jones, *Preparing Company Plans: A Workbook for Effective Corporate Planning* (New York: Wiley, 1974), 3; Richard G. Meloy, "Business Planning," *The CPA Journal* 63, no. 8 (March 1998): 74–75.

3. Robert G. Reed, "Five Challenges Multiple-Line Companies Face," *Market Facts* (January/February 1990): 5–6. For a recent article on minimizing risk, see "Prior Planning Is Key to Averting a Crisis," *Investor Relations Business,* July 23, 2001, 8.

4. C. W. Roney, "The Two Purposes of Business Planning," *Managerial Planning* (November/December 1976): 1–6; Linda C. Simmons, "Plan. Ready. Aim," *Mortgage Banking* 56, no. 5 (February 1996): 95–96. For an interesting account of the planning function in an international setting, see Gabriel Ogunmokun, "Planning: An Exploratory Investigation of Small Business Organizations in Australia," *International Journal of Management* 15, no. 1 (March 1998): 60–71.

5. Wendy Zellner, "Moving Tofu into the Mainstream," *BusinessWeek* May 25, 1992, 94.

6. Harold Koontz and Cyril O'Donnell, *Management: A Systems and Contingency Analysis of Management Functions* (New York: McGraw-Hill, 1976), 130.

7. For an interesting discussion on how the importance of planning relates to even day-to-day operations, see Teri Lammers, "The Custom-Made Day Planner," *Inc.,* February 1992, 61–62.

8. For other benefits of planning, see Scott Ransom, "Planning Is Vital New Skill for Physician Executives," *Physician Executive* 29 (2003): 59.

9. For a recent article on how planning can yield the advantage of improved quality in organizations, see Z. T. Temtime, "The Moderating Impacts of Business Planning and Firm Size on Total Quality Management Practices," *The TQM Magazine* 15 (2003): 52; see also Anita Lee, "Early Planning for Hazards Bring Benefits to Biloxi," *Planning* 70 (2004): 51.

10. Kenneth R. Allen, "Creating and Executing a Business Plan," *American Agent & Broker* (July 1994): 20–21.

11. For a discussion of how improper planning might result in a competitive disadvantage, see Yolanda Sarason and Linda Tegarden, "The Erosion of the Competitive Advantage of Strategic Planning: A Configuration Theory and Resource-Based View," *Journal of Business and Management* 9 (2003): 1.

12. This exercise was based on J. E. Mathieu and W. Schulze, 2006, "The influence of team knowledge and formal plans on episodic team process—performance relationships," *Academy of Management Journal* 3, 605–619.

13. For a discussion of U.S. shortsightedness in planning, see Michael T. Jacobs, "A Cure for America's Corporate Short-Termism," *Planning Review* (January/February 1992): 4–9. For a discussion of the close relationship between objectives and planning, see "Mistakes to Avoid: From a Business Owner," *Business Owner* (September/October 1994): 11.

14. For an overview of strategic planning, see Bryan W. Barry, "A Beginner's Guide to Strategic Planning," *The Futurist* 32 no. 3 (April 1998): 33–36.

15. For an example of a subsystem, see Sherry D. Ryan and David A. Harrison, "Considering Social Subsystem Costs and Benefits in Information Technology Investment Decisions: A View from the Field on Anticipated Payoffs," *Journal of Management Information Systems* 16, no. 4 (Spring 2000): 11–40.

16. For an excellent resource on mission statements, see Jeffrey Abrahams, *101 Mission Statements from Top Companies* (Berkeley, CA: Ten Speed Press, 2007).

17. James F. Lincoln, "Intelligent Selfishness and Manufacturing," *Bulletin* 434 (New York: Lincoln Electric Company).

18. John F. Mee, "Management Philosophy for Professional Executives," *Business Horizons* (December 1956): 7.

19. David J. Campbell and David M. Furrer, "Goal Setting and Competition as Determinants of Task Performance," *Journal of Organizational Behavior* 16, no. 4 (July 1995): 377–390.

20. Peter F. Drucker, *The Practice of Management* (New York: Harper & Bros., 1954), 62–65, 126–29. For an interesting discussion on objectives and innovation, see Barton G. Tretheway, "Everything New Is Old Again," *Marketing Management* 7, no. 1 (Spring 1998): 4–13. For a recent tribute to Drucker, see A. J. Vogo, "Drucker, of Course," *Across the Board* 37, no. 10 (November/December 2000): 1.

21. Robert D. Hof, "Back to the Future at Yahoo!" *BusinessWeek*, July 2, 2007, 34.

22. Charles H. Granger, "The Hierarchy of Objectives," *Harvard Business Review* (May/June 1964): 64–74; Richard E. Kopelman, "Managing for Productivity: One-Third of the Job," *National Productivity Review* 17, no. 3 (Summer 1998): 1–2. Reprinted with the permission of American Management Association International. New York, NY. All rights reserved; see also Robert Kaplan and David Norton, "How Strategy Maps Frame an Organization's Objectives," *Financial Executive* 20 (2004): 40.

23. Geoffrey Moore, "To Succeed in the Long Term, Focus on the Middle Term," *Harvard Business Review* 85, no. 7/8 (2007): 84–91. For another excellent review underscoring the importance of time when forming objectives, see Piers Steel and Cornelius J. Konic, "Integrating Theories of Motivation," 2006, *The Academy of Management Review* 31, no. 4 (2006): 889–913.

24. Robert A. Guth, "Behind Microsoft's Bid to Gain Cutting Edge," *Wall Street Journal*, July 30, 2007, A1.

25. See also Mike Deblieux, "The Challenge and Value of Documenting Performance," *HR Focus* (March 1994): 3. To better understand the role of setting objectives in compensation plans, see William J. Liccione, "Effective Goal Setting: A Prerequisite for Compensation Plans with Incentive Value," *Compensation & Benefits Management* 13, no. 1 (Winter 1997): 19–25.

26. Robert L. Mathis and John H. Jackson, *Personnel: Human Resource Management* (St. Paul, MN: West Publishing, 1985), 353–355.

27. Harry Levinson, "Management by Whose Objectives?" *Harvard Business Review* 81 (2003): 107.

28. For an interesting examination of goal specificity, see Gerard H Seijts, Gary P Latham, Kevin Tasa, and Brandon W Latham, "Goal setting and goal orientation: An integration of two different literatures," *Academy of Management Journal* 47, no. 2(2004): 227–239.

29. Robert Rodgers and John E. Hunter, "Impact of Management by Objectives on Organizational Productivity," *Journal of Applied Psychology* (1991): 322–335; Jerry L. Rostund, "Evaluating Management Objectives with the Quality Loss Function," *Quality Progress* (August 1989): 45–49; Peter Crutchley, "Management by Objectives," *Credit Management* (May 1994): 36–38; William J. Kretlow and Winford E. Holland, "Implementing Management by Objectives in Research Administration," *Journal of the Society of Research Administrators* (Summer 1988): 135–141.

30. MBO deals with objectives that are designed based on input from both managers and workers. Nonetheless, some workers may have some subconscious objectives that are not known to managers. For an interesting examination of such goals, see Alexander D Stajkovic, Edwin A Locke, and Eden S Blair, "A First Examination of the Relationships Between Primed Subconscious Goals, Assigned Conscious Goals, and Task Performance," *Journal of Applied Psychology* 91, no. 5 (2006): 1172–1180.

31. Charles H. Ford, "Manage by Decisions, Not by Objectives," *Business Horizons* (February 1980): 17–18. For an interesting description of how firms in Sweden employ MBO, see Terry Ingham, "Management by Objectives—A Lesson in Commitment and Cooperation," *Managing Service Quality* 5, no. 6 (1995): 35–38.

32. Henry Mintzberg, "A New Look at the Chief Executive's Job," *Organizational Dynamics* (Winter 1973): 20–40. For a recent interview with Mintzberg, see Stephen Bernhut, "In Conversation: Henry Mintzberg," *Ivey Business Journal* 65, no. 1 (September/October 2000): 18–23.

33. Another aspect of planning involves understanding who might become the firm's next CEO, a process that is known as CEO succession planning. For an interesting article examining CEO succession planning in entrepreneurial firms, see James P Marshall, Ritch Sorenson, Keith Brigham, Elizabeth Wieling, Alan Reifman, and Richard S. Wampler, "The paradox for the family firm CEO: Owner age relationship to succession–related processes and plans," *Journal of Business Venturing* 21, no. 3 (2006): 348–368.

34. For similar questions focusing on strategic planning, see Hans Hinterhuber and Wolfgang Popp, "Are You a Strategist or Just a Manager?" *Harvard Business Review* (January/February 1992): 105–113. For an example of how a CEO plans organizational change, see Peter Spiegel, "Old Dog, New Tricks?" *Forbes*, June 1, 1998, 47.

35. James M. Hardy, *Corporate Planning for Nonprofit Organizations* (New York: Association Press, 1972), 37. For an interesting article that describes how CEOs gain assistance from their boards of directors, see David Ravasi and Alessandro Zattoni, "Exploring the Political Side of Board Involvement in Strategy: A Study of Mixed–Ownership Institutions," *Journal of Management Studies* 43, no. 8 (2006): 1671–1702.

36. For a better understanding of how chief executives interact with other members of a top management team, see Stephen A Miles and Michael D Watkins, "The Leadership Team: Complementary Strengths or Conflicting Agendas?" *Harvard Business Review* 85, no. 4 (2007): 90–98.

37. For a discussion of outside consultants who develop plans for business clients, see Donald F. Kuratko and Arnold Cirtin, "Developing a Business Plan for Your Clients," *National Public Accountant* (January 1990): 24–27.

38. In many organizations, individuals holding the title of either *president* or *chief operating officer (COO)* also have planning responsibilities. For an intriguing study examining the role of these individuals in the planning process, see Yan Zhang, "The presence of a separate COO/president and its impact on strategic change and CEO dismissal," *Strategic Management Journal* 27, no. 3 (2006): 283–300; and Nathan Bennett and Stephen Miles, "Second in Command: The Misunderstood Role of the Chief Operating Officer," *Harvard Business Review* 84, no. 5 (2006): 70–79.

39. John Chong and Jaesun Park, "National Culture and Classical Principles of Planning," *Cross Cultural Management* 10 (2003): 29.

40. The section "Qualifications of Planners" is adapted from John Argenti, *Systematic Corporate Planning* (New York: Wiley, 1974), 126. For an interesting look at the role of power and politics in the planning process, see Renee Berger, "People, Power, Politics," *Planning* 63, no. 2 (February 1997): 4–9.

41. Michael Muckian and Mary Auestad Arnold, "Manager, Appraise Thyself," *Credit Union Management* (December 1989): 26–28.

42. Edward J. Green, *Workbook for Corporate Planning* (New York: American Management Association, 1970).

43. Z. A. Malik, "Formal Long–Range Planning and Organizational Performance," Ph.D. diss. (Rensselaer Polytechnic Institute, 1974).

CHAPTER 8

1. Kelly Nolan, "Toys' New Power Players," *Retailing Today* 46, no. 2 (February 12, 2007): 23–28; Francesco Guerrera and James Politi, "A private dose of tough love," *Financial Times*, May 15, 2007, 29.

2. For an excellent discussion of various decisions that managers make, see Michael Verespej, "Gutsy Decisions of 1991," *Industry Week*, February 17, 1992, 21–31. For an interesting discussion of decision making in government agencies, see Burton Gummer, "Decision Making under Conditions of Risk, Ambiguity, and Uncertainty: Recent Perspectives," *Administration in Social Work* 2 (1998): 75–93.

3. Abraham Zaleznik, "What Makes a Leader?" *Success*, June 1989, 42–45; Daphne Main and Joyce C. Lambert, "Improving Your Decision Making," *Business and Economic Review* 44, no. 3 (April/June 1998): 9–12.

4. Mervin Kohn, *Dynamic Managing: Principles, Process, Practice* (Menlo Park, CA: Cummings, 1977), 38–62.

5. William H. Miller, "Tough Decisions on the Forgotten Continent," *Industry Week* (June 6, 1994): 40–44.

6. John Christy and Lauren Silva, "Financial Insight: Starbucks Looks for a Jolt," *Wall Street Journal*, July 30, 2007, C8.

7. Marcia V. Wilkof, "Organizational Culture and Decision Making: A Case of Consensus Management," *R&D Management* (April 1989): 185–199.

8. Charles Wilson and Marcus Alexis, "Basic Frameworks for Decision," *Academy of Management Journal* 5 (August 1962): 151–164. To better understand the role of ethics in decision making, see Roselie McDevitt, Catherine Giapponi, and Cheryl Tromley, "A Model of Ethical Decision Making: The Integration of Process and Content," *Journal of Business Ethics* 73, no. 2 (2007): 219–229.

9. For a discussion of the importance of understanding decision makers in organizations, see Walter D. Barndt Jr., "Profiling Rival Decision Makers," *Journal of Business Strategy*, January/February 1991, 8–11; see also Bard Kuvaas and Geir Kaufmann, "Impact of Mood, Framing, and Need for Cognition on Decision Makers' Recall and Confidence," *Journal of Behavioral Decision Making* 17 (2004): 59.

10. "New OCC Guidelines for Appraising Management," *Issues in Bank Regulation*, Fall 1989, 20–22. For an interesting discussion of decision-making processes used in the United States versus those used in the United Kingdom, see Mark Andrew Mitchell, Ronald D. Taylor, and Faruk Tanyel, "Product Elimination Decisions: A Comparison of American and British Manufacturing Firms," *International Journal of Commerce & Management* 8, no. 1 (1998): 8–27.

11. For an extended discussion of this model, see William B. Werther Jr., "Productivity Through People: The Decision-Making Process," *Management Decisions*, 1988, 37–41.

12. These assumptions are adapted from James G. March and Herbert A. Simon, *Organizations* (New York: Wiley, 1958), 137–138.

13. William C. Symonds, "There's More Than Beer in Molson's Mug," *Business Week*, February 10, 1992, 108.

14. Chester I. Barnard, *The Function of the Executive* (Cambridge, MA: Harvard University Press, 1938).

15. For further elaboration on these factors, see Robert Tannenbaum, Irving R. Weschle, and Fred Massarik, *Leadership and Organization: A Behavioral Science Approach* (New York: McGraw-Hill, 1961), 277–278.

16. For more discussion of these factors, see F. A. Shull Jr., A. I. Delbecq, and L. L. Cummings, *Organizational Decision Making* (New York: McGraw-Hill, 1970).

17. For a worthwhile discussion of forecasting and evaluating the outcomes of alternatives, see J. R. C. Wensley, "Effective Decision Aids in Marketing," *European Journal of Marketing* (1989): 70–79.

18. This discussion was based on Ilan Yaniv and Maxim Milyavsky, "Using advice from multiple sources to revise and improve judgments," *Organizational Behavior and Human Decision Processes* 103, no. 1 (2007): 104–120. For more information about using the advice of others when making decisions, see Silvia Bonaccio and Reeshad S. Dalal, "Advice taking and decision-making: An integrative literature review, and implications for the organizational sciences," *Organizational Behavior and Human Decision Processes* 101, no. 2 (2006): 127–151.

19. H. A. Simon, *Models of Man: Social and Rational* (New York: Wiley, 1957).

20. K. E. Stanovich and R. F. West, "Individual differences in reasoning: Implications for the rationality debate," in T. Gilovich, D. Griffin, and D. Kahneman (Eds.), *Heuristics and Biases: The Psychology of Intuitive Judgment* (Cambridge: Cambridge University Press, 2002); Daniel Kahneman, "A Perspective on Judgment and Choice," *American Psychologist* 58, no. 9: 697–720. See also Jonathan St. B. T. Evans, 2008, "Dual-Processing Accounts of Reasoning, Judgment, and Social Cognition," *Annual Review of Psychology*, In press.

21. Erik Dane and Michael G. Pratt, "Exploring Intuition and Its Role in Managerial Decision Making," *Academy of Management Review* 32 (2007): 33–54.

22. Frank Knight, *Risk, Uncertainty, and Profit,* (Boston: Houghton Mifflin, 1921).

23. Truman F. Bewley, "Knightian Decision Theory, Part I," *Decisions in Economics and Finance* 25, no. 2 (2002): 79–110.

24. Steven C. Harper, "What Separates Executives from Managers," *Business Horizons* (September/October 1988): 13–19; to better understand the negative influence of poor decision making, see Joseph L Bower and Clark G Gilbert, "How Managers' Everyday Decisions Create or Destroy Your Company's Strategy," *Harvard Business Review* 85, no. 2 (2007): 72–79.

25. The scope of this text does not permit elaboration on these three decision-making tools. However, for an excellent discussion on how they are used in decision making, see Richard M. Hodgetts, *Management: Theory, Process and Practice* (Philadelphia: Saunders, 1975), 234–266.

26. For more information on probability theory and decisions, see Johannes Honekopp, "Precision of Probability Information and Prominence of Outcomes: A Description and Evaluation of Decisions Under Uncertainty," *Organizational Behavior and Human Decision Processes* 90 (2003): 124.

27. Richard C. Mosier, "Expected Value: Applying Research to Uncertainty," *Appraisal Journal* (July 1989): 293–296. See also Amartya Sen, "The Formulation of Rational Choice," *American Economic Review* 84 (May 1994): 385–390. For an illustration of how probability theory can be applied to solve personal problems, see Jeff D. Opdyke, "'Will My Nest Egg Last?'— Probability Theory, an Old Math Technique, Is Providing New—and Better— Answers to That Question," *Wall Street Journal,* June 5, 2000, 7.

28. For an example of how financial analysts use decision trees to reduce risk, see Joseph J. Mezrich, "When Is a Tree a Hedge?" *Financial Analysts Journal* 50, no. 6 (November/December 1994): 75–81.

29. John F. Magee, "Decision Trees for Decision Making," *Harvard Business Review* (July/August 1964). To better understand the relationships among decision trees, firm strategy, and financial analysis, see Michael Brydon, "Evaluating Strategic Options Using Decision-Theoretic Planning," *Information and Technology Management* 7, no. 1 (2006): 35–49.

30. Rakesh Sarin and Peter Wakker, "Folding Back in Decision Tree Analysis," *Management Science* 40 (May 1994): 625–628; Eric H. Sorensen, Keith L. Miller, and Chee K. Ooi, "The Decision Tree Approach to Stock Selection," *Journal of Portfolio Management* 27, no. 1 (Fall 2000): 42–52.

31. For a discussion of how decision trees can relate to ethics, see Constance Bagley, "The Ethical Leader's Decision Tree," *Harvard Business Review* 2 (2003): 18.

32. This section is based on Samuel C. Certo, *Supervision: Quality and Diversity Through Leadership* (Homewood, IL: Austen Press/Irwin, 1994), 198–202. See also Norbert L. Kerr and R. Scott Tindale, "Group Performance and Decision Making," *Annual Review of Psychology* 55 (2004): 623–655.

33. Clark Wigley, "Working Smart on Tough Business Problems," *Supervisory Management* (February 1992): 1.

34. Ferda Erdem, "Optimal Trust and Teamwork: From Groupthink to Teamthink," *Work Study* 52 (2003): 229.

35. Matthew Karnitschnig, "News Corp.'s Success Follows Delicate Dance Between Suitor and Target," *Wall Street Journal*, August 1, 2007, A1.

36. Joseph Alan Redman, "Nine Creative Brainstorming Techniques," *Quality Digest*, August 1992, 50–51.

37. For more information on idea generation, see Merry Baskin, "Idea Generation," *Brand Strategy* 172 (2003): 35.

38. David M. Armstrong, "Management by Storytelling," *Executive Female*, May/June 1992, 38–41.

39. Philip L. Roth, L. F. Lydia, and Fred S. Switzer, "Nominal Group Technique— An Aid for Implementing TQM," *CPA Journal,* May 1995, 68–69; Karen L. Dowling, "Asynchronous Implementation of the Nominal Group Technique: Is It effective?" *Decision Support Systems* 29, no. 3 (October 2000): 229–248.

40. N. Delkey, *The Delphi Method: An Experimental Study of Group Opinion* (Santa Monica, CA: Rand Corporation, 1969); Gene Rowe and George Wright, "The Delphi Technique as a Forecasting Tool: Issues and Analysis," *International Journal of Forecasting* 15, no. 4 (October 1999).

41. This case was based on Nick Wingfield, "Microsoft's Videogame Efforts Take a Costly Hit," *Wall Street Journal*, July 6, 2007, A3.

CHAPTER 9

1. This challenge case was based on James Covert, "Earnings Digest: Barnes & Noble Swings to a Loss," *Wall Street Journal*, May 25, 2007, B5; Mya Frazier, "Just You, Me, and Barnes & Noble," *Advertising Age* 78, no. 21(May 21, 2007): 16; Jim Milliot, "Chains Call Market Most Challenging Ever," *Publishers Weekly* 254, no. 15 (April 9, 2007): 4.

2. To better understand the different dimensions of strategic planning, see Peter Brews and Devavrat Purohit, "Strategic Planning in Unstable Environments," *Long Range Planning* 40 (2007): 64–83.

3. For an article on the importance of strategic planning, see Sarah Kaplan and Eric Beinhocker, "The Real Value of Strategic Planning," *MIT Sloan Management Review* 44 (2003): 71. To better understand the influence of strategic planning in developing countries, see Jose Santos, "Strategy Lessons from Left Field," *Harvard Business Review*, 2007, 20–21.

4. Tony Grundy and Dave King, "Using Strategic Planning to Drive Strategic Change," *Long-Range Planning* (February 1992): 100–108. For reasons why strategic thinking matters more to managers now than ever before, see Keith H. Hammonds, "Michael Porter's Big Ideas," *Fast Company*, March 2001, 150–156. For an interesting discussion of strategic planning in the context of service firms, see Povl Larsen, Richard Tonge, and Alan Lewis, "Strategic Planning and Design in the Service Sector," *Management Decision* 45, no. 2 (2007): 180–195.

5. Dyan Machan, "The Strategy Thing," *Forbes,* May 23, 1994, 113–114. For an example of a successful business strategy, see Laura Haller, "Target Reiterates Stable Strategy," *DSN Retailing Today,* June 4, 2001, 6.

6. For a detailed discussion of strategy formulation in small family-owned businesses, see Nancy Drozdow and Vincent P. Carroll, "Tools for Strategy Development in Family Firms," *Sloan Management Review* 39, no. 1 (Fall 1997): 75–88; see also Michael Beer and Russell Eisenstat, "How to Have an Honest Conversation about Your Business Strategy," *Harvard Business Review* 82 (2004): 82.

7. This section is based on Samuel C. Certo and J. Paul Peter, *Strategic Management: Concepts and Applications* (Chicago: Austin Press/Irwin, 1995), 3–27.

8. Samuel C. Certo and J. Paul Peter, *The Strategic Management Process*, 4th ed. (Chicago: Austen Press/Irwin, 1995), 32; William Drohan, "Principles of Strategic Planning," *Association Management* 49, no. 1 (January 1997): 85–87. For a recent study examining the interaction between organizations and environment, see Max Boisot and John Child, "Organizations as Adaptive Systems in Complex Environments: The Case of China," *Organization Science* 10, no. 3 (May/June 1999): 237–252.

9. This section is based on William F. Glueck and Lawrence R. Jauch, *Business Policy and Strategic Management* (New York: McGraw-Hill, 1984), 99–110.

10. John F. Watkins, "Retirees as a New Growth Industry? Assessing the Demographic and Social Impact," *Review of Business* (Spring 1994): 9–14.

11. Inga S. Baird, Marjorie A. Lyles, and J. B. Orris, "The Choice of International Strategies by Small Businesses," *Journal of Small Business Management* 32, no. 1 (January 1994): 48–60.

12. This discussion of Porter's model is based on chapters 1 and 2 of Porter's *Competitive Strategy* (New York: The Free Press, 1980); and chapter 1 of Porter's *Competitive Advantage: Creating and Sustaining Superior Performance* (New York: The Free Press, 1985). For an application of Porter's concepts, see William P. Munk and Barry Shane, "Using Competitive Analysis Models to Set Strategy in the Northwest Hardboard Industry," *Forest Products Journal* (July/August 1994): 11–18.

13. This research highlight is based on Vilmos Misangyi, Heather Elms, Thomas Grekhamer, and Jeffrey Lepine, "A New Perspective on a Fundamental Debate: A Multilevel Approach to Industry, Corporate, and Business Unit Effects," *Strategic Management Journal* 27, 571–590.

14. M. Klemm, S. Sanderson, and G. Luffman, "Mission Statements: Selling Corporate Values to Employees," *Long-Range Planning* (June 1991): 73–78. For a recent review of effective mission statements, see Shirleen Holt, "Mission Possible," *BusinessWeek,* August 16, 1999, F12.

15. Forest David and Fred Davis, "It's Time to Redraft Your Mission Statement," *Journal of Business Strategy* 24 (2003): 11.

16. Colin Coulson-Thomas, "Strategic Vision or Strategic Cons: Rhetoric or Reality," *Long-Range Planning* (February 1992): 81–89; Rhymer Rigby, "Mission Statements," *Management Today* (March 1998): 56–58; Jeffrey Abrahams, *101 Mission Statements from Top Companies* (Berkeley, CA: Ten Speed Press, 2007).

17. For an interesting discussion of holding leaders accountable for attaining the objective of developing organizational integrity as a strategic asset, see Joseph A. Petrick and John F. Quinn, "The Challenge of Leadership Accountability for Integrity Capacity as a Strategic Asset," *Journal of Business Ethics* 34 (2001): 331–343.

18. This section is based primarily on Thomas H. Naylor and Kristin Neva, "Design of a Strategic Planning Process," *Managerial Planning* (January/February 1980): 2–7; Donald W. Mitchell, "Pursuing Strategic Potential," *Managerial Planning* (May/June 1980): 6–10; Benton E. Gup, "Begin Strategic Planning by Asking Three Questions," *Managerial Planning* (November/December 1979): 28–31, 35; Rainer Feurer and Kazem Chaharbaghi, "Dynamic Strategy Formulation and Alignment," *Journal of General Management* 20, no. 3 (Spring 1995): 76–91.

19. For a practical example of SWOT applied in the business world, see Robert H. Woods, "Strategic Planning: A Look at Ruby Tuesday," *Cornell Hotel & Restaurant Administration Quarterly* (June 1994): 41–49; for a review of the advantages of SWOT analysis, see George Panagiotou, "Bringing SWOT into Focus," *Business Strategy Review* 14 (2003): 8.

20. Philip Kotler, *Marketing Management Analysis, Planning and Control,* 7th ed. (Upper Saddle River, NJ: Prentice Hall, 1991), 39–41.

21. See also J. Scott Armstrong and Roderick J. Brodie, "Effects of Portfolio Planning Methods on Decision Making: Experimental Results," *International Journal of Research in Marketing* (January 1994): 73–84; For an interesting description of how firms alter their product portfolios over time, see Chris Zook, "Finding Your Next CORE Business," *Harvard Business Review* 85, no. 4 (2007): 66–75.

22. For an interesting summary of the research examining Porter's generic strategies, see John A. Parnell, "Generic Strategies After Two Decades: A Reconceptualization of Competitive Strategy," *Management Decision* 44, no. 8 (2006): 1139–1154.

23. Ian C. MacMillan, Donald C. Hambrick, and Diana L. Day, "The Product Portfolio and Profitability—A PIMS-Based Analysis of Industrial-Product Businesses," *Academy of Management Journal* (December 1982): 733–755. For more information on establishing growth businesses, see Jeffrey G. Covin and Morgan P. Miles, "Strategic Use of Corporate Venturing," *Entrepreneurship Theory and Practice* 31, no. 2 (2007): 183–207.

24. Walecia Konrad and Bruce Einhorn, "Famous Amos Gets a Chinese Accent," *BusinessWeek,* September 28, 1992, 76.

25. Doron P. Levin, "Westinghouse's New Chief Aims to Push New Lines, Revitalize Traditional Ones," *Wall Street Journal,* November 28, 1983, 10.

26. For a practical discussion of strategy implementation, see Brooke Dobni, "Creating a Strategy Implementation Environment," *Business Horizons* 46 (2003): 43.

27. William Sandy, "Avoid the Breakdowns Between Planning and Implementation," *Journal of Business Strategy* (September/October 1991): 30–33.

28. Thomas V. Bonoma, "Making Your Marketing Strategy Work," *Harvard Business Review* (March/April 1984): 69–76. For an article illustrating the importance of strategy implementation, see Loizos Heracleous, "The Role of Strategy Implementation in Organization Development," *Organization Development Journal* 18, no. 3 (Fall 2000): 75–86.

29. For other useful articles on strategic control, see William B. Carper and Terry A. Bresnick, "Strategic Planning Conferences," *Business Horizons* (September/October 1989): 34–40; Stephen Bungay and Michael Goold, "Creating a Strategic Control System," *Long-Range Planning* (June 1991): 32–39; for a useful article on strategic control, see Pierre Kunsch, Alain Chevalier, and Jean-Pierre Brans, "A Framework for Strategic Control and Planning in Corporate Organizations," *Central European Journal of Operations Research* 10 (2002): 45.

30. For a detailed discussion of the characteristics of strategic and tactical planning, see George A. Steiner, *Top Management Planning* (Toronto, Canada: Collier-Macmillan, 1969), 37–39.

31. Russell L. Ackoff, *A Concept of Corporate Planning* (New York: Wiley, 1970), 4.

32. "The New Breed of Strategic Planner," *BusinessWeek,* September 17, 1984, 62–67.

33. This exercise was based in part on Marc Gunther, "Hard News," *Fortune,* August 6, 2007, 80–85.

CHAPTER 10

1. This Challenge Case was based on David Kiley, "The New Heat on Ford," *BusinessWeek,* June 4, 2007, 32–38 ; Bernard Simon, "Ford disposal marks an admission of failure," *Financial Times,* March 13, 2007, 20.

2. Charles B. Ames, "Straight Talk from the New CEO," *Harvard Business Review* (November/December 1989): 132–138.

3. Fremont E. Kast and James E. Rosenzweig, *Organization and Management: A Systems Approach* (New York: McGraw-Hill, 1970), 443–449. For a classic discussion on expanding this list of characteristics to 13, see P. LeBreton and D. A. Henning, *Planning Theory* (Upper Saddle River, NJ: Prentice Hall, 1961), 320–344. These authors list the dimensions of a plan as (1) complexity, (2) significance, (3) comprehensiveness, (4) time, (5) specificity, (6) completeness, (7) flexibility, (8) frequency, (9) formality, (10) confidential nature, (11) authorization, (12) ease of implementation, and (13) ease of control.

4. Jennifer A. Knight, "Loss Control Solution to Limiting Costs of Workplace Violence," *Corporate Cashflow* (July 1994): 16–17.

5. Gary McWilliams, "Wal-Mart to Crack Down on Young Shoplifters," *Wall Street Journal,* July 11, 2007, B4.

6. Kirkland Wilcox and Richard Discenza, "The TQM Advantage," *CA Magazine,* May 1994, 37–41.

7. This highlight was based on Karen Schnatterly, "Increasing Firm Value through Detection and Prevention of White-Collar Crime," *Strategic Management Journal* 24 (2003): 587–614. For more information on white-collar crime, see Gerhard Blickle, Alexander Schlegel, Pantaleon Fassbender, and Uwe Klein, "Some Personality Correlates of Business White-Collar Crime," *Applied Psychology* 55, no. 2 (2006): 220–233.

8. From "Seize the Future—Make Top Trends Pay Off Now," *Success* (March 1990): 39–45.

9. For an interesting article outlining the ethical and cultural challenges involved with budgeting, see Patricia Casey Douglas and Benson Wier, "Cultural and Ethical Effects in Budgeting Systems: A Comparison of U.S. and Chinese Managers," *Journal of Business Ethics* 60, no. 2 (2005): 159–174.

10. Kjell A. Ringbakk, "Why Planning Fails," *European Business* (July 1970). See also William G. Gang, "Strategic Planning and Competition: A Survival Guide for Electric Utilities," *Fortnightly,* February 1, 1994, 20–23.

11. For information that ranks U.S. cities on the possible site selection criterion of growth, see John Case, "Where the Growth Is," *Inc.,* June 1991, 66–79. See also Walt Yesberg, "Get a Grip on Building Costs," *ABA Banking Journal* 82 (March 1990): 90, 92.

12. Douglas P. Woodward, "Locational Determinants of Japanese Manufacturing Start-Ups in the United States," *Southern Economic Journal* (January 1992): 690–708.

13. Tom Murphy, "Toyota Redefines JIT with Tundra Program," *Ward's AutoWorld* 43, no. 7 (2007): 24.

14. Greg Nakanishi, "Building Business Through Partnerships," *HR Magazine,* June 1991, 108–112. For an interesting description of a company that performs human resource planning for other companies, see Eryn Brown, "PeopleSoft: Tech's Latest Publicly Traded Cult," *Fortune,* May 25, 1998, 155–156. For a study assessing the importance of human resource planning, see Senga Briggs and William Keogh, "Integrating Human Resource Strategy and Strategic Planning to Achieve Business Excellence," *Total Quality Management* 10, no. 4/5 (July 1999): S447–453.

15. For further ideas on the implementation of human resources planning, see Nen-Chen Hwang and Konstantin Kogan, "Dynamic Approach to Human Resources Planning for Major Professional Companies with a Peak-Wise Demand," *International Journal of Production Research* 41 (2003): 1255.

16. Jan Cienski and Christopher Condon, "Eastern Europe Hit by Shortage of Workers," *Financial Times*, June 5, 2007, 10.

17. Charles F. Kettering, "A Glimpse at the Future," *Industry Week* (July 1, 1991): 34.

18. Joanne Tokle and Dennis Krumwiede, "An Overview of Forecasting Error Among International Manufacturers," *Journal of International Business Research* 5, no. 2 (2006): 97–105.

19. William C. House, "Environmental Analysis: Key to More Effective Dynamic Planning," *Managerial Planning* (January/February 1977): 25–29. The basic components of this forecasting method, as well as of other methods, are discussed in Chaman L. Jain, "How to Determine the Approach to Forecasting," *Journal of Business Forecasting Methods & Systems* (Summer 1995): 2, 28. For information about software applications designed to help companies in their planning and forecasting, see Anonymous, "Planning and Forecasting," *Financial Executive* 17, no. 3 (May 2001): 14–15.

20. Marshall L. Fisher et al., "Making Supply Meet Demand in an Uncertain World," *Harvard Business Review* (May/June 1994): 83–89; Tony Dear, "Fast and Slow Approaches to Sales Forecasting," *Logistics Focus* 6, no. 4 (May 1998): 24–25.

21. Olfa Hemler, "The Uses of Delphi Techniques in Problems of Educational Innovations," no. 8499, RAND Corporation, December 1966. For an interesting article employing the Delphi method to analyze international trends, see Michael R. Czinkota and Ilkka A. Ronkainen, "International Business and Trade in the Next Decade: Report from a Delphi Study," *Journal of International Business Studies* 28, no. 4 (Fourth Quarter 1997): 827–844.

22. James E. Cox Jr., "Approaches for Improving Salespersons' Forecasts," *Industrial Marketing Management* 18 (November 1989): 307–311; Jack Stack, "A Passion for Forecasting," *Inc.*, November 1997, 37–38. For more information on forecasting, see Nassim N. Taleb, *The Black Swan: The Impact of the Highly Improbable* (New York: Random House, 2007).

23. For an application of time series analysis, see Lester Hunt and Yasushi Ninomiya, "Unraveling Trends and Seasonality: A Structural Time Series Analysis of Transport Oil Demand in the UK and Japan," *Energy Journal* 24 (2003): 63.

24. N. Carroll Mohn, "Forecasting Sales with Trend Models—Coca-Cola's Experience," *Journal of Business Forecasting* 8 (Fall 1989): 6–8. For an interesting article that describes the use of time series analysis in predicting the alcohol consumption of Europeans, see David E. Smith and Hans S. Solgaard, "Global Trends in European Alcoholic Drinks Consumption," *Marketing and Research Today* 26, no. 2 (May 1998): 80–85. For a historical perspective of time series analysis, see D. S. G. Pollock, "Statistical Visions in Time: A History of Time Series Analysis, 1662–1938," *Economica* 67, no. 267 (August 2000): 459–461.

25. For information on product life cycles, see George S. Day, "The Product Life Cycle: Analysis and Applications Issues," *Journal of Marketing* 45, no. 4 (1981): 60–67; David Rink and Harold Fox, "Using the Product Life Cycle Concept to Formulate Actionable Purchasing Strategies," *Singapore Management Review* 25 (2003): 73; see also Kuang-Jung Tseng, "Application of Thermodynamics on Product Life Cycle," *Journal of American Academy of Business* 4 (2004): 464.

26. For elaboration on these methods, see George A. Steiner, *Top Management Planning* (London: Collier-Macmillan, 1969), 223–227.

27. This discussion and accompanying table is based on Teresa M. McCarthy, Donna F. Davis, Susan L. Golicic, and John T. Mentzer, "The Evolution of Sales Forecasting Management: A 20-Year Longitudinal Study of Forecasting Practices," *Journal of Forecasting* 25 (2006): 303–324.

28. James Wilson, "Gantt Charts: A Centenary Appreciation," *European Journal of Operational Research* 149 (2003): 430. To better understand the sensitivity of Gantt charts, see S. A. Oke and O. E. Charles-Owaba, "A sensitivity analysis of an optimal Gantt charting maintenance scheduling model," *The International Journal of Quality & Reliability Management* 23, no. 2/3 (2006): 197–229.

29. Willard Fazar, "The Origin of PERT," *The Controller* (December 1962). For a discussion of software packages that draw preliminary PERT and Gantt charts, see Pat Sweet, "A Planner's Best Friend?" *Accountancy* (February 1994): 56, 58. Also see Curtis F. Franklin Jr., "Project Managers Toolbox," *CIO* 11, no. 2 (October 15, 1997): 64–70. For an extension of the Gantt chart, see Harvey Maylor, "Beyond the Gantt Chart: Project Management Moving On," *European Management Journal* 19, no. 1 (February 2001): 92–100.

30. See also H. M. Soroush, "The Most Critical Path in a PERT Network," *Journal of the Operational Research Society* 45 (March 1994): 287–300.

31. For insights about using PERT, see Jose Perez, Salvador Rambaud, and Jose Velasco, "Some Indications to Correctly Use Estimations of an Expert in the PERT Methodology," *Central European Journal of Operations Research* 11 (2003): 183. To better understand the dynamics involved with PERT, see Amir Azaron and Reza Tavakkoli-Moghaddam, "Multi-objective time-cost trade-off in dynamic PERT networks using an interactive approach," *European Journal of Operational Research* 180, no. 3 (2007): 1186–1200.

32. Avraham Shrub, "The Integration of CPM and Material Management in Project Management," *Construction Management and Economics* 6 (Winter 1988): 261–272; Michael A. Hatfield and James Noel, "The Case for Critical Path," *Cost Engineering* 40, no. 3 (March 1998): 17–18.

33. For extended discussion of these steps, see Edward K. Shelmerdine, "Planning for Project Management," *Journal of Systems Management* 40 (January 1989): 16–20.

34. This exercise was based on: Nick Wingfield, "Microsoft's Videogame Efforts Take a Costly Hit," *Wall Street Journal*, July 6, 2007, A3.

CHAPTER 11

1. Marc Gunther, "The Welshman, the Walkman, and the Salarymen," *Fortune*, June 12, 2006, 70–83.

2. A. Tacket, "Organizing and Organizations: An Introduction," *The Journal of the Operational Research Society* 53 (2002): 1401.

3. Douglas S. Sherwin, "Management of Objectives," *Harvard Business Review* (May/June 1976): 149–160. See also Lloyd Sandelands and Robert Drazin, "On the Language of Organization Theory," *Organizational Studies* 10 (1989): 457–77.

4. Tim Peakman, "Organizing the Organization," *Drug Discovery Today* 8 (2003): 673.

5. For a discussion emphasizing the importance of continually adapting organization structure, see Michael A. Vercspej, "When Change Becomes the Norm," *Industry Week*, March 16, 1992, 35–36.

6. Betsy Morris, "The GE Mystique," *Fortune* (March 6, 2006): 98–102.

7. Saul W. Gellerman, "In Organizations, as in Architecture, Form Follows Function," *Organizational Dynamics* 18 (Winter 1990): 57–68.

8. For an example of how organizing principles can be applied to the educational arena, see A. Georges Romme, "Organizing Education by Drawing on Organization Studies," *Organization Studies* 24 (2003): 697.

9. Max Weber, *Theory of Social and Economic Organization*, trans. and ed. A. M. Henderson and Talcott Parsons (London: Oxford University Press, 1947); Thomas A. Stewart, "Get with the New Power Game," *Fortune*, January 13, 1997, 58–62.

10. Sandra T. Gray, "Fostering Leadership for the New Millennium," *Association Management* (January 1995): L78–L82.

11. David Courpasson and Stewart Clegg, "Dissolving the Iron Cages? Tocqueville, Michels, Bureaucracy and the Perpetuation of Elite Power," *Organization* 13 (2006): 319–343.

12. Example based on Pui-Wing Tam, "System Reboot—Hurd's Big Challenge at HP: Overhauling Corporate Sales," *Wall Street Journal*, April 3, 2006, A1.

13. For a review focusing on division of labor, see "Division of Labor Welcomed," *Business Insurance* 34, no. 10 (March 6, 2000): 8.

14. Jeff Lewis and Walter Knott, "Division of Labor: To Gain the Benefits of a Team, Each Member Can't Do Everything," *On Wall Street*, August 1, 2003, 1.

15. Example based on "Painting by Numbers: China's Art Business," *The Economist*, June 10, 2006, 77.

16. Carol Ann Dorn, "Einstein: Still No Equal," *Journal of Business Strategy* (November/December 1994): 20–23.

17. C. R. Walker and R. H. Guest, *The Man on the Assembly Line* (Cambridge, MA: Harvard University Press, 1952). For an excellent example of how technology can affect division of labor, see John P. Walsh, "Technological Change and the Division of Labor: The Case of Retail Meatcutters," *Work and Occupations* 16 (May 1989): 165–183.

18. J. Mooney, "The Principles of Organization," in *Ideas and Issues in Public Administration*, ed. D. Waldo (New York: McGraw-Hill, 1953), 86. See also Peter Jackson, "Speed versus Heed," *CA Magazine*, November 1994, 56–57. For an application of the coordination principle, see Gail Karet and Tim Studt, "Managing Biotech Requires Cross-Functional Coordination," *Research & Development* 43, no. 3 (March 2001): 12–17; see also Jody Gittell and Leigh Weiss, "Coordination Networks Within and Across Organizations: A Multi-Level Framework," *The Journal of Management Studies* 41 (2004): 127.

19. Bruce D. Sanders, "Making Work Groups Work," *Computerworld* 24 (March 5, 1990): 85–89.

20. George D. Greenberg, "The Coordinating Roles of Management," *Midwest Review of Public Administration* 10 (1976): 66–76; Stephen Ackroyd, "How Organizations Act Together: Interorganizational Coordination in Theory and Practice," *Administrative Science Quarterly* 43, no. 1 (March 1998): 217–221.

21. Henry C. Metcalf and Lyndall F. Urwich, eds., *Dynamic Administration: The Collected Papers of Mary Parker Follett* (New York: Harper & Bros., 1942), 297–299; James F. Wolf, "The Legacy of Mary Parker Follett," *Bureaucrat Winter* (1988–1989): 53–57. For a recent discussion of the work of Mary Parker Follett, see David M. Boje and Grace Ann Rosile, "Where's the Power in Empowerment? Answers from Follett and Clegg," *Journal of Applied Behavioral Science* 37, no. 1 (March 2001): 90–117.

22. Lyndall Urwich, *Notes on the Theory of Organization* (New York: American Management Association, 1952). For a recent look at the implications of organizational structure on misbehavior, see Granville King III, "The Implications of an Organization's Structure on Whistleblowing," *Journal of Business Ethics* 20, no. 4 (July 1999): 315–326.

23. David Stamps, "Off the Charts," *Training* 34, no. 10 (October 1997): 77–83.

24. For an interesting discussion of a nontraditional organization structure, see David M. Lehmann, "Integrated Enterprise Management: A Look at the Functions, the Enterprise, and the Environment—Can You See the Difference?" *Hospital Material Management Quarterly* 19, no. 4 (May 1998): 22–26.

25. Leigh Buchanan, "Raising Revenue Building Blocks the Fastest-Growing Inner City Companies," *Inc.*, June 2007, 92–94.

26. Eric J. Walton, "The Persistence of Bureaucracy: A Meta-Analysis of Weber's Model of Bureaucratic Control," *Organization Studies*, 26, no. 4: 569–600.

27. S. R. Maheshwari, "Hierarchy: Key Principle of Organization," *Employment News* 21, no. 49 (March 8–14, 1997): 1–2.

28. Cass Bettinger, "The Nine Principles of War," *Bank Marketing* 21 (December 1989): 32–34; Donald C. Hambrick, "Corporate Coherence and the Top Management Team," *Strategy & Leadership* 25, no. 5 (September/October 1997): 24–29.

29. Leon McKenzie, "Supervision: Learning from Experience," *Health Care Supervisor* 8 (January 1990): 1–11. For a recent discussion of span of control, see "Span of Control vs. Span of Support," *Journal for Quality and Participation* 23, no. 4 (Fall 2000): 4.

30. For a look at the concept of span of management in public organizations, see Kenneth Meier and John Bohte, "Span of Control and Public Organizations: Implementing Gulick's Research Design," *Public Administration Review* 63 (2003): 61.

31. Harold Koontz, "Making Theory Operational: The Span of Management," *Journal of Management Studies* (October 1966): 229–43; see also John S. McClenahen, "Managing More People in the '90s," *Industry Week* 238 (March 1989): 30–38.

32. V. A. Graicunas, "Relationships in Organization," *Bulletin of International Management Institute* (March 1933): 183–187; L. F. Urwick, "V. A. Graicunas and the Span of Control," *Academy of Management Journal* 17 (June 1974): 349–354; Luther Gulick, Lyndall Urwick, James D. Mooney, Henri Fayol, et al. "Papers on the Science of Administration," *International Journal of Public Administration* 21, no. 2–4 (1998): 441–641.

33. For discussion about why managers should increase spans of management see Stephen R. Covey, "The Marketing Revolution," *Executive Excellence* 14, no. 3 (March 1997): 3–4.

34. John R. Brandt, "Middle Management: 'Where the Action Will Be,'" *Industry Week* (May 2, 1994): 30–36.

35. For a discussion of the benefits of tall structures, see Harold J. Leavitt, "Why Hierarchies Thrive," *Harvard Business Review* 81, no. 3 (2006): 96–102.

36. Philip R. Nienstedt, "Effectively Downsizing Management Structures," *Human Resources Planning* 12 (1989): 155–165.

37. Paul Glader, "It's Not Easy Being Lean," *Wall Street Journal*, June 19, 2006, B1.

38. Beth Herskovits, "If I Ran Pfizer," *Pharmaceutical Executive* 27, no. 3 (2007): 92–95.

39. Geary A. Rummler and Alan P. Brache, "Managing the White Space on the Organization Chart," *Supervision* (May 1991): 6–12.

40. Roderick E. White and Thomas A. Poynter, "Organizing for Worldwide Advantage," *Business Quarterly* 54 (Summer 1989): 84–89.

41. M. Lindgren and J. Packendorff, "What's New in New Forms of Organizing? On the Construction of Gender in Project-Based Work," *Journal of Management Studies* 43, no. 4 (2006): 841–866.

42. C. J. Middleton, "How to Set Up a Project Organization," *Harvard Business Review* (March/April 1967): 73. See also George J. Chambers, "The Individual in a Matrix Organization," *Project Management Journal* 20 (December 1989): 37–42, 50.

43. Y. K. Shetty and Howard M. Carlisle, "A Contingency Model of Organization Design," *California Management Review* 15 (1972): 38–45. For additional discussion of factors influencing formal structure, see Paul Dwyer, "Tearing Up Today's Organization Chart," *BusinessWeek*, November 18, 1994, 80–90.

44. For insights on how Ralph Larsen, CEO of Johnson & Johnson, views problems and how his view might influence the formal structure of his organization, see Brian Dumaine, "Is Big Still Good?" *Fortune*, April 30, 1992, 50–60.

45. Henri Fayol, *General and Industrial Administration* (Belmont, CA: Pitman, 1949).

CHAPTER 12

1. This case was based on the company's Web site as well as Susan Moran, "Meditate on This: Yoga Is Big Business," *New York Times*, December 28, 2006, C3.

2. Andre Nelson, "Have I the Right Stuff to Be a Supervisor?" *Supervision* 51 (January 1990): 10–12. For a recent responsibility-related trend, see "Office Professionals' Responsibilities Set to Soar," *British Journal of Administrative Management* (May/June 2001): 6.

3. Maria Bartiromo, "The Heat on Countrywide," *BusinessWeek*, September 10, 2007, 28.

4. J. E. Osborne, "Job Descriptions Do More Than Describe Duties," *Supervisory Management* (February 1992): 8. Charlene Marmer Solomon, "Repatriation Planning Checklist," *Personnel Journal* (January 1995): 32; Peggy Anderson and Marcia Pulich, "Making Performance Appraisals Work More Effectively," *The Health Care Supervisor* 16, no. 4 (June 1998): 20–27.

5. Robert J. Theirauf, Robert C. Klekamp, and Daniel W. Geeding, *Management Principles and Practices: A Contingency and Questionnaire Approach* (New York: Wiley, 1977), 334.

6. Deborah S. Kezsbom, "Managing the Chaos: Conflict Among Project Teams," *AACE Transactions* (1989): A4.1–A4.8. For an example of how overlapping responsibilities can impact a political organization, see Carolyn Ban and Norma Riccucci, "New York State Civil Service Reform in a Complex Political Environment," *Review of Public Personnel Administration* 14, no. 2 (Spring 1994): 28–40.

7. Richard Korman, "A Responsibility Gap Crashes at Location C3," *ENR* 250 (2003): 12.

8. Chuck Douros, "Clear Division of Responsibility Defeats Inefficiency," *Nation's Restaurant News* (February 21, 1994): 20.

9. Robert D. Melcher, "Roles and Relationships: Clarifying the Manager's Job," *Personnel* 44 (May/June 1967): 34–41.

10. This section is based primarily on John H. Zenger, "Responsible Behavior: Stamp of the Effective Manager," *Supervisory Management* (July 1976): 18–24.

11. Stephen Bushardt, David Duhon, and Aubrey Fowler, "Management Delegation Myths and the Paradox of Task Assignment," *Business Horizons* (March/April 1991): 37–43.

12. Max Weber, "The Three Types of Legitimate Rule," trans. Hans Gerth, *Berkeley Journal of Sociology* 4 (1953): 1–11. For a current illustration of this concept, see Gail DeGeorge, "Yo, Ho, Ho, and a Battle for Bacardi," *BusinessWeek*, April 16, 1990, 47–48.

13. John Gardner, "The Anti-Leadership Vaccine," *Carnegie Foundation Annual Report*, 1965.

14. Chester I. Barnard, *The Functions of the Executive* (Cambridge, MA: Harvard University Press, 1938).

15. To better understand the interplay between incentives and authority, see Jan Bouwens and Laurence Van Lent, "Assessing the performance of business unit managers," *Journal of Accounting Research* 45, no. 4 (2007): 667–697.

16. For an illustration of how line authority issues can impact the operation of the IRS, see "TEI Recommends Changes in IRS Appeals Large Case Program," *Tax Executive* 48, no. 4 (July/August 1996): 265.

17. Patti Wolf, Gerald Grimes, and John Dayani, "Getting the Most Out of Staff Functions," *Small Business Reports* 14 (October 1989): 68–70.

18. Harold Stieglitz, "On Concepts of Corporate Structure," *Conference Board Record* 11 (February 1974): 7–13.

19. Wendell L. French, *The Personnel Management Process: Human Resource Administration and Development* (Boston: Houghton Mifflin, 1987), 66–68.

20. Derek Sheane, "When and How to Intervene in Conflict," *Personnel Management* (November 1979): 32–36.

21. Robert Albanese, *Management* (Cincinnati: South-Western Publishing, 1988), 313; Michael T. McCue and John Gress, "Accountability: A New Commandment," *Managed Healthcare Executive* 11, no. 6 (June 2001): 14.

22. Anthony Buono, "Accountability: Freedom and Responsibility Without Control," *Personnel Psychology* 56 (2003): 546.

23. "How Ylvisaker Makes 'Produce or Else' Work," *BusinessWeek*, October 27, 1973, 112. For an interesting discussion of the importance of establishing an environment of accountability in a small women's specialty retail store, see Nan Napier, "Change Is Big Even for a Little Guy," *Business Quarterly* (Winter 1994): 21–27.

24. For a practical discussion related to the delegation process, see Kenneth Corts and Darwin Neher, "Credible Delegation," *European Economic Review* 47 (2003): 395; see also Massimo Colombo and Marco Delmastro, "Delegation of Authority in Business Organizations: An Empirical Test," *The Journal of Industrial Economics* 52 (2004): 53.

25. William H. Newman and E. Kirby Warren, *The Process of Management: Concepts, Behavior, and Practice,* 4th ed. (Upper Saddle River, NJ: Prentice Hall, 1977), 39–40; Dave Wiggins, "Stop Doing It All Yourself! Some Keys to Effective Delegation," *Journal of Environmental Health* 60, no. 9 (May 1998): 29–30. See also Kristin Gilpatrick, "Step Up to Delegation," *Credit Union Management* 24, no. 4 (April 2001): 18.

26. R. S. Drever, "The Ultimate Frustration," *Supervision* (May 1991): 22–23.

27. To better understand the intricacies of delegation in international contexts, see Zhen Xiong Chen and Samuel Aryee, "Delegation and employee work out-comes: An examination of the cultural context of mediating processes in China," *Academy of Management Journal* 50, no. 1(2007): 226–238.

28. For more recommendations regarding delegation, see Joni Youngworth, "Delegation dilemmas," *Journal of Financial Planning* 20 (September 2007): 10–12.

29. Ted Pollock, "Secrets of Successful Delegation," *Production* (December 1994): 10–11; Robert B. Nelson, "Mastering Delegation," *Executive Excellence* 7 (January 1990): 13–14.

30. Roz Ayres-Williams, "Mastering the Fine Art of Delegation," *Black Enterprise* (April 1992): 91–93.

31. Harold Koontz, Cyril O'Donnell, and Heinz Weihrich, *Essentials of Management,* 8th ed. (New York: McGraw-Hill, 1986), 231–233.

32. This highlight was based on David De Cremer and Tom R. Tyler, "The effects of trust in authority and procedural fairness on cooperation," *Journal of Applied Psychology* 92, no. 3 (2007): 639–649.

33. For a practical look at the process of centralization, see "Pros and Cons of Centralization," *Nature* 423 (2003): 787; see also Marco Adria and Shamsud Chowdhury, "Centralization as a Design Consideration for the Management of Call Centers," *Information and Management* 41 (2004): 497.

34. For an interesting discussion of whether to centralize the marketing function, see Richard Kitaeff, "The Great Debate: Centralized vs. Decentralized Marketing Research Function," *Marketing Research: A Magazine of Management & Applications,* (Winter 1994): 59; Charlotte Sibley, "The Pros and Cons of Centralization and Decentralization," *Medical Marketing and Media* 32, no. 5 (May 1997): 72–76; Christine Tierney and Katherine Schmidt, "Schrempp, the Survivor? To Tighten His Grip, He Will Centralize Decision-Making," *BusinessWeek,* March 5, 2001, 54.

35. Steve Weinstein, "A Look at Fleming's New Look," *Progressive Grocer* 74 (1995): 47–49. To understand the effects of globalization on decentralization, see Francesca Sanna-Randaccio and Reinhilde Veugelers, "Multinational knowledge spillovers with decentralized R&D: A game-theoretic approach," *Journal of International Business Studies* 38, no. 1 (2007): 47–63.

36. H. Gilman, "J.C. Penney Decentralizes Its Purchasing," *Wall Street Journal,* May 8, 1986, 6.

37. To better understand how decentralization influences innovation and new products, see Nicolaj Siggelkow and Jan Rivken, "When exploration backfires: Unintended consequences of multilevel organizational search," *Academy of Management Journal* 49, no. 4 (2006): 779–795.

38. Donald O. Harper, "Project Management as a Control and Planning Tool in the Decentralized Company," *Management Accounting* (November 1968): 29–33.

39. Information for this section is mainly from John G. Staiger, "What Cannot Be Decentralized," *Management Record* 25 (January 1963): 19–21. At the time the article was written, Staiger was vice president of administration, North American Operations, Massey-Ferguson, Limited.

40. This exercise was based on the company's Web site as well as Jena McGregor, "Room & Board Plays Impossible to Get," *BusinessWeek,* October 1, 2007, 80.

CHAPTER 13

1. This case was based on Bruce Einhorn, "The Shanghai Scramble," *BusinessWeek,* August 20, 2007, 53; and Bruce Einhorn, "Selling Cisco to China's Tech Talent Pool," *BusinessWeek Online,* September 18, 2007, 23.

2. To see how the performance of these steps can be shared in an organization, see Brenda Paik Sunoo, "Growing without an HR Department" *Workforce* 77, no. 1 (January 1998): 16–17. For a review of effective recruitment techniques, see Daniel Bates, "Do You Have Great People?: Roadshow Recruitment," *SBN Pittsburgh* 7, no. 10 (February 1, 2001): 32.

3. For a look at job descriptions, see Jeff Archer, "New Job Description?" *Education Week* 22 (2003): 18.

4. Bruce Shawkey, "Job Descriptions," *Credit Union Executive* 29 (Winter 1989–1990): 20–23; Howard D. Feldman, "Why Are Similar Managerial Jobs So Different?" *Review of Business* 11 (Winter 1989): 15–22.

5. "Job Analysis," *Bureau of Intergovernmental Personnel Programs,* December 1973, 135–52; Gundars E. Kaupins, "Lies, Damn Lies, and Job Evaluations," *Personnel* 66 (November 1989): 62–65; Jim Meade, "Identifying Criteria for Success Helps in Making Effective Hiring Decisions," *HR Magazine* 43, no. 5 (April 1998): 49–50.

6. James H. Martin and Elizabeth B. Franz, "Attracting Applicants from a Changing Labor Market: A Strategic Marketing Framework," *Journal of Managerial Issues* (Spring 1994): 33–53.

7. Fred K. Foulkes, "How Top Nonunion Companies Manage Employees," *Harvard Business Review* (September/October 1981): 90.

8. Walter S. Wikstrom, "Developing Managerial Competence: Concepts, Emerging Practices," *Studies in Personnel Policy,* no. 189, National Industrial Conference Board (1964): 95–105.

9. Richard Verrier and James Bates, "Eisner's Heir Far from Apparent at Disney," *Orlando Sentinel,* December 8, 2003: A1, A10.

10. Patricia Panchak, "Resourceful Software Boosts HR Efficiency," *Modern Office Technology* 35 (April 1990): 76–80.

11. Haig Simonian, "A new breed of private banker," *Financial Times,* August 14, 2007, 12.

12. For discussion of recent EEOC guidelines on discrimination, see Diane Hatch, James Hall and Mark Kobata, "New EEOC Guidance on National-Origin Discrimination," *Workforce* 82 (2003): 76.

13. For recent issues regarding affirmative action, see Glenn Cook, "A Victory for Affirmative Action," *American School Board Journal* 190 (2003): 7. For more infor-mation regarding the potential legal issues associated with discrimination, see Richard A. Posthuma, Mark V. Roehling, and Michael A. Campion. "Applying U.S. employment discrimination laws to international employers: Advice for scientists and practitioners." *Personnel Psychology* 59, no. 3 (2006): 705–739.

14. Ray H. Hodges, "Developing an Effective Affirmative Action Program," *Journal of Intergroup Relations* 5 (November 1976): 13. For a discussion of EEOC oper-ations, see Ellen Rettig, "EEOC Gets Tough with Employers," *Indianapolis Business Journal* 20, no. 46 (January 24, 2000): 1.

15. R. Roosevelt Thomas, Jr., "From Affirmative Action to Affirming Diversity," *Harvard Business Review* 68 (March/April 1990): 107–117. For a recent article supporting the notion of affirmative action, see Albert R. Hunt, "A Persuasive Case for Affirmative Action," *Wall Street Journal,* February 1, 2001, A23.

16. For an article describing the importance of careful employee selection, see Tim Fulton, "Firms shouldn't gamble on employee selection," *Atlanta Business Chronicle* 21, no. 42 (March 26, 1999): B3.

17. For more discussion of the stages of the selection process, see David J. Cherrington, *Personnel Management: The Management of Human Resources* (Dubuque, IA: Wm. C. Brown, 1987), 186–231. For an interesting study examining the perceived fairness of selection processes, see Deidra J. Schleicher, Vijaya Venkataramani, Frederick P. Morgeson, and Michael A. Campion. "So you didn't get the job. . . . Now what do you think? Examining opportunity-to-perform fairness perceptions," *Personnel Psychology* 59, no. 3 (2006): 559–590.

18. This section is based on Andrew F. Sikula, *Personnel Administration and Human Resource Management* (New York: Wiley, 1976), 188–190. For an overview of the potential errors involved with selection, see Herman Aguinis and Marlene A. Smith, "Understanding the impact of test validity and bias on selection errors and adverse impact in human resource selection," *Personnel Psychology* 60, no. 1 (2007): 165–199.

19. For an example of an aptitude test for accident proneness, see Hiroshi Matsuoka, "Development of a Short Test for Accident Proneness," *Perceptual and Motor Skills* 85, no. 3 (December 1997): 903–906.

20. Daniel P. O'Meara, "Personality Tests Raise Questions of Legality and Effectiveness," *HR Magazine,* January 1994, 97–100. See also Joyce Hogan, Paul Barrett, and Robert Hogan, "Personality measurement, faking, and employ-ment selection," *Journal of Applied Psychology* 92, no. 5 (2007): 1270–1285.

21. Clive Fletcher, "Testing the Accuracy of Psychometric Measures," *People Management* 3, no. 21 (October 23, 1997): 64–66. For a discussion of EEOC guidelines concerning appropriate pre-employment testing for Americans with disabilities, see Melanie K. St. Clair and David W. Arnold, "Preemployment Screening: No More Test Stress," *Security Management* (February 1995): 73.

22. David Littlefield, "Menu for Change at Novotel," *People Management* (January 26, 1995): 34–36; Susan O. Hendricks and Susan E. Ogborn, "Supervisory and

Managerial Assessment Centers in Health Care," *Health Care Supervisor* 8 (April 1990): 65–75.

23. Barry M. Cohen, "Assessment Centers," *Supervisory Management* (June 1975): 30. See also Paul Taylor, "Seven Staff Selection Myths," *Management* 45, no. 4 (May 1998): 61–65.

24. To examine the possible impact of assessment centers for inmates, see Ralph Fretz, "New Jersey's Assessment Centers Helping Inmates Take the Final Step Toward Release," *Corrections Today* 64 (2002): 78.

25. Ann Howard, "An Assessment of Assessment Centers," *Academy of Management Journal* 17 (March 1974): 177.

26. William Umiker and Thomas Conlin, "Assessing the Need for Supervisory Training: Use of Performance Appraisals," *Health Care Supervisor* 8 (January 1990): 40–45. For a look at innovative training techniques, see Rob Eure, "E-Commerce (A Special Report): The Classroom—On the Job: Corporate E-Learning Makes Training Available Anytime, Anywhere," *Wall Street Journal,* March 12, 2001, R33.

27. Richard Lowther, "Embracing and managing diversity at Dell," *Strategic HR Review* 5, no. 6 (2006): 16–19.

28. Bass and Vaughn, *Training in Industry.* For discussion on using technology to improve lecture effectiveness, see "Switches Offer Classroom Control," *Computer Dealer News* 14, no. 17 (May 4, 1998): 58.

29. David Sutton, "Further Thoughts on Action Learning," *Journal of European Industrial Training* 13 (1989): 32–35. For further information regarding the relationship between training and learning, see Andrew Neal, Stuart T. Godley, Terry Kirkpatrick, and Graham Dewsnap, "An Examination of Learning Processes During Critical Incident Training: Implications for the Development of Adaptable Trainees," *Journal of Applied Psychology* 91, no. 6 (2007): 1276–1291.

30. Anne Fisher, "Don't Blow Your New Job," *Fortune,* June 22, 1998, 159–162.

31. For an example of how training improves the effectiveness of consultants, see F. Lievens and J. I. Sanchez, "Can training improve the quality of inferences made by raters in competency modeling? A quasi-experiment," *Journal of Applied Psychology* 92, no. 3 (2007): 812–819.

32. Samuel C. Certo, "The Experiential Exercise Situation: A Comment on Instructional Role and Pedagogy Evaluation," *Academy of Management Review* (July 1976): 113–116. For a worthwhile discussion of the advantages of facilitation over lecturing for overcoming trainee resistance to learning, see Margaret Kaeter, "Coping with Resistant Trainees," *Training* 31 (1994): 110–114.

33. "Training Program's Results Measured in Unique Way," *Supervision* (February 1992): 18–19.

34. William Keenan Jr., "Are You Overspending on Training?" *Sales and Marketing Management* 142 (January 1990): 56–60.

35. For a review of the literature linking performance appraisal and training needs, see Glenn Herbert and Dennis Doverspike, "Performance Appraisal in the Training Needs Analysis Process: A Review and Critique," *Public Personnel Management* (Fall 1990): 253–270. See also Mike Deblieux, "Performance Reviews Support the Quest for Quality," *HR Focus* (November 1991): 3–4.

36. This highlight was based on Charlotte Fritz and Sabine Sonnentag. "Recovery, well-being, and performance-related outcomes: The role of workload and vacation experiences," *Journal of Applied Psychology* 91, no. 4 (2006): 936–945.

37. Douglas McGregor, "An Uneasy Look at Performance Appraisal," *Harvard Business Review* (September/October 1972): 133–134; David A. Waldman and David E. Bowen, "The Acceptability of 360 Degree Appraisals: A Customer-Supplier Relationship Perspective," *Human Resource Management* 37, no. 2 (Summer 1998): 117–129.

38. For information regarding the role of documentation in handling performance appraisals, see Brian Crawford, "Performance Appraisals: The Importance of Documentation," *Fire Engineering* 156 (2003): 100; see also Audrey Bland, "Motivate and Reward: Performance Appraisal and Incentive Systems for Business Success," *Human Resource Management Journal* 14 (2004): 99–100.

39. Linda J. Segall, "KISS Appraisal Woes Goodbye," *Supervisory Management* 34 (December 1989): 23–28. To see an example of how appraisal systems work for not-for-profits (in this case a police department), see Victor M Catano, Wendy Darr, and Catherine A. Campbell, "Performance appraisal of behavior-based competencies: A reliable and valid procedure," *Personnel Psychology* 60, no. 1 (2006): 201–230.

40. Robert M. Gerst, "Assessing Organizational Performance," *Quality Progress* (February 1995): 85–88. See also George A. Rider, "Performance Review: A Mixed Bag," *Harvard Business Review* (July/August 1973): 61–67; Robert Loo, "Quality Performance Appraisals," *Canadian Manager* 14 (December 1989): 24–26.

41. Michael Myser, "Bosses get a helping hand," *Business 2.0* 8, no. 6 (July 2007): 31.

42. This exercise was based on the company's Web site as well as Jena McGregor, "Room & Board Plays Impossible to Get," *BusinessWeek,* October 1, 2007, 80.

CHAPTER 14

1. "Wm. Wrigley Jr. Company Realigns Commercial Operations Structure," *PR Newswire,* February 26, 2007.

2. "Wrigley Is in a Sticky Spot; Firepower May Be Lacking to Counter the Big Threat of a Cadbury-Hershey Tie," *Wall Street Journal,* April 4, 2007, C.12

3. John H. Zimmerman, "The Principles of Managing Change," *HR Focus* (February 1995): 15–16.

4. For an in-depth analysis of effective change in the workplace, see Angela Mansell, Paula Brough, and Kevin Cole, "Stable Predictors of Job Satisfaction, Psychological Strain, and Employee Retention: An Evaluation of Organizational Change Within the New Zealand Customs Service," *International Journal of Stress Management,* 13 (2006): 84–107.

5. Rosabeth Moss Kanter, "The New Managerial Work," *Harvard Business Review* (November/December 1989): 85–92. For a review of planned change models as related to a nursing environment, see Constance Rimmer Tiffany et al., "Planned Change Theory: Survey of Nursing Periodical Literature," *Nursing Management* (July 1994): 54–59; see also William Kahn, "Facilitating and Undermining Organizational Change: A Case Study," *The Journal of Applied Behavioral Science* 40 (2004): 7.

6. John S. Morgan, *Managing Change: The Strategies of Making Change Work for You* (New York: McGraw-Hill, 1972), 99.

7. Bart Nooteboom, "Paradox, Identity, and Change in Management," *Human Systems Management* 8 (1989): 291–300.

8. For further information about handling organizational change, see Jeanette Bottitta, Alexia Idoura, and Lisa Pappas, "Managing the Effects of Organizational Changes," *Technical Communication* 50 (2003): 355.

9. Davis Balistracci, "Be a Change Agent," *Quality Progress* 36 (2003): 65.

10. For a discussion of the value of outside change agents, see John H. Sheridan, "Careers on the Line," *Fortune,* September 16, 1991, 29–30. See also John H. Zimmerman, "The Deming Approach to Construction Safety Management," *Professional Safety* (December 1994): 35–37.

11. For a recent article on being an effective change agent, see Shelley Cohen, "Change Agents Bolster New Practices in the Workplace," *Nursing Management* 37 (2006): 16–17.

12. Myron Tribus, "Changing the Corporate Culture—A Roadmap for the Change Agent," *Human Systems Management* 8 (1989): 11–22. For a review of the effects of structural change within an organization, see Shawn Young, "Structural Changes Pay Off in Profits for Top U.S. Long-Distance Carriers," *Wall Street Journal,* January 19, 1999.

13. Mara Der Hovanesian, "JPMorgan: The Bank of Technology," *BusinessWeek,* no. 3989 (June 19, 2006): 54.

14. For an interesting case illustrating the changing nature of organization structure at Procter & Gamble, see Aelita G. B. Martinsons and Maris G. Martinsons, "In Search of Structural Excellence," *Leadership & Organization Development Journal* 15 (1994): 24–28. See also Saul W. Gellerman, "In Organizations, as in Architecture, Form Follows Function," *Organizational Dynamics* 18 (Winter 1990): 57–68.

15. Frederick A. Goh and Merrill C Anderson, "Driving Business Value from Performance Management at Caterpillar," *Organization Development Journal* 25, no. 2 (Summer 2007): P219–P226.

16. This section is based primarily on R. Blake, J. Mouton, and L. Greiner, "Breakthrough in Organization Development," *Harvard Business Review* (November/December 1964): 133–155.

17. Blake, Mouton, and Greiner, "Breakthrough in Organization Development."

18. W. J. Heisler, "Patterns of OD in Practice," *Business Horizons* (February 1975): 77–84.

19. Martin G. Evans, "Failures in OD Programs—What Went Wrong," *Business Horizons* (April 1974): 18–22.

20. For one such article on organization development, see Jeana Wirtenberg, David Lipsky, Lilian Abrams, Malcolm Conway, and Joan Slepian, "The Future of Organizational Development: Enabling Sustainable Business Performance Through People," *Organization Development* 25 (Summer 2007): P11–P22.

21. David Coghlan, "OD Interventions in Catholic Religious Orders," *Journal of Managerial Psychology* 4 (1989): 4–6. See also Paul A. Iles and Thomas Johnston, "Searching for Excellence in Second-Hand Clothes?: A Note," *Personnel Review* 18

(1989): 32–35; Ewa Maslyk-Musial, "Organization Development in Poland: Stages of Growth," *Public Administration Quarterly* 13 (Summer 1989): 196–214.

22. For an interesting discussion of resistance to change from inherited staff, see Margaret Russell, "Records Management Program-Directing: Inherited Staff," *ARMA Records Management Quarterly* 24 (January 1990): 18–22.

23. For a recent article on resistance to change in the workplace, see David Stanley, John Meyer, and Laryssa Topolnytsky, "Employee Cynicism and Resistance to Organizational Change," *Journal of Business and Psychology* 19 (2005): 429–459.

24. For more information about internal resistance to change, see Robert Sevier, "Overcoming Internal Resistance to Change," *University Business* 6 (2003): 23.

25. This strategy for minimizing resistance to change is based on "How Companies Overcome Resistance to Change," *Management Review* (November 1972): 17–25. See also Hank Williams, "Learning to Manage Change," *Industrial and Commercial Training* 21 (May/June 1989): 17–20.

26. Angela J. Martin, Elizabeth S. Jones, and Victor J. Callan, "Status Differences in Employee Adjustment During Organizational Change," *Journal of Managerial Psychology* 21, no. 1–2 (2006): 145–162.

27. Newton Margulies and John Wallace, *Organizational Change: Techniques and Applications* (Chicago: Scott, Foresman, 1973), 14.

28. For a recent article on evaluating change within a pharmaceutical organization, see Bill Cowley, "Why Change Succeeds: An Organizational Self-Assessment," *Organization Development Journal* 25 (2007): P25–P30.

29. Edgar C. Williams, "Changing Systems and Behavior: People's Perspectives on Prospective Changes," *Business Horizons* (August 1969): 53.

30. Carrie Olsen, David White, and Iris Lemmer, "Career Models and Culture Change at Microsoft," *Organization Development Journal* Summer 25, no. 2 (2007): P31–P35, P236.

31. For an article on recent developments concerning stress in the workplace, see "Employers See Rise in Stress at Work," *Occupational Health* 55 (2003): 5; see also Patricia Sikora, David Beaty, and John Forward, "Updating Theory on Organizational Stress: The Asynchronous Multiple Overlapping Change (AMOC) Model of Workplace Stress," *Human Resource Development Review* 3 (2004): 3.

32. Hans Selye, *The Stress of Life* (New York: McGraw-Hill, 1956). See also James C. Quick and Jonathan D. Quick, *Organizational Stress and Preventive Management* (New York: McGraw-Hill, 1984).

33. James D. Bodzinski, Robert F. Scherer, and Karen A. Gover, "Workplace Stress," *Personnel Administrator* 34 (July 1989): 76–80.

34. For an article regarding the role of stress in the overall quality of life of employees, see Cary Cooper, "The Challenges of Managing the Changing Nature of Workplace Stress" *Journal of Public Mental Health* 5 (2005): 6–9.

35. For an article that describes the relationship between workplace stress and psychiatric disorders, see Carolyn Dewa, Elizabeth Lin, Mieke Kooehoorn, and Elliot Goldner, "Association of Chronic Work Stress, Psychiatric Disorders, and Chronic Physical Conditions with Disability Among Workers," *Psychiatric Services* 58 (2007): 652–658.

36. Corinne M. Smereka, "Outwitting, Controlling Stress for a Healthier Lifestyle," *Healthcare Financial Management* 44 (March 1990): 70–75.

37. J. Clifton Williams, *Human Behavior in Organizations* (Cincinnati: South-Western, 1982), 212–213; Thomas L. Brown, "Are You Living in 'Quiet Desperation'?" *Industry Week* (March 16, 1992): 17.

38. For more information about the relationship between stress, burnout, and depression, see A. Iacovides, K. Fountoulakis, S. Kaprinis, and G. Kaprinis, "The Relationship Between Job Stress, Burnout and Clinical Depression," *Journal of Affective Disorders* 75 (2003): 209.

39. Stewart L. Stokes Jr., "Life after Rightsizing," *Information Systems Management* (Fall 1994): 69–71. For a discussion of other stressors, see "Workplace Stress," *HR Magazine,* August 1991, 75–76.

40. J. Stebbing and T. Powles, "Stress in the Workplace Amongst Medical Professionals," *Journal of Postgraduate Medicine* 53, no. 2 (April–June 2007): 83–84.

41. For an interesting article addressing how managers can handle their own stress, see Thomas Brown, "Are You Stressed Out?" *Industry Week* (September 16, 1991): 21.

42. Fred Luthans, *Organizational Behavior* (New York: McGraw-Hill, 1985), 146–148. For one successful method of reducing workplace stress, see J. Michael Krivyanski, "Employer-Sponsored Programs Try to Keep Workplace Stress in Check," *Business Times Journal* 20, no. 38 (April 6, 2001): 34.

43. For a recent article outlining the advantages of workplace stress management classes, see Yoshio Mino, Akira Babazono, Toshihide Tsuda, and Nobufumi Yasuda, "Can Stress Management at the Workplace Prevent Depression? A Randomized Controlled Trial," *Psychotherapy and Psychosomatics* 75 (2006): 177–182.

44. Donald B. Miller, "Career Planning and Management in Organizations," *S.A.M. Advanced Management Journal* 43 (Spring 1978): 33–43.

45. This section is based upon Samuel C. Certo, *Supervision: Concepts and Skill-Building* (Burr Ridge, IL: McGraw-Hill Irwin, 2008), 376–381.

46. William H. Davidow and Michael S. Malone, *The Virtual Corporation* (New York: HarperCollins, 1992).

47. P. Maria Joseph Christie and Reuven R. Levary, "Virtual Corporations: Recipe for Success," *Industrial Management* (July/August 1998): 7–11.

48. Charles C. Snow, Raymond E. Miles, and Henry J. Coleman Jr., "Managing 21st Century Network Organizations," *Organizational Dynamics* (Winter, 1992): 5–20.

49. Judith R. Gordon, *Organizational Behavior: A Diagnostic Approach* (Upper Saddle River, NJ: Prentice Hall, 1999), 385.

50. Christopher Barnatt, "Virtual Organizations in the Small Business Sector: The Case of Cavendish Management Resources," *International Small Business Journal* 15, no. 4 (July/September 1997): 36–47.

51. Anthony M. Townsend, Samuel M. DeMarie, and Anthony R. Hendrickson, "Virtual Teams: Technology and the Workplace of the Future," *Academy of Management Executive* 12, no. 3 (August 1998): 17–29. For a recent article that examines the role of culture in the virtual workplace, see John Symons and Claudia Stenzel, "Virtually Borderless: An Examination of Culture in Virtual Teaming," *Journal of General Management* 32 (2007): 1–17.

52. For other examples of types of virtuality in organizations, see Daniel E. O'Leary, Daniel Kuokka, and Robert Plant, "Artificial Intelligence and Virtual Organizations," *Communication of the Ach* 40, no. 1 (January 1997): 52–59.

53. This section draws heavily from Thomas H. Davenport and Keri Pearlson, "Two Cheers for the Virtual Office," *Sloan Management Review* (Summer 1998): 51–65. For a further look at the advantages of a virtual office, see Stephen Roth, "Consultants Use a Virtual Office to Make New Services a Reality," *The Business Journal* 19, no. 20 (January 26, 2001): 8.

54. This exercise is based upon Jay Ericson, "Radical Change for a Small Business—To Remain Competitive, Ericson Manufacturing Needed to Do a Better Job of Business Forecasting," *Optimize* 5, no. 8 (August 2006): 55.

55. This exercise is based upon Dave Curtis, "Tebow, Retooled," *Orlando Sentinel,* August 20, 2007, C1.

CHAPTER 15

1. "Procter & Gamble stock reaches all-time high," Bizjournals.com, January 8, 2007.

2. For a recent article describing why some managers prefer certain influence tactics, see H. Steensma, "Why managers prefer some influence tactics to other tactics: A net utility explanation," *Journal of Occupational and Organizational Psychology* 80 (2007): 355.

3. Derek Torrington and Jane Weightman, "Middle Management Work," *Journal of General Management* 13 (Winter 1987): 74–89. For a useful discussion of how to influence people, see Martin Wilding, "Win Friends and Influence People by Being Sincere," *Marketing,* February 23, 1995, 16; Esther Bogin, "From Staff to Dream Team," *Financial Executive,* January/February 1995, 54–56.

4. For a recent article describing the most effective influencing tactics, see Joyce Leong, Michael Bond, and Ping Ping Fu, "Perceived Effectiveness of Influence Strategies Among Hong Kong Managers," *Asia Pacific Journal of Management* 24 (2007): 75–97.

5. Daniel Goleman, "Leadership that Gets Results," *Harvard Business Review* (March–April 2000): 78–90; Daniel Goleman, *Emotional Intelligence* (New York: Bantam Books, 1995); Daniel Goleman, *Working with Emotional Intelligence* (New York: Bantam Books, 1998).

6. Joseph Rode et al., "Emotional Intelligence and Individual Performance: Evidence of Direct and Moderated Effects," *Journal of Organizational Behavior* 28 (2007): 399–421.

7. "Why Emotional Intelligence Matters at Work," *Work & Family Life* 17, no. 4 (April 2003): 4.

8. For discussion of the importance of communication, see Terrence Coan, "Communication: The Key to Success," *Information Management Journal* (May/June 2002): 1.

9. Bernard Reilly and Joseph DiAngelo Jr., "Communication: A Cultural System of Meaning and Value," *Human Relations* 43 (February 1990): 29–40. Christine Clements, Richard J. Wagner, and Christopher Roland, "The Ins and Outs of Experimental Training," *Training & Development* (February 1995): 52–56. For a discussion of communication techniques, see "The Elements of Effective Communication," *Agency Sales* 30, no. 12 (December 2000): 45–46.

10. For a recent article describing the most important aspects of effective communication, see Donald English, Edgar Manton, and Janet Walker, "Human

Resource Managers' Perception of Selected Communication Competencies," *Education* 127 (2007): 410–419.

11. This section is based on the following classic article on interpersonal communication: Wilbur Schramm, "How Communication Works," *The Process and Effects of Mass Communication,* ed. Wilbur Schramm (Urbana, IL: University of Illinois Press, 1954), 3–10. For an innovative assignment on communication, see Karl L. Smart and Richard Featheringham, "Developing Effective Interpersonal Communication and Discussion Skills," *Business Communication Quarterly* 69 (2006): 276–283.

12. For more information regarding the elements of interpersonal communication, see Phyl Johnson, "Handbook of Interpersonal Communication," *Organization Studies* 24 (2003): 989.

13. David S. Brown, "Barriers to Successful Communication: Part I, Macrobarriers," *Management Review* (December 1975): 24–29. For a discussion of successful communication, see Jeanelle Barrett, "Successful Communication for Business and Management," *Business Communication Quarterly* 63, no. 4 (December 2000): 102.

14. James K. Weekly and Raj Aggarwal, *International Business: Operating in the Global Economy* (New York: Dryden Press, 1987).

15. "Increasing Pharmaceutical Sales Force Productivity Through Streamlined Internal Communications," *PR Newswire,* September 11, 2007.

16. For an interesting case study describing communication skills within the global arena, see Sabine Jaccaud and Bill Quirke, "Structuring Global Communication to Improve Efficiency," *Strategic Communication Management* 10 (2006): 18–21.

17. Davis S. Brown, "Barriers to Successful Communication: Part II, Microbarriers," *Management Review* (January 1976): 15–21. For study results having implications for e-mail as a communication microbarrier, see Norman Frohlich and Joe Oppenheimer, "Some Consequences of E-mail vs. Face-to-Face Communication in Experiment," *Journal of Economic Behavior & Organization* 35, no. 3 (April 15, 1998): 389–403.

18. Sally Bulkley Pancrazio and James J. Pancrazio, "Better Communication for Managers," *Supervisory Management* (June 1981): 31–37. See also John S. Fielden, "Why Can't Managers Communicate?" *Business* 39 (January/February/March 1989): 41–44.

19. Lydia Strong, "Do You Know How to Listen?" *Effective Communications on the Job,* ed. M. Joseph Dooher and Vivienne Marquis (New York: American Management Association, 1956), 28.

20. Robert E. Callahan, C. Patrick Fleenor, and Harry R. Knudson, *Understanding Organizational Behavior: A Managerial Viewpoint* (Columbus, OH: Charles E. Merrill, 1986). For a discussion of the process of generating feedback, see Elizabeth Wolfe Morrison and Robert J. Bies, "Impression Management in the Feedback-Seeking Process: Literature Review and Research Agenda," *Academy of Management Review* (July 1991): 522–541.

21. For more on nonverbal issues, see J. T. Sheppard, "Silent Signals," *Supervisory Management* (March 1986): 31–33.

22. For a recent study demonstrating the importance of feedback format, see L. Atwater and J. Brett, "Feedback format: Does it influence manager's reactions to feedback?" *Journal of Occupational and Organizational Psychology* 79 (2006): 517.

23. Verne Burnett, "Management's Tower of Babel," *Management Review* (June 1961): 4–11.

24. Reprinted by permission of the publisher from "Ten Commandments of Good Communication," by American Management Association AMA-COM et al., from *Management Review* (October 1955). © 1955 American Management Association, Inc. All rights reserved. See also Robb Ware, "Communication Problems," *Journal of Systems Management* (September 1991): 20; "Communicating: Face-to-Face," *Agency Sales Magazine,* January 1994, 22–23.

25. Ted Pollock, "Mind Your Own Business," *Supervision,* May 1994, 24–26; Joseph R. Bainbridge, "Joint Communication: Verbal and Nonverbal," *Army Logistician* 30, no. 4: (July/August) 40–42.

26. Paul Preston, "Nonverbal Communication: Do You Really Say What You Mean?" *Journal of Healthcare Management* 50 (2005): 83–86.

27. For a practical article emphasizing the role of gestures in communication, see S. D. Gladis, "Notes Are Not Enough," *Training and Development Journal* (August 1985): 35–38. See also Nicole Steckler and Robert Rosenthal, "Sex Differences in Nonverbal and Verbal Communication with Bosses, Peers, and Subordinates," *Journal of Applied Psychology* (February 1985): 157–163; W. Alan Randolph, *Understanding and Managing Organizational Behavior* (Homewood, IL: Richard D. Irwin, 1985), 349–350; Karen O. Down and Jeanne Liedtka, "What Corporations Seek in MBA Hires: A Survey," *Selections* (Winter 1994): 34–39.

28. Gerald M. Goldhaber, *Organizational Communication* (Dubuque, IA: Wm. C. Brown, 1983). For a discussion on the important role of organizational

29. communication within a corporation, see Bauke Visser, "Organizational Communication Structure and Performance," *Journal of Economic Behavior & Organization* 42, no. 2 (June 2000): 231–252.

29. For an article that describes how employees perceive different types of organizational communication, see Zinta S. Byrne and Elaine LeMay, "Different Media for Organizational Communication: Perceptions of Quality and Satisfaction," *Journal of Business and Psychology* 21 (2006): 149–173.

30. Kenneth R. Van Voorhis, "Organizational Communication: Advances Made During the Period from World War II Through the 1950s," *Journal of Business Communication* 11 (1974): 11–18.

31. Paul Preston, "The Critical 'Mix' in Managerial Communications," *Industrial Management* (March/April 1976): 5–9. For a discussion of implementing organizational communication reflecting a worldwide structure, see "Iridium Delays Full Start of Global System," *New York Times,* September 10, 1998, C6.

32. For a discussion of how to communicate failures upward in an organization, see Jay T. Knippen, Thad B. Green, and Kurt Sutton, "How to Communicate Failures to Your Boss," *Supervisory Management* (September 1991): 10.

33. For an article stressing the importance of upward and downward communication for managers, see W. H. Weiss, "Communications: Key to Successful Supervision," *Supervision* 59, no. 9 (September 1998): 12–14.

34. William V. Haney, "Serial Communication of Information in Organizations," in *Concepts and Issues in Administrative Behavior,* ed. Sidney Mailick and Edward H. Van Ness (Englewood Cliffs, NJ: Prentice Hall, 1962), 150. For a discussion involving implications of off-site patterns of communication, see Robert M. Egan, Wendy Miles, John R. Birstler, and Margaret Klayton-Mi, "Can the Rift Between Allison and Penny Be Mended?" *Harvard Business Review* 76, no. 4 (July/August 1998): 28–35.

35. Alex Bavelas and Dermot Barrett, "An Experimental Approach to Organizational Communication," *Personnel* 27 (1951): 366–371.

36. This highlight is based upon Jane Read, "Are We Losing the Personal Touch?" *British Journal of Administrative Management* (April/May 2007): 22–23.

37. Polly LaBarre, "The Other Network," *IndustryWeek* (September 19, 1994): 33–36.

38. For an article describing how to assess the existence of informal organizational communication, see R. Guimera, L. Danon, A. Diaz-Guilera, F. Giralt, and A. Arenas, "The Real Communication Network Behind the Formal Chart: Community Structure in Organizations," *Journal of Economic Behavior and Organization* 61 (2006): 653–667.

39. "Steelcase Workplace Index Survey Examines 'Water Cooler' Conversations at Work: Study Confirms Gossip Is Here to Stay, Which May Benefit Employers," *PR Newswire,* August 9, 2007.

40. Vesa Peltokorpi, "The Impact of Relational Diversity and Socio-Cultural Context on Interpersonal Communication: Nordic Subsidiaries in Japan," *Asian Business & Management* 5, no. 3 (September 2006): 333–356.

41. George de Mare, "Communicating: The Key to Establishing Good Working Relationships," *Price Waterhouse Review* 33 (1989): 30–37; Stanley J. Modic, "Grapevine Rated Most Believable," *IndustryWeek* (May 15, 1989): 11, 14.

42. Keith Davis, "Management Communication and the Grapevine," *Harvard Business Review* (January/February 1953): 43–49.

43. Linda McCallister, "The Interpersonal Side of Internal Communications," *Public Relations Journal* (February 1981): 20–23. See also Joseph M. Putti, Samuel Aryee, and Joseph Phua, "Communication Relationship Satisfaction and Organizational Commitment," *Group and Organizational Studies* 15 (March 1990): 44–52.

44. Ali Carruthers, "Listening to Company Stakeholders at McDonald's Restaurants," *The Business Communicator* 6, no. 4 (September 2005): 8–9.

45. This skills portfolio exercise draws from www.ericcson.com; Per Zetterquist and Bill Quirke, "Transforming Internal Communication at Ericsson," *Strategic Communication Management* 11, no. 1 (December 2006/January, 2007): 18–21.

CHAPTER 16

1. "Sales of Ink and Laptops Push HP Past Forecast," *New York Times,* August 17, 2007, C3.

2. Elise Goldman, "The Significance of Leadership Style," *Educational Leadership* 55, no. 7 (April 1998): 20–22. For a worthwhile look at the importance of instilling leadership in all members of a corporation, see Scott Payne, "Corporate Training Trend: Building Leadership," *Grand Rapids Business Journal,* November 13, 2000, B2; see also Dusya Vera and Mary Crossan, "Stragetic Leadership and Organizational Learning," *Academy of Management Review* 29 (2004): 222.

3. David Nadler and Michael L. Tushman, "Beyond the Charismatic Leader: Leadership and Organizational Change," *California Management Review* 32

(Winter 1990): 77–97; Peter R. Scholtes, *The Leader's Handbook: A Guide to Inspiring Your People and Managing the Daily Workflow* (New York: McGraw-Hill, 1998).

4. Abraham Zaleznik, "Executives and Organizations: Real Work," *Harvard Business Review* (January/February 1989): 57–64.

5. Theodore Levitt, "Management and the Post-Industrial Society," *Public Interest* (Summer 1976): 73.

6. Patrick L. Townsend and Joan E. Gebhardt, "We Have Lots of Managers . . . We Need Leaders," *Journal for Quality and Participation* (September 1989): 18–20; Craig Hickman, "The Winning Mix: Mind of a Manager, Soul of a Leader," *Canadian Business* 63 (February 1990): 69–72. For discussion of how successful executives place more importance and emphasis on leadership than management, see Michael E. McGrath, "The Eight Qualities of Success," *Electronic Business* 24, no. 4 (April 1998): 9–10.

7. For a recent study assessing the validity of traits theory, see Dean Gehring, "Applying traits theory of leadership to project management," *Project Management Journal* 38 (2007): 44–55.

8. Ralph M. Stogdill, "Personal Factors Associated with Leadership: A Survey of the Literature," *Journal of Psychology* 25 (January 1948): 35–64.

9. Cecil A. Gibb, "Leadership," in *Handbook of Social Psychology*, ed. Gardner Lindzey (Reading, MA: Addison-Wesley, 1954).

10. Valerie Sessa, "Creating Leaderful Organizations: How to Bring Out Leadership in Everyone," *Personnel Psychology* 56 (2003): 762.

11. J. Oliver Crom, "What's New in Leadership?" *Executive Excellence* 7 (January 1990): 15–16.

12. Geoff Colvin, "Leader Machines" *Fortune* 156, no. 7 (October 1, 2007): 98–106.

13. For an interesting application of the situational leadership model, see R. Vecchko, R. Bullie, and D. Brazil, "The utility of situational leadership theory: A replication in a military setting," *Small Group Research* 37 (2006): 407.

14. For a discussion of a leader in a military situation, see Sherrill Tapsell, "Managing for Peace," *Management* 45, no. 5 (June 1998): 32–37.

15. Robert Tannenbaum and Warren H. Schmidt, "How to Choose a Leadership Pattern," *Harvard Business Review* (March/April 1957): 95–101.

16. William E. Zierden, "Leading Through the Follower's Point of View," *Organizational Dynamics* (Spring 1980): 27–46. See also Tannenbaum and Schmidt, "How to Choose a Leadership Pattern."

17. Robert Tannenbaum and Warren H. Schmidt, "How to Choose a Leadership Pattern," *Harvard Business Review* (May/June 1973): 162–180.

18. Victor H. Vroom and Arthur G. Jago, *The New Leadership* (Upper Saddle River, NJ: Prentice Hall, 1988).

19. Gary A. Yukl, *Leadership in Organizations,* 2d ed. (Upper Saddle River, NJ: Prentice Hall, 1989).

20. For a recent application of the Vroom-Yetton model, see "The behaviour of managers in Austria and the Czech Republic: An intercultural comparison based on the Vroom/Yetton Model of leadership and decision making," *Journal of East European Management Studies* 9 (2004): 411–430.

21. Karen Yuan Wang and Gian Casimir, "How Attitudes of Leaders May Enhance Organizational Creativity: Evidence from a Chinese Study," *Creativity and Innovation Management* 16, no. 3 (September 2007): 229.

22. Charles S. Lauer, "In Each Other We Trust," *Modern Healthcare* 37, no. 37 (September 17, 2007): 20.

23. For an interesting discussion on the relationship between leadership and employee retention, see Pamela Ribelin, "Retention Reflects Leadership Style," *Nursing Management* 34 (2003): 18.

24. Vishwanath V. Baba and Merle E. Ace, "Serendipity in Leadership: Initiating Structure and Consideration in the Classroom," *Human Relations* 42 (June 1989): 509–25. For a further discussion of leadership style, see Maria Guzzo, "People to Watch: Mike Parton—Classic Leadership Style," *Pittsburgh Business Times Journal,* June 23, 2000, 14.

25. Rensis Likert, *New Patterns of Management* (New York: McGraw-Hill, 1961).

26. Harvey A. Hornstein, Madeline E. Heilman, Edward Mone, and Ross Tartell, "Responding to Contingent Leadership Behavior," *Organizational Dynamics* 15 (Spring 1987): 56–65.

27. A. K. Korman, "'Consideration,' 'Initiating Structure,' and Organizational Criteria—A Review," *Personnel Psychology* 19 (Winter 1966): 349–361. See also Rick Roskin, "Management Style and Achievement: A Model Synthesis," *Management Decision* 27 (1989): 17–22.

28. P. Hersey and K. H. Blanchard, "Life Cycle Theory of Leadership," *Training and Development Journal* (May 1969): 26–34.

29. Mary J. Keenan, Joseph B. Hurst, Robert S. Dennis, and Glenna Frey, "Situational Leadership for Collaboration in Health Care Settings," *Health Care Supervisor* 8 (April 1990): 19–25. See also Jane R. Goodson, Gail W. McGee, and James F. Cashman, "Situational Leadership Theory: A Test of Leadership Prescriptions," *Group and Organizational Studies* 14 (December 1989): 446–461.

30. Fred E. Fiedler, "Engineer the Job to Fit the Manager," *Harvard Business Review* (September/October 1965): 115–122.

31. For an interesting look at how different types of leaders and followers perform at different types of tasks, see R. Miller, J. Butler and C. Cosentino, "Followership effectiveness: An extension of Fiedler's contingency model," *Leadership and Organization Development* 25 (2004): 362.

32. F. E. Fiedler, *A Theory of Leadership Effectiveness* (New York: McGraw-Hill, 1967), 255–256. © 1967 by McGraw-Hill, Inc. Used with permission of McGraw-Hill Company.

33. L. H. Peters, D. D. Harike, and J. T. Pohlmann, "Fiedler's Contingency Theory of Leadership: An Application of the Meta-Analysis Procedures of Schmidt and Hunter," *Psychological Bulletin* 97 (1985): 224–285.

34. Brian W. T. Moffitt, "City Management Institute: A Blueprint for Leadership Succession," *Government Finance Review* 23, no. 4 (August 2007): 55–59.

35. Robert J. House and Terence R. Mitchell, "Path–Goal Theory of Leadership," *Journal of Contemporary Business* (Autumn 1974): 81–98; Gary A. Yukl, *Leadership in Organizations*.

36. For a recent article on the path–goal theory, see C. Schriesheim, S. Castro, X. Zhou and L. DeChurch, "An investigation of path–goal and transformational leadership theory predications at the individual level of analysis, *Leadership Quarterly* 17 (2006): 21.

37. For a worthwhile review of the path–goal theory of leadership, see Gary A. Yukl, *Leadership in Organizations*.

38. To learn how some managers are reacting to modern challenges, see Jaclyn Fierman, "Winning Ideas from Maverick Managers," *Fortune,* February 6, 1995, 66–80. For a fresh approach to leadership that modern managers are taking, see George Fraser, "The Slight Edge: Valuing and Managing Diversity," *Vital Speeches of the Day* 64, no. 8 (February 1, 1998): 235–40.

39. Andrew J. DuBrin, *Reengineering Survival Guide* (Cincinnati, OH: Thomson Executive Press, 1996), 115–129.

40. Karl W. Kuhnert and Philip Lewis, "Transactional and Transformational Leadership: A Constructive/Developmental Analysis," *Academy of Management Review* (October 1987): 648–657; Shirley M. Ross and Lynn R. Offermann, "Transformational Leaders: Measurement of Personality Attributes," *Personality and Social Psychology Bulletin,* October 1997, 1078–1086.

41. For a recent article describing the effects of this type of leadership, see J. Schaubroeck, S. Lam, and S. Cha, "Embracing transformational leadership: Team values and the impact of leader behavior on team performance," *Journal of Applied Psychology* 92 (2007): 1020.

42. For more discussion on specific steps that transformational leaders take, see Robert Miles, "Transformation Challenge," *Executive Excellence* 15, no. 2 (February 1998): 15.

43. Bernard M. Bass, *Leadership and Performance Beyond Expectations* (New York: Free Press, 1985).

44. For an in-depth look at the positive effects of coaching on employee productivity, see Bill Blades, "Great Coaching Can Increase Revenue," *Arizona Business Gazette,* January 18, 2001, 5.

45. For practical tips on developing this style of leadership, see M. Wakefield, "New views on leadership coaching," *The Journal for Quality and Participation* 29 (2006): 9–14.

46. For more information on empathy and leadership, see William G. Pagonis, "The Work of the Leader," *Harvard Business Review* (November/December 1992): 118–126.

47. Charles C. Manz, "Helping Yourself and Others to Master Self-Leadership," *Supervisory Management* (November 1991): 19–38; C. Manz and Henry P. Sims Jr., "SuperLeadership: Beyond the Myth of Heroic Leadership," *Organizational Dynamics* (Spring 1991): 28–40.

48. Robert K. Greenleaf, *Servant Leadership: A Journey into the Nature of Legitimate Power and Greatness* (Mahwah, New Jersey: Paulist Press, 1977).

49. To learn about how servant leadership is associated with trust, E. Joseph and B. Winston, "A correlation of servant leadership, leader trust, and organizational trust," *Leadership and Organization Development Journal* 26 (2005): 6–23.

50. Max E. Douglas, "Servant Leadership: An Emerging Supervisory Model," *SuperVision* 64, no. 2 (February 2003): 6–9.

51. Sen Sendjaya and James C. Sarros, "Servant Leadership: Its Origin, Development, and Application in Organizations," *Journal of Leadership and Organizational Studies* 9, no. 2 (Fall 2002): 57–64.

52. For a look at the personality characteristics of servant leaders, see R. Washington, C. Sutton, and H. Field, "Individual differences in servant leadership: The roles of values and personality," *Leadership and Organization Development Journal* 27 (2006): 700–716.

53. Ron Rowe, "Leaders as Servants," *New Zealand Management* 50, no. 1 (February 2003): 24–25.

54. Reylito A. H. Elbo, "In the Workplace," *BusinessWorld,* September 4, 2002, 1.

55. Keshavan Nair, *A Higher Standard of Leadership: Lessons from the Life of Gandhi* (San Francisco, California: Berrett-Koehler, 1994).

56. Robert F. Russell and A. Gregory Stone, "A Review of Servant Leadership Attributes: Developing a Practical Model," *Leadership and Organization Development Journal* 23, no. 3: 145–157.

57. Bernard M. Bass, "The Future of Leadership in Learning Organizations," *Journal of Leadership Studies* 7, no. 3 (2000): 18–40.

58. See R. Washington, C. Sutton, and H. Field, "Individual differences in servant leadership: The roles of values and personality," *Leadership and Organization Development Journal* 27 (2006): 700–716.

59. See R. Washington, C. Sutton, and H. Field, "Individual differences in servant leadership: The roles of values and personality," *Leadership and Organization Development Journal* 27 (2006): 700–716.

60. For a detailed review of entrepreneurial leadership, see L. W. Fernald, G. T. Solomon, and A. Tarabishy, "A new paradigm: Entrepreneurial leadership," *Southern Business Review* 30, no. 1 (2005): 1-10.

61. A profile of a successful female entrepreneurial leader in a multicultural situation is contained in Daniel J. McCarthy, Sheila M. Puffer, and Alexander I. Naumov, "Case Study–Olga Kirova: A Russian Entrepreneur's Quality Leadership," *International Journal of Organizational Analysis* 5, no. 3 (July 1997): 267–290.

62. Jane Horan, "Business Driven Action Learning: A Powerful Tool for Building World-Class Entrepreneurial Business Leaders" *Organization Development Journal* 25, no. 3 (Fall 2007): P75–P80.

63. This material based on James Fitzgerald, "Martha Stewart Arrives Home After Five-Month Prison Term to Begin Detention for Lying about Stock Sale," *Financial Times Information Ltd.*, March 5, 2005.

64. Barnet D. Wolf, "Breakfast Could Make a Return to Wendy's," *The Columbus Dispatch*, March 5, 2005.

CHAPTER 17

1. This description of the company Web site reflects data as of October 10, 2007.

2. Philip A. Rudolph and Brian H. Kleiner, "The Art of Motivating Employees," *Journal of Managerial Psychology* 4 (1989): i–iv; Carole L. Jurkiewicz, Tom K. Massey Jr., and Roger G. Brown, "Motivation in Public and Private Organizations: A Comparative Study," *Public Productivity & Management Review* 21, no. 3 (March 1998): 230–250.

3. For a useful discussion of motivation, see Thomas Wright, "What Every Manager Should Know: Does Personality Help Drive Employee Motivation?" *The Academy of Management Executive* 17 (2003): 131.

4. Mike DeLuca, "Motivating Your Staff Is Key to Your Success," *Restaurant Hospitality* (February 1995): 20; see also Sanford De Voe and Sheena Ivengar, "Managers' Theories of Subordinates: A Cross-Cultural Examination of Manager Perceptions of Motivation and Appraisal of Performance," *Organizational Behavior and Human Decision Processes* 93 (2004): 47.

5. Tyler Kepner, "Last Year's Quick Ouster Is This Year's Motivation for Yankees," *New York Times,* October 3, 2007, 3.

6. Craig Miller, "How to Construct Programs for Teams," *Reward & Recognition* (August/September 1991): 4–6; Walter F. Charsley, "Management, Morale, and Motivation," *Management World* 17 (July/August 1988): 27–28.

7. Victor H. Vroom, *Work and Motivation* (New York: Wiley, 1964); Thomas L. Quick, "How to Motivate People," *Working Women* 12 (September 1987): 15, 17.

8. J. Stacy Adams, "Towards an Understanding of Inequity," *Journal of Abnormal and Social Psychology* 67 (1963): 422–436. For a rationale linking expectancy and equity theories, see Joseph W. Harder, "Equity Theory Versus Expectancy Theory: The Case of Major League Baseball Free Agents," *Journal of Applied Psychology* (June 1991): 458–464. For group rewards as an alternative to individual rewards in human motivation, see Donald J. Campbell, Kathleen M. Campbell, and Ho-Beng Chia, "Merit Pay, Performance Appraisal, and Individual Motivation: An Analysis and Alternative," *Human Resource Management* 37, no. 2 (Summer 1998): 131–146.

9. Eric O'Keefe, "Executive Pay Proposals Rejected at AMR," *New York Times,* May 17, 2007, C5.

10. L. W. Porter and E. E. Lawler, *Managerial Attitudes and Performance* (Homewood, IL: Richard D. Irwin, 1968). For more information on intrinsic and extrinsic rewards, see Pat Buhler, "Rewards in the Organization," *Supervision* 50 (January 1989): 5–7.

11. Eunmi Chang, "Composite Effects of Extrinsic Motivation on Work Effort: A Case of Korean Employees," *Journal of World Business* 38 (2003): 70.

12. For a recent study that assesses the effectiveness of intrinsic and extrinsic rewards, see R. C. Mahaney and A. Lederer, "The effect of intrinsic and extrinsic rewards for developers on information systems project success," *Project Management Journal* 37 (2006): 42–54.

13. "Some Companies Pay Employees to Save Gas," *New York Times,* June 8, 2006, C16.

14. Eric G. Flamholtz and Yvonne Randle, "The Inner Game of Management," *Management Review* 77 (April 1988): 24–30.

15. Abraham Maslow, *Motivation and Personality,* 2d ed. (New York: Harper & Row, 1970). For an up-to-date discussion of the value of Maslow's ideas, see Edward Hoffman, "Abraham Maslow: Father of Enlightened Management," *Training* 25 (September 1988): 79–82.

16. "Maslow's Hierarchy of Needs Revisited," *Nursing Forum* 38 (2003): 3.

17. For a discussion of an empowerment tool managers can use to help employees satisfy esteem and self-actualization needs, see Chris Argyris, "Empowerment: The Emperor's New Clothes," *Harvard Business Review* 76, no. 3 (May/June 1998): 98–105.

18. For critiques of Maslow, see Jack W. Duncan, *Essentials of Management* (Hinsdale, IL: Dryden Press, 1975), 105; Hoffman, "Abraham Maslow: Father of Enlightened Management"; Dale L. Mort, "Lead Your Team to the Top," *Security Management* 32 (January 1988): 43–45.

19. For information about Maslow's revised hierarchy of needs, see M. Koltko-Rivera, "Rediscovering the later version of Maslow's hierarchy of needs: Self-transcendence and opportunities for theory, research, and unification," *Review of General Psychology* 10 (2006): 302–317.

20. Clayton Alderfer, *Existence, Relatedness, and Growth* (New York: Free Press, 1972). For a reconstruction of Maslow's hierarchy, see Francis Heylighen, "A Cognitive-Systemic Reconstruction of Maslow's Theory of Self-Actualization," *Behavioral Science* (January 1992): 39–58.

21. Chris Argyris, *Personality and Organization* (New York: Harper & Bros., 1957). See also Charles R. Davis, "The Primacy of Self-Development in Chris Argyris's Writings," *International Journal of Public Administration* 10 (September 1987): 177–207.

22. David C. McClelland and David G. Winter, *Motivating Economic Achievement* (New York: Free Press, 1969). See also Lawrence Holp, "Achievement Motivation and Kaizen," *Training and Development Journal* 43 (October 1989): 53–63; D. C. McClelland and David H. Burnham, "Power Is the Great Motivator," *Harvard Business Review* (January/February 1995): 126–139.

23. Michael Sanson, "Fired Up!" *Restaurant Hospitality* (February 1995): 53–64.

24. For an empirical investigation of the importance of a manager's ability to effectively communicate, see D. English, E. Manton, and J. Walker, "Human resource managers' perception of selected communication competencies," *Education* 127 (2007): 410–418.

25. Douglas McGregor, *The Human Side of Enterprise* (New York: McGraw-Hill, 1960). For an illustration of how Theory X–Theory Y relates to modern business, see Kenneth B. Slutsky, "Viewpoint: Why Not Theory Z?" *Security Management* 33 (April 1989): 110, 112. For a discussion of Theories X, Y, and Z as they relate to the adoption of new technology in organizations, see Richard T. Due, "Client/Server Feasibility," *Information Systems Management* (Summer 1994): 79–82.

26. For further information about McGregor's Theory Y, see C. Carson, "A historical view of Douglas McGregor's Theory Y," *Management Decision* 43 (2005): 450–462.

27. For further information about applying Theory Z in the workplace, see Richard Daft, "Theory Z: Opening the corporate door for participative management," *Academy of Management Executive* 18 (2004): 117.

28. For further information about the possible usefulness of Theory X, see Michael Bobic and William Davis, "A Kind Word for Theory X: Or Why So Many Newfangled Management Techniques Quickly Fail," *Journal of Public Administration Research and Theory* 13 (2003): 239.

29. For more information on reducing boredom in the workplace, see Z. Bhadury and Z. Radovilsky, "Job rotation using the multi-period assignment model," *International Journal of Production Research* 44 (2006): 4431.

30. For more discussion on the implications of job rotation in organizations, see Alan W. Farrant, "Job Rotation Is Important," *Supervision* (August 1987): 14–16; see also Wipawee Tharmmaphornphilas and Bryan A. Norman, "A Quantitative Method for Determining Proper Job Rotation Intervals," *Annals of Operations Research* 128 (2004): 251.

31. L. E. Davis and E. S. Valfer, "Intervening Responses to Changes in Supervisor Job Designs," *Occupational Psychology* (July 1965): 171–190.

32. This section is based on Frederick Herzberg, "One More Time: How Do You Motivate Employees?" *Harvard Business Review* (January/February 1968): 53–62.

33. For an understanding of how job enrichment relates to other workplace factors, see L. Lapierre, R. Hackett, and S. Taggar, "A test of the links between family interference with work, job enrichment, and leader-member exchange," *Applied Psychology* 55 (2006): 489.

34. Scott M. Meyers, "Who Are Your Motivated Workers?" *Harvard Business Review* (January/February 1964): 73–88; Matt Oechsli, "Million Dollar Success Habits," *Managers Magazine* 65 (February 1990): 6–14; J. Barton Cunningham and Ted Eberle, "A Guide to Job Enrichment and Redesign," *Personnel* 67 (February 1990): 56–61.

35. For an analysis of the strengths of implementing flextime in the workplace, see J. Haar, "Exploring the benefits and use of flextime: Similarities and differences" *Qualitative Research in Accounting and Management* 4 (2007): 69.

36. Bob Smith and Karen Matthes, "Flexibility Now for the Future," *HR Focus* (January 1992): 5.

37. D. A. Bratton, "Moving Away from Nine to Five," *Canadian Business Review* 13 (Spring 1986): 15–17.

38. Douglas L. Fleuter, "Flextime—A Social Phenomenon," *Personnel Journal* (June 1975): 318–319; Jill Kanin-Lovers, "Meeting the Challenge of Workforce, 2000," *Journal of Compensation and Benefits* 5 (January/February 1990): 233–236.

39. B. F. Skinner, *Contingencies of Reinforcement* (New York: Appleton-Century-Crofts, 1969).

40. For an interesting discussion of accounting as a means of rewarding employees, see Mahmoud Ezzamel and Hugh Willmott, "Accounting, Remuneration, and Employee Motivation in the New Organization," *Accounting and Business Research* 28, no. 2 (Spring 1998): 97–110.

41. For further information about the use of positive reinforcement in the workplace, see D. Wiegand and S. Geller, "Connecting positive psychology and organizational behavior management: Achievement motivation and the power of positive reinforcement," *Journal of Organizational Behavior Management* 24 (2004/2005): 3.

42. P. M. Padokaff, "Relationships between Leader Reward and Punishment Behavior and Group Process and Productivity," *Journal of Management* 11 (Spring 1985): 55–73.

43. For an understanding of the potential repercussions of excessive punishment, see Steven Schepman, and Lynn Richmond, "Employee Expectations and Motivation: An Application from the Learned Helplessness Paradigm," *Journal of American Academy of Business* 3 (2003): 405.

44. Karen Crouse, "Punishment Laps Help Jets Kick Penalty Habit," *New York Times* January 5, 2007, D2.

45. "New Tool: Reinforcement for Good Work," *Psychology Today* (April 1972): 68–69.

46. W. Clay Hamner and Ellen P. Hamner, "Behavior Modification on the Bottom Line," *Organizational Dynamics* 4 (Spring 1976): 6–8.

47. James K. Hickel, "Paying Employees to Control Costs," *Human Resources Professional* (January/February 1995): 21–24.

48. For more information about cognitive-behavior modification, see D. Boan, "Cognitive-behavior modification and organizational culture," *Consulting Psychology Journal: Practice and Research* 58 (2006): 51–61.

49. Rensis Likert, *New Patterns of Management* (New York: McGraw-Hill, 1961). For an interesting discussion of the worth of Likert's ideas, see Marvin R. Weisbord, "For More Productive Workplaces," *Journal of Management Consulting* 4 (1988): 7–14. The following descriptions are based on the table of organizational and performance characteristics of different management systems in Rensis Likert, *The Human Organization* (New York: McGraw-Hill, 1967), 4–10.

50. For an empirical investigation of the effectiveness of monetary incentives, see H. McGee, A. Dickinson, B. Huitema, and K. Culig, "The effects of individual and group monetary incentives on high performance," *Performance Improvement Quarterly* 19 (2006): 107–130.

51. For a discussion of a novel monetary incentive program, see Charles A. Cerami, "Special Incentives May Appeal to Valued Employees," *HR Focus* (November 1991): 17; see also Reginald Shareef, "A Midterm Case Study Assessment of Skill-Based Pay in the Virginia Department of Transportation," *Review of Public Personnel Administration* 18, no. 1 (Winter 1998): 5–22.

52. Harry J. Paarscha and Bruce S. Shearerb "Do Women React Differently to Incentives? Evidence from Experimental Data and Payroll Records," *European Economic Review* 51 (2007): 1682–1707.

53. Marilyn Moats Kennedy, "What Makes People Work Hard?" *Across the Board* 35, no. 5 (May 1998): 51–52.

CHAPTER 18

1. Nanette Byrnes, "Xerox New Design Team: Customers" *BusinessWeek*, May 07, 2007, 72.

2. For an article illustrating the importance of managing groups in organizations, see Gregory E. Kaebnick, "Notes from Underground: Walter Corbitt Talks about Monitoring Paperwork for 35,000 Underground Storage Tanks," *Inform* 3 (July/August 1989): 21–22, 48.

3. Edgar H. Schein, *Organizational Psychology* (Upper Saddle River, NJ: Prentice Hall, 1965), 67.

4. Dorwin Cartwright and Ronald Lippitt, "Group Dynamics and the Individual," *International Journal of Group Psychotherapy* 7 (January 1957): 86–102.

5. For insights into how to be more successful in dealing with people in groups, see Anonymous, "Becoming More Persuasive," *Association Management* 50, no. 7 (July 1998): 24–25.

6. Edgar H. Schein, *Organizational Psychology*, 2nd ed. (Upper Saddle River, NJ: Prentice Hall, 1970), 182.

7. For information on the role of gender in task groups, see S. Hysom and C. Johnson, "Leadership structures in same-sex task groups," *Sociological Perspectives* 49 (2006): 391–410.

8. For a study exploring diversity and task group processes, see Warren E. Watson, Lynn Johnson, and Deanna Meritt, "Team Orientation, Self-Orientation, and Diversity in Task Groups," *Group & Organization Management* 23, no. 2 (June 1998): 161–188.

9. To understand further the possible duties of a committee, see Stephanie Balzer, "Committee to Study $500M Civic Plaza Expansion," *The Business Journal* 21, no. 39. (June 22, 2001): 7.

10. Joseph Marks, "Committee May Diversify After All," *Grand Forks Herald,* June 28, 2007, A1.

11. Cyril O'Donnell, "Group Rules for Using Committees," *Management Review* 50 (October 1961): 63–67. For an example of problems created by committees not doing their jobs, see Joann S. Lublin and Elizabeth MacDonald, "Management: Scandals Signal Laxity of Audit Panels," *Wall Street Journal,* July 17, 1998, B1.

12. These and other guidelines are discussed in "Applying Small-Group Behavior Dynamics to Improve Action-Team Performance," *Employment Relations Today* (Autumn 1991): 343–353.

13. For an analysis of the symptoms associated with groupthink, see D. Henningsen, M. Henningsen, J. Eden, and M. Cruz, "Examining the symptoms of groupthink and retrospective sensemaking," *Small Group Research* 37 (2006): 36–64.

14. Robert McMrry, "The Tyranny of Groupthink," *Harvard Business Review* 81 (2003): 120.

15. See Irving L. Janis, *Groupthink* (Boston: Houghton Mifflin, 1982). For insights on how to avoid groupthink, see Peter Kay, "Group Think," *Philadelphia Business Journal,* July 2–8, 1999, 11.

16. For further information about independent work teams, see K. Roper and D. Phillips, "Integrating self-managed work teams into project management," *Journal of Facilities Management* 5 (2007): 22–36.

17. For suggestions on how to build a team, see "Teamwork Translates into High Performance," *HR Focus* 75, no. 7 (July 1998): 7; see also Sheila Webber and Richard Klimoski, "Crews: A Distinct Type of Work Team," *Journal of Business and Psychology* 18 (2004): 261.

18. Bernard Bass, *Organizational Psychology* (Boston: Allyn and Bacon, 1965), 197–198.

19. Raef T. Hussein, "Informal Groups, Leadership, and Productivity," *Leadership and Organization Development Journal* 10 (1989): 9–16.

20. Keith Davis and John W. Newstrom, *Human Behavior at Work: Organizational Behavior* (New York: McGraw-Hill, 1985), 310–312.

21. For the importance of determining such information, see Dave Day, "New Supervisors and the Informal Group," *Supervisory Management* 34 (May 1989): 31–33.

22. Homans, *The Human Group.*

23. For information regarding the role of culture in workplace teams, see M. Uday-Riley, "Eight critical steps to improve workplace performance with cross-cultural teams" *Performance Improvement* 45 (2006): 28.

24. William G. Dyer, *Teambuilding: Issues and Alternatives* (Reading, MA: Addison-Wesley, 1987): 4. See also Dawn R. Deeter-Schmelz and Rosemary Ramsey, "A Conceptualization of the Functions and Roles of Formalized Selling and

Buying Teams," *Journal of Personal Selling & Sales Management* (Spring 1995): 47–60.

25. For a recent article describing effective team problem-solving techniques, see V. Tran and H. Latapie, "Developing virtual team problem-solving and learning capability using the case method," *The Business Review, Cambridge* 8 (2007): 27–33.

26. J. H. Shonk, *Team-Based Organizations* (Homewood, IL: Irwin, 1922).

27. For a study exploring the relationship between leadership and self-managed teams, see Vanessa Urch Druskat and Jane Wheeler, "Managing from the Boundary: The Effective Leadership of Self-Managing Work Teams," *Academy of Management Journal* 46 (2003): 435.

28. Jack L. Lederer and Carl R. Weinberg, "Equity-Based Pay: The Compensation Paradigm for the Re-Engineered Corporation," *Chief Executive* (April 1995): 36–39.

29. Kevin R. Zuidema and Brian H. Kleiner, "Self-Directed Work Groups Gain Popularity," *Business Credit* (October 1994): 21–26.

30. Sami M. Abbasi and Kenneth W. Hollman, "Self-Managed Teams: The Productivity Breakthrough of the 1990s," *Journal of Managerial Psychology* 9 (1994): 25–30.

31. P. Robert Duimering and Robert B. Robinson, "Situational Influences on Team Helping Norms: Case Study of a Self-Directed Team," *Journal of Behavioral and Applied Management* 9, no. 1 (2007): 62–87.

32. For further information about the components of an effective cross-functional team, see Yvonne Athanasaw, "Team Characteristics and Team Member Knowledge, Skills, and Ability Relationships to the Effectiveness of Cross-Functional Teams in the Public Sector," *International Journal of Public Administration* 26 (2003): 1167.

33. For a recent article describing the role of positive feedback in cross-functional teams, see H. Peelle, "Appreciative inquiry and creative problem solving in cross-functional teams," *Journal of Applied Behavioral Science* 42 (2006): 447–467.

34. For more information on cross-functional teams, see D. Michael D. Hutt, Beth A. Walker, and Gary L. Frankwick, "Hurdle the Cross-Functional Barriers to Strategic Change," *Sloan Management Review* (Spring 1995): 22–30; John Teresko, "Reinventing the Future," *Industry Week* (April 17, 1995): 32–38; Margaret L. Gagne and Richard Discenza, "Target Costing," *Journal of Business & Industrial Marketing* 10 (1995): 16–22.

35. Bruce W. Tuckman and Mary Ann C. Jensen, "Stages of Small Group Development Revisited," *Group and Organizational Studies* 2 (1977): 419–427.

36. For an empirical analysis of how to effective develop a team, see E. Chong, "Role balance and team development: A study of team role characteristics underlying high and low performing teams," *Journal of Behavioral and Applied Management* 8 (2007): 202–217.

37. For further information on team effectiveness and leadership, see S. Baker and D. Gerlowski, "Team effectiveness and leader-follower agreement: An empirical study," *Journal of American Academy of Business, Cambridge* 12 (2007): 15–23.

38. Hans J. Thamhain, "Managing Technologically Innovative Team Efforts Toward New Product Success," *Journal of Product Innovation Management* (March 1990): 5–18.

39. For insights about motivation and teams, see Gerben van der Vegt, Ben Emans, and Evert van de Vliet, "Motivating Effects of Task and Outcome Independence in Work," *Group & Organization Management* 23, no. 2 (June 1998): 124–143.

40. Pete Engardio, "A Guide for Multinationals: One of the Great Challenges for a Multinational Is Learning How to Build a Productive Global Team," *BusinessWeek*, August 20, 2007, 48.

41. Jerre L. Stead, "People Power: The Engine in Reengineering," *Executive Speeches* (April/May 1995): 28–32.

42. For information on building trust in the context of teams, see P. Greenberg, R. Greenberg, and Y. Antonucci, "Creating and sustaining trust in virtual teams," *Business Horizons* 50 (2007): 325.

43. Fernando Bartolome, "Nobody Trusts the Boss Completely—Now What?" *Harvard Business Review* (March/April 1989): 114–131.

44. Peter Gumbel, "Burberry's New Boss Doesn't Wear Plaid," *Fortune*, October 15, 2007, 124–130.

45. Susan Berfield, "Bridging the Generation Gap: Employment Agency Randstad Teams Newbies with Older Staff to Great Effect," *BusinessWeek*, September 17, 2007, 60.

46. Information for this exercise based upon www.floridahospital.com

47. This exercise is from www.teambuildingportal.com.

CHAPTER 19

1. This case is based upon Jessica Marquez, "Creating a Culture of Safety: Out of Disaster Comes a Call for Creating a 'Safety Culture,'" *Workforce Management*, April 23, 2007, p. 1.

2. Data from www.BP.com (accessed November 25, 2007).

3. For notable research on the effects of organization culture on workplace performance, see Md Zabid Abdul Rashid, Murali Sambasivan, and Juliana Johari, "The Influence of Corporate Culture and Organizational Commitment on Performance," *The Journal of Management Development*, 22 (2003): 708; see also Lynn Waters, "Cultivate Corporate Culture and Diversity," *Nursing Management* 35 (2004): 36.

4. J. Chatman and D. F. Caldwell, "People and Organizational Culture: A Profile Comparison Approach to Assessing Person-Organization Fit," *Academy of Management Journal*, September, 1991, 487–516.

5. Mary G. Locke and Lucy Guglielmino, "The Influence of Subcultures on Planned Change in a Community College," *Community College Review* 34, no. 2 (October 2006): 108–128.

6. For an interesting study exploring African female executives and dominant culture organizations see: Patricia S. Parker, "Negotiating Identity in Raced and Gendered Workplace Interactions: The Use of Strategic Communication by African American Women Senior Executives within Dominant Culture Organizations," *Communication Quarterly* 50, no. 3/4 (Summer 2002) 251.

7. Stefan Stern, "Wake Up and Smell the Coffee on Your Corporate Culture," *Financial Times*, March 27, 2007, 12.

8. Victor S. L. Tan, "Transforming Your Organization," *New Straits Times*, June 16, 2007, 58.

9. Cass Bettinger, "Use Corporate Culture to Trigger High Performance," *Journal of Business Strategies* (March/April 1989): 38–42. For an article devoted to corporate culture, see J. Lee Howard, "Building a Corporate Culture," *The Business Journal* 14, no. 31. (November 5, 1999): 19.

10. Mike Foster, "Be positive!" *Construction Distribution* 10, no. 2 (October/November 2007): 80.

11. Julie Verity, "Understanding Success: Economics and Human Nature," *Business Strategy Series* 8, no. 5 (2007): 330.

12. "Finding the Right Fit: Nearly Half of Workers Have Misjudged an Employer's Culture," *PR Newswire*, May 23, 2007.

13. Patricia Karvelas, "Corporate Culture Bereft of Ethics," *The Australian*, November 28, 2006, 7.

14. Richard Coughlan, "Demystifying Business Ethics," *Successful Meetings* 52, no. 6 (May 2003): 33.

15. Kim S. Cameron and Robert E. Quinn, *Diagnosing and Changing Organizational Culture* (Reading, MA: Addison Wesley, 1999).

16. Southwest.com, http://southwest.com/about_swa/?ref=abtsw_fgn (accessed November 26, 2007).

17. www.google.com/corporate/culture.html (accessed November 26, 2007).

18. Kim S. Cameron and Robert E. Quinn, *Diagnosing and Changing Organizational Culture* (Reading, MA: Addison Wesley, 1999), 186–201.

19. Howard Risher, "Fostering a Performance-Driven Culture in the Public Sector," *Public Manager* 36, no. 3 (Fall 2007): 51–56.

20. Yi-Jen Chen, "Relationships Among Service Orientation, Job Satisfaction, and Organizational Commitment in the International Tourist Hotel Industry," *Journal of American Academy of Business* 1 no. 2 (September, 2007): 71.

21. L. W. Porter, R. M. Steers, R. T. Mowday, and P. V. Boulian, "Organizational Commitment, Job Satisfaction, and Turnover Among Psychiatric Technicians," *Journal of Applied Psychology* 59 (1974): 603–609.

22. Dirk De Clercq and Imanol Belausteguigoitia Rius, "Organizational Commitment in Mexican Small and Medium-Sized Firms: The Role of Work Status, Organizational Climate, and Entrepreneurial Orientation," *Journal of Small Business Management* 45, no. 4 (October 2007): 467–490.

23. Paul Basson, "How Ethics Can Help Establish Unified Corporate Culture," *Financial Times*, August 24, 2006, 8.

24. The remainder of this section is based upon Jean Thilmany, "Supporting Ethical Employees," *HR Magazine* 52, no. 9 (September 2007): 105.

25. Brian Hindo, "At 3M, a Struggle Between Efficiency and Creativity; How CEO George Buckley Is Managing the Yin and Yang of Discipline and Imagination," *BusinessWeek*, June 11, 2007, 8.

26. Mathew L. Sheep, "Nurturing the Whole Person: The Ethics of Workplace Spirituality in a Society of Organizations," *Journal of Business Ethics* 66, no. 4 (2006): 357–375.

27. Jean-Claude Garcia-Zamor, "Workplace Spirituality and Organizational Performance," *Public Administration Review* 63, no. 3 (May/June 2003): 355.

28. Jeff Mortimer, "Help Wanted: New Blood, Ideas Must Fuel Inclusive, Expanding Corporate Culture," *Automotive News*, October 29, 2007, T184.

29. Betsy Morris, "New Rule: The Customer Is King," *CNNMoney.com*, July 11, 2006.

30. The following section draws heavily from M. Higgins, Craig Mcallaster, Samuel C. Certo, and James P. Gilbert, "Using Cultural Artifacts to Change and Perpetuate Strategy," *Journal of Change Management* 6, no. 4 (December 2006): 397–415.

31. This discussion is based upon Harrison M. Trice and Janice M. Beyer (Upper Saddle River, NJ: Prentice Hall, 1993), 271–272.

32. J. Kerr and J. W. Slocum Jr., "Managing corporate culture through reward systems," *Academy of Management Executive* 19, no. 4 (2005): 130.

33. This section is based largely upon Catherine Filstad, "How Newcomers Use Role Models in Organizational Socialization," *Journal of Workplace Living* 16 (2004): 396–410.

34. "Use of Corporate Culture to Spur Growth in a Firm," *Africa News*, October 16, 2007.

35. This case is excerpted from Nelson D. Schwartz, "One Brick at a Time," CNNMoney.com, June 8, 2006, http://money.cnn.com/magazines/fortune/fortune_archive/2006/06/12/8379252/index.htm.

CHAPTER 20

1. This case based on Lauren R. Hartman, "Flat-Bottomed Pouch Is Oven-Ready," *Packaging Digest* 44, no. 5 (2007): 64–66; and Rod R. Kekkonen, "Hormel Gets Technical," *Industrial Engineer* 39, no. 7 (2007): 38–43.

2. For an excellent review of research on creativity, see Mark Runco, "Creativity," *Annual Review of Psychology* 55 (2004): 657–687.

3. Cameron M. Ford, "Creative Developments in Creativity Theory," *The Academy of Management Review* 25, no. 2 (April 2000): 284–285. For an interesting study examining creativity in the advertising industry, see Andrew Von Nordneflycht, "Is public ownership bad for professional service firms? Ad agency ownership, performance, and creativity," *Academy of Management Journal* 50, no. 2 (2007): 429–445.

4. David K. Carson, "The Importance of Creativity in Family Therapy: A Preliminary Consideration," *Family Journal* 7, no. 4 (October 1999): 326–334.

5. This section is based upon Theresa M. Amabile, "How to Kill Creativity," *Harvard Business Review* 76, no. 5 (September–October 1998): 77–89.

6. Teresa M. Amabile, Constance N. Hadley, and Steven J. Kramer, "Creativity Under the Gun," *Harvard Business Review* 80, no. 8 (August 2002): 52–61. See also Markus Baer & Greg R. Oldham, "The curvilinear relation between experienced creative time pressure and creativity: Moderating effects of openness to experience and support for creativity," *Journal of Applied Psychology* 91, no. 4 (2006): 963–970.

7. Jennifer M. George and Jing Zhou, "Dual tuning in a supportive context: Joint contributions of positive mood, negative mood, and supervisory behaviors to employee creativity," *Academy of Management Journal* 50, no. 3 (2007): 605–622.

8. John J. Kao, "The Art & Discipline of Business Creativity," *Strategy & Leadership* 25, no. 4 (July/August 1997): 6–11.

9. Jill E. Perry-Smith, "Social yet creative: The role of social relationships in facilitating individual creativity," *Academy of Management Journal* 49, no. 1 (2006): 85–101.

10. Howard Schlossberg, "Innovation: An Elusive Commodity with Many Definitions," *Marketing News* 25, no. 8 (April 15, 1991): 11.

11. James M. Higgins, *Innovate or Evaporate: Test & Improve Your Organization's IQ* (Winter Park, FL: The New Management Publishing Company, 1995). See also Shalini Khazanchi, Marianne Lewis, and Kenneth Boyer, "Innovation-supportive culture: The impact of organizational values on process innovation," *Journal of Operations Management* 25, no. 4 (2007): 871–884.

12. John Kao, *Innovation Nation* (New York: Free Press, 2007).

13. Jena McGregor, "Special Report: 25 most innovative companies," *BusinessWeek*, May 14, 2007, 52–60.

14. For more information on the link between creativity and innovation, see Bob Kijkuit and Jan van den Ende, "The Organizational Life of an Idea: Integrating Social Network, Creativity and Decision-Making Perspectives," *Journal of Management Studies* 44, no. 6 (2007): 863–882.

15. This discussion is based upon D. R. Nayak and J. M. Ketteringham, *Breakthroughs* (New York: Rawson Associates, 1986).

16. Olivier Toubia, "Idea generation, creativity, and incentives," *Marketing Science* 25, no. 5 (2006): 411–425.

17. James Higgins, *101 Creative Problem Solving Techniques: The Handbook of New Ideas for Business* (Winter Park, FL: The New Management Publishing Company, 1994), 9–10.

18. John C. Dvorak, "Razors with No Blades," *Forbes*, October 18, 1999, 168.

19. Claire Beale, "Strategic Thinking Will Never Rescue a Poor Creative Idea," *Campaign*, August 24, 2001, 14.

20. Tim Hanrahan, "New Cellphone Service Helps Find Friends and Place to Hang Out," *Wall Street Journal*, May 22, 2003, B1.

21. Bruce Orwall, "Universal's Anxious Summer," *Wall Street Journal*, May 22, 2003, B1.

22. Kristinha McCort, "Learning a New Definition," *Millimeter* 29, no. 11 (November 2001): 29–32.

23. Frances Horibe, "Innovation, Creativity, and Improvement," *The Canadian Manager* 28, no. 2 (Spring 2003): 20.

24. For more information on these three contributions, see Charles H. Fine and David H. Bridge, "Managing Quality Improvement," *Quest for Quality: Managing the Total System*, ed. by M. Sepheri (Norcross, GA: Institute of Industrial Engineers, 1987), 66–74. See also Klaus J. Zinc, "From total quality management to corporate sustainability based on stakeholder management," *Journal of Management History* 13, no. 4 (2007): 394–401.

25. For some of Crosby's more notable books in this area, see Philip B. Crosby, *Quality Is Free* (New York: McGraw-Hill, 1979); *Quality without Tears* (New York: McGraw-Hill, 1984); *Let's Talk Quality: 96 Questions You Always Wanted to Ask Phil Crosby* (New York: McGraw-Hill, 1989); and *Leading* (New York: McGraw-Hill, 1990).

26. "The Push for Quality," *BusinessWeek*, June 8, 1987, 131. For a study assessing the importance of total quality management in the workplace, see Thomas J. Douglas and William Q. Judge Jr., "Total Quality Management Implementation and Competitive Advantage: The Role of Structural Control and Exploration," *Academy of Management Journal* 44, no. 1 (February 2001): 158–169.

27. A. V. Feigenbaum, *Total Quality Control* (New York: McGraw-Hill, 1983).

28. For a broadening discussion of a positive image, see Susan Watkins, "A Positive Image Is Not Just the Business of Business," *Public Management* 82, no. 7 (July 2000): 8–10.

29. From Michael Schroeder, "Heart Trouble at Pfizer," *BusinessWeek*, February 26, 1990, 47–48.

30. For a discussion of companies that have recently won the Malcolm Baldrige National Award, see Karen Bemowski, "1994 Baldrige Award Recipients Share Their Expertise," *Quality Progress* (February 1995): 35–40.

31. Michael Hammer, "Reengineering Work: Don't Automate, Obliterate," *Harvard Business Review* (July/August 1990): 104–112.

32. See Deming's 14 Points (January 1990 revision) from W. Edwards Deming, *Out of Crisis* (Cambridge, MA: MIT Center for Advanced Engineering Study, 1986).

33. This case was based on information obtained from EASports.com.

CHAPTER 21

1. This Challenge Case is based on D. Foust, "Queen Of Pop," *BusinessWeek*, August 7, 2006, 44–53; and K. Parker, "ERP and SOA at the Coca-Cola Company," *Manufacturing Business Technology* 25, no. 5: 2.

2. For an illustration of the complexity of control in an international context, see Jean-Francois Hennart, "Control in Multinational Firms: The Role of Price and Hierarchy," *Management International Review*, Special Issue 1991, 71–96. See also "Defining Controls," *The Internal Auditor* 55, no. 3 (June 1998): 47.

3. For insights about control in the international arena, see John Volkmar, "Context and Control in Foreign Subsidiaries: Making a Case for the Host Country National Manager," *Journal of Leadership and Organizational Studies* 10 (2003): 93.

4. K. A. Merchant, "The Control Function of Management," *Sloan Management Review* 23 (Summer 1982): 43–55.

5. Robert L. Dewelt, "Control: Key to Making Financial Strategy Work," *Management Review* (March 1977): 18. For discussion relating planning and controlling to leadership, see Sushil K. Sharma and Savita Dakhane, "Effective Leadership: The Key to Success," *Employment News* 23, no. 10 (June 6–12, 1988): 1, 15.

6. For more discussion on Murphy's Law, see Grady W. Harris, "Living with Murphy's Law," *Research-Technology Management* (January/February 1994): 10–13.

7. Robert J. Mockler, ed., *Readings in Management Control* (New York: Appleton-Century-Crofts, 1970), 14.

8. For insights about the process that Delta Air Lines uses to control distribution costs, see Perry Flint, "Delta's 'Shot Heard 'Round the World,'" *Air Transport World* (April 1995): 61–62.

9. Francis V. McCrory and Peter Gerstberger, "The New Math of Performance Measurement," *Journal of Business Strategy* (March/April 1991): 33–38; L. Bielski, "KPI: Your metrics should tell a story," *ABA Banking Journal* 99, no. 10 (2007): 66–68; B. Hirtle, "The impact of network size on bank branch performance," *Journal of Banking & Finance* 31, no. 12 (2007): 3782–3805.

10. For an article focusing on challenges associated with measuring the performance of physicians, see T. G. Ferris, J. Marder, C. S. Sennett, and E. G. Campbell, "TRENDS: Physician Specialty Societies and the Development of Physician Performance Measures," *Health Affairs* 26, no. 6 (2007): 1712–1719.

11. For discussion of quality-oriented performance standards, see Perry Rector and Brian Kleiner, "Performance Standards: Defining Quality Service in Community-Based Organizations," *Management Research News* 26 (2003): 161.

12. James M. Bright, "A Clear Picture," *Credit Union Management* (February 1995): 28–29.

13. For a discussion of how standards are set, see James B. Dilworth, *Production and Operations Management: Manufacturing and Nonmanufacturing* (New York: Random House, 1986), 637–650. For more information on various facets of standards and standard setting, see Len Eglo, "Save Dollars on Maintenance Management," *Chemical Engineering* 97 (June 1990): 157–162.

14. For an example of a company surpassing performance standards, see Peter Nulty, "How to Live by Your Wits," *Fortune*, April 20, 1992, 19–20.

15. To better understand the importance of corrective action, see Zheng Gu, "Predicting Potential Failure, Taking Corrective Action Are Keys to Success," *Nation's Restaurant News* 33, no. 25 (June 21, 1999): 31–32.

16. For more about corrective action in developing countries, see Martin Brownbridge and Samuel Maimbo, "Can Prompt Corrective Action Rules Work in the Developing World?" *Journal of African Business* 4 (2003): 47.

17. For a review of other common problems in organizations, see Robert E. Quinn, Regina M. O'Neill, and Lynda St. Clair, *Pressing Problems in Modern Organizations (That Keep Us Up at Night): Transforming Agendas for Research and Practice*, (New York: AMACOM): 1999.

18. For an illustration of the problem/symptom relationship, see Elizabeth Dougherty, "Waste Minimization: Reduce Wastes and Reap the Benefits," *R&D* 32 (April 1990): 62–68.

19. To explore the relationship between nonverbal behavior and power, see Herman Aguinis, Melissa M. Simonsen, and Charles A. Pierce, "Effects of Nonverbal Behavior on Perceptions of Power Bases," *The Journal of Social Psychology* 138, no. 4 (August 1998): 455–469.

20. For more information on position power, see S. R. Giessner and T. W. Schubert, "High in the hierarchy: How vertical location and judgments of leaders' power are interrelated," *Organizational Behavior and Human Decision Processes* 104, no. 1 (2007): 30–44.

21. See Amitai Etzioni, *A Comparative Analysis of Complex Organizations* (New York: Free Press, 1961), 4–6. To better understand the potential negative outcomes associated with power, see T. B. Lawrence and S. L. Robinson, "Ain't Misbehavin: Workplace Deviance as Organizational Resistance," *Journal of Management* 33, no. 3 (2007): 378–394.

22. John P. Kotter, "Power, Dependence, and Effective Management," *Harvard Business Review* (July/August 1977): 128.

23. Kotter, "Power, Dependence, and Effective Management," 135–136. For a discussion on how empowering subordinates can increase the power of a manager, see Linda A. Hill, "Maximizing Your Influence," *Working Woman* (April 1995): 21–22.

24. Kotter, "Power, Dependence, and Effective Management," 131.

25. W. Jerome III, *Executive Control: The Catalyst* (New York: Wiley, 1961), 31–34. See also William Bruns Jr. and E. Warren McFarlan, "Information Technology Puts Power in Control Systems," *Harvard Business Review* (September/October 1987): 89–94.

26. For an article emphasizing the importance of management understanding and being supportive of organizational control efforts, see Richard M. Morris III, "Management Support: An Underlying Premise," *Industrial Management* 31 (March/April 1989): 2–3.

27. Garland R. Hadley and Mike C. Patterson, "Are Middle-Paying Jobs Really Declining?" *Oklahoma Business Bulletin* 56 (June 1988): 12–14; A. Essam Radwan and Jerome Fields, "Keeping Tabs on Toxic Spills," *Civil Engineering* 60 (April 1990): 70–72; Dean C. Minderman, "Marketing: Desktop Demographics," *Credit Union Management* 13 (February 1990): 26.

28. Henry Mintzberg, "The Myths of MIS," *California Management Review* (Fall 1972): 92–97; Jay W. Forrester, "Managerial Decision Making," in *Management and the Computer of the Future*, ed. Martin Greenberger (Cambridge, MA, and New York: MIT Press and Wiley, 1962), 37.

29. The following discussion is based largely on Robert H. Gregory and Richard L. Van Horn, "Value and Cost of Information." in *Systems Analysis Techniques*, ed. J. Daniel Conger and Robert W. Knapp (New York; Wiley, 1974), 473–489.

30. To better understand how information systems can improve the quality of an organization's information, see B. S. Butler and P. H. Gray, "Reliability, Mindfulness, and Information Systems," *MIS Quarterly* 30, no. 2 (2006): 211–224.

31. John T. Small and William B. Lee, "In Search of MIS," *MSU Business Topics* (Autumn 1975): 47–55.

32. G. Anthony Gorry and Michael S. Scott Morton, "A Framework for Management Information Systems," *Sloan Management Review* 13 (Fall 1971): 55–70.

33. Stephen L. Cohen, "Managing Human-Resource Data Keeping Your Data Clean," *Training & Development Journal* 43 (August 1989): 50–54.

34. Michael A. Verespej, "Communications Technology: Slave or Master?" *Industry Week* (June 19, 1995): 48–55; John C. Scully, "Information Overload?" *Managers Magazine*, May 1995, 2.

35. T. Mukhapadhyay and R. B. Cooper, "Impact of Management Information Systems on Decisions," *Omega* 20 (1992): 37–49. For more information on information systems in developing countries, see G. Walsham, D. Robey, and S. Sahay, "Foreword: Special Issue on Information Systems in Developing Countries," *MIS Quarterly* 31, no. 2 (2007): 317–326.

36. Robert W. Holmes, "Twelve Areas to Investigate for Better MIS," *Financial Executive* (July 1970): 24. A similar definition is presented and illustrated in Jeffrey A. Coopersmith, "Modern Times: Computerized Systems Are Changing the Way Today's Modern Catalog Company Is Structured," *Catalog Age* 7 (June 1990): 77–78.

37. Kenneth C. Laudon and Jane Price Laudon, *Management Information Systems: Organization and Technology* (New York: Macmillan, 1993), 38.

38. For an article discussing how a well-managed MIS promotes the usefulness of information, see Albert Lederer and Veronica Gardner, "Meeting Tomorrow's Business Demands through Strategic Information Systems Planning," *Information Strategy: The Executive's Journal* (Summer 1992): 20–27.

39. This section is based on Richard A. Johnson, R. Joseph Monsen, Henry P. Knowles, and Borge O. Saxberg, *Management Systems and Society: An Introduction* (Santa Monica, CA: Goodyear, 1976), 113–120; James Emery, "Information Technology in the 21st Century Enterprise," *MIS Quarterly* (December 1991): xxi–xxiii.

40. Robert G. Murdick, "MIS for MBO," *Journal of Systems Management* (March 1977): 34–40; see also A. S. Dunk, "Innovation budget pressure, quality of IS information, and departmental performance," *The British Accounting Review* 39, no.2 (2007): 115–124

41. The discussion is based on A. Rai, S. S. Lang, and R. B. Welker, "Assessing the Validity of IS Success Models: An Empirical Test and Theoretical Analysis," *Information Systems Research* 13, no. 1 (2002): 50–69.

42. For more information on the turnover of IT workers, see D. Joseph, K. Ng, C. Koh, and S. Ang, "Turnover of Information Technology Professionals: A Narrative Review, Meta-Analytic Structural Equation Modeling, and Model Development," *MIS Quarterly* 31, no. 3 (2007): 547–577.

43. C. O. Longenecker and J. A. Scazzero, "The Turnover and Retention of IT Managers in Rapidly Changing Organizations," *Information Systems Management* (Winter 2003): 58–63.

44. S. Overby, "The Future of Jobs and Innovation: Scenario One," *CIO* 17, no. 6 (2003): online.

45. J. King, "IT's Global Itinerary," *Computerworld* 37, no. 37: 36-X (online).

46. This discussion is based on M. K. Ahuja, K. M. Chudoba, C. J. Kacmar, D. H. McKnight, and J. F. George, "IT Road Warriors: Balancing Work-Family Conflict, Job Autonomy, and Work Overload to Mitigate Turnover Intentions," *MIS Quarterly* 31, no. 1 (2007): 1–17.

47. M. R. Gramaila and I. Kim, "An Undergraduate Business Information Security Course and Laboratory," *Journal of Information Systems Education* 13, no. 3 (2003): 189–196.

48. This exercise was based on www.merrilllynch.com, as well as Jena McGregor, "Room & Board Plays Impossible to Get," *BusinessWeek*, October 1, 2007, p. 80.

CHAPTER 22

1. C. Dade, "Changing Pilots," *Wall Street Journal*, October 4, 2007, A1; D. McDougall, "Hurry up and Wait," *CMA Management* 81, no. 5 (2007): 42–44.

2. James B. Dilworth, *Production and Operations Management: Manufacturing and Non-Manufacturing* (New York: Random House, 1986), 3.

3. For a better understanding of the relationship between employee knowledge and productivity, see M. R. Hass and M. T. Hansen, "Different knowledge, different benefits: Toward a productivity perspective on knowledge sharing in organizations," *Strategic Management Journal* 28, no. 11 (2007):1133–1153.

4. John W. Kendrick, *Understanding Productivity: An Introduction to the Dynamics of Productivity Change* (Baltimore: Johns Hopkins University Press, 1977), 114. For useful discussion on how to motivate people to do more to enhance productivity, see Geoffrey Colvin, "What Money Makes You Do," *Fortune,* August 17, 1998: 213–214. For a recent article assessing the role of productivity within a company, see Michael H. Moskow, "Productivity: Key to the Economic Future," *Executive Speeches* 15, no. 6 (June/July 2001): 24–28.

5. E. Magnani, "The Productivity Slowdown, Sectoral Reallocations and the Growth of Atypical Employment Arrangements," *Journal of Productivity Analysis* 20 (2003): 121.

6. Lester C. Thurow, "Other Countries Are as Smart as We Are," *New York Times,* April 5, 1981.

7. For an example of virtual offices created to increase worker productivity, see Michael K. Takagawa, "Turn Traditional Work Spaces into Virtual Offices," *Human Resources Professional* (March/April 1995):11–14.

8. This example is based on D. Clark, "Theory & Practice: Why Silicon Valley Is Rethinking the Cubicle Office," *Wall Street Journal,* October 15, 2007, B9.

9. For more information regarding the interplay between quality and production, see J. Voros, "The dynamics of price, quality and productivity improvement decisions," *European Journal of Operational Research* 170, no. 3 (2006): 809–823.

10. For more information on how customers might improve productivity, see I. Anitsal and D. W. Schumann, "Toward a conceptualization of customer productivity: The customer's perspective on transforming customer labor into customer outcomes using technology-based self-service options," *Journal of Marketing Theory and Practice* 15, no. 4 (2007): 349–363.

11. W. Edwards Deming, *Out of the Crisis* (Boston: MIT Centre for Advanced Engineering Study, 1986).

12. Gary McWilliams, "Wal-Mart Era Wanes Amid Big Shifts in Retail; Rivals Find Strategies to Defeat Low Prices; World Has Changed," *Wall Street Journal,* October 3, 2007, A.1.

13. John J. Dwyer Jr., "Quality: Can You Prove It?" *Fleet Owner* (April 1995): 36. For coverage of quality assurance, see "Quality Assurance," *Manufacturing Engineering* 125, no. 2 (August 2000): 270–291.

14. "Key Ratings: Developing a Quality Assurance Framework for In-Service Training and Development," *Measuring Business Excellence* 7 (2003): 99.

15. Gerry Davidson, "Quality Circles Didn't Die—They Just Keep Improving," *CMA Magazine,* February 1995, 6.

16. M. Beyer, F. Gerlach, U. Flies, and R. Grol, "The Development of Quality Circles/Peer Review Groups as a Method of Quality Improvement in Europe: Results of a Survey in 26 European Countries," *Family Practice* 20 (2003): 443.

17. John Peter Koss, "Plant Robotics and Automation," *Beverage World* (April 1995): 108; Rob Spencer, "A Driving Force: Use of Robotics Remains Strong in Auto Industry," *Robotics World* 19, no. 1 (January/February 2001): 18–21.

18. Robert E. Kemper and Joseph Yehudai, *Experiencing Operations Management: A Walk-Through* (Boston: PWS-Kent Publishing Company, 1991), 48.

19. Richard B. Chase and Nicholas J. Aquilano, *Production and Operations Management: A Life Cycle Approach* (Homewood, IL: Richard D. Irwin, 1981), 4. For a worthwhile discussion of forecasting product demand as a continual operations management activity, see Jim Browne, "Forecasting Demand for Services," *Industrial Engineering* (February 1995): 16–17.

20. Roger W. Schmenner, "Operations Management," *Business Horizons* 41, no. 3 (May/June, 1998): 3–4; M. Rungtusanatham, T. Choi, D. Hollingworth, Z. Wu, and C. Forza, "Survey Research in Operations Management: Historical Analyses," *Journal of Operations Management* 21 (2003): 475.

21. For a thorough discussion of product strategy, see Olav Sorenson, "Letting the Market Work for You: An Evolutionary Perspective on Product Strategy," *Strategic Management Journal* 21, no. 5 (May 2000): 577–592.

22. For an example of the kinds of layout issues that concern printers in Europe, see Jill Roth, "Molto Bene," *American Printer* (March 1994): 54–58.

23. For ways to ensure that human resource strategy is progressive, see Kevin Barksdale, "Why We Should Update HR Education," *Journal of Management Education* 22, no. 4 (August 1998): 526–530.

24. To appreciate the impact of job design, see M. Robinson, M. Peterson, T. Tedrick, and J. Carpenter, "Job Satisfaction on NCAA Division III Athletic Directors: Impact of Job Design and Time on Task," *International Sports Journal* 7 (2003): 46.

25. For a review of JIT and lean production, see M. Holweg, "The genealogy of lean production," *Journal of Operations Management* 25, no. 2 (2007): 420–437.

26. Lee J. Krajewski and Larry P. Ritzman, *Operations Management: Strategy and Analysis* (Reading, MA: Addison-Wesley, 1987), 573. Albert F. Celley, William H. Clegg, Arthur W. Smith, and Mark A. Vonderembse, "Implementation of JIT in the United States," *Journal of Purchasing and Materials Management* (Winter 1987): 9–15. See also, Y. Matsui, "An empirical analysis of just-in-time production in Japanese manufacturing companies," *International Journal of Production Economics* 108 (2007): 153–164.

27. John D. Baxter, "Kanban Works Wonders, but Will It Work in U.S. Industry?" *Iron Age* (June 7, 1982): 44–48.

28. Amy Chozick, "Toyota Sticks by 'Just in Time' Strategy After Quake," *Wall Street Journal,* July 24, 2007, A2

29. For discussion of cost control focusing on corporate jets, see Mel Mandell, "Why Sharing Jets Is Cost Effective," *World Trade* 11, no. 7 (July 1998): 85.

30. George S. Minmier, "Zero-Base Budgeting: A New Budgeting Technique for Discretionary Costs," *Mid-South Quarterly Business Review* 14 (October 1976): 2–8. See also Peter A. Phyrr, "Zero-Base Budgeting," *Harvard Business Review* (November/December 1970): 111–121; E. A. Kurbis, "The Case for Zero-Base Budgeting," *CA Magazine,* April 1986, 104–105; Linda J. Shinn and M. Sue Sturgeon, "Budgeting from Ground Zero," *Association Management* 42 (September 1990): 45–48; Gregory E. Becwar and Jack L. Armitage, "Zero-Base Budgeting: Is It Really Dead?" *Ohio CPA Journal* 48 (Winter 1989): 52–54.

31. Chris Argyris, "Human Problems with Budgets," *Harvard Business Review* (January/February 1953): 108.

32. This section is based primarily on J. Fred Weston and Eugene F. Brigham, *Essentials of Managerial Finance,* 7th ed. (Hinsdale, IL: Dryden Press, 1985). See also J. Pearce, "The Value of Corporate Financial Measures in Monitoring Downturn and Managing Turnaround: An Exploratory Study," *Journal of Managerial Issues* 19, no. 2 (2007): 253–270.

33. For an excellent discussion of ratio analysis and its alternatives, see W. Chen & L. McGinnis, "Reconciling ratio analysis and DEA as performance assessment tools," *European Journal of Operational Research* 178, no. 1 (2007): 277–291.

34. This highlight is based on K. C. Tan, V. R. Kannan, and R. Narasimhan, "The impact of operations capability on firm performance," *International Journal of Production Research* 45, no. 21 (2007): 5135–5156.

35. Lester R. Bittle, *Management by Exception* (New York: McGraw-Hill, 1964); Frederick W. Taylor, *Shop Management* (New York: Harper & Bros., 1911), 126–127.

36. These two rules are adapted from *Boardroom Reports* 5 (May 1976): 4.

37. Robert J. Lambrix and Surenda S. Singhvi, "How to Set Volume-Sensitive ROI Targets," *Harvard Business Review* (March/April 1981): 174.

38. For a listing and discussion of quantitative tools and their appropriate uses, see Kemper and Yehudai, *Experiencing Operations Management,* 341–355. For a clear discussion, illustrations, and examples of linear programming, break-even analysis, work measurement, acceptance sampling, payoff tables, value analysis, computer-aided design (CAD), computer-aided engineering (CAE), computer-aided manufacturing (CAM), manufacturing resource planning (MRP), program evaluation and review technique (PERT), capacity requirements planning (CRP), and input/output control, see Jay Heizer and Barry Render, *Production and Operations Management: Strategies and Tactics* (Needham Heights, MA: Allyn and Bacon, 1993).

PHOTO CREDITS

CHAPTER 15

Page 359: Courtesy of Daniel Bosler/Getty Images, Inc. *Page 361:* Courtesy of Al Behrman/AP Wide World Photos. *Page 367:* Courtesy of Jiang Jin/SuperStock, Inc. *Page 368:* Courtesy of Ellen Senisi/© Ellen B. Senisi.

CHAPTER 16

Page 385: Courtesy of Morry Gash/AP Wide World Photos. *Page 388:* Courtesy of Ted S. Warren/AP Wide World Photos. *Page 390:* Courtesy of Daniel Bosler/Getty Images, Inc. *Page 401:* Courtesy of Randy Pench/© 2003 Randy Pench/Sacramento Bee/Zuma Press. *Page 404:* Courtesy of Terry Vine/Getty Images Inc.–Stone Allstock.

CHAPTER 17

Page 415: Courtesy of Pearson Education/PH College. *Page 421:* Courtesy of AP Wide World Photos. *Page 424:* Courtesy of Ben Baker/Redux Pictures. *Page 427:* Courtesy of Getty Images–Stockbyte.

CHAPTER 18

Page 439: Courtesy of Michael Okoniewski/© Michael Okoniewski/The Image Works. *Page 443:* Courtesy of Bill Aron/ PhotoEdit Inc. *Page 449:* Courtesy of David Young-Wolff/PhotoEdit Inc. *Page 450:* Courtesy of AP Wide World Photos. *Page 455:* Courtesy of Georg Anderhub/Lebrecht Music & Arts Photo Library.

CHAPTER 19

Page 465: Courtesy of Pat Sullivan/AP Wide World Photos. *Page 471:* Courtesy of Paul Sakuma/AP Wide World Photos. *Page 475:* Courtesy of Richard Patterson/PRNewsFoto/KB Home/Newscom. *Page 480:* Courtesy of Daily Press, Buddy Norris/AP Wide World Photos.

CHAPTER 20

Page 491: Courtesy of Prentice Hall High School. *Page 495:* Courtesy of Eros Hoagland/© Eros Hoagland/ Redux. *Page 501:* Courtesy of Robert Sorbo/Corbis/Reuters America LLC. *Page 503:* Courtesy of Michael L. Abramson/Getty Images/Time Life Pictures.

CHAPTER 21

Page 515: Courtesy of Myrleen Ferguson Cate/PhotoEdit Inc. *Page 517:* Courtesy of Sergio Dorantes/Getty Images/Time Life Pictures. *Page 522:* Courtesy of Phanie/Photo Researchers, Inc. *Page 525:* Courtesy of Jeff Chiu/© Jeff Chiu /AP Wide World. *Page 529:* Courtesy of Susan Van Etten/PhotoEdit Inc.

CHAPTER 22

Page 543: Courtesy of Mike Simons/Newscom/Getty Images. *Page 546:* Courtesy of Maximilian Stock LTD/Phototake NYC. *Page 550:* Courtesy of Grant, Spencer/Photo Researchers, Inc. *Page 553:* Courtesy of Myrleen Ferguson Cate/PhotoEdit Inc. *Page 554:* Courtesy of Walter Hodges/Getty Images Inc.–Stone Allstock.

NAME INDEX

SUBJECT INDEX